Short Stories *for Students*

Short Stories for Students

Presenting Analysis, Context and Criticism on Commonly Studied Short Stories

Volume 3

Kathleen Wilson, Editor

Dorothea M. Susag, Simms High School, Simms, Montana
Bonnie Newcomer, Beloit Junior-Senior High School, Beloit, Kansas

Foreword by Nancy Rosenberger, Conestoga High School, Berwyn, Pennsylvania

GALE
DETROIT • NEW YORK • LONDON

Short Stories for Students

Staff

Copyright Notice

∞™ This book is printed on acid-free paper that meets the minimum requirements of American National Standard for Information Sciences—Permanence Paper for Printed Library Materials, ANSI Z39.48-1984.

ISBN 0-7876-2218-4
ISSN 1092-7735
Printed in the United States of America

10 9 8 7 6 5 4 3 2 1

Table of Contents

An Adventure in Reading

Sitting on top of my desk is a Pueblo storytelling doll. Her legs stick straight out before her and around her neck and flowing down into her lap are wide-eyed children. Her mouth is open as though she were telling the Zuni tale of the young husband who followed his wife to the Land of the Dead, a story strangely like the Greek myth of Orpheus and Euridice, as both teach the dangers of youthful impatience.

Although the Pueblo doll was created in New Mexico, she symbolizes a universal human activity. The pharaohs listened intently to tales of the goddess Isis, who traveled to foreign lands to rescue the dismembered body of her husband Osiris. Biblical narratives thrill the reader with stories like that of mortal combat between David and the giant Goliath. Greek and Roman myths immortalize the struggles of the wandering warriors Odysseus and Aeneas. In the Middle Ages, kings, queens and courtiers sat spellbound in drafty halls as troubadours sang of tragic lovers and pious pilgrims.

Around the world and down through the ages, myths, folktales, and legends have spoken to us about the human condition and our place in the world of nature and of spirit. Despite its ancient beginnings, however, there is no rigid criteria to which a story must adhere. It is one of the most protean literary forms. Though many scholars credit the nineteenth-century Romantic writers Edgar Allan Poe and Nathaniel Hawthorne with creating the modern short story, the form refuses to be frozen by a list of essential characteristics. Perhaps this is one of the reasons William Faulkner called it the "most demanding form after poetry." Jack London felt it should be "concrete, to the point, with snap and go and life, crisp and crackling and interesting." Eudora Welty wrote that each story should reveal something new yet also contain something "as old as time."

Below are some of the qualities you may observe as you explore the works discussed in *Short Stories for Students.* These characteristics also demonstrate some of the ways the short story differs from the novel:

1. Because time is compressed or accelerated, **unity** in plot, character development, tone, or mood is essential.
2. The author has chosen to **focus** on one character, event, or conflict within a limited time.
3. Poe wrote that **careful craftsmanship** serves unity by ensuring that every word must contribute to the story's design.
4. Poe also believed that reading should take place in **one sitting** so that the story's unity is not lost.
5. A character is **revealed** through a series of incidents or a conflict. The short story generally stops when it has achieved this purpose. A novel **develops** a character throughout its many chapters.

Now that we have briefly explored the history of the short story and heard from a few of its creators, let us consider the role of the reader. Readers are not empty vessels that wait, lids raised, to receive a teacher's or a critic's interpretation. They bring their unique life experiences to the story. With these associations, the best readers also bring their attention (a word that means "leaning towards"), their reading skills, and, most importantly, their imagination to a reading of a story.

My students always challenged me to discuss, analyze, interpret, and evaluate the stories we read without destroying the thrill of being beamed up into another world. For years I grappled with one response after the other to this challenge. Then one day I read an article by a botanist who had explored the beauty of flowers by x-raying them. His illustrations showed the rose and the lily in their external beauty, and his x-rays presented the wonders of their construction. I brought the article to class, where we discussed the benefits of examining the internal design of flowers, relationships, current events, and short stories.

A short story, however, is not a fossil to admire. Readers must ask questions, guess at the answers, predict what will happen next, then read to discover. They and the author form a partnership that brings the story to life. Awareness of this partnership keeps the original excitement alive through discussion, analysis, interpretation, and evaluation. Literary explorations allow the reader to admire the authors' craftsmanship as well as their artistry. In fact, original appreciation may be enhanced by this x-ray vision. The final step is to appreciate once again the story in its entirety—to put the pieces back together.

Now it is your turn. Form a partnership with your author. During or following your adventure in reading, enter into a dialogue with the published scholars featured in *Short Stories for Students.* Through this dialogue with experts you will revise, enrich, and/or confirm your original observations and interpretations.

During this adventure, I hope you will feel the same awe that illuminates the faces of the listeners that surround the neck of my Pueblo storyteller.

Nancy Rosenberger
Conestoga High School
Berwyn, Pennsylvania

Introduction

Purpose of the Book

The purpose of *Short Stories for Students* (*SSfS*) is to provide readers with a guide to understanding, enjoying, and studying short stories by giving them easy access to information about the work. Part of Gale's ''For Students'' Literature line, *SSfS* is specifically designed to meet the curricular needs of high school and undergraduate college students and their teachers, as well as the interests of general readers and researchers considering specific short fiction. While each volume contains entries on classic stories frequently studied in classrooms, there are also entries containing hard-to-find information on contemporary stories, including works by multicultural, international, and women writers.

The information covered in each entry includes an introduction to the story and the story's author; a plot summary, to help readers unravel and understand the events in the work; descriptions of important characters, including explanation of a given character's role in the narrative as well as discussion about that character's relationship to other characters in the story; analysis of important themes in the story; and an explanation of important literary techniques and movements as they are demonstrated in the work.

In addition to this material, which helps the readers analyze the story itself, students are also provided with important information on the literary and historical background informing each work. This includes a historical context essay, a box comparing the time or place the story was written to modern Western culture, a critical overview essay, and excerpts from critical essays on the story or author. A unique feature of *SSfS* is a specially commissioned overview essay on each story by an academic expert, targeted toward the student reader.

To further aid the student in studying and enjoying each story, information on media adaptations is provided, as well as reading suggestions for works of fiction and nonfiction on similar themes and topics. Classroom aids include ideas for research papers and lists of critical sources that provide additional material on the work.

Selection Criteria

The titles for each volume of *SSfS* were selected by surveying numerous sources on teaching literature and analyzing course curricula for various school districts. Some of the sources surveyed include: literature anthologies, *Reading Lists for College-Bound Students: The Books Most Recommended by America's Top Colleges; Teaching the Short Story: A Guide to Using Stories from Around the World,* by the National Council of Teachers of English (NTCE); and ''A Study of High School Literature Anthologies,'' conducted by Arthur Applebee at the Center for the Learning and Teaching of Literature and sponsored by the National Endowment for the Arts and the Office of Educational Research and Improvement.

Input was also solicited from our expert advisory board, as well as educators from various areas. From these discussions, it was determined that each volume should have a mix of ''classic'' stories (those works commonly taught in literature classes) and contemporary stories for which information is often hard to find. Because of the interest in expanding the canon of literature, an emphasis was also placed on including works by international, multicultural, and women authors. Our advisory board members—current high-school teachers—helped pare down the list for each volume. Works not selected for the present volume were noted as possibilities for future volumes. As always, the editor welcomes suggestions for titles to be included in future volumes.

How Each Entry Is Organized

Each entry, or chapter, in *SSfS* focuses on one story. Each entry heading lists the title of the story, the author's name, and the date of the story's publication. The following elements are contained in each entry:

- **Introduction:** a brief overview of the story which provides information about its first appearance, its literary standing, any controversies surrounding the work, and major conflicts or themes within the work.
- **Author Biography:** this section includes basic facts about the author's life, and focuses on events and times in the author's life that may have inspired the story in question.
- **Plot Summary:** a description of the events in the story, with interpretation of how these events help articulate the story's themes.
- **Characters:** an alphabetical listing of the characters who appear in the story. Each character name is followed by a brief to an extensive description of the character's role in the story, as well as discussion of the character's actions, relationships, and possible motivation.

  Characters are listed alphabetically by last name. If a character is unnamed—for instance, the narrator in ''The Eatonville Anthology''—the character is listed as ''The Narrator'' and alphabetized as ''Narrator.'' If a character's first name is the only one given, the name will appear alphabetically by that name.
- **Themes:** a thorough overview of how the topics, themes, and issues are addressed within the story. Each theme discussed appears in a separate subhead, and is easily accessed through the boldface entries in the Subject/Theme Index.
- **Style:** this section addresses important style elements of the story, such as setting, point of view, and narration; important literary devices used, such as imagery, foreshadowing, symbolism; and, if applicable, genres to which the work might have belonged, such as Gothicism or Romanticism. Literary terms are explained within the entry, but can also be found in the Glossary of Literary Terms.
- **Historical and Cultural Context:** This section outlines the social, political, and cultural climate *in which the author lived and the work was created.* This section may include descriptions of related historical events, pertinent aspects of daily life in the culture, and the artistic and literary sensibilities of the time in which the work was written. If the story is historical in nature, information regarding the time in which the story is set is also included. Long sections are broken down with helpful subheads.
- **Critical Overview:** this section provides background on the critical reputation of the author and the story, including bannings or any other public controversies surrounding the work. For older works, this section may include a history of how story was first received and how perceptions of it may have changed over the years; for more recent works, direct quotes from early reviews may also be included.
- **Sources:** an alphabetical list of critical material quoted in the entry, with bibliographical information.
- **For Further Study:** an alphabetical list of other critical sources which may prove useful for the student. Includes full bibliographical information and a brief annotation.
- **Criticism:** an essay commissioned by *SSfS* which specifically deals with the story and is written specifically for the student audience, as well as excerpts from previously published criticism on the work.

In addition, each entry contains the following highlighted sections, if applicable, set separate from the main text:

- **Media Adaptations:** where applicable, a list of film and television adaptations of the story, including source information. The list also includes stage adaptations, audio recordings, musical adaptations, etc.

- **Compare and Contrast Box:** an ''at-a-glance'' comparison of the cultural and historical differences between the author's time and culture and late twentieth-century Western culture. This box includes pertinent parallels between the major scientific, political, and cultural movements of the time or place the story was written, the time or place the story was set (if a historical work), and modern Western culture. Works written after the mid-1970s may not have this box.
- **What Do I Read Next?:** a list of works that might complement the featured story or serve as a contrast to it. This includes works by the same author and others, works of fiction and nonfiction, and works from various genres, cultures, and eras.
- **Study Questions:** a list of potential study questions or research topics dealing with the story. This section includes questions related to other disciplines the student may be studying, such as American history, world history, science, math, government, business, geography, economics, psychology, etc.

Other Features

SSfS includes ''An Adventure in Reading,'' a foreword by Nancy Rosenberger, chair of the English department at Conestoga High School in Berwyn, Pennsylvania. This essay provides an enlightening look at how readers interact with literature and how *Short Stories for Students* can help students enrich their own reading experiences.

A Cumulative Author/Title Index lists the authors and titles covered in each volume of the *SSfS* series.

A Cumulative Nationality/Ethnicity Index breaks down the authors and titles covered in each volume of the *SSfS* series by nationality and ethnicity.

A Subject/Theme Index, specific to each volume, provides easy reference for users who may be studying a particular subject or theme rather than a single work. Significant subjects from events to broad themes are included, and the entries pointing to the specific theme discussions in each entry are indicated in **boldface.**

Entries may include illustrations, including an author portrait, stills from film adaptations (when available), maps, and/or photos of key historical events.

Citing Short Stories for Students

When writing papers, students who quote directly from any volume of *SSfS* may use the following general forms to document their source. These examples are based on MLA style; teachers may request that students adhere to a different style, thus, the following examples may be adapted as needed.

When citing text from *SSfS* that is not attributed to a particular author (for example, the Themes, Style, Historical Context sections, etc.) the following format may be used:

''The Celebrated Jumping Frog of Calaveras County.'' *Short Stories for Students.* Ed. Kathleen Wilson. Vol. 1. Detroit: Gale, 1997. 19-20.

When quoting the specially commissioned essay from *SSfS* (usually the first essay under the Criticism subhead), the following format may be used:

Korb, Rena. Essay on ''Children of the Sea.'' *Short Stories for Students.* Ed. Kathleen Wilson. Vol. 1. Detroit: Gale, 1997. 42.

When quoting a journal essay that is reprinted in a volume of *Short Stories for Students,* the following form may be used:

Schmidt, Paul. ''The Deadpan on Simon Wheeler.'' *The Southwest Review* XLI, No. 3 (Summer, 1956), 270-77; excerpted and reprinted in *Short Stories for Students,* Vol. 1, ed. Kathleen Wilson (Detroit: Gale, 1997), pp. 29-31.

When quoting material from a book that is reprinted in a volume of *SSfS,* the following form may be used:

Bell-Villada, Gene H. ''The Master of Short Forms,'' in *Garcia Marquez: The Man and His Work* (University of North Carolina Press, 1990); excerpted and reprinted in *Short Stories for Students,* Vol. 1, ed. Kathleen Wilson (Detroit: Gale, 1997), pp. 90-1.

We Welcome Your Suggestions

The editor of *Short Stories for Students* welcomes your comments and ideas. Readers who wish to suggest short stories to appear in future volumes, or who have other suggestions, are cordially invited to contact the editor. You may write to the editor at:

Editor, *Short Stories for Students*
Gale Research
835 Penobscot Bldg.
645 Griswold St.
Detroit, MI 48226-4094

Literary Chronology

1776: The signing of the Declaration of Independence signals the beginning of the American Revolution.

1789: The French Revolution, marked by the violent Reign of Terror, shifts the balance of power in France.

1804: Nathaniel Hawthorne is born in Salem, Massachusetts, on July 4.

1834: Frank R. Stockton is born in Philadelphia.

1836: Bret Harte is born in Albany, New York, on August 25.

1850: *The Scarlet Letter,* Nathaniel Hawthorne's novel of a minister's involvement with a married woman, is published.

1853: "Bartleby the Scrivener, A Tale of Wall Street" by Herman Melville is published in *Putnam's* magazine.

1861: The U.S. Civil War begins when Confederate forces capture Fort Sumter in South Carolina.

1864: Nathaniel Hawthorne dies in Plymouth, New Hampshire, on May 19.

1865: The U.S. Civil War ends; Abraham Lincoln is assassinated.

1866: H. G. Wells is born in England on September 21.

1867: John Galsworthy is born in Surrey, England, on August 14.

1869: "The Outcasts of Poker Flat" by Bret Harte is published in *Overland Monthly* magazine.

1876: Susan Glaspell is born in Davenport, Iowa, on July 1.

1882: "The Lady, or the Tiger?" by Frank Stockton is published in *Century* magazine.

1883: Franz Kafka is born in Prague, Bohemia, on July 3.

1898: *The War of the Worlds,* H. G. Wells's early science fiction classic, is published.

1902: John Steinbeck is born in Salinas, California, on February 27.

1902: Frank Stockton dies in Washington, DC.

1902: Bret Harte dies in Surrey, England, on May 5.

1908: Richard Wright is born near Natchez, Mississippi, on September 4.

1910: "The Japanese Quince" by John Galsworthy is published.

1911: *The Door in the Wall and Other Stories* by H. G. Wells is published.

1912: The *R.M.S. Titanic* sinks on her maiden voyage from Southampton, England, to New York.

1914: Julio Cortazar is born in Brussels, Belgium, on August 26.

1914: With the assassination of Archduke Ferdinand of Austria, long-festering tensions in Europe erupt into what becomes known as the Great War.

1915: *The Metamorphosis,* Franz Kafka's novella about a man who wakes up and finds that he has been transformed into a cockroach, is published.

1917: ''A Jury of Her Peers'' by Susan Glaspell is published.

1918: World War I, the most deadly war in history, ends with the signing of the Treaty of Versailles.

1919: ''In the Penal Colony,'' written by Franz Kafka in 1914, is published. The first English translation of the story does not appear until 1948.

1920: The 18th Amendment, outlawing the sale, manufacture, and transportation of alcohol—known as Prohibition—goes into effect. This law led to the creation of ''speakeasies''—illegal bars—and an increase in organized crime. The law is repealed in 1933.

1922: *The Forsyte Saga,* John Galsworthy's novel with characters based on his own family members, is published.

1922: Grace Paley is born in New York City on December 11.

1924: Franz Kafka dies in Kierling, Austria, on June 3.

1928: Cynthia Ozick is born in New York City on April 17.

1929: The stock market crash in October signals the beginning of a worldwide economic depression.

1930: Chinua Achebe is born in Ogidi, Nigeria, on November 16.

1931: Donald Barthelme is born in Philadelphia on April 7.

1932: John Updike is born in Pennsylvania on March 18.

1933: John Galsworthy dies in London, on January 31.

1937: *Out of Africa,* Isak Dinesen's novel about plantation life in Kenya, is published.

1938: ''Flight'' by John Steinbeck is published in the collection *The Long Valley.*

1938: Raymond Carver is born in Oregon on May 25.

1939: World War II begins when Nazi Germany, led by Adolf Hitler, invades Poland; England and France declare war in response.

1939: *The Grapes of Wrath,* John Steinbeck's tale of the Joad family's displacement from the dust bowl of Oklahoma to the harsh farming life in California, is published.

1939: Margaret Atwood is born in Ottawa, Ontario, on November 18.

1940: *Native Son,* Richard Wright's novel about Bigger Thomas, a man condemned to death for the murder of a white woman, is published.

1940: Bobbie Ann Mason is born in rural Kentucky on May 1.

1940: Maxine Hong Kingston is born in Stockton, California, on October 27.

1942: ''The Man Who Lived Underground'' by Richard Wright is published in *Accent* magazine.

1942: ''Sorrow-Acre'' by Isak Dinesen is published in her collection *Winter's Tales.*

1945: World War II ends in August with the atomic bombing of Hiroshima and Nagasaki, Japan.

1946: H. G. Wells dies in London on August 13.

1948: Susan Glaspell dies in New York City.

1950: Senator Joseph McCarthy of Wisconsin sets off the ''Red Scare'' that leads to government hearings and blacklisting of suspected communists.

1954: Sandra Cisneros is born in Chicago.

1956: ''Axolotl'' by Julio Cortazar is published in *Final del juego.*

1958: *Things Fall Apart,* Chinua Achebe's classic novel about the Ibo society of Nigeria before British colonization, is published.

1960: Richard Wright dies in Paris on November 28.

1960: *Rabbit, Run,* John Updike's novel of a working-class man who constantly relives his high-school glory days, is published.

1961: ''A & P'' by John Updike is published in the *New Yorker.*

1963: President John F. Kennedy is assassinated in Dallas, Texas, on November 22.

1963: *Hopscotch,* Julio Cortazar's ground-breaking novel of 155 chapters, is published.

1968: ''Robert Kennedy Saved From Drowning'' by Donald Barthelme is published in his collection *Unspeakable Practices, Unnatural Acts.*

1968: John Steinbeck dies in New York City on December 20.

1971: ''Vengeful Creditor'' by Chinua Achebe is published in his journal, *Okike.*

1972: ''A Conversation with My Father'' by Grace Paley is published in the *New American Review.*

1974: President Richard Nixon resigns following the Watergate scandal.

1977: ''Rape Fantasies'' by Margaret Atwood is published in the Canadian edition of *Dancing Girls and Other Stories.*

1980: ''The Shawl'' by Cynthia Ozick is published in the *New Yorker.*

1980: ''On Discovery'' by Maxine Hong Kingston is published in her book *China Men.*

1982: ''Where I'm Calling From'' by Raymond Carver is published in the *New Yorker.*

1982: ''Shiloh'' by Bobbie Ann Mason is published in the *New Yorker.*

1984: Julio Cortazar dies in Paris on February 12.

1985: *In Country,* Bobbie Ann Mason's novel about the social effects of the Vietnam War, is published.

1986: *The Handmaid's Tale,* Margaret Atwood's novel about the futuristic dystopian society of Gilead, is published.

1988: Raymond Carver dies in Washington on August 2.

1989: Donald Barthelme dies in Houston on July 23.

1990: Soviet leader Mikhail Gorbachev's policy of *glasnost* results in the fracturing of the Iron Curtain. By December the Soviet flag is lowered from the Kremlin.

1991: ''Woman Hollering Creek'' by Sandra Cisneros is published in her collection, *Woman Hollering Creek and Other Stories.*

Acknowledgments

The editors wish to thank the copyright holders of the excerpted criticism included in this volume and the permissions managers of many book and magazine publishing companies for assisting us in securing reproduction rights. We are also grateful to the staffs of the Detroit Public Library, the Library of Congress, the University of Detroit Mercy Library, Wayne State University Purdy/Kresge Library Complex, and the University of Michigan Libraries for making their resources available to us. Following is a list of the copyright holders who have granted us permission to reproduce material in this volume of *SSFS*. **Every effort has been made to trace copyright, but if omissions have been made, please let us know.**

COPYRIGHTED EXCERPTS IN *SSFS,* VOLUME 3, WERE REPRODUCED FROM THE FOLLOWING PERIODICALS:

Bulletin of Hispanic Studies, v. LIV, April, 1977. Copyright ©1977 Liverpool University Press. Reproduced by permission.—***College Literature,*** v. 23, October, 1996. Copyright ©1996 by West Chester University. Reproduced by permission of the publisher.—***Comparative Literature Studies,*** v. 21, Winter, 1984. Copyright ©1984 by The Pennsylvania State University. Reproduced by permission of The Pennsylvania State University Press.—***Critique: Studies in Contemporary Fiction,*** v. XXXI, Fall, 1989. Copyright 1989 by Helen Dwight Reid Educational Foundation. Reproduced with permission of the Helen Dwight Reid Educational Foundation, published by Heldref Publications, 1319 18th Street, NW, Washington, DC 20036-1802.—***Delta,*** May, 1982 for "A Different Responsibility: Form and Technique in G. Paley's 'A Conversation with My Father'" by Nicholas Peter Humy. Reproduced by permission of the author.—***English Language Notes,*** v. XXX, December, 1992. ©copyrighted 1992, Regents of the University of Colorado. Reproduced by permission.—***The Explicator,*** v. XXIV, September, 1965; v. 45, Winter, 1987; v. 45, Winter, 1987; v. 51, Spring, 1993. Copyright 1965, 1987, 1989, 1993 by Helen Dwight Reid Educational Foundation. All reproduced with permission of the Helen Dwight Reid Educational Foundation, published by Heldref Publications, 1319 18th Street, NW, Washington, DC 20036-1802.—***Indian Journal of American Studies,*** v. 4, June & December, 1974. Copyright ©1974 by American Studies Research Centre. Reproduced by permission.—***Journal of Black Studies,*** v. 8, March, 1978. Copyright ©1978 by Sage Publications, Inc. Reproduced by permission of Sage Publications, Inc.—***The Journal of Narrative Technique,*** v. 15, Winter, 1985 for "Covert Plot in Isak Dinesen's 'Sorrow-Acre'" by David H. Richter. Reproduced by permission of the publisher and the author.—***Journal of the Short Story in English,*** Autumn, 1989. ©Université d'Angers, 1989. Reproduced by permission.—***Kentucky Romance Quarterly,*** v. 30, 1983. Copyright ©1983 Helen Dwight Reid

Educational Foundation. Reproduced with permission of the Helen Dwight Reid Educational Foundation, published by Heldref Publications, 1319 18th Street, NW, Washington, DC 20036-1802.—***Literature and Psychology,*** v. XXXX, 1994. ©Morton Kaplan 1994. Reproduced by permission.—***MELUS,*** v. 19, Spring, 1994; v. 21, Summer 1996. Copyright, *MELUS,* The Society for the Study of Multi-Ethnic Literature of the United States, 1994, 1996. Both reproduced by permission.—***Modern Fiction Studies,*** v. 35, Winter, 1989 The Johns Hopkins University Press. All rights reserved. Reproduced by permission of the Johns Hopkins University Press.—***Negro American Literature Forum,*** v. 4, July, 1970 for "The Identity of 'The Man Who Lived Underground'" by Shirley Meyer. Copyright ©1970 by the author. Reproduced by permission of the publisher.—***Partisan Review,*** v. XLVIII, 1981 for "Mrs. Hegel-Shtein's Tears" by Marianne DeKoven. Copyright ©1981 by Partisan Review. Reproduced by permission of the author.—***Shenandoah,*** v. XXXII, 1981 for an interview with Grace Paley by Joan Lidoff. Copyright 1981 by Washington and Lee University. Reproduced from Shenandoah with the permission of the Editor, The Literary Estate of Joan Lidoff, and Grace Paley.—***The Southern Literary Journal,*** v. 18, Spring, 1986. Copyright 1986 by the Department of English, University of North Carolina at Chapel Hill. Reproduced by permission.—***Southern Literary Review,*** v. 21, Spring, 1989. Copyright 1989 by the Department of English, University of North Carolina at Chapel Hill. Reproduced by permission.—***Studies in Short Fiction,*** v. 3, Summer, 1966; v. 17, Fall, 1980; v. 20, Spring-Summer, 1983; v. 25, Summer, 1988; v. 29, Winter, 1992; v. 30, Spring, 1993. Copyright 1966, 1980, 1983, 1988, 1992, 1993 by Newberry College. All reproduced by permission.—***Teaching English in the Two-Year College,*** v. 25, 1998 for "I Just Don't Understand It': Teaching Margaret Atwood's 'Rape Fantasies'" by Lisa Tyler. Copyright ©1998 by the National Council of Teachers of English. Reproduced by permission of the publisher and the author.—***Women's Studies,*** v. 12, 1986. Copyright ©1986 Gordon and Breach Science Publishers, Inc. Reproduced by permission.

COPYRIGHTED EXCERPTS IN *SSFS,* VOLUME 3, WERE REPRODUCED FROM THE FOLLOWING BOOKS:

Balogun, F. Odun. From ***Tradition and Modernity in the African Short Story: An Introduction to a Literature in Search of Critics.*** Greenwood Press, 1991. Copyright ©1991 by F. Odun Balogun. All rights reserved. Reproduced by permission of Greenwood Publishing Group, Inc., Westport, CT.—Berger, Alan R. From ***Crisis and Covenant: The Holocaust in American Jewish Fiction.*** State University of New York Press, 1985. ©1985 State University of New York Press. All rights reserved. Reproduced by permission State University of New York Press.—Bergonzi, Bernard. From ***The Early H. G. Wells: A Study of the Scientific Romances.*** Manchester University Press, 1961. ©1961 Bernard Bergonzi. Reproduced by permission of The Peters Fraser & Dunlop Group Limited on behalf of Bernard Bergonzi.—Brooks, Cleanth and Robert Penn Warren. From ***Understanding Fiction.*** Edited by Cleanth Brooks and Robert Penn Warren. Second edition. Appleton-Century-Crofts, 1959. Copyright 1959, renewed 1987, by Appleton-Century-Crofts, Inc. All rights reserved. Adapted by permission of Prentice-Hall, Inc., Upper Saddle River, NJ.—Buckley, Jerome Hamilton. From ***The Triumph of Time: A Study of Victorian Concepts of Time, History, Progress, and Decadence.*** Cambridge, Mass.: The Belknap Press of Harvard University Press, 1966. Copyright ©1966 by the President and Fellows of Harvard College. Reproduced by permission of the publishers.—Fetterley, Judith. From ***Gender and Reading: Essays on Readers, Texts, and Context.*** Edited by Elizabeth A. Flynn and Patrocinio P. Schweickart. The John Hopkins University Press, 1986. ©1986 The John Hopkins University Press. All rights reserved. Reproduced by permission of The Johns Hopkins University Press.—Greiner, Donald J. From ***The Other John Updike: Poems, Short Stories, Prose, Play.*** Ohio University Press, 1981. Copyright ©1981 by Ohio University Press. Reproduced by permission of the author.—Hammond, J. R. From ***H. G. Wells and the Short Story.*** St. Martin's Press, 1992. Copyright ©J. R. Hammond 1992. All rights reserved. Reproduced by permission of Macmillan Press Ltd. In North America with permission of St. Martin's Press, Incorporated.—Haynes, Roslynn D. From ***H. G. Wells: Discoverer of the Future: The Influence of Science on His Thought.*** New York University Press, 1980. ©R. D. Haynes 1980. Reproduced by permission.—Innes, C. L. From ***Chinua Achebe.*** Cambridge University Press, 1990. ©Cambridge University Press 1990. Reproduced by permission of the publisher and the author.—Jacobsen, Sally A. From ***Approaches to Teaching Atwood'sThe Handmaid's Tale and Other Works.*** The Modern Language Association of America, 1996. ©1996 by The Modern Language Association of America. All rights reserved. Reproduced by permission of the publisher.—Johannesson, Eric O. From ***The World of Isak Dinesen.*** University of Washington Press. ©copyright 1961 by the University of Washington Press. Renewed 1989 by Eric O. Johannesson. Reproduced by permission.—Molesworth, Charles. From ***Donald Barthelme's Fiction: The Ironist Saved from Drowning.*** University of Missouri Press, 1982. Copyright ©1982 by The Curators of the University of Missouri. All rights reserved. Reproduced by permission of the University of Missouri Press.—Oriard, Michael. From ***Sporting with the Gods: The Rhetoric of Play and Game in American Culture.*** Cambridge University Press, 1991. ©Cambridge University Press 1991. Reproduced with permission of the publisher and the author.—Shih, Shu mei. From ''Exile and Intertextuality in Maxine Hong Kingston's China Men'' in ***Studies in Comparative Literature: The Literature of Emigration and Exile.*** Edited by James Whitlark and Wendell Aycock. Texas Tech University Press, 1992. Copyright ©1992 Texas Tech University Press. All rights reserved. Reproduced by permission.—Thompson, Lee Briscoe. From ''Minuets and Madness: Margaret Atwood's Dancing Girls'' for ***The Art of Margaret Atwood: Essays in Criticism.*** Edited by Arnold E. Davidson and Cathy N. Davidson. Anansi, 1981. Copyright ©1981, House of Anansi Press Limited. All rights reserved. Reproduced by permission.—Timmerman, John H. From ***The Dramatic Landscape of Steinbeck's Short Stories.*** University of Oklahoma Press, 1990. Copyright ©1990 by the University of Oklahoma Press. All rights reserved. Reproduced by permission.—Trachtenberg, Stanley. From ***Understanding Donald Barthelme.*** University of South Carolina Press, 1990. Copyright ©University of South Carolina 1990. Reproduced by permission.

COMMISSIONED ESSAY(S) FOR *SSFS,* VOLUME 3, WERE RECEIVED FROM THE FOLLOWING SOURCES:

''Commentary on 'Shiloh','' by Bobbie Ann Mason. Copyright ©1997 by Bobbie Ann Mason. Reproduced by permission of the author.

PHOTOGRAPHS AND ILLUSTRATIONS APPEARING IN *SSFS,* VOLUME 3, WERE RECEIVED FROM THE FOLLOWING SOURCES:

An Albino Axolotl, from Mexico, photograph by Breck P. Kent. Breck P. Kent/JLM Visuals. Reproduced by permission.—A photograph of a doorway from ''The Door in the Wall'' by H. G. Wells, photograph by Alvin Langdon Coburn. Courtesy George Eastman House. Reproduced by permission.—A scene from the film ''Out of Africa,'' 1985, by Universal Studios, based on the novel by Isak Dinesen, photograph. Universal Studios. Courtesy of The Kobal Collection. Reproduced by permission.—A view of the rooftops of central Ibadan, Nigeria's second largest city, photograph by Paul Almasy. Paul Almasy/©Corbis. Reproduced by permission.—Achebe, Chinua, photograph. AP/ Wide World Photos. Reproduced by permission.—An A & P store on Northern Blvd., 62nd Street, photograph. Henry Hammond/ Archive Photos, Inc. Reproduced by permission.—An Old Household Kitchen, photograph. Hirz/ Archive Photos, Inc. Reproduced by permission.—Atwood, Margaret, photograph. The Library of Congress.—Barthelme, Donald, photograph by Jerry Bauer. ©Jerry Bauer. Reproduced by permission.—Carver, Raymond, photograph by Jerry Bauer. ©Jerry Bauer. Reproduced by permission.—Cisneros, Sandra, photograph. AP/Wide World Photos. Reproduced by permission.—Cortazar, Julio, photograph by Jerry Bauer. ©Jerry Bauer. Reproduced by permission.—Dinesen, Isak, photograph. Archive Photos, Inc. Reproduced with permission.—Galsworthy, John, photograph. Hulton-Deutsch Collection/ Corbis. Reproduced by permission.—Glaspell, Susan, photograph. AP/Wide World Photos. Reproduced by permission.—Gold Rush, photograph. Archive Photos, Inc. Reproduced by permission.—Harte, Bret, photograph. AP/Wide World Photos. Reproduced by permission.—Illustration of Chinese Women With Bound Feet, photograph by Leonard de Selva. Leonard de Selva/Corbis. Reproduced by permission.—Kafka, Franz, photograph. AP/Wide World Photos. Reproduced by permission.—Kennedy, Robert, photograph. John F. Kennedy Library.—Kingston, Maxine Hong, photograph by Miriam Berkley. Reproduced by permission of the photographer.—Map of Nigeria (showing major land formations and towns), illustration. Gale Research Inc. Reproduced by permission.—Mason, Bobbie Anne, photograph by Jerry Bauer. ©Jerry Bauer. Reproduced by permission.—Melville, Herman, (a painting), photograph. Archive Photos, Inc. Reproduced by permission.—Oliver E. Almis's Dairy Farm in Power, North Dakota, photograph. From the Potter Collection/ Archive Photos, Inc. Reproduced by permission.—Ozick, Cynthia, photograph by Thomas Victor. Copyright ©1986 by Thomas Victor. All rights reserved. Reproduced by permission of the estate of Thomas Victor.—Paley,

Grace, photograph. AP/Wide World Photos. Reproduced by permission.—Printing plant, photograph. Corbis-Bettmann. Reproduced by permission.—Shiloh National Military Park Cemetery, photograph. Archive Photos, Inc. Reproduced by permission.—Steinbeck, John, photograph. Archive Photos, Inc. Reproduced by permission.—Stockton, Frank R., photograph. Corbis-Bettmann. Reproduced by permission.—Survivors of the Dachau, WWII Concentration Camp, photograph. AP/Wide World Photos. Reproduced by permission.—The ripening greenish-yellow fruit of the quince tree, photograph by Patrick Johns. Patrick Johns/Corbis. Reproduced by permission.—Updike, John, photograph. AP/Wide World Photos. Reproduced by permission.—Wall Street, photograph. UPI/Corbis-Bettmann. Reproduced by permission.—Wells, H. G., photograph. AP/Wide World Photos. Reproduced by permission.—Wright, Richard, photograph. AP/Wide World Photos. Reproduced by permission.—Yukon Trail, photograph. UPI/Corbis-Bettmann. Reproduced by permission.

Contributors

BARKSDALE, Allen. Ph.D. candidate in American Culture Studies at Bowling Green State University and an instructor at Owens Community College. Entry: "The Outcasts of Poker Flat."

BARNHISEL, Greg. Ph.D. in English from University of Texas at Austin and instructor of English. Entry: "Vengeful Creditor."

BILY, Cynthia. Instructor of writing and literature at Adrian College in Michigan. Contributor to reference publications, including *Feminist Writers, Gay and Lesbian Biography,* and *Chronology of Women Worldwide.* Entry: "The Man Who Lived Underground."

CHANDLER, Gregory. Story analyst for TriStar Pictures, with degrees from UCLA and Columbia University. Entries: "Axolotl" and "The Door in the Wall."

DOMINIC, Catherine. Editor of *Shakespeare's Characters for Students* and a freelance writer. Entries: Compare and contrast sections for many entries.

ELLIOT, Mark. Ph.D. candidate in history at New York University. Editor of the "New England Puritan Literature" section for the *Cambridge History of American Literature.* Entry: "Bartleby the Scrivener."

GARDINER-SCOTT, Tanya. Associate professor of English at Mount Ida College in Newton, Massachusetts. Entry: "The Lady, or the Tiger?"

GRIFFIN, Tery. Faculty member of Trinity College in East Hartford, Connecticut, and author of several short stories, plays, and essays. Entry: "The Shawl."

HENNINGFELD, Diane Andrews. Assistant professor of English at Adrian College in Michigan and contributor to reference works for Salem Press. Entry: "Shiloh."

HENRY, Richard. Assistant professor of English at State University of New York at Potsdam. Entry: "Robert Kennedy Saved from Drowning."

HICKS, Jennifer. Freelance writer on literature and founder of a writing firm specializing in Web content. Entry: "Woman Hollering Creek."

KIPPEN, David. Ph.D. in English from State University of New York at Stony Brook and a specialist in British colonial literature and twentieth-century South African literature. Entries: "Sorrow-Acre," "Vengeful Creditor," and "The Japanese Quince."

KORB, Rena. Freelance writer and editor specializing in English literature and education. Entry: "Conversation with My Father."

LEVERICH, Jean. Ph.D. in literature from University of Michigan. Instructor of English at

University of Michigan, New York University, and Georgetown University. Entry: ''On Discovery.''

MADSEN HARDY, Sarah. Ph.D. in English from University of Michigan. Entries: ''Axolotl'' and ''The Lady, or the Tiger?''

MUNRO, Joyce. Lawyer with UAW-Ford Legal Services and Ph.D. candidate in British and American literature and Wayne State University in Detroit. Entry: ''Flight.''

ORTIZ, Lisa. Ph.D. candidate in English and literature at Wayne State University, instructor of writing and composition. Entry: ''A Jury of Her Peers.''

PELTIER, Robert. Instructor of English at Trinity College in East Hartford, Connecticut. Entry: ''A & P.''

PIEDMONT-MARTON, Elisabeth. Ph.D. in English from University of Texas at Austin and coordinator of the university's writing center. Entry: ''Vengeful Creditor.''

ROUSTER, William. Ph.D. in composition from Wayne State University in Detroit, and instructor of composition and rhetoric at Wayne State University, Oakland University, and Eastern Michigan University. Entry: ''Woman Hollering Creek.''

SMITH, Barbara. Designer and facilitator of multicultural workshops for educators. Entry: ''Woman Hollering Creek.''

SONKOWSKI, Mike. Director's assistant at the Temple University Center for Intergenerational Learning. Instructor of English at the University of Pennsylvania. Entry: ''Where I'm Calling From.''

SPEIRS, Kenneth. Ph.D. candidate in English at New York University. Entry: ''The Japanese Quince.''

THORN, Michael. Author of *Tennyson* (1992), a biography of the English poet, and a reviewer for the *Times Educational Supplement.* Entry: ''In the Penal Colony.''

TRUBEK, Anne. Ph.D. candidate in English at Temple University in Philadelphia, and instructor of English and literature. Entry: ''A Conversation with My Father.''

WALTER, Catherine. Instructor of English as a second language at Temple University in Philadelphia, and instructor of English at Pennsylvania State University, Drexel University, and Pierce College. Entry: ''Rape Fantasies.''

WILLIAMS, Deborah. Freelance writer and former instructor at Rutgers University. Entry: ''The Door in the Wall.''

WILSON, Kathleen. Editor and freelance writer. Entries: ''The Lady, or the Tiger?,'' ''Rape Fantasies.''

A & P

John Updike

1961

John Updike's short story "A & P" was first published in the July 22, 1961 issue of the *New Yorker,* and was published again the following year in the author's collection *Pigeon Feathers and Other Stories.* Arthur Mizener's review of the collection in the *New York Times Book Review* exalted Updike in terms that soon became commonplace for the writer: "his natural talent is so great that for some time it has been a positive handicap to him." Almost forty years later, "A & P" remains Updike's most anthologized story and one of his most popular.

Sammy's encounter with a trio of swimsuited girls in the grocery store where he works encompasses many of the themes central to adolescence, including accepting the repercussions of one's choices. When Sammy quits in protest of how the girls are treated by the store's manager, he knows that from now on, the world will be a more difficult place.

Critics have responded enthusiastically to "A & P," and readers' identification with Sammy's predicament has contributed to the story's popularity. Though little action occurs in the story, Sammy's character is finely drawn in the space of a few pages, and his brush with authority has large implications. He has been compared to Holden Caulfield, J. D. Salinger's protagonist in *Catcher in the Rye,* and Walter Wells has suggested that Sammy's moment of protest is similar to the "epiphany" of the

narrator in James Joyce's story "Araby," a comment that places Updike in the pantheon of the most accomplished writers of the twentieth century. Negative reactions to the story center on what some readers perceive as Sammy's misogynist views. Other critics consider "A & P" a slight story, though one into which a lifetime of dignity, choices, and consequences is compressed.

Author Biography

John Updike is one of America's most prolific authors. He has written novels, short stories, essays, poetry, reviews, articles, memoirs, art criticism, and even a play. His work has been adapted for television and film, and he has won numerous awards, including a National Book Award and two Pulitzer Prizes. Since 1959 he has published nearly fifty books.

Updike was born on March 18, 1932, in Reading, Pennsylvania and lived in nearby Shillington until he was thirteen. Many of Updike's stories exhibit autobiographical elements, and his fictional town of Olinger is patterned after Shillington. When he was thirteen he moved with his parents and grandparents to a farm in Plowville, Pennsylvania, where his mother had been born. His father was a junior high school math teacher, and his mother a writer who, as her son later did, wrote stories for the *New Yorker* magazine. Updike did well in school, graduated from Shillington High School as co-valedictorian, and attended Harvard University on a scholarship. In college, he wrote for the *Harvard Lampoon.*

In 1953 Updike married Mary Pennington, and the couple traveled to England on a Knox Fellowship. He enrolled in the Ruskin School of Drawing and Fine Art at Oxford, and for a while he considered drawing cartoons for Walt Disney or the *New Yorker.* In 1955 his daughter Elizabeth was born. For the sake of his growing family, Updike took a job at the *New Yorker* which he held for two years before deciding to move to Ipswich, Massachusetts, and devote himself to fiction writing as an independent author. He and Mary eventually had four children before the couple divorced in 1977. He subsequently married Martha Bernhard.

The years 1958 and 1959 were productive, as Updike published his first novel, *Poorhouse Fair,* a collection of short stories, *The Same Door,* and a book of poems, *The Carpentered Hen and Other Tame Creatures.* The following year, the first of his "Rabbit" books, *Rabbit, Run,* introduced the world to Harry Angstrom, a man whose life peaked at eighteen when he was a high-school basketball star. To Harry's continued amazement and sorrow, he lives his life as a shadow of what he used to be.

Critics have praised the character of Harry Angstrom highly, and Updike has won two Pulitzer Prizes for his "Rabbit" books; one in 1982 for *Rabbit Is Rich,* and one in 1991 for *Rabbit at Rest.* Another of Updike's most popular novels is *The Witches of Eastwick,* the story of three divorced women in New England who gain magical skills to attract men. Their enticements backfire when a devilish man moves into the neighborhood. The book was made into a film in 1987 starring Jack Nicholson, Michelle Pfeiffer, Susan Sarandon, and Cher. Throughout the many forms Updike's writing takes—novels, stories, poems, and essays—the author's primary concerns are Protestant, middle-class, contemporary American life, and the roles that marriage, divorce, sexuality, and religion play in it.

Updike told *SSfS* that he wrote "A & P" "in 1961, when I was living in Ipswich, Massachusetts. Driving past the local A & P, I asked myself, 'Why are there no short stories that take place inside an A & P?' I proceeded to write one, based on a glimpse I had had of some girls in bathing suits shopping in the aisles. They looked strikingly naked." Updike added: "Originally the story went on, past the ending it now has: Sammy goes down to the beach to find the girls, and never does find them. But the story's editor at the *New Yorker* thought that the story ended where it now does, and I agreed with him."

Plot Summary

Sammy, the teenaged narrator, begins the story by describing the three girls who have walked into the A & P grocery store where he works. They are wearing nothing but bathing suits. He is so distracted by them that he cannot remember if he rang up a box of crackers or not. As it turns out, he did ring them up, a fact that his customer, "a witch about fifty," lets him know quickly and loudly.

He finishes ringing up the customer's items as the girls, who have disappeared down an aisle, circle back into view. He notices that they are barefoot. He describes each: there's a ''chunky one . . . and a tall one [with] a chin that was too long'' and the ''queen,'' whom he imagines is their leader. She catches his eye for a number of reasons, not the least of which is the fact that the straps of her bathing suit have fallen off her shoulders.

Sammy watches the reactions of the other shoppers to the girls. He refers to the store's other customers as ''sheep'' and ''a few houseslaves in pink pin curlers.'' Another clerk, Stokesie, a married twenty-two year old with two children, trades innuendoes with him. Sammy notes that the store, in a town north of Boston, is five miles from the nearest beach.

The narrator announces that he has come to what his family deems ''the sad part'' of the story, though he does not agree. The girls come to his checkout station, and Queenie puts down a jar of herring snacks and pulls a dollar from her bathing-suit top, a motion that makes Sammy nearly swoon. The store's manager, Lengel, spots the girls and reprimands them for their attire. Lengel further tells them that they should be decently dressed when they shop at the A & P.

Sammy rings up the girls' items, carefully handling the bill that just came from between Queenie's breasts. Other customers appear nervous at the scene Lengel has made at the check-out, and the girls are embarrassed and want to leave quickly. Sammy, in a passionate moment, tells Lengel that he quits. The girls, however, fail to notice his act of chivalry and continue walking out of the store. Lengel asks him if he said something, and Sammy replies, ''I said I quit.'' Lengel, a longtime friend of Sammy's parents, tries to talk him out of it, but Sammy folds his apron, puts it on the counter, punches ''No Sale'' on the cash register, and walks out. He realizes that the world will be a harder place for him from now on.

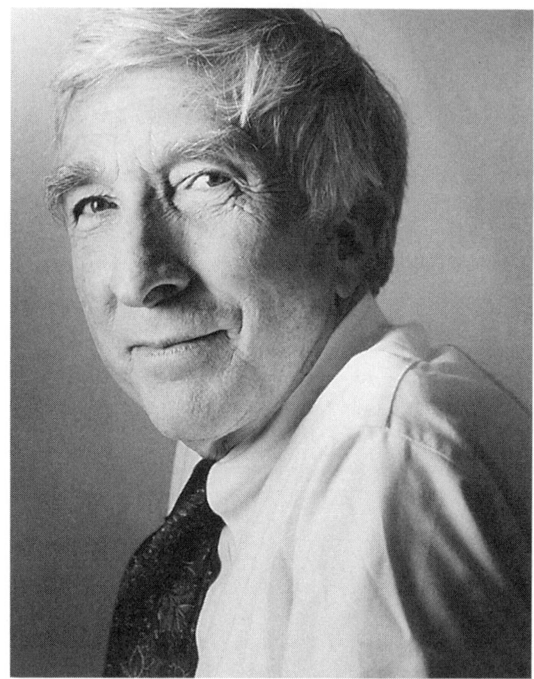

John Updike

Characters

Lengel

Manager of the local A & P, Lengel is a man who spends most of his days behind the door marked ''Manager.'' Entering the story near the end, he represents the system: management, policy, decency, and the way things are. But he is not a one-dimensional character. He has known Sammy's parents for a long time, and he tells Sammy that he should, at least for his parents' sake, not quit his job in such a dramatic, knee-jerk way. He warns Sammy that he will have a hard time dealing with life from now on, should he quit. He seems truly concerned even while he feels the need to enforce store policy.

Queenie

''Queenie'' is the name Sammy gives to the pretty girl who leads her two friends through the grocery store in their bathing suits. He has never seen her before but immediately becomes infatuated with her. He comments on her regal and tantalizing appearance. She is somewhat objectified by nineteen-year-old Sammy, who notes the shape of her body and the seductiveness of the straps which have slipped off her shoulders. When the girls are chastised for their attire by Lengel, Queenie, who Sammy imagines lives in an upper-middle-class world of backyard swimming pools and fancy hor d'oeuvres, becomes ''sore now that she remembers her place, a place from which the crowd that runs the A & P must look pretty crummy.'' Sammy becomes indignant at Lengel's treatment of the girls and tries to help them save face by quitting his job. Queenie, however, appears not to notice and leaves

Media Adaptations

- "A & P" is read by the author on the audiocassette *Couples and Pigeon Feathers,* published by Caedmon Audio Cassette. The cassette also includes the other stories from both collections.

the store promptly, diminishing the impact of Sammy's gesture.

Sammy

Readers do not learn Sammy's name until the end of the story, even though he is the first-person narrator of the story. He is a checkout clerk at an A & P supermarket. His language indicates that, at age nineteen, he is both cynical and romantic. He notes, for instance, that there are "about twenty-seven old freeloaders" working on a sewer main up the street, and he wonders what the "bum" in "baggy gray pants" could possibly do with "four giant cans of pineapple juice." Yet, when Queenie approaches him at the checkout, Sammy notes that "with a prim look she lifts a folded dollar bill out of the hollow at the center of her nubbled pink top. . . . Really, I thought that was so cute." He vacillates back and forth between these extremes of opinion during the story, calling some of his customers "houseslaves in pin curlers," yet he is sensitive enough that when Lengel makes Queenie blush, he feels "scrunchy inside." At the end of the story, he quits his job in an effort to be a hero to the girls and as a way of rebelling against a strict society. In a sudden moment of insight—an epiphany—he realizes "how hard the world was going to be to me hereafter" if he refuses to follow acceptable paths.

Stokesie

Stokesie is twenty-two, married, and has two children. He works with Sammy at the A & P checkout. He has little to say or do in this story, though, like Sammy, he observes the girls in the store with interest. He is a glimpse of what Sammy's future might be like; Stokesie's family "is the only difference" between them, Sammy comments.

Themes

Choices and Consequences

An important theme in "A & P" is that of choices and consequences. All of the main characters in the story must make a choice and endure the consequences of that choice. The consequences of these choices are not always apparent to the characters. Sammy, the cashier, makes the most obvious and most painful choice, and on some level he is aware of the consequences. When he chooses to quit his job, he knows that this decision will have ramifications in his life that will last for a long time. His family is affected, and it causes him to recount the situation as "sad." Because he has stood up for something on principle—he was protesting the manager's chastisement of the girls—he knows life will be difficult for him. If Sammy quits his job every time he encounters a situation he dislikes, his life will become extremely complicated. In the short term, the consequence of quitting is having to find another job, and with his rash decision comes the possibility he will be branded a troublemaker or misfit by the community in which he lives.

The three girls must suffer the consequences of having gone to the grocery store in their bathing suits. It is hard to believe that they had no idea they were improperly dressed. In the early 1960s, women still wore dresses, hats, and gloves most of the time when they were in public. In their youthful exuberance to push the limits of propriety, the girls have been reprimanded by an adult. They have also made quite an impression on two young men, Sammy and Stokesie, which was, perhaps unconsciously, their intention in the first place. Nevertheless, because of their choice to violate community standards, they suffer embarrassment by being reprimanded by an authority figure. Even Sammy's attempt at solidarity with them is not enough to salvage the situation; they make a hasty retreat from the store and disappear without taking a stand, unlike Sammy. From the girls' meek reaction, one can surmise that the girls will not take many more risks of the same sort in the future. Such a brush with authority will likely hem them in, successfully socializing them to accept community norms. Sammy, however, because of his quick defiance, is less likely to blindly adhere to arbitrary rules for the sake of maintaining peace.

Lengel, too, makes a choice, and for him the consequences are entirely unforeseen. When he comes into the store after ''haggling with a truck full of cabbages,'' he could have ignored the three girls. They were, after all, standing in the check-out line, and he is ''about to scuttle into that door marked MANAGER.'' Instead, he makes the choice to confront the girls in front of Sammy. If he considers any consequences to his actions, he does not show it. He is merely enforcing the social codes of his time and place. He expects that the girls will comply and that Sammy, and anyone else within hearing, will agree with him.

The girls inevitably stop their protestations, as Lengel expected they would, but Sammy quits—an act that Lengel could not have imagined ahead of time. To Lengel's credit, in spite of his stuffiness and self-importance, he shows Sammy patience. He does not yell or order him immediately out of the store, but warns him of the very real consequences of his act. Yet, it is Lengel's adherence to the social code—which says that this behavior must go into Sammy's personnel file and dog him for the rest of his life—that cause those consequences. It is, in a small way, like Greek tragedy. The players in this drama are helpless to act other than the way they do, but it is not the gods who set the parameters of their behavior, but society, with its written and unwritten list of expected behaviors and consequences for deviating from that list.

Individualism

Sammy asserts his individuality when he quits. He knows that Lengel has every right, according to the standards of his time, to speak to the girls as he does. But by standing up for the girls, Sammy questions those standards and asserts that there is a higher standard of decency that says one should not embarrass others. In deciding which rules of conduct are more important, he asserts his individuality, unlike the girls who slink away because they know they have violated the rules of conduct.

Sammy is the only character in this story who asserts his individuality. Two of the girls are simply following their leader, and Queenie is easily embarrassed and capitulates to Lengel. The other shoppers in the A & P are only ''sheep,'' nervously herding together at Stokesie's cash register to avoid the confrontation. Lengel is the enforcer of policy, a term often used for rules that cannot be easily explained with any degree of rationality. He blindly follows the dictates of society, unable to articulate the reasons for those dictates beyond saying that the A & P ''isn't the beach,'' an observation so obvious and so lacking in reason that it causes Sammy to smile—a small, but definite step toward his rebellion.

Topics for Further Study

- Rewrite the first paragraph of this story in the third person. Why do you think Updike wrote it in the first person? Which version do you think is better? Why?
- If three girls in bathing suits walked into your local supermarket, what do you think the reaction would be today? Has society's attitude towards such issues as dress changed or remained essentially the same in the past forty years?
- If you were to make this story into a film that takes place today, what song would you have playing over the store's speakers? Think of the themes involved in both the story and the song as you make your decision.
- At the end of the story, Sammy says ''I felt how hard the world was going to be to me hereafter.'' Do you think he is insightful or naive about his own character and the future?

Style

Point of View and Narration

Sammy, a checkout clerk, narrates this story in the first person. His voice is colloquial and intimate. His speech is informal, a factor that highlights his individuality and propensity to question authority. Terms of slang, like describing a dollar bill that had ''just come from between the two smoothest scoops of vanilla I had ever known'' characterize him as a fairly typical teenage boy. Using the present tense to make the story seem immediate, he speaks as if to a friend—''I uncrease the bill, tenderly as you may imagine''—drawing the reader immediately to his side. Everything that happens, the reader sees through his eyes. When the girls in bathing suits disappear from his view, they disappear from the reader's view, as well.

Sammy's diction indicates that he is probably not a well-educated person. ''In walks these three girls,'' he says at the very beginning of the story. He also uses a kind of wisecracking slang when talking to Stokesie. Yet, because of the immediacy of his voice, he seems to be a reliable narrator, telling the truth even when it does not flatter him.

Symbolism

''A & P'' is rich in symbolism. The HiHo crackers Sammy is ringing up are an exclamation. When he rings them up the second time, he is saying ''Heigh-ho! Something out of the ordinary is happening!'' And the older woman takes him to task for it. The other shoppers are ''sheep'' who follow blindly up and down the aisles, finally entering the chutes where they will check out. Near the end of the story, they bunch up in Stokesie's chute, crowding together like the nervous sheep they are.

The girls themselves are associated with bees, from the moment that Sammy notices one of them is the ''Queen,'' leading the others around the store. Shortly after that, he wonders what goes on in their minds, if it is ''just a little buzz like a bee in a glass jar.'' Like buzzing bees, they make everyone just a little bit nervous. They are the catalyst in the story, stirring things up as they buzz around the store. Of course the girls, especially Queenie with her shoulder straps hanging loosely, symbolize sexual freedom as they walk around the store. It is a sexual freedom that is bottled up rather quickly when Lengel arrives. At the end, Lengel tries to talk Sammy into staying, but Sammy cannot get the picture of the girls' embarrassment out of his mind, so he rings up *No Sale* on the cash register. He is not buying.

Epiphany

An epiphany is an instance of sudden truth brought about by a mundane event. What began for Sammy as an ordinary day results in a the realization of an important truth: ''I felt how hard the world was going to be to me hereafter.'' This final statement of ''A & P'' is the culmination of the fairly minor event of witnessing three inappropriately dressed girls reprimanded for their appearance. In presenting this epiphany, Updike illustrates how average people grow and change. Ordinary events become pivotal as people examine their motives and reasons for their decisions and behavior. At nineteen, Sammy is ripe for experiences that will start to define who he is going to be. He discovers, as ''his stomach kind of fell,'' that he prefers not to be a sheep who blindly follows the dictates of society.

Another well-known literary instance of epiphany occurs in James Joyce's story ''Araby.'' A boy realizes shamefully that he has been idolizing a friend's sister after embarking on a quest to a church carnival to bring her a present, a token of his affection. Once he realizes that the carnival is nothing but an excuse to sell people cheap trinkets, and that his friend's sister is merely an ordinary girl with no special interest in him, his eyes ''burned with anguish and anger.'' The similarity between the epiphany in ''Araby,'' in which an adolescent realizes the futility of romantic quests, and the one in ''A & P'' is explored by Walter Wells in his essay ''John Updike's 'A & P': A Return Visit to Araby.'' He notes that both protagonists become ''smitten . . . distracted, agitated, disoriented'' by pretty, unattainable girls. Furthermore, ''both protagonists have come to realize that romantic gestures—in fact, that the whole chivalric world view—are, in modern times, counterproductive.''

Historical Context

No Shirt, No Shoes, No Service

Today it is common for businesses to post signs stating the rules of their premises: ''No Shirt, No Shoes, No Service,'' or for movie theaters to constantly remind people not to talk during a film. Society has become so informal that reminders of basic decency and courtesy are commonplace. This is in sharp contrast to a generation or two ago, when standards of appearance and behavior were more rigid and more accepted. Women were required to wear hats in church, and men were required to take theirs off. In the office, rules were largely unwritten, but rarely broken. Women wore dresses, nylons, and girdles. Men wore gray, blue, or black suits and never left home without a tie.

This era was the 1950s and early 1960s, when conservative dress mirrored conservative social values. Conformity was the measure of popularity as well as a measure of moral rightness. Most people, particularly members of the middle-class, wanted to fit in with their neighbors. Suburbs were con-

Compare & Contrast

- **1959:** Although only 10 percent of all grocery stores are large enough to be considered supermarkets, they account for almost 70 percent of all food sold in the United States. (The A & P, a long-standing concern originally called the Great Atlantic and Pacific Tea Company, is one of these supermarkets.) This statistic mirrors the trend towards suburbanization, since most supermarkets are located in fast-growing suburbs.

  1993: Sears Roebuck stops publishing the Sears Catalogue, which for almost a hundred years has enabled people to mail order everything from groceries to prefabricated houses. In addition, Sears closes over a hundred stores nationwide. The decision is impacted by the rising popularity of so-called "category killer" stores, huge warehouse-like structures that specialize in certain niche markets, like housewares, and can offer the public deep discounts because of bulk buying.

- **1961:** FCC chairman Newton Minow declares television "a vast wasteland" filled with "blood and thunder . . . mayhem, violence, sadism, murder . . . more violence, and cartoons . . . and, endlessly, commercials—many screaming, cajoling, and offending."

  1997: Bowing to pressure from parents concerned about the effects of violence and sex on their children, television networks agree to a system of ratings for television programs, which will allow parents to gauge whether or not a program's content is suitable for their children.

- **1960s:** According to Alfred Kinsey's study of female sexuality, one-third of all 25-year-old unmarried women are sexually active. Other studies claim that 75 percent of young unmarried women are virgins. An estimated 40 percent of unmarried men are virgins.

  1990s: According to most surveys, a majority of females are sexually active by the age of 17. Thirty percent of all children in the United States are born out of wedlock. Eighty percent of all teenage mothers are unmarried, and eighty percent of them go on welfare to support their babies.

structed of identical houses, and the American dream was to have a family, car, and the other modern conveniences that would make them equal to others of their social standing. Those who bucked the trends were frequently labeled eccentric or bohemian. The rebellion of many young people from the mid-1960s onward stemmed from what they perceived as the oppression of the staunch rules their parents imposed upon them. Sammy is a good example of this. He knows what the rules are, but he does not admire the "sheep" who so willingly follow them. When he quits his job at the grocery store, he has upset the status quo, an event that Sammy's parents deem "sad." In refusing to smooth over his behavior and return to his job, Sammy takes a stand that makes him aware of "how hard the world was going to be . . . hereafter." In such a rigid society, he knows he may be relegated to the status of an outsider or troublemaker for disagreeing with the unwritten code of acceptable behavior.

There was little positive incentive for Sammy to act as he did. In the late 1950s, the culture had its iconoclasts, but they were never sanctioned by the mainstream. In Nicholas Ray's 1955 film *Rebel Without a Cause,* a teenager's quest for love and warmth, played by James Dean, in a cold and loveless world turns to tragedy. All movies were subject to censorship from the Hayes Office before the current rating system was devised in the late 1960s. Not only was sex, obscene language, and violence strictly curtailed, but characters of low morals were required to suffer negative consequences of their actions within the course of the film. Jack Kerouac's seminal novel *On the Road,* published in 1957, tells of beatnik outcasts Sal

Paradise and Dean Moriarty who drive across the United States listening to jazz and smoking marijuana while trying to find something authentic in American culture. It was also during this era that Allen Ginsberg's poem *Howl* was published. In it, Ginsberg condemns a conformist culture for crushing the creative spirit of artists: ''I saw the best minds of my generation destroyed by madness, starving hysterical naked, dragging themselves through negro streets at dawn looking for an angry fix.'' Such strong language was not received warmly by mainstream society. The poem became the subject of a landmark obscenity trial, and the poem's publisher, Lawrence Ferlinghetti of City Lights Books, was jailed by the San Francisco Police Department and charged with obscenity.

Rock 'n' roll music got its start in the 1950s. At best, it was dismissed as a fad, at worst, it was considered the devil's work. The new music was filled with a sensuality that middle America vehemently condemned, if only because it was causing young people to swoon with emotions previously kept largely in check. Elvis Presley, Little Richard, and Chuck Berry were considered suspicious for their wild movements, flashy clothes, and for beguiling American youth away from the path of safe, decent, sexually modest entertainment. This is the world into which Updike introduces the three teenage girls in bathing suits in ''A & P.''

Critical Overview

Updike was only in his twenties when he wrote ''A & P,'' but he had already gained a reputation for his concise and elegant prose. In a *New York Times Book Review* article on *Pigeon Feathers,* the collection in which ''A & P'' was reprinted, Arthur Mizener called him ''the most talented writer of his age in America . . . and perhaps the most serious.'' Having already published two novels and a collection each of stories and poems, Updike had familiarized reviewers with his propensity for capturing small moments in his fiction. Though many claimed he did so with grace, others criticized Updike because the moments *were* small, and in their opinion, insignificant. ''A & P'' originally suffered from this view. An anonymous reviewer in *Time* magazine remarked that ''this dedicated 29 year old man of letters says very little and says it well,'' echoing the sentiment of many of his contemporaries. The reviewer went on to say that ''even the book's best story—a young A & P food checker watches three girls in bathing suits pad through the store and quits his job impulsively when his boss reproaches them for their immodesty—is as forgettable as last week's *New Yorker.*''

Yet, ''A & P'' has become Updike's most popular story over the years and has appeared in more than twenty anthologies. Young people especially seem to identify with Sammy and respond to the way he tells his story. Robert Detweiler surmised in his book, *John Updike*, that Sammy's popularity is due to his ''integrity, one that divorces him from his unthinking conservative environment.'' M. Gilbert Porter, in an essay for *English Journal,* noted that Sammy's overreaction ''does not detract from the basic nobility of his chivalric intent, nor does it reduce the magnitude of his personal commitment.'' Ronald E. McFarland, in an essay for *Short Studies in Fiction* claimed that the story's enduring popularity was due in part to the ambiguity of the narrator's actions. This sentiment was first proposed by Suzanne Uphaus, who stated in her book, *John Updike*, that Sammy's behavior is an attempt by Updike to reflect on his conviction that ''the heroic gesture is often meaningless and usually arises from selfish rather than unselfish impulses.''

Other critics are similarly interested in the character of Sammy. In an essay titled ''Irony and Innocence in John Updike's 'A & P','' Lawrence Jay Dessner lauded the story's ''brevity and its outrageously naive yet morally ambitious teen-age hero,'' whom he called ''boisterously inventive and rebellious.'' Walter Wells discussed the story as a modern interpretation of James Joyce's classic tale of adolescent initiation, ''Araby.'' Calling Sammy's ''the more ambivalent epiphany,'' Wells drew comparisons between the sudden realizations of the narrator of ''Araby'' and that of Updike's story, and speculated that the author's purpose in updating Joyce's story was ''to contrast the spiritual value-systems and the adolescent sexual folkways of Joyce's Dublin with those of suburban New England in the Atomic Age.'' Donald J. Greiner, in *The Other John Updike: Poems, Short Stories, Prose, Play,* summarized the attraction many readers feel to Sammy: ''The end of the story suggests that all is not self-righteousness and slang. Sammy has sympathy and a sense of outrage. However ironic, his sacrificial gesture is as refreshing as his colloquial candor. . . . An observer of his social world, he resolves not just to record but also to act upon his impressions.''

An A & P grocery store from the 1950s, a prototype for the modern supermarket.

Criticism

Robert Peltier

Peltier is an English instructor at Trinity College and has published works of both fiction and nonfiction. In the following essay, he argues that Updike's story presages the youthful rebellion of the 1960s.

John Updike has been accused of writing extremely well about matters of very little importance. His prose, sentence to sentence, paragraph to paragraph, does read beautifully, perhaps more beautifully than anyone writing today. Erica Jong says, in an essay in Robert Luscher's *John Updike: A Study of the Short Fiction,* that his detractors are "transparently envious" of him. I agree with Jong. Updike's prose style is not separable from the content of his works, and that content is not trivial. The story we are examining here, "A & P," is a fine example, especially since many critics consider it a slight work describing an ultimately insignificant moment in a young man's small life.

A reader skating along the smooth ice of Updike's prose might be quite content to simply watch the approaching horizon, but the careful reader who looks below the surface will see all sorts of interesting, and sometimes frightening things lurking there. In "A & P," it seems that a grocery checkout clerk named Sammy quits his job to impress a pretty girl in a bathing suit. But just below the surface, we can see that Sammy has made a conscious choice to protest his manager's bad treatment of the girl. And if we get close and look even deeper, we can see that this story, informed by the social and cultural currents of the times, is an early harbinger of the youthful rebellion of the 1960s, which was in its embryonic stage at the time Updike wrote "A & P."

The 1950s were to some extent years of conformity, of marching in step, and also (it is said) years of sexual repression. Married couples portrayed on television and in the movies had to have twin beds. Censors dictated that bedroom scenes involving man and wife had to have at least one partner with a foot on the floor at all times. On the political front, a few influential people believed there were communists everywhere—or so it would seem from the headlines and speeches of the day. At times Hollywood seemed obsessed with communists and troubled teenagers, with films like *I Married a Communist* and *Runaway Daughter.* To be different in any significant way was to be suspect. In short, some Americans believed that there existed

What Do I Read Next?

- *Pigeon Feathers and Other Stories* (1962) by John Updike. "A & P" is one of the stories in this collection which contains stories about characters making choices and living with those choices as they grow.
- *The Catcher in the Rye* (1951) by J. D. Salinger, a classic—and controversial—coming-of-age story. Holden Caulfield is kicked out of school—again—and decides to take a few days vacation before heading home
- *25 & under Fic* edited by Susan Ketchin and Neil Giordano. A collection of stories by writers who are twenty-five years old or younger. It includes one story about the extraordinary outcome of an ordinary event that happens to a woman walking away from an A & P.
- *The Children of Perestroika Come of Age: Young People of Moscow Talk about Life in the New Russia* (1994) by Deborah Adelman. What is it like to be a teenager in Moscow? Adelman interviews a cross-section of young people and finds that Russian youth face many of the same problems as their American counterparts.
- *Coming of Age: Short Stories About Youth & Adolescence* (1993), edited by Bruce Emra. A collection of short stories about coming of age.
- *Minor Characters* (1983) by Joyce Johnson. In this memoir, Johnson writes of what life was like for a woman in the company of the Beat writers during the 1950s.

people "out there" who would seduce the nation's children, turn the country communist, and play rock and roll music all day in order to arouse the base, sexual longings of the populace. These people were more afraid of being labeled outsiders than they were afraid of the outsiders themselves.

Most people, of course, were not so dogmatic in their thinking. Most lived productive, normal lives, unrecognized and basically content. There were other people who spoke out in various ways against the uniformity of American society. But they were, by and large, on the periphery of the culture.

Among those who spoke out, the bi-coastal Beat Movement, centered around Jack Kerouac, Allen Ginsberg, Gregory Corso, William S. Burroughs, Neal Cassady, and various friends, fans, and hangers-on, came to the fore in the mid-1950s with the publication of Kerouac's *On the Road* and Ginsberg's *Howl.* Although neither work might seem dangerous to us in the 1990s, they were roundly condemned by mainstream society at the time for being too sexually explicit, encouraging the mixing of the races, promoting drug use, and instigating a host of other immoral and illegal acts. Combining a fear of sex, race, drugs, communism, and freedom of dress and self-expression, society labeled the Beats "beatniks." In fact, *anyone* who challenged the status quo was labeled, humiliated, criticized, and denounced everywhere, from the Oval Office at the White House to the pulpit of the local Congregational Church, from the halls of Congress, to the halls of Shillington High School.

It is into this rigid world that John Updike sends three young girls wearing nothing but bathing suits.

Youth is significant in this story. Sammy is only nineteen, and the girls are younger than he. Lengel and the shoppers are, one assumes, much older. Stokesie, the other checkout clerk, has already crossed the great divide. He is twenty-two, an age at which it is legal to vote, to drink, to marry and to have children. He is vested in the system. It is only the young who have not been indoctrinated, who still have the freedom—and perhaps the courage—to make choices.

The choice the girls make is to walk into an A & P with nothing on but their bathing suits. Make no mistake; this is a conscious decision. They are young, but they are also sexual beings, proud, in that often confused way that teenagers are, of their sensuality. They are aware of Sammy watching them, and they are half self-conscious and half exhilarated by his attention.

The other shoppers nervously tend to their shopping as the girls pass them by. There is something amiss, something out of the ordinary and therefore frightening but, as Sammy notes, "I bet you could set off dynamite in an A & P and the people would by and large keep reaching and checking oatmeal off their lists and muttering 'Let me see, there was a third thing, began with A, asparagus, no, ah, yes, applesauce!' or whatever it is they do mutter." Sammy sees the dogmatic, rote way people lead their lives, alphabetizing their purchases, buying by the letter instead of by the food itself. What could be further apart in terms of taste and texture than asparagus and applesauce? Yet the shoppers force them together in their lists under the letter "A."

Sammy also knows that no matter what happens, these shoppers will not visibly react. They just want to get along, follow the cart in front of them up and down the aisles without incident. If dynamite were to go off, they would ignore it, go about their business as usual. It would have nothing to do with them. They want only to get their shopping done and get home. They do not want to stick out in a crowd. It is as if they are praying, "Get me through life without incident, Lord. Let me feel no pain and, if taking away feeling means I'll feel no joy, so be it." They have made their choices, and they are faced with the consequences of those choices.

Lengel, too, makes a choice. He is the manager, the person charged with enforcing policy, and so he chooses to chastise—and embarrass—the three girls. They are checking out when he sees them, so he could easily let them go, but he feels deeply his responsibilities as the representative of the Establishment. Managers, of large and small institutions alike, are there, in large part, to make sure that the social codes are enforced within that institution.

He brushes aside their argument that they aren't "doing any real shopping," but merely picking up one item. "That makes no difference. . . . We want you decently dressed when you come in here," Lengel says, and one can hear this voice spring from our youthful memories of teachers and parents and clergy and other grownups who knew so much about right and wrong. But Queenie does not address his comment directly, because he has addressed the wrong issue. "We *are* decent," she says. She knows the difference between appearances and a deeper truth. Dressing decently and being decent are different things. She knows she is a decent girl, and to judge her by her appearance is itself indecent.

"I think it important that students read a story (or a poem, or essay) for themselves, and get what they can out of it. For a writer or a teacher to tell students what a story means is to clip the story's wings."—John Updike

Sammy, of course, makes the most drastic choice, a choice some critics have charged is charmingly romantic, but naive. But, as it foreshadows the choices an entire generation is about to make, I think it is of great importance. Sammy chooses to quit his job. He first says this to Lengel when the girls are still in the store, and one might be tempted to dismiss such a gesture as silly and romantic. But Lengel, perhaps wishing to give Sammy a chance to recant or even pretend he had said something else or nothing at all, asks, after the girls are gone, "Did you say something, Sammy?" This is what raises this story above the superficial; this simple interrogative sentence changes everything, for Sammy then says, "I said I quit."

Sammy had several alternatives, but he chose the straight and true one. He knew that he was quitting not to impress the girls now, but in protest over Lengel's action. He had an epiphany that it was an indecent thing to do to embarrass three young, vulnerable girls in public. He saw the unyielding "policy" of the "kingpins" as a doctrine that was cold and callous and amoral. He agrees with Lengel that he'll "feel this for the rest of [his] life," for he knows that he has just gone against "policy," too, and a world run by policy will not be easy on him.

By the end of the story, Updike has foretold of the coming revolution when sex will be sprung from its monastic cell, when the Establishment will have

"All the elements in American society that led to the free-spirited, often naive, romanticism of the 1960s are present in Updike's 'A & P.'"

to justify each and every rule (and war), when appearances will not place one outside of society's gates. All the elements in American society that led to the free-spirited, often naive, romanticism of the 1960s are present in Updike's "A & P."

Source: Robert Peltier, for *Short Stories for Students,* Gale, 1998.

Walter Wells

Wells is Professor of English at California State University, Dominguez Hills. As a literary scholar, he is known primarily for his Tycoons and Locusts: Hollywood Fiction in the 1930s *and* Mark Twain's Guide to Backgrounds in American Literature. *In the following essay, Wells draws comparisons between Updike's "A & P" and James Joyce's famous story of adolescent epiphany, "Araby."*

John Updike's penchant for appropriating great works of literature and giving them contemporary restatement in his own fiction is abundantly documented—as is the fact that, among his favorite sources, James Joyce looms large.

With special affinity for *Dubliners,* Updike has, by common acknowledgment, written at least one short story that strongly resembles the acclaimed "Araby," not only in plot and theme, but in incidental detail. That story, the 1960 "You'll Never Know, Dear, How Much I Love You"—like "Araby"—tells the tale of a poor, romantically infatuated young boy who, though obstructed by parental slowness, journeys with innocent urgency, coins in hand, to a seemingly magical carnival—only to find there, behind its facades, just a sleazy, money grasping, sexually tinged reality that frustrates and embitters him. Both stories draw on the Christian imagery of Bunyan's Vanity Fair episode to trace a modern boy's passage from innocence to experience, and to expose some of the pains and complexities of that passage. Notwithstanding "Araby"'s cachet as one of the great short stories in the English language, at least two critics have found "You'll Never Know, Dear" to be "a far more complex story."

What remains unacknowledged, I think, is that shortly after writing "You'll Never Know, Dear," Updike made a second fictional excursion to Araby. This time he transformed Joyce's latter-day Vanity Fair, not into a cheaply exotic destination for a starry-eyed youngster, but into the richly resonant single setting for an older adolescent's sad tale: a tale of the modern supermarket. The resulting story, since its publication in 1962, has been Updike's most frequently anthologized: the popular "A & P." Updike even signals his intention for us at the outset, giving his story a title that metrically echoes Joyce's: Araby . . . A & P. (Grand Union or Safeway would not suffice.)

Like "Araby," "A & P" is told after the fact by a young man now much the wiser, presumably, for his frustrating infatuation with a beautiful but inaccessible girl whose allure excites him into confusing his sexual impulses for those of honor and chivalry. The self-delusion in both cases leads quickly to an emotional fall.

At 19, Updike's protagonist, Sammy, is a good bit older than Joyce's—at the opposite end of adolescence, it would seem. While in Joyce's boy we readily believe such confusion between the gallant and profane, I think we needn't assume that Sammy is likewise unable to distinguish between the two quite normal impulses. His attraction to the girl in the aisle is certainly far more anatomically and less ambiguously expressed than that of Joyce's boy to Mangan's sister. But it is Beauty that confounds the issue. When human aesthetics come into play, when the object of a young man's carnal desire also gratifies him aesthetically, that is when the confusion arises. In Irish-Catholic Dublin of the 1890s, such youthful beauty not surprisingly invokes analogies between Mangan's sister and the Queen of Heaven (though the swinging of her body and "the soft rope of her hair toss[ing] from side to side," which captivate the boy, hint at something less spiritual than Madonna worship). And while beauty's benchmarks in Sammy's more secular mid-century America *are* more anatomical than spiritual, Updike does have Sammy call his young *femme fatale* "Queenie," and he does make her the center of a "trinity" of sorts, showing her two friends at one point ''huddl[ing] against her for relief.''

Once smitten, both young protagonists become distracted, agitated, disoriented. Joyce's turns impatient ''with the serious work of life.'' His teacher accuses him of idling. His heart leaps, his thoughts wander, his body responds ''like a harp'' to the words and gestures of Mangan's sister, which run ''like fingers . . . upon the wires.'' Similarly, Updike's young hero can't remember, from the moment he spots Queenie in the aisle, which items he has rung up on the cash register.

Even details in the two stories are similar, Updike clearly taking his cues from ''Araby.'' Both boys are excited by specified *whiteness* about the girls—Joyce's boy by ''the white curve of her neck'' and ''the white border of [her] petticoat'' in the glow of Dublin lamplight, Sammy by the ''long white prima-donna legs'' and the white shoulders to which he refers repeatedly. ''Could [there],'' he wonders, ''have been anything whiter than those shoulders[?].'' Joyce's boy also observes a nimbus surrounding Mangan's sister, ''her figure defined by the light from the half-opened door.'' True, Mangan's sister comports herself more humbly than her American counterpart. Queenie walks, heavy-heeled and head high, with the haughty pride of the affluent, secularized American upper middle class. But her enticing whiteness, in Updike's sly parody, is also given a luminous, halo-like quality: ''around the top of the cloth,'' says Sammy of the bathing suit that ''had slipped a little on her . . . there was this shining rim.''

Both girls, remote as they are from their ardent admirers, also engage in some subtly seductive posturing. In the supermarket aisle, Queenie turns so slowly that Sammy's stomach is made to ''rub the inside of [his] apron.'' It's the same sensation, we suspect, that Joyce's protagonist feels when Mangan's sister ''turn[s the] silver bracelet round and round her wrist'' and bows her head toward him in the lamplight in front of her door. Queenie bows to no one, but the ''clear bare plane of the top of her chest . . . [is] like a dented sheet of metal tilted in the light.'' Her beauty, too, like that of Mangan's sister, is incandescent as it inclines toward her aspiring young knight.

Certainly one artistic motive for Updike's second reworking of ''Araby'' must be to contrast the spiritual value-systems and the adolescent sexual folkways of Joyce's Dublin with those of suburban New England in the Atomic Age. (The disillusionment of little Ben, who is only ten in ''You'll Never Know, Dear,'' is clearly presexual.) ''A & P'' holds the secular materialism of Updike's own day up for comparison against the slowly imploding, English-dominated Irish Catholicism of the mid-1890s—and, behind it, the fervor of Protestant evangelism in Bunyan's seventeenth century. As critics have often noted, few non-Catholic writers in America make issues of religious faith and doubt as important in their fictions as does Updike. In Victorian Dublin, redolent with the musty odor of incense, parochial schools, and the litter of dead priests, the Araby bazaar, a romanticized, pseudo-Oriental pavilion created by the fund raisers of the Jervis Street Hospital, stands incongruously pagan and temporary. It is there briefly, soon to be gone. Updike's supermarket, on the other hand, is permanently planted in the light of day near Boston, precisely where the church used to be: ''right in the middle of town.'' ''[From its] front doors,'' says Sammy, ''you can see two banks and the Congregational church and the newspaper store and three real estate offices . . .''—quite the satellites to material abundance they've become. The temple of modern consumerism has supplanted the house of worship at the heart of things. It is also an era in which Sammy (and hardly Sammy alone) takes for granted that the godless communists will take control sooner or later (as the British had long since assumed control in Joyce's Ireland). Sammy looks ahead quite assuredly to a time when the A & P (the Great Atlantic and Pacific Tea Co., that bedrock American institution) will be ''called the Great Alexandrov and Petrooshki Tea Company or something.''

Updike heightens the story's skepticism over the destiny of American Christianity by having his

"One artistic motive for Updike's second reworking of 'Araby' must be to contrast the spiritual value-systems and the adolescent sexual folkways of Joyce's Dublin with those of suburban New England in the Atomic Age."

three girls stroll through the aisles of the A & P inappropriately clad, in reductive parody of Bunyan's pilgrims in Vanity Fair:

> [E]ven as they entered into the fair, all the people in the fair were moved, and the town it self as it were in a Hubbub about them; and that for several reasons: For, First, the pilgrims were cloathed with such kind of Raiment as was diverse from the Raiment of any that Traded in that fair. The people therefore of the fair made a great gazing upon them. Some said they were fools, some they were Bedlams, and some they are Outlandish-men.
>
> The sheep pushing their carts down the aisle—the girls were walking against the usual traffic . . .—were pretty hilarious. You could see them, when Queenie's white shoulders dawned on them, kind of jerk, or hop, or hiccup, but their eyes snapped back to their own baskets and on they pushed. I bet you could set off dynamite in an A & P and the people would by and large keep reaching and checking oatmeal off their lists. . . . But there was no doubt this jiggled them. A few houseslaves in pin curlers even looked around after pushing their carts past to make sure what they had seen was correct.

Contrast these two sets of "pilgrims" in the marketplace. Bunyan's proudly ignore exhortations that they partake of the bounty of the fair, insisting instead that the wares of the marketplace are nothing but stimuli to vanity. They will, they say, buy only the Truth. Queenie and her pals, on the other hand, do buy: one jar of Kingfish Fancy Herring Snacks in Pure Sour Cream.

Queenie's approach to the checkout stand, Sammy warns us, begins "the sad part of the story." Lengel, the store's manager, a self-appointed moral policeman who also teaches Sunday school, confronts the girls at the register—just as Bunyan's pilgrims are confronted by "the Great One of the fair" (i.e., Beelzebub) "Girls, this isn't the beach," Lengel tells them, echoing the Devil's demand in Vanity Fair that the pilgrims account for "what they did there in such an unusual Garb." Queenie and her friends, like Bunyan's pilgrims, protest that they "weren't . . . shopping," only buying the snacks that Queenie's mother asked them to get on their way home from the beach. Bunyan's pilgrims explain to *their* inquisitor that they are just passing through on their way to the Heavenly Jerusalem. Sammy imagines, in fact, that the girls *are* returning to their own latter-day heavenly city, the affluent beach set where folks eat "herring snacks on toothpicks off a big glass plate and . . . [hold] drinks the color of water with olives and sprigs of mint in them"—this by comparison to the lemonade and Schlitz beer crowd, whence Sammy comes, where the suds are drunk from glasses with stenciled cartoons. In Bunyan's world, the choice was earthly vanity or heavenly salvation; in Updike's, it's just one level of class vanity or another.

To Queenie's protest, Lengel replies that it "makes no difference. . . . We want you decently dressed when you come in here." Queenie snaps back, insisting that she and her friends "*are* decent." But they are nonetheless (after Lengel allows Sammy to ring up the herring snacks) quietly banished from the store. Bunyan's pilgrims, of course, are more harshly persecuted, thrown in a cage and forced to assert their dignity much more protractedly than Updike's girls. The difference, however, is only one of degree.

At the checkout stand, Sammy witnesses Queenie's mortification up close with profound, if complicated, sympathy. He tenderly unfolds the dollar bill she hands him ("it just having come," he says, "from between the two smoothest scoops of vanilla I had ever known"), puts her change "into her narrow pink palm," hands her the jar of herring in a bag, then blurts out "I quit"—quickly enough, he hopes, for the girls to hear, so they will stop and acknowledge "their unsuspected hero."

It's pure impetuousness on Sammy's part, a gallant gesture, a promise of sorts. Like Joyce's boy in Dublin, when face to face with the object of his adoration, not knowing what else to say or do, Sammy offers a gift. Where the Irish boy, in his comparatively poor working-class milieu, wants (perhaps needs) to offer something material to Mangan's sister to show his adoration, Sammy, who inhabits an affluent American world cut loose from the consolations of Christian faith, a world of largely material values, offers instead an assertion of principle as his gift. His Queenie has been wronged, and he will stand by her; in an age when the supermarket has replaced the church as the community's central institution, "principle" is the nearest equivalent one has to spiritual commitment. But before we anoint Sammy's act as one of pure principle, however imprudent, we should ask ourselves whether he would have done the same had one of the other girls—maybe Big Tall Goony-Goony—borne the brunt of the reprimand, with Queenie out of the picture. I doubt it.

The promises of both young men prove futile, of course. Joyce's boy gets to Araby too late, and recognizes in the flirtatious banter there between the salesgirl and her two English admirers, and in the two men counting money, something uncomfortably close to the nature of his own longing: his dream, he later sees, was actually sexual, and money would not buy it. In the A & P, Queenie and her friends disappear out the door. Sammy's promise is also in vain; but, like Joyce's young protagonist, he's stuck with it. "It seems to me," says Sammy, "that once you begin a gesture it's fatal not to go through with it." He removes his apron and bow tie, and leaves the market. Once outside, he looks back woefully through the store windows and sees Lengel replacing him behind the cash register. Business goes on, and—as at Araby—the money must be collected. Like Joyce's boy peering into the darkened rafters of the Araby bazaar and lamenting the vanity of his impulsive act, Sammy says at the end of *his* story, "My stomach kind of fell as I felt how hard the world was going to be to me hereafter."

Hereafter . . . it's an oddly formal word with which to conclude for Sammy, who is otherwise a most colloquial storyteller. Does Updike mean to hint that Sammy's epiphany bears intimations of immortality?—and not very positive ones at that? Joyce's boy would seem simply to have matured as a result of his insight, to have become better equipped for life as an adult. Though convinced as a youth that his devotion to Mangan's sister was divinely driven, he has come to realize—as his older, more articulate narrative voice makes clear—that he had, back then, been "a creature driven and derided by vanity." Looking backward, Joyce's narrator has resolved his earlier confusion of spirit and libido, and can recount for us, however wistfully, how that resolution came about. Updike's Sammy, by comparison, speaks less retrospectively. He is still 19 at the end of his story, and still looking around for the girls in the parking lot, though "they're gone, of course." Sammy looks ahead—into the life that lies before him, even perhaps (given that including word) at his own uncertain path to the Hereafter. And he sees nothing very clearly, only indefiniteness.

Both protagonists have come to realize that romantic gestures—in fact, that the whole chivalric world view—are, in modern times, counterproductive. That there are, however, for American adolescents in post-atomic, Cold War New England, any viable alternatives is less assured. Sammy's is the more ambivalent epiphany.

Source: Walter Wells, "John Updike's 'A & P': A Return Visit to Araby," in *Studies in Short Fiction,* Vol. 30, No. 2, Spring, 1993, pp. 127–33.

Lawrence Jay Dessner

Dessner is Professor of English at the University of Toledo. He specializes in Victorian literature and creative writing. In the following essay, Dessner presents insight into the character of Sammy, whom the critic believes does not realize what his real *troubles in life will be.*

John Updike's short story "A & P" first published in *The New Yorker* and then in *Pigeon Feathers and Other Stories* (1962), has become something of a classic of college literature anthologies, and no doubt the story's brevity and its outrageously naive yet morally ambitious teen-age hero have much to do with that status. Part of the story's appeal, too, derives from the fact that the wild comedy of its boisterously inventive and rebellious narrator modulates at its end into a gentle but benign sobriety. Moments after Sammy dramatically surrenders his job at the cash register to protest the unchivalrous treatment of the three girls in swim suits who have broken the store's unwritten dress code, we may rejoice in the condescending yet charming irony of his naive conclusion: "I felt how hard the world was going to be to me hereafter." Sammy surely overrates the harm he has done to his prospects. We chuckle at his groundless apprehension and at Updike's momentarily convincing if mischievous pretense that the world is benign. We are gladdened to have had our disbelief suspended.

But this analysis of the tonal satisfactions of the ending overlooks its deeper irony and the story's more considerable structural design on which that irony depends. The running theme which links the bulk of the story's incidents repeatedly demonstrates Sammy's inability to imagine himself personally at risk. The expectation this motif awakens in us is that Sammy will continue to underrate the world's dangers. At the story's end, however, he surprises us by *overrating* them—although with ludicrous and touching selectivity.

The first of these dangers to present itself to Sammy is either penury or a neurotic meanness of spirit. The middle-aged customer who gives Sammy "hell" for ringing up her box of crackers twice is in Sammy's quick calculation, "about fifty," and a "witch" of the sort he's learned once flourished in nearby Salem. He notices the "rouge on her cheekbones and no eyebrows" but nothing else that might stir him in the direction of sympathy. That the malicious intent he silently accuses her of, and the "sheep"-like behavior, "like scared pigs in a chute," of the other "houseslaves in pin curlers" who draw his sarcastic ire, might have sources in something other than the one's motiveless malignity and the others' dullness of character, does not occur to Sammy. He calls the "pigs" "scared" as if he himself had never known fear, as if no one ever had, as if "scared" were a term of opprobrium. He blames the customers of his A & P for being "houseslaves" without any sensitivity to the misfortunes of literal or metaphoric slavery the epithet points to. The thought that his mother, or his wife to be, might herself deserve something more generous than loathing for having "varicose veins [like those] mapping [the shoppers'] legs" does not break the shell of the boy's innocence.

Nor does he know, or care about, the circumstances that might lead one—himself for instance—to a career as a laborer in the city's Department of Streets and Sewers. The men who have come to such employment are to him nothing more than "old freeloaders." Similarly, the "old party in baggy gray pants who stumbles up [to his checkout lane] with four giant cans of pineapple juice" evokes in Sammy nothing more than the thoroughly self-satisfied question, "what do these bums *do* with all that pineapple juice? I've often asked myself." There is no malice in that "bums," merely the guileless narcissism of youth. We laugh with Sammy more than we laugh at him. How grand it must be to know nothing at all about marginal employment or implacable constipation!

Sammy sneers at the store manager for "haggling with a truck full of cabbages"—and by extension sneers at all those who grow, transport, even eat, such mundane stuff. He is entranced and made enviously defensive by his notion that the underclad younger shoppers inhabit a higher social station than his own. His reflections on this topic permit him a kindly smirk not only at his own family's lower middle-class predilections but also at their better's sartorial usages. "Ice-cream coats" is his mocking name for their formal summer attire. Of his own eventual settling into or battling to gain or retain a standing in the social hierarchy, he is merrily unaware.

Sammy shamelessly ogles the three girls and reports on his sudden bodily weakness when one of them hands him a dollar bill taken from her bodice, but when McMahon, who works behind "the meat counter," follows them with his eyes while "patting his mouth" in the embarrassed simulation of yawning boredom, Sammy watches without an iota of masculine fellow feeling. McMahon *is* what Sammy doesn't realize he may someday consider himself fortunate to have become: McMahon is "old." To Sammy *his* ogling the girls is absurd, ludicrous, grotesque, even distasteful, a response Sammy neatly expresses when he says that McMahon, the butcher, is "sizing up their joints."

Sammy's tenure at the check-out counter at the A & P has exposed him to a fair sampling of the ordinary range of insult and indignity with which adults are forced to compromise. The fact that his observations, so marvelously acute and so precisely and delightfully expressed, have not led him to the slightest insight into his own membership in the family of the sons of Adam culminates in the surprising double irony of the story's conclusion. While enormously overrating the world's subsequent interest in his own employment history, Sammy enormously underrates the range and reach of the adult world's terrors, those necessities which do indeed lie in wait for him, the exhibition of which has comprised the essential bulk of his narrative.

Sammy renounces his allegiance to the A & P for their sake, but the girls are gone when he seeks them on the street; and when he looks back through the store's "big windows," he "could see Lengel," the offending store manager, standing in for him at the cash register. "His face was dark gray and his back stiff," says Sammy, "as if he'd just had an injection of iron. . . ." We know that Lengel had "been a friend of [Sammy's] parents for years" and that he had asked Sammy to reconsider quitting for their sakes. Surely the "dark gray" of his face is the sign of something other than the proud obstinacy Sammy believes it to be. But from the story's beginning to here at its very end, Sammy gets it wrong. The payoff of this theme ought to be Sammy's *lack* of concern for the consequences of his precipitous renunciation of his job. The irony turns in on itself when he doesn't even get *that* right. Our chuckles at his overestimation of the trials which await him are seasoned with a soupcon of kindly concern for him that has been prompted by his underestimation of all those ordeals of which his narrative has so forcefully and comically reminded us—but not him. Sammy, like the frightened child in Philip Levine's poem "To a Child Trapped in Barber Shop," thinks that his "life is over." The poem's narrator, like our story's, reminds his protagonist with wistful affection that "it's just begun."

Source: Lawrence Jay Dessner, "Irony and Innocence in John Updike's 'A & P'," in *Studies in Short Fiction,* Vol. 25, No. 3, Summer, 1988, pp. 315–17.

Ronald E. McFarland

McFarland is Professor of English at the University of Idaho. In the following essay, he discusses the reasons he sees for the enduring popularity of Updike's story and theorizes about the symbolism of the story's brand names.

During the twenty years since its appearance in *Pigeon Feathers* (1962), "A & P" has been established as John Updike's most widely read short story. Its popularity among anthologists, as recourse to the listings in *Studies in Short Fiction* demonstrates, has made the story standard reading for thousands of college and high school students. It has appeared in over twenty anthologies since its inclusion in Douglas and Sylvia Angus's *Contemporary American Short Stories* in 1967. What accounts for the continuing popularity of this particular story?

The reviewers greeted *Pigeon Feathers* with that peculiar damnation-by-hyperbolic-praise which continues to plague Updike. Arthur Mizener began his page-one review in *New York Times Book Review* by hailing Updike as "the most talented writer of his age in America (he is 30 today) and perhaps the most serious," only to warn later of the dangers of Updike's Joycean "verbal brilliance" and of the sometimes awkward conflict in his work between "wit and insight." He did not mention "A & P." J. M. Edelstein, who made a passing comment on "A & P" but focused on "Lifeguard," found Updike's work "rewarding," but also "terribly frustrating." Along with the stories' "glitter and shine," occasional "dazzle," their "irony" and "neat felicity," Edelstein also detected "a cleverness and an obvious mannerism that becomes tiresome." Granville Hicks did not mention the story in his lead review for *Saturday Review,* though his praise of Updike ("bold, resourceful, and intensely serious") was more unstinting than that of other reviewers. Only the unsigned reviewer for *Time,* who began, "John Updike is a brilliant writer who has so far failed to write a brilliant book," reflected upon "A & P." But here, too, the damning with exaggerated praise was evident. Lauding "A & P" as the best story in *Pigeon Feathers,* the reviewer concluded that "it is as forgettable as last Week's *New Yorker.*"

Regardless of this indifferent reception, "A & P" has emerged as Updike's best known story. One reason that anthologists have embraced the story is probably their awareness of audience. Sammy, the 19-year-old check out boy, has natural appeal to a classroom full of 18- and 19-year-olds. His colloquial usages make him "accessible" to college-age readers, and the frequently remarked similarities with J. D. Salinger's Holden Caulfield have probably added to his appeal.

In his instructor's handbook, R. V. Cassill characterizes Sammy as "a good-natured, average boy" with "a vague preference for beauty, liberty, youth, and recklessness as against the stultifying cant of a stodgy civilization." This has been the main trend of the critical response to Sammy as a character. "He will not always be understood," Rachael C. Burchard writes, "but he refuses to be captured by conformity and monotony." Hailing "A & P" as "one of the brilliant pieces" in *Pigeon Feathers,* Robert Detweiler finds that with his act Sammy "achieves a new integrity, one that divorces him from his unthinking conservative environment." The most effusive admiration of Sammy, however, is provided in M. Gilbert Porter's essay, which discovers Emersonian qualities of various sorts in the protagonist and which argues that the "histrionic" aspect of his gesture "does not detract from the basic nobility of his chivalric intent, nor does it reduce the magnitude of his personal commitment." Sammy, Porter concludes, "has chosen to live honestly and meaningfully." This decision, presumably, makes him an Emersonian character rather than an ordinary fellow who, one may surmise, elects to live dishonestly and meaninglessly. Porter admits that Sammy's view of the adult world is "harsh," but he also finds it "essentially true."

An important reason for the continuing attractiveness of "A & P," however, as is often the case with stories which prove to be of interest to literary critics and other serious readers, is its ambiguity, or, more narrowly, the ironic doubleness with which the protagonist is presented. Caught up in the colloquial comedy of Sammy's narration, the reader tends to view the story (and especially the protagonist) uncritically, thus discovering in Sammy at least a Quixotic type of nobility. Shortly after it was published, William Peden described the story as "trivial rather than significant, and more dull than delightful," perhaps because he could detect little besides adolescent arrogance in the protagonist, though he did not elaborate. More recently, Donald J. Greiner, noting that the girls in the story, ironically, are not in need of Sammy's help, observes: "Sammy learns that no one welcomes or even tolerates idle idealism. Rather than insist on principle, he has merely shown off." Suzanne Uphaus also detects the "ironic distance" between what

Sammy intends and what he accomplishes, "which reflects Updike's conviction ... that the heroic gesture is often meaningless and usually arises from selfish rather than unselfish impulses." Much of the impact of the story, as I shall demonstrate, derives from the ambiguity, the ironic doubleness, with which Updike has invested his protagonist.

In order to illustrate (in a couple senses of the word) this story, Updike creates what I will call "brand-name symbolism." From the HiHo crackers to the Falcon station wagon. Updike's brand names are more than simply appropriate projections of the setting. They are symbols, comical, if only because of their nature and context, which have meaningful associations when properly considered. They also contribute to the ironic portraits offered throughout the story.

Sammy associates himself at the outset with HiHo crackers, and they are a fitting symbol for him—an ordinary, middle-class (not Ritz crackers) snack item. How seriously, then, ought one to take Sammy? How seriously does he take himself? The brand name connotes light-heartedness and high spirits. The movement of the story, and of Sammy's perspective, is from the easy gaiety and freedom of youth toward the "hard" realities of adult societal judgment. As Sammy observes, his parents think what has happened is "sad," but, although he sees that life hereafter will be hard for him, he doesn't yet see how unfortunate is his fall from boyhood.

The girl Sammy calls "Queenie" is associated with "Kingfish Fancy Herring Snacks in Pure Sour Cream: 49¢." (I recently priced a similar product at $1.98 for an 8-ounce jar.) The brand name not only fits the imperial Queenie, but also suggests the social class, the upper crust, to which she belongs. The incongruity of the common HiHo crackers and a luxury hors d'oeuvres like herring snacks anticipates one aspect of the hard lesson that Sammy will learn. Queenie's brand-name symbol represents a world completely alien to that of Sammy, who visualizes her parents and their stylish friends "picking up herring snacks on toothpicks off a big glass plate." As X. J. Kennedy observes in his instructor's manual, the unsophisticated Sammy "thinks martinis are garnished with mint." The brand name that Sammy refers to as symbolic of his own family is Schlitz.

In the confrontation itself there are several ironies. The A & P, after all, is the subsuming brand name in the story. It is a democratic melting pot of sorts, a typically American institution where, just as the Atlantic and Pacific come together, so do crackers and herring snacks, and so do the proletarian (the "bum" in his baggy pants who buys pineapple juice), the bourgeois, and the patrician. All are equal, one might suppose, at the supermarket. Yet it is here that a standard of social decorum is asserted, so the irony cuts at the upper class girls. Sammy is no kinder to his reflections on the proletariat (including the streetworkers) and the bourgeoisie than Lengel, the manager, is in his treatment of the patricians. At the same time, the social code itself is undercut, for though it is distinctly bourgeois in nature, its aim is to sustain the appearance of "class" (the patrician). The code of decorum keeps the store from being what it would pretend to be. The supposedly elite upper class is, in fact, very casual, too casual, under the circumstances, for the snobbish middle-class manager.

Some less central brand-name symbols also figure in the story. McMahon, the butcher is mentioned in the context of Diet Delight peaches, an ironic anti-product to that of his department. The only brand name (of a sort) associated with the town besides the A & P is the Congregational church, a standard, Protestant, middle-class denomination, which is virtually surrounded by such non-spiritual businesses as two banks, a newsstand, and three real estate offices. Finally, although the company is not named, record albums which denote a particular middle-class brand of music are alluded to: the Caribbean Six and Tony Martin Sings. The common name of the popular singer contrasts with the presumably exotic sextet.

The ironic doubleness and ambiguity are most obvious, however, with the last brand-name symbol in the story, the "powder-blue Falcon station wagon." Associated with "some young married screaming with her children" and being a station wagon, the vehicle relates to the sheeplike customers, the women with varicose veins and six children, and the fifty-year-old cash-register-watchers. But the vehicle's model name, "Falcon," suggests predatory aggressiveness. Falconry is traditionally a sport of aristocrats, and poetically the falcon has been connected with the power of Christ (a sort of antitype to the dove). The vehicle itself, therefore, is a sort of self-contradiction. It is small wonder that the confused Sammy anticipates a hard life ahead. The world which he is entering creates just such confusing, ambiguous symbols for itself.

Some readers, as I have indicated above, have asserted confident and even dogmatic readings of

Sammy's character. He is commonly seen as "standing for" youth (naive, but "right"), beauty, sensitivity, nonconformity, individualism, honesty, and excitement. It appears that the story has been promoted largely by those who read the protagonist in that way. Like Holden Caulfield, then, the altruistic (even chivalric) Sammy learns a hard lesson about reality, the "sad wisdom of compromise," as Detweiler calls it. But Sammy lacks several essentials of the worthy hero. For one thing, he has no perspective on his situation. He can judge the effects of his "gesture," apparently, only from a brief passage of time. Furthermore, despite what some readers have said, Sammy appears to have very little sensitivity, except, of course, to the obvious nubile beauty of Queenie and her friends (although they respond to it differently, both Stokesie and McMahon also perceive that beauty). Sammy's reaction to the angry customer early in the story and his lack of sympathy for the varicose-veined mothers simply indicate his immaturity and failure of compassion. His descriptions of customers as sheep, or as "scared pigs in a chute" may be funny, but a moment's reflection shows them to be simply jejune. Finally, by his own account, Sammy's "gesture" (the word is used advisedly, for it is a mere gesture) is intended to impress the girls who have, ironically, missed the whole show.

If my antithetical portrait of Sammy were the whole story, however, he would be no more engrossing as a protagonist than what I might call "Sammy the altruist," as portrayed by other readers. Sammy, in fact, achieves a certain degree of heroism not so much by his gesture, which initially appears to be selfishly motivated rather than a defense of principle, but by his insistence upon going through with it even after the girls have left. At the end, the reader perceives Sammy as both victor and victim. Against the many instances of his insensitivity and immaturity, the reader finds some signs at the end that Sammy is growing up. In short, it is only partly correct to say that Sammy is noble or chivalric, and it is only partly correct to say that he is acting on selfish impulses. Much of the continued popularity of the story derives from Updike's refusal to guide the reader to an easy solution.

At this writing, I can account for ten books or monographs published on the works of John Updike, a writer who, at fifty, may have his best work ahead of him. His facility with language and what David Thorburn describes as his "unmannerly fertility" may always be held against him. The charges (particularly of his facile style) are reminiscent of those

"The incongruity of the common HiHo crackers and a luxury hors d'oeuvres like herring snacks anticipates one aspect of the hard lesson that Sammy will learn."

one encounters from time to time against F. Scott Fitzgerald. Robert E. Spiller wrote: "Fitzgerald's strength—and his weakness—lay in the sincerity of his confession and in the gift of words in which it was expressed." Like Fitzgerald, Updike concentrates on a specific social milieu. Updike's subject, Thorburn writes, "is always some variation on the spiritual and communal enfeeblement of contemporary American society, particularly among the suburban middle class." Like Fitzgerald's, Updike's reputation will have to wait a generation or two to be properly measured, but I think he will prove to be the major spokesman of a longer and more complex era (the 1960's through the 1980's) than the Jazz Age.

Source: Ronald E. McFarland, "Updike and the Critics: Reflections on 'A & P'," in *Studies in Short Fiction,* Vol. 20, Nos. 2–3, Spring-Summer, 1983, pp. 95–100.

Donald J. Greiner

Greiner is the chair professor of English at the University of South Carolina. He has published extensively on the works of Updike and Robert Frost, among other American authors. In the following excerpt, Greiner discusses "A & P," focusing particularly upon the character of Sammy.

"A & P" is one of Updike's most popular and anthologized tales. Told in the first person from Sammy's point of view, the story calls attention not to the tone of nostalgia but the brashness of his colloquialism. The first sentences suggest his confidence: "In walks these three girls in nothing but bathing suits. I'm in the third check-out slot, with my back to the door, so I don't see them until they're over by the bread. The one that caught my eye first was the one in the plaid green two-piece." Sammy's sympathy with the teeny boppers is established immediately by the contrast between the girls and the typical cash-register watcher, "a witch

"Sammy initially seems so confident that he may irritate some readers. Surveying the three girls as they wander the aisles, he assumes that his perspective and judgment are naturally correct."

about fifty with rouge on her cheekbones and no eyebrows'' who gives him a hard time for ringing up a box of HiHo crackers twice. Admiring the three girls for daring to enter the grocery store dressed in bathing suits, he especially likes the one who wears her straps down and her head high. He also enjoys the shock on the faces of the housewives in pin curlers who do a double take to corroborate this breach in decorum: ''these are usually women with six children and varicose veins mapping their legs . . . there's people in this town haven't seen the ocean for twenty years.''

The sketch turns on the offhand comment that his parents think the outcome sad. We know then that despite the colloquial immediacy of the tale, ''A & P'' is the record of an incident which Sammy has already lived through but not forgotten. His response to the situation has made an impact upon him which he continues to ponder. When Lengel, the store manager who teaches Sunday school, criticizes the three girls with the comment, ''this isn't the beach,'' Sammy's sense of heroism is aroused. Lengel utters his sarcasm as if the A & P were a great sand dune and he the head lifeguard, but no one is saved. Like a hero in a story by J. D. Salinger performing a quixotic gesture, Sammy accepts the role of the girls' unsuspected hero and announces to Lengel that he quits.

He does not agree with his parents that the outcome is sad. Someone must stand up for embarrassed teen-agers in bathing suits with straps down. But this quixotic gesture does him no good. The girls never hear him declare himself their protector, and they do not wait for him in the parking lot with favors and thanks. Indeed, when he steps outside, he is in the ugly world of harried housewives with varicose veins: ''There wasn't anybody but some young married screaming with her children about some candy they didn't get by the door of a powder-blue Falcon station wagon.'' Sammy does not want to quit his job, but he believes that he must go through with the gesture. His protest throws him out of the artificially ordered world of the A & P, where the third checkout slot looks directly up the row to the meat counter, and into the parking lot where mothers yell at children while pretty girls in bathing suits do not notice small acts of heroism. Worse, they do not care.

Sammy's brash slang covers his sentimental act which neither the teen-agers nor the world accepts. His sacrificial action is incongruous but nevertheless mildly moving. The irony is that the girls never need his help. They stand up well under the Victorianism of Lengel and the stares of the other shoppers. As one of the girls retorts, ''We *are* decent.'' Sammy learns that no one welcomes or even tolerates idle idealism. Rather than insist on a principle, he has merely shown off: ''My stomach kind of fell as I felt how hard the world was going to be to me hereafter.'' . . .

In both ''A & P'' and ''Lifeguard,'' the first-person narrators are defined largely by their tones and vocabularies. No one else supplies background information or details to round out character. Updike experiments with opposite extremes of voice, for Sammy is casual and colloquial while the lifeguard is pompous and pedantic. Sammy initially seems so confident that he may irritate some readers. Surveying the three girls as they wander the aisles, he assumes that his perspective and judgment are naturally correct. When he describes the girls, we wonder if his lyrical flights of language expose the inadequacy of his slang as he stretches to show why these teen-agers deserve his sacrifice: Breasts, for example, become two smooth scoops of vanilla. We can see him longing to ring up the purchase of *that* ice cream. Yet the end of the story suggests that all is not self-righteousness and slang. Sammy has sympathy and a sense of outrage. However ironic, his sacrificial gesture is as refreshing as his colloquial candor. We finish the story sensing that he is more than just another A & P employee with an eye for cute behinds. An observer of his social world, he resolves not just to record but also to act upon his impressions.

Source: Donald J. Greiner, in his *The Other John Updike: Poems, Short Stories, Prose, Plays,* Ohio University Press, 1981, 297 p.

Sources

Detweiler, Robert. *John Updike,* Twayne, 1972, p. 68.

Luscher, Robert M. *John Updike: A Study of the Short Fiction,* Twayne, 1993.

Mizener, Arthur. "Behind the Dazzle Is a Knowing Eye," in the *New York Times Book Review,* March 18, 1962.

Porter, M. Gilbert. "John Updike's 'A & P': The Establishment and the Emersonian Cashier," in *English Journal,* Vol. 61, November, 1972, p. 1157.

A review of *Pigeon Feathers* in the *Times Literary Supplement,* February 1, 1963, p. 73.

A review of *Pigeon Feathers,* in *Time,* March 16, 1962, p. 86.

Uphaus, Suzanne, *John Updike,* Ungar, 1980, pp. 125-26.

Further Reading

Macnaughton, William R. *Critical Essays on John Updike,* G. K. Hall, 1982.
A longer collection of essays and criticism. Authors include fellow fiction writers as well as Updike scholars.

Javna, John and Gordon Javna, *60s!,* St. Martin's, 1988.
A catalogue of 1960s popular culture, from toys to television shows. It also includes a look at some '60s fads that have made a comeback.

Axolotl

Julio Cortazar

1956

Julio Cortazar's short story "Axolotl," from his collection *Final del juego* (*End of the Game, and Other Stories*), has disturbed, perplexed, and delighted a growing number of devoted readers and critics since its publication in 1956. One of Cortazar's most famous stories, it is told by a man who has been transformed into an axolotl, a species of salamander, after spending many hours watching axolotls in an aquarium. As an axolotl, the man still sees the human he used to be and hopes the human will write a story about a man who becomes an axolotl. Many critics find the axolotl's final comment to be the pervading theme of Cortazar's short fiction—that through art one can become another and communicate on behalf of all creatures, so that none may feel the terror of isolation and imprisonment.

Cortazar's fiction unites fantastic and often bizarre plots with everyday events and characters. This method urges readers to look beyond the commonly held conviction of Western thought that life is guided by fact. Instead, Cortazar wants readers to understand that reality is in the eye of the beholder. Cortazar is one of the seminal figures of magic realism, an movement in Latin American literature that began in the 1950s. Cortazar's contemporaries, Gabriel Garcia Marquez and Carlos Fuentes, also combine fantastic and ordinary situations and characters in an attempt to create new ways in which literature can represent life.

Author Biography

Cortazar was born to an Argentinian family living in Brussels, Belgium, in 1914. In 1918 he moved with his parents to their native Argentina. After earning a teaching degree, he taught high school from 1937 to 1944. During this time Cortazar began writing short stories, and in 1938, under the pseudonym Julio Denis, he published *Presencia,* a book of sonnets exhibiting the influence of French Symbolist poet Stephane Mallarme. In 1944 and 1945 Cortazar taught French literature at the University of Cuyo in Mendoza, but he resigned from his post after being arrested for participating in demonstrations against Argentine president Juan Peron. He then moved to Buenos Aires, where he began working for a publishing company. In that same year he published his first short story, ''Casa tomada'' (''House Taken Over''), in *Los anales de Buenos Aires,* an influential literary magazine edited by fellow Argentinian Jorge Luis Borges. Between 1946 and 1948 Cortazar studied law and languages to earn a degree as a public translator. Cortazar has stated that the arduous task of completing this three-year course in less than a year produced temporary neuroses that are reflected in his fiction. One of his phobias, a fear of eating insects hidden in his food, inspired the short story ''Circe,'' a tale about a woman who feeds her suitors cockroaches in the guise of candies.

In 1951 Cortazar published *Bestiario,* his first collection of short stories and also received a scholarship to study in Paris, where he became a translator for the United Nations Educational, Scientific, and Cultural Organization (UNESCO). Paris remained his base until his death. In 1953, collaborating with his wife, Aurora, Cortazar completed translations into Spanish of Edgar Allan Poe's prose works, which were a major influence on his work. Like the characters in his stories and novels, Cortazar was constantly crossing national as well as philosophic boundaries. Throughout his life the author traveled extensively—primarily between France, Argentina, Cuba, Nicaragua, and the United States—often lecturing for social reform in Latin America. He believed that art and writing could bridge gaps between different ways of seeing the world and experiencing reality. By challenging readers to question their individual conceptions of reality and to think beyond them, Cortazar encouraged a better understanding of all people as the only hope for resolving the world's conflicts. A number of Cortazar's works explicitly reflect his strong concern for political and human rights causes. For example, the novel *Libro de Manuel* (1973; *A Manual for Manuel*) is in part an expose of the torture of political prisoners in Latin America. Both in his fiction and in his essays, he was an advocate of socialism and a vocal supporter of the Cuban and Nicaraguan revolutions. Cortazar was a poet, amateur jazz musician, and movie buff. His story ''Blow-Up,'' from the collection *Las armas secretas* was the basis for Michelangelo Antonioni's 1966 film of the same name. Cortazar died of the combined effects of leukemia and a heart attack in Paris in 1984.

Plot Summary

''Axolotl'' opens with a blunt summary of its own plot: ''There was a time when I thought a great deal about the axolotls. I went to see them in the aquarium at the Jardin des Plantes and stayed for hours watching them, observing their immobility, their faint movements. Now I am an axolotl.'' An axolotl, the narrator later explains, is the larval stage of a type of salamander.

The rest of the story recounts how this fantastic transformation took place. The narrator, a man living in Paris, has grown bored with the lions and panthers he usually observes at the zoo, the Jardin des Plantes. He decides to explore the aquarium and unexpectedly ''hits it off with the axolotls.'' A sign above the tank tells him they are Mexican, but he already knows this because their pink faces remind him of Aztecs. He begins to visit the axolotls several times a day. He peers through the glass for hours, studying them closely. He becomes particularly fascinated by their golden eyes, which suggest to him ''the presence of a different life, of another way of seeing.''

As time goes on he feels a growing sense of relationship with the axolotls. One day, as he is pressing his face against the glass, he suddenly realizes that he is no longer looking at the face of an axolotl inside the tank but at his own face, staring into the tank from outside. At that instant he realizes that it is impossible for the man to understand the world of the axolotl: ''He was outside the aquarium, his thinking was a thinking outside the tank. Recognizing him, being him himself, I was an axolotl and in my world.'' He is initially horrified at the idea of being ''buried alive'' in the midst of ''unconscious creatures,'' but his feeling of horror ends as he

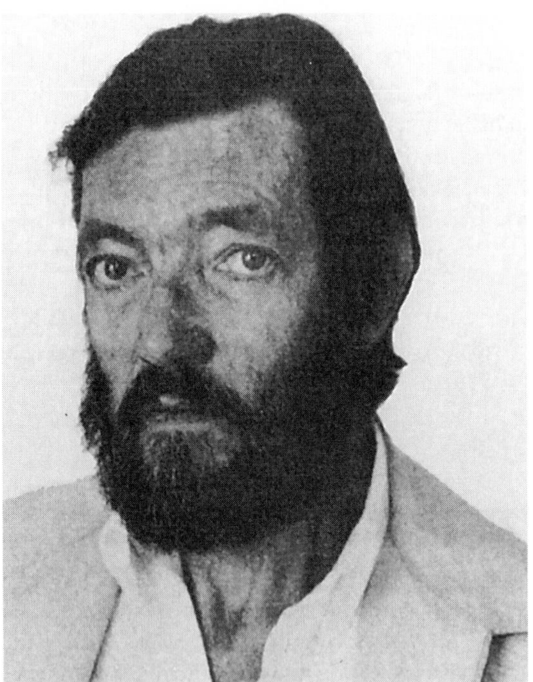

Julio Cortazar

realizes that although the axolotls cannot communicate, they all share his knowledge.

The man visits the tank less and less frequently, and the axolotl-consciousness eventually realizes that the connection between them is broken. In the ''final solitude'' to which the man ''no longer comes,'' the axolotl offers himself the consolation that the man may write a story that will tell ''all this about axolotls.''

Characters

Narrator

The unnamed narrator of ''Axolotl'' is a lonely man who becomes so obsessed with axolotls (Mexican salamanders) that he becomes one—or at least, believes that he does. Cortazar provides few details about the narrator, but the details he does provide are revealing. It is a spring morning, and Paris is ''spreading its peacock tail after a wintry Lent,'' when the narrator visits the Jardin des Plantes. He remarks that he is (or ''was'') a friend of the lions and panthers and had never before entered the ''dark and humid'' aquarium. This suggests that the narrator is attracted to all that is beautiful and assertive in nature: the morning, spring days, lions, and panthers. In fact, it is only when he finds that the lions are ''ugly and sad'' and that the panthers are sleeping—in other words, when they do not measure up to his image of them—that he decides to go into the aquarium. In choosing the beautiful and assertive he has avoided another side of nature, that represented by the dark aquarium. The narrator desperately wants to get inside the mind of the axolotls. He believes their golden eyes speak to him ''of the presence of a different life, of another way of seeing.'' Some critics think that the narrator represents the modern individual in search of self-realization and spirituality.

Themes

Change and Transformation

On one level, the narrator has been transformed into an axolotl. On another, deeper, level he has become a more enlightened being. The literal transformation of man into animal can be understood as a metaphor (a word, thing, or action applied to a distinctly different kind of word, thing or action, without asserting a direct comparison) for a kind of spiritual transformation. In other words, the narrator was unable to think beyond his rational conception of himself until he entered the mind of the axolotl and realized that there were other ways of experiencing existence. The transformation, however, is not complete, since the physical man still exists outside the tank and eventually stops visiting it and his axolotl-self. The existence of the story, however, seems to confirm that some permanent change in the man outside the tank has taken place, since he has presumably retained enough of his insights to write the story.

Consciousness

The man's consciousness struggles against his unconscious. Contemporary studies of human behavior suggest that all people have in the unconscious mind a primitive and instinctual side that they repress more and more deeply as they grow from infancy into adulthood. In contrast, animals never bury these forces. Many psychologists believe that accessing the unconscious can provide a person with a more complete way of living and perceiving the world. This is why psychologists sometimes use hypnosis to help their patients solve problems. For the narrator, the axolotl comes to represent the unconscious portion of his mind. The narrator recalls that before his transformation he "had found in no animal such a profound relation with myself." He was particularly fascinated with the creatures' eyes, which suggested to him the existence of "another way of seeing." "I knew that we were linked," he recalls, "that something infinitely lost and distant kept pulling us together." After his transformation, he overcomes his initial horror at feeling "buried alive" in an unconscious creature as he realizes that the axolotls share an awareness that does not need to express itself. By becoming an axolotl, he bridges the conscious part of his mind with the unconscious. A lasting union of the two aspects of consciousness is, however, impossible. The man still exists "outside the tank," while the part of his consciousness that has made this leap in perception is inside the tank: "I was an axolotl and in my world." As time goes by, the man outside the tank separates himself from his moment of perception: "the bridges were broken between him and me, because what was his obsession is now an axolotl, alien to his human life." Nonetheless, the story ends on a note of hope that the man will carry with him some memory of his perception and will express it in a story.

Passivity

Although the axolotls are capable of moving, they rarely do. The narrator notes that as a rule the only parts of their bodies to move are three small gills on each side of the head. Occasionally a foot moves, but just barely. By observing the axolotls in their transparency and quietness, the narrator becomes aware of what he calls "their secret will, to abolish space and time with an indifferent immobility." The narrator-axolotl comments that this immobility allows the axolotls to avoid "difficulties . . . fights, tiredness." The immobility of the axolotls contrasts with the mobility of the man outside the tank, who rides a bicycle, who comes and goes, and who eventually distances himself from the axolotls and his thoughts about them.

Time

The concept of a realm of consciousness that exists outside of time is reinforced by the continual shifts in the sense of time in the story. The story begins in the past ("There was a time when I thought a great deal about the axolotls"). The narrator then recounts, in the past tense, the events and thoughts leading up to his transformation, occasionally breaking into the present tense to comment from his perspective after the transformation. After the transformation the story ends in the present as the narrator-axolotl reflects on what has happened. Finally, he imagines that the man will, in the future, write a story about axolotls—presumably the story the reader has just read. The constant shifting of temporal planes serves to undermine the reliability of rational thought as opposed to spiritual existence.

Topics for Further Study

- Investigate some of the myths, legends, stories, novels, and films in which humans turn into animals. Have people in real life ever claimed this has happened to them? Are there nonfiction accounts of this phenomenon? What features do these works have in common with "Axolotl"?
- Research the government of Argentina during the 1950s as led by Juan Peron. How did it treat artists and writers? From Cortazar's story, can you conclude what his political opinions may have been?
- What is magic realism? Could "Axolotl" be labeled magic realism ? Explain why or why not. Also, some writers object to the term magic realism; why do you think this is?

The Rational vs. The Spiritual

For Cortazar, the spiritual refers to a person's deepest self, instincts, unconscious, and soul. Humans pass most of their conscious existence grounded in a rational mode of thinking whereby they accept reason as the only authority in determining their opinions and actions. The axolotls in the story are described in a way that makes them a metaphorical expression of a different, non-rational experience. Immobile and inexpressive, they suggest to the narrator, before his transformation, "the presence of a different life, of another way of seeing." The man cannot understand the axolotls; his thinking is "a thinking outside the tank." Nonetheless, the axolotl's comment at the end of the story, "he's going to write all this about axolotls," suggests that the man will not entirely lose touch with the world he sensed but could not understand. Through writing, the man will be able to revisit the axolotl's mind, or, in other words, the unconscious and spiritual side of his nature.

Style

Point of View

The story's narration blurs the line between reality and fantasy. The story is narrated by a first-person narrator, some part of whose consciousness or physical being is transformed into an axolotl. This creates considerable ambiguity, because the "I" and "me" of the narrator may at any point refer to the man before the transformation or to his axolotl-self who is telling the story. The musings of the first are juxtaposed with the insights of the second. While the ambiguous "I" emphasizes the connection between the man and the axolotl, the two contrasting points of view that it represents also serves to highlight the division between the man who remains outside the tank and that part of his consciousness that migrates into the tank. The reader's need to follow the continual shifts between the two viewpoints may also be said to mirror the protagonist's own shift from a limited human perspective to his widened understanding after his transformation. The constant interchange of perspectives undermines the reliability of rational thought and underscores the multiplicity of reality.

Structure

The structure of "Axolotl" is different from that of most short stories because it is circular rather than linear. The major events of the story take place over a period of a few days during which the narrator focuses on the most important phases of his transformation. The opening paragraph is in itself a closed circle which functions as the center of the larger circle of the story: "There was a time when I thought a great deal about the axolotls. I went to see them in the aquarium at the Jardin des Plantes and stayed for hours watching them, observing their immobility, their faint movements. Now I am an axolotl."

Four distinct parts can be found in this cyclical structure. The first involves the narrator's gradual approach to the fascinating but foreign world of the axolotls. He observes and describes them from outside the aquarium glass: "I saw from very close up the face of an axolotl immobile next to the glass." The second deals with the metamorphosis process: "No transition, no surprise," says the narrator, "I saw my face against the glass, I saw it on the outside of the tank, I saw it on the other side of the glass." At this point, the man believes himself to have metamorphosed into an axolotl with his human mind intact—"buried alive," as he puts it—"condemned to move lucidly among unconscious creatures." In the third division, the feeling of horror stops as he becomes so immersed in his new world that he is able to sense what he could not perceive on the other side: "a foot grazed my face, when I moved just a little to one side and saw an axolotl next to me who was looking at me." A fourth part to the story is found in its last paragraph, which functions as an epilogue. Here there is a definite separation between two worlds. Although the narrator had achieved a kind of unity in his knowledge of both the man's perspective and an axolotl's, he cannot communicate that understanding to the man who still remains outside the glass. There is a division between the man who became an axolotl and the man whose visits to the aquarium have ceased. Nonetheless, the axolotl believes "that all this succeeded in communicating something to him in those first days, when I was still he." The axolotl's hope that the man will write "all this about axolotls" completes the circle, since the story the man will write is apparently the story readers have just read.

Symbols

Cortazar is known for employing many symbols in his fiction. A symbol is a word or phrase that suggests or stands for something else without losing its original identity. In literature, symbols combine their literal meaning with the suggestion of an abstract concept. In the story "Axolotl," the axolotl may be interpreted as a symbol of the narrator's unconscious mind. His transformation—or the transformation of a part of his consciousness—into an axolotl functions on a symbolic level. This means that Cortazar is trying to do more than simply tell a story about a man who turns into a salamander. The axolotl further symbolizes basic drives and appetites, which include the urge for self-fulfillment. Like the snake, the axolotl is a symbol of the instinctual self. Struggling for understanding, the narrator mentions "the mystery," "nonexistent consciousness," "mysterious humanity," "secret will," and "diaphanous interior mystery," which were all claiming him. These references underscore the need for symbols to communicate something that cannot be fully expressed in rational terms.

Other prominent images in the story that can be interpreted symbolically include the glass wall of the aquarium, which functions at various times as a mirror, as a barrier, and as a gateway; the golden eyes of the axolotls, which appear to the man as both blank and expressive; and the enclosed and watery world of the aquarium itself.

Magic Realism

Cortazar is one of the seminal figures of magic realism. Magic realism (sometimes called magical realism) is a term applied to the prose fiction of Julio Cortazar, Jorge Luis Borges (Cortazar's mentor), Carlos Fuentes, Gabriel Garcia Marquez, Juan Rulfo, Mario Vargas Llosa, and many other writers who combine the fantastic with ordinary situations in an attempt to create new ways in which literature can represent life. Their work violates, in a variety of ways, standard novelistic expectations by its drastic experiments with subject matter, form, style, temporal sequence, by fusions of the everyday, the fantastic, the mythical, and the nightmarish, and by writings that blur traditional distinctions between what is serious or trivial, horrible or ludicrous, tragic or comic.

Historical Context

Existentialism's Influence on Cortazar

"Axolotl" was first published in 1956. At that time, Cortazar no longer lived in his native Argentina, but in Paris, France. The story is set in Paris and appears to take place in the time it was written. Critic Terry J. Peavler says that the existentialism of Jean-Paul Sartre, an important philosophical movement of the day, influenced Cortzar's "Axolotl." In fact, existentialism, which began in France, inspired many authors of the 1950s, including Irish playwright Samuel Beckett, and French authors Albert Camus and Jean Genet. Peavler draws a comparison between "Axolotl" and Sartre's book *Being and Nothingness,* which was published the same year. Sartre felt that individuals create their own identities through their choices and actions. While people should not think of themselves as comprised of a fixed set of characteristics or categories, neither should they go to the other extreme and conceive of themselves as pure nothingness. At the conclusion of Cortazar's story, the axolotl hopes the narrator will "write all this about axolotls" as a means of finding the existential balance between being (the rational mind idealized in most Western philosophies) and nothingness (the unconscious mind, symbolized by the axolotl's primitive nature). The story suggests that to reach this balance, one must experience both extremes, as the narrator has done, before this kind of self-awareness becomes possible.

World War II and the Absurd

The horror of World War II (1939-45) left Western culture in a state of moral confusion. In a world gone mad, most artists found earlier norms and traditions to be insufficient models of expression. All manner of experimentation took hold in art, theater, philosophy, literature, and film. This violent new world manifested itself in works of an absurdist nature. Eugene Ionesco, a leading writer of the drama of the absurd, states in an essay on Franz Kafka: "Cut off from his religious, metaphysical, and transcendental roots, man is lost; all his actions become senseless, absurd, useless." Peavler believes Ionesco's comment could just as well be applied to the characters in Cortazar's stories of the 1950s. Absurdism is an aspect of magic realism, or the "boom," an innovative movement in Latin and South American literature that began in the 1950s and continues into the late twentieth century, of which Cortazar is one of the seminal figures. However, magic realists do not often use the term "absurdist" to describe their writing; instead, they prefer the term "fantastic." Both terms denote a shift in literature after World War II toward a new definition of reality that rejected rational, convenient, and limiting interpretations of the everyday world. Cortazar uses the word "fantastic" in defining his fiction and his own special way of understanding reality. By "fantastic" he means the alternative to what he calls "false realism" or the view that "everything can be described and explained in line with the philosophic and scientific optimism of the eighteenth century, that is, within a world governed by a system of laws, of principles, of causal relations, of well-defined psychologies, of well-mapped geographies." Cortazar, through his use of fantastic elements, aims to defy the man-made formulae and simplistic explanations of reality that give rise both to the

Compare & Contrast

- **1950s:** Zoos are popular destinations for children and adults alike. Animals are captured in the wild and live the rest of their lives in captivity.

  1990s: Zoos commonly breed captive animals instead of capturing them from the wild since the U.S. Endangered Species Act was passed in 1973. Less than one percent of large mammals in U.S. zoos are captured from the wild. In order to encourage breeding of captive animals, most zoos have upgraded the animals' habitats so that the environment more closely resembles their natural habitats.

- **1950s:** Literature by Latin American authors following the end of World War II becomes characterized by magic realism. The absurd or the fantastic marks the postwar Latin American writing, and a rational view of reality is rejected.

  1997: Gabriel Garcia Marquez, considered a master of magic realism, recieves critical attention for his new book, *News of a Kidnapping,* about the Colombian drug trade of the 1980s.

repression of the unconscious, and, in a political sense, to totalitarianism (the oppression of peoples). When a group or nation is forced to think a certain way by those in power, bloodshed is usually the outcome. In 1956, Soviet troops crushed uprisings in Poland and Hungary because these ''satellite nations'' chose to reinterpret well-defined laws of Soviet communism. During the 1950, many artists, Cortazar included, used absurdist or fantastic elements in their work to open up the mind, liberate repressed thoughts and feelings, and combat restrictive thinking, in an effort to heighten self-awareness and generate a greater tolerance of differing viewpoints.

President Juan Peron of Argentina

Juan Domingo Peron (1895-1974) was president (Cortazar referred to him as a dictator) of Argentina from 1946 to 1955 and from 1973 to 1974. He was one of the most important twentieth-century political figures in South America. When the civilian government was overthrown in 1943, Peron, a career military officer and leader of a politically active military club, became head of the labor department. Supported primarily by the working class and various labor unions, Peron was elected president in 1946 and again in 1951. The Peronist program of economic nationalism and social justice eventually gave way to monetary inflation and political violence, and Peron was ousted by a military coup in 1955. Peron, in exile, continued to be a powerful force in Argentine politics, and he was re-elected in 1973 by a clear majority. Cortazar, a writer with outspoken political beliefs, was defiantly anti-Peronist. In 1945 he was arrested and as a result was forced to relinquish his academic career in Argentina. He became a translator, and in 1951, disgusted with Argentina's tyrannical government, he moved to Paris. ''Axolotl'' was written in Paris around the same time Peron was ousted by a military coup. Some critics see Cortazar's short story as a symbol of rebirth, not of the spiritual self, but of a new Argentine generation replacing a corrupt, fascist one.

Critical Overview

Cortazar is generally acknowledged as one of the most important authors of the mid-century literary ''boom'' in Latin and Central America. A handful of writers, among them Jorge Luis Borges (Argentina), Alejo Carpentier (Cuba), Mario Vargas Llosa (Peru), Jose Donoso (Chile), Gabriel Garcia Marquez (Colombia), and Carlos Fuentes (Mexico), brought

Latin American literature to international prominence in a span of less than thirty years in a literary flowering that has not been matched in Spanish literature since the ''Siglo de Oro'' (the golden century—the seventeenth).

The history of the critical reception of ''Axolotl'' is similar to that of Cortazar's other stories and novels: an immediate popular success, followed by a delay of some years by critical success. Enrique Anderson Imbert, a fellow Argentinian writer and critic, thought Cortazar's early stories, such as ''Axolotl,'' which is now considered to be one of his best, were unsuccessful and disappointing. When ''Axolotl'' was translated and published in English in 1967, American readers enjoyed its idiosyncratic style and bizarre elements, but again critics were not initially impressed. In the 1980s and 1990s, however, critical interest grew.

Like most of the other members of the ''boom,'' Cortazar was deeply involved in politics. In many instances, politics has been as important as aesthetics in determining an author's reception in Latin America, and Cortazar's case is as complex as any. In the early 1960s, Cortazar, like many Latin American intellectuals, became a strong supporter of Fidel Castro's Cuban Revolution and of other nations that were experiencing Marxist or leftist revolutions. Readers in these countries, however, attacked his work for being too concerned with fantasy and not providing ''revolutionary'' content. In rebuttal, Cortazar argued that so long as an artist's ideological position has been established and is well known (everyone was well aware of Cortazar's avowal of socialism), no directives and no critical dogma should be allowed to curb his creative freedom. He particularly stressed the need to create lasting works of art: ''The most serious error we could commit as revolutionaries would be to want to adjust literature or art to suit immediate needs.'' Furthermore, he insisted, any truly creative act is revolutionary, for it advances the present state of art and works toward the future.

Criticism

Sarah Madsen Hardy

Madsen Hardy has a Ph.D. in English and is a freelance writer. In the following essay, she considers Cortazar's use of foreign-language words as a way of understanding how his experience as an expatriate may have shaped the story's style and its themes.

I once took a class in Latin American fiction in which my professor described Cortazar's book as not the sort with which one wants to curl up in bed. There is something cold and distant about Cortazar's style. Plus, one needs to be quite alert to keep up with him. ''Axolotl'' is a story that makes its readers think hard, and such hard thinking is also the story's major theme. ''Axolotl'' is, after all, a story about immobility, thus the protagonist's action entails almost nothing but the laborious processes of his/its/their consciousness. It is this set of qualities, I believe, that leads most readers to either love Cortazar's writing or to hate it. The story is named ''Axolotl'' and reading it, one has an experience not unlike that of the protagonist. Zoo visitor and readers alike encounter the cold, paralyzing, un-human world of the axolotls, the imaginary world of ''Axolotl.'' For those who love it, ''Axolotl'' is an intellectual carnival ride, a mind game, a thrill of perspective. But other readers may feel frustrated with the initially distant protagonist who grows even less familiar and less accessible as the story proceeds—or circles, as the case may be. What's my way into the strange world of this story, they may wonder, and what's at stake in understanding it anyway?

Cortazar's revolutionary Latin American political allies also questioned what was at stake in his writing. They criticized it as too intellectual, too detached from social reality. On the other hand, scholars tend to adore Cortazar for this very same reason. Because Cortazar's writing is so abstract, it is easy to apply theories to it, as theories, too, are by nature abstract. In the few slender pages of prose that make up ''Axolotl,'' Cortazar raises questions about myth and reality, God and man, mind and body, death and rebirth, time and timelessness, being and nothingness. My list is not exhaustive. It is impressive how scholars have managed to interpret ''Axolotl'' by applying many of the most important schools of philosophical thought of the twentieth century, and it is also a little overwhelming. Just what is Cortazar saying about all of these big philosophical questions? Many readers may agree with Doris T. Wight's opening claims in her essay ''Cortazar's 'Axolotl': Contradiction Is All One Can Cling to in the Short Tale,'' ''deception is

An axolotl, a type of salamander indigenous to Mexico and the western United States.

all one can count on,'' ''purposeful obfuscation is all one can grasp,'' and ''confusion is all that appears trustworthy.''

It is helpful, first, to acknowledge, as Wight has, the difficulty of getting a grasp on any one philosophical interpretation before its validity starts to melt away, given the enigmatic nature of the story. It is also helpful to step back from the heady philosophizing and to focus on the concrete, descriptive words on the page. Immediately, the story starts to seem simpler. It is really quite straightforward. While the transformation he describes is fantastical and mysterious, Cortazar goes out of his way to describe it in the most direct and specific way possible.

It is through Cortazar's exquisitely precise use of language that I can find a way into the real and magical world of ''Axolotl.'' Within the context of Cortazar's relationship to the various languages he spoke and the various contexts in which he spoke them, I will explore the use of ''foreign'' language within the story—the non-Spanish words that appear within what was an originally Spanish text (Spanish being Cortazar's native language). I am particularly interested in how such use of different languages can shed light on the *idea of foreignness* —so extreme and abstractly symbolic in the narration of a nameless man's transformation into a larval salamander—as part of Cortazar's social reality, his cultural identity, and his life story.

Cortazar's relationship to his native land and native language was complicated from the start. Since he was born in French-speaking Brussels to Argentinean parents, where he lived until age four, Cortazar's first home was a place where he was, paradoxically, a foreigner. He returned with his family to Argentina, and later, as a young adult, became very active in Latin American politics, identifying strongly with continental, pan-Latino causes, particularly the struggles of the common and poor people. But all the while Cortazar was studying and teaching French, and he was very much engaged with the elite European literary and philosophical discourse associated with this language. In both his life and in his writing, Cortazar moved back and forth between the languages, traditions, and cultures of Europe and Latin America. His familiarity with both gave him a new perspective on each, an ability to translate the terms of one onto the other, such as (Latin) magic and (European) realism. But it also left him nowhere to feel fully at home.

In Spanish the word for foreigner, *extranjero,* is derived directly from the word for strange, *extrano.*

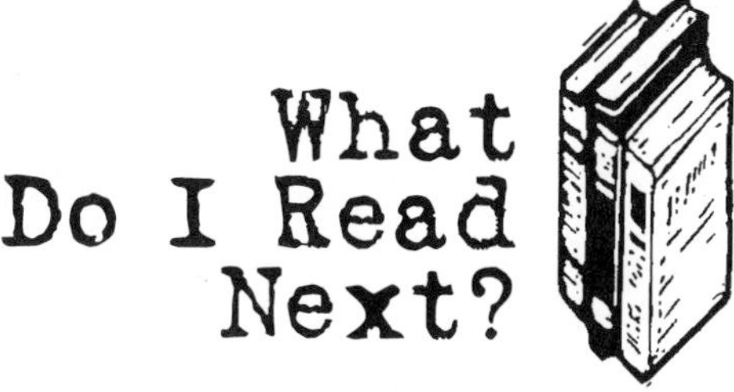

- *The Metamorphosis,* Franz Kafka's 1915 novella. One day a man wakes up to find that he has been transformed into an insect.
- *Labyrinths, Selected Stories and Other Writings,* Jorge Luis Borges's 1962 collection. Recognized all over the world as one of the most original and significant figures in modern literature, Borges was also Cortazar's mentor.
- Evelyn Picon Garfield's 1975 critical study, *Julio Cortazar,* begins and ends with personal interviews that she conducted with Cortazar at his home in Provence, France. An invaluable guide to Cortazar's philosophies, his preferences, and even his nightmares, which illuminate much of the symbolism found in his work.
- Cortazar's 1966 novel *Hopscotch* is recognized as a modern literary classic. Its main character, Horacio Oliveira, has an ambition: to so fragment his personality that his life will become a series of present moments, which never cohere into a perceptible whole. He leaves Argentina to join a floating, loose-knit circle known as "the Club," then returns to Buenos Aires, working by turns as a salesman, as keeper of a mathematically proficient circus cat, and as an attendant in a mental asylum owned by his friends. His is a life truly fragmented—a life of aloof sensuality and empty pleasure over which he has lost control.
- Cortazar's 1960 novel *The Winners* is the story of the winners of a mystery cruise in a special state lottery. Not long after they leave the jubilant dockside cafe in Buenos Aires, tensions emerge among the widely varying personalities. Quarantined from a certain part of the ship, served by a silent and forbidding crew, and treated more like prisoners than winners, they split into two groups: those who want to know what's really going on, and those who prefer to let sleeping dogs lie.

Cortazar wrote "Axolotl" as an expatriate, a political self-exile from his native country of Argentina. He was fired from his job as a professor of French Literature in Argentina because of his opposition to the rising politician Juan Peron, after which he undertook a rigorous, accelerated course of study to work as a public translator. The combination of stresses brought on a period of great emotional instability, precipitating a move to France, where he continued to study, write, and translate. Paris was a place where many cosmopolitan intellectuals gathered, and Cortazar stayed there until his death. But he wrote "Axolotl" in Paris shortly after his arrival, when it was probably most apparent to him that, despite his fluency in French, he was an *extranjero*—a foreigner and a "stranger." Interpreting the very strangeness of the story as an expression of Cortazar's status as an expatriate illuminates a complex cultural and psychological dimension. Approaching the story as in some way autobiographical is narrower than the philosophical interpretations, which have the admitted appeal of addressing big, timeless questions—but I think it warms the story up a bit.

Early in "Axolotl" the issue of foreign language presents itself. The story is set in a real and specific place, the Jardin des Plantes in the city of Paris. In the story, French is the language of locations. Cortazar specifies that the protagonist "was heading down the boulevard Port-Royal," then "took Saint-Marcel and L'Hospital" on the day he first decides to go into the aquarium. The library—the only other setting of the story—is also specified as being "at Sainte-Genevieve." The Paris streets—the "real world" of the protagonist in his human form—are, in this way, set apart from the rest of the fictional world of "Axolotl." This indicates that, as Cortazar writes in his native language, the Parisian environment he moves through and writes of remains foreign. Language creates a distance, a barrier, between the protagonist and the place where he lives.

> "The protagonist knew, before seeking out the scientific facts, that the salamanders were Mexican, simply by looking at their faces."

A use of foreign language that is both more striking and more subtle, is, of course, the story's title and main subject: axolotl. Whether one reads the original Spanish or an English translation, the world *axolotl*—a word Cortazar repeats frequently—stands out as strange and rare. It has a distinctly different sound from any other word in the story, and readers may be unsure how to pronounce it (AK-seh-LOT-l). The reason for this is that axolotl is a word from the Aztec language of Nahuatl. While French and Spanish are closely related as romance languages, both deriving from the ancient European language of Latin, Nahuatl is one of the many native languages of Latin America, predominant before its colonization in the sixteenth century. (Confusingly, Mexico, Central, and South America are designated Latin America, despite the fact that there is nothing ''Latin'' about them except for the fact that they were colonized by the Latinate Spaniards, French and Portuguese.) Cortazar is conscious of how he uses this single Nahuatl word. He offers an alternative, the Spanish *ajolate*—a word that would not have stood out as ''foreign'' in the original Spanish text—suggesting that, like the French location names, the world of the axolotl is set apart from familiar and spontaneous, ''native'' ways of thinking and perceiving. Both the real Paris setting and the magical caged amphibians are somehow strange. This quality of strangeness renders them paradoxically similar and opposite.

Cortazar also gives the Latin name for the salamander's genus, *Ambystoma.* Latin is a ''dead'' language, no longer spoken but used in science for purposes of categorization. Thus, it is associated with empirical facts. Latin is also the language that ties Cortazar, through his native Spanish, to the continent of Europe and the language of French. One might say that it stands for the Western/rational ''real'' of magic realism. The Nahuatl *axolotl,* on the other hand, is mysterious and magical. For the protagonist knew, before seeking out the scientific facts, that the salamanders were Mexican—that is, native to his own native Latin America—simply by looking at their faces. The foreign, set-apart quality of the Nahuatl word is associated with the special kinds of perception accessible only through the salamanders' ''little pink Aztec faces'': ''the eyes, two orifices wholly transparent gold, lacking any life but looking, letting themselves be penetrated by my look, which seemed to travel past the golden level and lose itself in a diaphanous interior mystery,'' and ''the rosy stone of the head, vaguely triangular, but with curved and irregular sides which gave it a total likeness to a statue corroded by time.'' It is through such looking that the protagonist finds another sort of knowledge, not only about the animals but about himself. ''After the first minute I knew that we were linked, that something infinitely lost and distant kept pulling us together.'' Could it be, at least in part, Cortazar's bond with his homeland—the broader, pan-Latino homeland of Cortazar's politics—that is the ''something'' in the axolotl's eye that is paradoxically ''infinitely lost and distant'' and ''pulling us together''? Cortazar never spoke Nahuatl. That, to him, is infinitely lost and inaccessible—nothing like the streets of Paris which he negotiates so ''fluently.'' The axolotls represent the loss of an imagined home (or, more precisely perhaps, a feeling of being ''at home'') that he never had and never will have. Despite being profoundly out of place, trapped and immobile in their tank, the axolotls are so alluring because they represent the only possible link to that imagined home, even through its absolute loss.

The glass at the Paris zoo that separates the Mexican salamanders from the protagonist literally reflects him, and reflects upon his cultural predicament. ''I saw from very close up the face of an axolotl immobile next to the glass. No transition and no surprise, I saw my face against the glass, I saw it on the outside of the tank, I saw it on the other side of the glass.'' It is the very real, concrete barrier of the glass that makes the foreign world of Paris and the foreign world of the tank perform this strange translation, this contradictory melding and splitting that is, on the one hand, a magical feat of double perspective, and, on the other, a reflection of displacement, alienation, and loneliness.

Source: Sarah Madsen Hardy, ''Foreign Worlds and Foreign Languages,'' for *Short Stories for Students,* Gale, 1998.

Doris T. Wight

In the following essay, Wight offers her view of the theme of contradiction in ''Axolotl,'' focusing on Cortazar's narration.

Contradiction is all one can cling to in the short tale ''Axolotl,'' which takes place in the aquarium at the Jardin des Plantes in Paris one spring after a wintry Lent; deception is all one can count on in this story of a tiny animal that is not yet really even an animal; purposeful obfuscation of fact is all one can grasp in this artistic fabrication by Julio Cortazar; confusion is all that appears trustworthy.

Perhaps its very being is an impossibility—the existence of this impossible object, although some first-person narrator (Cortazar? highly unlikely) has called the creature an ''axolotl'' and has even described it. The reader sees, thrown before him by the magic lantern of precise, vivid description, the little rosy translucent body six inches long that looks rather like a lizard's and ends in a fish's tail of marvelous delicacy. Along the back, a transparent fin joins onto the tail. ''Feet of the slenderest nicety'' end in ''tiny fingers with minutely human nails,'' and ''eyes two orifices, like brooches, wholly of transparent gold, each ringed with a very slender black halo'' are painted with the improbable clarity of a Salvador Dali work. The excruciatingly meticulous description goes on and on, its purpose that of persuading someone of the real existence of a tiny being. Yet, there is always something subtly wrong somewhere, everything is too exact and perfect, so determinedly exotic that some force within us makes us resist the slick-glistening words, and we grasp desperately to subterranean denial, we cling to contradiction, we insist on deception, we silently shout ''purposeful obfuscation of fact!'' and trust only to our sense of confusion that we might be spared the face of the narrator, whose madness we sense in horror from the start. For from the very beginning we know that the narrator is insane: how else could one interpret this opening paragraph?

> Hubo un tiempo en que yo pensaba mucho en los axolotl. Iba a verlos al acuario del Jardin des Plantes y *me quedaba* horas mirandolos, observando su inmovilidad, sus oscuros movimientos. Ahora soy un axolotl.
>
> There was a time when I thought a great deal about the axolotls. I went to see them in the aquarium at the Jardin des Plantes and stayed for hours watching them, observing their immobility, their faint movements. Now I am an axolotl.

"Though axolotls think like humans, humans refuse to think like axolotls."

It is precisely because the narrative implies from the very beginning that it is the raving of a lunatic that we reject the explanation that this is but a madman's tale. Or perhaps one should put it this way: we never believe a liar more than when he tells us bluntly that he is lying. Similarly, when we are told that what we are encountering is nothing but nonsense, meaningless fancy, emptily delusionary dreams, then we become intensely, immediately convinced that before us, behind the facade, lies Truth. Thus Cortazar captures us from the start of his tale, and never looses his grip on our credulity and helpless curiosity about the forbidden—for we cannot help interpreting claims to Untruth as glorious opportunities to find the dazzling light, the Secret!

Along with the narrator we become enchanted immediately with the mysterious axolotl and convinced of its importance to our own destinies. That little rosy stone-headed, golden-eyed creature in the aquarium at the Jardin des Plantes that huddles on the floor of moss and stone in the water tank with its eight fellows receiving visits morning after morning by the human visitor: what is it? The entranced visitor who observes it has learned in the library at Sainte-Genevieve, we are told, that:

> los axolotl son formas larvales, provistas de branquias, de una especie de batracios del genero amblistoma.
>
> axolotl are the larval stage (provided with gills) of a species of salamander of the genus Abystoma.

The visitor had already learned by reading the placard at the top of the tank and ''by looking at them and their pink Aztec faces'' that axolotls are Mexican, that ''specimens of them had been found in Africa capable of living on dry land during the periods of drought,'' etc.

Here might lie an almost inaccessible, perhaps truly inaccessible allegory: the Aztec, slave of his body in a world-culture that has left him behind historically, exists as an artifact in a museum or aquarium or library's encyclopedia for middle-class Europeans or Americans to visit and perhaps become infatuated by. For the ''blind gaze, the diminutive gold disc without expression and nonetheless terribly shining'' sends forth, the narration tells us, a message: ''Save us, save us.'' Marxists might identify instantly the impossible object as a Third or Fourth World victim of capitalist exploitation. . . .

But no. Even yet the analysis is not ringing quite true to the text. The analysis, self-assured, does not match the contradictions of the text itself. After telling us in paragraph three, for instance, that he has learned that axolotls are animals, the narrator (the *narration,* to be more exact) denies that facile identification in paragraph six and explicitly states, ''They were not *animals,*'' for axolotls are discovered to have existed much farther back in the evolutionary chain than animals—perhaps justifying their existence in the Garden of Plants. Again, in paragraph seven the larvae are identified as ''witnesses of something, and at times like horrible judges,'' but of a ''something'' increasingly elusive. Then the word ''larva'' slips away from us too, for we are told, very pointedly, that ''larva means disguise and also phantom.'' Meaning has slipped away, and now contradiction is all that we can cling to, an oxymoronic confusion that describes the tiny Aztec faces as ''without expression'' but simultaneously ''of an implacable cruelty.'' And how could we know of that cruelty except through expression on the closely observed Aztec faces, since axolotls cannot speak? The mystery grows and grows, leading to the question that the narrative asks at paragraph's end, ''What semblance was awaiting its hour?''

Perhaps the answer to that frightening question comes shortly. At the conclusion of paragraph nine, the classical ''discovery'' of narratives seems to occur with these words: ''Then my face drew back and I understood.'' What the man watching the axolotls in their tank—and one central axolotl in particular—apparently ''understands'' becomes clear in the next paragraph: he grasps the incredible identification/exchange with the object before him:

> Afuera mi cara volvia a acercarse al vidrio, vera mi boca de labios apretados por el esfuerzo de comprender a los axolotl. Yo era un axolotl y sabia ahora instantaneamente que ninguna comprension era posible.
>
> Outside, my face came close to the glass again, I saw my mouth, the lips compressed with the effort of understanding the axolotls. I was an axolotl and now I knew instantly that no understanding was possible.

Again, contradiction. The man has just said that he understands; but what he understands is that no understanding is possible. Reversal and confusion continue:

> Conociendolo, siendo el mismo, yo era un axolotl y estaba en mi mundo. El horror viia—lo supe en el mismo momento—de creerme prisionero en un cuerpo de axolotl, transmigrado a el con mi pensamiento de hombre, enterrado vivo en un axolotl, condenado a moverme lucidamente entre criaturas insensibles.
>
> Recognizing him, being him himself, I was an axolotl and in my world. The horror began—I learned in the same moment—of believing myself prisoner in the body of an axolotl, metamorphosed into him with my human mind intact, buried alive in an axolotl, condemned to move lucidly among unconscious creatures.

Now consciousness seems clearly located in the axolotl, for the narrator speaks (and here we must repress a smile, even through our terror) from the tank, from among other axolotls. What was told in paragraph five as from the human-narrator's stance has come true, that ''the eyes of the axolotls spoke to me of the presence of a different life, of another way of seeing.'' This other way of seeing appears to involve contradiction as its very essence. As an axolotl, the narrator sees another axolotl next to him looking at him, one who understands him, the narrator assures us, for he ''can tell''; yet the narration also assures us that despite that communication of understanding between these two tiny creatures, there was ''no communication possible.'' All the axolotls look at the face of the man outside the tank now, including presumably the man-turned-axolotl himself, all these tiny brilliantly drawn primeval forces questioning and confronting the human condition; but the modern-day God, man, grows less and less interested in the axolotls from which he once sprang, and to whose species he still belongs, since he is both down inside the tank looking up at the exalted human, and also up above staring hypnotically at his past self.

One must halt again. The man grows disinterested in those creatures of his own primeval being, the axolotls from which he evolved. This should mean—though apparently it does not—a corresponding lessening of interest of the axolotls in the man since, as the man-axolotl narrator informs us, ''every axolotl thinks like a man inside his rosy stone resemblance.'' Contradiction, contradiction. Bafflement again.

All attempts at rational comprehension of this tale, all efforts to make it mirror an actual, coherent, believable world, again resist our pleas, yet the more we deny understanding, the more we seem to be on the verge of capturing it. For of course the narrator was not mad at the moment of his identification with the larval salamander, the primitive creature who stepped out of the waters to live in a wholly new environment, the land, the creature that prophesied the coming of humans in its very form: the feet ending in tiny *fingers* with minutely *human* nails, the little pink *Aztec faces,* the "handsome eyes so similar to our own," in which the human observer read at last "that liquid hell they were undergoing" because it was his own. That moment of identification, rather than a plunge into madness, was the human's one instant of enlightenment, his realization that "Thou art That" and "That art Thou," his simultaneous grasp of Darwinian evolution and the counter-truth of the Buddhistic doctrine of Nothingness, that progress and regression alike are illusory.

In the end, however, the only world this tale agrees to present on the surface is a language world. The situation is as if the manifest content of a dream has been cut off from the latent content, repressed underworlds are denied the chance to surface, and an artistically inclined, self-indulgent dreamer busily and engagingly works on processes of secondary elaboration, spinning a tale of words by words about words.

"I console myself by thinking that perhaps he is going to write a story about us, that, believing he's making up a story, he's going to write all this about axolotls," says the forlorn object, the subject that has gone over completely into the mirror image, the man/axolotl. Alas, the severed subject, the man above the tank, never thinks the desired message, "Save us, Save us"; for though axolotls think like humans, humans refuse to think like axolotls. The man, having left the tank in boredom, is now too busy analyzing his experience, rationalizing, conjuring words, words, words, trying to describe logically, and thus contradictorily, the impossible historical event that never took place in the aquarium at the Jardin des Plantes in Paris one spring after a wintry Lent.

Source: Doris T. Wight, "Cortazar's 'Axolotl'," in *The Explicator,* Vol. 45, No. 2, Winter, 1987, pp. 59–63.

Harry L. Rosser

Rosser is a professor at Boston University. In the following essay, he examines the theme of transformation in "Axolotl," relating it to the psychology of Carl Jung.

In the narratives of Julio Cortazar there is an intense preoccupation with the unexplainable phenomena which invade individual and collective experience. This restless, self-exiled Argentine rejects the rational, convenient, and limiting interpretations of the every-day world. He defies man-made formulae and simplistic explanations of reality. Cortazar believes that human beings can change and act upon their limitless potential for self-realization, for spiritual fulfillment, for a totality of life.

> "The salamander in Cortazar's story may be seen as an archetypal representation of basic drives and appetites which include the urge for self-fulfillment."

Cortazar uses the word "fantastic" in defining his fiction and his own special way of understanding reality. By "fantastic" he means the alternative to what he calls "false realism" or the view that "everything can be described and explained in line with the philosophical and scientific optimism of the eighteenth century, that is, within a world governed by a system of laws, of principles, of causal relations, of well-defined psychologies, of well-mapped geographies." He has emphasized that for him there exists "the suspicion of another order, more secret and less communicable" in which the true study of reality is found in the exceptions to the laws rather than in those laws themselves. For Cortazar, the approach to this order requires a loosening of the mind in order to make it a more receptive instrument of knowledge to stimulate authentic transformations in man. This approach is evident in many of the short stories of this imaginative non-conformist.

Of the several stories that reflect Cortazar's fascination with fantastic incursions into the rational world of the self, "Axolotl" most memorably portrays a transformation experience and raises questions about the nature of that experience. While the story can be read as a direct narration of novelistic events, it lends itself to elucidation on another level as well. The purpose here is to offer an interpretation of Cortazar's narrative within the context of his unusual view of reality. This first requires a brief synthesis of the plot and an examination of the literary techniques which make the story work.

''Axolotl'' is the autobiographical account of a lonely man, Cortazar's anonymous narrator-protagonist, who frequents the city zoo and one day wanders into an aquarium where he has never been before. There he feels a peculiar attraction toward a group of translucent, rose colored *axolotls,* a species of Mexican salamander with large golden eyes. He returns day after day to be drawn into hypnotic contemplation of the fishy creatures. He senses that they are endowed with a special intelligence and project an inexplicable power which he finds irresistible. He perceives that he has some remote link with the salamanders. Time and space disappear for him in the presence of these beings belonging to a different life.

Gradually a metamorphosis takes place as the man becomes convinced that he has been transformed into one of the tranquil salamanders looking at him from inside the aquarium. He feels alarmed but also strangely comforted. He senses that his human mind is inside the body of the amphibian. At the same time he feels a oneness with the other salamanders which glide about him inside the tank. The salamander element in the man has left him to establish a separate kind of existence. The expanded ego of the narrator goes from one side of the glass to the other. The salamander is no longer simply the object of the narrator's observation, it now becomes engaged in the act of observing.

The enigmatic communication between man and salamander, it becomes clear, cannot be sustained. A rupture of sorts occurs. Silence invades the atmosphere. By the end of the story, the narrator-protagonist is the salamander and comments on the man who had previously been the narrator. On one side of the glass the man, no longer the person he used to be, stops visiting the aquarium. On the other side remains the salamander, consoled by the possibility that the man will write a story about this unsettling experience.

Cortazar uses a variety of literary techniques in ''Axolotl.'' The events of the story take place over a period of a few days during which the narrator-protagonist focuses on critical phases of the transformation process. There is no linear sequence or spatial constancy. There appears to be no plot development, an impression conveyed by a circular kind of narrative procedure. The central idea established in the first few lines of the story is regularly reiterated: ''There was a time when I thought a great deal about the axolotls. I went to see them in the aquarium at the Jardin des Plantes and stayed for hours watching them, observing their immobility, their faint movements. Now I am an axolotl.''

The opening paragraph is in itself a closed circle which, as one critic has pointed out, functions as the center of the larger circle of the story. For Antonio Pages Larraya [in *Homenaje a Julio Cortazar,* 1972] three distinct parts can be found in this cyclical structure. The first involves the protagonist's gradual approach to the fascinating but foreign world of the salamanders. He observes and describes them from outside the aquarium glass: ''I saw from very close up the face of an axolotl immobile next to the glass.'' The second deals with the metamorphosis process: ''No transition, no surprise,'' says the narrator, ''I saw my face against the glass, I saw it on the outside of the tank, I saw it on the other side of the glass.'' At this point, the man believes himself to have metamorphosed into a salamander with his human mind intact—''buried alive,'' as he puts it, ''condemned to move lucidly among unconscious creatures.'' In the third division, the feeling of horror stops as he becomes so immersed in his new world that he is able to sense what he could not perceive on the other side: ''. . . a foot grazed my face, when I moved just a little to one side and saw an axolotl next to me who was looking at me. . . .''

It should be added that a fourth part to the story is found in its last paragraph, which functions as an epilogue. Here there is a definite separation between two worlds. The narrator-protagonist had achieved a kind of unity. There is now, however, a division between the man who became a salamander and the man whose visits to the aquarium have ceased. The salamander declares: ''I am an axolotl for good now, and if I think like a man it's only because every axolotl thinks like a man inside his rosy stone semblance. I believe that all this succeeded in communicating something to him in those first days, when I was still he.''

As in a number of Cortazar's stories, suspense in ''Axolotl'' is not dependent upon the element of surprise but upon the particular experience described and upon the atmosphere of tension in which that experience takes place. Cortazar has stated that it is of utmost importance to him to hold the attention of his reader-accomplices, as he likes to call them, and to widen their horizons. Thus he advocates a style that, in his words, ''consists of those elements of form and expression that fit the thematic nature of the story in a precise fashion, elements that give it its most penetrating and original visual and auditory form, that make it unique, unforgettable, that fix it forever in its time, in its atmosphere and in its most primordial sense.'' ''Axolotl'' is typical of Cortazar in other ways: it introduces a protagonist in a situation characterized by a routine existence; it recounts the way in which an alien presence interrupts that routine; and it reveals—at least partially—the consequences of that intervention.

''Axolotl'' is a story in which the line between reality and fantasy gradually blurs in the reader's mind. It is narrated from several different perspectives that shift unpredictably and whose sources are somewhat ambiguous. Intentional confusion is caused by the skillful use of personal pronouns, verbal suffixes, and several verb tenses that are associated with the varying points of view. The fact that pronouns can be readily abandoned in Spanish in favor of implications carried by the verb makes for even more subtle variations in perspective (e. g., *''era''* can mean ''I was,'' ''you were'' [formal singular], ''he was,'' ''she was,'' or ''it was''). In addition to this, the reader must keep track of to whom the first person singular refers as well as of the function of the first person plural and the third person singular and plural. There is the ''ego I'' of the man before and after the metamorphosis; there is the collective ''we'' of the man and the salamanders, and of the salamanders as a group; there is the use of the third person singular ''he'' and plural ''they'' by the man, both before and after the change, as well as by a kind of omniscient narrator.

The multiple perspectives established through the use of various pronouns and verbal suffixes are developed even further by a constant change in the temporal context. Several verb tenses appear in the same short paragraph or even in the same sentence: ''The axolotls huddled on the wretched, narrow (only I can know how narrow and wretched) floor of stone and moss.'' The story begins in the past (''There was a time when I thought a great deal about the axolotls.''), skips back and forth in time and then draws to a close in the present. The use of the present tense imbues the account with a sense of open-endedness. The last words of the salamander are: ''And in this final solitude, to which he no longer comes, I console myself by thinking that perhaps he is going to write a story about us, that, believing he's making up a story, he's going to write all this about axolotls.''

Taken together, these literary techniques underscore the multiplicity of reality which Cortazar is so intent upon conveying through his fiction. The constant interchange of perspectives and temporal planes that the techniques create undermines the reliability of rational thought. Cortazar's innovative methods are meant to revitalize language as well as people. ''I've always found it absurd,'' he says, ''to talk about transforming man if man doesn't simultaneously, or previously, transform his instruments of knowledge. How to transform oneself if oneself continues to use the same language Plato used?''

In ''Axolotl'' Cortazar has sought to express something for which there is no verbal concept within the realist mode of writing. He rejects writing on the basis of logical conceptualizations, for the mode he refers to as ''fantastic'' is not practiced from an intellectual standpoint. In fact, he has explained that, for the most part, writing just happens to him. It is a kind of literary exorcism. By his own admission it is a process by which he attempts to deal with the products of his own imagination which resist control and upset a carefully, albeit precariously, established way of life. On occasion it is as though he were a medium receiving a force over which he has no conscious control. The story under analysis, therefore, can be seen as a metaphor because it clearly has that mysterious quality of suggesting meaning beyond the mere anecdote of the narrative.

The meanings implied in the transformation may be numerous. The interpretation offered here is that the significance of the event described in ''Axolotl'' closely coincides with Carl Gustav Jung's views on the dynamics and development of the self. Indeed, the similarities are remarkable between Cortazar and the Swiss psychologist, particularly in regard to the concept of reality. ''The distinctive thing about real facts,'' writes Jung [in *The Undiscovered Self,* tr. R. F. C. Hall, 1958], ''is their individuality. Not to put too fine a point on it, one could say that the real picture consists of nothing but exceptions to the rule, and that, in consequence, absolute reality has predominantly the character of irregularity.'' What happens in ''Axolotl'' strongly suggests that Cortazar means to represent an ego-conscious personality striving for wholeness, or what Jung describes [in ''On the Nature of Dreams''] as ''the ultimate integration of conscious and unconscious, or better, the assimilation of the ego to a wider personality.''

Throughout the narrative it is suggested that Cortazar is actually portraying aspects of a process of self-realization. The solitary, routine existence in which the protagonist is mired is interrupted by an unexpected obsession for the salamanders. He is unable to think of anything else. Through the function of intuition he senses the attractive power of a collective image: ''I knew that we were linked, that something infinitely lost and distant kept pulling us, together.'' In Jungian terms the unconscious component of the self—that is, those personal psychic activities and contents which are ''forgotten, repressed or subliminally perceived, thought, and felt''—erupts into consciousness. It does this on its own accord, requiring the ego somehow to assimilate the new content. [Jung, ''Psychological Types'']. Cortazar's protagonist describes psychic associations which suggest that the activity originates in the unconscious, not only on a personal but on a collective level as well. In the unconscious, as Jung explains, there is interaction between ''the acquisitions of the personal existence'' and ''the inherited possibility of psychic functioning in general, namely, in the inherited brain structure.'' Being the base of the psyche of every individual, the collective unconscious is a kind of heritage passed on to all human beings, and maybe even to all animals as well.

With these concepts in mind, the salamander in Cortazar's story may be seen as an archetypal representation of basic drives and appetites which include the urge for self-fulfillment. Like the snake, the salamander is a symbol of what Jung calls ''the undifferentiated instinctual world in man'' [Jolande Jacobi, *The Psychology of C. G. Jung,* 1975]. Struggling for understanding, the protagonist makes mention of ''a diaphanous interior mystery,'' ''a secret will,'' ''a mysterious humanity,'' ''nonexistent consciousness,'' ''the mystery,'' etc. which were all claiming him. Such references underscore the need for symbols to communicate something that cannot be fully expressed in rational terms.

The narrator-protagonist gives even more weight to the primordial image that amphibians convey by his persistent attention to the eyes of the salamanders: ''Above all else, their eyes obsessed me,'' he reveals. They are referred to as ''eyes of gold,'' ''golden eyes,'' and ''diminutive golden discs.'' Apart from the hypnotic effect that is suggested through the man's reaction to the eyes, they may be understood to have psychological meaning as well. The eye is traditionally considered to be a window to the soul. Like sparks and stars, it is an artistic motif associated with the illumination of consciousness. Indeed, consciousness has commonly been described in terms related to light. With regard to ''Axolotl'' it is worth noting that references to fishes' eyes can be found readily in medieval texts. Apparently they are meant to represent the introspective intuitions which in some way apprehend the state of the unconscious. Clearly, the eyes of the salamanders serve a similar purpose and evoke analogous associations in Cortazar's text.

There is further and more telling evidence that the metamorphosis in this story has to do with a creative transformation, reflecting the archetypal experience of an inner rebirth. The protagonist overcomes his initial horror at feeling submerged in unconscious creatures. He conveys the idea of achieving a kind of complete unity, at least temporarily, in such statements as: ''It would seem easy, almost obvious, to fall into mythology. I began seeing in the axolotls a metamorphosis which did not succeed in revoking a mysterious humanity. . . . They were not human beings, but I had found in no animal such a profound relation with myself.'' The man's consciousness had been struggling against the primitive unconsciousness of unmitigated instinctuality. Jung eloquently describes this kind of conflict: ''The closer one comes to the instinct world, the more violent is the urge to shy away from the murks of the sultry abyss. Psychologically, however, the archetype as an image of instinct is a spiritual goal toward which the whole nature of man strives; it is the sea to which all rivers wend their way, the prize which the hero wrests from the fight with the dragon. '' [Jung, ''On the Nature of the Psyche''].

It is understood that what the man in ''Axolotl'' has undergone is not only fantastic but primitive and symbolic as well. The more primordial the experience seems, the more it represents the potentiality of being. The contents of the unconscious can provide a more complete way of living and perceiving. The salamanders' eyes speak to the man ''of the presence of a different life, of another way of seeing.'' Such subjective perception and introverted sensation have been discussed at length by Jung. He believes that primordial images, in their totality, constitute a ''psychic mirror world'' that represents the present contents of consciousness, not in their familiar form but in the way a million-year old consciousness might see them. [Jung, ''Psychological Types''].

More primordial imagery can be found in ''Axolotl.'' The narrator protagonist reiterates that to his way of thinking the salamanders are not human beings, but that they are not animals either. In comparing the two, he insists on the positive value of the animal. This is a recurring theme in

Cortazar's fiction. "The intention is not to degrade man," as [Antonio Pages Larraya] has put it, "but to do away with certain ill-founded pretensions regarding the nature of mankind." The protagonist's sense of a superior perceptive faculty is alluded to at the end of the story. The transformed protagonist asserts that the salamander next to him "knew also, no communication possible, but very clearly knew." This observation seems to point to the idea of a world-soul which pervades all living creatures, enabling them to have a special sense of things, including those that are yet to be.

Jung's psychology of the unconscious provides for the specific kinds of instinctual patterns in human biology. The existence of these patterns, however, is difficult to establish through the empirical approach to knowledge. Cortazar deals with this very point in "Axolotl." He develops the idea that the ways for apprehending these patterns in man are characterized by an inherent duality. This kind of duality has been discussed by Jung, who explains that consciousness itself is a transformation of the original instinctual image while at the same time it is the transformer of that image. The man in Cortazar's story feels conflicts between conscious and unconscious contents, between knowledge and faith, and between spirit and nature. His psychic situation has disrupted him to the point where he admits, on the one hand, that he is frightened by a compulsive force within him. On the other hand, he implies that his consciousness has deepened and broadened, allowing him to deal with the instincts which he feared would make him a prisoner within the salamander.

Cortazar's protagonist, then, has been caught up in an unsettling development process which leads to a kind of synthesis of conscious and unconscious elements. As it is explained in the story "what was his obsession is now an axolotl." In other words, the narrator's momentous transformation signifies that he has become consciously aware of the effects of an instinctual side that he had neglected or suppressed. He has now integrated its valuable elements into his being. He no longer yields entirely to his rational conception of himself. He has discovered that he has a larger capacity for self-awareness. The details of what the hidden mind and spirit reveal to the narrator-protagonist are not disclosed specifically to the reader, but it is suggested that he has gained a deeper understanding of life. In relating to the amphibious creatures of the aquarium he acquires the insights, the means of comparison, that he needed for self-knowledge and for a sense of continuity as a living being. "Only the person who can consciously assent to the power of the inner voice becomes a personality," Jung has written [Jacobi, *The Psychology of Jung*]. The man in "Axolotl" has heard that voice in the salamander and has gained the psychological advantage of a larger sense of life and of a reaffirmation of the spirit. He is now a changed, more complete being.

There may be disagreement over whether or not the transformation experience depicted in "Axolotl" has positive connotations. Some readers are of the opinion that Cortazar has told a story about a personal failure, about a defeat. The argument is that the salamander abandons the man, that a lack of communication ensues, and that at the end the man is left impoverished by the experience. "The 'I' is denied the possibility of living on two planes," concludes one critic [Malva Filer in *Homenaje a Julio Cortazar*]. The interpretation that has been presented here views the transformation as positive. The conflicts over the matter arise from the enigmatic qualities of Cortazar's fiction, which reflects the inherent ambiguities of reality itself. Most likely, debate over the issue will go on. In any event, what is clear is that the readers of Cortazar's "Axolotl" are left with a heightened sense of awe regarding the potentialities of biological, spiritual and, most of all, literary realities.

Source: Harry L. Rosser, "The Voice of the Salamander: Cortazar's 'Axolotl' and the Transformation of the Self," in *Kentucky Romance Quarterly,* Vol. 30, No. 4, 1983, pp. 419–27.

Daniel R. Reedy

Reedy is a professor at the University of Kentucky. In the following excerpt, he presents his views on the mythic structure of "Axolotl," focusing on its theme of rebirth.

One of the threads common to the fabric of *Rayuela* [*Hopscotch*] and several of Cortazar's short stories is the looking-glass image which functions symbolically as the aperture through which the author reveals a recurrent mythic process involving many of his characters. These moments of revelation, which allow the perception of the essential nature of something or the intuitive grasp of a hidden reality, are akin to [James] Joyce's epiphanies which have been described as 'the single word that tells the whole story . . . the simple gesture that reveals a complex set of relationships. What seem trivial details to others may be portentous symbols to him'

"The unanswered questions in this work relate to the circumstances of how, by metamorphosis, transmigration, or some other transformation, he has become an axolotl."

[Henry Levin, *James Joyce: A Critical Introduction,* 1941].

In one of the Expendable Chapters of *Rayuela,* Cortazar's alter ego, Morelli, describes the genetic archetype of the mirror image:

> No podre renunciar jamas al sentimiento de que ahi, pegado a mi cara, entrelazado en mis dedos, hay como una deslumbrante explosion hacia la luz, irrupcion de mi hacia lo otro o de lo otro en mi, algo infinitamente cristalino que podria cuajar y resolverse en luz total sin tiempo ni espacio. Como una puerta de opalo y diamante desde la cual se empieza a ser eso que verdaderamente se es y que no se quiere y no se sabe y no se puede ser.

This crystalline door appears in Cortazar's early works in several related forms, as a crystal ball, the porthole of an airplane, the glass wall of a formicarium, the lens of a camera, or the refracted glass of a kaleidoscope. Each image has its own unique qualities, yet collectively their symbolic function is to shed light on the more recondite significance of the works in which they appear. It is worth while observing, as well, that they all share a certain kinship in form and substance with the mirror which may symbolize '. . . the mythic form of a door through which the soul may free itself "passing" to the other side. . . .' [J. E. Cirlot, *A Dictionary of Symbols,* translated by Jack Sage, 1962]. Such is the case of the mirror-door, for example, in [Lewis] Carroll's *Through the Looking-Glass. . . .*

The emphatic statement by the protagonist of 'Axolotl' (*Final del juego,* 1964) in the first line of the work—'Ahora soy un axolotl'—leaves little mystery about his physical form. The unanswered questions in this work relate to the circumstances of how, by metamorphosis, transmigration, or some other transformation, he has become an axolotl. The protagonist's dual nature (man/axolotl) is further accentuated by his use of the first person plural, not as an editorial 'we,' but to denote his oneness with all axolotls. Yet he continues to describe them from a third-person objective, albeit emphatic point of view.

The inordinate attraction of these larval, embryonic creatures for the protagonist-narrator prompts his daily visits to the aquarium in the Jardin des Plantes. He is motivated in part by intellectual curiosity, by a desire to understand their *voluntal secreta,* and by what one critic [Antonio Pages Larraya, in *Homenaje a Julio Cortazar,* 1972] calls 'la busqueda de solidaridad y comprension'—sentiments which he appears not to have found in his own world. Each day he takes his station at the glass pane of the aquarium which separates, yet serves to join him to the captive axolotls which in their silence seem to communicate the promise of a world where temporal and spatial limitations do not exist. His problem is to find the passageway which will lead him into their midst.

Finally, as the protagonist contemplates the reflection of his own face in the glass of the aquarium with his axolotl counterpart on the other side, his spirit transmigrates into the body of the axolotl:

> Mi cara estaba pegada al vidrio del acuario, mis ojos trataban una vez mas de penetrar el misterio de esos ojos de oro sin iris y sin pupila. Veia de muy cerca la cara de un axolotl inmovil junto al vidrio. Sin transicion, sin sorpresa, vi mi cara contra el vidrio, en vez del axolotl vi mi cara contra el vidrio. Entonces mi cara se aparto y yo comprendi.
>
> Solo una cosa era extrana: seguir pensando como antes, saber. Darme cuenta de eso fue en el primer momento como el horror del enterrado vivo que despierta a su destino. Afuera, mi cara volvia a acercarse al vidrio, veia mi boca de labios apretados por el esfuerzo de comprender a los axolotl. Yo era un axolotl y sabia ahora instantaneamente que ninguna comprension era posible.

The glass pane functions both as a reflector of his physical state as a man and as the doorway leading to the other side, to the reality of the axolotls. Dr Pages Larraya's observation is pertinent that 'La insistencia en el uso de la palabra "vidrio" subraya a la vez la transferencia de planos que separa realidad e irrealidad.' The glass becomes an avenue of transcendence through which the protagonist passes into another reality.

While he does not bring the fact to the fore, Cortazar obviously had in mind a structure based on Aztec myth when he chose the axolotl as a counterpart of the protagonist of this work. One of the earliest versions of the transformation myth of the god Xolotl is recorded by Padre Bernardino Sahagun [in *Historia general de las cosas de Nueva Espana,* 1938], who points out that Xolotl was one of the twin brothers of the god Quetzalcoatl and a deity of dual phenomena, having existed in several dual forms:

> . . . dicese que uno llamado Xolotl rehusaba la muerte, y dijo a los dioses: '¡Oh dioses! ¡No muera yo!' Y lloraba en gran manera, de suerte que se le hincharon los ojos de llorar; y cuando llego a el el que mataba echo a huir, y escondiose entre los maizales, y convirtiose en pie de maiz que tiene dos canas, y los labradores le llaman *xolotl;* y fue visto y hallado entre los pies del maiz; otra vez echo a huir, y se escondio entre los magueyes, y convirtiose en maguey que tiene dos cuerpos que se llama mexolotl; otra vez fue visto, y se echo a huir y metiose en el agua, y hizose pez que se llama axolotl, y de alli le tomaron y le mataron.

Of particular importance in the myth is the fact that the god Xolotl was the larval form assumed by Quetzalcoatl in the Land of the Dead, out of which he was born as spirit. For the protagonist of 'Axolotl,' the material, corporal state remains outside the aquarium glass as the spiritual self transmigrates through the glass medium to take its place within an axolotl where a sense of eternal entrapment results; nonetheless, the myth of Xolotl and the spiritual rebirth of his twin Quetzalcoatl suggest the promise of rebirth in a spiritual sense for the protagonist, as well, even though he is unaware of the fact.

There is an appropriate correspondence between the function of the aquarium glass as the medium through which the transmigration occurs and the water-filled aquarium with the embryonic axolotls representing the womb from which rebirth may take place. In his discussion of this type of myth, Mircea Eliade explains [in *Myth and Reality,* tr. Willard R. Trask, 1963] that 'the *regressus ad uterum* is accomplished in order that the beneficiary shall be born into a new mode of being or be regenerated. From the structural point of view, the return to the womb corresponds to the reversion of the Universe to the "chaotic" or embryonic state.' And he explains further the spiritual significance of the process: 'the "return to the origin" prepares a new birth, but the new birth is not a repetition of the first, physical birth. There is properly speaking a mystical rebirth, spiritual in nature. . . .'

The significance of mythic structure in 'Axolotl' is found in the culmination of the protagonist's search which imitates the pattern of search for spiritual rebirth. His apparent fate as a prisoner in the body of an axolotl does not suggest necessarily a negative destiny for the central character; rather, his transformation promises a new state of being instead of the solitude and isolation of the aquarium. Like Quetzalcoatl, he must await the time of spiritual rebirth which will come from his present chrysolic form. Laurette Sejourne's observation that 'Xolotl . . . is simply the seed of the spirit enclosed in matter, the dark region of Death' reinforces the idea that the protagonist's ultimate fate is not an eternal hell, but the promise of rebirth out of matter into spirit. In fact, this concept is at the centre of Man's desire to attain the paradisiacal state. Even though his protagonist seems unaware of his final destiny, Cortazar knows that passage to the other side awaits.

Source: Daniel R. Reedy, "Through the Looking-Glass: Aspects of Cortazar's Epiphanies of Reality," in *Bulletin of Hispanic Studies,* Vol. LIV, No. 2, April, 1977, pp. 125–34.

Sources

Rabassa, Gregory. "Lying to Athena: Cortazar and the Art of Fiction." *Books Abroad,* Vol. 50, No. 3, Summer, 1976, pp. 542-7.

Further Reading

Alazraki, Jaime, and Ivan Ivask, eds. *The Final Island.* Norman: University of Oklahoma Press, 1978.

The Final Island is a collection of essays, including two by Cortazar himself, about the role of magic as it works alongside what appears to be realism in Cortazar's fiction. The essays are helpful, though advanced and complex in language and concept.

Garfield, Evelyn Picon. "An Encounter With Julio Cortazar." In her *Julio Cortazar,* pp. 1-11. New York: Frederick Ungar Publishing Co., 1975.

Garfield begins and ends her study with personal interviews she conducted with Cortazar at his home in Provence, France. An invaluable guide to Cortazar's philosophies, his preferences, and even his nightmares, which illuminate much of the symbolism found in his work.

Neyenesch, John G. "On This Side of the Glass: An Analysis of Cortazar's 'Axolotl'," in *The Contemporary Latin-American Short Story,* edited by Rose S. Minc, Senda Nueva De Ediciones, 1979, pp. 54–60.

Discusses "Axolotl" in the framework of Latin-American literature, especially in regards to imagery and themes.

Peavler, Terry J. *Julio Cortazar,* pp. 1-23. Boston: Twayne Publishers, 1990.

Peavler argues that analyzing Cortazar's works as ''psychological'' or ''political'' produces a superficial understanding of his intent, which is to study the nature of fiction itself. A thorough and accessible study.

Bartleby the Scrivener, A Tale of Wall Street

Herman Melville

1853

''Bartleby the Scrivener'' was written by Herman Melville in 1853 and was first published in *Putnam's Magazine* in the November/December issue of that year. The plot involves one man's difficulty in coping with his employee's peculiar form of passive resistance. One day, Bartleby the scrivener announces that he ''would prefer not to'' follow his employer's orders or even to be ''a little reasonable.'' The resulting tragedy follows from Bartleby's inability or unwillingness to articulate the reasons for his rebellion and from his employer's inability to comprehend Bartleby's reasons for resisting and ultimate unwillingness to accommodate him. The story has been interpreted by critics in numerous ways. Most have viewed it as a work of social criticism dealing with the psychological effects of capitalism as it existed in the 1850s. Others have viewed it as a philosophical meditation on the human condition, or as a religious parable on religion itself. However one interprets its ultimate meaning, the story provides an exploration into such universal issues of the human experience as alienation, passivity, nonconformity, and psychological imprisonment. The story's enduring appeal largely stems from its well-crafted ambiguity. It is highly admired for its remarkable ability to accommodate multiple interpretations.

Author Biography

Herman Melville was born in New York City on August 1, 1819. He was the son of Allan Melville, a successful merchant, and Maria Gansevoort Melville, who came from an old New York family of distinction and wealth. Although their family name was well respected, the Melvilles went bankrupt in 1830. Allan Melville tried to re-establish his business in Albany, New York, but his financial burdens drove him to a mental and physical breakdown. In 1832, when Herman was twelve, his father died, leaving the Melville family heavily burdened by debt. The experience of his father's financial ruin and mental collapse left a deep impression on the young Melville, who later explored issues of sanity and the pressures of capitalism in such stories as "Bartleby the Scrivener."

After his father's death, Melville left school and worked odd jobs. Melville briefly considered becoming a legal scrivener but was unable to secure a job. In 1839 he signed on as a sailor and spent the next five years at sea. In 1842 he jumped ship in the Marquesas Islands of the South Pacific during a whaling voyage and spent several months living among a tribe of cannibals in the Taipi Valley. While traveling en route to Tahiti after being picked up by an Australian whaler, Melville was imprisoned by the British Consul for refusing duty on the ship. He then escaped from Tahiti and made his way on various whaling ships to Honolulu, Hawaii, where he was mustered into the United States Naval Service. In 1844 Melville was discharged from the Navy and returned to New York, where he soon embarked on a literary career.

In the 1840s, Melville began writing novels based on his sea adventures, and his books proved to be extremely popular with readers and critics. Titles included *Typee* (1846), *Omoo* (1847), *Redburn* (1849), and *White-Jacket* (1850). In 1847, at the height of his popular success, he married Elizabeth Shaw, the daughter of Massachusetts Chief Justice Lemuel Shaw. As Melville's literary ambitions grew, he soon resented the reputation he had earned as "the man who lived among the cannibals." Encouraged by his friendship with writer Nathaniel Hawthorne, Melville began to publish more serious and philosophical novels, including *Mardi* (1849) and his greatest achievement, *Moby Dick* (1851). While disheartened by the poor reception of these novels, Melville stubbornly persisted in challenging the public with experimental works like *Pierre* (1852) and *The Confidence Man* (1857). To sustain an income, he published short stories in monthly periodicals. Unfortunately, the harsh criticism and commercial failure of his later novels forced a severely depressed Melville to abandon his literary career by the late 1850s. At the urging of Justice Shaw, Melville traveled to Europe and the Near East to restore his mental health and then returned to New York in 1866 to become a customs inspector—a job he held for the next twenty years. Adding to the tragedy of his later years, Melville's oldest son, Malcolm, committed suicide in 1867. On September 28, 1891, Herman Melville died a bitter and forgotten writer at the age of seventy-two. An unpublished story, "Billy Budd," was found among his personal papers and published to critical acclaim in 1924.

Plot Summary

The Law Office on Wall Street

The narrator of "Bartleby the Scrivener" begins the story by introducing the reader to the law office on Wall Street of which he was the manager when he first met Bartleby. The narrator describes himself as an unambitious, elderly lawyer who has enjoyed a comfortable tenure as Master in Chancery. Before hiring Bartleby, the narrator—henceforth referred to as the lawyer—employed two law-copyists, or scriveners, and one office boy. The lawyer describes each of his employees in turn. The elder scrivener, nicknamed Turkey, is nearing sixty and it is implied that he drinks heavily on his lunch hour. The other scrivener, who goes by the nickname Nippers, is younger and considered overly ambitious by the narrator. The office boy is called Ginger Nut after the cakes which he brings to the two scriveners.

Bartleby's Peculiar Resistance

Because of an increased work load at his office, the lawyer is forced to hire a third scrivener. He hires Bartleby mostly on account of his sedate and respectable demeanor, which he hopes will temper the manners of his other two scriveners. The lawyer situates Bartleby behind a high folding screen and in front of a window that looks out upon a wall. Bartleby is quietly industrious in his work until the third day, when he is asked to proofread some documents. To the lawyer's astonishment, Bartleby responds to his request with the simple reply, "I would prefer not to." The lawyer feels the urge to dismiss Bartleby instantly, but he finds himself unnerved by Bartleby's perfect composure. A few days later, the lawyer asks Bartleby again to proofread some documents with the other scriveners. Once again, Bartleby declines with the curt refusal, "I would prefer not to." This time the narrator attempts to reason with Bartleby and demands a fuller explanation of his unwillingness. When Bartleby will not respond, the lawyer points to the reasonableness of his request and appeals to Bartleby's common sense. Failing to sway him, the lawyer entreats Turkey, Nippers, and even Ginger Nut to attest to the reasonableness of the request. They comply, but Bartleby remains unmoved. Vexed by Bartleby's resistance, the lawyer carries on with business, unwilling to take any action. The next day, Bartleby again refuses to proofread and also refuses to run an errand, each time explaining softly, "I would prefer not to." While Turkey offers to "black his eyes," the lawyer instead chooses to tolerate Bartleby's disobedience without punishment.

The lawyer stops by the office on a Sunday on his way to church. To his surprise, he discovers that Bartleby has been living in the office, apparently because he has no other home. At first the lawyer pities Bartleby's state of loneliness, but upon reflection his feelings turn to fear and repulsion. He observes that Bartleby does not read or converse with people and sometimes stands for long periods staring blankly out at the walls. Finally, the lawyer resolves to ask Bartleby about his history and his life and to dismiss him if he will not answer.

The Lawyer Attempts to Rid Himself of Bartleby

The next morning, the lawyer questions Bartleby about his personal life. Bartleby replies that he prefers not to answer. The lawyer begs Bartleby to cooperate and be reasonable, but Bartleby responds that he prefers not to be reasonable. The lawyer resolves that he must rid himself of Bartleby before the rebellion spreads to the other scriveners—who, he notes, have begun to use the expression "prefer" for the first time—but he takes no immediate action. The next day, Bartleby informs the lawyer that he has given up copying—the one task that he had been willing to perform previously. Several more days pass. Finally, the lawyer is satisfied that Bartleby will never resume his work. He tells Bartleby that he must vacate the premises by the end of six days. At the end of the sixth day, the lawyer reminds Bartleby that he must leave, gives him his wages plus twenty dollars, and tells him goodbye. The next

Herman Melville

day Bartleby is still there. Exasperated, the lawyer decides that he will not use physical force or call the police, remembering the Bible's injunction "that ye love one another." Instead, he attempts to conduct his business as usual, ignoring the fact that Bartleby inhabits his office without working and refuses to leave. This state of affairs lasts until the lawyer becomes aware that Bartleby's presence in his office has become the subject of much gossip which has jeopardized his professional reputation. Unable to convince Bartleby to leave and unwilling to bear the whispers about him, the lawyer decides to move his office to a new location. When a new office space has been secured, the lawyer removes all of his possessions from the old office, leaving Bartleby standing in an empty room. He again gives Bartleby money and abandons him with some regret. A few days later, a stranger visits the lawyer's new office and insists that he come and get Bartleby. The lawyer refuses. Several days later a small crowd entreats him to do something about Bartleby, who is still inhabiting the old office. Fearing exposure in the papers, the lawyer speaks to Bartleby and tries to induce him to leave. He interrogates Bartleby as to what he would like to do and suggests several occupations. Finally, the lawyer invites Bartleby to come home with him and live there until he can decide what he would like to do. Bartleby declines this offer, and the lawyer flees from the scene, telling himself that there is nothing more he can do to help. After a short vacation, the lawyer returns to work to find a note from his previous landlord stating that Bartleby has been taken to prison. This decisive action satisfies the lawyer, who agrees in retrospect that there was no other alternative.

Bartleby Dies in Prison

The lawyer visits the prison, where he makes a sympathetic report about Bartleby to the police and asks that Bartleby be removed to the poor house. The lawyer then visits Bartleby, who is unwilling to speak with him and stares blankly at the prison wall. When he discovers that Bartleby has not been eating, the lawyer tips the grub-man a few dollars to be sure that Bartleby gets dinner. The lawyer returns to the prison a few days later and finds Bartleby lying dead in the prison courtyard. Apparently having starved himself to death, Bartleby's withered body is found curled up, eyes open, facing the prison wall. To conclude his tale, the lawyer offers the reader a vague rumor about Bartleby as a possible explanation of his behavior. This famous passage concludes the story: ''Ah, Bartleby! Ah, humanity!''

Characters

Bartleby

The title character of the story, Bartleby, is hired by the lawyer as a scrivener, whose job is to copy out legal documents by hand. Bartleby is described as neat, pale, and forlorn. Although Bartleby's demeanor suggests sadness or discontent, he never expresses any emotion in the story and is described by the lawyer as ''mechanical'' in his actions. The plot of the story revolves around Bartleby's enigmatic refusal to carry out his employer's orders. When asked to perform a task, Bartleby frequently responds, ''I would prefer not to.'' This peculiarly passive form of resistance causes his employer much consternation. Eventually, Bartleby refuses to do anything at all and simply stares vacantly at the wall. Bartleby is finally carried off to prison, where he starves himself to death. The reason for Bartleby's disturbed state of mind is never revealed, although the lawyer believes it may have something to do with a previous job that Bartleby may had held in the dead letter office of the U.S. Post Office. Because so little is learned about Bartleby in the story, critics have tended to interpret him in purely symbolic terms.

Ginger Nut

Ginger Nut is the nickname of the twelve-year-old boy hired to run small errands around the law office for a dollar a week. His name is derived from the ginger nut cakes that he brings every day to the two scriveners, Turkey and Nippers. Ginger Nut's father hopes that his job will one day help him enter a legal career. The lawyer describes him as quick-witted.

Lawyer

Although he is not the title character, the lawyer, who narrates the story, is arguably the key figure in ''Bartleby the Scrivener.'' He is approximately sixty years old and holds the prestigious position of Master in Chancery. His job is widely viewed as a sinecure—a profitable position requiring little actual work that is given to relatives or friends of the very powerful. The lawyer describes himself as a ''safe'' and ''unambitious'' man. He seems to pride himself on his even temper, prudence, and gentility. Because the story is told from his point of view, determining the lawyer's prejudices and social outlook is crucial to an interpretation of the story. The narrative revolves around the lawyer's reactions to Bartleby's behavior. Some critics contend that the lawyer empathizes on some level with Bartleby's despair and find his intentions toward Bartleby generally admirable. Others view him as a pathetic figure whose supposedly ''liberal'' outlook only serves to mask (even from himself) his self-interest in exploiting and controlling the Bartlebys of the world.

Nippers

Nippers is the nickname of the younger scrivener in the law office. Nippers is described as a well-dressed young man about twenty-five years of age. The lawyer believes that Nippers suffers from indigestion in the mornings, which causes him to be restless and discontented. In the afternoon, his work is more steady. Nippers seems dissatisfied with his position as a scrivener. The lawyer believes him to be overly ambitious because he displays an unusual interest in the lawyer's business affairs, and he is often visited by suspicious-looking men to whom

Media Adaptations

- *Bartleby* is a 1970 film adaptation of Melville's story starring Paul Scofield, John McEnery, Thorly Walters, and Colin Jeavons, and directed by Anthony Friedman. The film was produced by Pantheon, distributed by British Lion, and is 78 minutes.
- The film *A Discussion of Herman Melville's Bartleby* was produced by Encyclopaedia Britannica Educational Corp. in 1969, and accompanies the film *Bartleby by Herman Melville,* produced by the company that same year.
- *Bartleby,* a motion picture by Audio-Visual Services, 1962, is also based on Melville's story.
- *Bartleby the Scrivener* is available on audiocassette read by Milton R. Stern as part of the Everett Edwards 1971 series, 19th-Century American Writers. 39 minutes.
- A filmstrip and cassette of *Bartleby the Scrivener* was produced by Prentice-Hall Media in 1977.

he refers as "clients" but who appear to be bill collectors.

Turkey

Turkey is the nickname of the elder scrivener in the law office. He is identified as an Englishman of approximately sixty years of age who wears dirty clothes. In the mornings, Turkey is industrious and able to ingratiate himself with his employer with his charming manners. In the afternoons, Turkey becomes irritable and insolent and his work becomes very sloppy. It is implied, but never stated, that Turkey's lunch hour is spent drinking alcohol.

Themes

Individualism/Peer Pressure

One of the primary themes of the story involves the pressure toward conformity in American business life that inhibits the creative development of the individual. It is not coincidental that the story is set on Wall Street, which is the center of American financial and business affairs. By choosing legal scriveners as his subject, Melville emphasizes the intellectually stultifying atmosphere of the business world, since scriveners create nothing of their own but instead mechanically copy the ideas and work of others. In fact, the lawyer is initially attracted to Bartleby because he seems to lack a strong personality and independent will, making him seem like a model employee. Significantly, when Bartleby resists, he is either unable or unwilling to explain the reason for his discontent. Perhaps Bartleby's ability to think independently has been so damaged that he does not even have the words to express his own vague desires. In keeping with this theme, the lawyer himself fears nonconformity so much that he is moved to take action regarding Bartleby only when he hears that people are gossiping about his office arrangements.

Freedom and Imprisonment

Related to the theme of individualism in "Bartleby the Scrivener" is the issue of freedom. Walls are pervasive in the story. Symbolically, the office is located on Wall Street, and the office's windows look out onto walls on all sides. Bartleby has a tendency to stare blankly at the wall, lost in what the lawyer calls "a dead-wall reverie." Bartleby seems to feel imprisoned in his life, and it is significant that he eventually dies in prison. Through the character of Bartleby, Melville seems to be questioning the nature of human freedom. In a historical sense, it could be argued that Bartleby is

Topics for Further Study

- Because of Bartleby's obvious maladjustment to society, many critics have used the character as a case study for psychoanalysis. How would you diagnose Bartleby's behavior? How would you diagnose the behavior of the lawyer?
- Investigate the social conditions of New York City during the 1850s. How did class conflict play a role in the day-to-day life of most New Yorkers? What were conditions like for office workers on Wall Street?
- Melville is considered by many to be a deeply philosophical novelist. Using the story of "Bartleby the Scrivener," examine Melville's attitude toward one of the following philosophical movements: the Enlightenment, transcendentalism, Romanticism, idealism, nihilism.
- Research attitudes about conformity in American business life by relying on sociological studies or literary works. How have such attitudes changed over time?

trapped by the emerging capitalist economy which demands that he sell his time and labor in exchange for low wages. At the time, capitalism was often condemned by those suspicious of economic independence and referred to as "wage-slavery." In a philosophical sense, Bartleby may be trapped by the inability to grasp with certainty the underlying reason or meaning of existence.

Apathy and Passivity

Another theme of the story involves the apathy and passivity of both Bartleby and the lawyer. Bartleby's rebellion is one of inaction. He passively resists his employer's instructions and chooses instead to do nothing. Bartleby displays a disturbing degree of apathy about his own fate. When questioned by the lawyer as to what he would prefer to do if given the choice, Bartleby responds that he is not particular. In fact, nothing appeals to him. Eventually, Bartleby's inaction leads to his own death by starvation, which seems to be less the result of self-hatred than of a most profound indifference toward his own life. The lawyer in turn finds himself unable to take decisive action regarding Bartleby's behavior, opting to procrastinate in hopes that the problem will solve itself. This attitude may indicate a level of coldness to Bartleby's suffering, since the lawyer appears to be concerned primarily with Bartleby's performance at work. In their own way, both characters are seized by an overpowering apathy towards their fellow men that paralyzes them.

Class Conflict

One of the primary tensions in the story involves the conflict of interest between the lawyer and his three scriveners. As an employer and the holder of a distinguished legal position, the lawyer inhabits a very different social world from the scriveners. Since the story is told through his eyes, part of the irony of "Bartleby the Scrivener" stems from the lawyer's inadvertent revelation of his class prejudices through his narration. For instance, at one point the lawyer describes his annoyance at Turkey's ragged wardrobe. He remarks condescendingly that he supposed one of "so small an income" probably could not afford a new coat, yet it never occurs to him that if he wished him to appear more respectable he could simply raise Turkey's wages. Also, the lawyer never considers the mind-numbing monotony of copying legal documents as a cause of his scriveners' eccentricities. Instead, he continually focuses on improving the productivity of his office at the expense of considering the well-being of his employees. The lawyer's insensitivity to the suffering of his employees foreshadows his inability to fathom Bartleby's discontent with his job.

Style

Setting

The setting of "Bartleby the Scrivener" is a crucial element in the story because it underscores Melville's concern about the effects of capitalism on American society. Significantly, the story is set on Wall Street in New York City, which had become the center of American financial and business life by the 1850s. The values of Wall Street are central to the story. The lawyer, who serves as the narrator, has an unabashed reverence for "the late John Jacob Astor," who was regarded as the most successful businessman of his time. The lawyer also reflects the values of Wall Street in his concern over such relatively superficial aspects of his employees as their appearance and dress. The work-oriented atmosphere of the office is devoid of friendliness and a sense of community. Indeed, the environment of Wall Street itself, Melville points out, is so business-oriented that after working hours it is reduced to an empty space "entirely unhallowed by humanizing domestic associations." Melville's descriptions of Wall Street convey a cold and alienating setting where the forging of close human ties is difficult.

Point of View

Melville's use of an unreliable narrator is the stylistic technique most remarked upon by literary scholars who have examined "Bartleby the Scrivener." By relating the narrative from the lawyer's point of view, Melville adds a level of complexity to the story that greatly enhances the number of ways it can be interpreted. As a narrator, the lawyer is unreliable because the reader cannot always trust his interpretation of events. The lawyer, as he himself admits, is a man of "assumptions," and his prejudices often prevent him from offering an accurate view of the situation. This becomes clear early in the story when the lawyer's description of Turkey's unpredictable behavior in the afternoons begs the obvious conclusion that he drinks during his lunch hour. Yet the lawyer is evasive about the matter, perhaps intentionally so. Thus, when the lawyer interprets Bartleby's behavior, the reader must decide carefully whether or not the lawyer is accurately perceiving events. The story is full of ironic scenes, among them when the lawyer compliments himself on his deft handling of Bartleby's dismissal after it has become clear to the reader that his efforts have been futile. Some critics argue that the story is really more about the lawyer than about Bartleby. Certainly the narrator's clouded perspective makes it all the more difficult to unlock the mystery of Bartleby's behavior.

Symbolism

The two most significant symbols in "Bartleby the Scrivener" are walls and dead letters. Walls are pervasive in the story. The office is located on Wall Street, and its windows look out onto walls on all sides. Bartleby has a tendency to stare blankly at the wall, lost in what the lawyer calls "a dead-wall reverie." The walls symbolize Bartleby's psychological imprisonment. Significantly, his fate is to die in prison. Why does Bartleby feel trapped, or "walled off" from society? There are perhaps many answers to this question, but one is suggested by the intriguing symbol of "dead letters" which the lawyer offers at the end of the story. The lawyer believes that the depressing experience of having worked in the United States Dead Letter Office may have affected Bartleby's state of mind. To the lawyer, the "dead letters" represent words of comfort or charity that arrived too late to serve their purpose; as he puts it, "pardon for those who died despairing; hope for those who died unhoping." These symbols of failed communication reflect Bartleby's sense of isolation from society and the failure of the lawyer, or anyone else, to reach him.

Ambiguity

The works of Herman Melville are famous for being deliberately ambiguous, or unclear. Once considered a stylistic flaw, ambiguity is now recognized as a literary device in which the author employs words, symbols, or plot constructions that have two or more distinct meanings. By constructing multiple layers of possible meaning within his story, Melville frustrates those readers who seek an obvious message. Typically, Melville forces his readers to consider his characters and events from more than one perspective. For instance, not only is Bartleby's behavior never fully explained, but it is filtered through the distorted perspective of the lawyer, whose own behavior is somewhat mysterious. Moreover, the lawyer's unexpected concluding words, in which he compares the plight of Bartleby to the plight of all humankind, offers another possible meaning to the events that have passed and causes the reader to reevaluate the entire story. The result is a narrative that remains open to many interpretations.

Historical Context

The Triumph of Capitalism

At the time Melville wrote ''Bartleby the Scrivener,'' New York City was firmly entrenched as the financial center of the United States's economy. It had been the nation's leading port during the colonial era, and by the mid-nineteenth century, New York overflowed with banks, credit institutions, insurance companies, brokerage houses, and a thriving stock exchange—all of which put its business community at the forefront of the ''organizational revolution'' in American economic institutions. By the 1850s, the development of capitalism in New York had matured to the extent that open conflict emerged between wage laborers and capitalists in the form of strikes and street violence. As early as the 1830s, artisans and skilled workers formed trade unions to resist the methods of factory production and wage labor. These craftspeople resented being run out of business by rich capitalists who undercut their trade by selling cheap, mass-produced goods. In addition, wage workers lamented the disappearance of the old relationship between master craftsmen and apprentices. Before the advent of factory production, most skilled workers learned their trade under a master craftsman, who usually took them in and paid for their room, board, and education. This close bond between employer and employee became defunct when machine-oriented factory production eliminated the need for skilled workers, requiring instead a large supply of hourly paid, unskilled laborers. Whereas they had once inhabited the same quarters, now an immense social divide had arisen between laborers and their capitalist employers. New York's merchants and financiers formed the most conspicuous aristocracy of wealth in the country. These businessmen, like the famous John Jacob Astor and Andrew Carnegie, dominated the city's political and social life and became notorious for their opulence. In ''Bartleby the Scrivener,'' Melville's narrator comments wistfully on how the very name John Jacob Astor ''rings like unto bullion.'' Melville's intimate legal office, with its three scriveners (who can be classified as semi-skilled workers), contains elements of both the old and new economic systems.

The Coming of the Civil War

The most pressing political concern of the United States in the 1850s involved the growing conflict between the North and the South, which culminated in 1861 into the Civil War. The Compromise of 1850 had not only failed to settle fundamental disputes over slavery but had worsened them. *Uncle Tom's Cabin* by Harriet Beecher Stowe was published in 1853, one year before ''Bartleby the Scrivener'' appeared in *Putnam's Magazine.* Stowe's immensely popular novel expressed the deep repulsion that many Northerners felt toward the institution of slavery and implicitly celebrated the ''free'' society of the North. Southern politicians responded to Stowe's attack by condemning what they referred to as the ''wage slavery'' of the Northern factory system. These Southerners claimed that the condition of a wage laborer was worse than enslavement on a Southern plantation. In debates over slavery, politicians and intellectuals were often faced with the difficult task of defining the meaning of freedom in America. Melville addressed the theme of freedom vs. slavery in several works, including *Benito Cereno,* ''The Paradise of Bachelors and the Tartarus of Maids,'' and ''Bartleby the Scrivener.'' Abraham Lincoln suggested that freedom meant the ''right to rise and better [one's] conditions in life.'' By 1856, pitched battles had broken out in Kansas between slaveholders and non-slaveholders, which increased the likelihood of a full-scale civil war. This fate was sealed when a reputed abolitionist, Abraham Lincoln, was elected President in 1860.

Philosophical Trends

In April of 1853, a few months before Melville wrote ''Bartleby the Scrivener,'' the first English translation of the works of German philosopher Arthur Schopenhauer appeared in a respected English periodical. Schopenhauer believed that the human will is superior to knowledge. He suggested, however, that the only way for the will to free itself from society and human law is to practice an asceticism that demanded a total withdrawal from society. Schopenhauer imagined that the ideal man destroys life's illusions through inaction. Only by gradually extinguishing all connection with the world around him can Schopenhauer's hero perform the supreme act of individual will. It is unknown whether Melville was acquainted with this idea.

Critical Overview

''Bartleby the Scrivener'' was first published in *Putnam's Magazine* in the November and Decem-

Compare & Contrast

- **1850s:** Conflicts between labor and management are not uncommon. The U.S. economy is growing rapidly, largely at the expense of unskilled and semi-skilled laborers. Unions are beginning to form on the national level. Local unions also gain more power and represent workers from a variety of crafts and trades. During this period of development, labor organizers begin to make distinctions between skilled and unskilled workers.

  1990s: Though not as powerful as they were in previous decades, labor unions continue to exert their power in order to improve working conditions and wages for their members. In 1997, United Parcel Service (UPS) goes on strike and cripples many other industries that rely on UPS for delivery of their products. Teamsters President Ron Carey describes the strike's settlement as "a victory over corporate greed."

- **1850s:** The narrator states that Ginger Nut, the office boy, earns one dollar a week. Wages during this time are quite low. In 1860, the average farmer makes 88 cents per day and works 66 hours a week.

  1990s: While the position of law copyist held by Bartleby, Turkey, and Nippers no longer exists, similar modern professions include legal secretaries and paralegals. A legal secretary helps prepare legal documents for lawyers and earns between $16,400 and $36,000 a year. Paralegals do much of the background work for lawyers, including legal research, and earn between $14,000 and $39,000 a year.

---

ber issue of 1853. It was republished three years later in Melville's collection of short stories titled *The Piazza Tales.* Written during Melville's decline in popularity, "Bartleby the Scrivener" attracted little attention when it first appeared. Since the rebirth of Melville scholarship in the twentieth century, however, this story has become widely considered a great work of short fiction.

Although contemporary critics have been unanimous in their praise of "Bartleby the Scrivener" as a work of genius, there has been little agreement about the meaning of the story. Leo Marx's 1953 article "Melville's Parable of the Wall" argues that the character of Bartleby was autobiographical in nature. In Marx's opinion, Melville saw himself as a nonconformist who preferred not to copy the conventional fiction of his day, much as Bartleby refused to copy legal documents. Alternatively, in his 1962 essay, "Melville's Bartleby as Psychological Double," Mordecai Marcus suggests that the character of Bartleby functions to remind the lawyer of his repressed hatred of his own life. Marcus believes that the story was meant as a devastating criticism of the sterile and monotonous business world inhabited by men like the lawyer, who responds with horror to witnessing his "psychological double" act out his hidden desires.

Many critics of "Bartleby the Scrivener" have attempted to psychoanalyze the title character. Bartleby has been interpreted variously as schizophrenic, neurotic, manic depressive, and autistic. Bartleby has also been compared to Jesus Christ. Donald M. Fiene's 1970 essay "Bartleby the Christ" suggests that Bartleby is a Christ figure because his death results from the lawyer's failure to extend Christian charity to him. In "Dead Letters and Dead Men: Narrative Purpose in 'Bartleby the Scrivener'," (1990) Thomas Mitchell argues that the story is really about the lawyer. Mitchell offers an interpretation that is sympathetic to the lawyer's point of view and suggests that the lawyer ultimately rejects Bartleby's nihilism, or belief in nothing. Finally, David Kuebrich's 1996 article, "Melville's Doctrine of Assumptions: The Hidden Ideology of Capitalist Production in 'Bartleby'," argues that the story is about class conflict and demonstrates the

Photograph of Wall Street, New York City, in the 1860s.

inhumane attitude of the capitalist class in New York in the 1850s.

Criticism

Mark Elliott

Elliot is a Ph.D. student in history at New York University and a former editor of "New England Puritan Literature" for the Cambridge History of American Literature. In the essay that follows, he examines the multiple meanings and interpretations that can be applied to the title character of "Bartleby the Scrivener."

Almost one hundred and fifty years since it was first published, Herman Melville's "Bartleby the Scrivener" remains one of the most elusive short stories in all of American literature. What is the reason for Bartleby's strange behavior in the story? This is the question that plagues the story's narrator, and it has plagued the readers of "Bartleby the Scrivener" as well. While many intriguing hypotheses have been offered over the years, no single interpretation dominates critical opinion or seems to

What Do I Read Next?

- Nathaniel Hawthorne's short story "The Celestial Railroad" (1843) is a nineteenth-century retelling of John Bunyan's *Pilgrim's Progress.* Hawthorne parodies Americans' self-confident belief in progress without moral consequences. Hawthorne's work had a significant influence on Herman Melville and dealt with many similar themes.
- Melville's 1855 story "The Paradise of Bachelors and The Tartarus of Maids" takes another look at the social effects of capitalism, emphasizing shifting gender roles. Melville's repulsion toward the New England paper factories is explicit, and his descriptions of dehumanized factory workers can be compared to his descriptions of Bartleby.
- Tom Wolfe's 1987 novel *Bonfire of the Vanities* concerns greed and moral corruption on Wall Street in the prosperous 1980s. In recounting the protagonist's downfall, Wolfe examines the class structure and justice system of New York City.
- Melville's 1857 novel *The Confidence-Man: His Masquerade* explores the psychological and philosophical aspects of human relations in a heterogeneous, capitalist society. Like "Bartleby," this highly experimental work presents numerous difficulties to the reader but remains a powerful meditation on American society in the 1850s.
- Karen Halttunen's historical study *Confidence Men and Painted Women: A Study of Middle-Class Culture in America, 1830-1870* examines the fears of middle-class Americans about the dangers of a capitalist society. Using Melville's "Confidence-Man" as her central model, Halttunen shows how American attitudes toward honesty and deception have changed over time. See especially her chapter "The Confidence-Man in Corporate America" for an interpretation of American business culture.
- David Riesman, Nathan Glazer, and Reuel Denny's *The Lonely Crowd: A Study of the Changing American Character* (1950) is a sociological study of the complex relationship between economics and personality development. This work traces the "dominant personality types" that have corresponded to the three major phases of American economic history. The issue of conformity vs. character development in business life is central to their analysis of American history.
- In his prize-winning study *Chants Democratic: New York City and the Rise of the American Working Class, 1788-1850* (1984), Sean Wilentz traces the rise of capitalism and the creation of an industrial working class in New York City. He examines of the role of working-class radicals and their resistance to the capitalist system in the early years of the Industrial Revolution.
- "The Beast in the Jungle," a 1903 story by American writer Henry James, provides an interesting comparison to Melville's literary techniques in "Bartleby the Scrivener." The story presents a psychological drama from the viewpoint of an unusually unreliable narrator who attempts to interpret the actions of those around him.
- "The Secret Sharer" (1909) by Joseph Conrad is the story of a sea captain who harbors a possibly murderous stowaway on his ship. The story concerns the theme of the "doppelganger," or psychological double, that some critics have suggested is evident in Melville's work.

---

fully explain the author's intention. Indeed, part of "Bartleby's" enduring appeal comes from its well-crafted ambiguity and denial of easy interpretation. Such an enigmatic story by one of America's great-

"In Bartleby Melville created a highly ambiguous symbol that cannot be reduced to a single meaning or interpretation."

est writers has proved an irresistible challenge to scholars in numerous fields, including literature, history, philosophy, psychology, and religion. These various approaches to "Bartleby" have deepened our understanding of the issues in the story, even if they have not solved the riddle of Bartleby's behavior. Perhaps to understand the story one must first accept that there is no single meaning to the character of Bartleby. This essay will consider Bartleby's actions in light of the possibility that his ultimate meaning is not meant to be understood by the reader.

Let us briefly examine one of the most influential interpretations of "Bartleby the Scrivener." In a 1953 essay Leo Marx argued that the character of Bartleby symbolically represents Melville himself, who resisted the pressure to write the kind of unoriginal, formulaic fiction that could provide him with a comfortable living. Marx believed that "Bartleby" was Melville's testament to the misunderstood artist who refuses to "copy" popular forms—as Bartleby refused to copy legal documents—and who suffers rejection and alienation from society on account of his independence. It is tempting to interpret the story in this fashion because, undoubtedly, Melville was something of a Bartleby. Throughout his life, Melville felt himself an outcast from society and looked askance at America's self-confident republic. His innocence was shaken by his father's financial ruin and early death, which led to Melville's years of aimlessness as a sailor. Even after he obtained a good reputation and a steady income as a writer, Melville remained unfulfilled. He constantly challenged his readers with difficult works that betrayed an unpopular degree of pessimism about the state of humanity. Melville refused to change his message despite the consequences, as he complained to author Nathaniel Hawthorne: "Dollars damn me. . . . What I feel most moved to write, that is banned—it will not pay. Yet . . . write the *other* way I cannot." Or, as Marx would have it, Melville would *prefer* not.

Like many who have interpreted "Bartleby," Marx sheds some important light on the story, but he does not explain enough. Unlike Melville's, Bartleby's resistance is entirely passive. Bartleby takes no action and offers no overt criticism of society or even a reason for his actions. Bartleby cannot communicate his ideas or feelings in any form except the inadequate statement, "I prefer not to." Bartleby's strange unwillingness to articulate his feelings casts serious doubt on the argument that he represents the uncompromising artist. Bartleby is described as eerily "mechanical" and "inhuman." Unlike Bartleby, Melville never became mentally or socially paralyzed. Moreover, his feelings of pessimism about society never reached the tragic depths that appear to affect Bartleby. The effort it took to create Melville's works of fiction demonstrate that he must have had at least a glimmer of hope that they could somehow make a difference to the world. Bartleby's alienation seems somewhat greater and more universal than Melville's, yet his silence ensures that the meaning of his resistance will remain ambiguous to the end. Considering Melville's ability as a writer, it is fair to say that the difficulties presented by the character of Bartleby are there for a reason. Why did Melville create this inscrutable character? Some clues can be gathered from a recognition of Melville's own philosophical angst and his use of symbolism.

Bartleby functions in the story not as a character but as a symbol. It may be useful to compare Bartleby the symbol to another highly ambiguous creation of Melville's imagination—Moby Dick. Of all of Melville's characters, only the white whale, Moby Dick, presents the same interpretive difficulties as Bartleby and has been construed in as many different ways. In the novel *Moby Dick,* each of Melville's characters interprets the white whale differently, and its ultimate meaning seems both awesome and unknowable. The inscrutability of the white whale reflects Melville's own skepticism about the inability of human beings to fully comprehend and control the forces in the universe at a time when faith in science and human reason were rarely questioned. Ahab, who accepts no limits on man's ability to know, sums up the white whale's elusive meaning when he explains his hatred of the whale: "How can a prisoner reach outside except by thrusting through the wall? To me, the white whale is that wall, shoved near to me. Sometimes I think there is naught beyond. But 'tis enough. . . . That inscrutable thing is chiefly what I hate; and be that white whale agent, or be that white whale principal, I will wreak that hate upon him.'' It is significant that Ahab compares Moby Dick to a wall. Ahab desires to know the ultimate meaning of all things, but he is frustrated because he cannot penetrate beyond the surfaces of the tangible world. For Ahab, existence in this world is but a prison because he cannot know, and sometimes doubts, that any deeper meaning exists. Thus, all that is left to Ahab is to attack and destroy the inscrutable surfaces which he has personified in the white whale.

In ''Bartleby the Scrivener,'' Melville explores similar philosophical issues in a different kind of setting. In a striking parallel with Ahab, Bartleby is also transfixed by walls, a pervasive symbol in the story. The office is located on Wall Street, and its windows look out onto walls on all sides. Bartleby has a tendency to stare blankly at the wall, lost in what the lawyer calls ''a dead-wall reverie,'' and his fate is to eventually die in prison, his face turned to the wall. It could be argued that, like Ahab, the walls symbolize Bartleby's sense of imprisonment within the limits of human knowledge, but we can never know this for sure. Like Moby Dick, Bartleby himself is also a kind of wall. To others he presents an inscrutable facade beyond which ultimate meaning is unknown. Bartleby, in fact, assumes the same symbolic function as Moby Dick, and the drama unfolds in the narration of the lawyer, who tries to comprehend him. No grand egotist like Ahab, the lawyer confronts the inscrutable Bartleby from the perspective of a typical genteel American whose comfortable existence has given him no reason for philosophical angst. As Bartleby's behavior causes his ordinary world of routine and unshaken ''assumptions'' to collapse, the lawyer is forced to confront issues about the human condition from which he had been previously sheltered.

All the reader knows about Bartleby is learned through the point of view of the lawyer. Thus, it may be worth considering that what Bartleby ''really means'' is not as important as what he means to the lawyer. At first, the lawyer is miffed at Bartleby's refusal to proofread documents, and he attempts to make him aware of the traditional practices and ''common usages'' of the office. Throughout the story, the lawyer continually attempts to explain Bartleby's behavior within a rational framework. The lawyer supposes in turn that Bartleby does not understand the rules of the office; Bartleby's resistance is just a minor eccentricity that can be controlled like Turkey's and Nipper's; Bartleby ails physically from a poor diet or bad light; and, finally, Bartleby has been deeply affected by a previous job experience. None of his explanations are satisfactory, however. The lawyer himself reacts with growing horror and confusion as the seriousness of the problem becomes clear, especially when considering Bartleby's total solitude. At this point, it becomes evident that Bartleby's behavior has begun to take on deeper symbolic significance for the lawyer. ''How can a person exist without communication with others?'' he wonders when he realizes that Bartleby neither converses with other people nor reads. ''Is it possible to be so utterly alone in the universe?'' Bartleby's actions and demeanor suggest to the lawyer, perhaps for the first time, that existence has no meaning or purpose and it is possible that we live in a cold and indifferent universe.

Once the lawyer has contemplated the meaning of Bartleby, he begins to make an effort to dispel the mystery and establish some human connection that will restore confidence in his optimistic view of life. He begins by trying to discover something about Bartleby's past, assuring Bartleby that he ''feels friendly'' towards him. This fails, but later in the story the lawyer tries again to reach Bartleby when he points out that life offers him choices and questions him as to what he would ''prefer'' to do with his life. Yet this tactic also fails, as Bartleby refuses to differentiate between the ''choices'' he is offered, saying with indifference that he is not particular. Finally, the lawyer offers to take Bartleby in and care for him. Again, this offer of kindness and human sympathy fails to impress Bartleby, who would rather remain in the doorway. In these scenes a conflict emerges between the lawyer's optimistic and reassuring view of the universe and what he perceives as Bartleby's nihilism. The fact that the lawyer perceives a profound meaninglessness and existential despair in Bartleby's actions may suggest that buried deep within his own optimistic and superficial world view there exists (at least) a lingering doubt.

Many critics have regarded Melville's lawyer as a buffoonish parody of the American middle class. Yet if the philosophical conflict between the lawyer and Bartleby is taken seriously, then one must reconsider whether Melville really views his lawyer with contempt. Melville, as I have argued, never totally succumbed to his pessimism, as Bartleby seems to. Is there something of value, then, in the lawyer's critique of Bartleby? In one of the most significant passages in the story, the lawyer visits Bartleby at the prison. He finds Bartleby standing alone in the prison courtyard, staring intently at the stone wall. The lawyer attempts to tear Bartleby's attention from the wall, stating, ''see, it is not so sad a place as one might think. Look, there is the sky, and here is the grass.'' Without looking, Bartleby responds, ''I know where I am.'' The contrast between their value systems is made clear: even if it is true that the human condition is a prison, the lawyer will optimistically focus his attention on the sky and the grass, while all Bartleby can think of are the walls that shut him in. Unable to accept what he perceives as Bartleby's point of view, the lawyer eventually decides that Bartleby must have been adversely affected by an experience which forced him to constantly contemplate the hopelessness and sad ironies of life. By ''assorting for the flames'' those dead letters which lawyer imagines would bring ''hope to the unhoping'' and comfort for the ''despairing,'' Bartleby somehow lost faith. This conclusion suggests that the lawyer will carry on believing in something, however superficial, despite his contact with Bartleby.

In Bartleby Melville created a highly ambiguous symbol that cannot be reduced to a single meaning or interpretation. Melville thus places the reader in much the same position as the lawyer in the story. It is somewhat ironic that most critics of the story have dismissed the lawyer's interpretation of Bartleby as inaccurate while advancing their own as correct. It may be that the lawyer's interpretation is the only one that matters. When confronted with an experience that shakes his comfortable world view, the lawyer becomes anxious and fearful but finally regards Bartleby sentimentally as a fellow ''son of Adam'' who has mysteriously lost his way. It is not unlikely that Melville had some sympathy for the lawyer's resolution of the matter. By finally leaving questions of ultimate meaning unresolved, the lawyer restores his own faith through a simple expression of empathy for Bartleby's suffering. It is not philosophically profound, but it is undeniably human.

Source: Mark Elliott, ''An Overview of 'Bartleby the Scrivener','' in *Short Stories for Students,* Gale, 1998.

R. K. Gupta

In the following excerpt, Gupta concludes that it was Melville's intention in ''Bartleby the Scrivener'' to show the limits of reason and to emphasize the importance of imagination and intuition.

> *''Say now, that in a day or two you will begin to be a little reasonable:—say so, Bartleby.''*
>
> *''At present I would prefer not to be a little reasonable,'' was his mildly cadaverous reply.*

The unnamed narrator of ''Bartleby'' is an apostle of reason. His outlook on life is clear, unambiguous, and uncluttered by mysticism or imagination. Reason and common sense are his deities, and he looks upon them as infallible guides to human conduct.

All goes well with the narrator until he decides to engage as his new scrivener an inscrutable and ''motionless'' young man named Bartleby. For two days, Bartleby diligently does ''an extraordinary quantity of writing.'' But on the third day, when the narrator calls him to compare a copy sheet, Bartleby, ''in a singularly mild, firm voice,'' replies: ''I would prefer not to.'' The narrator is stunned by what he considers to be the unreasonableness of Bartleby's conduct and briefly argues with him. But Bartleby remains unmoved.

A few days later, the narrator again solicits Bartleby's help, and Bartleby again replies: ''I would prefer not to.'' This time, the narrator is so amazed at Bartleby's intransigence that for a few moments he is ''turned into a pillar of salt.'' The first thing he does on recovering his composure is to ask the ''reason'' for it: ''*Why* do you refuse?'' (italics Melville's). When Bartleby simply repeats the refrain: ''I would prefer not to,'' the narrator begins to ''reason with him.'' His appeal is to ''common usage and common sense.'' But even this appeal goes unheeded and Bartleby tells him that his decision—or shall I say preference—is irreversible. This greatly upsets the narrator, particularly because Bartleby's refusal is ''unprecedented'' and ''unreasonable.''

Several days pass. But Bartleby shows no sign of relenting, and continues in his course of passive resistance. Again and again, the narrator asks him to do something ''perfectly reasonable,'' and again and again his only reply is: ''I would prefer not to.'' The narrator is not so much annoyed at the inconvenience that Bartleby's conduct causes him as he is flabbergasted by its ''perverseness'' and ''unreasonableness.'' He has spent his whole life shutting out whatever is unpleasant or inconvenient. His mind has, therefore, fallen into a groove it cannot easily get out of. Bartleby's advent, however, creates a situation with which he can cope effectively only if he can break out of his routine and think in unaccustomed ways. Since nothing in his life and experience has prepared him for such an eventuality, he feels helpless and lost. The story dramatizes how tragically the narrator fails to deal with Bartleby in an effective manner and how Bartleby's steady and compulsive refusal gradually undermines the norms by which he has lived so far.

In course of time, the narrator becomes sufficiently interested in Bartleby to want to know the details of his life and the source of his malady. But even here he is frustrated, and Bartleby prefers not to tell him anything about himself. The narrator is now completely nonplussed: what "reasonable objection," he wonders, can Bartleby have to speak to him. After all, he feels "friendly" towards him. Even now, he clings tenaciously, although somewhat precariously, to his hope that given time, Bartleby may be brought round to see reason, and in a highly significant scene, he addresses Bartleby thus:

> "Bartleby, never mind, then, about revealing your history; but let me entreat you, as a friend, to comply as far as may be with the usages of this office. Say now you will help to examine papers to-morrow or next day: in short, say now that in a day or two you will begin to be a little reasonable—say so, Bartleby."
>
> "At present I would prefer not to be a little reasonable," was his mildly cadaverous reply.

Critics have shown great ingenuity trying to determine the cause of Bartleby's malady. But to look for a rational explanation of Bartleby's conduct is to repeat the narrator's mistake and to miss the whole point of the story. The most significant aspect of Bartleby's behavior is that it is not only unexplained but also inexplicable, and that it is therefore futile to invoke reason and common sense in dealing with it or in trying to understand it. Melville carefully refrains from identifying the source of Bartleby's problem, because Bartleby's very irrationality is the point of his story. In "Bartleby" Melville clearly suggests what is confirmed by modern psychology: that men are not primarily creatures of reason, but are controlled by dimly perceived instinctual drives and obscure impulsions, and that this being so, one needs much more than reason and common sense to deal effectively with human problems.

Herein, I think, lies the failure—or should we call it the limitation of the narrator. He pitches reason's claims exceptionally high and over-estimates the range of the results that can be achieved by an exclusive reliance on it. He has too much confidence in the efficacy of intellectual processes. Unaware of the merits of unreflecting spontaneity, he has committed himself to the slow pace, the qualifications and hedging of rational thought. For a long time, critics have debated what the narrator could or should have done, and some have gone to the extent of showing annoyance with Bartleby and considerable respect for the narrator. That the narrator is benevolent and well-intentioned is undoubtedly true, but it is also completely irrelevant. What is relevant is his flatulence and evasion, and his application of only compromises and half-measures to what is an extreme malady—"innate and incurable disorder" as he himself calls it. But the "disorder" is "incurable" only in terms of the palliatives that the narrator, with his limited vision, can think of. Because he has boundless faith in the efficacy of unaided reason as an instrument of action, he is totally helpless when exposed to a reason-defying situation. When faced with Bartleby's unreasonable wilfulness, the best that he can do is to try to reason him out of it through appeals to tradition, authority, and common usage. . . . But the situation calls for more than reason; it calls for intuition and imagination, which the narrator has eschewed all his life. Henri Bergson remarks that the surest way to attain the truth is by perception and intuition, by reasoning to a certain point, then by taking a "mortal leap." The narrator, however, can go only so far as reason takes him. Not being gifted with imagination and intuition, he is incapable of taking the "mortal leap" that might have enabled him to cope with his problem successfully.

"The situation calls for more than reason; it calls for intuition and imagination, which the narrator has eschewed all his life."

From the standpoint of conventional morality, of course, no guilt attaches to the narrator. His guilt, as Maurice Friedman points out [in his "'Bartleby' and the Modern Exile"], is "existential guilt," the guilt of "human existence itself, the guilt that every man feels when his responsibility for another is unlimited while his resources are limited." He is, to be sure, more tolerant than most people would have been in his situation, and he was constitutionally incapable of the kind of sympathy that was required. But the narrator in "Bartleby" is not judged from the viewpoint of conventional morality. He is judged from the viewpoint of idealistic Christian morality, from standards which, to use Plotinus Plinlimmon's phrase in *Pierre,* are "chronometrical" rather than "horological." The attorney in Murray's ["'Bartleby' and I"] complains thus:

> But my profoundest, all-embracing grievance comes from an uneasy feeling, or suspicion, that Mr. Melville was out to flog me with the Sermon on the Mount, as if to say, you should have given the full measure of your love to Bartleby, all of it, every atom's atom of it, without reservations, qualifications, or reflections as to the consequences of so selfless a commitment of compassion. You should have sacrificed your profession, deserted your clients, set aside your duties to the High Court of Chancery, and taken Bartleby to live with you at home. Is not the author implying this and nothing less? If he is, I'd like to ask, what right has he to judge me from that unearthly and inhuman pinnacle of ethics?

The narrator's morality, however, is firmly rooted in expediency, and his self-interest tends to supplant altruistic considerations. Even his kindness is not entirely a product of compassion but is often motivated by prudence. When faced with spiritual crises, he responds with his usual stance of reason and common sense, a stance admirably suited to his own utilitarian world, but hopelessly ineffectual in relation to Bartleby's situation. As an apostle of reason, he so desperately seeks rational explanations for Bartleby's conduct that he is driven to read "Edwards on the Will" and "Priestley on Necessity" in the vain hope that these writers might shed light on it. The rumored explanation of Bartleby's conduct that he offers in the epilogue is again an attempt on his part to account in a tidy and rational manner, for what is essentially above and beyond reason. Even after having undergone the experience, the narrator has not understood its full purport. Although he has had glimpses into hitherto unexplored aspects of life, he has not assimilated his experience fully. In fact, he is still bewildered by it, and his recounting of the experience might well be the result of his compulsive need to rationalize it, and thus to exorcise it out of his system where it has for long festered as a sore, upsetting his precise and measured ways of life.

In the final analysis then, the story focuses on the narrator's failure of perception and judgment. His unswerving faith in reason and common sense renders him unfit for dealing effectively with Bartleby's situation. He tries to cure Bartleby's spiritual paralysis by tentative acts of charity, and fails to realize that Bartleby's problem could not be fathomed by logic but only by imaginative understanding. He is thus one of those mundane men who reduce everything to what Carlyle's Teufelsdrockh calls "Attorney-Logic." Spiritual insight is not granted to such as he. Ministering utilitarian solutions to spiritual problems, he becomes what Teufelsdrockh calls a "sandblind pedant":

> whoso recognizes the unfathomable, all-pervading domain of Mystery, which is everywhere under out feet and among our hands; to whom the Universe is an Oracle and Temple, as well as a Kitchen and Cattle stall,—he shall be a delirious Mystic; to him thou with sniffing charity, wilt protrusively proffer thy handlamp, and shriek, as one injured, when he kicks his foot through it—*Armer Teufel* . . . Retire into private places with thy foolish cackle; or what were better, give it up, and weep, not that thy reign of wonder is done, and God's world all disembellished and prosaic, but that thou hitherto art a Dilettante and sandblind pedant.

Thus in "Bartleby" Melville brings out the limits of reason as a guide to human conduct and as a controlling factor in human behavior and stresses the need for understanding and imagination. He shows in unmistakable terms that intellectual and analytical processes are not the most decisive determinants of the beliefs and conduct of men, and that human behavior, therefore, cannot be fully grasped by reason but only by imagination. Although Melville did not share the Transcendentalist belief in the supremacy and infallibility of intuition, he recognized its need and its value in establishing meaningful human relationships. The need for human interdependence is, after all, a recurrent theme in Melville's fiction, and in "Bartleby" Melville shows a full awareness of how lack of insight and intuition and an exclusive reliance on reason can block channels of communication. No wonder, then, that the story should seem teasingly modern in rhythm, idiom, and controlling vision, and that critics should seek—and find—its analogues, not in Melville's contemporaries, but in such Russian masters as Gogol, Goncharov, and Dostoievsky, and in the modern existentialists such as Sartre, Camus, and Kafka.

Source: R. K. Gupta, "'Bartleby': Melville's Critique of Reason," in *Indian Journal of American Studies,* Vol. 4, Nos. 1–2, June and December, 1974, pp. 66–71.

Mordecai Marcus

In the following essay, Marcus argues that Bartleby is a psychological double for the lawyer-narrator of "Bartleby the Scrivener."

Most interpreters of Melville's haunting story "Bartleby the Scrivener" (1853) have seen it as a somewhat allegorical comment on Melville's plight as a writer after the publication of *Moby-Dick* and *Pierre.* Others have suggested that the story dramatizes the conflict between absolutism and free will in its protagonist, that it shows the destructive power of irrationality or that it criticizes the sterility and impersonality of a business society. The last of these interpretations seems to me the most accurate, and the others suffer either from an inability to adjust the parts of the story to Melville's experience (or that of any serious writer), or to adjust the parts to one another.

I believe that the character of Bartleby is a psychological double for the story's nameless lawyer-narrator, and that the story's criticism of a sterile and impersonal society can best be clarified by investigation of this role. Melville's use of psychological doubles in *Mardi, Moby-Dick,* and *Pierre* has been widely and convincingly discussed. Probably Melville's most effective double is Fedallah, Ahab's shadowy, compulsive, and despairing counterpart. Bartleby's role and significance as a double remain less evident than Fedallah's, for the lawyer is less clearly a divided person than is Ahab, and Bartleby's role as double involves a complex ambiguity. Bartleby appears to the lawyer chiefly to remind him of the inadequacies, the sterile routine, of his world.

Evidence that Bartleby is a psychological double for the lawyer-narrator is diffused throughout the story, in details about Bartleby and in the lawyer's obsessive concern with and for Bartleby. The fact that Bartleby has no history, as we learn at the beginning of the story and in a later dialogue, suggests that he has emerged from the lawyer's mind. He never leaves the lawyer's offices and he subsists on virtually nothing. After he refuses to work any longer, he becomes a kind of parasite on the lawyer, but the exact nature of his dependence on the lawyer remains mysteriously vague. His persistent refusal to leave despite all inducements and threats implies that he cannot leave, that it is his role in life not to leave the lawyer's establishment. Bartleby's compulsive way of life, calm determination, and otherwise inexplicable tenacity suggest that he is an embodiment of the kind of perverse determination we might expect to flower in the rather gentle and humane lawyer should he give over to an unyielding passivity as a protest against his way of life.

> "Bartleby's role as a psychological double is to criticize the sterility, impersonality, and mechanical adjustments of the world which the lawyer inhabits."

The behavior of the lawyer gives stronger evidence that Bartleby is his psychological double. The screen which the lawyer places around Bartleby's desk to "isolate Bartleby from my sight, though not remove him from my voice" so that "privacy and society were conjoined" symbolizes the lawyer's compartmentalization of the unconscious forces which Bartleby represents. Nevertheless, Bartleby's power over the lawyer quickly grows as the story progresses, and it grows at least partially in proportion to Bartleby's increasingly infuriating behavior. Towards the beginning of the story the lawyer feels vaguely that "all the justice and all the reason" may lie with Bartleby's astonishing refusal to check his copy. Later the lawyer confesses to being "almost sorry for my brilliant success" when he thinks he has succeeded in evicting the now wholly passive Bartleby; and when he finds that he is mistaken, he admits that Bartleby has a "wondrous ascendancy" over him. Growing used to Bartleby's amazing tenacity, he feels that Bartleby has been "billeted upon me for some mysterious purpose of an all-wise Providence," and he muses about Bartleby: "I never feel so private as when I know you are here."

The lawyer finally accepts Bartleby's presence as a natural part of his world, and he admits that without outside interference their strange relationship might have continued indefinitely. But the crisis of the story arrives when his professional friends criticize him for harboring Bartleby and thus lead him to his various struggles to be rid of him. The professional friends represent the rationality of the "normal" social world, an external force which recalls the lawyer from his tentative acceptance of the voice of apparent unreason represented by Bartleby. When he finally resorts to moving out of his offices in order to leave Bartleby behind, he declares "Strange to say—I tore myself from him whom I had so longed to be rid of."

The lawyer's intermittently vindictive responses to Bartleby's passivity, which are combined with acceptance of and submission to Bartleby, suggest an anger against a force which has invaded himself. The last action which suggests identification of the two occurs when in the prison yard Bartleby behaves as if the lawyer is responsible for his imprisonment and perhaps for his hopeless human situation as well.

Bartleby's role as a psychological double is to criticize the sterility, impersonality, and mechanical adjustments of the world which the lawyer inhabits. The setting on Wall Street indicates that the characters are in a kind of prison, walled off from the world. The lawyer's position as Master of Chancery suggests the endless routine of courts of equity and the difficulty of finding equity in life. The lawyer's easygoing detachment—he calls himself an "eminently safe man"—represents an attempt at a calm adjustment to the Wall Street world, an adjustment which is threatened by Bartleby's implicit, and also calm, criticism of its endless and sterile routine. Although the humaneness of the lawyer may weaken his symbolic role as a man of Wall Street, it does make him a person to whom the unconscious insights represented by Bartleby might arrive, and who would sympathize with and almost, in a limited sense, yield to Bartleby.

The frustrating sterility and monotony of the world which Bartleby enters is further shown in the portraits of the lawyer's two eccentric scriveners, Turkey and Nippers. These men display grotesque adjustments to and comically eccentric protests against the Wall Street world. Both of them are frustrated by their existences. Turkey spends most of his money for liquor, imbibing heavily at lunchtime, presumably to induce a false blaze of life which will help him to endure but which makes him useless for work during each afternoon. Nippers, on the other hand, needs no artificial stimulant; he possesses a crude radiance of his own, and in the mornings is "charged . . . with an irritable brandy-like disposition," but at this time of day his work is poor. Nippers can get through life in the office only with the aid of endless re-adjustments of his writing table; no matter how he places it, he is still uncomfortable. Both of these men are least serviceable when they are, in a sense, most alive. Turkey and Nippers combine automaton behavior, self-narcosis, and awkward attempts to preserve their individuality.

Entering this world of mildly smug self-satisfaction and mechanical behavior, Bartleby begins his work eagerly, "as if long famishing for something to copy." This action probably represents both a hunger for life and a desperate attempt to deaden his sensibilities among such sterile surroundings. Very soon, however, Bartleby evinces the first of his many refusals: he will not help to verify his copy against the original. Apparently Bartleby is willing to act within the lawyer's world, but he refuses all personal contact because it is spurious. His refusal is paradoxical, for he rejects the illusion of personality in an impersonal world by retreating to another kind of impersonality which alone makes that world endurable. His insistence that he "prefers not" to conform reflects both his gentleness and the profundity of his rejection of impersonality masking itself as personal contact. As such, it appropriately represents a voice deep within the lawyer himself, a desire to give up his way of life. As the story progresses, Bartleby rejects all activity and refuses to leave; he has discovered that impersonality is not enough to help him endure this world. Bartleby clings to the lawyer because he represents a continuing protest within the lawyer's mind, whom he makes "stagger in his own plainest faith."

As Bartleby's passivity picks up momentum, he moves from the impersonality of copying to the impersonality of contemplating the dead, blind wall which fronts the window near his desk. This wall, and the prison walls "of amazing thickness" at the base of which Bartleby finally lies dead, parallel the images of the whale as "that wall shoved near to me" (Chapter 36) and of the whale's head as a "dead, blind wall" (Chapters 76 and 125) in *Moby-Dick.* Noting this parallel [in his "Melville's Parable of the Walls"], Leo Marx takes these images to represent the wall of death. I believe, however, that in both story and novel, they represent chiefly the terror and implacability of existence, against which Ahab actively and Bartleby passively revolt. Both men suggest that, in Ahab's words, "The dead, blind wall butts all inquiring heads at last'' (Chapter 125). The wall may also symbolize those limitations which give every individual his personal identity, for Ahab's unwillingness to accept his limitations as a suffering man motivates his vindictive drive to pierce the wall.

The parallel between another image in ''Bartleby'' and a significant symbol in *Moby-Dick* adds to the likelihood that Bartleby represents a force in the lawyer's unconscious mind: Bartleby, ''like the last column of some ruined temple . . . remained standing mute and solitary in the middle of the otherwise deserted room.'' This passage resembles a series of remarkable images which symbolize the unconscious part of Ahab: ''those vast Roman halls of Thermes,'' where man's ''awful essence sits . . . like a Caryatid . . . upholding on his frozen brow the piled entablature of ages'' (Chapter 41).

The wall in ''Bartleby'' symbolizes the human condition in the society within which Bartleby feels trapped, and by extension the burden of his own identity within the limitations of such a society. The lawyer's establishment on Wall Street, and the wall which is ten feet from his window (Bartleby's is three feet from his), suggest his slighter awareness of his trapped human condition. When at the end Bartleby lies dead within the prison walls ''of amazing thickness,'' he has succumbed to the impersonality of his society and to his inability to resist it actively. His assuming the foetal position in death, ''his knees drawn up, and lying on his side, his head touching the cold stones,'' suggesting a passive retreat to the womb, seems the opposite of Ahab's desire to be a superman who will pierce the wall of limitations and identity.

However, the symbol of the prison walls is complicated by the appearance within them of a green turf and by the lawyer's exclamation to Bartleby, within the prison, ''There is the sky, and here is the grass.'' These images of grass symbolize the creative possibilities of life. Bartleby's response to the lawyer's declaration is, ''I know where I am,'' which is an accusation that the lawyer is responsible for Bartleby's incarceration in the prison of the world. The lawyer's sensitivity to both the validity of Bartleby's general protest and to the creative possibilities which it neglects indicates, I believe, that Bartleby represents a protest within the lawyer which has at least partially taken the form of a death drive. Parallel to this paradox is the fact that Bartleby's protest also resembles the protests of Turkey and Nippers, who combine self-effacement, self-assertion, and self-narcosis.

The concluding section of the story in which the lawyer seeks for a rational explanation of Bartleby's actions by reporting a rumor that he had worked in the dead letter office in Washington and so had become obsessed with human loneliness seems to me an artificial conclusion tacked on as a concession to popular taste. The lawyer's otherwise final statement that Bartleby lies asleep ''with kings and counselors'' is probably the story's authentic conclusion, for—despite the hopelessness of Bartleby's position—it attributes profundity and dignity to Bartleby's protest against the sterility of a spiritless society.

Melville, however, appears to intend further metaphysical speculation. The embodiment of a protest against sterility and impersonality in the passive and finally death-seeking Bartleby may suggest that man is hopelessly trapped by the human condition in an acquisitive society. Thus the lawyer may feel wisdom in Bartleby's final resignation as well as in his protest. The situation, however, is complicated by the likelihood that Bartleby appears as a protest within the lawyer's mind against his way of life, but this protest leads to death, and only the lawyer perceives the creative possibilities that Bartleby ignores.

I do not believe, however, that Melville was suggesting that the lawyer's way of life contained promises of creativity which Bartleby could not see. Rather he was suggesting the negative course which impulses represented by Bartleby might take, particularly when they emerge in a rather thoroughly sterile environment. Thus the story lacks a thematic resolution. Its conclusion creates not so much a counter-criticism of Bartleby's passivity as an expression of quiet despair about the human predicament. The lawyer is not visibly changed after a struggle with his double, as are Dostoyevsky's Raskolnikov or Conrad's young sea captain in ''The Secret Sharer.'' Neither does he succumb to an intense and destructive despair, although Bartleby has partially represented a subliminal death drive within him. However, the standstill to which the lawyer's insights have brought him does show Melville's imagination moving in the direction of the intense despair found in much contemporary literature.

Source: Mordecai Marcus, ''Melville's Bartleby as Psychological Double,'' in *College English,* Vol. 23, No. 5, February, 1962, pp. 365–68.

Sources

Marx, Leo. ''Melville's Parable of the Wall,'' *The Sewanee Review,* Vol. LXI, No. 4, Autumn, 1953, pp. 102-27.

Mitchell, Thomas R. ''Dead Letters and Dead Men: Narrative Purpose in 'Bartleby the Scrivener','' *Studies in Short Fiction,* Vol. 27, No. 3, Summer, 1990, pp. 329-38.

Further Reading

Fisher, Marvin. '''Bartleby,' Melville's Circumscribed Scrivener,'' *The Southern Review,* Vol. X, No. 1, Winter, 1974, pp. 59-79.

Fisher surveys several critical interpretations of ''Bartleby'' and concludes that Bartleby is intended to represent humankind generally.

Kaplan, Morton, and Kloss, Robert. ''Fantasy of Passivity: Melville's 'Bartleby the Scrivener','' in *The Unspoken Motive: A Guide to Psycho-analytic Literary Criticism,* Free Press, 1973, pp. 63-79.

This article diagnoses Bartleby as a manic depressive and insists that the lawyer's passivity is a neurotic attempt to repress aggressive and violent impulses.

Kuebrich, David. ''Melville's Doctrine of Assumptions: The Hidden Ideology of Capitalist Production in 'Bartleby,''' *The New England Quarterly,* Vol. LXIX, No. 3, September, 1996, pp. 381-405.

This article argues that ''Bartleby'' is about class conflict and demonstrates the false ideology of the capitalist class in New York in the 1850s.

Morgan, Winifred. ''Bartleby and the Failure of Conventional Virtue,'' in *Renascence,* Vol. LXIX, No. 3, September, 1996, pp. 381-405.

A long essay that concentrates on how Bartleby's actions reveal the psychological composition of his boss.

Perry, Dennis R. '''Ah, Humanity': Compulsion Neuroses in Melville's 'Bartleby','' *Studies in Short Fiction,* Vol. 24, No. 4, Fall, 1987, pp. 407-15.

Perry contends that the character of Bartleby suffers from neuroses because he cannot deal with the social conventions of Wall Street.

A review of *The Piazza Tales,* in the *New York Tribune,* June 23, 1856. Reprinted in *Melville: The Critical Heritage,* edited by Watson G. Branch, Routledge and Kegan Paul, 1974. p. 357

Brief review that offers some favorable comments about ''Bartleby.''

Stempel, Daniel, and Stillians, Bruce M. '''Bartleby the Scrivener': A Parable of Pessimism,'' in *Nineteenth-Century Fiction,* Vol. 27, No. 1, 1972-1973, pp. 268-82.

This article demonstrates the parallels with, and possible influence of, Schopenhauer's philosophy in ''Bartleby.''

A Conversation with My Father

Grace Paley

1972

Grace Paley's "A Conversation with My Father" was originally published in the *New American Review* in 1972. It was subsequently included in Paley's second collection of short stories, *Enormous Changes at the Last Minute,* published in 1974. On one level, the story is about women's relationships with their fathers and sons. Paley recounts a visit between a middle-aged woman and her elderly, bedridden father, who suffers from heart disease. The father reproaches his daughter, a writer, for not constructing straightforward narratives. He encourages her to emulate the nineteenth-century writers Anton Chekhov and Guy de Maupassant, who wrote sparsely realistic tragedies. The daughter attempts to do so, telling him a story about some neighbors, a drug-addicted mother and son. She does not write a tragic ending, but ultimately both mother and son overcome their addictions. Her father rejects her ending, stating that she is unable to face tragedy in life and in fiction. On another level, the story is about storytelling. Within the larger story of the father and daughter, Paley includes two versions of another story, the story about the drug-addicted family. The presence of two stories, the portrayal of a writer writing a story, and the conversation about fiction between the narrator and her father make "A Conversation with My Father" a metafictional work, a story about stories and story-writing.

One of Paley's most critically acclaimed stories, "A Conversation with My Father" exemplifies Paley's efforts to combine realism with experi-

mentation. The similarities between Paley and her protagonist highlight the story's self-reflexive commentary on the author's own narrative techniques. A further connection between Paley's own life and writing and her fiction is found in the disclaimer included in the beginning of *Enormous Changes at the Last Minute:* "Everyone in this book is imagined into life except the father. No matter what story he has to live in, he's my father, I. Goodside, M.D., artist, and storyteller.—G. P." "A Conversation with My Father" not only deals with the possibilities of fiction, but it also explains Paley's own fictional processes and aims.

Author Biography

Grace Paley was born in New York City in 1922. Her parents, Isaac and Mary Goodside, were Russian Jewish immigrants who supported socialist and Zionist causes. Paley credits her parents' intellectual interests and political activism for encouraging her own feminist and leftist beliefs. The predominately Jewish area of the Bronx in which she grew up and the immigrant experiences of her parents also influenced Paley's concern with Jewish protagonists and Jewish-American life.

Paley attended Hunter College in New York City but dropped out without receiving a degree. In 1942, at the age of twenty, she married a photographer and cameraman, Jess Paley, with whom she had two children, a son and a daughter. Paley separated from Jess three years later and subsequently married the poet and playwright Robert Nichols. In 1942, Paley studied poetry with W. H. Auden at the New School for Social Research. During her early career as a writer, Paley wrote only poetry. At age thirty-three, she turned to writing short stories. Many of her short stories can be found in her collections *The Little Disturbances of Man* (1959), *Enormous Changes at the Last Minute* (1974), *Later the Same Day* (1985), and *The Collected Stories* (1995).

Today, Paley is known for her innovative short stories that combine realism with experimentation and reflect her political commitments. Her stories often deal with feminist and political themes, such as the oppression of women, the working-class lives of New Yorkers, and relationships between generations. These same issues motivate her public activism: Paley has been an outspoken supporter of the feminist movement, and during the 1960s and 1970s was arrested for her involvement in anti-Vietnam War demonstrations. A mother of two, an activist, and a professor of creative writing at Sarah Lawrence College, Paley's full life has limited her literary output. Of her relatively small body of work and her decision not to write a novel, Paley has commented: "Art is too long and life is too short. There is a lot more to do in life than just writing."

Paley told *SSfS,* "I don't like to write about my stories. On the other hand, I am glad to demystify their sources and meanings." She further commented on the story "A Conversation with My Father": "My father and I often talked about books, not so frequently about my stories. We also argued about my life, my ideas about my friends' lives. The truth is that I had said good night to my father, kissed him, placed his pills by his bedside, saw him insert the oxygen tubes into his nostrils, closed the apartment door, settled into the long subway trip from the north Bronx to my home downtown in Greenwich Village and began, in my head, a paragraph, 'My father is 86 and in bed. . . .' When I reached home (my kitchen table), I wrote much of the rest of what is now the first page of that story, maybe the second as well. So you see, I had no grand theme in mind, in fact no story—only a dreamed and imagined conversation with my father that is true but not a fact.

Plot Summary

"A Conversation with My Father" recounts a discussion between the narrator and her bedridden father, who is eighty-six years old and dying. He asks his daughter to write a "simple story," the kind that Maupassant or Chekhov wrote, "Just recognizable people and then write down what happened to them next." The daughter says yes because she wants to make him happy. She does not like stories that follow a plot line from start to finish because they remove all hope—there is no room for something different to happen.

She tells her father this story: A woman had a son. The son became a junkie, and to preserve their relationship, the woman became a junkie, too. After awhile, the son gave up heroin and broke with his mother, who now disgusted him. The woman missed her son.

Her father is not happy with the story. He claims that she left out all the important details, such as descriptions, occupations, and family. The daughter tells the story a second time, adding more details. But the father is still unhappy with the story, but he is pleased that she put the words *The End* in it, because, he says, it is the end of the woman as a person. The daughter protests, saying that her protagonist is only forty and still has lots of things she could do with her life. Her father disagrees, saying that his daughter simply chooses not to recognize the tragedy of her protagonist's life. "No hope," he says. "The end." The daughter has promised her family to let her father have the last word, so she only revises the end of the story: The woman's son never comes home again, but the woman finds a job as a receptionist in a clinic in a neighborhood with a lot of drug users. The doctors tell her that her experiences are a great asset for this job.

The father does not believe this new ending and insists that the woman will slide back to her bad habits since she has no character. The daughter then says that her new ending is the end, that the woman will stay working as a receptionist. The story ends with the father wondering out loud how long the woman will last in her job and how long it will take his daughter to accept that life is inherently tragic.

Grace Paley

Characters

Daughter

See Narrator

Father

As the title makes clear, the story recounts a conversation between the protagonist, the daughter, and the antagonist, her father. The father is described in the story's opening as an eighty-six year old man who is confined to his bed. Despite his health problems, he is mentally alert. A former doctor who became an artist in retirement, he is still interested in "details, crafts, [and] technique." He asks his daughter to write a "simple story" about "recognizable people," like the stories written by Guy de Maupassant and Anton Chekhov, nineteenth-century European writers whose stories were realistic and often tragic. The narrator tries to comply, but her father is critical of both versions of the story she made up for him. In the story's final line, he asks his daughter how long it will be before she faces up to the tragedy in life. According to a note included in *Enormous Changes at the Last Minute,* a collection in which this story appeared, the father in the story represents Paley's real-life father, Isaac Goodside.

Narrator

The narrator is a writer who is visiting her elderly, bedridden father. She talks with him about fiction and attempts to create a simple, direct story of the sort her father admires. While the narrator wants to please her father, she cannot fulfill his request to compose a straightforward, tragic story. The narrator believes that in both literature and life, a plot that follows "the absolute line between two points . . . takes all hope away." In the story she recounts to her father, she leaves open a possibility for change at the end. Her dying father wonders when she will face up to the tragic realities of fiction and life.

Pa

See Father

Media Adaptations

- *Enormous Changes at the Last Minute* is a 1983 film based on the short story collection in which "A Conversation with My Father" appeared. The film was directed by Mirra Bank and stars Kevin Bacon, Ellen Barkin, and Maria Tucci. The script was written by John Sayles and Susan Rice.
- An audiocassette from American Audio Prose Library, *Grace Paley Reads "A Conversation with My Father" and "Friends,"* was released in 1987.

Themes

Art and Experience

The substance of the conversation between the daughter and her father concerns the way real life should be represented in fiction. The major conflict between the two resides in their different experiences of life and, therefore, different expectations for fiction. The father wishes his daughter would write stories like those of Guy de Maupassant and Anton Chekhov, nineteenth-century European writers whose works reflect more structured societies and whose characters struggle within those societies' limited opportunities. The father, as Paley explains in a note accompanying *Enormous Changes at the Last Minute,* represents her real father, a Russian who immigrated to the United States at the age of twenty. His experience leads him to desire and appropriate stories about the tragic events of "recognizable people." In an interview with Joan Lidoff published in *Shenandoah,* Paley states that her father "came from a world where there was no choice, where you couldn't really decide to change careers when you were forty-one years old." The father is expressing his "own time in history."

The narrator, though, comes from another historical era, and thus her fiction differs from that of Maupassant and Chekhov. As Paley says in the same interview, "she really lives at a time when things have more open possibility." The narrator believes that the drug-addicted mother in her story might change. She refuses to "leave her there in that house crying." So the narrator has her character get off drugs and become a receptionist in a clinic for drug addicts. For the narrator, a child of post-World War II America, fiction should reflect the opportunities of life not available to previous generations.

Limitations and Opportunities

Closely related to the theme of art and experience is the theme of opportunity. The daughter abhors the kind of story her father wants because it is limiting. For this reason, she hates "plot, the absolute line between two points." Her hatred of plot stems not from "literary reasons, but because it takes all hope away. Everyone, real or invented, deserves the open destiny of life." While her father believes that the woman has no "character" and is destined to a tragic end, the daughter believes that a happy ending might very well ensue. She says of her invention: "She's only about forty. She could be a hundred different things in this world as time goes on." The different attitudes of the two towards the possibility of opportunities and change, fictional or real, stem from their different world views and experiences. As Paley says in the *Shenandoah* interview, the story is "about generational attitudes towards life, and it's about history. . . . [The narrator] was really speaking for people who had more open chances. And so she brought that into literature, because we just don't hop out of our time so easy."

Style

There are two stories contained within "A Conversation with My Father." One story is about a visit between a middle-aged woman and her sick, elderly father. Together, they discuss fiction and the daughter's attitude toward tragedy in literature and, by implication, in life. The second story is the narrative the daughter tells her father. This story is about a mother who, to be close to her drug-addicted son, becomes a drug-addict herself, only to be abandoned by the son when he overcomes the habit.

Metafiction

"A Conversation with My Father" is a metafictional story; that is, a fiction about fiction. The inclusion of a story within a story, the descriptions of the narrator writing that story, and the narrator and her father's conversation about fiction are all elements of metafiction. Metafictional stories prompt the reader to think about how stories are structured, why writers develop their stories as they do, and what expectations readers might bring to stories. These issues make up the content of the discussion between the narrator and her father. Why, the father asks, does the narrator not write simple narratives about people who are familiar to us, rather than writing about "people sitting in trees talking senselessly, voices from who knows where?"—a reference to one of the narrator's (and Paley's) earlier stories. But to the narrator, fiction should reflect one's experience in life, and the two versions of the story she writes reflect her less conventional views both of narrative and of life experience. The overall narrative of "A Conversation with My Father" also invites a consideration of these two viewpoints. Is it itself a simple, tragic story, as her father would like it to be, or an open-ended story without a straightforward plot, as the narrator prefers? Paley's metafictional technique causes readers to reflect not only on the story's theme and structure, but also on the themes and structures of all fiction—and, by extension, on the themes and the structure that people perceive in their own lives.

Plot

One of the major elements of metafiction in "A Conversation with My Father" is the way Paley plays with the concept of plot. Near the beginning of the story, the narrator states her opinion about plot. Although she wants to please her father, she feels passionately about the constraints of plot, "the absolute line between two points which I've always despised. Not for literary reasons, but because it takes all hope away. Everyone, real or invented, deserves the open destiny of life." The two plots in Paley's story, then, are open-ended. The story of the drug-addicted mother and son is left hanging. After finishing one version with the words "The End," the narrator revises the story to extend the ending, and ellipses, three dots signifying uncertain continuation, ambiguously conclude the story. The story of the conversation between the narrator and her father is also incomplete, ending with a question. Finally, taken together, the two stories which comprise "A Conversation with My Father" frustrate attempts to identify with certainty specific plot elements of the story, such as the rising action, the climax, or the denouement.

Topics for Further Study

- The narrator's attitudes and the events in her story-within-a-story reflect the mood of the early 1970s in the United States, particularly the issue of generational differences and the "generation gap." For example, the mother in the story wants to be part of "youth culture." Research youth culture in the 1960s and 1970s and compare your findings with the attitudes expressed by the narrator and the events recounted in her story.
- Paley calls herself "a feminist and a writer." How are her feminist beliefs and concerns evident in this story?
- Compare both stories within "A Conversation with My Father" with a short story by Anton Chekhov or Guy de Maupassant. How do the differences between their stories and Paley's relate to the different attitudes towards fiction expressed by the daughter and her father?
- One topic of conversation within the story is tragedy. Do you think "A Conversation with My Father" is a tragic story?

Historical Context

Political Upheaval Leads to Generation Gap

The early 1970s followed a time of great social upheaval in the United States. In the 1960s, the country was divided over issues that affected nearly everyone in some capacity: civil rights, the Vietnam War and the women's movement were among the most important. The broad-based civil rights movement of the early 1960s gave way, in the wake of the deaths of Nation of Islam leader Malcolm X in 1965 and civil rights activist Martin Luther King Jr. in

Compare & Contrast

- **1970s:** The Equal Rights Amendment, a proposal to change the constitution to guarantee women's rights, particularly equal pay for equal work, becomes a central issue of political debate.

  1990s: Although efforts to ratify the Equal Rights Amendment failed in 1982, women have earned greater political, social and cultural authority in the United States. In 1988, more than 56 percent of women held jobs. On the other hand, government guarantees of equal access and treatment to public and private occupations have increasingly been challenged in an era of shrinking government. For instance, in 1996, the largest university system in the country, the University of California, ended an affirmative action program for student admissions and faculty hiring.

- **1970s:** The broadly based civil rights movement of the early 1960s gives way to the more radical politics of a younger generation of activists. The militant Black Power organizations fade from prominence when it is revealed that government agencies infiltrated and pursued the leaders of these groups.

  1990s: The Nation of Islam claims millions of followers, and its leader, Louis Farrakhan, despite his controversial views, speaks to a gathering of hundreds of thousands of men at the Million Man March in Washington, DC, in 1995.

- **1970s:** A full range of government guaranteed services to the poor, known as entitlements, are instituted to guarantee a minimum standard of living for all U. S. citizens, continuing reforms of the 1960s.

  1996: President Clinton signs the Welfare Reform Bill, limiting recipients to five years of benefits and ending a federal guarantee of a sustainable income through the use of food stamps, medical assistance and cash grants.

- **1970s:** Judges begin interpreting Civil Rights legislation as requiring full racial integration of public school systems. Many efforts to integrate schools result in violence.

  1990s: Debates over the quality and equity of education continue. Many school districts remain segregated, despite twenty years of efforts at integration. New proposals for education reform include school choice, school vouchers, home schooling, charter schools, and a federal guarantee of access to higher education.

1968, to the more radical politics of a younger generation of activists epitomized by the Black Power movement associated with Angela Davis, the Black Panthers, and others. Likewise, protests over the United States's role in Vietnam (Paley was arrested in several antiwar demonstrations) became more acrimonious as the war continued. In 1970, four students were killed by the National Guard on the campus of Kent State University in Ohio during a peaceful protest. During this period of protest, many women assumed public roles of leadership. As a consequence, the women's movement revived a century-long attempt to gain an Equal Rights Amendment to the U. S. Constitution. Consciousness-raising groups, the legalization of birth control and abortion, and affirmative action laws fueled their progress, though the Equal Rights Amendment, passed by Congress, eventually failed to be ratified.

In many ways, these conflicts were played out within families as a struggle between generations. Children fought with their more conservative, Depression-era parents over issues of race, politics, and morality. Throughout this period, college campuses became centers of protest and spawned what Paley and others called ''youth culture.'' In ''A Conversation with My Father,'' the mother and son become addicted to drugs and their kitchen becomes a center for ''intellectual addicts,'' many of whom follow the teachings of Timothy Leary, a psychology professor who advocated the use of the hallucinogenic drug LSD. The mother and son in the daughter's story reflect the widespread experimentation with drugs during the 1960s and 1970s, which was often seen as part of a social revolution involving the development of a new consciousness and freedom from the constraints of tradition.

Critical Overview

"A Conversation with My Father" is Paley's most critically discussed work, perhaps because it is also her most overtly metafictional one. When it was first published in 1972, critics hailed it as one of the best stories about storytelling ever, since it is a story which reflects the complexities of life through the complexities of fiction. It has also been commended for its articulation of feminist themes.

The question of Paley's relationship to her characters has been a matter of critical debate. The disclaimer at the beginning of *Enormous Changes at the Last Minute* states that "Everyone in this book is imagined into life except the father. No matter what story he has to live in, he's my father, I. Goodside, M.D., artist, and storyteller." This statement leads one to assume that the unnamed narrator is Paley herself. Further proof is Paley's discussion elsewhere about visiting her father when he was terminally ill, and the reference within the story to Paley's other fiction, namely the comment her father makes about people talking in trees which refers to the short story, "Faith in the Trees." But, as Neil Isaacs notes in a study of Paley's short fiction, readers should refer to the narrator as Paley only "as long as we understand that we are talking about a Grace imagined into life as the Paley storytelling persona." According to Isaacs, critics such as Rose Kamel, who refer to the narrator as Faith (a central character in many of Paley's stories) are mistaken. Marianne DeKoven, writing in the *Partisan Review,* distinguishes between the narrator and Paley. She argues that Paley the writer is committed to a political and moral role for the storyteller, in "not only . . . a nonlinear vision of life's events, but also, ultimately, in a profound commitment to freedom as a primary value."

In an essay published in *Delta,* Nicholas Peter Humy agrees that responsibility for one's creative writing is a central theme of the story. For Humy, the conversation is a struggle over patriarchal demands upon language. The narrator, by refusing to tell the story her father wants to hear, refuses to alter "the lives of her inventions to his given end and meaning, to his law." D. S. Neff, writing in *Literature and Medicine,* offers a very different reading of the story. For him, the physician-father is struggling to make his daughter accept his impending death. He wants her to write, as a sort of therapy, a traditional tragedy with an unambiguous conclusion. The narrator, by refusing to end her stories, is trying to overcome death.

In *Grace Paley: Illuminating the Dark Lives,* Jacqueline Taylor argues that one reason critics misread Paley is due to their failure to recognize her "boldly female" voice. Paley, Taylor argues, "manifests a willingness to speak the unspeakable; she is irreverent, comic, compassionate and wise." Taylor argues that "A Conversation with My Father" might be titled "A Conversation with the (Literary) Patriarchs," because it serves as a meditation on Paley's subversion of male narrative conventions. The narrator's decision to write a new, hopeful ending to the drug-addicted mother's story reveals her "recognition of the fluidity of life and her resistance to narrative resolutions." While the father might protest, the narrator-daughter has, nonetheless, written her own story.

Criticism

Rena Korb

Korb has a master's degree in English literature and creative writing and has written for a wide variety of educational publishers. In the following overview of Paley's "A Conversation with My Father," she focuses on the relationship between life and fiction in the story.

Known as an innovative, "one-of-a-kind" writer, Grace Paley writes stories that are deceptively simple. At first they seem uncomplicated, but a closer reading reveals Paley's careful craftsmanship. She began her writing life as a poet but came to find that she could not express in poetry the ideas that she and her women friends were discussing, so she turned to fiction. Many of her stories center on the specific concerns of women and the roles society places upon them. Paley's stories, while relating everyday matters, always have social or political motives, yet they never moralize. Paley simply presents a world filled with people who, like herself, are aware of the world around them.

What Do I Read Next?

- The themes of ''A Conversation with My Father'' also figure in the other pieces of short fiction in the collection in which the story was first published in 1974, Paley's *Enormous Changes at the Last Minute.*
- Metafiction, or fiction about writing fiction, was an innovative form in the 1970s, and Paley's fiction is part of this interest in experimentation. Another metafictional collection of short stories is Robert Coover's *Pricksongs and Descants* (1969).
- Another feminist writer who published during the 1970s, Marge Piercy explores women's lives, patriarchal structures, and the Jewish-American experience in her novels and poetry. *Small Changes* (1973) and *Woman on the Edge of Time* (1976) offer illuminating comparisons with Grace Paley's works.
- Todd Gitlin's *The Sixties* is a cultural history written by a participant in the social upheavals of the decade.

''A Conversation with My Father'' is one of Paley's best-known and most critically discussed stories. It is trademark Paley, not only in its concern for issues of female identity, but in its use of a narrative technique that has strong elements of postmodernism. The narrator in ''A Conversation with My Father'' is also a writer. She relates the story of a conversation with her father during which she tells him two versions of another story. She is a self-aware, self-referential narrator, placing herself in the story she tells her father, continually commenting on her relationship with the stories she has created. The narrator presents her own—and Paley's—view of what constitutes a story. The story itself defies traditional literary conventions such as a linear plot; there is no ''end,'' just the assertion that life will continue with unknown twists and turns. Because the story so clearly merges Paley's beliefs with those of her narrator, some critics have pointed to the narrator's dismissal of a linear plot in ''A Conversation with My Father'' as evidence that nothing happens in Paley's fiction. Paley, however, maintains, ''Plot is nothing. Plot is only movement in time. If you move in time, you have a plot.''

In many ways, ''A Conversation with My Father'' is a comment on both the open-endedness of life and the freedom a writer has in narration. The story relates a conversation between a middle-aged woman and her father, who, breathing from an oxygen tank and giving ''last minute advice,'' presumably is dying. The father wants his daughter to tell him a ''simple story . . . the kind de Maupassant wrote, or Chekhov.'' Though the woman wants to please her father, she finds it impossible to tell him what he wants to hear. Paley's narrator has ''always despised'' stories in which there is an ''absolute line between two points,'' for such a fixed line ''takes all hope away.'' When the narrator vocalizes these beliefs to her father, however, he asserts that by maintaining a belief in hope, she is simply trying to deny the tragedy that exists in life—the tragedy of the character she creates for him and, by implication, the tragedy of his own imminent death.

Paley has acknowledged the autobiographical slant of much of her fiction—her narrator shares many similarities with Paley—so it is no surprise to find that the narrator also echoes many of Paley's own beliefs about writing. The narrator of the story, like Paley's authorial voice, constantly merges fact and fiction. In keeping with this, the narrator chooses to tell a story that ''had been happening for a couple of years right across the street,'' of a woman who became a junkie to keep her teenage son company. The son kicked his habit and left his mother alone and grieving. The narrator's father accuses his daughter of having ''left everything out'' and asks for such details as the mother's appearance, her family background, and her marital status. In her book *Grace Paley: Illuminating the Dark Lives,* Jacqueline Taylor notes, ''The questions are notable for their preoccupation with defining the woman of the story according to key patriarchal categories for women: looks, social status, and marital status.'' In an article published in *Delta,* Nicholas Humy points out that the father's choices ''happen to be the traditional ones, those that are usually made inadvertently by writers of fiction, and so seem not to be choices at all, but necessary to the form which will convey what the work is about.'' Though these critics differ in their reasons why the father needs the answers to these questions, their positions are not in reality contradictory; their insights show how questions of what defines a woman are intertwined with traditional viewpoints, even on seemingly unrelated matters.

The narrator's response to her father also highlights this connection. Her protest—''Oh, Pa, this is a simple story about a smart woman who came to N.Y.C. full of interest love trust excitement very up to date. . . . Married or not, it's of small consequence''—shows that what is important to the narrator is the woman's *life,* not her definition through appearance or relationships. The narrator does answer her father's questions but makes sure that any inclusion of these details in the revised story does not enrich it. The woman in the story changes from being simply ''a woman'' to being a ''fine handsome woman,'' yet neither her behavior nor her outcome changes. The narrator is determined to appease her father because he is ill, but still not give up her own set of beliefs, both about women and about writing. She remains true to her own artistic vision. It is interesting to note, as well, that in her fiction Paley does not generally provide details of appearances or relationships. So in ''A Conversation with My Father'' there is another connection: one between author and narrator. Paley's narrator asserts Paley's own social and literary beliefs.

In the revised story, the narrator keeps the same sequence of events but fleshes them out with details. These details border on the absurd, however—''[The woman] had a son whom she loved because she'd known him since birth (in helpless chubby infancy, and in the wrestling, hugging ages, seven to ten, as well as earlier and later).'' Her father knows that these details are added only for the sake of his ideas of what should be included in a story—they are not sincere—and only comments that his daughter has ''a nice sense of humor.'' The narrator allows

"The daughter and father embark on another debate, not on what constitutes good writing but, by implication, on how she is or is not accepting the fact that he is going to die soon."

her own character to intrude further, mentioning neighbors who also witness the woman's fall into drug addiction and grief; the opening ''Once in my time'' becomes ''Once, across the street from us.'' Through inclusion of the neighbors, the narrator subtly reminds the listener that the story of this woman is, in fact, based on a real one, thus admonishing against adding extra or glamorous details simply to make a story more exciting or fulfilling. The ending of the revised story also alludes to another falsity—it finishes with those dramatic words that really only signify that the *telling* of the story is over, *The End.* Her father, while expressing his continuing dissatisfaction that his daughter has failed to tell a ''plain story,'' approves at least of one thing: ''The end. The end. You were right to put that down. The end,'' he says.

Thus the daughter and father embark on another debate, not on what constitutes good writing but, by implication, on how she is or is not accepting the fact that he is going to die soon. They continue to couch their dialogue in a discussion of the life of the woman in the story. When her father declares that his daughter has depicted a tragedy, or ''the end of a person,'' she protests, '''No, Pa,' I begged him. 'It doesn't have to be. She's only about forty. She could be a hundred different things in this world as time goes on.''' The woman feels it is her duty to interact with her story. After all she has a responsibility because ''that woman lives across the street,'' and she changes the story again, giving the woman a job in a community clinic in the drug-ridden East Village where her experience as a junkie makes her invaluable. The daughter fully believes that her feelings should influence her creation, which is really an extension of her beliefs. She does not acknowledge, however, that her father also allows his own feelings to influence his interpretation of the creation, and that at eighty-six, it makes utter sense that his feelings may differ from her own. Her father believes some things already to be fixed, like the fact of his death. He asks his daughter, ''Tragedy! You too. When will you look it in the face?'' He is not referring only to what becomes of the woman in the story, crying her ''terrible, face-scarring, time-consuming tears''—he is referring to his own death.

Victoria Aarons has noted, in an article in *Studies in Short Fiction,* that ''the line between fiction and reality is precarious [in Paley's prose]. . . for her characters, identity is a continual process.'' Aarons also states that dialogues in Paley's fiction are a source of power because they give the characters possibilities for the future by preventing any one resolution. Her analysis could very well have been written for ''A Conversation with My Father.'' The line, always difficult to draw, becomes invisible by the end as the two stories merge into one. The narrator's story blends into the story of her dialogue with her father. The revised ending is not set apart from the rest of the text as were the two previous versions of the story, and the woman works at the clinic in the present tense; in fact ''right now, she's the receptionist.'' The narrator, in her retelling of the life of her neighbor, shows the infinite number of things that can happen in a life, the choices and the opportunities; instead of working at the community clinic, she could have been a ''teacher or a social worker. An ex-junkie! Sometimes it's better than having a master's in education!'' The narrator also implies that the meaning of a life is not simply to be summed up at its end, for every person will indeed die. She refuses to accept her father's belief that what is most important in his future is his death. By changing the woman's story at the end, she asserts a powerful statement—that most important is the living, and in the mere fact of living rests renewed hope for a future.

Source: Rena Korb, ''Overview of 'A Conversation with My Father','' in *Short Stories for Students,* Gale, 1998.

Nicholas Peter Humy

In the following essay, Humy discusses the disagreement between the narrator and her father about what a story should be, and how this disagreement relates to their differing views of freedom and predetermination.

''I would like you to write a simple story just once more. . . .''

It seems a straightforward request to the narrator's aging father, although he does ask specific qualities of his story: ''the kind de Maupassant wrote, or Chekhov, the kind you used to write. Just recognizable people and then write down what happened to them next.''

This request is made in the second paragraph of ''A Conversation with My Father,'' but we are already aware of the difference between the sort of story the father wants to hear and that which the narrator is in the process of telling. The father, like all aging fathers, is concerned with the past. His request is for a story like those of the past, like those the narrator ''used to write.'' His story is to be peopled with ''recognizable'' characters, those he is familiar with, and is to tell ''what happened to them next.'' The narrator's story, ''A Conversation with My Father,'' [exists] not in the past, but in the present. Its events and characters do not exist prior to the writing of their story.

> My father is eighty-six years old and in bed. His heart, that bloody motor, is equally old and will not do certain jobs any more. It still floods his head with brainy light. But it won't carry the weight of his body around the house. Despite my metaphors, this muscle failure is not due to his old heart, he says, but to a potassium shortage.

In these first five sentences we are shown how the narrator wishes to tell her father's story. He and his condition are not described with language, but created in it. The metaphors which the narrator uses do not help to make her father ''recognizable'' to the reader, rather, they call attention to the language and testify that the act of writing will intrude upon the tale. The father protests. It is a description of him, after all, and, ''despite [her] metaphors,'' he and his ''potassium shortage,'' would like to be found within it. It would seem to the father that his daughter has forgotten the responsibilities of the writer.

These responsibilities seem to be derived from Aristotle's theory of tragedy as it appears in *Poetics,* which is to say that, whether or not the father has read *Poetics,* he is one of those who have been made to expect, by the various wrappings which are used to package art in our culture, that literature will provide a purgative arousal of fear and pity brought about by the description or imitation of an action, culminating in the demise of the flawed hero. The father also asks that the story be neatly contained within its bounds consisting of beginning, middle, and end, and, in order to ensure its status as bearer of truth, that the protagonist be faceless enough to be universal ("recognizable"), while maintaining consistent enough character to go from one action to the next according to the laws of probable cause.

When she agrees to tell her father his story, one "that begins: 'There was a woman. . .' followed by plot, the absolute line between two points," the narrator agrees to repress those intrusions which her writing makes on the tale, to take "all hope away," denying her own beliefs that "everyone, real or invented, deserves the open destiny of life." At this point, as though to close the lid on the matter, "A Conversation with My Father" switches from the present to the past tense.

But the lid is not quite closed, for the narrator has "misunderstood [her father] on purpose." She chooses as the center figure of her story a woman, who cannot properly be a "tragic" character, and, while claiming to simply write down the story she has thought of, implying that the roles of writer and writing are no more than the chroniclers of the action, she "lays bare" the arbitrary nature of the elements of a causal progression in any fiction.

Her "unadorned and miserable tale" does seem to move in "an absolute line between two points," and yet the narrator demonstrates that the line exists only as her creation, and that, as William Gass points out, "its telling is a record of the choices, inadvertent or deliberate, the author has made from all possibilities of language" [*Fiction and the Figures of Life,* (1971)].

It is precisely those choices to which she makes her father attend. By maintaining her claim on the tale ("Once in my time. . ."), by failing to give it a proper end, allowing it to seep into the present ("We all visit her"), by describing neither compelling causes ("which is not unusual," "for a number of reasons"), nor "recognizable" characters, she forces her father to ask her to fill in what he feels is absent. "You know there's a lot more to it. You know that. You left everything out."

His main concern is for a more complete knowledge of the woman's character, for he knows, as do all Aristotelians, that character is the servant of dramatic action, that without it the action will not reveal the moral purpose of its agents, and hence, the meaning of the tale.

The greater part of any character in a given fiction is always left unstated. The reader of "A Conversation with My Father" is comfortable in attributing to the character of the father a certain life-in-words, though he has almost none of the necessary organs for life-on-earth, as it were, with only his legs, heart/motor, and brain somewhat resembling a lightbulb. What of his bowels? to say nothing of his nose, throat and ears. In the narrator's "unadorned and miserable tale" the mother and her son are not described physically, historically, or emotionally at all. When the father asks for details of the woman's hair and heritage, he is making choices, his choices, of what is "of consequence." His choices happen to be the traditional ones, those that are usually made inadvertently by writers of fiction, and so seem to him not to be choices at all, but necessary to the form which will convey what the work is about.

> "This piece is the story of a conversation and it traces for us the struggle that we all encounter when we acquire language, the tool of the father, and use it with, for, or against him."

Harold Bloom, in "The Breaking of Form," reminds us that the word "about" means "to be on the outside of" something. "All that a poem can be about, or what a poem *is* other than trope, is the skill or faculty of invention or discovery, the heuristic gift." The narrator shares this sense of her work, and does not see herself as relating to her father his story, history, but as *telling* a story. She wants him to see the process of storytelling anew, to see how, in the telling, the story becomes defamiliarized, becomes, not what it is about, but what it *is.* And what it is is a form which, according to Shklovsky, reveals the experience of its making.

What the father sees as unmotivated events in the narrator's first attempt are unmotivated only in the referential sense of what the story is about. They are perfectly motivated in the technical sense of calling attention to the telling of the tale.

But the telling of the tale is not of primary interest to the father, for the creation of "telling" subverts the disclosure of "told." The daughter is aware that a story is no more and no less than the language in which it is created, and the desire by which it is formed. The father's demands for disclosure of what went before the telling of the tale are attempts to halt the free flow of desire, to reentangle his daughter in the incestuous net of Oedipus, where her telling would become told, would become the law of the father. And the narrator's father invokes law when he demands disclosure of what was not spoken of the woman:

> ''For Godsakes, doesn't anyone in your stories get married? Doesn't anyone have the time to run down to City Hall before they jump into bed?''
>
> ''No,'' I said. ''In real life, yes. But in my stories, no.''
>
> ''Why do you answer me like that?''

In order to explain her choices the narrator, in exasperation, steps outside of the tale and tells her father what her fiction is ''about,'' and in so doing, undercuts to a certain extent, the very freedom, the very hope and desire, she had maintained in its telling.

> ''Oh, Pa, this is a simple story about a smart woman who came to N.Y.C. full of interest love trust excitement very up to date, and about her son, what a hard time she had in this world. Married or not, it's of small consequence.''

But to the father, it is ''of great consequence,'' for he senses the woman in the story as though she were flesh, as though he has somehow reached through the artifice of fiction to shake the hand of this person ''with heavy braids, as though she were a girl or a foreigner,'' and wants better to understand her, understand the character, not the artifice: ''. . . but listen. I believe you that she's good-looking, but I don't think she was so smart.'' Character and action do not correspond as the rules state they should. Intelligence would have prevented her from acting as she did.

And, in a sense, the narrator agrees with her father that the woman she has created has a life, though not one of flesh. As an invention in language the woman is alive and responsive to language, to its intrusions, to its metaphors. The narrator has already expressed her dislike for any portion of a fiction which is predetermined, outside of language, for such predetermination ''takes all hope away,'' and, in agreeing with her father that her explanation of what the story was ''about'' may have precluded a portion of her character's ''life,'' she reiterates her sense of the relation between character and language in fiction.

> Actually that's the trouble with stories. People start out fantastic.
>
> You think they're extraordinary, but it turns out as the work goes along, they're just average with a good education. Sometimes the other way around, the person's a kind of dumb innocent, but he outwits you and you can't even think of an ending good enough.

The father, ''still interested in details, craft and technique,'' accuses his daughter of ''talking silly'' when she explains that sometimes the end is not predetermined by traits attributed to the character and wholly controlled by the author. She suggests that sometimes it is reached in ''some agreement'' between the writer and the invention, mediated by the language.

In the second attempt to please her father, the narrator begins her story as though to include her father. Instead of ''Once in my time. . .'' the new story opens, ''Once, across the street from us. . . .'' She has also kept the story entirely in the past tense and given it an end (''The End''), in capital letters, closing the tale from any reverberation into the present. It is at this point that we are presented with the most marked contrast between written text and speech. It is here that we see the tension in the concessions the narrator makes in this text within a conversation. The narrator has provided her father with an end, has filled out the causal relationships between one event and the next, has even given her character a hint of a tragic flaw (''She would rather be with the young, it was an honor, than with her own generation''), and yet her father is not entirely satisfied. He has three comments.

''Number One: You have a nice sense of humor.'' Here he is referring to the way in which his daughter chose to explain the juxtaposition of various events. The story exposes probable cause for what it is—a convention—by using irony to systematically undo our understanding and belief in causality. The mother becomes a junkie like her son ''in order to keep him from feeling guilty.'' She wants to prevent him from feeling guilty ''because guilt is the stony heart of nine tenths of all clinically diagnosed cancers in America today.'' And in double irony, she explains that the mother loved her son ''because she'd known him since birth (in helpless chubby infancy and in the wrestling, hugging ages, seven to ten, as well as earlier and later). ''The father, by insisting on determining factors for all events in the fiction, is given an explanation for drug addiction and mother love which seems to him to be a joke.

''Number Two: I see you can't tell a plain story. So don't waste time.'' This comment echoes the conclusion of the second story, (''she would cry out, My baby! My baby! and burst into terrible face-scarring, time-consuming tears''), and comments upon the different demands father and daughter make on a story. The daughter wishes her father to *hear* her story. Instead he discounts the tale as unrecognizable, unwilling to listen to that which is new.The narrator shares with Shklovsky the belief that "the purpose of art is to impart the sensation of things as they are perceived and not as they are known" ["Art as Technique," in *Russian Formalist Criticism,* edited by Paul A. Olson, (1965)]. She does not feel that failure to arrive at an anticipated end is a waste of time, but that it is rather an exercise in the process of perception, which "is an aesthetic end in itself and must be prolonged."

But the father still desires an end to the story, both in the sense of conclusion and purpose. A "plain story" would provide this but his daughter's tale, while seeming to come to a proper end, has already undermined, through irony, the means she has used to arrive there. Nonetheless, the father will try to salvage that which he so desires.

> "Number Three: I suppose that means she was left like that, his mother. Alone. Probably sick?"
>
> I said, "Yes."
>
> "Poor woman. Poor girl, to be born in a time of fools, to live among fools. The end. The end. You were right to put that down. The end."

But the narrator knows that the telling of a story is the creating of a story is the creating of a form, and she will not let her father impose the end which the tragic form dictates.

> I didn't want to argue, but I had to say, "Well, it is not necessarily the end, Pa."

Her father is insistent. "You don't want to recognize it. Tragedy! Plain tragedy! Historical tragedy! No hope. The end." He feels that the form of tragedy is a given truth, just as he feels his eventual death to be. He urges his daughter to face the dictates of form just as we are told to brave death. His daughter's life, like his, will teach the lesson of death. "In your own life, too, you have to look it in the face." And, in speaking those words, he demonstrates his own desire to delay that end, while still entrenching himself in the conviction of its meaning.

> He took a couple of nitroglycerin. "Turn to five," he said, pointing to the dial on the oxygen tank. He inserted the tubes into his nostrils and breathed deep. He closed his eyes and said, "No."

Though the narrator "had promised the family to always let him have the last word when arguing," she recognizes "a different responsibility" towards him. She will demonstrate to him that it is not in the end that meaning is found by changing the ending of the woman's story. Believing that form dictates the limits of perception, the father is convinced that meaning resides in the end, in death, in the summing up of life. His daughter, believing that perception gives rise to the possibilities of form, and knowing that all stories and lives must eventually come to an end of some kind, at some point, plays Scheherazade to her father, dislocating the end from the tale, trying to save her father's death from meaning. Life might have no pity; it does not commute the sentence of death, but that sentence is only the last of the tale, and its connection to the body of the story is no more secure than that between the creation and its conception. The woman in the story exists for the telling, fathers for the living. The daughter knows this, and, as she moves her tale out of the stasis of the end, as she shifts the story of the woman out of the past and into the present tense, she reminds us that she has also played Scheherazade to the reader. She begins her new ending as she did the second version of the story, with a colon. But the addition has the same spacing as the body of "A Conversation with My Father" has had and is not indented. The father has closed his eyes; the narrator is addressing the reader. The doctor's speech is presented in quotation marks, which have appeared before only in dialogue between the father and his daughter, so that the two stories merge into one. When the father breaks in, "The doctor said that?" we are made aware of the play between past and present tense, made aware of the weaving together of the two stories. The intrusion of the father's voice at this point lays bare the device of the contrasting forms of the stories within a story, and transfers our perception of the father's story "into the sphere of a new perception," where, ironically, written text becomes speech, speech a written text. This piece is the story of a conversation and it traces for us the struggle that we all encounter when we acquire language, the tool of the father, and use it with, for, or against him. Grace Paley is perfectly aware of the relationship she is entering into with the father when she is telling a story. On the page facing the table of contents of the collection in which the story appears, she informs us: "Everyone in this book is imagined into life except the father." The father cannot be imagined into life in words for he dwells in them already. The narrator, by telling the stories within the father's story, has demonstrated what the responsibility of the storyteller is not. She has not formed the lives of her inventions to *his* given end and meaning, to *his* law. And, in the telling of her father's story, she has commuted the sentence, and, like the narrator of "Debts," fulfilled her true responsibility: ''That is, to tell their stories as simply as possible in order, you might say, to save a few lives.''...

Source: Nicholas Peter Humy, ''A Different Responsibility: Form and Technique in G. Paley's 'A Conversation with My Father','' in *Delta,* May, 1982, pp. 87–92.

Marianne DeKoven

In the following excerpt, DeKoven examines the reconciliation of postmodern form with traditional subjects in Paley's works, particularly in ''A Conversation with My Father'' and ''Faith in the Afternoon.''

... Though Paley has published only two collections of stories, *The Little Disturbances of Man* and *Enormous Changes at the Last Minute,* she is nonetheless an important writer—important in the significance of the fictional possibilities she realizes rather than in the uniform merit of her published work. She is not always at her best. But when she is, Paley reconciles the demands of avant-garde or postmodern form for structural openness and the primacy of the surface with the seemingly incompatible demands of traditional realist material for orchestrated meaning and cathartic emotion.

''A Conversation with My Father,'' in *Enormous Changes,* makes of this seeming incompatibility an argument between father and daughter, from which emerges the statement, crucial to Paley's work, that traditional themes can no longer be treated *truthfully* by formally traditional fiction: formal inventiveness and structural open-endedness not only make fiction interesting, they make it ''true-to-life.'' Paley's concern is not mimesis or verisimilitude, but rather the problem of creating a literary form which does not strike one as artificial; which is adequate to the complexity of what we know. Her narrator in ''A Conversation with My Father,'' calls traditional plot ''the absolute line between two points which I've always despised. Not for literary reasons, but because it takes away all hope. Everyone, real or invented, deserves the open destiny of life.'' Her father, arguing that plot is the truth of tragedy, wants her to write like Chekhov or Maupassant: ''Tragedy! Plain tragedy! Historical tragedy! No hope. The end.'' Paley's narrator-surrogate, arguing for open-ended hope and change, clearly bests her father in the conversation. But in the story, Paley gives him the last word: the setting is his hospital room, and he speaks from what we may assume is his deathbed. His lecture on writing is ''last-minute advice,'' and the closing speech, from father's pain to daughter's guilt, is his: '''How long will it be?' he asked. 'Tragedy! You too. When will you look it in the face?'''

The assertion of hope through change and open-endedness is therefore neither easy nor unambiguous. As the literary father sees, an inevitable component of optimistic belief in saving the situation through ''enormous changes at the last minute'' is evasion of genuine and unavoidable horror, the father's tragedy. As Faith herself says in ''Living'' (*Enormous Changes*), ''You have to be cockeyed to love, and blind in order to look out the window at your own ice-cold street.''...

The people Paley's narrator in ''A Conversation with My Father,'' would accuse of having merely ''literary reasons'' for rejecting traditional plot might explain the ''enormous change'' as an interesting substitute for outworn, tedious literary convention (linear plots are stale and boring), infusing new life into fiction. But Paley's structures are more than that. They are rooted not only in an assertion of open-endedness and possibility, and in a nonlinear vision of life's events, but also, ultimately, in a profound commitment to freedom as a primary value (nonlinearity is not as alien to Paley's politics as it might appear). For many postmodernists, that freedom is problematic; tangled with fear of chaos on one hand and of authority on the other.... But the freedom implied for Paley by ''enormous changes,'' the freedom from inevitability or plot, is synonymous with hope; hence her larger assertion that open-endedness in fiction is the locus of ''the open destiny of life,'' to which everyone is ''*entitled*''—a strongly political statement.... Tentatively and comically, Paley offers fiction's ''enormous changes'' as a warbling counter-note to the tragic gong, even in twentieth century political life, that notoriously unredeemed domain.

The tragic subject matter of Paley's work reaches the reader emotionally as pathos, a tricky entity because it so easily becomes sentimental. However, pathos remains pathos in Paley's work: she jerks no tears but neither does she freeze them. Instead, she distracts the reader from pathos at dangerous moments, when sentimentality threatens, by calling attention to her wildly inventive, comic language and imagery. In those moments when her language takes on the burden of simultaneously communicating and distracting from pathos, Paley creates a unique and fascinating literary object....

At the heart of Paley's engagement with everyday life is her deep empathy with her characters.

Even the deserters and betrayers she allows their "reasons," as she might say, and the rest she actively likes—a stance even more unusual in serious postmodern fiction than her assertions of hope in the face of our despair. It is not surprising that this uncommon empathy, which is really the condition of adherence to subjects of everyday life, is the province of a woman. Empathy and compassion are legacies of sexism that women do well to assert as privileged values rather than reject as stigmata of oppression. Uncomfortable as it makes her to write in such a predominantly male tradition, as a woman in the avant-garde, Paley is in an especially propitious position to unite interesting forms with important themes. She uses innovative form much as she uses innovative activism, to make new the endlessly dreary and shameful moral-political world we inhabit. . . .

Source: Marianne DeKoven, "Mrs. Hegel-Shtein's Tears," in *Partisan Review,* Vol. XLVIII, No. 2, 1981, pp. 217–23.

Joan Lidoff and Grace Paley

Lidoff was an American educator and critic who wrote extensively on women writers. The interview excerpted below is a composite of private conversations and classroom discussions held while Paley visited the University of Texas in 1981. In the excerpted portion of the interview, Paley discusses storytelling, "A Conversation with My Father," and her feelings regarding feminism.

[Lidoff]: *At your reading last night, you said that all story tellers are story hearers. Would you tell us some more about that?*

[Paley]: If you're a person who doesn't pay attention, and who isn't listening, you won't be a writer, you won't even be a story teller. Those of you who are writers from the very beginning of your lives were probably unusually attentive children. You heard things that the other kids on the block really weren't listening to. You may not have known it; you didn't go around when you were six years old saying "Oh, what I heard today!" but you probably did tend to come home from school with more stories for your mother or for whoever your afternoon-listener was. If they were there, if there were people to listen, you tended to be a very talkative child. You were an extremely good listener also, which everybody doubted, always saying to you, "Will you listen?" when you knew that you heard four times as much as anybody. If there was no one to listen to you, you probably heard anyway. You were a listener and you felt crummy because you were storing up all this information all the time. There's an example in that really wonderful story in Chekhov where the son dies and the father is a coachman and he keeps going around looking for people to tell "My son, my boy died" to, to tell them what happened. And nobody is listening to him at all. Finally he just takes his horse and tells the story to the horse. I think there are a lot of story hearers that nobody listens to. I think the world is full of people that nobody listens to who have a lot to say. And then I think there are people who aren't saying anything, who are storing it all up for some moment.

> "At the heart of Paley's engagement with everyday life is her deep empathy with her characters. Even the deserters and betrayers she allows their 'reasons,' as she might say, and the rest she actively likes."

Is there anyone in particular in your family who was a story teller who influenced you?

When I say a story hearer, that doesn't mean that you just listen to people tell stories. Sometimes you really are extracting them from people. You say, "Well, what happened?" And they say "Nothing." That happens in a lot of families. And it takes you years sometimes to extract stories from people in your family. But no, my father was a very good talker. And my mother as a result was somewhat more quiet. But he really was a good talker, and he spoke well about lots of things. A lot of people told stories: my grandmother, aunts, mother, sister. I don't think they thought of themselves as storytellers, but neither do most people. But almost everybody in this room, in this school, is a story teller. You tell stories all the time. So it's really one of the

"'A Conversation with My Father' is about story telling, but it's also really about generational attitudes towards life, and it's about history."

things that almost anybody can do. It's something that's natural. I have a little grandchild and I just know that from the first time she can put half a sentence together she's going to tell me some little story. She's already telling jokes. People tell stories everywhere in the world. When you and I were sitting around having coffee we must have told each other fourteen stories. . . .

In your story "A Conversation with My Father," the characters discuss the problem of plot. People are sometimes critical of your stories, and say nothing happens in them, there is no plot. I wonder if perhaps that's a peculiarly woman's form of story, where a lot happens, but it's not always what's called plot.

Well, I think by writing that story I sort of screwed myself up, because people really don't read. I mean, a great deal happens in almost any one of those stories, really sometimes more than in lots of other peoples', enough to make a novel or something. When people say, well, she really doesn't care much about plot, all they're doing is repeating what I said in my story. Plot is nothing. Plot is only movement in time. If you move in time you have a plot, if you don't move in time, you don't have a plot, you just have a stand-still, a painting maybe, or you have something else. But if you move in time you have a plot.

Your stories move around in time—almost Einsteinian time; there's long time and short time. Do you intentionally compress time and spread it out?

That's the way I think. I say it has to move in time but that doesn't mean it moves dead ahead in time. It can curl around on itself, it can just fall down and slip out through one of the spirals and go back again. That's the way I see. I see us all in a great big bathtub of time just swimming around; everything's in this ocean called time and it's a place. . . .

Going back to "A Conversation with My Father,". . .

Well, actually the story's about a couple of things. It's about story telling, but it's also really about generational attitudes towards life, and it's about history. I tend not to look at things psychologically so much, but historically, I think. And for him, he was quite right, from his point of view. He came from a world where there *was* no choice, where you couldn't really decide to change careers when you were forty-one years old, you know. You couldn't decide to do things like that. Once you were a junkie, that was the end of everything. Once you were anything, that was it. Who you were was what you were. And she was speaking really from her own particular historical moment, and in another country besides, where things were more open. So it wasn't that she was giving some philosophical attitude, or some attitude close to her own optimistic disposition, although both of those things were true. That's also true, but she was also really (although neither of them knew it, only the writer knew this), they were really speaking from their own latitude and longitude, and from their own time in history when they spoke about these things. So that's really, I think, what was happening there. And her feeling which she talked about in terms of stories was pretty much exactly the same. I mean she really lives at a time when things have more open possibility, and for a group or a class that had more possibilities and a generation in that line, because he was an immigrant and he just about got here and did all right by the skin of his teeth. So she was really speaking for people who had more open chances. And so she brought that into literature, because we just don't hop out of our time so easy. . . .

Did you ever look for women writers, in particular, or look to find your own experience in your reading?

No, not when I was very young. It's not so much that I looked for women writers, but I had sense enough to know that, like Henry Miller, he wasn't writing for me. That's as far as I went. I knew that these guys, even the Beats—I thought they were nice, nice to see all those boys, and nice to see all the sexual feelings, but I knew it really wasn't written for me at all. It's not so much that I looked for women writers, as that I understood certain much admired writers, like Burroughs, weren't talking to me. There was nothing to get from them. Though at the same time I did get stuff from Proust. That talked to me, but all those ballsy American heroes had nothing to say to me, though my friends thought they were just hot shit, excuse me. . . .

Do you consider yourself a feminist writer?

I'm a feminist and a writer. Whatever is in here comes from the facts of my life. To leave them out would be false. I do write a lot about women and the men they know. That's who the people are and what they think about. . . .

Source: Grace Paley with Joan Lidoff, in an interview in *Shenandoah,* Vol. XXXII, No. 3, 1981, pp. 3–26.

Sources

Isaacs, Neil. *Grace Paley: A Study of the Short Fiction,* Twayne, 1990.

Kamel, Rose. "To Aggravate the Conscience: Grace Paley's Loud Voice," in *Journal of Ethnic Studies,* Fall, 1983, pp. 29-49.

Neff, D. S. "'Extraordinary Means': Healers and Healing in 'A Conversation with My Father,'" in *Literature and Medicine,* Vol. 2, 1983, pp. 118-24.

Taylor, Jacqueline. *Grace Paley: Illuminating the Dark Lives.* University of Texas Press, 1990.

Further Reading

Aarons, Victoria, "A Perfect Marginality: Public and Private Telling in the Stories of Grace Paley," in *Studies in Short Fiction,* Vol. 27, No. 1, Winter, 1990, pp. 35–43.

Aarons explores the development of identity and the precarious line between fiction and reality in Paley's stories.

Arcana, Judith. *Grace Paley's Life Stories: A Literary Biography,* University of Illinois Press, 1993.

Arcana's work is a study of Paley's life and art. She argues that "much of what Grace Paley asserts in her stories, as in political action, is the strength and force of individual character embodied in human presence."

The Door in the Wall

H. G. Wells

1911

H. G. Wells's short story "The Door in the Wall" was first published in 1911 as part of a collection titled *The Door in the Wall, and Other Stories.* The conflict between science and imagination is the major theme of the story, which was enormously popular when it first appeared. Today Wells's reputation rests almost entirely upon his science fiction novels, which include *The Time Machine* (1895), *The Island of Dr. Moreau* (1896), *The Invisible Man* (1897), and *The War of the Worlds* (1898), all of which are acknowledged classics of the science fiction genre and continue to be widely read and adapted into other media. "The Door in the Wall" is considered by both readers and critics to be Wells's finest short story.

"The Door in the Wall" examines an issue to which Wells returned repeatedly in his writing: the contrast between aesthetics and science and the difficulty of choosing between them. The protagonist, Lionel Wallace, possesses a vivid imagination but goes into politics, where he is considered extremely rational. Wells himself was both a trained scientist and a writer of fiction, and this theme recurs in several guises in Wells's work. The story suggests both the magic and the danger of a nostalgia for a buried time. It is a story about politician Wallace who, while growing up in a joyless home, discovers a door in a wall leading to an enchanted garden. Wells's recurrent theme of science versus art is part of a wider contrast between the rational and the imaginative elements of experience. Wells

has often been seen as being caught on an intellectual battleground between his scientific training in rational thought and his gift of a vivid imagination. Wallace's inability to bridge the gap between his imagination and his rational, scientific side leads to his death.

Author Biography

H. G. Wells was a scientific visionary and social prophet. One of the most widely read British writers of his generation, he explored the new territory of science fiction and crusaded for a new social order in more than forty-four novels and social and historical books.

Herbert George Wells was born into a poor family in Bromley, Kent, a suburb of London, on September 21, 1866. He sought to escape poverty by receiving an education at London University and the Royal College of Science, where he studied zoology. One of his professors, the noted biologist T. H. Huxley, instilled in Wells the belief in social and biological evolution that Wells later cited as the single most influential aspect of his education. After graduating, Wells wrote a biology textbook and began submitting fiction to various magazines, determined to fulfill his dream of being an author. His childhood fascination with science, coupled with his science education, found expression in *The Time Machine,* the first of several enormously popular novels of scientific mythmaking, which was followed by *The Island of Dr. Moreau, The Invisible Man, The War of the Worlds,* and *The First Men in the Moon.*

Fame brought Wells an invitation to join the socialist Fabian Society, an alliance that later turned sour despite Wells's great enthusiasm for the socialist cause. In his personal life, he sought the ideal woman, one who would combine passion and intellect, and this led to a stormy ten-year love affair with the young English author Rebecca West. (Their union resulted in a son, Anthony West, who grew up to become a distinguished writer himself.) Wells's ambivalence about the benefits of science and technology contained in his earlier novels increasingly gave way to a sense of himself as a social architect and cautionary prophet. Throughout the 1930s he took center stage in warning that humankind was on the brink of disaster, while zealously planning the reconstruction of society. Throughout this time his fiction took on an instructional tone, reflecting the author's increasingly bitterness about humanity and its prospects for perfectibility. Wells died in 1946 at the age of eighty.

Plot Summary

Confiding to his friend Redmond who narrates "The Door in the Wall," Lionel Wallace relates that a preoccupation is gradually coming to dominate his life, one that is even affecting his career as a successful politician. Long ago as a lonely child of five he had wandered out of his home into the streets of West Kensington in London, where he noticed a green door set in a white wall. It was very attractive to him, and he wanted to open it, but at the same time he felt that his father would be very angry if he did. Wallace's father is described as "a stern preoccupied lawyer, who gave him little attention and expected great things of him." Wallace's mother was dead, and he was being raised by a governess. Nevertheless, the young Wallace gives in to the temptation and finds himself in an enchanted garden. Wallace describes the garden as a children's paradise with an inspiring atmosphere. The garden's colors are clean and bright, and the child is filled with happiness. There are various animals, including two tame panthers, beautiful flowers, and shady trees. Wallace meets a tall, fair girl who "came to meet me, smiling, and said 'Well?' to me, and lifted me and kissed me, and put me down and led me by the hand." He meets other children and they play games together, although he cannot remember the games, a fact which later causes him much distress.

A woman begins to read a book to the boy, and soon it becomes apparent that the story she is telling is that of his own life. When the book reaches the point in his life at which Wallace finds himself outside the green door, the enchanted world vanishes, and the boy finds himself once more on the dismal West Kensington street in London.

Wallace tells his father about the garden—and is punished for telling what his father assumes is a lie. In time, and as a result of this punishment, Wallace succeeds in suppressing the memory. But he can never quite forget it completely and often dreams of revisiting the garden. Throughout his life he unexpectedly comes upon the door in the wall in different parts of London, but each time he is rushing to an important commitment of one sort or another and does not stop to open it.

H. G. Wells

Wallace tells his friend Redmond that three times in the past year he has seen the door, and on each occasion he has passed it by: once because he was on his way to a vital division in the House of Commons; once, significantly, because he was hurrying to his father's deathbed and once because he wished, for reasons of personal ambition, to continue a discussion with a colleague. Now his soul "is full of unappeasable regrets," and he is barely capable of working. One morning a few months later, Wallace is found dead, having apparently mistaken a door at a dangerous construction sight for the elusive door in the wall.

Characters

Redmond

Redmond, the narrator of "The Door in the Wall," meets his old friend Wallace for a dinner one night. Wallace tells Redmond the story of the door in the wall. At first, Redmond does not know if he should or should not believe his friend's wild tale: "But whether he himself saw, or only thought he saw, whether he himself was the possessor of an inestimable privilege, or the victim of a fantastic dream, I cannot pretend to guess." This unwillingness to judge his friend displays his sense of sympathy. Redmond represents the voice of reason, making Wallace's story more believable because it is told by what readers assume is a reliable narrator. Furthermore, because Redmond is relating the tale, readers also learn of Wallace's strange death, which seems to verify the tale Wallace tells him at dinner. Redmond's account of the story also lends it a tragic tone because it is related after Wallace's death—a feat not possible if Wallace himself was the narrator.

Lionel Wallace

Politician Lionel Wallace is the protagonist of "The Door in the Wall." As a child living in a joyless home, he discovers a door to a visionary garden of happiness. His cautious nature is shown by his trepidation upon encountering the door, because he knows his father will be angry if he opens it. A child of a strict, Victorian upbringing, Wallace has been conditioned to deny his imagination and put all his effort into becoming successful. Nevertheless, the young Wallace gives in to the temptation—not yet having mastered self-control—and opens the door in the wall, and finds himself in an enchanted garden filled with beautiful flowers, tamed panthers, and friendly children. When Wallace tells his father about the garden, his father punishes him for lying, causing Wallace to suppress the memory of the garden.

Throughout his life, Wallace sees a similar door a few times, but he is too driven by his ambition for worldly success to stop and open it. Now, at age 39 and very successful, Wallace regrets passing up the garden and vows to stop the next time he sees the door. This regret illustrates his desire to give in to imagination and to break free from his rational life. Wallace's inability to distinguish between reality and fantasy, however, is demonstrated at the story's end when he is found dead at a construction site, having apparently mistaken a workmen's door for the door to his garden.

Themes

Alienation and Loneliness

Whether Wallace's fantastic tale about the garden is true is of less significance than the fact that it

Topics for Further Study

- Research three scientific advances of the first decade of the twentieth century, when Wells was at the peak of his popularity. How did these advances affect people's everyday life? Write about other scientific advances that have been made since Wells's time.
- Wells is regarded as one of the most prominent champions of the early twentieth-century spirit of British liberal optimism. Find out what British liberal optimism was. You may want to consult David Daiches's *New Literary Values,* (1936), specifically the chapter ''Literature and Belief''; G. K. Chesterton's *The Victorian Age in Literature* (1912), especially the chapter ''The Breakup of the Compromise''; or William H. Marshall's *The World of the Victorian Novel* (1967). What events have taken place since the early 1900s that have eroded British liberal optimism?
- Do some biographical research on Wells. You may want to consult your school's encyclopedias, *H. G.: The History of Mr. Wells,* by Michael Foot (1995), or *The Importance of H. G. Wells,* by Don Nardo (1992). How did Queen Victoria's political views influence Wells?

is a metaphor for his alienation and loneliness. Wallace's mother died when he was born, and his father was stern and expected great things of him. The treatment Wallace received as a child forced him to retreat into a private world of imagination. The only place where he could find love and attention was through the door in the wall. Wallace was forced as a child to repress his imagination: ''I tried to tell them, and my father gave me my first thrashing for telling lies. When afterwards I tried to tell my aunt, she punished me again for my wicked persistence. Then . . . everyone was forbidden to listen to me, to hear a word about it.'' Because he had to retreat into a private world just so he could use his imagination, alienation and loneliness became familiar feelings for Wallace. These feelings persist throughout his life and make it difficult for him to connect with other people.

Sanity and Insanity

At first, Redmond does not know if he should believe his friend's wild tale: ''But whether he himself saw, or only thought he saw, whether he himself was the possessor of an inestimable privilege, or the victim of a fantastic dream, I cannot pretend to guess.'' The reader is more willing to believe Wallace's fantastic story because it is filtered through the sensible, ''sane'' voice of the narrator. Redmond fits the preconceived notion of a sane person in that he seems to have a normal, healthy mind, makes sound, rational judgments, and shows good sense. Wallace seems just as sane at first; he does not fit the stereotype of an insane person because he holds a prestigious job and seems successful. Wells's intention was not to develop an insane character but to show the consequences of having to separate the various components of one's personality. As a child, Wallace is forced to suppress his imagination, and he carries this into adulthood. He has been made to think that imagination is a terrible thing. Therefore, Wallace begins to view his childhood experience not as imaginary but as real, and this is the only way Wallace can accept this part of himself. In a Freudian interpretation, he no longer has the ability to differentiate between real and imaginary, since the imaginary is off limits to him. In the end, it may seem that Wallace has gone insane—mistaking a door at a railway construction site for the magical door in the wall—but he is merely trying to return to that brief time in the garden when he was allowed to be himself.

Public vs. Private Life

In his public life, Wallace is an extremely successful Cabinet Minister in the British government. He is trusted and respected. Redmond, the narrator, holds Wallace in the highest esteem. The morning after Wallace tells Redmond the fantastic story, Redmond says, "I lay in bed and recalled the things he had told me, stripped of the glamour of his earnest slow voice, denuded of the focused shaded table light, the shadowy atmosphere that wrapped about him." Because Wallace is a politician, he is skillful at speaking and presenting himself, which is why Redmond believes him. It is not until Redmond is alone that he begins to question the tale. In private, Wallace is not so competent; he longs for the enchanted garden, that special place behind the wall that he has never known in his public life. His father has raised him to be rational and dull, cold and interested only in his career. Redmond says "what a woman once said of him—a woman who had loved him greatly. 'Suddenly,' she said, 'the interest goes out of him. He forgets you. He doesn't care a rap for you—under his very nose.'" Wallace, like many people raised in such repressive environments as Victorian England, is unable to unite his public and private selves into one balanced person.

Science and Technology

"The Door in the Wall" poses an issue which Wells returned to repeatedly in his writing: the conflict between aesthetics and science. Wells himself was both a scientist and a writer of fiction; similarly, Wallace possesses a vivid imagination but goes into politics, where he is considered extremely rational. This theme recurs in Wells's work and is part of a wider contrast between tangible and imaginative elements of experience. Wells has often been considered a participant in the debate between the virtues of science and the necessity of imagination. Wallace's inability to bridge the gap between his imagination and his rational, scientific side leads to his death.

Style

Point of View

"The Door in the Wall" is told from the point of view of Redmond, Wallace's friend. Redmond speaks in the first person ("I") as he relates Wallace's story. At first, Redmond does not know if he should believe his friend's wild tale: "But whether he himself saw, or only thought he saw, whether he himself was the possessor of an inestimable privilege, or the victim of a fantastic dream, I cannot pretend to guess." The reader is more willing to believe Wallace's fantastic story because it is filtered through the sensible, trustworthy voice of Redmond, the narrator. This particular point of view also allows the reader to find out about Wallace's demise, something that would not have been possible if Wallace told the story himself, although it prevents readers from knowing what Wallace's final thoughts were.

Symbols

"The Door in the Wall" relies heavily on symbols. A symbol is something that is used to represent or refer to something else. Many of Wells's symbols are dreamlike and represent masculine and feminine forces: "'There was,' he said, 'a crimson Virginia creeper—all one bright uniform crimson, in a clear amber sunshine against a white wall. That came into the impression somehow . . . and there were horse-chestnut leaves upon the clean pavement outside the green door. They were blotched yellow and green, you know, not brown nor dirty, so that they must have been new fallen.'" The white wall is a feminine symbol representing Wallace's desire for nurturing, which he has repressed since the death of his mother. The white wall is contrasted with the "clear amber sunshine," a symbol for the masculine ego—for the dominant and logical as opposed to the passive and emotional. The symbolic colors in this passage reinforce the contrasting masculine/feminine symbols on which so much of the story hinges. The amber sunshine and red creeper (masculine, virile, dominant) is juxtaposed with the whiteness of the wall (moon, feminine). The green door symbolizes fertility; it is the color associated with the Roman and Greek goddesses of love, Venus and Aphrodite. In opening the door and entering the world beyond his father's domain, Wallace passes into the feminine realm of imagination and sympathy. The door itself is a common literary symbol that represents the passageway between the conscious and the unconscious.

Psychologists who study dreams note that leaves are a symbol of happiness. The leaves Wallace describes are "blotched yellow and green," suggesting that his happiness is short-lived. Although Wallace is exceptionally happy inside the garden, he never regains his sense of delight outside of it, and for the remainder of his life he is tormented with "the haunting memory of a beauty and happiness that filled his heart with insatiable longings, that made all the interests and spectacle of worldly life seem full and tedious and vain to him.''

Metaphor

It is irrelevant whether or not Wallace's fantastic tale is true; more importantly, the tale serves as a metaphor for Wallace's alienation and loneliness. Wallace spends his life longing to return to the enchanted garden, where he knew love and the joy that comes with using one's imagination. In his everyday life, these things were frowned upon. Therefore, the story is a metaphor for Wallace's desire to return to an innocent, beautiful time and place.

Fantasy

Fantasy literature is intended to leave the reader in a state of uncertainty as to whether events are due to natural or supernatural forces. This is the case in ''The Door in the Wall,'' in which five-year-old Wallace visits an enchanted garden. He has utmost confidence in his story's truth. His friend Redmond is not so sure. Fantasy literature usually begins in an unremarkable, everyday setting. In Wells's story, the men meet for dinner and conversation. Readers are slowly pulled into the fantastic story. By gradually easing them into it, readers are more apt to believe the fantasy. In ''The Door in the Wall,'' readers are never quite sure if Wallace really did visit the magical garden or if it was purely a fantasy invented by his imagination.

Historical Context

Optimism in the Edwardian Age

Wells is regarded as one of the most prominent champions of the early twentieth-century spirit of British liberal optimism—the belief that scientific advances have made life almost perfect and that there is nothing left to discover. At the Royal College of Science, Wells studied zoology with noted biologist T. H. Huxley, who instilled in the young scientist the belief in social as well as biological evolution that Wells later cited as the single most influential aspect of his education. His works are ranked with those of playwright Bernard Shaw as exemplary of the era's exuberant sense of release from strict Victorian convention and the belief in the escalating benefits of scientific progress.

A photograph by Alvin Langdon Coburn, taken to illustrate a recent edition of Wells's A Door in the Wall and Other Stories.

''The Door in the Wall'' was published at a time of great change in England; rapid cultural change had been taking place since the death of Queen Victoria in 1901. Victoria had ruled Great Britain since 1837, and her reign was known for its conservative outlook on sex, politics, and the arts. In the years following Victoria's death, the English people embraced the possibilities of a new, modern era.

The Schism between Art and Science

Great strides in art and science were taking place at the turn of the century. As inventions such as the automobile, the airplane, and motion pictures began to transform everyday life, the unsettling pace of progress began to affect the arts, which questioned the wisdom of such unbridled growth. Wells, who was both an artist and a scientist, however, was excited by both imagination and technology. Some of the scientific advances that sparked Wells's imagination during these years were Orville and Wilbur Wright's first airplane flight in 1903, the discovery of gamma rays by Paul Villard in 1900, Max Planck's proposition of the

Compare & Contrast

- **1900s:** ''The Door in the Wall'' is written in a time when the British are concerned with domestic matters. King Edward VII begins his reign following the death of Queen Victoria in 1901. In Parliament, the Conservatives are divided on several issues and the general election of 1906 puts the Liberals in power by a significant majority. As the ruling party, the Liberals create Britain's early welfare program. The Labour Party is formed during this time as well, with 29 original members.

  1997: In May, after eighteen years of Conservative rule, the Labour Party wins the majority of seats in the House of Commons, and the Party's leader, Tony Blair, becomes Britain's youngest prime minister since 1812. The Conservatives, or Tories, suffer their worst defeat since 1906. Blair is said to represent a new Britain, a more liberal, multicultural society.

- **1900s:** A prevalent attitude in Britain is one of liberal optimism, the belief that scientific advancements have vastly improved the quality of life, and that there is little, if anything, left to discover. In 1905, Albert Einstein publishes a paper that outlines his theory of relativity. The incandescent electric light bulb, invented by Thomas Edison in 1879, proves to have an enormous impact on how people spend their time by the turn of the century.

  1990s: Scientific advancements are made in a number of fields, most notably in medical research dealing with cancer and AIDS, and in space exploration. In 1996, scientists successfully clone a sheep, causing great debate concerning bioethics. In 1997, the plutonium-powered Cassini space probe is launched to explore Saturn.

quantum theory, and the theory of relativity published in 1905 by Albert Einstein.

At the same time, new ideas about art were gaining popularity. Wells was influenced by these as well. For example, he read *Creative Evolution* (1907), a book by French philosopher Henri Bergson that stressed the importance of change through a creative life force, in opposition to a scientific view of nature. This view stresses intuition as superior to scientific or intellectual perception. Wells was also interested in the visual arts; he saw that the traditional forms and concepts of art were starting to break down dramatically after 1900 as a variety of alternative aesthetic principles, particularly Cubism, began to develop. Cubism began in 1907 with Pablo Picasso's painting *Demoiselles d'Avignon* and attempted to break away from the conventions of perspective that had ruled European art since the Renaissance.

The first decade of the twentieth century saw enormous changes, and Wells reacted to much of it in his writing. It was the conflict between art and science, however, that Wells primarily explored in his fiction. The contrast between imagination and science and the difficulty of choosing between them is dramatically illustrated in ''The Door in the Wall.''

Critical Overview

Since its first publication, ''The Door in the Wall'' has been recognized by critics as one of Wells's most accomplished stories. In 1924, Alfred C. Ward published a short interpretation of the symbolism of the garden in his *Aspects of the Modern Short Story,* paying particular attention to the theme of the deceptive natures of time and happiness. Among other critics, Bernard Bergonzi, in his *The Early H. G. Wells* (1961), has also examined the symbolism of ''The Door in the Wall.'' Such critics as Roslynn D. Haynes and J. R. Hammond have studied the story's themes, focusing on the conflict between science and the imagination, and between reality and the projections of the imagination—noting that the difference between them is often hard to distinguish. Jerome Hamilton Buckley, in an essay in his *The Triumph of Time* (1969), has suggested that the story's ending is open to interpretation by the reader. Because of its ambiguity, ''The Door in the Wall'' remains a much-examined and widely read short story.

Criticism

Deborah Williams

Williams was previously an instructor at Rutgers University and is currently a freelance writer. In the following essay, she offers an overview of the psychoanalytic interpretations of Wells's ''The Door in the Wall,'' suggesting that Wells warns of the dangers of ignoring the value of imagination.

In ''The Door in the Wall,'' H. G. Wells explores what Roslynn D. Haynes has called a characteristically Wellsian concern: the relationship between imagination and reason, or between the aesthetic and the practical. As a boy, Lionel Wallace, now a prominent politician and man of the world, stumbled across a green door in a white wall. Entering, even though he felt certain ''his father would be very angry,'' Wallace found a fantastic garden. He sees the green door several more times during his life, but always at times when stopping to enter the garden would mean sacrificing worldly success.

The symbolic garden at the center of this difficult story has been read differently by critics throughout the years. Early in this century, critics such as Alfred C. Ward, writing in *Aspects of the Modern Short Story: English and American,* saw the garden simply as an emblem of ''any one of those fine aspirations by which men are moved and from which they are debarred by the fret and wear and tear of the workaday world.'' In other words, this is a story about the many beautiful dreams we neglect because of our mundane preoccupation with our jobs. Later psychoanalytical critics, such as the Freudian critic Bernard Bergonzi and the Jungian critic J. R. Hammond, read the garden and its imagery and symbolism as part of a complex psychological drama enacted between the conscious and unconscious elements of Wallace's psyche.

Psychoanalytic literary criticism first became popular in the 1940s, and it remains a strong influence on many critics today. Sigmund Freud set forth the basic tenets of what he called psychoanalysis in his *Introduction to Psychoanalysis* in 1920. He continued to expand upon his original ideas until his death in 1939, creating the tenets of what is today known as classical psychoanalytic criticism—a methodology for interpreting literature by seeing it as wish-fulfillment. For a classical Freudian, literature (like dreams, according to Freud) acts as an arena for playing out unconscious (often sexual) wishes that cannot be realized in everyday life because of our social standards. These wishes are often hidden (or sublimated) in the story. For a psychoanalytic critic, then, the story has both its obvious content (what the story *seems* to be about), and the suppressed, hidden meanings that can be revealed by examining and translating the story's language, imagery, and symbolism.

In his book *The Early H. G. Wells: A Study of the Scientific Romances,* Bergonzi argued that the green door through which Wallace enters the garden is ''an obvious womb symbol'' and that Wallace's trip to the garden is ''a return in fantasy to a prenatal state.'' Wallace never knew his mother, so the tall fair girl and the somber woman in the garden are, according to Bergonzi, stand-ins for his real mother. Wallace's trip to the garden and his long-cherished wish to return are aspects of a revolt against his father and his father's authority. Bergonzi reads ''The Door in the Wall'' as a classic Oedipal myth.

Oedipus, a character from Greek mythology, kills his father and marries his mother. Freud coined the phrase ''Oedipal complex'' to represent what he felt was a unconscious desire in young boys to compete with the father for the mother's affection, and their wish to dispose of their fathers in order to be the sole object of their mothers' attention, like Oedipus. Because these desires are repressed in order for the boys to exist successfully within society, the desires appear instead in literature, dreams, and other acceptable forms. One stumbling block for this interpretation of ''The Door in the Wall,'' however, is that fact that, since his mother is already dead, Wallace cannot be said to be in competition, in any meaningful way, with his father for his mother's love (though it does seem clear that

What Do I Read Next?

- Wells's 1895 novel *The Time Machine* gives a glimpse of the distant future, suggesting that the evolution of humankind is not necessarily progressing toward a more refined species.
- Wells's nonfiction book *A Modern Utopia* (1905) established him as a leading proponent of socialism, world government, free thought, and free love, and as an enemy of the entrenched English establishment.
- Charles Darwin's monumentally important study, *The Origin of Species* (1859), was a huge influence on Wells. The book asserts that Homo Sapiens have evolved from other creatures.
- Edward Bellamy's classic novel *Looking Backward* (1888) describes an ideal social and industrial system of the future. Wells was ambivalent about such notions of progress, at times embracing them and at other times suspecting that Bellamy's embrace of the concept of scientism—progress driven by science—was shallow and not in balance with human nature.
- ''The Bungalow House,'' a story by Thomas Ligotti, published by Carroll & Graf in *The Nightmare Factory* (1996), concerns the fracturing of a man's mind and his preoccupation with a house he sees every day while riding the bus.
- William Morris's famous novel *News from Nowhere* (1890) describes an idyllic utopia of social and ethical progress. Wells felt the same way about this book as he did about Bellamy's.
- Frances Hodgson Burnett's *The Secret Garden* (1909) tells the story of ten-year-old orphan, Mary Lennox, who gains the key to a mysterious walled rose garden at her uncle's mansion. The book is considered the first modern novel for children.
- Lewis Carroll's *Alice in Wonderland* (1865) is a story of a logical girl who falls down a rabbit hole into a strange land. It is considered a premier example of fantasy literature by an author who also had an extensive background in mathematics.

---

he has an unconscious desire to rebel against his father's wishes). Bergonzi recognizes this, remarking that the ''picture is not exclusively Freudian in its implications.''

Carl G. Jung, originally a student of Freud's, broke with Freud and developed his own theories of psychology. Jung's work has had as great an impact on literature and anthropology as that of his teacher and mentor. For Jung, the collective unconscious—unconscious elements shared by all humans—contains primordial images and patterns of experience he calls archetypes. Because they are universal, these archetypes appear again and again in literature, religious stories, and mythology—in all cultures and in all times. Jung felt that truly great writers are able to tap into the experiences of the collective unconscious and create literature that, by using archetypes, revitalizes us by ''integrating'' or bringing into balance, different warring aspects of the psyche.

The work of a Jungian critic such as Hammond, then, consists of identifying the archetypal elements in a given work of literature and determining whether (or how) integration occurs. Hammond, in ''Lost Orientations'' in *H. G. Wells and the Short Story,* reads the garden Wallace enters as a symbol for the unconscious, and argues that the door is a ''familiar psychological metaphor for the threshold between conscious and unconscious.'' Wallace's conflict is between the masculine, rational world represented by his father and his career and the feminine, imaginative realm represented by the garden; but it is also a conflict between the two sides of his psyche—the masculine persona and the feminine anima, a Jungian term that represents the unconscious feminine aspect of any given man. To achieve psychic wholeness, Wallace needs to integrate the two. Because he cannot, he becomes miserable. Whether or not Wallace finally succeeds in integrating these two warring aspects of his psyche is a matter still open to the interpretation of the individual reader. He does come to recognize and value the world the garden represents; but we never really know for sure if he succeeds in returning to the garden.

"Wallace does come to recognize and value the world the garden represents; but we never really know for sure if he succeeds in returning to the garden."

The conflict between aesthetic and practical or scientific concerns was one that Wells knew from firsthand experience. Throughout his life, he felt the pull of competing interests. Wells escaped the lower-middle-class life of his parents by winning a scholarship to the London University, where he studied biology. While writing his first book—a biology textbook—Wells was already writing fiction and publishing short stories. At the time he wrote ''The Door in the Wall,'' Wells was deeply involved in politics himself and had just finished a nonfiction book called *A Modern Utopia.* Wells returned to the conflict between imagination and reason repeatedly in his writing. On the one hand, Wells had a profound faith in scientific progress to create an ever-better society. On the other, he was well-aware of the dangers of divorcing progress from social responsibility. His famous novel, *The Island of Dr. Moreau,* published in 1896, depicts a misguided exponent of scientific progress who tries to turn beasts into humans. In *The Invisible Man,* Wells again raises the question of whether science and humane interests are compatible. An outcast scientist discovers a way to make himself invisible and plans to use the knowledge to terrorize the world.

Of course, Wells was neither the first nor the only writer to take up the conflict between the aesthetic/imaginative side of human nature and the rational/scientific side. These are age-old concerns. In his *Republic* (upon which Wells based his *A Modern Utopia*), Plato derided all artists, especially writers, because he thought they served no purpose other than to inflame emotions and make people unreasonable. What is remarkable about the different ways writers have approached this conflict, from Plato to Wells, is that they all see these two ''worlds'' as irreconcilable opposites. Wells poses the problem as an either/or question. There seems to be no possibility to have both worlds; no chance, for example, that Wallace might leave the garden door ajar and mix the two worlds together. This is odd because in our everyday lives we mix the two, just as Wells himself most certainly did in his time. Insisting on seeing the garden as irreconcilably opposed to the everyday practical world makes for a more dramatic story, but it means there is no possible ending to this story that is not pessimistic. Wallace must choose one world or the other; he cannot have both. In the end he has either escaped the rational, practical world of his father and politics by returning to the garden, or he has been killed by the dream of it.

So what are we to make of this story? Lionel Wallace has worked hard, has done good things, and has tried to serve his country honorably. At least twice when he turns away from the green door it is in service to others; and he has frequently sacrificed his own desires to please his father and others. The work of people like Wallace is indispensable; it builds societies. And yet the garden appears in his life because it is something Wallace needs. Whether we read it as Freudian manifestation of a desire to rebel against his father or Jungian need to integrate the masculine and feminine aspects of his psyche, it seems clear that the garden represents something necessary to Wallace, even if the value of the garden can never be measured by the standards of the practical world. And perhaps that is the point. Plato banished the artists out of his ideal Republic; perhaps Wells warns us that we do so at our own peril.

Source: Deborah Williams, ''An Overview of 'The Door in the Wall','' in *Short Stories for Students,* Gale, 1998.

J. R. Hammond

''I have been greatly influenced in my life, work, and attitudes by the writings of H. G. Wells,'' Hammonds has written. An English writer, he has published several important works about Wells. In the following excerpt, Hammond analyzes the imagery in ''The Door in the Wall'' and illustrates

> "If one takes the garden as a metaphor for the imagination, the theme of the story can be read as Wallace's recognition of his true nature."

how it contributes to the theme of opposition between reality and imagination.

'The Door in the Wall,' one of Wells's most deservedly familiar short stories, is the story of a prominent politician, Lionel Wallace, who is haunted by the vision of an enchanted garden glimpsed in childhood. The story makes extensive use of archetypal and dream imagery and interweaves within its narrative a pattern of leitmotivs characteristic of Wells as man and writer.

The door and the wall are described in such unforgettably vivid terms that the image is fixed indelibly on the imagination:

> 'There was,' he said, 'a crimson Virginia creeper in it—all one bright uniform crimson, in a clear amber sunshine against a white wall. That came into the impression somehow . . . and there were horse-chestnut leaves upon the clean pavement outside the green door. They were blotched yellow and green, you know, not brown nor dirty, so that they must have been new fallen.'

The imagery of this passage becomes clearer when it is expressed in the following form:

> white wall
> fallen leaves
> red creeper
> green door
> amber sunshine.

The white wall is a feminine symbol, representing the gentle, motherly aspects of Wallace's (and, by implication, Wells's) nature. This is contrasted with the 'clear amber sunshine', a symbol for the masculine ego, for the dominant and logical as opposed to the passive and emotional. The door is a familiar psychological metaphor for the threshold between conscious and unconscious. In passing through the door and entering the enchanted garden Wallace leaves behind him the conscious, rational world of his daily life and enters the domain of imagination and dreams, a world in which the longings of his innermost self come to the fore. In the language of dreams leaves are an allegory for happiness. The leaves Wallace describes are 'blotched yellow and green', suggesting that his happiness is transitory. Though Wallace is blissfully happy inside the garden he never regains his sense of delight outside it and for the remainder of his life is tormented with 'the haunting memory of a beauty and happiness that filled his heart with insatiable longings, that made all the interests and spectacle of worldly life seem full and tedious and vain to him'. The symbolism of colour in this passage reinforces the contrasting masculine/feminine imagery on which so much of the story hinges. The whiteness of the wall (= moon, feminine, the anima) is juxtaposed against the amber sunshine and red creeper (= masculine, virile, dominant). The green door suggests femininity, the colour of Venus and Aphrodite. In opening the door and entering the domain beyond, Wallace passes into the feminine realm of imagination and sympathy, leaving behind him the worlds of duty, career and ambition. . . .

And it is at the moment when he returns to his moment of hesitation—'so at last I came to myself hovering and hesitating outside the green door in the long white wall'—that he loses sight of the beautiful garden. This element of ambiguity recurs throughout the narrative. At each crucial stage in the story Wallace is torn between conflicting desires.

This dichotomy is aptly symbolized by the contrasting female figures who befriend him in the garden. The first is described as 'a tall, fair girl' who takes him by the hand and fills him with 'an impression of delightful rightness, of being reminded of happy things that had in some strange way been overlooked'. This girl with her 'sweet kind face', pleasant voice and classical features is recognisably an anima figure, the embodiment of those qualities of femininity, allurement and mystery which haunt so much of English literature (cf. Estella in Dickens's *Great Expectations,* Beatrice Normandy in Wells's *Tono-Bungay* and Sarah Woodruff in John Fowles's *The French Lieutenant's Woman).* It is she who initiates Wallace into the enchanted garden, who leads him into conversation and guides him through the paradisal domain. She is contrasted with 'a sombre dark woman, with a grave, pale face and dreamy eyes . . . wearing a soft long robe of pale purple'. This enigmatic figure shows him a book containing scenes from his life up until the moment of entering the garden. When, in his eagerness to learn what happens next, he attempts to turn the pages Wallace remembers that '*she bent down upon me like a shadow and kissed my brow* (my italics)'. This dark woman with a grave bearing and sombre expression can be seen as the Shadow, a personification of the unconscious, instinctive aspects of his make-up. It is she who looks at him sadly while he follows the story of his life and she who resists his fingers while he struggles to look into the future. She recognises his nature and is aware that, though fascinated by the garden, he is destined to leave it behind him in his quest for career and influence. The two figures symbolise the contradictory drives which pull him throughout his life: the one happy, beckoning, mysterious; the other austere, emotionless, dutiful. The dichotomy haunts him throughout his career. When, later in life, he suddenly catches sight of the door in the wall he experiences '*a queer moment, a double and divergent movement of my will* (my italics)'. He is filled with a sense of 'unforgettable and still unattainable things':

> Those dear friends and that clear atmosphere seemed very sweet to me, very fine but remote. My grip was fixing now upon the world. I saw another door opening—the door of my career.

It is significant that when he looks back to the moment of first seeing the door, he remarks: 'I forgot the sort of gravitional pull back to the discipline and obedience of home, I forgot all hesitations and fear, forgot discretion, forgot all the intimate realities of this life.' Discipline, obedience, discretion, reality—it is these which are momentarily laid aside in the quest for beauty and enchantment.

'The Door in the Wall' is built up on this pattern of opposites, a very characteristic feature of Wells's fiction. The enchanted garden with its beautiful people and aura of peace and happiness is continually contrasted with the 'grey world' outside the wall—with the bullying at school, the tawdry world of politics, the demands of career and ambition. The garden is described in terms which convey an unmistakable echo of the Garden of Eden:

> There was something in the very air of it that exhilarated, that gave one a sense of lightness and good happening and well-being; there was something in the sight of it that made all its colour clean and perfect and subtly luminous. In the instant of coming into it one was exquisitely glad—as only in rare moments, and when one is young and joyful one can be glad in this world. And everything was beautiful there. . . .

What is so striking about these descriptive passages is the extensive use of contrasting imagery: masculine—feminine; conscious—unconscious; life—death; inner—outer; immortality—transience. It is as if Wells is deliberately posing a series of contradictions. The hard, masculine spikes and the gentle doves; the cold marble and the brightly coloured paraquets. The broad red steps and the great avenue of trees symbolise Wallace's journey through life, his progression to higher levels of consciousness. At the climax of his journey he arrives at a spacious palace filled with fountains, an apt metaphor for the unconscious, for the centre of his imaginative life: full of the promise of beauty and desire. The 'grass-covered court' suggests the enclosed quality of Wallace's life, the fact that the only real happiness he ever knows takes place within the confines of the garden. But the delightful games with his companions are played against a backcloth of 'very old trees', and a sun-dial surrounded by flowers. Always one is reminded of time, of the transience of beautiful things. In the 'marble seats of honour and statuary' can be detected a precognition of his worldly ambitions, his successful political career. But what are we to make of the 'old man musing among laurels'? The laurel is traditionally an emblem of victory, of a triumph over odds. The venerable figure musing among these symbols of conquest reinforces the ambiguity of Wells's parable: which is Wallace to conquer—his ambitions or his dreams? It is this element of doubt which pervades the story to the end.

If one takes the garden as a metaphor for the imagination, the theme of the story can be read as Wallace's recognition of his true nature. On the one hand, imagination and wonder ('I became in a moment a very glad and wonder-happy little boy'); on the other hand, reality and conformity. These are the competing drives which pull him in opposite directions throughout his life.

Source: J. R. Hammond, "Lost Orientations," in *H. G. Wells and the Short Story,* St. Martin's Press, 1992, pp. 125–31.

Roslynn D. Haynes

In the following excerpt, Haynes examines Wells's depiction of the conflict between science and imagination in "The Door in the Wall."

'The Door in the Wall' . . . partakes very largely of the aura of fairy tale, even of myth, albeit one that is psychologically valid. It concerns the politician Lionel Wallace, who once, as a child of a joyless, inhibiting home, discovered a door to a visionary garden of happiness. This door presented itself to him as simultaneously attractive and illicit, and it

> "Wells has often been seen as being caught on an intellectual battle-ground between his scientific training in rational thought and his native gift of a vivid imagination. He himself was apparently aware of this conflict."

has reappeared temptingly at critical moments throughout his distinguished public career. Hitherto he has remained true to the latter, passing by 'the door that goes into peace, into delight, into a beauty beyond dreaming, a kindness no man on earth can know.' Wallace is subsequently found dead in an excavation, having one night apparently mistaken the workmen's door in the hoarding for the door in the wall of his garden. The story poses a question to which Wells returned repeatedly in his writing—the contrast between the aesthetic and the practical, scientific inclinations of man and the difficulty of choosing between them.

> I am more than half convinced that he had, in truth, an abnormal gift, and a sense, something—I know not what—that in the guise of wall and door offered him an outlet, a secret and peculiar passage of escape into another and altogether more beautiful world. At any rate, you will say, it betrayed him in the end. But did it betray him? There you touch the inmost mystery of these dreamers, these men of vision and the imagination. We see our world fair and common, the hoarding and the pit. By our daylight standard he walked out of security into darkness, danger and death.
>
> But did he see like that?

This theme recurs in several guises in Wells's work, being part of a wider contrast between tangible and imaginative elements of experience, or between science and aesthetics, a conflict which was all too pertinent to Wells's own experience. Wells has often been seen as being caught on an intellectual battle-ground between his scientific training in rational thought and his native gift of a vivid imagination. He himself was apparently aware of this conflict intermittently during his science course at South Kensington, when poetry seduced attention from geology practical work, [*Experiment in Autobiography*] and he portrayed a similar struggle in several student characters—in Lewisham and in William Hill of 'A Slip Under the Microscope'—and at greater length in George Ponderevo's dalliance with art. Thus even in a manifest fairy story, 'The Door in the Wall,' Wells is preoccupied with a question, partly psychological, partly sociological, raised by his own experiences as a science student. It is certainly conceivable that this divided intellectual allegiance still beset Wells in the literary field—how far was his imagination justified in leaping beyond the limits of the scientifically acceptable postulates of his day? Or alternatively, how far did a desire to put forward a point of view as scientifically as possible emasculate his potential literary gifts?

Source: Roslynn D. Haynes, "Scientific Method and Wells's Credentials," in *H. G. Wells: Discoverer of the Future: The Influence of Science on His Thought,* New York University Press, 1980, pp. 49–50.

Jerome Hamilton Buckley

Buckley is a distinguished American educator and literary scholar whose studies focus primarily upon Victorian literature. In the following excerpt, he briefly outlines Wells's "The Door in the Wall" and suggests that the ending is open to interpretation.

Early in the new century H. G. Wells suggested through a compelling short story both the spell and the menace of a nostalgia for a buried time. "The Door in the Wall"—patently sexual in much of its symbolism and implication—describes a lonely child's vision of an enchanted garden, behind a green door in a high white wall, where the intruder feels instant joy and "a keen sense of homecoming," and where a benevolent somber woman, "very gentle and grave," shows him a picture book of his own life. Before opening the door, the boy has had not only the strong desire to do so, but also "the clearest conviction that either it was unwise or it was wrong of him—he could not tell which—to yield to this attraction," and he has known instinctively that "his father would be very angry." Afterwards, when his father, who is a lawyer and a grim rationalist, punishes him for telling lies about the garden, he succeeds in suppressing the memory. But he can never quite forget, and now and again throughout his career he catches glimpses of the strange familiar door in the wall: once when his eagerness not to be late for school overcomes his wish to stop, once when he cannot afford to let anything interfere with his arrival at Oxford for a fellowship, once when he does not care to keep a lady waiting. Eventually he achieves distinction in politics and is even asked to join the Cabinet; but he is dissatisfied always with his successes and tortured by increasingly frequent thoughts of the by-passed door. In the end his dead body is found at the bottom of a deep excavation; he has apparently wandered through an unlocked gate in the hoarding. It remains a question whether the dream of a lost peace and security has ultimately released him from the distractions of the world or merely betrayed him.

Source: Jerome Hamilton Buckley, ''The Passion of the Past,'' in *The Triumph of Time: A Study of Victorian Concepts of Time, History, Progress, and Decadence,* Cambridge, MA: The Belknap Press of Harvard University, 1966, pp. 113–14.

Bernard Bergonzi

Bergonzi is an English literary critic and writer of fiction and poetry who has written full-length critical studies on the works of H. G. Wells, T. S. Eliot, and Gerard Manley Hopkins. In the following excerpt, he provides an overview of Wells's ''The Door in the Wall,'' offering his interpretation of the symbolism of the door.

The politician Lionel Wallace is, in the eyes of the world, a successful man; but, as he confides to the friend who tells the story, he has a 'preoccupation' that is gradually dominating his life and even affecting his efficiency. As a child of five he had wandered out of his home and through the streets of West Kensington, where he had noticed a green door set in a white wall. It was immensely attractive to him, and he had a very strong desire to open it and pass through (he somehow knew that it would be unfastened), but at the same time he felt an equally strong conviction that this would be wrong or unwise: in particular he felt his father would be very angry if he did so. Nevertheless, he yields to the temptation and finds himself in a beautiful garden. (One is reminded here of the garden which Alice sees through the little door in Chapter I of *Alice in Wonderland.*) Wells's account of the garden tries to give the sense of a child's paradise but is scarcely satisfactory; nevertheless, it can be accepted as shorthand for a type of *locus amoenus.* It has a rare and exhilarating atmosphere, its colours are clean and bright, and the child is filled with joy. There are rich flower-beds and shady trees, and various animals, including two splendid tame panthers. He meets a tall fair girl who 'came to meet me, smiling, and said ''Well?'' to me, and lifted me and kissed me, and put me down, and led me by the hand. . . .'

"It remains a question whether the dream of a lost peace and security has ultimately released Lionel Wallace from the distractions of the world or merely betrayed him."

He meets other children and they play games together, though he cannot remember the games (a fact which later causes him much distress).

> Then presently came a sombre dark woman, with a grave, pale face and dreamy eyes, a sombre woman, wearing a soft long robe of pale purple who carried a book, and beckoned and took me aside with her into a gallery above a hall—though my playmates were loth to have me go, and ceased their game and stood watching as I was carried away. 'Come back to us!' they cried. 'Come back to us soon!' I looked up at her face, but she heeded them not at all. Her face was very gentle and grave. She took me to a seat in the gallery, and I stood beside her, ready to look at her book as she opened it upon her knee. The pages fell open. She pointed, and I looked, marvelling, for in the living pages of that book I saw myself; it was a story about myself, and in it were all the things that had happened to me since ever I was born. . . .

When the record of the book reaches the point at which he had found himself outside the green door, the whole enchanted world vanishes, and the little boy is once more in the dismal West Kensington street.Throughout his later life he dreams of revisiting the garden, and at long intervals he has unexpected glimpses of the door in the wall, in different parts of London, but always when the exigencies of his immediate circumstances make it impossible—or at least, highly inconvenient—for him to stop and open the door. The child's vision, as Wells presents it, has all the marks of a return in fantasy to a prenatal state: the door is an obvious womb-symbol. This suggestion is emphasized when we recall that Wallace's mother had died when he was two: the tall fair girl who greets him when he arrives in the garden, and the sombre dark woman who initiates him into the events of his life after birth (and who is referred to as 'the grave mother') can both be taken as aspects of the mother he had scarcely

"The child's vision, as Wells presents it, has all the marks of a return in fantasy to a prenatal state: the door is an obvious womb-symbol."

known. Yet Wells's picture is not exclusively Freudian in its implications; it also has elements of an older mode of regarding prenatal existence—the Wordsworthian. This is apparent in the reference to the children with whom the little boy plays, and who call him back when the dark lady draws him aside:

> Hence in a season of calm weather
> Though inland far we be,
> Our Souls have sight of that immortal sea
> Which brought us hither,
> Can in a moment travel thither,
> And see the Children sport upon the shore. . . .

After his mother died Wallace had been brought up by a governess; his father is described as 'a stern preoccupied lawyer, who gave him little attention and expected great things of him'. In the sphere of public life his father's expectations are fulfilled, for Wallace has an unusually successful career. Yet his constantly cherished secret desire to return to the garden represents a potential revolt against his father's authority; had he not, as a boy of five, felt that his father would be very angry if he went through the green door? We have here the elements of an Oedipus situation: ultimately Wallace destroys himself in daring to risk, for the second time, his father's displeasure, by opening the door and returning to the delectable world which he identified with his dead mother.

This fate is, in a sense, predictable, but on the narrative level the way in which Wells brings it about is extremely adroit. Wallace tells his friend that three times in the past year he has seen the door, and on each occasion he has passed it by: once because he was on his way to a vital division in the House of Commons, once, significantly, because he was hurrying to his father's death-bed, and once because he wished, for reasons of personal ambition, to continue a discussion with a colleague. And now his soul 'is full of unappeasable regrets', and he is barely capable of working.

A few months later he is dead:

> They found his body very early yesterday morning in a deep excavation near East Kensington Station. It is one of two shafts that have been made in connection with an extension of the railway southward. It is protected from the intrusion of the public by a hoarding upon the high road, in which a small doorway has been cut for the convenience of some of the workmen who live in that direction. The doorway was left unfastened through a misunderstanding between two gangers, and through it he made his way.

On the next apparition of the door, we may assume, Wallace resolved, at whatever cost, to open it and rediscover his garden; this represented a virtual and perhaps an actual abandonment of his career (and so struck, symbolically, at his father). At this point Wallace's visions—or hallucinations, if we prefer it—and the physical world around him were in fatal conjunction. There is a certain grim irony in the fact that the deep pit into which Wallace fell can be seen as just as much of a womb-symbol as the enclosed garden he was seeking.

Source: Bernard Bergonzi, "The Short Stories," in *The Early H. G. Wells: A Study of the Scientific Romances,* University of Toronto Press, 1961, pp. 84–7.

Alfred C. Ward

In the following excerpt, Ward offers his interpretation of the symbolism of the garden in Wells's "The Door in the Wall," paying particular attention to the deceiving nature of time and happiness.

Turning to the Parables in *The Country of the Blind,* we find three stories that can be thus designated: "The Door in the Wall," "The Beautiful Suit," and "The Country of the Blind." The first describes how Lionel Wallace, when a little fellow between five and six years old, wandered through West Kensington streets one day, and came to a green door set in a white wall. The door attracted the child, as it were magnetically, so that he opened it and discovered a wonderful and beautiful garden stretching far and wide, with distant hills. He found delightful playmates there; and, afterwards, a grave and sombre woman who took him to a seat and showed him a book:

> The pages fell open. She pointed, and I looked, marvelling, for in the living pages of that book I saw myself; it was a story about myself, and in it were all the things that had happened to me since ever I was born.

In a while the grave woman stooped to kiss the boy's brow, and at that moment he found himself crying in a long grey street in Kensington. He thought he would be able to find that door again whenever he went to look for it; but he could not. He did see it again, several times in his life, but it was always in some different locality; and Wallace was always prevented by some immediately urgent worldly call from passing again through the door. A time came when he determined that nothing whatever should keep him away from the wonderful garden whenever next he should see the green door in the white wall; and one morning his body was found in a railway excavation near East Kensington Station, beyond a hoarding in which a small doorway was cut. . . . The advantage of both this story and "The Beautiful Suit" is that they may be interpreted according to the temper of the individual mind. Wallace's mysterious garden might be any one of those fine aspirations by which men are moved, and from which they are debarred by the fret and wear and tear of the workaday world. Men cry: "We have no time for the beauty that lies beyond the door in life's wall. We are too busy to-day; let our time for rest and the sweet things of life be to-morrow." And when that remote to-morrow dawns at last, the wonderful garden of which they had the freedom in childhood, eludes them after all, and in the hour of delusion they walk behind a hoarding—into the pit beyond.Yet that is not all, maybe. H. G. Wells says of Lionel Wallace:

> I am more than half convinced that he had, in truth, an abnormal gift, and in sense, something—I know not what—that in the guise of wall and door offered him an outlet, a secret and peculiar passage of escape into another and altogether more beautiful world. At any rate, you will say, it betrayed him in the end. But did it betray him? . . . By our daylight standard he walked out of security into darkness, danger, and death.
>
> But did he see like that?

Source: Alfred C. Ward, "H. G. Wells," in *Aspects of the Modern Short Story: English and American,* University of London Press, Ltd., 1924, pp. 139–41.

Further Reading

Batchelor, John. *H. G. Wells,* pp. 4-107. Cambridge: Cambridge University Press, 1985.

Provides an overview of Wells's "The Door in the Wall," offering an interpretation of the door's symbolism and commenting on the narrative style of the story.

Huntington, John. *The Logic of Fantasy: H. G. Wells and Science Fiction,* pp. 50-91. New York: Columbia University Press, 1982.

Analyzes the imagery in Wells's "The Door in the Wall" and illustrates how the imagery contributes to the theme of opposition between reality and imagination.

Wood, James Playsted. *I Told You So! A Life of H. G. Wells,* pp. 109-22. New York: Pantheon, 1969.

Examines Wells's style of depicting the conflict between science and imagination, and contends that the theme of conflict between the two is paramount in "The Door in the Wall."

Flight

John Steinbeck

1938

John Steinbeck's short story ''Flight'' was published in 1938 in *The Long Valley,* a collection of stories set in the Salinas Valley in California. The book appeared just three years after Steinbeck first received critical acclaim for his novel *Tortilla Flat* and one year before the publication of what many consider his greatest work, *The Grapes of Wrath.* ''Flight'' is generally considered one of Steinbeck's best works of short fiction, written at the height of his career. It is the story of young Pepe Torres, an unsophisticated youth from an isolated farm along the California coast. He wants very much to be considered a man. On his first trip alone to town, he kills a drunken man in an argument and flees to the mountains, only to succumb to thirst, infection, and the bullets of his pursuers. Critics have interpreted the story as a parable of the journey from youth to manhood. In writing the story, Steinbeck drew on his own experiences growing up in the Salinas Valley to give a vivid portrayal of the arid, rocky mountains east of the valley, which are filled with wild animals and danger. His energetic narrative style gives ''Flight'' its suspense and dramatic power. Steinbeck's sympathy for the struggles of the peasant against the forces of nature and wealthy landowners, which forms the basis for *The Grapes of Wrath* and many of his other works, is apparent in this story.

Author Biography

Winner of the 1940 Pulitzer Prize in literature for his novel *The Grapes of Wrath,* the 1937 New York Drama Critics Circle Award for his theatrical adaptation of his novella *Of Mice and Men,* and the 1962 Nobel Prize for literature, Steinbeck enjoyed popular as well as critical success during his lifetime and beyond. Although Steinbeck's romantic portrayals of dignified and noble common folk are now seen by some as simplistic, his works continue to appeal to critics and readers of the present day, supporting Steinbeck's enduring reputation as one of the most important twentieth-century American writers.

John Ernst Steinbeck was born on February 27, 1902, in Salinas, California. He grew up in the Salinas Valley and used it as the setting for many of his works, including "Flight." He used this familiar terrain as a setting in which to test his characters' relationship to their environment. Peter Shaw comments that "[T]he features of the valley at once determined the physical fate of his characters and made symbolic comment on them." Steinbeck's studies at Stanford University in California, where he became interested in biology, led him to take an evolutionary view of human society. He referred to this as his "biological" approach to understanding and writing about human behavior. This placed him in philosophical alignment with other naturalist writers who were influenced by Charles Darwin's theories of evolution and natural selection. In naturalistic works, the characters are products of their heredity as it acts upon their environment. Such stories end usually with the destruction of the main character, who by acting in response to his impulses and instincts, is crushed by the forces of the environment. However, Steinbeck is not strictly naturalistic, as he frequently casts his stories in mythic frameworks, giving them romantic or spiritual dimensions lacking in much naturalistic fiction.

Steinbeck's greatest achievement was *The Grapes of Wrath,* published in 1939. It is the story of the migration of an Oklahoma family during the Great Depression of the 1930s from their drought-destroyed farm to the dream of prosperity in California. When the Joad family reaches California, they find many others like them, all competing for low wages to pick fruit on corporate-owned farms. Steinbeck's epic and sympathetic presentation of this story led to charges that he was a communist. In the resulting controversy, the book was both banned and praised. Steinbeck continued to write, in 1952 publishing *East of Eden,* a novel paralleling the biblical story of Cain and Abel. He also served briefly as a war correspondent during the Vietnam conflict. Steinbeck died in New York City on December 20, 1968.

Plot Summary

"Flight" opens at an unspecified time, probably in the 1930s, on the Torres farm on the California coast, fifteen miles south of Monterey. Nineteen-year-old Pepe Torres is amusing his younger brother and sister, Emilio and Rosy, by skillfully throwing his switchblade at a post. The knife is his inheritance from his father, who died ten years earlier after being bitten by a rattlesnake. Their mother scolds Pepe for his laziness and tells him he must ride into Monterey to buy salt and medicine. He is to spend the night in Monterey at the home of a family friend, Mrs. Rodriguez. Pepe is surprised that he will be allowed to go alone, and he asks to wear his father's hat, hatband, and green silk handkerchief. He tells his mother that he will be careful, saying, "I am a man." His mother responds that he is "a peanut" and "a foolish chicken."

Before sunrise the next morning, Pepe returns unexpectedly to the farm. He tells his mother he must go away to the mountains. He tells his mother that he had drunk wine at Mrs. Rodriguez's, and that a few other people had shown up as well. He tells her about a quarrel he had with a man. His knife seemed to fly on its own, and the man was stabbed. Pepe concludes by saying, "I am a man now, Mama. The man said names to me I could not allow."

Mama Torres agrees that Pepe is now a man, but she also has her doubts. She has worried about Pepe's knife-play and where it might lead him. She gives him his father's black coat and rifle, as well as a water bag and some provisions. Dressed in his father's garments, Pepe hurries off to the mountains. Mama Torres starts the formal wail of mourning for the dead. Emilio asks Rosy if Pepe is dead, and Rosy replies, "He is not dead. . . . Not yet."

Pepe rides into the mountains, and as he climbs, the trail changes from soft black dirt beside a stream

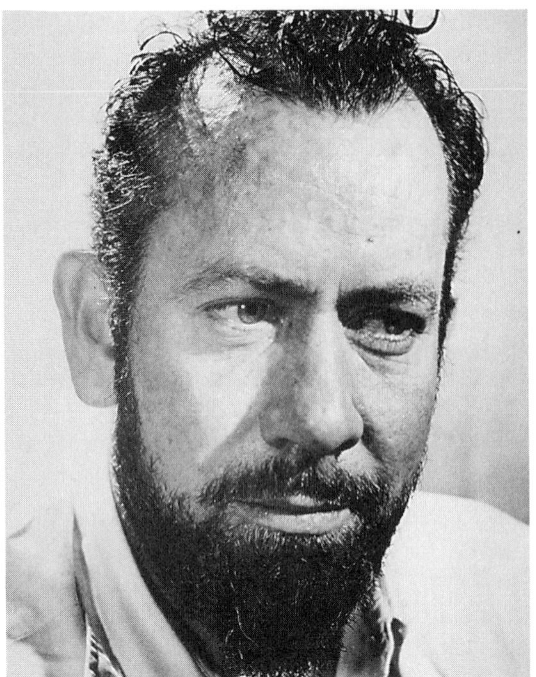

John Steinbeck

to redwood forest to rough, dry, rocky open country. He avoids a mounted man on the trail. As he rides higher toward the pass, he glimpses a dark figure on the ridge ahead, then looks quickly away. He stops in the evening by a small stream, tying the horse. A wildcat comes to the stream and stares at Pepe, who does not use the rifle for fear of revealing his location to his pursuers. He sleeps, then wakes suddenly in the night when his horse whinnies to another horse on the trail. After hastily saddling his horse and going up the hill, he realizes that he has left his hat behind.

He continues riding into the dry waste country. Then, without warning, his horse is shot dead from under him. Pepe, under fire, crawls up the hill, moving "with the instinctive care of an animal." He worms his way up, running only when there is cover, otherwise "wriggling forward on his stomach." He waits as wild animals go about their business, the buzzards already circling over his dead horse below. When he sees a flash below him, he aims and fires. In the return fire, a chip of granite embeds itself in his right hand. Pepe takes the stone out and the cut bleeds. He stuffs a dusty spider web into the wound to stop the bleeding, then slides and crawls slowly up the hill. He is almost bitten by a rattlesnake, and lizards scatter before him as he crawls upward. He sleeps in the bushes until night. His arm is infected and swollen tight inside the sleeve of his father's coat. He leaves the coat behind. He is very thirsty and his tongue is swollen.

That night he comes to a damp stream bed and digs frantically for water. Exhausted, he falls asleep until late the next afternoon. He awakens to find a large mountain lion staring at him. The big cat moves away at the sound of horses and a dog. Pepe crouches behind a rock until dark, then moves up the slope before he realizes he has left his rifle behind. He sleeps, then awakens to find his wound swollen and gangrenous. He clumsily lances the wound with a sharp rock and tries to drain the infection from his hand. He climbs near the top of a ridge only to see "a deep canyon exactly like the last, waterless and desolate."

He sleeps again in the daylight, awakening to the sound of pursuing hounds. He tries to speak, "but only a thick hiss came to his lips." He makes the sign of the cross with his left hand and struggles to his feet. Standing tall, he allows his pursuers to take aim. Two shots ring out and Pepe falls forward down the rocky cliff, his body causing a "little avalanche."

Characters

Mama

See Mrs. Torres

Papa

See Mr. Torres

Mrs. Rodriguez

Mrs. Rodriguez lives in Monterey and is a friend of the Torres family. Although she does not appear in the story, it is at her home that Pepe becomes drunk and stabs the drunken stranger. Her home is the only location of social gathering in the story.

Mr. Torres

Mr. Torres is Pepe's father who, ten years prior to the time of the story, died when he tripped over a stone and fell on a rattlesnake. The switchblade Pepe now owns was inherited from his father.

Although the story says nothing about the father other than his manner of death, his presence is constantly felt.

Mrs. Torres

Mrs. Torres is Pepe's widowed mother. She lives on the family's seaside farm with her two sons and her daughter and is determined to maintain her home without the help of a man. She keeps the two younger children home from school so they can fish and bring in food for the family. She believes that Pepe is "fine and brave," though there is little evidence to substantiate her opinion. In fact, she constantly tells Pepe how lazy he is, and says that he is foolish when he asserts that he is a man.

When Pepe returns from an errand in Monterey and tells his mother he must flee, she helps him pack, admitting that she had been worried about his quick reflexes with the knife. Despite the fact that he has failed to stay out of trouble while on his errand, she believes that Pepe's experience in Monterey has made him "a man now," for "[h]e has a man's thing to do."

Pepe Torres

Nineteen-year-old Pepe Torres is the main character in "Flight." He is tall, thin, gangly, and lives on the family farm with his widowed mother and a younger brother and sister. While his mother believes that he is "fine and brave," there is no indication that he is anything but lazy. He is very skilled in throwing his father's switchblade, however, and wants to prove that he is a man.

In Monterey, Pepe gets drunk and knifes a man who quarrels with him. He tries to explain to his mother how much of a man he is now, but refuses to accept full responsibility for his actions. He even claims that, at one point, "[T]he knife—it went almost by itself." Pepe then flees to the mountains, taking only his father's coat, rifle, and a few provisions. In his flight, he loses the hat, the provisions, the rifle, and his horse—everything he needs to survive. Such carelessness shows how much Pepe still has to learn about being a responsible adult.

With no skills to aid him and with an infected hand becoming gangrenous, Pepe becomes exhausted, hungry, thirsty, and is reduced to crawling away from his pursuers like an animal. His parched mouth can no longer form words. In his degradation, he is able to stand up—like a man—to his pursuers, and face his death.

Media Adaptations

- "Flight" was adapted as a film by Barnaby Conrad, starring Efrain Ramirez and Ester Cortez and produced by Columbia Pictures in 1960.

Themes

Growth and Development

At the beginning of "Flight" Pepe Torres is a nineteen-year-old youth living on an isolated farm with his mother and two younger siblings. He keeps insisting to his mother that he is a man, but she dismisses him with belittling names. Pepe does not understand what it means to be a man. When he is given the responsibility of riding to town to buy medicine and salt for the family, like a child he excitedly asks if he can wear his father's hatband and handkerchief. The clothing makes him appear to be an adult, but his idea of maturity is very superficial. In town he gets drunk and argues with a drunken man who insults him. He does not accept responsibility for knifing the man. He tells his mother that "the man started toward [him] and then the knife—it went almost by itself. It flew, it darted before [he] knew it." He insists that because he is now a man he cannot allow himself to be insulted. While Pepe does appear changed—his eyes are sharp and bright and purposeful, with no laughter or bashfulness in them anymore—he is not mature. When his mother tells his brother and sister he is a man now, Pepe's appearance changes "until he looked very much like Mama."

The ride into the wilderness is a test of Pepe's maturity. However, he loses his hat, his horse, his father's coat, his father's rifle, and his water supply. These are all necessary to protect him from the heat of the sun and the cold nights as well as the dry desert mountains while he tries to escape punishment for his crime. Injured by a chip of granite which his pursuers' bullet drove into his right hand, Pepe becomes more and more debilitated as the infection spreads. He is described as an animal, as

Topics for Further Study

- Based on what Mama Torres says to Pepe in the story, what do you think she believes about his level of maturity at the beginning of the story? Does her opinion of him change when he returns from Monterey, or just her expectations of him?
- Before going to Monterey, Pepe is eager to wear the black hat with the leather hatband and the green silk handkerchief. How does he look and feel while wearing these? How does he look when he puts on his father's black coat before he rides into the mountains? What is the significance of his losing the hat, the coat, and the tools and supplies his mother sends with him?
- Who or what are the ''dark watchers''? What does their presence add to the atmosphere and feeling of the story?
- Think of some other folk tales you have read or heard. How is this story similar to them? How is it different?
- Explain how Steinbeck's biological view of human nature can be applied to the character of Pepe.

he crawls on his stomach, wriggling and worming toward the top of the next ridge. Because he is so thirsty, he loses the ability to talk. At the end of the story, he manages to stand on his two legs again at the top of the ridge and face his pursuers. Most critics see this stand as proof that Pepe has finally matured and now, like a man, is able to accept the consequences of his actions.

Change and Transformation

The central idea of ''Flight'' is Pepe's transition from boy to man. In the course of running from his crime, Pepe starts as a youth fleeing responsibility. As he loses the tools that define his humanity, he is reduced to crawling on the ground like an animal, wriggling like a snake and ''worming'' his way along. This recalls his father's death ten years earlier from a rattlesnake bite. Pepe first changes not from boy to man but from human to animal. He even loses the most distinctive trait of his humanity—the ability to speak. After suffering with thirst, a wound which becomes gangrenous, and the effects of being without shade in the hot sun, Pepe pulls himself to his feet to face his pursuers. Most critics see this as the point where Pepe becomes a man. Maturity is not a condition which comes at a certain age; it must be learned and earned through suffering. It is this suffering which changes Pepe into a man. Other critics, however, maintain that Pepe fails in his quest for manhood.

Individual versus Nature

When Pepe flees to the wilderness to escape from the consequences of his crime, he also flees from his humanity. The wilderness tests not just his maturity but also his place in the natural world. It is no longer just a question of whether he will become an adult but whether he will become human. He loses the marks of his humanity when he loses his tools and the ability to speak. He is just one animal among others in the natural world. He is reduced to digging for water and struggling to find shelter from the hot sun. But instead of dying like an animal among animals, Pepe stands up like a man in both senses of the word to face his punishment for his crime.

Style

Narrator and Point of View

''Flight'' is told from a third-person point of view. The narrator, the person telling the story, is outside the story and relates events as an observer would see them. For most of the story, the narrator is not omniscient, or ''all-knowing,'' about the characters in the story. When a narrator's point of view is limited, the reader is not told a character's thoughts or feelings during the course of the story. Instead, the reader must determine what a character is thinking or feeling from what the character does or says. One exception to this limited point of view appears near the beginning of the story, when the narrator says, ''Mama thought [Pepe] fine and brave, but she never told him so.'' The narrator is stepping into Mrs. Torres' mind and telling readers what she thinks. For most of the story, however, the reader can tell what a character is thinking or feeling only from the external clues which the narrator gives provides. For example, when Pepe is dressed up in his father's hat and green silk handkerchief, readers know he is feeling proud and happy because the narrator says that "Pepe grinned with pride and gladness" as he rode off to Monterey. As Pepe crawls up the mountain, thirsty and without his hat or horse, the narrator does not say that Pepe is feeling uneasy. Instead, the narrator says, "[h]is eyes were uneasy and suspicious," and this description of Pepe provides a clue to readers about how he is feeling.

The use of the limited third-person point of view in this story puts the reader in the same position as an observer. This makes the reader infer Pepe's motives from what he says and does. If the narrator were all-knowing, the reader would be told the reason why Pepe stands up on the ridge at the end of the story. Because the narrator does not know what Pepe is thinking, readers do not have access to Pepe's thoughts. Consequently, the reader can never be sure why Pepe stands up to certain death. The limited point of view contributes to the story's ambiguity.

Setting

"Flight" is set in an indeterminate time on the coast of central California as well as further inland in the coastal mountains. The story could have taken place any time between the late 1800s and the mid-1900s. The Torres farm is located on the cliffs overlooking the Pacific coast, at the edge of the continent. The country to the east, toward which Pepe flees, is a wilderness first of redwood forest and then dry, rocky hills and mountains. It is the ideal setting for the confrontation of man against nature.

Imagery

Animal imagery dominates "Flight." Pepe's mother compares him to a big coyote, a foolish chicken, a descendant of "some lazy cow," and a big sheep. He is described as grinning "sheepishly." His wrist flicks like the head of a snake. After his horse is shot underneath him, Pepe crawls, worms his way, wriggles, darts, and flashes like an animal. As he is crawling away after his hand is cut, he slides "into the brush on his stomach" and crawls close to a rattlesnake. His movements are those of a rattlesnake. These images evoke his father's death as a result of falling onto a rattlesnake. On his final day, Pepe moves toward the top of the ridge "with the effort of a hurt beast." He tries to speak, but can only make a "thick hissing noise." When he lances and drains his infected hand, he whines "like a dog" at the pain. He again tries to speak, but can produce only a "thick hiss." Only at the very end is he able to stand erect on his feet, like a human.

Structure

"Flight" is a short story which can almost be read as a folktale. It is set in an indeterminate time, almost a "once upon a time." Pepe is the hero who is sent out into the world on an errand, much as Jack of "Jack and the Beanstalk" was sent to sell the cow. Pepe encounters a problem, and he must flee for his life. His mother is his helper, and she gives him his father's coat and rifle for warmth and protection on the journey, as well as advice on how to survive. Pepe is, like many folktale heroes, a peasant. He passes into the wilderness and is tested. However, Pepe loses his horse and his father's rifle. He loses his power of speech and is reduced to the level of an animal. The "dark watchers" provide an element of the supernatural; it is never explained whether they are some type of imaginary power or just the men pursuing Pepe.

Naturalism

Although "Flight" is similar in tone and form to a folktale, it is written in a highly naturalistic style. Naturalism is a style of fiction which developed from the ideas of Charles Darwin's mid-nineteenth century theories of evolution and natural selection. Naturalist writers, according to M. H. Abrams's *Glossary of Literary Terms,* "held that a human being belongs entirely in the order of nature and does not have a soul or any other mode of participation in a religious or spiritual world beyond nature; that such a being is therefore merely a higher-order animal whose character and fortunes are determined by two kinds of forces, heredity and environment."

Steinbeck was influenced by such naturalist writers as Theodore Dreiser, as well as by his study of biology at Stanford. "Flight" is considered a masterpiece of naturalist writing. This story is a combination of a folktale form and a scientific attitude toward the human condition. The folktale and naturalistic short story are conflicting forms and styles, and this conflict emphasizes the ambiguity of the story's ending. Did Pepe simply die, as a failure and an animal, or did he succeed in his quest for manhood by standing up before his enemies?

Historical Context

California Geography

Steinbeck's "Flight" is set on the mid-California coast about fifteen miles south of Monterey and in the coastal mountains to the east. This was familiar terrain to Steinbeck, who was born and raised in Salinas. The Salinas Valley is the valley to which the title *The Long Valley* refers. As an adult, Steinbeck lived in Pacific Grove, a short distance from Monterey. He was very familiar with the terrain, from the rocky cliffs above the Pacific south of Monterey to the redwood forest inland to the dry, saw-tooth mountains to the east, then to the fertile Salinas Valley further east. This is the country through which Pepe passes on his flight from his pursuers.

In the 1930s, when Steinbeck was writing many of his works, the valley was a fertile farming region. During the Great Depression, however, many of the area's inhabitants were forced to sell their land to wealthy industrialists, who compelled those who worked the land to work hard for little in return. The people in the area who had farmed for generations were often Mexicans or descendants of the pioneers who had settled the land in the mid-nineteenth century. Pepe's Indian features could be attributed to earlier intermarriage between Mexican settlers and Native Americans from the area.

The dialogue in the story highlights the area's Spanish influences. Not only do specific phrases in Spanish appear in the dialogue, but the family uses the familiar form of the personal pronouns, "thee" and "thou," instead of the formal "you" when speaking with each other. Spoken English no longer makes these distinctions, unlike other languages. The resulting archaic feeling to the language helps place the characters in another, mythical time, or the indeterminate era in which folktales take place.

The Labor Movement

Steinbeck studied biology at Stanford in the 1920s. He developed a biological view of the human condition based on Darwinian ideas of evolution, natural selection, and adaptation. He liked to set man against nature in his writing, as he does in "Flight," and to examine how well man can survive in the wild. In addition, he was sympathetic to the poor and the exploited, who often became the central characters in his writings. He supported the labor movement, and he despised the exploitation of workers by corporate farms and large ranches. In novels like *The Grapes of Wrath* and *In Dubious Battle,* his clear sympathy for dispossessed farmers and striking workers led to accusations from some critics that he was a communist. Steinbeck addressed the political and economic stresses of the 1930s by writing of the effects on the poor, but he did not subscribe to a specific ideology.

"Flight" was written during the Great Depression, which began in 1929 and lasted through the 1930s. During that time, many people lost their jobs, homes, and became itinerant, often moving their entire families westward in hopes of finding work on farms that had not become part of the Midwestern "dustbowl" region. The poor became a viable political group because they had very little to lose. In this atmosphere, many labor unions, both in the industrialized North and the agricultural West, formed and became powerful. By exerting their political clout, and with the assistance of President Franklin Roosevelt's activist relief agenda, unions were able to compel Congress to enact laws establishing a minimum wage, worker's rights to organize and bargain collectively, and safe practices in the workplace.

Critical Overview

Well received by critics and the reading public when published in *The Long Valley* in 1938, "Flight" is considered one of Steinbeck's best stories. It was written at the height of his powers and published a year before *The Grapes of Wrath.* However, Steinbeck's views have declined in popularity in the decades since he first published these works. His romantic portrayals of dignified and noble common men are now seen by some as simplistic. In spite of this, his forceful and energetic writing style continues to earn him readers.

Critics still debate the meaning of "Flight." Most see it as a parable of what it means to be human, or in terms of the story, a man. Some see the story as showing how Pepe earns the right to call himself a man by suffering on his flight from his crime. Edward J. Piacentino in *Studies in Short Fiction,* catalogs the many animal references in the story and concludes that "the patterns they form give 'Flight' a richly suggestive texture that is often characteristic of some of the more artistically impressive short stories of twentieth-century literature." He notes that while Pepe is still at home on the farm, his mother refers to him in the imagery of

Compare & Contrast

- **1930s:** Many street gangs that arose during the 1920s in order to take advantage of Prohibition move on to other illegal ventures. The romanticized ''Dead End Kids'' (also known as the East Side Kids and the Bowery Boys) star in a number of movies during this time.

  1990s: Gang members range from grade-school children to adults. Drug dealing and related crimes are a major activity and means of profit for gangs. In Los Angeles alone, there are an estimated 70,000 gang members. In 1997, a new California program attempts to curtail gang violence by bringing criminal charges against parents of gang members. The program makes use of a 90–year-old law requiring the reasonable care and supervision of children.

- **1930s:** During the Great Depression, murder rates are considered high. They peak in 1933 at 9.7 murders per 100,000 people annually.

  1990s: Murder rates begin to fall in urban areas after skyrocketing in the 1970s and 1980s. In 1996, the murder rate hovers near 10 per 100,000 people.

- **1930s:** During the Great Depression, many farmers lose their farms because they are unable to pay their mortgages. Part of the problem is that farmers produce more than people are able to buy. President Roosevelt creates the Agricultural Adjustment Agency in 1933 to address this problem. The agency is declared unconstitutional in 1936 but is redeveloped and reinstated in 1939. Other programs developed by the government during the same time seek to protect farmland from being misused or overused. These are eventually taken up by the Farm Security Administration.

  1990s: Many farmers in the 1980s and 1990s go bankrupt. Musicians such as John Mellencamp and Willie Nelson organize the Farm Aid concerts to assist families who have lost their livelihood. Other farmers struggle to remain profitable and become increasingly involved in environmental land issues, including prevention of soil erosion and runoff and contamination of crops from insecticide and herbicide residues.

---

domestic animals. For example, an ancestor of his must have been ''a lazy cow,'' and Pepe is ''a big sheep,'' and a ''foolish chicken.'' Twice she also refers to him or his ancestors as having the traits of a ''lazy coyote.'' This and several references to his skill with the knife as being ''snakelike,'' are indications of his ''primitive animalism'' underneath his domesticity.

Piacentino finds that this use of domestic animal imagery in the first part of the story is in contrast to the imagery of wild animals used to describe Pepe's predicament and behavior in the mountains. Doves and quail are stalked by a wildcat ''creeping toward the spring, belly to the ground.'' Lizards on the trail slither away from Pepe and his horse. At night owls hunt rabbits. After his horse is shot out from under him, Pepe himself must act like an animal, ''worming,'' ''wriggling,'' ''crawling,'' ''slithering,'' and ''hissing.'' At the end, Pepe climbs to the top of the ridge ''with the effort of a hurt beast,'' and though unable to speak, stands like a man. His fall is not just a fall from grace; it is also the fall from youthful innocence in attaining maturity.

John H. Timmerman sees ''Flight'' as a story of ''an exploration of one individual's flight into unknown regions—a spiritual odyssey into the high, arid regions far from the nurturing sea.'' Timmerman uses letters written by Steinbeck and selections from Steinbeck's notebooks and other published works to supply a background to Steinbeck's philosophy of life. Steinbeck's passionate interest in marine biology and the sea was, in the 1930s, a strong influence on his work. The metaphor of the sea as a nurturing mother is evidenced in ''Flight'' as the secluded Torres farm by the sea. Pepe's flight from this protected environment for the dry, unknown mountains is not only, as Timmerman says, a story of "a modern man in search of his manhood and finding the animal within," it is also "a devolution, paced by a divestment of civilized tools and in incrementally intensifying animal imagery." In a notebook entry about the humanity's evolutionary development from lower forms which lived in the sea to an organism able to stand on dry land, Steinbeck had written, "Oh man who in climbing up has become lower.... What nobility except from pain, what strength except out of anger, what change except from discomfort." When Pepe loses his tools, his water, and his protective clothing, he is stripped down to himself alone. As his thirst takes away his human speech, his movements are described as those of a snake. Although Pepe has lowered himself to the level of a snake, he finally regains his humanity. In standing up to his responsibility, he becomes a man.

Dan Vogel, in an article in *College English,* finds that "Flight" shows characteristics of myth and tragedy. Pepe's flight is an "ordeal of transformation from innocence to experience, from purity to defilement." The physical pain of the festering cut to his right hand and the psychological pain of being the hunted are the components of his ordeal. Pepe must separate himself from the mother and lose the knife, gun, hat, and coat of the father before he can stand alone. Vogel sees "Flight" as telling the myth "of the natural miracle of entering manhood."

In contrast to most critics, Walter K. Gordon asserts that Pepe's flight is not the story of a youth leaving behind his mother and the tools of the father to become a man, but rather the opposite. In *Studies in Short Fiction,* Gordon argues that the story shows "man's moral deterioration and regression that inevitably results when he abandons responsibility for his actions." While Pepe and his family believe that the experience in Monterey has made him a man, the story demonstrates that he is unable to utilize the tools he has been given to help him succeed in his flight. He does not learn and grow and attain a sense of maturity from his experiences. For Gordon, "Flight" is a journey away from manhood.

As these various critical interpretations show, the ambiguity of the story itself lends it to conflicting interpretations of what it means. The value of "Flight" is that it is complex and does not yield easy answers to the human condition.

Criticism

Joyce Munro

Munro is an lawyer who works for UAW—Ford Legal Services. She is pursuing a doctorate in British and American literature at Wayne State University. In the following essay, she provides an overview of several critical interpretations of "Flight," but gives special focus to it as a work in which Steinbeck combines a naturalistic outlook with what could almost be called a folktale, with Pepe featured in the role of a Trickster.

Most of the criticism of Steinbeck's "Flight" discusses the story as Pepe Torres's journey from childhood to maturity. Nineteen-year-old Pepe wants very much to be considered a man and not a child. However, when he is given the responsibility of going to Monterey alone, he is unable to complete his errand without getting into trouble. He drinks too much wine, then knifes a drunken man who insults him. His flight into the mountains and the hardships he endures reduce him to the level of an animal. At the very end, Pepe stands up on the ridge to face his pursuers. He is shot and falls. To Edward J. Piacentino, Pepe's fall from the ridge is a fall from childhood into maturity. By standing up to his pursuers, Pepe finally faces responsibility for his actions in Monterey. Dan Vogel, in an essay in *College English,* sees the story as mythic and tragic. Pepe's flight is an ordeal taking him from innocence to experience, and Pepe's death is the death and burial of childhood. John H. Timmerman suggests that the central theme of "Flight" is that Pepe discovers, tragically, "that indomitable, spiritual consciousness of himself as human that separates him from the animals."

Other critics also see a spiritual dimension in Pepe's journey. Not only does Pepe move from childhood to maturity, he also grows from reacting like an unthinking animal to acting like a responsible human. John Antico writes of the animal-like, crawling Pepe that "[i]t is only by standing up on two feet and *facing death* that the sub-human Pepe can give birth to Man." In an article on "Flight" in the *Explicator,* William M. Jones sees Pepe's major

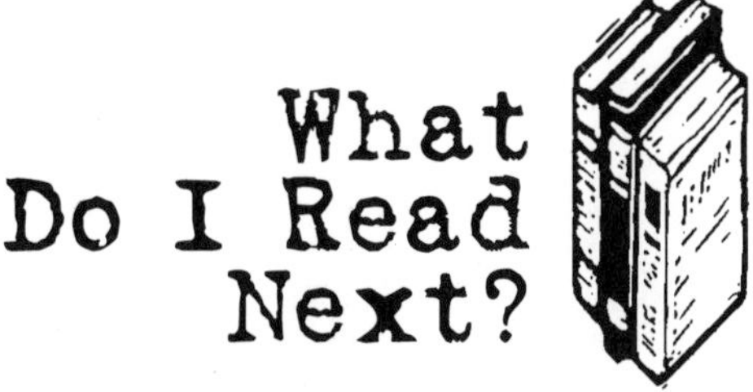

- *The Red Pony,* also by Steinbeck, was first published in 1937 and revised in 1945. It is the story of a boy's confrontation with death and his resulting maturation.
- *The Pearl,* Steinbeck's last work of short fiction, was published in 1947. It is a parable of a poor fisherman who discovers a pearl of great value which brings evil to his family. Like "Flight," it is told in almost the tone and form of a folktale.
- "The Bear," by William Faulkner, is included in *Go Down, Moses,* first published in 1940. This story is really a novella in a collection of short stories, all set in a particular place, Faulkner's fictional Yoknapatawpha County, Mississippi, and featuring characters who appear in more than one story. "The Bear" is the story of a sixteen-year-old boy who is finally allowed to hunt with the men. The main character seeks "to earn for himself the name and state of hunter." The novella displays the complex interrelationships among different races and social classes when a group of men go into the wilderness to hunt.
- *The Old Man and the Sea* by Ernest Hemingway was published in 1952. This novella is told in the form of a fable that chronicles an old fisherman's struggle to land a legendary fish. The tone, like that of "Flight," is almost mythic.
- Toni Morrison's *The Bluest Eye*, first published in 1970, is the chilling tale of a young girl's flight from her own identity in response to the pressures of racism, poverty, and brutality.
- *Ceremony* by Leslie Marmon Silko was published in 1977. It traces the efforts of Tayo, a young Native American soldier released from a Japanese prisoner-of-war camp after World War II, to evade the memories and nightmares of his captivity. As he realizes that the country he fought for during the war has no place for him and that he has no role in his home pueblo, he is compelled to begin a quest to find—and heal—himself.

flaw as being the sin of pride. "The details of Pepe's flight show how Pepe gradually conquered the family pride that caused his original sin and how through suffering he expiated that sin." By undergoing the hardships in the mountains and by being reduced to the level of an animal, Pepe makes amends both for his own impulsive action of stabbing a man who insulted him and for his condition of being born with original sin.

However much the reader wants a satisfying ending to this dramatic story, "Flight" refuses to give one. Walter K. Gordon argues in *Studies in Short Fiction* that Pepe actually flees *from* maturity. Pepe is first broken down in the story "from boy to animal, then from animal to an inanimate part of nature." How can one story generate such different interpretations?

Because the story itself refuses to give Pepe either a clear triumph or a defeat at the end, it remains open to interpretation. This lack of closure at the end keeps the reader thinking about what the story means long after it has been read. The critics who interpret Pepe's stand at the end of the story as redemptive overlook the particular features of the story itself. Perhaps this is why their arguments do not explain the story satisfactorily. The story is more ambiguous than these readings suggest.

Another look at the animal imagery in the story opens up further interpretations of "Flight." The narrator describes Pepe as having "sharp Indian cheek bones and an eagle nose." As he throws the switchblade, "Pepe's wrist flicks like the head of a snake." The comparisons of Pepe to wild animals and the reference to his Indian heritage invite the

"The folktale and the naturalistic story are very different, almost opposite, styles. For Steinbeck to superimpose them in the same story is for him to write a story which is based on a built-in contradiction."

reader to consider the significance of the coyote in Native American folklore. The fact that Mrs. Torres makes two references to the coyote suggests that the coyote has a special meaning in the story. The coyote is not just a wild animal or a sly, lazy animal, but a form of the Trickster in some Native American traditions. A Trickster is a ''disruptive character appearing in various forms in the folklore of many cultures,'' according to *Merriam Webster's Tenth Collegiate Dictionary.* The Trickster is part divine and part animal. He has a skill or magic power which he uses sometimes to benefit humankind but which sometimes backfires on him. Often he can change his shape. He freely crosses the boundaries both between human and animal and between the divine and the human.

During both his nights on the mountain, Pepe hears a coyote. Like Coyote the Trickster, Pepe has a dual nature. Mama Torres is certainly aware of this. Her son is both boy and man, and human but with potential to act with animal-like instinctive reflexes. Each time he asserts to her that he is a ''man,'' she refuses to acknowledge it, responding that he is a ''peanut'' or ''a foolish chicken.'' At the same time, she thinks of him as ''fine and brave.'' After Pepe rides off to Monterey, her younger son Emilio asks her, ''Did Pepe come to be a man today?'' She replies, ''A boy gets to be a man when a man is needed.'' She thinks Pepe is ''nearly a man now.'' When Pepe returns from Monterey changed, he again asserts, ''I am a man now, Mama,'' and this time she nods and says, ''Yes, thou art a man, my poor little Pepe. Thou art a man. I have seen it coming on thee. I have watched you throwing the knife into the post, and I have been afraid.'' For her, Pepe is at the same time both a man and her ''poor little Pepe.'' But the man she acknowledges is the one who too easily throws the knife, the one she has feared he might become. The distinction between ''man'' versus ''child'' and ''man'' versus ''animal'' is made early in the story.

When Pepe begins his flight to the mountains, ''his face was stern, relentless and manly.'' But as he goes on, he is gradually reduced from riding to walking to crawling like an animal up the dry mountains. Pepe, the man-boy and the man-animal slides on his stomach, wriggles, and squirms his way forward, much like the rattlesnake he encounters. He gets up on his feet ''[w]ith the effort of a hurt beast.'' When he tries to speak, he can only make ''thick hissing'' sounds. When he drains his infected hand, ''he threw back his head and whined like a dog.''

The terrain itself almost seems to take on human characteristics. The trail ''staggers'' down. The granite is ''tortured.'' The oak trees ''whisper.'' The mountain has ''jagged rotten teeth'' and ''granite teeth.'' Pepe begins by observing the animals, but later, they are observing him. After the mountain lion watches him for hours, then slinks away into the brush, ''Pepe took his rifle in his left hand and he glided into the brush almost as quietly as the lion had. Only when the dark came did he stand up.'' Pepe has become more animal than man.

As the plot of the story resembles a folktale concerning a Trickster, other aspects of the story also resemble a folktale. The story is set in an indeterminate time, almost a ''once upon a time.'' Pepe rides to Monterey like a youth in search of his fortune or his manhood. When his manhood is challenged, he reacts unthinkingly and with fatal results, and he must flee for his life. His mother gives him talismans of his dead father, the coat and the rifle, and he rides into the wilderness. ''The dark watchers'' in the wilderness add a supernatural element to the story. In the folktale, anything can happen. Frogs change into princes and men into toads. On his flight, Pepe is ''changed'' into an animal who crawls, wriggles, and worms his way along. At the end, he seems to change back into a man, depending on how the reader interprets his stand against his pursuers.

But while the story has some elements of a folktale, it is at the same time a naturalist work of fiction. Naturalism refers to a style of writing fiction which is almost scientific in its attempt to portray characters and how they react to their environment. This approach to fiction is, according to M. H.

Abrams in *A Glossary of Literary Terms,* "a product of post-Darwinian biology in the mid-nineteenth century," which holds that "a human being belongs entirely in the order of nature and does not have a soul or any other mode of participation in a religious or spiritual world beyond nature; that such a being is therefore merely a higher-order animal whose character and fortunes are determined by two kinds of forces, heredity and environment." The folktale and the naturalistic story are very different, almost opposite, styles. For Steinbeck to superimpose them in the same story is for him to write a story which is based on a built-in contradiction.

This type of contradiction may be the story's major strength. It helps to explain why the ending is ambiguous. Is Pepe a man or an animal? Or, like the Trickster, is he two things at once, animal and divine? Perhaps the story resolves this question by refusing to resolve it. This leaves the reader to draw his or her own conclusions as to whether Pepe succeeds in becoming a man.

Source: Joyce Munro, "Overview of 'Flight'," in *Short Stories for Students,* Gale, 1998.

John H. Timmerman

Timmerman is affiliated with the Department of English at Calvin College. In the following excerpt, he discusses how Steinbeck's use of thematic patterns and images in "Flight" effectively portrays the main protagonist as a person "in search of his manhood," whose powerful and enduring spirit enables him to rise above "the animal in man."

Steinbeck's interest in marine biology was inflamed to a passion in the early 1930s. The sea, with its endless surgings and its proliferation of life, would remain a powerful influence upon his life and art throughout his career. We can acknowledge the homing quiet and clashing of dubious battles in his valleys; we can celebrate the high, sun-splashed reaches of his mountains; but we must return over and over to the timeless swell of life and death in the sea as a metaphorical pattern as well as a geographical place in his work.

The sea represents, at once, life and death. For Steinbeck it is the mother: the bringer of life in swarming generation. It is also, beneath its unruly and deceptive surface, a place of primeval violence. That uneasy juxtaposition is captured superbly in *Cannery Row.* In chapter six, Doc surveys the sea, from quiet tidal pools to the deep reaches. His vision moves from the serene grace of the shallows to the primeval undertows. There a chaotic world of ferocity reigns, a feral world. For Steinbeck, probing into the sea is a probing into the origins of life itself, a descent into the mythic subconsciousness of human nature. From *The Log from the Sea of Cortez* to *The Winter of Our Discontent,* the sea functions powerfully in Steinbeck's prose.

> "While the story has some elements of a folktale, it is at the same time a naturalist work of fiction."

The sea also functions metaphorically in "Flight"—by its absence. In one of his notebooks of the early 1930s, during one of his frequent breaks from writing stories to pen personal reflections, Steinbeck turned his attention to the sea. "Man is so little removed from the water," he observes. "When he is near to the sea near the shore where the full life is, he feels terror and nostalgia." There we find our evolutionary predecessors, our lost memory: "Come down to the tide pool, when the sea is out and let us look into our old houses, let us avoid our old enemies."

Having paused to look into the tidal pools, Steinbeck recounts the course of humanity:

> We came up out of the water to the barren dry, the desert dry. It's so hard to get used to the land. It is a deep cry. Oh man who in climbing up has become lower. What good thing but comes out of the depths. What nobility except from pain, what strength except out of anger, what change except from discomfort. We are a cross race so filled with anger that if we do not use it all in fighting for a warm full body, we fight among ourselves. Animals fight nature for the privilege of living but man having robbed nature of some of its authority must fight man for the same right.

It is precisely that movement into the dry reaches, where we fight like animals "for the privilege of living," that marks the thematic pattern of "Flight." The story is a fictionalization of the idea Steinbeck expressed in this notebook entry; Pepe is very much modern man in search of his manhood and finding the animal within. But, as Steinbeck discovered in telling the story, Pepe also discovers something more, a human spirit that is inviolable and

"The story changes from a simple narration of a posse's manhunt to an exploration of one individual's flight into unknown regions—a spiritual odyssey into the high, arid regions far from the nurturing sea."

undefeatable, possessing an enduring power that lies below and rises above the animal in man.

The change in the title of the story from "Manhunt" to "Flight" is in itself significant. The story changes from a simple narration of a posse's manhunt to an exploration of one individual's flight into unknown regions—a spiritual odyssey into the high, arid regions far from the nurturing sea. Like the change in title, the story itself changed dramatically in the writing. As it first developed, far more attention was given to the knifing itself. After buying the necessary things in Monterey, Pepe stops at a church to light a candle for his father and then visits the house of Mrs. Rodriguez and her two daughters. After affirming that Pepe has grown to be a man, Mrs. Rodriguez tells him that the surly Carlos is drunk in the kitchen. Pepe, avowing that he is a man, says he will send the troublesome Carlos away. He enters the kitchen to confront him.

The passage that follows, from the *Long Valley* notebook, amplifies the scene. In a fashion he adopted to conserve ink and paper during this penurious time, Steinbeck did not pause in his writing to observe minor paragraph breaks:

> "Awaken!" said Pepe. He shook a pan. A big black face arose from the table, and sullen sleepy eyes looked at him. "Who are you?" "I am Pepe Torres. Mrs. Rodriguez wants you to go away now." Behind him, Mrs. Rodriguez said helplessly, "This is the son of Jose Torres. You know him, Carlos." The sullen eyes looked at her and then back at Pepe. "I know Jose Torres. He was a thief." The sentence was uttered as an insult, was meant to be insulting. Pepe stepped back. "I am a man." He looked inquiringly at Mrs. Rodriguez. She shook her head. Pepe's stomach was sad and then ice got into his stomach and then the ice grew up to his beard. His hand went into his pocket and came out and hung listlessly in front of him. He was surprised at the sound of his voice. "Thou art a liar and a pig." Carlos stood up. "Dirty naked Indian. You say that to me?" Then Pepe's hand flashed. The blade seemed to bloom from the black knife in midflight. It thudded into the man's chest to the handle. Carlos' mouth was open in amazement. His two black hands came up and found the knife and half pulled it out. And then he coughed, fell forward on the table and drove it in again. Pepe looked slowly around at the woman. His sweet girlish mouth was quizzical, "I am a man," he said. "I will go now."

While Steinbeck conveyed the entire scene indirectly in the final version, having Pepe report what happened in several quick sentences, the excised portion shows that the act of killing is allied with Pepe's manhood, and death itself is attended by blackness, both of the knife and of Carlos.

The opening line of the next paragraph in the first draft, inked out in a heavy line, indicates one direction the story might have taken: "They found him in the church sitting in a pew and looking at the lights on the altar. He had said many [undecipherable word] Ave Marias." After the crossed-out line, Steinbeck wrote, "Pepe's movements were swift but unhurried." He heads back to his house, covering the same route through Point Lobos that he had taken earlier. From here the final version follows with a few exceptions. In the first draft, Pepe shoots one of the trackers; in the final version he does not. Most of the revisions were the ones Steinbeck typically made, changing passive verbs to active constructions and sharpening details. The materials included in the two-page notebook entry, "Addenda to Flight," written several days after the first draft, are incorporated into the conclusion of the final version.

With its riveting power as a story, its feral imagery that stalks nearly every paragraph, and its mystical ambiguity, "Flight" has both enchanted and puzzled critics. It has occasioned some of the very best literary criticism of Steinbeck's work as scholars match their wits against a compelling drama. For its sheer, evocative power, few of Steinbeck's short stories match it.

Artistically, the tale is a tour de force, with layer upon layer of craftsmanship revealed in close reading. The ostensible plot and conflict—Pepe's quest for manhood against intractable odds of humanity and nature—appear simple enough. Since his father's death from a rattlesnake bite, Pepe inherits the place of manhood in the family. The one legacy from his father is the black-handled knife, with which Pepe demonstrates a fluid grace. But Mama Torres is reluctant to allow Pepe the place of manhood, berating him incessantly as a "peanut," "lazy coyote," or "big sheep." Nonetheless, she "thought him fine and brave, but she never told him so."

As Pepe leaves for Monterey to buy some medicine, his parting words are, "I will be careful. I am a man." The trip is allied with his manhood, and indeed he will acquire the adult knowledge of death on the trip. When a drunken man at Mrs. Rodriguez's house calls him a name—in the first draft he called Jose Torres a thief—Pepe's sense of manly honor will not permit it. The knife, says Pepe, "went almost by itself."

Many readers have focused exclusively upon that action and the subsequent flight to the exclusion of suggestive imagery patterns undergirding the tale. Thus, Dan Vogel sees the tale as "the ordeal of transformation from innocence to experience, from purity to defilement." In a brief note on the story ["Steinbeck's 'Flight,'" *Explicator* 18 (Nov. 1959)], William M. Jones suggests,

> The details of Pepe's flight show how Pepe gradually conquered the family pride that caused his original sin and how through suffering he expiated that sin. Not only does he subdue the proud flesh . . . but in so doing he regained a place in nature that his family, scratching away to get what they could out of the world, had failed to find. This progress seems to be Steinbeck's explanation of the maturing process.

Walter K. Gordon argues, "What is important in 'Flight' is not the crime itself but Pepe's mental and physical response to it, how he deports himself when the circumstances are propitious for a boy to become a man," an effort at which, in Gordon's view, Pepe ultimately fails. Like Steinbeck's note in the *Tortilla Flat* notebook, detailing humanity's trek from the sea to the arid heights, however, the story bears a yet more supple richness and probing of what it means to be human than these views suggest.

In Flannery O'Connor's "The Life You Save May Be Your Own," Mr. Shiftlet, spellbound by his own empty phrases, asks Mrs. Lucynell Crater, "What is a man?" The answer comes some time later: "a moral intelligence." The same question puzzled John Steinbeck. Is humanity the product of evolutionary eons, the offspring of the dark sea's surging?

The Log from the Sea of Cortez suggests as much:

> "A third pattern is woven into the loss of civilized tools and the heavy use of animal imagery—the increasing images of darkness."

> There is tied up to the most primitive and powerful racial or collective instinct a rhythm sense or "memory" which affects everything and which in the past was probably more potent than it is now. It would at least be more plausible to attribute these profound effects to devastating and instinct-searing tidal influences during the formative times of the early race history of organisms.

Or, in Steinbeck's view, is humanity also a moral intelligence? His answer unfolded steadily throughout his literary career. In *The Grapes of Wrath,* he speculates,

> For man, unlike any other thing organic or inorganic in the universe, grows beyond his work, walks up the stairs of his concepts, emerges ahead of his accomplishments. This you may say of man—when theories change and crash, when schools, philosophies, when narrow dark alleys of thought, national, religious, economic, grow and disintegrate, man reaches, stumbles forward, painfully mistakenly sometimes. Having stepped forward, he may slip back, but only half a step, never the full step back.

And in a letter to John O'Hara written a decade later, he asserted,

> The great change in the last 2,000 years was the Christian idea that the individual soul was very precious. Unless we can preserve and foster the principle of the preciousness of the individual mind, the world of men will either disintegrate into a screaming chaos or will go into a grey slavery. And that fostering and preservation seem to me our greatest job.

Steinbeck's own answer to the question is that humanity is unique by virtue of mind and spirit.

In the hot, sun-blasted world of "Flight," however, when a lazy boy asserts his manhood with a knife, when civilization's code of conduct is violated and the posse mounts, man is very much reduced to an animal. One recalls Steinbeck's reflection in his notebook: "Oh man who in climbing up has become lower." Pepe's flight into the mountains is also a devolution, paced by a divestment of civilized tools and in incrementally intensifying animal imagery. He loses gun and knife, saddle, horse, and food. John Ditsky notes the pattern of loss [in ''Steinbeck's 'Flight': The Ambiguity of Manhood'']:

> Beyond the simple deterioration of his possessions—as when his clothing tears away or his flesh is ripped—leading to a contemplation of man's naked state like that in *King Lear,* there is the importance of the fact that the objects just named are Pepe's from his father; they are, as the knife is in fact described, ''his inheritance.'' Pepe's attempt to sustain the manhood he has claimed in a single violent act—by means of the tools which were his father's badge of manhood and his estate—fails; he is finally stripped down to what he brings with him *within* himself: his own gifts, his own courage.

Stripped of civilized tools, Pepe's movements are increasingly described in verbs that suggest a primordial or serpentine creature. Pepe ''crawled,'' ''wormed,'' ''wriggled,'' ''darted,'' ''flashed,'' ''slid,'' ''writhed,'' and ''squirmed'' in the final stages. Furthermore, his paralyzing thirst strips him of the one thing that separates humanity from animals—speech: ''His tongue tried to make words, but only a thick hissing came from between his lips.'' Even his tongue becomes infected with blackness—''Between his lips the tip of his black tongue showed''—and the only sound of which he is capable is a ''thick hiss.''

As several critics have mentioned, a third pattern is woven into the loss of civilized tools and the heavy use of animal imagery—the increasing images of darkness. From his early fascination with the lights on the altar and the sun-swept cliffs of his home, Pepe's world is subsumed by blackness, culminating in the Dark Watchers. He leaves for his flight on a morning when ''Moonlight and daylight fought with each other, and the two warring qualities made it difficult to see.'' Louis Owens observes,

> The theme of death is woven on a thread of blackness through the story. It is Pepe's black knife which initiates the cycle of death. When Pepe flees he wears his dead father's black coat and black hat. It is the two ''black ones,'' Rosy and Emilio, who prophesy Pepe's death. The line of gangrene running the length of Pepe's arm is black, foreshadowing his death, and it is the ''dark watchers'' who finally symbolize death itself. From the beginning of the story, Pepe grows increasingly dark, until in the end he will be black like the watchers.

The climactic final portrait is thick with darkness, and even as a new morning breaks the sky, the eagle, which has been present from the start, is replaced by predatory black vultures.

Yet that progression is incomplete. Too many readers confine their attention to that stripping and figurative pattern. At his moment of most profound abnegation, wandering a black wasteland, stripped of civilized tools, an animal contending with animals, Pepe reclaims a uniquely human attribute, the power at once to defy and to submit to his own death. It is the conscious decision of a human, not an animal, and it is accompanied by spiritual awareness: ''Pepe bowed his head quickly. He tried to speak rapid words but only a thick hiss came from his lips. He drew a shaky cross on his breast with his left hand.'' When the first bullet misses him, Pepe hauls his broken body straighter still to receive the death blow.

John Antico is one of the few scholars to pay attention to that scene and the story's religious dimension. He observes [in ''A Reading of Steinbeck's ' Flight',' ' *Modern Fiction Studies* 11 (Spring 1965)], ''It is only by standing up on two feet and *facing death* that the sub-human Pepe can give birth to Man. An animal does not face death; death happens to it. A man is aware of what he is facing, and it is this awareness that makes him a man.'' Yet, Antico wonders what exactly enables Pepe to get up and face death. What is this quality of manhood that he has discovered? It is not a miracle in response to his sign of the cross. Rather, it arises from an indomitable power within Pepe himself:

> Indeed it was a long struggle for Man to emerge, and what prompts this sub-human to get up from all fours and stand on two feet is the inexpressible quality within him which later developed into what we call religion. To attempt to name or define this quality would, however, falsify it. It is not God or religion as civilized man knows them, but that inner quality which eventually leads to religion and the concept of God.

Many have read the story as a supreme document of literary naturalism—as indeed it is. Stripped of all civilized customs and tools, man engages in an animalistic struggle for survival. In the naturalist tradition, ''Flight'' ranks with London's ''To Light a Fire'' and Crane's *Maggie: A Girl of the Streets* as among the best of a kind. But the story is not only that. It is a discovery of what separates humankind from the animals.

In the article ''Cutting Loose,'' Michael Ratcliffe provides a narrative account of an interview with Steinbeck in 1962 on the occasion of his receiving the Nobel Prize. Steinbeck reflected on the Nobel speech he had made, pointing out, ''A story is a parable; putting in terms of human action the morals—and immorals—that society needs at the time. Everyone leaves the bullfight a little braver because one man stood up to a bull. Isaiah wrote to meet the needs of his people, to inspire them. It is a meeting of needs.'' Ratcliffe asked what kinds of needs, and Steinbeck responded, ''Needs of beauty, courage, reform—sometimes just pure pride.'' It may well be that Pepe's response in ''Flight'' is pure, indomitable pride. His standing to receive the fatal bullet is the asseveration his speechless tongue can no longer make: I am a man! But it is signaled by religious signs, and that too is a pattern of the story. Antico correctly notes, however, that

> One hesitates to mention the numerous triads with all their Biblical overtones throughout the story, for then one is tempted to find or seek out strict Biblical parallels or a rigid sort of symbolism or religious allegory which twists the significance of these details all out of proportion. Steinbeck's method is not symbolism or allegory; he merely *suggests* religion and Biblical overtones; he actually seems to blur the edges of his analogies so that one feels a religious atmosphere but not a strict and limited Christian reference.

Antico's caution is well observed. The religious references do not suggest that the story is a parable, a modern crucifixion of a saintly man. Rather, the imagery supports the central premise—that Pepe, finally, is not an animal but a man discovering, albeit tragically, that indomitable, spiritual consciousness of himself as human that separates him from the animals.

While Steinbeck changed the title of his story from ''Manhunt'' to ''Flight'' to draw attention from the civilization that pursues to the individual that flees, there is an applicable irony in the first title. Pepe also hunts his manhood, and in his act of knowing acceptance, he finds it. While the story bears all the trappings of a naturalistic document, or to use the terminology Steinbeck was becoming fond of, a nonteleological telling, the flight of Pepe does arrive at a goal.

Source: John H. Timmerman, '''Flight': What Is Man That Thou Art Mindful of Him?'' in *The Dramatic Landscape of Steinbeck's Short Stories,* University of Oklahoma Press, 1990, pp. 189–98.

Edward J. Piacentino

Piacentino is an Associate Professor of English at High Point College. In the following essay, he ''attempt[s] to demonstrate [that] there are a significant number of animal references which seem to function either to define features of Pepe Torres' character or to accent some of the physical challenges he experiences during his flight for survival and the resulting psychological traumas of this ordeal.''

"Dubbed a sheep, a cow, and then a chicken, Pepe, at least in his mother's eyes, is, at this stage of his innocent life, much like a domesticated farm animal that needs to be fed, sheltered, and generally watched over by others."

Published initially in *The Long Valley* (1938), ''Flight,'' a work that one of Steinbeck's most discerning critics [Warren French, in *John Steinbeck,* 1975] has called a tale of ''frustrated young manhood,'' a ''depressing account of an unprepared youth's failure to achieve maturity,'' has often been regarded as one of John Steinbeck's best stories. Peter Lisca, in his analysis of the story [in *The Wide World of John Steinbeck,* 1958], sees Pepe Torres' flight as reflecting two levels of meaning. ''On the physical level,'' Lisca observes, ''Pepe's penetration into the desert mountains is directly proportional to his increasing separation from civilized man and reduction to the state of a wild animal. . . . The symbolic meaning of Pepe's flight moves in the opposite direction. On this level, the whole action of the story goes to show how man, even when stripped of all his civilized accouterments . . . , is still something more than an animal.''

Other critics have also given notice to the story's animal references. Joseph Fontenrose, for instance, in correcting an erroneous comment made by Edmund Wilson about *The Long Valley,* generally interprets the plants and animals of the stories in this collection as having a ''symbolic function, helping us to understand the human characters who are really central and really human.'' John M. Ditsky, who sees the meaning of Pepe's manhood as ambivalent—''the contradictions inherent in a situation in which a man gains his life only to lose it''—generally perceives that Pepe must revert to brute animalism as an essential stage in becoming a man, or at any rate must use animal mannerisms to ''preserve his manhood.'' Ditsky goes on to offer only brief support for this claim by citing in the last part of the story Pepe's movements, his primitive way of treating his wounded hand, his lancing of his infection, and his desperate digging in an attempt to find water.

The most cogent and perceptive treatment of animal references in ''Flight'' yet to appear is a brief article by Hilton Anderson, which persuasively demonstrates that ''by repeated references to snakes, by the use of such words as *crawl, wiggle, wriggle, zig-zag,* and *hiss,* and by his physical descriptions of Pepe, Steinbeck has suggested a rather strong kinship between Pepe and a snake.'' Anderson's interpretation of Pepe as exhibiting snake-like traits is, however, too reductive, for it fails to take into account the diversity and suggestiveness of the other animal references in the story. In other words, some of the characteristics Anderson cites seem to be more related to animal-like behavior generally than to the mannerisms of a snake exclusively. But more will be said about this later.

Animal imagery abounds in ''Flight,'' from the reference in the first sentence to ''hissing white waters'' of the Pacific Ocean to the ''thick hiss'' that comes from Pepe's lips as he tries desperately to speak just before he is shot and killed at the end. In characterizing Pepe near the outset, Steinbeck points out his ''sharp Indian cheek bones'' and his ''eagle nose,'' the latter a suggestive image which serves to establish Pepe's primitive, animal-like nature. Mama Torres, Pepe's mother, likewise uses animal imagery in describing her son's laziness. As she tells Pepe, '''Some lazy cow must have got into thy father's family, else how could I have a son like thee'.'' And at an earlier time, while she was pregnant with Pepe, she playfully and simplistically points out to him, '''. . . a sneaking lazy coyote came out of the brush and looked at me one day. That must have made thee so'.'' The coyote mentioned here is, of course, a wild animal, an appropriate reference to highlight Pepe's primitive animalism.

Pepe's animal-like nature is further emphasized by the repetition of his somewhat snake-like appearance (He has a ''tall head, pointed at the top.''), and also as he throws his big black knife into a redwood post, his wrist, it is noted, ''flicked like the head of a snake.'' This last image, while reinforcing Pepe's quick, seemingly instinctive manner of reacting, should perhaps also be viewed in the broader context in which the snake is a universal emblem of evil. In this context, the snakelike quickness that Pepe displays in this basically carefree activity of knife throwing importantly reflects his impetuous nature and foreshadows the ease with which he succumbs to evil in murdering a man in Monterey. As Steinbeck describes Pepe's rash, seemingly instinctive action during the quarrel scene that leads to the murder, one can see a first-hand manifestation of the youth's latent animalism: ''. . . the man started toward Pepe and then the knife—it went almost by itself. It flew, it darted before Pepe knew it.'' From the apparent noncommittal manner with which Steinbeck recounts Pepe's spontaneous, unthinking action, one may get the distinct impression that the author does not wish to call the reader's attention to the fact that the youth is morally culpable, anymore than any cornered, enraged animal would be under similar perilous circumstances.

Another way of interpreting the snake in the image used to describe Pepe's wrist action when he throws his knife, particularly if one is willing to think in terms of the snake as being poisonous, is to see it as a force potentially destructive to human life. This is especially true when the snake senses his security is in jeopardy. After all, a snake, whether it be poisonous or not, will, by its very nature, usually attack potentially threatening elements that come within its striking range. And in fact this is almost precisely what Pepe, who exhibits snake-like traits, seems to do in Monterey in the fatal quarrel scene. In this scene, which Pepe himself describes to his mother after the fact, he strikes out to defend himself when, in the kitchen of Mrs. Rodriquez, a man, whom he senses to be his adversary, starts toward him in anger, threatening his security. Thus the affinity between the quick movement of Pepe's wrist and the defensive reaction of a distracted snake becomes functionally appropriate in the quarrel scene for defining another significant facet of Pepe's character.

There are other animal references in the first part of the story that accent Pepe's primitive animalism. When Mama Torres orders Pepe to go to Monterey to have the medicine bottle refilled, she calls him a ''big sheep,'' which by conventional association can be interpreted as an established symbol of primitive, gentle innocence (the lamb being a universal symbol of innocence). Yet, in retrospect, this reference becomes ironic, for Pepe's nature, as his murderous behavior forthrightly demonstrates, is not that of any submissive domesticated farm animal but rather that of a wild beast. Also, before he begins his journey to the town, Mama

Torres calls him a "big coyote," that will probably sit, she tells him, in the church in Monterey, "flapping . . . [his] mouth over Aves all day while . . . [he] looked at the candles and the holy pictures." The coyote reference here seems to take on a different meaning from that discussed previously. Initially, it should be remembered, Mama Torres had seen the appearance of a coyote as a sign prefiguring Pepe's laziness. In this later scene, however, the coyote Mama Torres uses to characterize her son suggests Pepe's primitive animalism as reflected in the fact that he has been conditioned to respond through very basic, repetitive, mechanical behavioral patterns—which in this instance are evidenced in prayer by rote. Finally, just before Pepe, who claims at this time to be a man, departs, Mama Torres—who is not as convinced of Pepe's manhood as he himself is—calls him a "foolish chicken," an apt and degrading metaphor to designate Pepe's weakness, instability, and immaturity. Dubbed a sheep, a cow, and then a chicken, Pepe, at least in his mother's eyes, is, at this stage of his innocent life, much like a domesticated farm animal that needs to be fed, sheltered, and generally watched over by others.

The sheep reference is reintroduced soon after Pepe's departure for Monterey in the description of Emilio and Rosy, his younger brother and sister who remain at home in the relatively safe, secluded environment of their farm home, sleeping, we are told, in boxes "full of straw and sheepskins." This reference to sheepskins is thematically functional as a counterpoint, for it serves to recall by symbolic association the primitive, innocent, and largely protected environment which the boy Pepe has left. As far as we know Mama Torres does not tell Emilio and Rosy specifically why Pepe will have to flee to the mountains after his return from Monterey, and if this conjecture is correct then most of the animal references which have been employed up to this point in describing Pepe, who as a carefree and lazy youth remained on the farm, reinforce the notion of the Torres' home as a place mainly of sheltered innocence. Yet this innocence, Steinbeck implies, is only for children.

The second part of the story which focuses on Pepe's flight to the mountains in an effort to escape his mysterious pursuers also contains numerous suggestive animal references. In fact, an important pattern emerges here when late on the first day of his flight, Pepe moves farther and farther away from sheltered domesticity into the unpredictable and unprotected realm of primitive nature. As Pepe's horse makes his way slowly and cautiously along a steep mountain trail of broken rock, it is pointed out that lizards "scampered away into the brush as the horse rattled over the little stones." This seemingly incidental event may actually be viewed as a microcosm of Pepe's repeated response to his predicament: that is, the lizards flee the potential and uncertain danger of the large and intruding horse as Pepe himself flees his inimical pursuers.

This pattern of using animals to accent Pepe's flight is repeated several other times. As Pepe's horse continues to proceed along the trail, the sound of his hooves also frightens vigilant birds and rabbits that sense the danger. Moreover, on the evening of the first day of Pepe's flight, doves and quail that gather near a spring are stalked by a wildcat that "was creeping toward the spring, belly to the ground . . . ". This situation, like the two previously cited, parallels Pepe's own and provides another illustration of withdrawal from danger as fitting behavior when the circumstances of survival depend on man's ability to resort to strategies of primitive animalism. And finally on the night of the first day, the pursuit and flight pattern is further illustrated when the owls hunt the slopes, looking for rabbits. This incident like the others recreates through remarkably similar animal actions the tremendous fear and tension that Pepe's flight from danger has caused him. In short, the similarly patterned behavior of the animals in this series of scenes serves to reinforce quite blatantly the primitive animalism of Pepe Torres.

As Pepe progresses farther into the mountains, an environment of uncertainty and hostility, he seems to feel even more compelled to act in the manner of a hunted wild beast. When his horse is shot by one of his pursuers, Pepe, Steinbeck observes in the scene that follows, moves with the "instinctive care of an animal," "worming" and "wriggling" his way to safety behind a rock. The point Steinbeck seems to be making here is certainly not vague, for he emphasizes it throughout the story—namely, the naturalistic view that man must resort to behaving like a brute animal in his struggle to survive. Even though Pepe spots a single eagle flying overhead, free and unencumbered, just before his horse is shot, this eagle becomes ironic when viewed in retrospect and within the context of Pepe's own greatly restricted and reduced mobility, the result of the untimely loss of his horse and a painful, near maiming injury to his right hand.

Other animal references also serve a functional thematic purpose during the period of Pepe's flight. In fact, it might be argued that nearly every successive animal image becomes more threatening and sinister than the ones that preceded it. Soon after the injury to his hand, Pepe views a number of wild animals in the following order of appearance: a small brown bird, a high-soaring eagle that "stepped daintily out on the trail and crossed it and disappeared into the brush again," a brown doe, a rattlesnake, grey lizards, a "big tawny mountain lion," that sits watching him, and last circling black birds, presumably buzzards, a universal portentous sign of disaster, in this case Pepe's own approaching death.

It is curious and perhaps significant to note that Pepe displays an almost animal-like cautiousness and vigilance during this time. Though he crawls very near to a rattlesnake before actually seeing it, he, nevertheless, manages to avoid its deadly fangs (unlike his father, who tripped over a stone and fell on a rattlesnake which fatally bit him). Though the grey lizards may not be as formidable a threat as a poisonous rattlesnake, still Pepe, in his animal-like urge to survive, does not want to take any chances and consequently crushes one of these unsuspecting lizards with a stone as it creeps near him. Interestingly, this action seems to anticipate Pepe's own sudden destruction at the end of the story. The mountain lion, the largest and possibly the most dangerous of the animals Pepe observes during his ordeal, watches Pepe for a long time and in turn is viewed by Pepe at a safe distance before it finally slinks away into the thick brush.

Just after the lion departs, Pepe, hearing the sounds of horses' hooves pounding loudly on the rocks and the sharp yelp of a dog, and sensing danger to be near, instinctively glides quickly into a nearby brush "almost as quietly as the lion had" and then crouches "up the hill toward the next ridge," where he stays until dark. Pepe's withdrawal for self-preservation and the emphasis on his distinct crawling and crouching movements aptly complement his many other previously observed animal-like mannerisms. Then, a short time later, when greatly bothered by the excruciating pain in his infected arm and very much dismayed by having carelessly lost his gun, Pepe, whose state again resembles that of a wild animal, climbs to the top of a ridge "with the effort of a hurt beast." And finding he cannot speak, the only sound that he utters from his lips is an unintelligible hissing noise, an utterance that is another striking manifestation of his transformation into animalism, a sound, moreover, that he repeats on the next day, the final day of his life, when he realizes that his pursuers (he hears the "crying yelp" of their hounds) are still following his trail.

In observing Pepe's hissing and crawling and several other of his mannerisms, one may be inclined to accept the view of Hilton Anderson, cited previously, that Steinbeck seems to be consciously emphasizing close affinities between Pepe and a snake. To draw such a connection seems quite logical, except that Anderson tries to push his analogy too far outside the bounds of reasonable credibility. When Pepe crosses himself with his left hand just before the start of the final scene in the story, Anderson, recalling the always readily accessible Edenic myth, sees Pepe's action as an exorcism of his "serpent qualities." This observation, though ingenious, is not entirely accurate, however; for as noted earlier in this essay, Pepe is portrayed in the last section of the story as exhibiting several other animal-like traits, such as the dog-like whine he makes when he scrapes his infected arm with a sharp stone or his withdrawing into the brush as the mountain lion had done, neither of which relates to the snake analogy or to the Edenic archetype.

Furthermore, though Pepe Torres stands erect, apparently transcending his animalism in exhibiting some degree of manliness at the story's conclusion, the sense of his fall or loss must not be interpreted exclusively within the limited context of the Edenic myth but in the more general sense of a human being's loss of youthful innocence as represented here in Pepe's death.

The final animal reference that should be commented on is the circling, scavenging buzzards, a foreboding reminder that the end of Pepe's flight is inevitable death. As the ending of "Flight" clearly indicates, Pepe can flee no farther (He finally reaches the top of the big rock on the ridge's peak), and importantly his subsequent stoicism and courage, reliable indicators of his maturity, reveal he realizes this: "Once there, he arose slowly, swaying to his feet, and stood erect"—this time as a man, but a man on the verge of losing the precious sense of living he has only recently acquired through the dual acts of murder and the ordeal of flight.

Thus in "Flight," as I have attempted to demonstrate, there are a significant number of animal references which seem to function either to define features of Pepe Torres' character or to accent some of the physical challenges he experiences during his flight for survival and the resulting psychological traumas of this ordeal. One set of these references establishes a readily discernible pattern wherein before his journey to Monterey Pepe's innocence is complemented through descriptions of selected domestic farm animals while later his frenzied flight, which, as we have seen, becomes a jungle-like struggle for survival, is complemented through descriptions of wild, potentially dangerous animals. In the mannerisms of these wild, predatory animals, moreover, a second pattern emerges as they become imposing threats to weaker, smaller animals, which at the sign of danger are compelled to withdraw to safety. This pattern, it should be noted, can be conveniently viewed as a close parallel to Pepe's own precarious predicament after he commits murder in Monterey. In addition, there are references in which animals seem to be consciously employed as ominous signs, prefiguring Pepe's inevitable doom. Viewed within the context of the story, then, the various animal references and the patterns they form give ''Flight'' a richly suggestive texture that is often characteristic of some of the more artistically impressive short stories of twentieth-century literature.

Source: Edward J. Piacentino, ''Patterns of Animal Imagery in Steinbeck's 'Flight',''in *Studies in Short Fiction,* Vol. 17, No. 4, Fall, 1980, pp. 437–43.

Walter K. Gordon

Gordon is affiliated with Rutgers University in New Brunswick, New Jersey. In the following essay, he discusses Pepe's moral deterioration in ''Flight.''

Critics have generally agreed with Peter Lisca's contention [in *The Wide World of John Steinbeck,* 1958] that ''Flight'' describes ''the growth of a boy to manhood and the meaning of that manhood,'' thereby identifying Pepe Torres' experience with that of Huck Finn, Henry Fleming, George Willard, and Eugene Gant in one of the most familiar intellectual odysseys in American literature. I should like to suggest, however, that Steinbeck's short story is not really in the Bildungsroman tradition at all; for rather than depicting the spiritual evolution of an adolescent developing and struggling toward manhood, the story, I think, portrays just the opposite—man's moral deterioration and regression that inevitably results when he abandons responsibility for his actions. Pepe, then, begins as a child and becomes by running away less than an animal rather than a man.

Steinbeck's parable of crime and punishment is not vitally concerned with either but merely em-

"Rather than depicting the spiritual evolution of an adolescent developing and struggling toward manhood, the story, I think, portrays just the opposite—man's moral deterioration and regression that inevitably results when he abandons responsibility for his actions."

ploys the archetypal pattern of the chase as a framework for psychological delineation of character. Steinbeck, for instance, never explicitly tells us that Pepe did *kill* his victim, nor do we know the specific circumstances out of which the crime evolved. What is important in ''Flight'' is not the crime itself but Pepe's mental and physical response to it, how he deports himself when the circumstances are propitious for a boy to become a man. It is true that Pepe, his mother, brother, and sister all think that his drunken quarrel in Mrs. Rodriguez' kitchen initiates him into manhood. Mrs. Torres even says in this connection, ''Pepe goes on a journey. Pepe is a man now.'' But it is patently evident that Steinbeck does not accept this primitive ethic, for at no time thereafter does he portray Pepe as an adult with any of the duties, obligations, or responsibilities that adulthood implies. Nor does Steinbeck show any growth or intellectual change in his protagonist—no enlightenment, no increased perception of his world—which normally accompany the process of growing up. Indeed, we can measure Pepe's intellectual, physical, and moral deterioration from that night when he returns from Monterey to tell his mother of his decision to escape retribution for his crime by fleeing into the mountains.

Steinbeck attempts to illustrate this deterioration on the symbolic as well as the narrative level and incorporates into his story several objects associated with Pepe's father—the long, black-handled knife, the black coat, and the saddle. It is significant that each of these symbols of adulthood is lost or abandoned in Pepe's flight from responsibility. Dan

"Only when having been separated from his mother and having cleansed himself of all the accoutrements and artifacts of his father, can the youth stand alone."

Vogel interprets this as a divesting of the artifacts of the father because the youth, now a man and able to stand alone, no longer needs them. But is not the point here precisely that Pepe is *not* able to stand alone? Does he not sorely need these objects to survive, their loss putting him at the mercy of a hostile environment that makes of him more a thing than an adult?

Also supporting this view of Pepe's flight is its structure, which is oriented around the two-stage dehumanization of the protagonist, first from boy to animal, then from animal to inanimate part of nature, an indistinguishable part of the barren landscape. Pepe begins the first stage of his regression by shunning humankind in his avoidance of the red-cheeked fat man on the trail, then by later losing the outer trappings (his hat and the tear in his jeans) that distinguish him from the animals. When his horse is shot, he is forced to walk, then crawl, then wriggle forward on his stomach. Steinbeck describes him at this point as moving ''with the instinctive care of an animal.''

The second stage of his retrogression, his progressive identification with a physical waste land that symbolizes his increasing moral and spiritual degeneration, begins when one of the posse's bullets slivers a piece of granite that pierces Pepe's hand. At this point Pepe becomes one with the setting of the story. Here the union is only temporary, and he is able to remove the sliver of stone from his hand. In order to stop the bleeding, however, he gathers spider webs on two occasions and presses them into his wound. Later, in order to assuage his thirst, he eats mud; and as he retreats further, those faculties which separate man from lower forms of nature disappear, and Pepe loses the power of speech, his tongue being unable to articulate words and giving rise to hissing sounds only. The final degradation takes place when after being struck by two bullets, he rolls down a hill, starting a small avalanche that covers only his head, an action symbolic of the obliteration of all reasoning powers. The identification with nature and the journey *from* manhood and its compelling responsibilities are complete!

Source: Walter K. Gordon, ''Steinbeck's 'Flight': Journey to or from Maturity?'' in *Studies in Short Fiction,* Vol. 3, No. 4, Summer, 1966, pp. 453–55.

Dan Vogel

Vogel is chairman of the Department of English at the Jerusalem College for Women in Israel. He is the author of The Three Masks of American Tragedy *(1974) and a critical biography of poet Emma Lazarus. In the following excerpt, Vogel examines the mythical elements of Steinbeck's ''Flight.''*

More than a mere allegory, ''Flight'' reveals characteristics of myth and tragedy. A myth is a story that tries to explain some practice, belief, institution, or natural phenomenon, and is especially associated with religious rites and beliefs. The natural phenomenon, for Steinbeck, is not the facts of nature, with which historical myths deal; rather, it is . . . the development of innocent childhood into disillusioned manhood. The myth that Steinbeck wrought also contains another quality of myth, the rite. The plot of ''Flight'' narrates symbolically the ritual: the escape from the Mother, the divestiture of the Father, and the death and burial of Childhood. To discern these mythic symbols, it is necessary to review the narrative facts.

At the beginning of the story, Pepe, though 19 years of age, has all the innocence of the ''toy-baby'' his mother calls him. . . .

When his rather domineering mother—who constantly taunts him with his inability to be ''a man''—asks him to go to Monterey, ''a revolution took place in the relaxed figure of Pepe.''. . . He is asked, surprisingly, to go alone; he is permitted to wear his father's hat and his father's hatband and to ride in his father's saddle. . . .

When Pepe returns, he has killed a man with his father's knife, left behind him at the scene of the crime. The look of innocence is gone; he has been shocked by a fact of life, an extreme independent act. His mother quickly understands and helps him outfit himself for the flight into the mountains. She gives him especially his father's black coat and rifle. Weighted down by the accoutrements of his father, Pepe separates himself from his mother. She recognizes the change. She tells the little boy, "Pepe is a man now. He has a man's thing to do." . . . Logically, however, this is not necessarily so. A man might possibly have been expected to give himself up and pay for his crime. It seems to me, then, that Pepe's mother perceived that her son is entering manhood and must stand alone. This he must do.

The ordeal of transformation from innocence to experience, from purity to defilement begins. There is the physical pain of the ordeal, symbolized by a cut hand that soon becomes gangrenous. There is the psychological pain—the recognition of a strangeness in this life that is omnipresent, silent, watchful and dark—the sense of Evil, or Tragedy, or Retribution. This realization is symbolized by the narratively gratuitous, unrealistic presence of the black figures, the "dark watchers" who are seen for a moment on the tops of ridges and then disappear. . . . These are the silent inscrutable watchers from above, the universal Nemesis, the recognition of which signals a further step into manhood. . . .

Only [when] having been separated from his mother and having cleansed himself of all the accoutrements and artifacts of his father, can the youth stand alone. But to Steinbeck this is far from a joyous or victorious occasion. It is sad and painful and tragic. Pepe rises to his feet, "black against the morning sky," . . . astride a ridge. He is a perfect target and the narrative ends with the man against the sky shot down. The body rolls down the hillside, creating a little avalanche, which follows him in his descent and covers up his head. Thus innocence is killed and buried in the moment that Man stands alone.

Thus the myth ends, as so many myths do, with violence and melodrama. What the myth described is the natural miracle of entering manhood. When serenity of childhood is lost, there is pain and misery. Yet there is nevertheless a sense of gain and heroism which are more interesting and dramatic. It is a story that has fascinated many from [William] Wordsworth to [Ernest] Hemingway, and what Steinbeck has written is a myth that describes in symbols what has happened to each of us.

Source: Dan Vogel, "Steinbeck's 'Flight': The Myth of Manhood," in *College English,* Vol. 23, No. 3, December, 1961, pp. 225–26.

Sources

Antico, John. "A Reading of Steinbeck's 'Flight'," in *Modern Fiction Studies,* Vol. 11, Spring, 1965 pp. 45- 53.

Gordon, Walter K. "Steinbeck's 'Flight': Journey to or from Maturity?," in *Studies in Short Fiction,* Vol. III, No. 4, Summer, 1966, pp. 453-55.

Jones, William M. "Steinbeck's 'Flight'," in *The Explicator,* Vol. 18, November, 1959, Item 11.

Further Reading

French, Warren. "Adventures in the Long Valley," in *John Steinbeck,* pp. 80–94. New York: Twayne Publishers, 1961.

Discussion of Steinbeck's short fiction which finds "Flight" comparable to Theodore Dreiser's novel *An American Tragedy,* "since Pepe, like Dreiser's Clyde Griffiths, is an impetuous but not too intelligent young man who is destroyed when a social situation places upon him responsibilities he is unequipped to assume."

McCarthy, Paul. "The Steinbeck Territory," in *John Steinbeck,* pp. 23–45. New York: Frederick Ungar Publishing Co., 1980.

Discusses "Flight" as a story which is enriched by its successful blend of several important elements. McCarthy notes that the story's symbolism, imagery, and setting combine with "such traditional themes as the flight from society into the wild, and passage from innocence to experience" to form an "excellent story" which is richer and more complex than other Steinbeck stories, such as "The Chrysanthemums" and "The White Quail."

Young, Stanley. "The Short Stories of John Steinbeck," in *The New York Times Book Review,* September 25, 1938, p. 7.

Review of *The Long Valley* which finds "Flight" a story concerned primarily with Pepe's struggle with the primitive emotion of raw fear. Young considers the story "as terrifying and as vivid as the flight of Reynard the Fox as [John] Masefield set it down."

In the Penal Colony

Franz Kafka

1919

Franz Kafka wrote the novella-length story "In the Penal Colony" while he was writing his novel *The Trial* in 1914, and it was first published in 1919. The story of an explorer's tour of an island known for its unusual capital punishment machine, "In the Penal Colony" took just two weeks to complete, although Kafka was dissatisfied with the ending and rewrote it several times in later years. Since the story's publication in English translation in 1948, it has come to be seen, along with *The Metamorphosis,* as one of Kafka's most significant shorter works. Critical responses to the story have largely been concerned with interpreting its allegorical aspects, and with placing such interpretations in the context of Kafka's other writings and of certain biographical issues, such as his relationship with his father. There has been no agreement on the allegory it presents, and recent criticism has come to accept this fact. There is agreement, however, that the story's theme is religious, and that it is a story which sets out to examine a shift in the relationship between human existence and divine law. Accordingly, Kafka's Jewish heritage, and in particular the Jewish traditions of the parable and kabbala, have been considered important issues in interpreting the story. Kafka's detached narrative style—in which character description is minimal and the author's presence unobtrusive—is one of the admired qualities of this story, and it is a strong factor in its haunting effect. "In the Penal Colony" is considered by many critics to be an allegory comparing the Old

and New Testaments of the Bible, with the officer's willing sacrifice serving as an analogy to Jesus Christ's suffering and death. Others have viewed the story as prophetic of the Nazi death camps of World War II.

Author Biography

Franz Kafka's father was a successful businessman in Prague, Czechoslovakia. The city's elite was German-speaking, and for this reason the young Kafka was educated at German rather than Czech schools. He eventually graduated with a law degree from the German University in Prague in 1906. He took a position in a workers' accident insurance firm which he held for fifteen years. Diagnosed as suffering from tuberculosis in 1917, Kafka continued working at the company until ill health forced him to retire in 1922. He died two years later at a sanatorium in Vienna.

These brief facts of Kafka's life conceal much of the emotional turmoil he suffered. His diaries and correspondence show that he was obsessed with a perceived conflict between family life and artistic integrity. A diary entry from 1912 reads: "When it became clear in my organism that writing was the most productive direction for my being to take, everything rushed in that direction and left empty all those abilities which were directed towards the joys of sex, eating, drinking, philosophical reflection, and above all music." Nine years later he was still reflecting, fatalistically, on marriage: "I do not envy particular married couples, I simply envy all married couples together; and even when I do envy one couple only, it is the happiness of married life in general, in all its infinite variety, that I envy—the happiness to be found in any one marriage, even in the likeliest case, would probably plunge me into despair." Kafka was twice engaged to Felice Bauer, and the start to his failed relationship with her coincided with the writing of *The Judgment,* considered by most critics to mark the beginning of his writing career. He had already completed several impressionistic sketches, but *The Judgment,* written in 1912, established both a key theme (a troubled father-son relationship) and what was to be a characteristic narrative technique for Kafka: writing from the point of view of an unreliable narrator. Both *The Metamorphosis,* a story in which the central character wakes up to find that he has turned into an insect, and *Amerika,* his first novel, were written in the same year.

Kafka's second novel, *The Trial,* and the story "In the Penal Colony" were written in 1914. The works share common themes, both being meditations on guilt and punishment. In 1917 Kafka finished a series of stories known as the "Country Doctor Cycle." These are surreal tales told in a low-key, realistic style . His third novel, *The Castle,* was published in 1922, the year in which Kafka retired from the insurance office. The last book to be published before his death was *A Hunger-Artist,* which contained stories about extreme cases of alienation, one of his most common themes.

Plot Summary

"In the Penal Colony" opens with an officer showing an explorer a remarkable apparatus, a capital punishment machine. The explorer has been invited to witness an execution due to take place in a dry and desolate valley on a remote island. Four characters are present: the officer, the explorer, the condemned man, and a soldier. Also mentioned is a fifth character, a Commandant, who is responsible for inviting the explorer to witness the execution.

Although he has accepted the invitation, the explorer is unenthusiastic about the apparatus and initially indifferent to the plight of the condemned man. The officer busies himself making last minute adjustments to the machine. He is dressed in a heavy uniform, which the explorer considers quite unsuitable for the tropical climate. The officer agrees but explains that the uniform reminds him of home. He is a serving officer in a colonial military.

The officer explains the machine in great detail to the explorer. He also discusses that the present Commandant's predecessor was the machine's inventor. The plans, which he shows to the explorer, consist of an unintelligible "labyrinth of lines crossing and recrossing each other." The former Commandant is responsible for more than the execution apparatus. "The organization of the whole penal colony is his work," the officer tells the explorer. This is the first time, apart from in the story's title, that readers are made aware that this is a *penal* colony. The explorer has a hard time listening to the officer, who is speaking in French, a language which neither the soldier nor the prisoner understand. In this foreign tongue the principle parts of

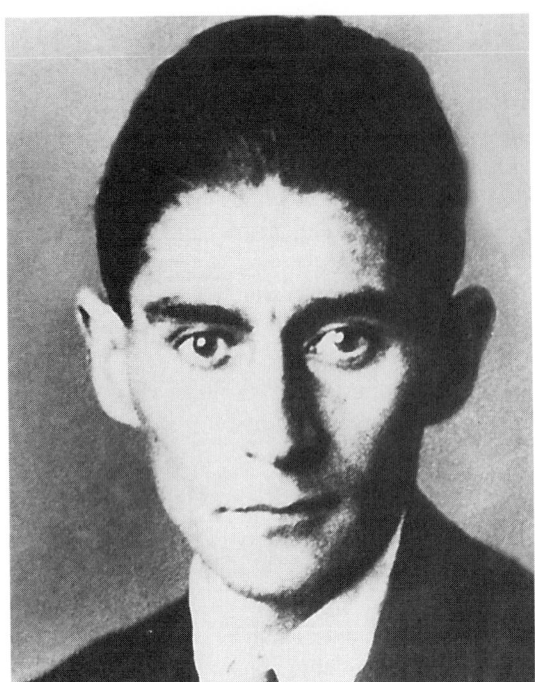

Franz Kafka

the machine—the Bed, the Designer and the Harrow—and their actions are explained. The Designer contains the cogs which drive the machine. The Harrow, made of glass, is set with needles designed to pierce the condemned man's skin in such a way that they write on his body the nature of his crime. The Bed, layered with cotton wool, is where the condemned man lies.

In the course of explaining the workings of the machine, the officer relates his dissatisfaction with the new Commandant, who shows little interest in the execution process and seems intent on seeing the machine slip slowly into disuse. No spare parts have been ordered for some time. However, the officer claims to have been appointed the penal colony's sole judge. ''My guiding principle is this: Guilt is never to be doubted.'' In the case of the present prisoner, the reported crime is that he was found asleep on duty while in the employment of a captain.

The time comes for the prisoner to be placed upon the machine. By now the explorer, knowing the extraordinary nature of the machine, feels some impulse to intervene on the condemned man's behalf. However, he thinks to himself: ''It's always a ticklish matter to intervene decisively in other people's affairs.'' He is further inhibited by the fact that he is a foreigner. Nevertheless, the officer sees the explorer as a potential ally. He continues to criticize the present Commandant, a man who surrounds himself with women and ignores the executions. In previous times, an execution was a great public spectacle, and children were given a place in the viewing gallery. He seems to think that the sight of the present execution will persuade the explorer to lobby the Commandant for the machine's preservation. ''Help me against the Commandant!'' the officer implores.

The explorer eventually declares his disapproval of the procedure but also states, ''Your sincere conviction has touched me, even though it cannot influence my judgement.'' The officer, having failed to procure an ally, abruptly releases the prisoner and takes his place on the bed after readjusting the machine to inscribe the sentence ''BE JUST'' on his body. The officer's self-execution does not go according to plan. Cogwheels begin tumbling from the machine, and the needles, rather than writing with slow but repeated pricking, jab uncontrollably, and soon the officer is dead.

When the explorer sees the face of the dead officer, ''no sign was visible of the promised redemption.'' Leaving the valley with the soldier and the prisoner, the explorer is brought to a teahouse, one of many dilapidated buildings in the town. The soldier shows him the grave of the old Commandant, under a teahouse table. The patrons of the teahouse, poor laborers, move away to let the foreigner view the grave. An inscription speaks of a prophecy that the old Commandant will rise again. Having read this, the explorer passes out a few coins and then boards a ferry that takes him back to his steamship. The soldier and prisoner stand on the harbor steps, but the explorer refuses to let them board with him.

Characters

Colonel

See Officer

Condemned man

See Prisoner

Explorer

The narrative of ''In the Penal Colony'' primarily recounts the explorer's experiences. Typical of Kafka's protagonists, the explorer is a somewhat tenuous character, with little will of his own.The explorer has accepted an invitation to view an execution. Initially, he is a disinterested bystander, but the means of execution and the officer's behavior lead the explorer to question the present Commandant's motives in issuing the invitation. He wonders if he is expected to play a decisive role in the execution process. The ambiguity of his role unsettles him.

The explorer is a foreigner, that is, he does not share the nationality of those who live in the penal colony. He may be French: French is the language in which he speaks to the officer. The explorer arrives at the penal colony with "recommendations from high quarters" and is known there as "a famous Western investigator." With this reputation preceding him, it is startling to observe how ineffectual he is. Ultimately, the injustice and inhumanity of what he witnesses compel him to voice his disapproval. He is "fundamentally honorable and unafraid," but he does not intervene during the execution or when the officer takes his own life. After viewing the grave of the old Commandant, he leaves the colony without comment and without offering assistance to the prisoner and the soldier who run after him to the water's edge, apparently hoping to leave with him.

New Commandant

Though he does not appear in the story, the new Commandant's presence is felt because he has invited the explorer to the island and because the officer speaks of him to the explorer. The new Commandant has inherited the penal colony's organizational structure and execution machine from the former Commandant, who originated the system. The new Commandant, however, shows signs of wanting to institute reform and has allowed the machine to fall into a state of disrepair. Unlike the old Commandant, the new Commandant rarely attends the colony's executions and never explains the torture devices to visitors. According to the officer, the new Commandant has jeopardized the system of law and justice established by his predecessor. Critics who interpret the story as a religious allegory often surmise that the new Commandant represents religious reform or the New Testament.

Officer

The officer was the technical assistant of the penal colony's previous Commandant, who was responsible for designing the execution machine—a "remarkable apparatus." Serving under the new Commandant, the officer continues to oversee the machine, but he also acts as the colony's judge, taking as his guiding principle the belief that "Guilt is never to be doubted." The officer tries to turn the presence of a foreign visitor to his own advantage, asking the explorer to make a public statement in defense of the execution machine. Much of the early part of the story is taken up with the officer's loving description of the machine's working parts. His devotion to this mechanical instrument of death is total.

After he fails to enlist the explorer's support in his desire to have the machine properly fixed and its continued use endorsed, the officer frees the prisoner, straps himself to the machine. and is killed quickly as the machine malfunctions. His self-chosen sentence, "BE JUST," is not properly inscribed on his body. Although he dies with a "calm and convinced" expression on his face, there is no trace of the "promised redemption" that other victims of the machine's justice have purportedly experienced.

Old Commandant

The old Commandant invented the execution machine as well as the organizational structure of the penal colony. During his time, he had many supporters and the colony seemed to thrive. The officer claims that the few remaining supporters of the old Commandant's ways are afraid to declare themselves; it is possible that the officer is the only one remaining. The old Commandant's gravestone lies under a table in a teahouse. The grave's unsigned inscription holds out the promise of his triumphant return. Critics who interpret the story as a religious allegory often surmise that the old Commandant represents orthodox religious tradition or the Old Testament.

Prisoner

The prisoner, or condemned man, is described in the story as being stupid and bewildered. He is entirely submissive and does not resist his impending execution. He cannot understand the explanation of the machine that the officer gives to the explorer in French, but is sufficiently curious to direct his gaze "wherever the officer pointed a finger." The prisoner has been arrested for disobeying and insulting an officer. After he fell asleep on duty, his captain lashed him across the face with a riding whip. When the prisoner fought back, the captain reported the incident to the officer. The machine has been programmed to engrave in his body the words: ''HONOR THY SUPERIORS!''

When the officer realizes that the explorer does not intend to commend the method of execution to the new Commandant, he releases the prisoner from the machine and grants his freedom. The prisoner subsequently engages in horseplay with the soldier who had been guarding him, demonstrating his own ridiculous appearance in the clothing that the soldier had earlier cut from his body with a knife to prepare him for execution. After taking the explorer to the tea room beneath which the old Commandant is buried, and chatting there with some friends, he and the soldier chase after the explorer, apparently wanting to leave the island on his boat, but they make only a half-hearted attempt to escape and are left behind as the explorer is ferried to his steamship.

Scientist

See Explorer

Soldier

The soldier's role is to guard the prisoner and strap him onto the machine. He appears, however, to be somewhat incompetent. At one point, half-asleep, he allows the prisoner to lean too close to the machine during the officer's explanation and gets a handful of dirt thrown at him. The dexterity with which he slashes the prisoner's shirt and trousers so that they instantly fall off suggests he has been the officer's assistant for some time. The soldier does not understand the French spoken by the officer and the explorer, nor does he speak the same language as the condemned man. Nevertheless, he and the prisoner share a moment of joviality when he retrieves the prisoner's torn clothing from the pit with the point of his bayonet. Their relationship is further established when they spend time together at the teahouse after the prisoner is released and then both run after the explorer as he is ferried to his ship.

Traveller

See Explorer

Themes

Justice and Injustice

The story concerns the administration of justice in a penal colony. A time has recently passed when the operation of the colony's judicial system received popular support and approval. But this approval was gained by the popularity of the architect of the justice system and the execution machine, the Commandant. The new Commandant shows no enthusiasm for his predecessor's social order. Rather than trying to actively reform the system, it appears he is hoping to change things through benign neglect. In the meantime the old judicial system still operates, thanks to the dedication of the old Commandant's assistant, an officer who sees it as his duty to preserve the machine which inflicts the same fatal punishment on all who are charged, regardless of their crime. The colony's judicial system does not recognize the concept of injustice. Prisoners are not allowed to defend themselves. They are accused by word of mouth—in the case of the condemned man in the story, by his superior officer—and then executed without a judicial hearing or any chance to defend themselves. It is significant, and an example of irony, that when the guardian of the machine gives up his own life at the end of the story, the sentence which was supposed to have been inscribed on his body, had the machine worked properly, was ''BE JUST.''

Guilt and Innocence

The officer who oversees the execution machine considers one of the main merits of the colony's judicial system to be the fact that guilt is never questioned. ''My guiding principle is this: Guilt is never to be doubted. Other courts cannot follow that principle, for they consist of several opinions and have higher courts to scrutinize them. This is not the case here.'' If the story were merely about the methods of dealing with isolated acts of criminal behavior—petty theft, for example—the plot could be read as an exaggerated comment on the harsh and inhumane punitive methods of fundamentalist systems of law. However, the condemned man's crime is a fairly minor one: he fell asleep on duty and shouted back at his captain. His death sentence suggests that a point is being made about the inherent sinfulness of human nature. The execution machine becomes a symbol for the judgement that all people must eventually face. Due to the machine's twelve-hour cycle, victims become conscious of their sinfulness before the end comes. Guilt is written on the body while the body clings to life, and in the time remaining the prisoner must face his loss of innocence.

Punishment

Another feature of the colony's judicial system is that there is no gradation of punishment. The punishment—death—is the same no matter what the crime, except in one regard. The Harrow's needles inscribe a different sentence on the body of each condemned person. The words comprise both a linguistic sentence (a series of words) and a penal sentence (the condemned person's punishment). This sentence is programmed into the machine at the start of the execution process by the operating officer. The prisoner is not told what it is before the machine is switched on. "He'll learn it on his body." The sentence is directly related to whichever commandment has been broken. Readers are given two examples. The prisoner who fell asleep on duty and shouted at his captain "will have written on his body: HONOR THY SUPERIORS!" The officer, in a bizarre act of sudden self-condemnation, selects his own sentence: "BE JUST."

Choices and Consequences

The explorer and the officer are the only characters in the story who act decisively, in accordance with their own beliefs. The soldier and the condemned man are submissive and merely play the roles assigned to them by the judicial process. They make a half-hearted attempt to take control of their lives at the end of the story, but they do not strongly assert their desire to leave the colony enough to make it happen. The explorer, as an outsider, is placed in the position of critical commentator. He knows this, and likewise the officer seeks his help because he sees the explorer's presence as one more ploy of the new Commandant in his efforts to destabilize the old order. The explorer's Western European background is repeatedly emphasized. The explorer chooses to declare his position to the officer, but also chooses not to report his views to the new Commandant. The officer, realizing that even without a formal and public declaration of criticism from the explorer that his efforts to prop up the old system of justice are doomed to failure. In light of this, he chooses to accept the consequences of his own system and throws himself at the mercy of the machine.

Science and Technology

The execution machine is a grotesque torture apparatus. Its workings are described in great detail in the story. Though it is not highly technical, it emphasizes the mechanical, no-room-for-error nature of the punishment process, as meted out by its operator, the officer. The explorer, who comes from a more enlightened background, seems at first uninterested in the machine. The officer, so proud of the old Commandant's invention, is apparently unaware that the machine, although horrifically efficient in its execution, is also comically grotesque. It is like the brainchild of a mad professor, as might be found in a traditional horror story, and Kafka provides it with the conventional demise for such machines. It breaks apart while in the process of dispatching its last victim, possibly symbolizing humankind's misplaced reliance on machines to perform perfectly. At the end of the story the explorer leaves the island by rowing to his steamer, another technical invention of the modern age, but one without the punitive overtones of the killing machine.

Topics for Further Study

- In literature, irony refers to an instance of something happening that is the opposite of what is expected. How is the official's death an example of irony?
- From information in the story, produce a diagram of the execution machine.
- Gershom Scholem, historian of Jewish mysticism, has identified Kafka as a neo-kabbalist. Find out what you can about *kabbalah* and identify two ways in which it could relate to Kafka's story.
- Imagine that in his old age the explorer writes his memoirs and looks back at his own behavior at the penal colony. Which, if any, of his actions does he affirm or regret?
- Why do you think Kafka was dissatisfied with the ending to the story? How might it be improved?

Style

Setting

The island colony is supervised by uniformed soldiers of various ranks. Although their heavy, ornate uniforms are unsuitable for the tropical climate of the colony, they are worn as reminders of home. "We don't want to forget about home," the officer explains to the explorer. The geographical and the political setting are only hinted at by Kafka. Readers know that the valley in which the execution machine is located is a hot and sandy place, surrounded by "naked crags." Readers know that the colonial force is probably not European, but that the officer is able to communicate with the explorer in French. However, there is much that is unexplained. Strictly speaking, a penal colony would be an outpost used by a governing country for the expulsion of criminals. The luxury of exiling wrong-doers to a faraway place is only an option for a great power. This particular colony seems to have an indigenous population. The women who surround the new Commandant and the dock laborers who sit at the teahouse tables may also have been imported by the colonial power. But their presence makes the island much more than simply a storehouse for convicts. It is a mixed society requiring its own codes of social behavior and own system of law and order. There is no reference to the customs and way of life of the home country, other than that they are not European and the Commandant is not bound by them. Indeed, the old Commandant set up the penal colony according to his own plan. "The organization of the whole colony is his work," the official tells the explorer.

Point of View

Kafka employs a detached, neutral narrative technique in which each character acts without comment from the narrator. The point of view, though third person, tends to be closely aligned with the explorer's experience. The story opens in the valley because that is where the explorer is. Readers accompany him to the teahouse at the end of the story, and it ends as he departs the island for his steamship. Because of this relationship between the point of view and the explorer, readers identify with his intellectual and emotional predicament. Does he, as a guest of the colony, speak his mind about the execution process? Should he make a report to the new Commandant, or should he say nothing? The officer has the most to say, and spends much time trying to read the new Commandant's intentions. Until the very end of the story readers know about the old and the new Commandants from what the officer has said, and he cannot be considered a wholly reliable source of information. He claims to be "the sole advocate of the old Commandant's tradition." Others, called "adherents," he despises for their mealy-mouthed ambiguities and unwillingness to be open about their loyalties. Nevertheless, this "objective" point of view does not clarify the author's intentions. Kafka detaches himself from his characters in order to prevent being too obvious in his message.

Symbols and Symbolism

It is generally agreed that "In the Penal Colony" is a parable with meanings beyond the literal episodes described. Kafka was Jewish, and there is strong consensus among critics for interpreting the story as a commentary on orthodox versus reformed Judaism. The officer represents the traditional orthodox wing of Judaism. The former Commandant's guiding plans—"my most precious possessions"—consist of "a labyrinth of lines crossing and recrossing each other" and symbolize the script in which the Commandments were written. The officer does not speak of laws being broken. He speaks of Commandments disobeyed. The number of biblical images that crop up throughout the story makes it impossible to determine a precise allegorical reading. Although the method is very different, the setting and the duration of the execution process certainly invite the reader to think about the crucifixion of Jesus Christ. This comparison is made more compelling by the imagery used—the blood and water being washed into the pit and the rice pap fed to the dying man. Finally, the officer sacrifices himself to the machine, and in doing so causes it to fall apart. By dying he destroys the very symbol of law and order he had purported to conserve.

Historical Context

World War I Gives Rise to Expressionism

The psychological discord evident in Kafka's writing was influenced in part by the chaos in Europe prior to World War I. Nowhere were the period's social, religious, and nationalistic conflicts greater than in his birthplace, Prague. By 1914 the Austro-Hungarian empire was coming to an end and World War I engulfed all of Europe. The war, which had been brewing for years, began when Archduke Franz Ferdinand and his wife, members of the ruling Habsburg family of the Austro-Hungarian empire, were killed by a Serbian assassin protesting the Austro-Hungarian empire's claim

Compare & Contrast

- **1914:** World War I begins in eastern Europe with the assassination of Archduke Ferdinand and his wife, members of the ruling family of the Austro-Hungarian empire. Following the assassination by a Serb, Austro-Hungarians declare war on Bosnia.

  1990s: Bosnia is torn by war between Muslims, Croats, and Serbs. Turmoil continues following the 1992–95 war in Bosnia, with the country divided between Serbian and Muslim-Croat zones.

- **1900s:** A penal colony is essentially a prison. In the early 1900s, prison rates in the United States range from a rate of 121.2 per 100,000 people in 1910 to 99.7 people per 100,000 people in 1923.

  1990s: In the United States, the prison rate is 311 per 100,000 people in 1990 and 429 per 100,000 people in 1995. Rates vary among European nations. For example, in Austria in 1990, 68,092 adults and 3,630 are convicted. In 1997, the prison rate for the Russian Federation, 700 per 100,00 people, is considered to be the highest in the world.

- **1919:** The gulag, the Soviet system of forced labor camps, is established in Siberia. Prisoners include common criminals, thieves, murders, as well as political and religious dissidents. Death rates are high, due to the prisoners' lack of clothing, food, warmth, and shelter.

  1998: Following *glasnost,* Mikhail Gorbachev's new policy of openness, the gulag system is dismantled. After the collapse of the Soviet Union, all remaining prisoners are freed and the camps are destroyed.

over his country. The Austro-Hungarians declared war on Bosnia after they failed to comply with their demands for an investigation into the murders. This war's brutality was unlike anything the world had ever seen, and millions of casualties were caused by technical advances such as poison gas, guns mounted on airplanes, and trench warfare. Militarism, hedonism, and nationalism reflected the attitudes of Kafka's day. The cruelty and futility of these events fueled Expressionism in art and increased Kafka's own anxiety and dread.

The key characteristic of Expressionism—a literary movement which spanned approximately fifteen years (1910-1925), the same period as Kafka 's productive life—is said to be the shriek, an ''expression'' of interior terror. Kafka is not, strictly speaking, an Expressionist writer, but his work shares many Expressionist themes: hatred of authority and the father-figure; a belief that the universe and natural world are hostile to mankind; the knowledge, made graphic by the outbreak of World War I, that an old order was passing. Max Brod's autobiographical novel, *The Kingdom of Love,* includes a portrayal of his friend Kafka as an Expressionist saint.

Prague, A Divided City

Kafka was a German-speaking Jew. For centuries, Jews had lived in a ghettoized area of Prague. As a result, the tight-knit community gave rise to its own legends, the most famous being that of the Golem, a man made of clay who comes to life to destroy the enemies of the city's Jewish citizens. Living in Prague, Kafka thus felt doubly different from the Czech-speaking, non-Jewish population. His diaries and letters reveal a personality that was deeply neurotic and self-analytical. His family and personal relationships were difficult. Internalizing much of his surroundings, Kafka began to write his own tales of horror in which the monsters were modernity, bureaucracy, and the alienation caused by an industrial, mechanized age. Martin Seymour-Smith wrote, ''Kafka was above all a realist: the most precise realist of his century. Of course he is a symbolist. But those who cannot find their unhappily true selves in the not unaggressive bewilderments of his protagonists are insensitive indeed.'' Kafka's dying wish was that his work be destroyed. The image of the self-destructing and disintegrating execution machine in ''In the Penal Colony'' is therefore suggestive of both a toppling social order evident in the destruction caused by World War I and Kafka's own will to destroy his legacy.

Critical Overview

Although Kafka wrote ''In the Penal Colony'' in 1914, and it was published in German in 1919, there was no English translation until 1948. Accordingly, little criticism in English appeared before the 1950s. Austin Warren, in ''An Exegetical Note on 'In the Penal Colony','' published in the *Southern Review* was one of the first critics to identify the allegory in the story as dealing with religion in the modern world. He theorized that the penal colony represents the whole earth where all people await judgement. In times past there was a systematic theology which meant that everyone knew his place. There was no question or argument about the fact that men and women were sinners and in due course they would be judged. The machine in the story stands for the religious framework that once held sway. The official is still faithful to this system, and he represents an orthodox theologian. The explorer represents secular humanitarianism. ''In its tone,'' Warren wrote, ''the story is a matter-of-fact description of an elaborate method of punishment, no longer believed in by the 'enlightened'.'' His reading of the story sees Kafka as sympathetic towards the machine, wanting to support the place of religion in the modern world. The machine is cruel, costly, and difficult to maintain, but these are prices which have to be paid if the religion is to survive.

In his 1962 book *Franz Kafka, Parable and Paradox,* Heinz Politzer agreed that the story is supposed to represent a universal view of life. ''The lunar landscape surrounding [the machine] and the sea cutting off the island from the civilized world fortify this impression.'' Politzer was more inclined than Warren to see social and political resonances as well as religious ones in the story. ''The machine . . . is Kafka's prime symbol during these years. If his purpose was to concentrate in one universally valid image the process of dehumanization characteristic of the time of the First World War, then he found it here in this symbol of man's self-destructive ingenuity.'' Politzer's reading differs from Warren's especially in its application of the religious allegory. For Politzer the machine does not represent some highly developed religious structure but: ''In its primitiveness the torture machine points to an archaic stage of religious development. . . . The Bed of the torture machine is an altar, on which a man is slaughtered in honor of the monstrous idol. . . . In spite of its mechanical sophistication the apparatus seems to be a relic from the times of primordial savagery.''

Kurt J. Fickert, in a 1965 essay on this short story, took issue with Warren's tightly allegorical interpretation. For Fickert ''In the Penal Colony'' is an existential story following the same pattern of presentation of a crisis and dilemma followed by a decision, which is to be found in Kafka's other work. ''The machine's function in the story is to precipitate a crisis, to lure the mind into a trap, a decision.'' An existential reading focuses attention on the explorer and his predicament and provides a commentary for the characters' speedy departure from the island. ''The traveller flees, like all mankind, with the instinct of self-preservation,'' in response to a fear-and-flight syndrome brought on by a perceived hostility in the environment.

Wilhelm Emrich, in his critical study of Kafka's writings published in translation in 1968, gives a reading which is more in tune with Warren's tightly allegorical interpretation. He believes the story is about the ''total guilt of existence,'' not about a crucial moment when a decision is called for. Like Warren he sees the story as being critical of the new order. ''The new law is the law of the Devil. The old order, for the sake of redemption, sacrificed man; the new order, for the sake of man, has sacrificed redemption.''

In *The Terror of Art, Kafka and Modern Literature,* Martin Greenberg argued that the story is essentially about the conflict between morality and spirituality. The story is disturbing because of the central character's flight from the conflict. ''Before this conflict between the moral and the spiritual, the explorer retreats into a neutrality which has nothing to do with his old scientific detachment. His neutrality now expresses the troubled state of mind of someone who has had a glimpse into hitherto undiscerned depths.''

Kafka was dissatisfied with the ending of the story, and his papers contained variant endings which have been taken into account by some critics. These critics have written about how such variant endings might affect the basic allegorical meaning of the story.

Criticism

Michael Thorn

Thorn is the author of Tennyson *(1993), a biography of the English poet, and a reviewer for the* Times Educational Supplement. *In the following essay, he examines "In the Penal Colony" and asserts that "first and foremost the story is a dream or a parable."*

For most of his life as a writer Kafka was employed at a workers' accident insurance company. He wrote at night, on weekends, and on the holidays. It was a routine which made the writing of a novel an arduous business. He did not enjoy writing novels. Indeed, he never succeeded in finishing one. But he did enjoy writing short stories. In 1912 he confided to his diary, having just completed a story called "The Judgment" in a single sitting, writing from ten o'clock at night to six o'clock in the morning: "with my novel-writing I am in the shameful lowlands of writing. Only *in this way* can writing be done, only with such coherence, with such a complete opening out of the body and the soul." It was a similar opening out of body and soul, two years later, that produced "In the Penal Colony," written quickly during a two-week holiday while he was in the middle of writing *The Trial.*

"In the Penal Colony" has the ghoulish intensity and enigmatic atmosphere of a dream. Immediately before Kafka wrote the passage quoted above in his diary, he stopped to consider the appearance of his undisturbed bed, "as though it had just been brought in." It is as if all the tossing and turning, all the normally secret brain activity of the night, has found an outlet onto the written page. By "coherence" he means a creative coherence, a flow of ideas, which he found it nearly impossible to achieve in the stop-start nature of novel-writing.

"In the Penal Colony" has been considered a difficult story. Some have argued that it is too difficult to teach, and that its underlying meanings are either too arcane or too incoherently presented to make them accessible to anyone but the most sophisticated reader. This may well be the case if one approaches the story in a stern endeavor to unravel its secret and establish the key to its allegorical meaning. Those who read Kafka in the original language have been more inclined to consider him a comic writer than those who read him in translation. Probably a degree of wit and wordplay is lost in translation, but there are surely sufficient comic touches, even in a story such as "In the Penal Colony" to make us aware that we are not dealing with a dry, message-oriented allegorist.

First and foremost the story is a dream or a parable. A parable is always open to a number of interpretations, and a dream does not follow human logic. The beings which people dream about are sometimes recognizable as people they know, but they are rarely fully rounded characters, and they do not behave as if they inhabit the real world. Their motives are inexplicable, or barely explicable. In the final paragraph of this story the soldier and the condemned man, having been chatting away to some people that they each know at the teahouse, suddenly decide to run along to the harbor in pursuit of the explorer. "Probably they wanted to force him at the last minute to take them with him." Kafka's use of the word "probably" in this sentence indicates a double meaning to the story. The sentence describes what is going through the explorer's mind as he sees them coming after him. "Now, what do those two want?" But the sentence can also be read to mean that Kafka, the author, is unsure why they are pursuing the explorer. He compounds this narrative uncertainty by writing: "the two of them came headlong down the steps, in silence, for they did not dare to shout." Similarly, the explorer does not call out to them, but he lifts a "heavy knotted rope from the floor boards, threatened them with it and so kept them from attempting the leap." There is something uncanny about this noiseless denouement. Something which makes the blood run cold more than any of the blood-thirsty machine descriptions which have filled the earlier part of the story. In just such a silent tableau do many dreams and nightmares end, on a note of narrow escape.

The atmosphere of dreams is evoked by a good number of short story writers. What makes "In the Penal Colony" so unsettling is its air of menace—that quality which has become known as "Kafkaesque," having a nightmarishly complex, bizarre, or illogical quality. Several years after the original draft of the story was finished, Kafka began to play around with the ending, particularly with the role of the explorer. Of several experimental paragraphs which he wrote into his 1917 diaries, the following pose certain questions for those who interpret the story as an allegory:

Machines in an early twentieth-century printing plant, which bear some resemblance to the capital punishment machine in "In the Penal Colony." Through his job with a workers' accident insurance company, Kafka had some familiarity with the increasingly large and complex machines being used in factories of the time.

The explorer felt too tired to give commands or to do anything. He merely took a handkerchief from his pocket, gestured as if he were dipping it in the distant bucket, pressed it to his brow, and lay down beside the pit. He was found in this position by the two men the Commandant had set out to fetch him. He jumped up when they spoke to him as if revived. With his hand on his heart he said, "I am a cur if I allow that to happen." But then he took his own words literally and began to run around on all fours. From time to time, however, he leaped erect, shook the fit off, so to speak, threw his arms around the neck of one of the men, and tearfully exclaimed, "Why does all this happen to me!" and then hurried to his post.

As though all this were making the explorer aware that what was still to follow was solely his and the dead man's affair, he dismissed the soldier and the condemned man with a gesture of his hand; they hesitated, he threw a stone at them, and when they still deliberated, he ran up to them and struck them with his fists.

"What?" the explorer suddenly said. Had something been forgotten. A last word? A turn? An adjustment?

What Do I Read Next?

- *The Trial*, the novel Kafka was working on in the same year that "In the Penal Colony" was written, concerns a man, Josef K., who is arrested, tried, convicted, and executed, though he never learns what his crime is.
- *Jewish Folk Tales* (1989), selected and retold by Pinhas Sadeh, contains over two hundred stories which document the Jewish tradition of humor and magic in fiction.
- *The Book of Lights* by Chaim Potok (1981) is a contemporary novel which concerns the conflict between age-old secrets of Jewish mysticism and the new scientific horizon of nuclear physics.
- *The Unbearable Lightness of Being* (1984) by Milan Kundera, a Czechoslovakian writer based in Prague during the 1960s and influenced by Kafka, concerns the hardships and limitations that can result from commitment and the meaningless of life without responsibility.
- *The Collected Stories of Isaac Bashevis Singer* (1982) contains stories colored by an East European tradition, all originally composed in Yiddish. Kafka and Singer are, on first consideration, very different writers. Examining the nature of their differences will help clarify the characteristics of Kafka's work which stem from his Jewishness and those that stem form his individual personality.

> Who can penetrate the confusion? Damned, miasmal tropical air, what are you doing to me? I don't know what is happening. My judgement has been left back at home in the north.

In the story as it was published the explorer is simply "greatly troubled" when the machine begins to go to pieces. "Almost against his will" he has to force himself to look into the face of the corpse, while putting the soldier and the prisoner into position, ready to lift the officer's dead body off the needles of the Harrow. It is clear from the above alternatives that Kafka thought the explorer's agitation needed greater emphasis. The story is much better for not being altered. The explorer's coolness is in keeping with his character in the earlier part of the story. Would a man who can say plainly, and without any high-handedness or sense of bluster, "I do not approve of your procedure," later run around on all fours, or even throw stones and punches?

The explorer is consistently humorless and colorless. Earlier in the story when the officer is in full flight about the glory days of the former commandant the reader is treated to a typical example of Kafka's ironic black humor. Speaking about the public executions, and the previous clamor for good viewing positions, the officer explains: "The Commandant in his wisdom ordained that the children should have the preference; I, of course, because of my office had the privilege of always being at hand; often enough I would be squatting there with a small child in either arm." At the end of this effusion, creepily amusing in its "suffer the little children to come unto me" connotations, the officer "had embraced the explorer and laid his head on his shoulder." The explorer, embarrassed, does nothing but stare straight over the officer's head. Kafka's sense of humor as expressed in this passage has its roots in Jewish lore.

Kafka's fiction examines the fate of individual characters subjected to humiliating, embarrassing, bewildering, or sinister situations. The explorer is the quintessentially Kafkaesque character in "In the Penal Colony." Hence, the author's later alterations. It is the explorer who is discomforted, who is made to feel he has lost his senses. It is the explorer who takes flight.

Many of the essential ingredients of this story are lifted from horror tales of the nineteenth century, but stripped of Gothic trappings and placed in a sun-scorched dreamscape, they are reinvented by Kafka and injected with a sense of anxiety and

> "Many of the essential ingredients of this story are lifted from horror tales of the nineteenth century, but stripped of Gothic trappings and placed in a sun-scorched dreamscape, they are reinvented by Kafka and injected with a sense of anxiety and alienation."

alienation. "In the Penal Colony" has few trappings which tie it to a particular historical period, and those that there are—the steamer, for example—can be used to date it at least half a century earlier than 1914. Yet it is clearly a twentieth-century story, one which asks questions that have not been resolved in the last decades of the century.

Who stands in judgement over us? If it is to be neither God nor machine, are we to judge one another? If left to judge ourselves, might not the verdict, as it was in Kafka's own case, be mercilessly harsh?

Source: Michael Thorn, "Overview of 'In the Penal Colony'," in *Short Stories for Students,* Gale, 1998.

Martin Greenberg

In the following excerpt, Greenberg offers his interpretation of Kafka's "In the Penal Colony," claiming that the story, although powerful, is not successful due to its lack of subjectivity and inability to reach the truth.

Kafka failed in *Amerika* for lack of a suitable narrative mode, the subjective mode of the dream story. In the short novel "In the Penal Colony," which he wrote in the fall of 1914, about the same time he began *The Trial,* again he seems to me to fail to master his material. Now, however, the failure is not due to artistic immaturity—now it is the failure of the mature artist to stick with sure instinct to the formal requirements of his own vision. Failure however is too strong a word here. One cannot call such a powerful story a failure. But neither is it a success.

Ideas obtrude in the story with unusual distinctness and in the end the reader is confronted with an intellectual dilemma rather than a living mystery—but not for want of a unitary image through which to tell the story. The image is there, and a very powerful one it is, in the shape of the penal island with its dreadful execution machine squatting in the middle of it—the image of a world under the judgment of the law. Nevertheless, as Austin Warren observes, "this story [is] pretty persistently and consistently allegorical"; that is, it refers one *directly* to ideas. If we examine what the allegory consists in and how it is presented, I think we shall find that the power of the story to disturb is not only due to its artistic power.

The world discovered in the story is in a state of schism, a world divided between the Old and the New. That is the essential allegory. On one side stands the traditional machine of judgment under the law, invented and built by the patriarchal old Commandant, now dead. By an ingenious mechanism of vibrating needles it writes a condemned man's sentence deeper and deeper into his flesh till at the sixth hour "enlightenment comes even to the most dull-witted"; at the twelfth hour he dies. The priest of this cruel rite is the officer-judge, a disciple of the old Commandant; he describes the workings of the machine with enthusiastic pedantry to the visiting explorer. On the other side stands the new Commandant, "always looking for an excuse to attack [the] old way of doing things"; his "new, mild doctrine" prefers humane judicial methods, but he hesitates to affront a venerable institution directly and therefore tries to subvert it by harassment and deliberate neglect.

The old law judged according to the principle that "guilt is never to be doubted"—the guilt of mankind was never to be doubted. Therefore no trial needed to take place. "Other courts cannot follow that principle, for they consist of various opinions and on top of that have higher courts over them." The old court then was absolute—the highest court. In the new, liberal order there is no highest court, only "various opinions."

The old law aimed at being eternal law: "We who were [the old Commandant's] friends," says the officer, "knew even before he died that the organization of the colony was so perfect that his successor, even with a thousand new schemes in his head, would find it impossible to alter anything, at least for many years to come.'' But the new Commandant cares nothing about eternity; what he cares about, as a man of progress and the times, is ''harbor works, nothing but harbor works!'' A womanizer, he swims in the atmosphere of a crowd of admiring females; through the ''women who influence him'' the world is womanized. The old Commandant had ''his ladies'' too, but there was no petticoat government.

The condemned man vomits when he is strapped down in the machine and takes the felt gag in his mouth, because ''the [new] Commandant's ladies stuff the man with sugar candy before he's led off. He has lived on stinking fish his whole life long and now he has to eat sugar candy!'' The ''new, mild doctrine'' is effeminate and, by causing the condemned man to vomit over himself, degrading. But the condemned man vomits too because the felt gag has been chewed by hundreds rather than being changed for every execution as it used to be. So the new regime is callous as well as sentimental.

''How different an execution was in the old days!'' exclaimed the officer-judge. Then the whole island gathered together in the true ceremony of belief and the Commandant himself laid the condemned man under the Harrow.

> No discordant noise spoilt the working of the machine. Many did not care to watch it but lay with closed eyes in the sand; they all knew: Now Justice is being done. In the silence one heard nothing but the condemned man's sighs, half muffled by the felt gag. Nowadays the machine can no longer wring from anyone a sigh louder than the felt gag can stifle; but in those days the writing needles let drop an acid fluid, which we're no longer permitted to use. Well, and then came the sixth hour! It was impossible to grant all the requests to be allowed to watch it from near by. The Commandant in his wisdom ordained that the children should have the preference often enough I would be squatting there with a small child in either arm. How we all absorbed the look of transfiguration on the face of the sufferer, how we bathed our cheeks in the radiance of that justice, achieved at last and fading so quickly! What times there were, my comrade!

Under the old law, *Justice was done.* All shared ritually in the redemption which the condemned man found under the law in death. All stood under the same law and could look forward to the same redemption. Death redeemed. Of course, all this is according to the officer's point of view. But the point is that his is the point of view that excludes ''points of view''—he lives the conviction of absolute justice.

"The world discovered in the story is in a state of schism, a world divided between the Old and the New. That is the essential allegory."

That is how things were in the old days. Now, however, the sea of faith has ebbed. When the officer is unable to persuade the explorer, who remains convinced ''that the injustice of the procedure and the inhumanity of the execution were undeniable,'' to side with him against the new Commandant, he lies down with devout determination in the judgment machine to execute himself. But execution according to the old law is no longer possible, a new dispensation has succeeded; the machine can no longer ''do Justice.'' Negated, it spits out its parts and goes to pieces, murdering the officer indecently instead of executing him: ''. . . [T]his was no [ceremonial] torture such as the officer desired, this was plain murder.'' Death no longer redeems:

> [The face of the corpse] was as it had been in life; no sign was visible of the promised redemption; what the others had found in the machine the officer had not found; the lips were firmly pressed together, the eyes were open, with the same expression as in life, the look was calm and convinced, through the forehead went the point of the great iron spike.

As Professor Emrich comments, ''The age of redemption is no more. The dead man remains stuck in life. He no longer can cross the boundary into the liberating Beyond. Man is consigned entirely to the earth.''

Lawless sentimentality takes the place of implacable judgment, turning with satisfaction how the officer takes his place in the machine:

> So this was revenge. Although he himself had not suffered to the end, he was to be revenged to the end. A broad, silent grin now appeared on his face and stayed there all the rest of the time.

Justice no longer holds sway, but revenge—an internecine warfare of each against each, in a never-ending pursuit of the upper hand.

In the cavernous, blackened interior of the teahouse, which makes on the explorer "the impression of some historical memory or other," so that he feels "the power of past times," the old Commandant lies buried. All that remains of the old order is a prophecy, written on his gravestone, that he "will rise again and lead his adherents from this house to recover the colony. Have faith and wait!"

"In the Penal Colony" takes place in historical time—the colony is a more or less recognizable possession of a European power of the late-nineteenth or early-twentieth century—rather than in the timeless subjective dimension into which the protagonists of Kafka's dream narratives awaken out of historical time. Its subject matter is the religious history of the world, which it recapitulates in terms of the old times and the new times of a penal colony. Like most of Kafka's stories, it is concerned with spiritual need, but it treats this subject in historical terms rather than through an individual who experiences the despair of spiritual darkness in the timelessness of his soul. It is an historical allegory.

It would be a mistake, however, to read too-specific references into the allegory. The old regime of the old Commandant does not, for example, pointedly refer to Old Testament days, it only embraces them in its meaning, along with all the other old regimes that based their authority on a transcendent religious absolute. As an ancient idol which is at the same time a piece of modern machinery, the execution machine reaches from the present all the way back to the most barbarous times of Dagon and the other stocks and stones in whose name our worshiping fathers did absolute justice. The old ends and the new begins at the point at which justice based on supreme authority yields to justice based on "various opinions."

So far I have said little about the explorer, yet as the one through whose eyes the story is narrated and the embodiment of its moral point of view, his role is crucial for the way in which the allegory is presented. A dispassionate observer of the "peculiarities of many peoples," an enlightened modern relativist and naturalist, from first to last he condemns the injustice and the inhumanity of the old law—so much so indeed that he is moved to abandon his attitude of scientific neutrality for once and intervene against the execution. Mixed, however, with his disapproval of the old judicial procedure is a growing admiration for the officer, even though he cannot but deplore his narrow-mindedness. Touched in the end by the officer's "sincere conviction," the explorer decides to do nothing to hinder the operation of the old law, although, by refusing the officer's plea to join forces with him against the new Commandant, he will do nothing to help it either. When the officer lies down under the Harrow to execute himself, he can only approve his decision: "the officer was doing the right thing; in his place the explorer would not have acted otherwise."

What the explorer is confronted with on the penal island is a moral choice between the old law and the new—the story arranges itself as a kind of contest between the two regimes to win his concurrence. The old law is primitive and cruel, yet the explorer must admire the spiritual unity and conviction it begets in its adherents; a conviction which is able to attain ultimate spiritual knowledge in redemption through final judgment under the law. On the other hand, it is just precisely ultimateness that the new law lacks. He despises its effeminate sentimentality, laxity and shallow worldliness. Nevertheless, he must approve its superior humanity: "The injustice of the [old] procedure and the inhumanity of the execution were undeniable." So actually it is not a moral choice that the explorer is faced with, since there is never any question of what his moral judgment is. The choice he faces is between morality and spirituality. The two have come apart. Before this conflict between the moral and the spiritual, the explorer retreats into a neutrality which has nothing to do with his old scientific detachment. His neutrality now expresses the troubled state of mind of someone who has had a glimpse into hitherto undiscerned depths.

And yet the glimpse he gains is historical rather than religious. It is not insight into religious truth but into the religious past. The explorer does not and cannot believe in the truth of the old law; what he sees is the way it was when mankind was ruled by the idea of supreme truth. The execution machine is an historical demonstration to him of the primitive unity of absolute justice and human society, spirit and the world. But that unity explodes under his very eyes when the officer dies unredeemed ("murdered") in the disintegrating machine—redemption under the old law is an exploded (literally exploded!) religious idea. What the explorer feels toward the old law is a mixture of horror and nostalgia: horror at its cruelty, nostalgia for its spirituality. The story is painfully divided between the moral and the religious (or rather between the moral and the religious regarded nostalgically) and in the end the explorer must flee the dilemma the colony presents him with in dismayed haste.

"In the Penal Colony" is not *about* the conflict between the moral and the religious; it falls victim to that conflict. The explorer's dilemma is only a dilemma because the question of the old law's truth has been left aside. Leaving aside the question of truth casts an obscurantist shadow over the whole story, introduces a moral and intellectual equivocation. When the question of truth is not left aside there can be only one choice: we can only choose to be modern and go on from there. There is no going back to the old law, even if only to the extent of choosing to be neutral toward it as the explorer does. One of the reasons why the story is disturbing is this negative one: because it is morally and intellectually equivocal. The allegory teeters on the edge of a familiar snobbery, which was so strong in Prague among the sons of the Jewish middle class at the beginning of the century—the snobbery, as Werfel puts it in a quotation already cited, of "those . . . who run around as mystics and orthodox believers only because every tailor, schoolteacher and journalist is a believing atheist." But working against the impression of snobbish obscurantism is the mute, unpalliated horror of the execution machine. Never do we lose sight of the fact that "the injustice of the procedure and the inhumanity of the execution were undeniable." The positive power of the story to disturb is owing to the image of the execution machine; its finicky details testify incontrovertibly to injustice. The authentic power of the story lies in its image of a religiosity which is as wicked and destructive as it is spiritual.

In the more or less historical framework of the story, on its level of rational consciousness, the old Commandant's religion, as a relic of the past, can only move the explorer nostalgically, it cannot compel him at the center of his being. An outside observer, an onlooker rather than a participant, he is impressed by the old law's spiritual appearance—aesthetically. The explorer does not face a true dilemma in the penal colony, he is spectator at an allegorical confrontation.

The failure of the story is a failure to be subjective—and through subjectivity to reach the truth.

Source: Martin Greenberg, "The Failure to Be Subjective," in *The Terror of Art: Kafka and Modern Literature,* Basic Books, Inc., 1968, pp. 92–112.

Kurt J. Fickert

In the following excerpt, Fickert discusses the protagonist's escape at the end of Kafka's "In the Penal Colony," and contends that his escape "reveals his inability to deal with the paradoxes of truth; but more importantly, the traveler flees . . . with the instinct of self-preservation."

At the end of Franz Kafka's story "In the Penal Colony" the protagonist, variously called traveler, explorer, scientist, is in full flight: "When they [the soldier and the condemned man] arrived down below, the traveler was already in the boat, and the boatman was casting off from shore. They could still have leapt in the boat, but the traveler picked up a heavy, knotted rope from the bottom of the boat, threatened them with it and thus kept them from jumping." Explanations of the traveler's escape and indeed of his entire role have not been completely satisfying; e.g., Satish Kumar identifies the traveler with Kafka himself and interprets his retreat to the boat as "nothing else but the transition from dream life to reality." ("Franz Kafka: In der Strafkolonie," *Deutschunterricht fur Auslander,* XIII (No. 5/6, 1963), 154; my translation.) An earlier explication by Austin Warren depicts the traveler as a convert to the machine and the religion it represents; "he excludes from his boat those who wish to escape from the penal colony." (See Cleanth Brooks and Robert Penn Warren, *Understanding Fiction,* New York, 1943, p. 391.)

The difficulty with these surmises lies in the fact that they fit too readily into the over-all pattern, the allegory, which the interpreters insist upon finding in "In the Penal Colony." Of the several kinds of unity in Kafka's stories, however—method, purpose, style—a consistency in the use of symbols seems most conspicuously lacking. The heavy, knotted rope, for example, will not necessarily recur elsewhere. On the other hand, the theme of "In the Penal Colony" is not appreciably different from that in most of Kafka's stories and novels: man in a dilemma, called upon to solve the insoluble. For the protagonist here has no name but a philosophical label: scientist, explorer, traveler. He is called upon to make a decision in the matter of the execution machine; he must be either for it or against it. But the machine, described with a plethora of realistic detail, remains insubstantial and can actually be seen only as a number of philosophic tenets, the horns of the protagonist's dilemma. The machine's function in the story is to precipitate a crisis, to lure the mind into a trap, a decision.

"Of the several kinds of unity in Kafka's stories, however—method, purpose, style—a consistency in the use of symbols seems most conspicuously lacking."

With this framework, "In the Penal Colony" follows the pattern of the existentialist literary work, deftly traced by Helmut Kuhn in *Begegnung mit dem Nichts* (Munchen, 1950): "The word crisis is derived from a Greek verb which means to separate (as with a sieve), to choose, to test, or to judge. Through the crisis man is tested. Testing, however, requires a standard—no crisis without a criterion. The only philosophically valid crisis is the crisis of criteria. Philosophy is this crisis. But this crisis itself demands a criterion, and if we omit it, we dissolve the crisis itself. Existentialism, which claims to be a philosophy of crisis, destroys the crisis" (p. 173; my translation). Thus the execution machine faces the protagonist with the problem of injustice (also a religious problem, of course), but since the problem occurs in an existentialist framework, it predicates insolubility. The nature of the machine is such that no basis exists on which it may be judged, and Kafka abandons the problem; the traveler flees. Helmut Kuhn analyzes this kind of retreat as the usurpation of the role of conscience by primitive fright (p. 156).

Fear in the face of the inexplicable and resultant flight appear again and again in Kafka; e.g., Karl Rossmann in *Amerika* finds refuge in an illogical utopia and never grows up; in "Die Verwandlung" the escape is the entire story. Although the flight of the protagonist may have been an obvious device, since Kafka assumed that man's dilemma had no solution, he nevertheless exposed a deep root in man's emotional network in an act of psychological probing which makes his work compelling in spite of its self-defeating argumentativeness. Constant fear and incipient flight have been described in an article by Heini Hediger ("Die Angst des Tieres," *Universitas,* XIV, No. 9, September, 1959) as the primary motive force in animal life (before hunger and sex); "quick and purposive flight of the individual is the first duty toward preservation of the species" (p. 929; my translation). The dissolution of the existentialist's philosophic pretensions in panic flight becomes a key to an understanding of man's true nature: his fear of an ever-present though concealed hostility in his environment and his one weapon against the dark unknown—flight. When the traveler escapes at the end of "In the Penal Colony" he reveals his (and Kafka's and anybody else's) inability to deal with the paradoxes of truth; but, more importantly, the traveler flees, like all mankind, with the instinct of self-preservation.

Source: Kurt J. Fickert, "Kafka's 'In the Penal Colony'," in *The Explicator,* Vol. XXIV, No. 1, September, 1965, item #11.

Cleanth Brooks and Robert Penn Warren

Brooks and Warren were central figures in the New Criticism movement in America in the 1930s and 1940s. In the following excerpt, the critics use Austin Warren's interpretation of Kafka's "In the Penal Colony" to demonstrate that the story is "an allegory concerning the state of religion in the modern world."

One realizes that this story is not intended to be a realistic account of events which are to be judged by ordinary notions of probability. It is a fantasy. The strangeness of the situation, the unusual behavior of the condemned man and the soldier, the mysterious nature of the machine, all indicate that we are dealing with fantasy, just as we are in "The Lottery."

But are we to take the story to be merely fantastic? Do we not, rather, expect that the unrealistic and fantastic elements in such a piece of fiction as "In the Penal Colony" shall have some bearing, finally, on real human experience? The violation of our ordinary notions of probability, which is characteristic of fantasy, seems to promise an imaginative escape from ordinary experience, but in the end we discover that the intention of the creator of the fantasy is not to provide us with an escape from our ordinary experience but to provide us with an interpretation of our experience. In other words, fantasy as a type of fiction differs from other types of fiction merely in method and not in its basic intention.

The specific method employed by "In the Penal Colony" is allegorical. In an allegory, one finds a surface narrative the items of which—characters, objects, and events—stand for ideas and relations among ideas. That is, in so far as the allegory is strictly maintained, there is a point-to-point equating of the surface narrative with the background meaning. This method of communicating meaning is essentially different from that of ordinary realistic fiction. For instance, in ''The Lament'' the persons do not stand for ideas, and events do not indicate relationships among ideas. The old man does not stand for grief, for example, but is simply himself, an old man who is suffering from grief and loneliness. The meaning of the story, then, does not come from our grasp of particular concepts and relations as exemplified, item by item, in the narrative, but as a result of the total story: in so far as the character and situation of the old man work on our imagination, we become aware of the unthinking callousness of the world, and our comprehension of, and our sympathy for, the lonely and outcast are awakened. That is, we arrive at the meaning of a realistic story much as we arrive at the meaning of an event in real life.

This leads to a second distinction between allegory and realistic fiction. In realistic fiction, we are convinced by the logic of character and event, by our notion of probability. But in allegory the principle of organization does not finally depend upon the logic in the surface narrative, but upon the logic of the relationships among the ideas represented. Though the surface narrative may be more or less realistic, and in so far as it is realistic possess an independent logic, the emphasis is always upon the logic of the background.

''In the Penal Colony'' as interpreted by one critic, Austin Warren, is an allegory concerning the state of religion in the modern world. We know that the characteristic beliefs of the modern world are primarily founded on science. Science is concerned with the realm of the natural and not with the realm of the supernatural. Its assumption is that the events of the world are in accord with natural laws, and that by the use of his reason man may become acquainted with natural law and can, in so far as his knowledge of that law is perfect, predict the course of nature. It pictures a completely rational world, in which there is no place for the irrational, the miraculous, the supernatural. It assumes that miraculous and supernatural manifestations would, if man's scientific knowledge were adequate, be seen to be merely natural phenomena. Associated with this belief in science is the belief in progress: as man learns more his control of nature increases and he can improve his world. That is, perfect knowledge,

"'In the Penal Colony' is an allegory concerning the state of religion in the modern world."

in the scientific sense, would bring perfect control of nature, including human nature. And associated with this purely natural or secular view of the world we find the belief in humanitarianism. Pain is the great evil, according to such a belief, and the conquest of pain becomes the greatest good. Furthermore, the idea of natural law as applied in human affairs leads to an emphasis on the idea of determinism—people are good or bad as a result of heredity and environment and not as a matter of responsible moral choice. Over against these beliefs which are characteristic of modernism as it is popularly understood are the traditional religious beliefs: that there is a supernatural realm, that God's will is finally inscrutable and that man must have faith, that the salvation of the soul is the greatest good, and that men are free moral agents. According to Austin Warren's interpretation, ''In the Penal Colony'' is an allegory of the conflict between these two sets of beliefs:

> ''The earth is a penal colony, and we are all under sentence of judgment for sin. There was once a very elaborate machine, of scholastic theology, for the pronouncement of sentence, and an elaborate ecclesiastic system for its administration. Now it is in the process of disappearance: the Old Commander (God) has died, though there is a legend, which you can believe or not, that He will come again. Meanwhile the 'machine' seems antiquated and inhuman to ladies, who are sentimental about criminals, and to the new governor, who is a humanitarian.
>
> ''Important is the setting of the machine's draughtsman. The first victim suffers under 'Honor your Superior,' the moral law which he has broken: this is a law appropriate to his caste of servant. For his own use, the old officer adjusts the sentence to 'Be just.' Has he violated this injunction? Not consciously; but a judge of his fellowmen should be 'just' and no mortal man can be: 'none is Good save God': the old officer can be sure that, whatever his intentions, he has been unjust in the sight of Justice.
>
> ''At the end of the story, the explorer has become converted to the doctrine of the machine: he excludes from his boat those who wish to escape from the penal

island. 'Converted' is too strong: if really converted, he would stay on the island—at least if the machine still operated. But at least he makes no report to the new commander; and he takes the Prophecy of Return seriously: when the men about him ridicule the inscription, he does not join in their laughter: the Prophecy may be true. Like Pilate, he refuses to judge; he finds no fault in the just manipulators of the machine.

''In its tone, the story is a matter-of-fact description of an elaborate method of punishment, no longer believed in by the 'enlightened.' kept going a little longer by the devotion of an old man who doesn't understand it very well and can't repair it. Narration is from the point of view of, through the eyes of, the explorer, who is shocked by what he sees and yet who, unlike the present management of the penal colony, can understand the possible use of the machine in what is, after all, a penal colony; and who becomes increasingly sympathetic as he sees that the operator of the machine believes in it for himself as well as for others. But it is essential to Kafka's purpose that there shall be no suppression of the difficulties in accepting the gospel of the machine: it is cruel; it makes errors; it is costly to keep up; people have ceased to believe in it; its inventor has died, and it is generally thought ridiculous to credit the pious legend that he will come again. 'My ways are not your ways, neither my thoughts as your thoughts,' saith the Lord. . . . Kafka, fearful of softening religion, wants to present it in all its rigor, its repellence to the flesh—in its irrationality and inscrutability and uncertainty, too. We must put up with the professional pride and the pedantry of the old officer: religionists are always forgetting ends in absorption with means, taking human (and impious) pride in the details of their theological and ecclesiastical systems. Nothing is simple, nothing unmixed. We never get reality straight, but always through a veil of illusion. If we are determined to be scrupulously positivistic and 'accept no illusion,' then we shall have to content ourselves with no more than statistics: we shan't find reality.''

If Mr. Warren's interpretation of ''In the Penal Colony'' is acceptable, then one sees that the allegory of the story is strict rather than loose—that most of the details of the surface narrative have specific parallels at the level of ideas. One sees also that here we have a contrast between the fantastic surface—which cannot be judged in terms of the logic of actual experience—and the represented argument—which can be judged in terms of actual experience. That is, the argument in the background is a possible view of the subject under discussion, and is held by many intelligent people. There is an ironical contrast between the fantastic way of representing the ideas and the ideas themselves, which are not fantastic, which are one way of interpreting an actual situation; in other words, the fantasy may, ironically, be logical after all.

A similar irony is indicated in the contrast between the fantastic events and the style in which they are narrated. The style is a rather bare, factual style—the style of a person who is trying to be scrupulously accurate and does not wish to color the truth by indulging in any literary and rhetorical devices. It implies that the narrator is willing to let the case rest on the facts alone. It does not try, we might say, to provoke the reader to horror or sympathy.

This contrast between the fantastic events and setting and the particular style is commented on by Mr. Warren: ''Its [the story's] powerful effect is indeed produced by its complete absence of fantasy in detail: The story offers, by its method, the sense of a fact which you can interpret as you like, of which you can make what you will: I'm telling you, as a sober scientist, what I saw.'' The style, then, has a dramatic function, in connection with the total story, just as it does in ''The Killers'' or ''I Want to Know Why'' or any other successful piece of fiction. It here indicates a fusion, an interpenetration, of the fantastic and realistic elements of experience, an idea which is to be associated with the basic meaning of the story.

Source: Cleanth Brooks and Robert Penn Warren, ''Franz Kafka,'' in *Understanding Fiction,* second edition, edited by Cleanth Brooks and Robert Penn Warren, Appleton-Century-Crofts, Inc., 1959, pp. 368–93.

Sources

Bloom, Harold, editor. *Gershom Scholem,* Chelsea House, 1987, 240 p.

Brod, Max, editor. *The Diaries of Franz Kafka 1910-23,* Schocken Books, 1948-49.

Emrich, Wilhelm. ''The Construction of the Objective World and the Binding Law,'' in *Franz Kafka: A Critical Study of His Writings,* translated by Sheema Zeben Buehne, Frederick Ungar, 1968, pp. 268-75.

Politzer, Heinz. ''Parable and Paradox: 'A Country Doctor' and 'In the Penal Colony','' in *Franz Kafka: Parable and Paradox,* Cornell University Press, 1962, pp. 83–115.

Seymour-Smith, Martin. *The Macmillan Guide To Modern World Literature,* 3rd edition, Macmillan, 1985, 1396 p.

Warren, Austin. ''An Exegetical Note on 'In The Penal Colony,''' in *The Southern Review,* Vol. VII, No. 2, 1941, pp. 363-369.

Further Reading

Brod, Max, trans. by G. Humphreys Roberts and Richard Winston, *Franz Kafka: A Biography,* Schocken Books, 1960, 267 p.

An important work by Kafka's personal friend. Brod preserved and edited Kafka's manuscripts after his death.

Hayman, Ronald. *Kafka: A Biography,* Oxford University Press, 1982, 349 p.

A experienced biographer provides insights into Kafka's personal and family relationships.

Kafka, Franz, ed. by Max Brod. *The Diaries of Franz Kafka, 1910-23,* Schocken, 1948-49.

Kafka kept extensive diaries throughout his life. The entries for the period during which he wrote ''In the Penal Colony'' focus on his difficulties in writing his novels.

Neumeyer, Peter. ''Do Not Teach Kafka's 'In The Penal Colony.''' *College Literature,* Vol. VI, No. 2, Spring, 1979, pp. 103-112.

Neumeyer makes several forceful criticisms of the John Muir translation of Kafka's works.

Tauber, Herbert. *Franz Kafka: An Interpretation of His Works,* Haskell House Publishers, 1968, 252 p.

This book provides accessible readings of all Kafka's major texts.

The Japanese Quince

John Galsworthy

1910

Since its first publication in 1910 in the collection *A Motley,* John Galsworthy's ''The Japanese Quince'' has been popular with readers for its richly suggestive, yet subdued, narrative. The story recounts an episode from the life of Mr. Nilson, who is momentarily diverted by the sights, sounds, and smells of an early spring morning. Seized by the beauty of the natural world, Mr. Nilson is briefly lifted out of his highly regimented, well-ordered life. Born to wealth and having lived his entire life in the Victorian English world of the upper middle class, Galsworthy wrote about what he knew. The hollow lives of his patrician characters provide the matrix for the primary pathos of his work. He once stated that ''The Japanese Quince'' was his attempt to ''produce in the reader the sort of uneasy feeling that now and then we run up against ourselves.'' Like much of Galsworthy's fiction, this story has been commended for its complex insights into the ambivalence of human nature, and for its glimpse into a world that reveals its shortcomings while suggesting the possibilities for its redemption.

Author Biography

A prolific novelist, playwright and short-story writer, Galsworthy is considered one of the most successful English authors of the early twentieth century. Born 14 August 1867 at his wealthy family's estate near London, Galsworthy was a member of the upper-class Victorian society he later challenged in his fiction. His work is admired for capturing the proud but declining spirit of upper-class society from the 1880s to the years following World War I. While revealing the shortcomings of society, particularly its material and consumer values, Galsworthy's best work also manages to communicate the possibility of change for the better, or the poignant reality that the possibility for betterment has passed unacknowledged before the eyes of his characters.

Educated at Oxford to be a lawyer, Galsworthy never took up the practice, choosing instead to travel. In 1891, at the age of twenty-four, Galsworthy sailed to Russia, South Africa, Australia, and Fiji. During his voyages he met Joseph Conrad, the novelist best known for *Lord Jim* and *Heart of Darkness,* who encouraged Galsworthy to pursue his own literary efforts. In rejecting a prosperous living to be gained from practicing law, and in carrying on an illicit love affair with a married woman (who would later become his wife), Galsworthy was somewhat of a rebel against the conventions of his time. Such testing and questioning of English bourgeois values is a prominent feature in Galsworthy's writing.

By publishing short stories, novels, and plays, Galsworthy gradually made himself into a successful man of letters. He was remarkably generous with his fortune; over the years he gave large sums of money to charity, supporting such causes as slaughterhouse reform and aid to the poor. His writings reflect this socially conscious spirit by portraying the dreadful plight of prostitutes and prison inmates, whom Galsworthy thought suffered under an unfair social and political system. For example, his play *Justice* (1910), which examines the practice of solitary confinement in prisons, has been credited with prompting Winston Churchill to introduce legislation for prison reforms before the House of Commons. Although a few critics consider Galsworthy's social plays his most important works, his accomplishments as a dramatist have been largely overshadowed by the renown of "The Forsyte Chronicles."

Publication of *The Forsyte Saga* (1922) established Galsworthy's reputation as a novelist. The works known as "The Forsyte Chronicles" include the novels and short fiction collected in *The Forsyte Saga* and *A Modern Comedy* (1929); the short story volume *On Forsyte 'Change* (1930); and several pieces of short fiction published in other works. Galsworthy modeled many of the characters in these works upon his ancestors and immediate family members. (Soames Forsyte, the central figure of the "Chronicles," is based on Galsworthy's cousin Arthur.) Commentators have noted that while Galsworthy satirized the wealthy in his early works, his later works, especially those collected in *A Modern Comedy,* present a more sympathetic view of the Forsytes.

The recipient of numerous awards, Galsworthy also founded PEN, the important international writers' society, and served as its first president for twelve years. (The acronym stands for poets, playwrights, editors, essayists, and novelists.) Offered knighthood for his literary and social achievements, Galsworthy declined the honor, perhaps his country's highest, claiming that such a title was incompatible with the identity he had worked to construct as a socially conscious writer. Shortly before his death in 1932, Galsworthy was awarded the Nobel Prize in literature. Although his works were highly regarded during his lifetime, Galsworthy's reputation declined abruptly after his death. In 1967 the British Broadcasting Corporation aired for television a twenty-six hour adaptation of *The Forsyte Saga.* Syndicated in more than forty countries, this adaptation is credited with rekindling interest in Galsworthy's life and works.

Plot Summary

The action of "The Japanese Quince" appears at first glance quite simple and straightforward, perhaps deceptively so. On a beautiful spring morning, Mr. Nilson opens his dressing room window, only to experience "a peculiar sweetish sensation in the back of his throat." Descending to his dining room and finding his morning paper laid out, Mr. Nilson again experiences that peculiar sensation as he takes the paper in his hand. Hoping to rid himself of this uncomfortable feeling, Mr. Nilson determines to take a walk in the nearby gardens before breakfast.

With paper firmly in hand behind him, Mr. Nilson notes with some alarm that even after two laps around the park, the unsettling sensation has

John Galsworthy

not ceased. Breathing deeply only exacerbates the problem. Mr. Nilson is unable to account for the way he feels, until it occurs to him it might possibly be ''some smell affecting him,'' a scent evidently emanating from the budding bushes of spring. When a blackbird begins singing, Mr. Nilson's attention is drawn to a nearby tree.

Mr. Nilson pauses to enjoy the flowering tree. He congratulates himself on having taken the time to enjoy the beautiful morning. He then wonders why he is the only person who has bothered to come out and enjoy the square. Just then he notices that he is, in fact, not alone. Another man is standing quite near to him, likewise ''staring up and smiling at the little tree.'' At the sight of the man, Mr. Nilson ceases to smile and regards the ''stranger'' cautiously. The man, as it turns out, is Mr. Nilson's neighbor, Mr. Tandram. His presence causes Mr. Nilson to perceive ''at once the awkwardness of his position, for, being married, they had not yet had occasion to speak to one another.''

Unsure of how to respond to Mr. Tandram's presence, Mr. Nilson finally murmurs a greeting before continuing on his way. When Mr. Tandram responds, Mr. Nilson detects ''a slight nervousness in his neighbor's voice.'' A glance reveals that his neighbor is remarkably similar to him in appearance, both possessing ''firm, well-colored cheeks, neat brown mustaches, and round, well-opened, clear grey eyes.'' Both clasp newspapers behind their backs.

Feeling that he has been ''caught out,'' Mr. Nilson asks his neighbor the name of the tree they have both been admiring. A nearby label reveals that the tree is a Japanese Quince. Both men remark on the beauty of the day and the blackbird's song. They gaze again in silence at the beautiful tree before them, until Mr. Nilson suddenly, in a moment of self-recognition, regards Mr. Tandram as appearing a little foolish, ''as if he had seen himself,'' and Mr. Nilson bids farewell to his neighbor.

The neighbors retrace their steps to their respective homes. As he approaches the doorstep, Mr. Nilson's attention is drawn to the sound of Mr. Tandram's cough. He sees his neighbor standing ''in the shadow of his French window . . . looking forth across the Gardens at the little quince tree.'' Mr. Nilson returns to his newspaper, ''unaccountably upset.''

Characters

Mr. Nilson

''The Japanese Quince,'' by some definitions, is a character sketch of Mr. Nilson. In a brief scene, Galsworthy paints a fairly complete portrait of a well-to-do man who is out of touch with himself and others. His wealth and class is established in the first sentence: He is ''well known in the City''—the financial center of London—and though he right away notices the spring morning, he prefers to contemplate the price of Tintos—stock shares. While looking in an ivory-backed mirror, he is described physically as exhibiting ''a reassuring appearance of good health,'' despite the aching feeling beneath his fifth rib. His life is rigid and ordered, a fact that can be deduced from the striking of the cuckoo clock that tells him he has exactly a half-hour to breakfast. When he goes out to the square to enjoy the morning, he walks around the circular path two times. He marvels at the blooming quince tree but is also quite concerned about the sensation of ''some sweetish liquor in course within him.'' This illness suggests a disparity between the appearance of Mr. Nilson's life—the way it looks from the outside—and the reality of his inner life.

Mr. Nilson's true character is exposed when he confronts Mr. Tandram, who functions as his counterpart, or doppelganger. Their brief conversation, though their thoughts echo one another's almost perfectly, leaves Mr. Nilson ''unaccountably upset.'' The men's exchange creates the tension between appearance and reality—between the outer world of the City and the inner world of Mr. Nilson's soul—in various ways. Appearing at times uncertain and at other times resolved, Mr. Nilson moves through the story in a series of stops and starts. Several times he begins to achieve an action or utter a thought, only to halt abruptly before revealing his feelings.

Mr. Tandram

Mr. Tandram functions as a mirror-image of Mr. Nilson. Both men are well-to-do London financiers who are married and live in the same neighborhood. Both men are strolling through the Garden Square with their newspapers before breakfast. Both prefer the song of the blackbird to the thrush. They are also moved in similar ways by the blossoming quince tree. Though he responds to the natural beauty of the morning, the fact that he is not able to give himself over to this world underscores Mr. Nilson's similar adherence to a safe, familiar, well-ordered, and illness-inducing life.

Topics for Further Study

- Galsworthy's story is, in part, a meditation on peoples' relationships to each other. What does he mean by saying that Mr. Nilson was ''visited somehow by the feeling that he had been caught out''? Why is this statement important?
- How does the author impart to readers that Mr. Nilson is a financially well-off man? Do you think that it is harder for wealthy people than others to appreciate beauty? What might some of Galsworthy's reasons be for suggesting so?
- The story ends with Mr. Nilson ''unaccountably upset.'' Speculate on the reasons for this feeling. Imagine the rest of Mr. Nilson's day—do you think he will give any more thought to the blackbird or the quince tree?
- Consider the extent to which spontaneity is encouraged or valued in society. On what occasions might you have wished to give yourself over more fully to the beauty of the natural world? What prevented you?
- Identify another work you have read that can be linked with the experience Galsworthy describes or the ideas he explores. How are the two works similar? How are they different? What can be learned by comparing them with one another?

Themes

Alienation

Mr. Nilson is alienated from both nature and humankind. Although he praises himself for taking a walk in the square on a beautiful morning, he takes his newspaper with him. Still, the strange sensation does not abate, and he suspects it might be caused by something he ate. Upon encountering the quince tree, his first instinct is to find out exactly what species it is, rather than simply enjoy the flowers. Towards the end of the story, when the blackbird resumes its singing, ''that queer sensation, that choky feeling in his throat'' returns, further underscoring his alienation from nature.

Related to Mr. Nilson's alienation from nature is the alienation he feels from humankind, which is demonstrated by his stilted exchange with Mr. Tandram. Though they have been next-door neighbors for five years, they have not yet introduced themselves to one another. Mr. Nilson blames this on his marital status—inferring that one of his wife's duties is to protect him from unnecessary social intrusions. The men's exchange in front of the quince tree is indirect and somewhat empty; it also suggests the desire on the part of both Mr. Nilson and Mr. Tandram for something more: ''Nice fellow, this, I rather like him,'' thinks Mr. Nilson. These successful businessmen seem to yearn, at some level, for more meaningful connection. Yet, both fear appearing foolish for exhibiting the feelings that nature has produced in them: ''It struck him suddenly that Mr. Tandram looked a little foolish . . . as if he had seen himself.'' Even as they part awkwardly, Mr. Nilson takes precautions to make sure he does not encounter Mr. Tandram on the way back to his house. The exchange has left him ''unaccountably upset,'' and he returns to the solitary, hermetic world of his newspaper. Likewise, Mr. Tandram resorts to contemplating the quince tree from ''the shadow of his French window.''

Illness as Metaphor

As a result of his alienation from the environment and his own humanity, a ''feeling of emptiness'' at times comes over Mr. Nilson. Described variously as a ''queer sensation,'' a ''faint aching just above the heart,'' and a ''choky feeling in his throat,'' Mr. Nilson's ailments are the effects of a dissatisfaction with his life that he attempts to bury beneath order and affluence. Although he reassures himself while gazing in a mirror that his eyes exhibit ''a reassuring appearance of good health,'' the ''queer'' feeling within him only increases as he enjoys the nice morning. The ''emptiness just under his fifth rib'' hints at a figurative ''hole in his heart,'' which he tries to explain away as indigestion. Mr. Tandram, who is heard coughing at the end of the story, may well be suffering the same malaise.

Beauty

Hovering near the surface of ''The Japanese Quince'' is the theme of beauty. In a review published in the *New York Times Book Review* in 1920, Louise Maunsell Field remarks that if she ''were to try to sum up in a single word that for which John Galsworthy stands, both in the matter of expression and of creed, it would seem inevitable that the word should be 'beauty.''' The events of ''The Japanese Quince'' support such a claim. A reverence for beauty permeates the story through the descriptions of the spring morning, the flowers of the quince tree, and the song of the blackbird. Galsworthy's implication, according to some interpretations, is that people will remain divided and isolated as long as they neglect the beauty that the world offers them. No matter what other qualities they possess or what possessions they secure, an inability to appreciate nature—even in small ways—is to deny the senses and to be deprived of a force that has the power to heal.

Style

Omniscient Narrator

An third-person omniscient narrator relates the events of the story. Galsworthy's choice in narrative technique is an important feature of ''The Japanese Quince'' and contributes to the ultimate meaning of the story. Permitted access to unspoken thoughts, an omniscient narrative traces the workings of Mr. Nilson's mind as he moves through his morning. Although Mr. Nilson says nothing out loud, readers are privy to his health concerns and his uneasiness around Mr. Tandram. Likewise, readers are aware that he is doing his best to appreciate the morning, whereas a third-person limited narrator would not be able to impart much more than the fact that he took a walk around the square while holding his newspaper.

Doppelganger

''Doppelganger'' is the literary term sometimes used to describe a character who functions as a double for the protagonist. In ''The Japanese Quince'' Mr. Tandram is Mr. Nilson's doppelganger, a man of ''about Mr. Nilson's own height, with firm, well-colored cheeks, neat brown mustaches, and round, well-opened, clear grey eyes; and he was wearing a black frock coat.'' Mr. Nilson's neighbor is also strolling the square with a newspaper clasped behind his back. Even Mr. Tandram's name, which is similar to the term ''tandem,'' meaning working in conjunction with, seems to imply his role as Mr. Nilson's doppelganger. The purpose of the doppelganger is to reveal what happens when the narrator encounters someone with the same characteristics that he or she possesses. In the case of Mr. Nilson, such an encounter fails to rouse him from his hermetic world. Both men, after failing to connect in any significant way during their brief conversation, return to ''the scrolled iron steps'' of their houses.

The Senses

The language of ''The Japanese Quince'' includes terms that evoke all five senses. Through such vivid language, Galsworthy reveals his appreciation for the natural world and attempts to spark similar appreciation in the reader. The imagery used to evoke sight includes the description of the quince tree, with its "young blossoms, pink and white, and little bright green leaves" on which "the sunlight glistened." Sound is represented by the cuckoo clock, the song of the blackbird—whose voice has "more body in the note" than a thrush, according to Mr. Tandram—and the cough that attracts Mr. Nilson's attention at the end of the story. The sense of touch is prefigured by the use of such adjectives as "spiky" to describe the leaves of the quince tree and the "faint ache" that ails Mr. Nilson. Smell rendered in the phrase "faint sweet lemony scent, rather agreeable than otherwise," which Mr. Nilson notices coming from the blooming bushes. Finally, taste is evoked by the narrator's description of Mr. Nilson's ailment, which courses through him like "some sweetish liquor."

Historical Context

Modernism in Art and Literature

In the decade immediately before World War I, the constraints of the Victorian Age were slowly shed, and new styles of art and literature began to appear. Surrealism, a style of art that depicted dreamlike landscapes scattered with objects of symbolic importance, became popular through the works of Giorgio de Chirico, a young Italian painter, whose *Enigma of an Autumn Afternoon* was one of several works who exhibited notably new styles in art. Ferdinand Leger, a French painter who was influenced by the Cubists, became known for his "mechanical" paintings like *Nudes in the Forest,* and Henri Matisse, because of his bold colors and broad shapes, became known as one of the "Fauves," a term meaning "wild beast." In 1910 Wassily Kandinsky painted the first nonrepresentational painting, an act that paved the way for many twentieth-century art movements, most notably Abstract Expressionism. In literature, James Joyce had written and would soon publish *A Portrait of the Artist as a Young Man* (1916), a book that would signal a break from old literary styles in its stream-of-consciousness style and in its rejection of society in an era in which old beliefs and traditions no longer seemed to make sense. Other English-language works published in 1910 reflected the world that was about to disappear amid the upheaval of World War I, an event that would leave no facet of Western society untouched. E. M. Forster's novel *Howard's End* was an Edwardian love story set in upper-class British society; Rudyard Kipling and Frances Hodgson Burnett also published books that year which, in less than a decade, would come to be seen as invariably old-fashioned. Galsworthy was seen as a writer of the old order, and following World War I, when the Bloomsbury Group, led by Virginia Woolf, gained literary prominence, he was chastised as being out of touch with the ideas of the day, and was relegated to minor status in the literary canon.

British Imperialism

On May 6, 1910, King Edward VII died, and within four years the period of relative peace and prosperity known as the Edwardian Era came to a close with the onset of World War I. Edward's reign had followed the Boer War, fought from 1899 to 1902 to gain control over the Boer Republics of South Africa, which had resulted in bloody losses among British forces. As a result, many Britons begin to seriously question whether the nation's imperialism was worth the cost in lives and resources. Over time, the British Empire was gradually transformed into the British Commonwealth, an association of self-governing countries, a process which continued throughout the first half of the twentieth century. Galsworthy is often considered emblematic of the era of British imperialism, during which the ruling classes, made up of landed gentry, lived in prosperity and benefited greatly from the country's industrialization and imperialism, relatively oblivious to the wretched conditions of many in the city, particularly children.

Critical Overview

Galsworthy's first works can be seen as studies or apprentice work, and perhaps for this reason he published his first works under the pseudonym John Sinjohn. Significantly, after his father's death in 1904, Galsworthy began publishing under his own name. *The Man of Property,* the first novel in his acclaimed *Forsyte Saga,* was published in 1906; and the year also saw the critical and commercial success of his play *The Silver Box.* From this year onward Galsworthy was an important figure in English literary life, receiving numerous awards and honors. He continued to publish prodigiously; in the first two decades of the twentieth century he wrote fifteen novels, thirteen plays, and numerous essays, poems and volumes of short stories. Galsworthy had been writing and publishing for over a decade when he wrote "The Japanese

Compare & Contrast

- **1910:** On May 31, the Republic of South Africa is formed after the region gains independence from Great Britain.

  1997: On July 1, Hong Kong is ceded back to China, ending over a hundred years' rule by Great Britain. In the handover, Great Britain relinquishes control of its last important colony. A rude jibe holds that Britain's influence has been reduced from an empire upon which the sun never set to a small island upon which the sun seldom shines.

- **1910s:** With the advancement of modern medicine, people come to realize the link between exercise, diet, and good health. John Harvey Kellogg's Battle Creek Sanitarium in Michigan is a fashionable resort where wealthy patrons partake of the latest fitness and diet fads.

  1990s: People are increasingly conscious about fitness and nutrition. Low-fat foods and exercise devices are a billion dollar industry. Still, over 25 percent of the U.S. population is overweight.

- **1910s:** Britain's public schools, serving the empire's boys, place a heavy emphasis upon rough-and-tumble games, especially rugby football and cricket. Boys who exhibit sensitivity, bookishness, or a contemplative nature are marked as contemptibly peculiar and frequently become the target of bullies.

  1990s: British public schools still place a heavy premium upon sports. But the schools are now coeducational and a much greater emphasis is placed upon academic achievement across disciplines.

Quince.'' Although his early works are considered derivative, influenced heavily by English writer Rudyard Kipling, ''The Japanese Quince'' exhibited his talents as an original writer. In addition to addressing themes of love and beauty, much of Galsworthy's fiction challenges the standards of upper-class Victorian society; both ideas are prevalent in ''The Japanese Quince.'' Noted as much for his short stories as for his novels, particularly *The Forsyte Saga,* Galsworthy has long been regarded as a representative of an outworn narrative tradition, but in recent years his reputation has been enhanced as critics have come to appreciate pre-World War I fiction as a product of its times.

In J. Henry Smit's essay from *The Short Stories of John Galsworthy,* appears a letter from Galsworthy explaining to a reader his purpose in writing ''The Japanese Quince'':

> ''The Japanese Quince'' attempts to convey the feeling that comes to all of us—even the most unlikely—in the spring. It also attempts to produce in the reader the sort of uneasy feeling that now and then we run up against ourselves. It is also a satire on the profound dislike which most of us have of exhibiting the feelings which Nature produces in us, when those feelings are for one quite primitive and genuine.

Smit characterizes ''The Japanese Quince'' as one of the ''few short stories by Galsworthy written in the modern undramatic manner.'' He also notes that many fail to see the point of the story.

In his essay ''Another Way of Looking at a Blackbird'' (*Research Studies,* Vol. 39, June, 1971), Roger Ramsey quotes Laurence Perrine, who analyses the story as a comment on social class. Perrine interprets the characters of Mr. Nilson and Mr. Tandram as men who are ''clearly meant to be representative of a social class'' and the quince tree as ''a radiant symbol for beauty, joy, life, growth, freedom, ecstasy.'' Ramsey summarizes the story as a tale in which ''the reader is left with the pathos of life missed, life . . . understood as dark, mysterious, dangerous, not quite proper.'' He also quotes Herbert J. Muller, who wrote in *Modern Fiction: A Study of Values* (1937) that Galsworthy's ''melancholy is a gentle melancholy, quite lacking in wild, strange, rebellious moments.'' As ''the dark place of his heart continues to sing,'' Ramsey summa-

A quince tree. Its fruit is often used to make preserves.

rizes, ''Mr. Nilson returns to his morning paper, to an 8:30 breakfast, and to that other, safer bird song—the cuckoo clock.'' Appraising the collection *A Motley* in his study *John Galsworthy* (1987), Sanford Sternlicht calls the story ''a charming vignette in which a flowering tree attracts two very conservative business men. . . . The tree brings them together, but alas, their inbred reticence prevents friendship for these mirror-image men, and they return to relating to life through their newspapers.

Impressive for its quantity and its high quality, Galsworthy's body of work won him much praise until the author's death in 1932, when his reputation declined steeply. Targeted by Virginia Woolf and D. H. Lawrence as an outmoded figure of the past—a writer of hackneyed narratives and techniques—Galsworthy's influence remained slight through much of the mid twentieth century. But with the BBC production of *The Forsyte Saga* for television in 1967, coupled with a gradual shift in taste, interest in Galsworthy has rekindled. Above and beyond the shifts in the winds of taste, critics and readers have registered similar criticisms in their observations on Galsworthy's fiction. Expressing the reservations of many, the American poet and critic Conrad Aiken has remarked, ''One has the feeling, occasionally that [Galsworthy] is describing his characters rather than letting them live; that when they face a crisis, he solves it for them *intellectually:* and that again and again he fails to sound the real truth in the situations which he himself has evoked.'' Few would deny that Galsworthy is a skilled technician. Yet, for his indirect observation of life, his reliance on cliche and stock characters, and his use of tidy plots that depend rather heavily on contrivance, Galsworthy is widely deemed a writer with evident limitations, though a writer of astonishing productivity capable of illuminating moments. As a first-rate chronicler of a particular time and a particular class of people, Galsworthy will always hold the interest of readers.

Criticism

David Kippen

Kippen is an educator and specialist on British colonial literature and twentieth-century South African fiction. In the following essay, he examines the many symmetrical reflections in Galsworthy's story and argues that they, together, create a larger rhetorical mirror directed outward at the reader.

What Do I Read Next?

- "The Apple Tree" (1934) is one of Galsworthy's most popular stories. A man returns to the moors of Devonshire, where many years before he had loved and abandoned a farm girl. He learns that she was so distraught at having been jilted by him that she drowned herself. He thus comes to resent his sterile and conventional life and evokes her as a figure of both Aphrodite and Eve, recalling their time together as having been Edenic in its beauty and innocence.
- "Miss Brill" (1922) by Katherine Mansfield is a story of an elderly woman who enjoys a crisp fall day in the park. Her contentment and illusions of community are shattered, however, when she becomes an object of derision by two young lovers.
- "The Secret Sharer" (1909) by Joseph Conrad is the tale of a young ship's captain who harbors a stowaway. The stowaway is the captain's doppelganger, and the ship's journey becomes a journey toward self-knowledge and identity for the captain.
- "The Door in the Wall" (1911) by H. G. Wells tells of a successful, busy English businessman who is fascinated by recurrent glimpses of a mysterious door he first saw and passed through in his childhood. After that initial experience, as he grows to adulthood, he is always too busy to return to the door and pass through to the paradise—he supposes—he found as a child.

At first blush, Galsworthy's "The Japanese Quince" seems quite simple; however, the story's superficial simplicity is deceptive. Mr. Nilson, a well-to-do man of commerce walks out, one fine spring day, into the Garden Square adjacent to his home. He ruminates on spring, meets and converses with a neighbor indistinguishable from him in all but name, becomes self-conscious, and returns to his home. Though this summary fails to describe Nilson's concerns about his heart, which motivate his stroll, and the Japanese quince and blackbird at the story's linear and gravitational center, it is nonetheless a reasonable summation of what happens. What is remarkable about Galsworthy's story is clearly not the originality of his plot nor the depth of his characterizations; he is neither an O. Henry nor a James Joyce. What sets "The Japanese Quince" apart is the nearly perfect formal balance between elements within the story, and the story's mimetic representation of itself in its rhetorical function: the story's smooth surfaces are intended to mirror its reader.

"The Japanese Quince" can be conveniently divided into two halves. In the first, the story follows Nilson's motion toward Tandram. In the second, it follows his retreat back into his house, a retreat mirrored by Tandram's retreat to his home. Now, if one overlooks the preamble to these events in Nilson's house (I shall have more to say about the preamble later), these halves are evenly balanced in length and thematic shape, mirroring each other's content and motion as closely as Nilson is mirrored by Tandram. An important effect of this near-perfect symmetry is that it directs the reader's attention toward the middle, or the fulcrum, upon which the halves balance, toward Nilson and Tandram's closest point of approach:

> Tandram reads the tree's label: "Japanese Quince!"
>
> "Ah!" said Mr. Nilson, "thought so. Early flowerers."
>
> "Very," assented Mr. Tandram, and added: "Quite a feelin' in the air today."
>
> Mr. Nilson nodded.
>
> "It was a blackbird singin'," he said.
>
> "Blackbirds," answered Mr. Tandram. "I prefer them to thrushes myself; more body in the note." And he looked at Mr. Nilson in an almost friendly way.
>
> "Quite," murmured Mr. Nilson. "These exotics, they don't bear fruit."

Two important things happen in this brief passage, each of which demonstrates that Tandram is not only "like" Nilson, but is a perfect reflection of him. The more obvious point is that both men drop a terminal "g" in their sentences (feelin'; singin'). Though this might escape the modern American reader, it certainly would not have passed the eye of an English reader—particularly a reader from Nilson's and Tandram's class background. In turn-of-the-century London, dropping a terminal "g" was briefly popular among the well-to-do; the intended signification was perhaps similar to wearing the same university tie, or offering a Masonic handshake: it said, "we're in the same club." However, within the world depicted in "The Japanese Quince," the dropped consonants signify an even closer kinship. They are best understood as Galsworthy giving the reader a subtle nudge, in effect saying "notice this—they're exactly alike!"

"When the reader looks into this text, Galsworthy asks the reader to see, through the many reflections of Nilson, a reflection of the reader's better self, a self uncorrupted by the world: a self unafraid to sing."

Nilson's and Tandram's exact likeness is expressed with more subtlety in the same passage, this time in Tandram's preference of blackbirds to thrushes. Tandram says "I prefer them to thrushes myself; more body to the note," and Nilson agrees. Interestingly, their agreement goes against the conventional wisdom that says the thrush is a far lovelier singer than the blackbird. Compare, for example, this description from the 1910 *Encyclopedia Britannica* with Tandram's observation: "the notes of the blackbird are rich and full, but monotonous as compared to those of the song-thrush." Why, then, do both men prefer the blackbird's song?

The more obvious answer would be that this unconventional choice underscores that Nilson and Tandram are not similar, but the same. (While it might not say a great deal to observe that two people like cream in their coffee, it says much if they both like it in their beer.) This point has more to yield. Galsworthy could have underscored their likeness with almost any vehicle—as he does with the paper they carry, their outfits, their identical features, even a shared preference for dry toast to buttered—but he chooses to demonstrate it with a shared preference for blackbirds to thrushes. Why?

The blackbird and thrush are both members of the thrush family (*turdidae:* the blackbird's Latin name is *turdis merula,* while the song-thrush is aptly named *turdis musicus*). For my purposes here, the important distinctions between these closely related birds are two: their coloration and their habit. In each regard, Nilson and Tandram prefer the blackbird to the thrush not because of any viable aesthetic theory, but because the blackbird's coloration and habit are so like their own. Unlike the thrush, with arresting, colorful brown back and spotted breast, the blackbird's coloration is—like Nilson's and Tandram's—somber and, among birds, conservative. And while the thrush is commonly seen hopping, robin-like, through grass and field in search of snails, the blackbird's habit is "of a shy and restless disposition, courting concealment, and rarely seen in flocks, or otherwise than singly or in pairs." These habits, as the story shows, are Nilson's, too. So rather than being a distinction without a difference, the men's shared preference for one bird to another demonstrates yet another level at which Nilson's external world reflects and illuminates his internal reality. (A similar point can be drawn from Nilson's comment about the Japanese quince: "these exotics, they don't bear fruit." The quince family is in fact comprised of two groups, both of which blossom, but only one of which produces fruit—a fruit Nilson and Tandram would certainly be familiar with in the form of quince jam. Again, the preference for the less-spectacular fruiting quince to the magnificent flowering quince again shows the text's mirroring of Nilson's unexamined self.)

There is, however, an extremely important distinction to be made between the habits of the blackbird, the quince, and Nilson: while bird and tree recognize and revel in the arrival of spring, he, finally, cannot. At the story's opening, Nilson feels a "peculiar sweetish sensation" at the back of his throat, "a feeling of emptiness just under his fifth rib" (at his heart). Though the opening page and a half paint a convincing portrait of a man on the verge of a heart attack, the reader soon realizes that it is the coming of spring which has Nilson feeling peculiar. Unlike the blackbird, he cannot burst into song, but instead, must search for a reasonable, preferably medical, explanation for his feelings.

In the final analysis, then, Galsworthy's portrait is of a pathology: of a living creature unable to recognize the joyous resurrection that spring brings. And taken at this level alone, the story does what it sets out to do quite well. But ''The Japanese Quince'' also has a rhetorical dimension. Galsworthy's textual mirror is not confined to Nilson, its apparent subject. Just as the fruiting quince, blackbird, Tandram, and even his own ivory-backed mirror serve to reflect Nilson's inner and surface selves back to him; just as he recognizes some of these reflections (his face; Tandram) and does not recognize others (blackbird; quince; and finally, the reflection of his own life in the bird's song), so the text itself mirrors its reader. When the reader looks into this text, Galsworthy asks the reader to see, through the many reflections of Nilson, a reflection of the reader's better self, a self uncorrupted by the world: a self unafraid to sing.

Source: David Kippen, ''The Blackbird's Song,'' for *Short Stories for Students,* Gale, 1998.

Doris Lanier

Lanier is an educator at Georgia Southern University. In the following essay, she discusses the blackbird of Galsworthy's story as a symbol of ''the call to spontaneity,'' a concept that is difficult for Mr. Nilson to accept.

According to Laurence Perrine and Thomas Arp, the blackbird in John Galsworthy's ''The Japanese Quince'' is not symbolically significant: it is ''simply'' a ''part of the tree symbol,'' the ''song at the tree's heart, the expression of lyric ecstasy.'' Galsworthy, they say, ''has chosen a blackbird simply because the English blackbird . . . is a rich singer and would be found in London in the spring.'' In the June 1971 issue of *Research Studies,* Roger Ramsey presents ''another way of looking at [the] blackbird'' in ''The Japanese Quince.'' Ramsey relates the blackbird to the ''empty feeling in Mr. Nilson's heart,'' saying its call is a ''call to the darker places of the heart for which [Mr. Nilson] finds no place in his regulated world.'' To Ramsey, the ''darkness of the heart's recesses, the bird's blackness, and the black frock coat worn by Mr. Tandram imply ''the world of unknowns.'' He even goes so far as to say that ''blackness may suggest nothingness,'' a ''destructive principle or element'' or ''even . . . evil'' but that Mr. Nilson rejects the unknown world and fails ''to immerse himself in this destructive element.'' An even more implausible interpretation of the story is Nathan Cervo's in a 1989 issue of *The Explicator.* Cervo attempts to ''explicate the word 'five''' in ''The Japanese Quince'' ''within the 'Trismegistan' context of [Sir Thomas Browne's] remarks on decussation and 'the Quincunciall Ordination' that Sir Thomas perceives to pervade nature.''

Of the three readings of ''The Japanese Quince,'' Perrine's has the most merit, but it still leaves the reader unsatisfied about the role of the blackbird, which is obviously more than a part of the tree symbolism. On the other hand, Ramsey goes too far in suggesting that the bird's blackness suggests ''evil'' and ''destruction'' and is tempting the darker side of Mr. Nilson, and Cervo's complex interpretation leads the reader through a maze of circles and numbers, the outcome of which is confusion rather than enlightenment. Thus, to understand the role of the blackbird in the story, one must look beyond the interpretations already offered. In doing so, the reader should first fix upon the major problem that is being addressed in the story. In ''The Japanese Quince,'' Galsworthy's main concern is with Mr. Nilson's alienation from man and nature, a condition that is the result of his living in an ordered and structured world where his every action, the way he dresses, his friends, and his lifestyle are dictated by the rules of his society. Mr. Nilson's formal and regulated life, in which everything is identified, labeled, and in place, is reflected in his black frock coat, the clock, his morning ritual, the thermometer, and even the name tag on the quince tree: nothing unexpected or out of place in his ordered world; however, in conforming to a life that is governed by rules and regulations, Mr. Nilson has lost the ability to react spontaneously to life—to react to life freely, without undue concern for others' opinions of his actions or for rules that govern behavior. The story focuses on a moment in his life when he becomes aware of the oppression, the artificiality, and the emptiness of his existence and is tempted to break away from it, a temptation he resists. The blackbird's call, which is clearly directed toward Mr. Nilson, is a call to spontaneity, the quality most lacking in Mr. Nilson's life—a call to the natural life, unencumbered by duty, rules, etiquette.

One sign of approaching emotional and mental illness in a person is a lack of spontaneity—the inability to react instantly and naturally to situations without premeditation or restraint—mainly because the person has become suspicious and afraid of others and is, thus, reluctant to reveal himself to them. Because he is abnormally afraid of doing something wrong, his every word and action becomes calculated, his whole life structured to avoid being "caught out." This is the situation of Mr. Nilson in "The Japanese Quince."

At first glance it is difficult to understand Mr. Nilson's apprehensions. He is clearly a successful person, at least by the standards of his world. He is "well-known in the City," he lives in a comfortable house that has French windows, scrolled iron steps and a garden. Dressed in a black frock coat, with his "neat brown mustaches," his "clear grey eyes," and "the reassuring appearance of good health," his very image says to the world that he is a prosperous man; his feeling of success is intruded on only by an imagined illness, "a peculiar sweetish sensation in the back of his throat, and a feeling of emptiness just under his fifth rib"; yet, his illness isn't physical as a glance in his ivory-backed mirror reveals. And this peculiar feeling is certainly not enough to keep him from his morning walk in the gardens. The residents of Campden Hill, where he lives, can rest assured that Mr. Nilson is one of them.

Mr. Nilson's remarks to himself when alone are spontaneous enough. After noticing the bright blossoms of the quince tree, he says to himself, "Perfect morning. . . . spring at last," as if he has looked forward to such a day. Still talking to himself, he says, "Half an hour to breakfast . . . I'll take a turn in the Gardens." Afterwards, with no one else around, he smiles at the blossoming tree, it is "so alive and pretty!" As he continues to "[smile] at the tree," he begins to look with disdain on others, seeing himself as somewhat superior even though he is unable to understand just what it is that makes him superior. "Morning like this!" he thinks to himself, "and here I am the only person in the Square who has the—to come out and—!" Though it isn't clear what Mr. Nilson is thinking, he obviously believes that he is different from the other residents of Campden Hill in that he has appreciation enough, nerve enough and takes time enough to enjoy the beauty of the morning.

Though proud of himself for being slightly different from his neighbors, he completely freezes when Mr. Tandram, a mirror image of himself, comes on the scene. Even his thoughts are affected by the presence of another. He immediately becomes defensive, "[ceases] to smile," and "[looks] furtively" at "the stranger," (a neighbor for five years!), feeling that he is in an awkward position, that he has "been caught out." Finally, "doubtful as to his proper conduct," he murmurs a very proper, "Fine morning." It is only when Mr. Nilson notices that Mr. Tandram, who is also uncomfortable at the meeting, has a "slight nervousness in his . . . voice," that he is "emboldened to regard him openly." After that, since both feel "caught out," they focus their attention on the tree to avoid looking directly at each other. Then unwilling to share their rejoicing at the beauty of the morning or to admit that, as Emerson says, "beauty has its own excuse for being," they turn the conversation from the beauty of the tree to its label, as if concerned with the technicalities of the physical world rather than with its beauty. On safe ground, they then identify the tree and the bird. Mr. Nilson, wanting to appear practical, points out that the tree is not fruit-bearing, in spite of its pretty blossoms. After this they are both more at ease, almost casual. "Nice fellow," Mr. Nilson thinks, "I rather like him." And for a moment, at least, it appears that they will bridge the gap between them; but in the end both men fail to yield to the spontaneous impulse to be open and friendly and to share the beauty of the day.

"Though he went on to become the foremost critic of the smug, stuffy world he lived in, like Mr. Nilson and Mr. Tandram, Galsworthy was unwilling or unable to forsake his comfortable world and give up its privileges, even for freedom and an unfettered and more joyous life."

The blackbird's reaction to life, to spring, to nature contrasts sharply to that of the two men. If the two men represent a lack of spontaneity, the blackbird, one of the most common creatures of nature and, by the way, very sociable, symbolizes the spontaneous response of a living being to life and nature. The blackbird appears at three strategic positions in the story, indicating that Galsworthy meant for it to have a special function. It first appears shortly after Mr. Nilson enters the garden and begins his "promenade." After two revolutions of the circular path in the garden, he, again, feels the sensation of "some sweetish liquor in course within him" and "a faint aching just above his heart." Although somewhat concerned about his condition, he is about to continue his "promenade," when "a blackbird close by [bursts] into song." Interestingly, though Mr. Nilson has seen the quince tree from his dressing room window, after going outside he does not notice the tree until the blackbird's call directs him to it. Seeing the tree's beauty, Mr. Nilson "smiles," probably for the first time that morning, and, instead of passing on, "[stays] there smiling at the tree." At this point Mr. Nilson sees his neighbor, whose close resemblance to him suggests that Mr. Nilson for the first time confronts himself, realizes something is wrong in his life, and hears the call to a different life.

The blackbird calls the second time at the end of the short conversation between Mr. Nilson and Mr. Tandram after Mr. Nilson thinks, "Nice fellow, this, I rather like him." At the moment when he is obviously about to drop his guard and offer Mr. Tandram his friendship, the blackbird, perched in the heart of the tree, "[gives] a loud, clear call"—a call to Mr. Nilson to respond from his heart; but Mr. Nilson rejects the call, drops his eyes, and suddenly sees Mr. Tandram as "a little foolish," as if "he [has] seen himself." A "shade" also [passes] over Mr. Tandram's face. Even though the call to life is "loud" and "clear," when faced with the choice between their world and the world of freedom, the two men deliberately choose the smug, comfortable and ordered world with which they are familiar.

As the two men retreat to their homes, the blackbird appears the third time, "chanting out his heart," while Mr. Nilson pauses "on the top step" of his home, his song unsung, again feeling "that queer sensation, that choky feeling in his throat." It is clear that he will go inside, deliberately rejecting the call to live a more spontaneous life, even though his sigh and his peculiar feelings indicate that he is not happy with his life as it is.

It is of interest to note that Galsworthy himself would have identified with the two men in "The Japanese Quince," who were torn between conforming to their world or rebelling against it. Born in 1867 to a prosperous family in Surrey, England, Galsworthy grew up in a home with many servants and gardeners, who tended the beautiful grounds where Galsworthy played cricket, croquet, and tennis with his friends, most of whom were as privileged as he. While he was getting an education at Harrow and Oxford, his circle of friends included mostly others from his class. Always "elegant in the extreme," he has been described as "a stuffed shirt," who lived in a "stuffy, selfish world" governed by rules and concern for appearances. Galsworthy broke away from his conventional life briefly as a young man, when he met and fell in love with his cousin's wife, whom he later married. But, according to David Holloway's book on Galsworthy, "Galsworthy was too conventional a man ever to be able to break entirely free from his birth and upbringing," and was, in fact, "a prisoner of his class." Though he went on to become the foremost critic of the smug, stuffy world he lived in, like Mr. Nilson and Mr. Tandram, he was unwilling or unable to forsake his comfortable world and give up its privileges, even for freedom and an unfettered and more joyous life.

Source: Doris Lanier, "The Blackbird in John Galsworthy's 'The Japanese Quince'," in *English Language Notes,* Vol. XXX, No. 2, December, 1992, pp. 57–62.

Nathan Cervo

Cervo is an educator at Franklin Pierce College, in Rindge, New Hampshire. In the following essay, he delineates the similarities between Galsworthy's "The Japanese Quince" and the works of Sir Thomas' 1716 book Christian Morals.

John Galsworthy (1867–1933) won the Nobel Prize for Literature in 1932. He had been educated at Harrow and Oxford. He graduated from Oxford with honors in law. It is therefore highly likely that he not only read Sir Thomas Browne, whose works were considered of crucial importance in the liberal arts program of that day, but brought a fine and attentive mind to his perusal of Sir Thomas's writings. In what follows, I shall explicate the word "five," as it appears in Galsworthy's short story "The Japanese Quince" (first published in 1910), within the "Trismegistan" context of Sir Thomas's remarks on decussation and "the Quincunciall Ordination" that Sir Thomas perceives to pervade nature. The similarity between "quince" and "quincunciall" is immediately apparent.

In *Christian Morals* (1716), "Part the Third," Sir Thomas speaks of Hermes Thrice-Great (Hermes Trismegistus) thus: "*Trismegistus* his Circle, whose center is everywhere, and circumference nowhere, was no hyperbole." In "The Japanese Quince," "Mr. Nilson, well known in the City, opened the window of his dressing room" and looked out at the Japanese quince. "Nilson" suggests nil, "nothing," and the name in this light means "son of nothing." Further, although on the literal level "the City" refers to the financial and commercial center of London, the English Wall Street, on the evocative level "the City" resonates Dante's Inferno, *"la citta dolente"* ("the doleful city of Dis"). In "The Japanese Quince," it is not Galsworthy who is "nihilistic" but Mr. Nilson, for whom, as soulless capitalist—this is not to say that all capitalists are soulless—time is not the medium for the message of spiritual salvation but a mechanism for making money: time is money. Galsworthy regards this view, or obsession, as "cuckoo," no matter how unselfconscious or urbane it may seem to be. He thus tells us that "A cuckoo clock struck eight," whereupon Mr. Nilson leaves his mausoleumlike apartment "and proceeded to pace the circular path." He makes "two revolutions," the effect of which is to bear in upon him the fact that he is dead, although he is not aware of his demise. Earlier, scrutinizing his image in "an ivory-backed handglass," he admires the "reassuring appearance of good health," the details of which, as the reader recognizes, constellate nothing more than the undertaker's cosmetic art and augment the morbid aura exhaled by the "peculiar sweetish sensation in the back of his throat, and a feeling of emptiness just under his fifth rib," details that translate to embalming fluid, the surfeiting scent of flowers of a distinctly mortuary cast, and to the fact that his heart has stopped beating. Ironically, Mr. Nilson's "meditations on the price of Tintos" is reprised in and given existential dimension by his mirror image in "the ivory-backed" glass.

The "eight" that the cuckoo clock strikes and the "two revolutions" on "the circular path" that Mr. Nilson ("son of zero," so to speak) makes introduce and sustain, when taken in tandem with the mirror, ideas concerning decussation and the quincunx presented and discussed by Sir Thomas Browne about two centuries earlier. Decussation, derived from the Latin *decem* ("ten"), means the crossing of lines in the form of the figure X (Roman sign for "ten"). Looking at X, we can see two V (Roman sign for "five") figures comprising it, one inverted, as if the mirror image of the top one. For Sir Thomas, it is highly significant that the ancient

"Galsworthy calls attention to the crucial importance of the number five in his story thus: 'Mr. Nilson saw at a distance of perhaps five yards a little tree'; and, upon the appearance of Mr. Tandram: 'It was his next-door neighbor, Mr. Tandram, well known in the City, who had occupied the adjoining house for some five years.'"

Egyptians decussated the arms of their dead. A critical part of the undertaker's art was to arrange the arms of the corpse in a figure "ten" ("X"). In this figure, the ancient Egyptians perceived the meaning of the pyramid and its completed mirror image in eternity. The line that divided (if division were possible in so spiritualized an ideogram) the tips of the pyramid signified death, or what passes for death in the world. Basically, one's earthly sojourn, considered solely as time, defined itself as nullity for the ancient Egyptians. The upper inverted pyramid signified omneity. As Sir Thomas puts it in *Religio Medici* (1643), in the completed decussation ideogram "Omneity informed Nullity into an Essence."

In "The Japanese Quince," Mr. Nilson does not so much persevere in his nothingness as *perseverate* it. Another pun is possible, since the fruit of the Japanese quince is in the main considered ornamentable, that is, uneatable, though the quince may be used in preserves to delightful effect. The cuckoo's "eight" takes on the spectral character of the decussation motif, with the pyramids giving way to the two chambers of an hourglass. Mr. Nilson gives an edge to both hourglass chambers as symbols for time when he makes his "two revolutions" in "the Square Gardens." Like a necromancer tracing mystical signs in the dust or on the floor, his "two revolutions" draw Mr. Tandram toward him. Mr. Tandram, Nilson's mirror image in every detail, joins Mr. Nilson. They contemplate the Japanese quince in tandem. Instead of allowing its supernal meaning to affect them, they resort to a label to reduce the peculiar fascination that the tree exercises over them to a "name." The name Tandram not only suggests "tan" (as in "I've been to Bermuda," so to speak) and "dram" (a small amount of liquor, as in a dram of brandy) but serves as an anagram (symbolic, in Christian terms, of the mutilated and jumbled Word) for damn rat, nard mat, mad rant, and man dart (this latter distinctly penile in its suggestiveness and explaining why Mr. Nilson uneasily "dropped his eyes" in the company of Mr. Tandram). It would appear that one may be in a maze when one's human nature is radically thwarted by routine (damn rat), that Mr. Nilson will always be coming out into "the Square Gardens" to meet Mr. Tandram uneasily (just as the phoenix, according to myth, was supposed to incinerate itself every five hundred years and rise renewed from it nard mat consisting of cinnamon, unguents, and other spices and ointments), and that when the calm jargon of "the City" is translated into human value, it amounts to nothing more than mad rant.

In *The Garden of Cyrus* (1658), Sir Thomas Browne, expatiating on the "Quincunciall order" that pervades the universe, writes:

> Lastly, it is no wonder that this Quincunciall order was first and is still affected as gratefull unto the eye: For all things are seen Quincuncially; for at the eye the Pyramidal rayes, from the object, receive a decussation, and so strike a second base upon the Retina or hinder coat, the proper organ of Vision; wherein the pictures from objects are represented, answerable to the paper, or wall in the dark chamber; after the decussation of the rayes at the hole of the horny-coat, and their refraction upon the Christalline humour, answering the *foramen* of the window, and the *convex* or burning-glasses, which refract the rayes that enter it.

In "The Japanese Quince," just as the cuckoo's "eight" is tipped on its side by the emergence of another generic "son of nothing" (Mr. Tandram) and thus forms with Mr. Nilson the symbol of infinity, so Galsworthy tilts the X of the decussation of the ancient Egyptians over on its side. His finer optics thus reveal two V-figures facing each other in tandem. It is no longer a question of omneity and nullity but of two nullities. Time does not ascend to eternity in order that eternity may grace existence with essence. Time is curtailed as time, and this is the quality of Mr. Nilson's damnation. The "blackbird," which Mr. Tandram fails to recognize as a "thrush" (the English blackbird is every bit as much a thrush as is the nightingale), singing in the tree evokes the nursery rhyme:

> Four and twenty blackbirds
> Baked in a pie.
> When the pie was opened,
> The birds began to sing.
> Now wasn't that a dainty dish
> To set before the King!

The twenty-four blackbirds suggest the twenty-four hours that make up a day. Within a Christian context, the King would clearly refer to Christ, to Sir Thomas's "Christalline humour." In addition, the blackbird is a sociable bird. In Galsworthy's story, a single blackbird sings amid fruit fit for marmalade, for preserves (symbolically, as in self-preservation and delimiting one's preserves, insisting upon them even to the point of war). The blackbird thus signifies Mr. Nilson's own isolation, which is only frustratingly and lubriciously tempered by the "shade" of an equally exploitive, autoerotic alter ego (Mr. Tandram). Soul functions as "hole" in this lateral or horizontal (time-oriented, time-saturated) mock-decussation of "Vision." The face-off of the two purely timeous halves of the knocked-over decussation are two horizontal five-figures or V's touching each other like the mirror image of the beak of a solitary "blackbird." Galsworthy calls attention to the crucial importance of the number five in his story thus: "Mr. Nilson saw at a distance of perhaps five yards a little tree"; and, upon the appearance of Mr. Tandram: "It was his next-door neighbor, Mr. Tandram, well known in the City, who had occupied the adjoining house for some five years."

Source: Nathan Cervo, "Galsworthy's, 'Japanese Quince'," in *The Explicator,* Vol. 47, No. 2, Winter, 1989, pp. 38–41.

Sources

Field, Louise Maunsell. "Mr. Galsworthy in War and Peace," in *The New York Times Review of Books,* March 28, 1920, p. 139.

Ramsey, Roger. "Another Way of Looking at a Blackbird," in *Research Studies,* Vol. 39, No. 2, June, 1971, pp. 152-54.

Smit, J. Henry. An excerpt from *The Short Stories of John Galsworthy,* Haskell House, 1966, pp. 43-6, 56-60, 143-46.

Sternlicht, Sanford. "The Short-Story Writer," in *John Galsworthy,* Twayne, 1987, pp. 87-100.

Further Reading

Bradbury, Malcolm and James McFarlane, editors. *Modernism: 1890-1930,* Penguin, 1991.

A study considering the critical movement known as Modernism, which emerged in the years 1890-1930. Providing a comprehensive survey of the various art forms expressive of Modernism, this study examines the defining features of the movement.

Cox, C. B. and Dyson, A. E., editors. *The Twentieth-Century Mind: History, Ideas, and Literature in Britain,* Oxford University Press, 1972.

This collection invites a number of well-known scholars to write about the climate of thought in the early twentieth-century in Britain. The essays address, among other things, the social, political, economic, and religious conditions of life in the first quarter of the twentieth century.

Dupre, Catherine. *John Galsworthy: A Biography,* Collins, 1976.

An authoritative, thorough look at the events of Galsworthy's life.

"John Galsworthy," in *Short Story Criticism,* Vol. 22, edited by Margaret Haerens, Gale, 1996, pp. 55-103.

Contains excerpts of previously published criticism on Galsworthy's works. Included are excerpts from critical works by Sheila Kaye-Smith, L. P. Hartley, Isabel Paterson, and Sanford Sternlicht, among many others.

Ginden, James. *John Galsworthy's Life and Art,* University of Michigan Press, 1979.

Contextualizing its discussion through historical material, this study considers the ways in which the social and cultural conditions of Galsworthy's life came to influence his life's work.

Perrine, Laurence. *Literature: Structure, Sound, and Sense,* 5th ed., Harcourt, Brace, Jovanovich, 1988, pp. 61–4.

Argues that "The Japanese Quince" is a commentary upon social class. Perrine interprets the characters of Nilson and Tandram as men who are representatives of their social class, and the quince tree as "a radiant symbol for beauty, joy, life, growth, freedom, ecstasy."

A Jury of Her Peers

Susan Glaspell

1917

Susan Glaspell's "A Jury of Her Peers," first published in 1917, is a short story adaptation of her one-act play *Trifles.* Since their first publication, both the story and the play have appeared in many anthologies of women writers and playwrights. Although *Trifles* was written first and performed in 1916 by Glaspell's theater troupe, the Provincetown Players, the play was not published until three years after the short story appeared in the March 5, 1917 edition of *Everyweek* magazine. Inspired by events witnessed during her years as a court reporter in Iowa, Glaspell crafted a story in which a group of rural women deduce the details of a murder in which a woman has killed her husband. Understanding the clues left amidst the "trifles" of the woman's kitchen, the women are able to outsmart their husbands, who are at the farmhouse to collect evidence, and thus prevent the wife from being convicted of the crime. The play was received warmly, and Glaspell made only minor changes in adapting the play into a short story.

Glaspell claimed that "A Jury of Her Peers" was based on an actual court case she covered as a reporter for the *Des Moines Daily.* On December 2, 1900, sixty-year-old farmer John Hossack was murdered in Indianola, Iowa. His skull was crushed by an ax while he and his wife were asleep in bed. His wife, Margaret, was tried for the crime and eventually released due to inconclusive evidence. Like Minnie Wright, the main character of Glaspell's story, Mrs. Hossack claimed not to have seen the

murderer. The trial was attended many of the town's women. Among them was the sheriff's wife, who showed much sympathy to Mrs. Hossack throughout the trial despite having initially testified against her. Critics believe that Glaspell based the character of Mrs. Peters on this woman. Because women were not allowed to be jurors at the trial, Glaspell created a jury of those female peers in her short story.

Author Biography

Playwright, novelist, and short story writer Susan Glaspell was born July 1, 1876, in Davenport, Iowa, though some sources cite her birth year as 1882. She received a rural, middle-class public school education. Eventually she attended Drake University in Des Moines, Iowa, and graduated in 1899 with a degree in journalism. In college Glaspell acquired several awards and made a name for herself as a competitive student. Following her graduation, she began work as a reporter for the *Des Moines Daily,* writing on local crime and politics, an unusual occupation for a woman of her time.

In 1913 Glaspell married playwright George Cram Cook. The couple never had children together, but she became stepmother to his two children from a previous marriage. They spent summers at their East Coast property and in 1915 founded the Provincetown Players, an organization of playwrights and actors, in Provincetown, Massachusetts. Recognized as a dramatist in her own right, Glaspell often acted in her own productions and provided artistic support for other young writers and performers, most notably Eugene O'Neill. Glaspell was widowed in 1924 and married playwright Norman Matson. They divorced in 1932.

In her lifetime, Glaspell wrote thirteen plays, fourteen novels, and more than fifty essays, articles, and short stories. In 1931 she became only the second woman playwright to win the Pulitzer Prize. *Trifles,* the play upon which ''A Jury of Her Peers'' is based, is Glaspell's most anthologized work and accounts for much of her popularity as a twentieth-century American playwright. She died in Provincetown of pleural embolism in 1948. Glaspell had lived and worked during a time when ambition and independence characterized many women, whose newfound political power was a driving force behind the suffrage and the temperance movements. This strong sense of female identity challenged the perceptions of many who viewed the public realm as a ''man's world'' only.

Plot Summary

The story begins with Mrs. Martha Hale being hurried along by her husband, Lewis Hale. She leaves her kitchen in the middle of making bread, hating the fact that she is leaving things half done. She accompanies George Henderson, the county attorney, Sheriff Henry Peters, and his wife, Mrs. Peters, to the scene of a crime at the home of the Wrights, a couple they all knew. Mrs. Hale has been asked along to keep Mrs. Peters company, even though the two women have met only once before. The crime they are investigating is the murder of Mr. John Wright. His wife, Mrs. Minnie Wright, whom the women refer to by her maiden name, Minnie Foster, is being held at the jail as a suspect. The Hales, the Peters, and Attorney Henderson all meet at the scene to determine what might have happened the day before.

Mr. Hale and his son, who are the Wrights' closest neighbors, were the first to see Minnie and her dead husband. Mr. Hale tells how they arrived at the Wright home to find Minnie in her rocking chair looking ''queer'' and pleating her apron. When Mr. Hale asked to see John, she calmly told him he was upstairs and had been strangled to death; she claimed that someone had slipped a rope under her husband's neck and killed him while they were sleeping. Mr. Hale explained that he was there to inquire if John wanted a telephone installed; a request that caused Minnie to laugh. Shortly afterward, the coroner arrived with the sheriff to begin investigating the scene and Minnie was taken away to jail as a suspect.

The men are slightly appalled at Minnie's messy kitchen and criticize her housekeeping. Convinced that there is ''nothing here but kitchen things,'' the men search for clues upstairs where the body was found and outside in the barn, while the women stay in the kitchen and gather some items to take to Minnie. Among the unfinished and badly sewn quilting, the jars of preserves that have burst due to the cold, and the dirty pots and cooking area, they begin to uncover their own clues about why Minnie might have wanted to kill her husband. They uncover evidence that the men overlook, such as the crooked stitch of the quilt, Minnie's old and drab clothing, the rundown kitchen in which she had to

Susan Glaspell

cook, and her beloved canary that had been strangled and saved in a box. Mrs. Hale has known Minnie since they were young girls. She discusses with Mrs. Peters how Minnie had been more cheerful and sociable before she was married. She notices that she had changed into a more serious, lonely, and introverted person after she became Mrs. Wright. Mrs. Hale recalls what a strict and cold person Mr. Wright was. She remarks that he was too selfish and somber a person to match Minnie's lively and generous spirit. Over and over Mrs. Hale remarks that she should have visited Minnie more often—it was a crime not to have seen her in over a year. Mrs. Peters tries to comfort her by stating that "somehow, we just don't see how it is with other folks till—something comes up."

Both Mrs. Hale and Mrs. Peters imagine what it must have felt like to live in such a horrible environment. Mrs. Peters sadly remembers the solitude of her farmhouse after her only child died. Mrs. Hale recalls the hurry in which she left her kitchen earlier that day, with her cooking and cleaning half done. The women discuss how only a distracted woman could leave her housework unfinished, her kitchen untidy, and her stitching crooked.

Together, they determine that such a lonely household could only make Minnie "lose heart." Seeing the broken hinge on the bird cage, they speculate that the canary may have been killed by her husband, much the way they believe he killed Minnie's spirit with his overbearing manner. They blame Mr. Wright for Minnie not having nice clothes to wear in public and for having to live and cook in a rundown home without even a telephone to keep her connected to the outside world. Both women put themselves in Minnie's place to try and feel what she may have been feeling. All the while they exchange knowing, uncomfortable glances.

The women repair her poor quilting and concoct a story of a runaway cat to explain the disappearance of the canary. In doing so, they conceal clues that might reveal Minnie's motive for murder. Neither one is able to say for certain who they believe is guilty of the murder, but they suggest that all of this information about Minnie, her marriage, and the dead canary holds the answer to who committed the crime. The women do not tell the men about the canary or about their assumptions about Minnie's unhappy marriage. The story ends with Mrs. Hale and Mrs. Peters nervously removing the canary and the unfinished quilting from the premises.

Characters

Minnie Foster

See Minnie Wright

Lewis Hale

Lewis Hale is an Iowa farmer and a neighbor of the Wrights. He is called on the day after John Wright's murder to participate in the investigation as a witness. He tells the police how he found the body in the upstairs bedroom and of Minnie's peculiar behavior that day. Through his narrative the reader and the other characters learn about Minnie's state of mind after the murder. He tends to be long-winded when he speaks, and his wife is frequently worried that he will not get the story straight. Along with the other male characters, Mr. Hale searches for clues in all the obvious places, yet misses some of the most crucial evidence in the kitchen.

Martha Hale

Martha Hale is the only character visible for the entire story. The narrator follows her from her own kitchen to Wright's kitchen. While waiting for the detective to investigate the premises, she conducts her own examination of the scene. Rather than search Minnie Wright's home with the critical eye of the law, Mrs. Hale observes it with the sympathetic eye of a farm wife. As an acquaintance of Minnie's for over twenty years, she provides the reader with background on what Minnie was like before and after marriage. She represents loyalty and female solidarity by concealing evidence that would implicate Minnie in the death of her husband.

George Henderson

George Henderson is the young county lawyer who intends to prosecute Minnie Wright for the murder of her husband. As part of the investigating party, he asks questions and take notes. His sarcasm about the women's attention to minor domestic details aggravates the women and shows him to be narrow-minded.

Henry Peters

As a man of the law, the sheriff's main goal is to convict John Wright's murderer. He is described as the perfect example of a sheriff—heavy and big-voiced. He is driven by the belief that he and his assembly of men can solve the crime of their own accord without the help of the women. He dismisses the women's observations as a silly waste of time.

Mrs. Peters

Mrs. Peters's first name is never revealed in the story. She is the sheriff's wife, and the county prosecutor reminds her that she is "married to the law." Her first tendency is to discourage Mrs. Hale from rushing to conclusions and tampering with the evidence they uncover in the kitchen. Later, Mrs. Peters's female sensibility causes her to pardon Minnie of her possible crime, and she assists Mrs. Hale in concealing evidence. For the greater part of the story, she is clearly undecided about whether to side with the men, who want to prosecute Minnie, or with Mrs. Hale, who is sympathetic to Minnie's predicament. Hers is the "swing vote" on whether or not to "convict" Minnie.

Sheriff Peters

See Henry Peters

John Wright

John Wright is Minnie's husband, and his murder sets in motion the action of the story. Like Minnie, he does not appear in the story and, thus, cannot defend himself. He is described by both the men and the women as a selfish, cold, unsociable man who did not care much for his wife's needs and opinions. Mrs. Hale and Mrs. Peters assume that he strangled Minnie's canary, which they find tucked away in Minnie's sewing basket. Since Mr. Wright has been strangled himself, the women hypothesize that Minnie murdered him in retaliation for what he did to her pet bird.

Minnie Wright

Minnie Wright is the main suspect in her husband's murder, but she does not appear in the story. Thus, she is not allowed to speak for herself; and the reader comes to know her solely by what Mrs. Hale says about her and by the "clues" she left in the kitchen that reveal her lifestyle and her frame of mind at the time of the murder. Mrs. Hale's reminiscence of Minnie Foster, the girl she was before she married John Wright, tells readers that she was a lively and pretty young woman who always dressed well and sang in the church choir. Mr. Hale's account of the Mrs. Wright he found after the murder indicates a "queer" woman who rocks in her chair while her husband lies dead upstairs.

Media Adaptations

- "A Jury of Her Peers" was adapted into a thirty minute motion picture of the same title in 1981, directed by Sally Heckel and produced by Texture Films in New York.

Themes

Gender Roles

Much of the tension in "A Jury of Her Peers" results from what the women understand and what the men are blind to. The kitchen, during the time the story takes place, was the sole domain of the wife. Wives themselves, Mrs. Hale and Mrs. Peters are able to determine Mrs. Wright's frame of mind from how she left her kitchen. The men are scornful of the messy kitchen, and ultimately dismissive of

Topics for Further Study

- "A Jury of Her Peers" is based on Glaspell's own one-act play *Trifles*. Consider what reasons the author may have had for rewriting the play in short story form. What are the main differences between telling a story through narration and telling it through drama? How might the story be different if it were adapted as another form, such as a poem or a film?
- Read *Trifles* and write an essay comparing the differences between the short story and the play. Which gives you a better idea of who Minnie is? Are there any improvements that you find notable in the short story? Any distractions?
- Think about the significance of the title "A Jury of Her Peers." What images might it evoke for a reader? What might it represent in relation to the story?
- Glaspell's story demonstrates the domestic roles women were expected to live by at the turn of the century. Research how most women lived back then. What things have changed and how? What has remained the same? Why might some things have changed while others have not?
- In what ways does "A Jury of Her Peers" resemble a classic murder mystery? In what ways does it differ from one? What do these similarities and differences say about justice and the duty of law-abiding citizens?
- Suppose the situation in "A Jury of Her Peers" were reversed: Suppose John Wright had been a pleasant man, full of the love of life until his marriage to Minnie Foster, at which point he found himself thoroughly dominated by someone who specialized in non-stop belittling remarks and verbal abuse. Suppose John were reduced to an emotional wreck after several years of this treatment, to the point that he killed Minnie; and suppose a handful of John's similarly dominated friends covered up the crime by removing small pieces of circumstantial evidence from the crime scene. How would your view of John's crime and his friends' "male solidarity" differ from your view of Minnie's crime and her friend's "female solidarity" in "A Jury of Her Peers"? Why?

what it contains. The sheriff comments that there's "nothing here but kitchen things," and when Mrs. Peters laments that the jars of preserves have burst from the cold, Mr. Hale says that "women are used to worrying over trifles." Yet the women know that Mrs. Wright would not choose to have such a shabby or ill-kept kitchen. When the attorney notices the filthy dish towels and says, "Not much of a housekeeper, would you say, ladies?" Mrs. Hale replies that "Those towels get dirty awful quick. Men's hands aren't always as clean as they might be."

Because both women have been farmer's wives themselves, they understand the loneliness of living in isolation on a farm, and they can understand how upset Mrs. Wright would be over the death of her canary. They also recognize that the erratic stitching on her quilting squares, which contradicts her earlier, neater stitching was the result of a distracted mind. Eventually, the men leave the women in the kitchen to search for clues in "more important" areas of the house, but not before telling Mrs. Peters and Mrs. Hale to keep their eyes open. The attorney's comment—"you women might come upon a clue to the motive" indicates that he does not think they could deduct a motive, but only stumble on to evidence by mistake. Mr. Hale takes this line of reasoning even farther by asking "would the women know a clue if they did come upon it?" Such an attitude towards women in the room of the house they know best highlights not only the differences between men's and women's household roles, but also that the women's role is devalued by men. The stark divisions between men's and women's roles is noted by Mrs. Hale, who says "I'd hate to have men comin' into my kitchen . . . snoopin' round and criticizin'."

The story makes it clear that men have obligations in the home as well. The women note that Mrs. Wright's clothing was worn and shabby. "You don't enjoy things when you feel shabby," Mrs. Hale says by way of explaining why she probably had not seen much of Minnie Wright in public since she had gotten married twenty years ago. They also note the decrepit state of the stove. When contemplating what they should do about the clues, Mrs. Hale says that "The law is the law—and a bad stove is a bad stove," and thinks about "what it would mean, year after year, to have that stove to wrestle with." Mr. Hale originally went to the Wrights' house to ask if John Wright would install a telephone, "all the women-folks like the telephones," he says, but by the way Minnie had laughed at his proposition, it is inferred that John Wright would have denied his wife even that bit of comfort in her own home.

Deception and Loyalty

As Mrs. Peters and Mrs. Hale piece together a probable scenario for Mr. Wright's murder, they become torn between deceiving the men, particularly Mrs. Peters' husband, who is the sheriff, and maintaining their loyalty to a woman with whom they identify. Because the men are so reluctant to consider the quilting, the preserves, and the state of the kitchen to be significant details of the crime, the women may feel that any attempts to convince them of how important these "trifles" really are will only be met with more dismissive sarcasm. "The law is the law—and a bad stove is a bad stove," says Mrs. Hale, succinctly summarizing their quandary. Their deception is borne of their loyalty to another woman—even if it is someone neither of them knew well. Even after the men have searched the grounds and are returning to the kitchen, their minds are not made up. At the end, the attorney tells Mrs. Peters that "a sheriff's wife is married to the law." when asked if she sees it that way, and she replies "Not—just that way."

Public vs. Private Life

The men investigating the crime are unsuccessful in determining a motive that would have prompted Minnie to kill her husband because the are in unfamiliar territory. The division of public and private life in the early twentieth century was very clear. Women remained isolated in the private sphere as homemakers, and men were required to function in the public world as breadwinners. Women did not commonly have knowledge of the more male-dominated institutions of law or business, and men were generally unaware of what was involved in homemaking and raising children. Since the domestic realm of the kitchen is so foreign to the sheriff and his male companions, they do not view its contents with the same understanding that the women do. To them, a dirty towels and dishes can signify only one thing—sloppy housekeeping. But the women know that most homemakers are conscientious and that dirty towels and dishes may be symptoms of an unsettled or disrupted mind. Because they are unfamiliar with women's work, the men are quick to dismiss it.

Style

Omniscient Narrator

The third-person omniscient narrator in "A Jury of Her Peers" is capable of relating the thoughts of each character. It differs from a first-person narrator in that it does not tell the story from only one character's point of view but sees things from a central vantage point. Omniscient narration allows readers to witness the physical actions and often the mental and emotional states of more than one character. It provides readers with information about things that the characters themselves do not say aloud, or that they are unaware of. In the story, Mrs. Hale's husband says that "women are used to worrying over trifles." The omniscient narrator relates that he says it in a tone of "good-natured superiority." It is not likely that Mr. Hale realized he was demeaning the women, but the narrator comments on it.

The narrator, however, does focus on the women in the kitchen. When the men leave to do the police work of searching the barn and the bedroom upstairs, the narrator does not report what they are doing. One reason could be that whatever they found or did not find could not be as significant to the story as what the women uncovered. The narrative perspective calls attention to what is most important for the reader to know. It reflects the decision of the author to foreground some details and events and to overlook others.

Symbolism

Symbolism is a literary technique in which something comes to represent something else, without losing its original meaning. It is an important device used by writers who want to impart an added dimension of meaning to a character or some element of the plot. The two main symbols in "A Jury of Her Peers" are the canary and the quilt pieces. The canary is a symbol for Minnie, who used to sing in the church choir. Mrs. Hale confronts the comparison directly: "come to think of it, she was kind of like a bird herself. Real sweet and pretty, but kind of timid and—fluttery." But the women find the bird dead; strangled, a symbol for Minnie's squelched liveliness in a drab house. Just as Mr. Wright had clipped his wife's wings and left her to toil alone in an insufficient kitchen, Mr. Wright killed the bird, "a bird that sang. She used to sing. He killed that too." Both the bird's song and Minnie's happiness have been eliminated.

The women's discovery of Minnie's haphazard quilting opens up another interesting symbolic interpretation. The squares can be said to be symbolic of John Wright. Though Minnie at first was dutiful towards her quilting, making sure the stitches were meticulous, her most recent squares exhibit angry, sloppy stitches that reveal inner torment. Mrs. Hale and Mrs. Peters question whether or not Minnie intended to knot or quilt the squares together. When they tell the men that they believe she intended to knot the quilt, that knot becomes symbolic for the other knot that Minnie made—in the noose around her husband's neck. Mrs. Hale's final remark that Minnie did, in fact, intend to knot the quilt symbolizes her belief that Minnie is guilty.

Historical Context

Turn of the Century Images of Womanhood

The era between 1914 and 1939 is sometimes referred to the modernist period of literary history. During this time, the social climate of many Western countries began to change dramatically. In 1917 the United States entered World War I. This international event threw many accepted social traditions into chaos. While the men were off fighting in the war and dying in greater numbers than ever before, women remained on the home front and increased independence was necessary for their survival. In order to support themselves and their families, mothers, sisters, wives, and daughters began to move into the work force and take charge of their family's well-being. Modernism in literature was a movement characterized by a rejection of traditional literary methods and values. Gone was the adherence to bourgeois values, and in its place was an often pessimistic sense of foreboding and questioning.

The poet W. H. Auden characterized the national sentiment of this era and its response to women's increasing independence as the "Age of Anxiety." The rise of women's suffrage challenged the male world of politics and government and ended their absolute power over the public realm. In 1918 women in England were granted the legal right to vote and suffrage for American women followed in 1920. Political power and economics were now shared—at least somewhat—between the sexes, and the preexisting gender divide between public man and private woman no longer provided the security of male mastery. English writer D. H. Lawrence's essay "Matriarchy" exaggerated a picture of these times by theorizing that a matriarchy, or woman-centered society, was growing out of the modernist era and taking control, and destroying the "mastery" of the patriarchy, or male-centered society.

In rural parts of the country, however, change was slow in coming. Away from the cities, farmers continued to toil the land like they always had. The coming of the automobile, motorized farm equipment, and the telephone began to break down some of the forces of isolation on the farm, but many farmers were not wealthy enough to take advantage of these new technologies. The spirit of the pioneers, for those who had lost touch with their rural roots, became a popular topic for literature. Laura Ingalls Wilder's *Little House on the Prairie* books romanticized the simplicity of rural and small town life, and Willa Cather's *O Pioneers!* and *My Antonia* celebrated the resolve of the Midwest's first pioneers. In stark contrast to this trend was Glaspell's "A Jury of Her Peers," an unromantic look at the

A kitchen from a turn-of-the-century farmhouse. All cooking and baking was done from scratch, and homemakers had to contend with such limitations as small ovens and rudimentary iceboxes.

loneliness, isolation, and desperation that can result from the harsh life of the prairie.

Critical Overview

Little criticism of ''A Jury of Her Peers'' dates from the time of its initial publication or from 1927 when it was collected with Glaspell's other stories in the collection *A Jury of Her Peers.* Only after the story gained acclaim during the 1970s did critical interest in it grow. However, theater reviews of *Trifles,* performed in 1916, one year before the publication of ''A Jury of Her Peers,'' relate that critics found the performance to be the Provincetown Players' finest to date.

In *Susan Glaspell: A Research and Production Sourcebook,* Mary Papke lists six reviews of the play, only one of which did not enthusiastically

Compare & Contrast

- **1910s:** The average salary for farm workers is $830 a year.

  1990s: The average farm laborer makes approximately $22,000 a year.

- **1917:** The United States enters World War I. Women are prohibited by law from fighting in the battlefield, but nearly 9,000 Red Cross nurses, including many women, serve with the Army and Navy Nurse Corps in Europe.

  1991: During the Persian Gulf War, 13 American women soldiers are killed and two are taken prisoner.

- **1880s:** Approximately 2.5 million U.S. women engage in paid work.

  1990s: Over 3 million U.S. women work at least two jobs to make ends meet.

- **1917:** The homicide rate is 6.9 per 100,000 people in the United States.

  1992: The homicide rate is 9.3 per 100,000 people in the United States.

---

recommend it. Early critiques from the *New York Dramatic Mirror* gave it high praise as a drama of mystery and suspense and *Theatre Magazine* found the female actors in their interpretation of women's intuition ingenious. On the other hand, the *New York Times* critic found both its acting and dialogue unsatisfactory. Later reviews of European productions agreed that the play's appeal was for an exclusively American audience because it addressed a historical milieu specific to early twentieth-century America. No reviewers noted the story's strong feminist statement; that reading was formulated by feminists involved in the women's movement of the 1970s.

Over fifty years after the first performance of *Trifles,* feminist critics appropriated the short story version as a critique of male-dominated society. It is now considered a feminist classic. In her essay ''Small Things Reconsidered: Susan Glaspell's 'A Jury of Her Peers',' ' Elaine Hedges notes that Mary Anne Ferguson's 1973 anthology entitled *Images of Women in Literature* reintroduced *Trifles* to readers as the forgotten text of an extraordinary writer. The recognition of women's artistic ability and intellect challenged the stereotype of women as concerned with the ''trifles'' of life. Thereafter, a number or critics, including Annette Kolodony, began to consider ''A Jury of Her Peers'' and include it in their work in hopes that the story would become popular in classrooms and anthologies of women's literature.

In her 1986 essay ''Reading About Reading,'' Judith Fetterly's criticism of ''A Jury of Her Peers'' exposes what she feels is a contradiction in reading it as a feminist short story. She states, ''Minnie is denied her story and hence her reality . . . and the men are allowed to continue to assume that they are the only ones with stories. So haven't the men finally won?'' Fetterley finds that because the women in the story allow the men to continue to believe their version of the truth, and they never assert their side of the story, that Minnie is not really let off the hook. Although she may never be convicted of the crime, it is not a victory since she cannot have her say and defend her actions. Fetterly's suspicion is that this sense of feminism comes at the expense of allowing men to continue to devalue a woman's story. Her point is that choosing to remain silent is not a feminist act if it encourages male superiority.

A different perspective of ''A Jury of Her Peers'' comes from the 1995 introduction to Linda Ben-Zvi's edited collection of critical essays on Glaspell titled *Susan Glaspell: Essays on Her Theater and Fiction.* In it, Ben-Zvi states that ''Susan Glaspell's writing is marked by strong women, personae whose consciousness of themselves and

A dairy farm at the turn of the century in North Dakota, illustrating the isolation forced upon wives whose sole domain was the home.

their world shapes her plays and fiction.'' Not only did Glaspell's female persona shape her fiction, Ben-Zvi theorizes, but her strong female characters also shaped the situations in which they were introduced. Today, readers can appreciate Glaspell's work for its historical place in the long tradition of literature written by women in the United States.

Criticism

Lisa Ortiz

Ortiz has a master's degree in English Literature and teaches at Wayne State University in Detroit, Michigan. In the following essay, she addresses the significance of women's subjective experience in Glaspell's portrayal of legal justice in ''A Jury of Her Peers.''

When Mrs. Hale says to Mrs. Peters, ''We all go through the same things—it's all just a different kind of the same thing! If it weren't—why do you and I understand? Why do we know—what we know this minute?'' she was talking about a shared female subjectivity.

A good way to understand subjectivity is to imagine that all people are subjects. As subjects of their particular environments, their identities are constructed by the times, geography, gender, age, and any number of things that make them who they are. People's actions, thoughts, and feelings are informed by all these circumstances. This individual perspective is the person's subjectivity. This subjectivity is the root of an individual's epistemology, or the way they know what they know.

Objectivity would be the opposite of this. An objective perspective or way of thinking relies on a person's ability to put aside his or her own subjective experience and view a situation from a standard or formulaic point of view. This point of view is removed from what the person thinks for him or herself and is based on a general set of assumptions.

People share a certain subjective viewpoint if they have enough common experiences. Mrs. Hale, Mrs. Peters, and Minnie Wright all share a certain female subjectivity as wives of farmers. They live in the same town and have very similar lives, therefore knowing themselves is similar to knowing one another. It is this shared understanding of their lives that allows Mrs. Hale and Mrs. Peters to reconstruct a picture of what Minnie's life might have been like.

It is a lack of this subjective approach that keeps their husbands unaware of the circumstances of the crime. The men's objective approach to the crime is informed not by their own ideas of what might have happened, but by a set of assumptions of what most people agree constitutes a crime.

While looking for a certain set of clues like forced entry, a murder weapon, and signs of intruders around the barn, they are not open to other interpretations of the crime, interpretations that perhaps only a woman who shared Minnie's experiences might see. When the men disregard the women's attention to the kitchen, they are favoring an objective approach. Upon briefly surveying the kitchen, the sheriff decides to move the investigation upstairs. His cynical assessment of the scene is, "Nothing here but kitchen things."—"Nothing," as the county attorney suggests "that would point to any motive." In fact, the men openly doubt the women's ability to read a crime with their subjective experience. The assumption that the women are prone to do so places them under suspicion of being blinded by this subjectivity and thus unable to come up with any useful information. Mr. Hale sums up this theory by asking, "But would the women know a clue if they did come upon it?"

Female subjectivity is crucial in comprehending the story because it is the only way in which readers come to have a sense of who Minnie is. It is through the shared experiences of Mrs. Hale and Mrs. Peters that the reader comes to understand what Minnie's life might have been like. Only when the women synthesize their observations at the crime scene with what they know about their own lives as rural housewives do they achieve a shared concept of married rural womanhood. This shared sense of identity is the basis for their shared subjectivity.

Minnie does not have to tell them that she was lonely or unhappy. They use memories of their own experiences to sympathize with her isolation and to defend her against the accusations of the law. To Sheriff Peters's attempt to sway Mrs. Hale's loyalty to her sex, "Not much of a housekeeper, would you say, ladies?" Mrs. Hale reminds him that it takes two to dirty a house and only one is expected to clean it: "Men's hands aren't always as clean as they might be." The dual meaning of the phrase "clean hands" implies that husbands are not always as free from guilt as they could be. As housewives, Mrs. Hale and Mrs. Peters know this to be true. Perhaps their own homes have been dirtied by similarly careless hands. Mrs. Hale also understands the anxiety of housework interrupted, "Things begun—and not finished." The question of what might have interrupted Minnie's work comes to Mrs. Hale's mind after placing herself in Minnie's shoes. A housewife would not leave her work undone if not for some disturbance. This insight points Mrs. Hale in the direction of a motive.

Critic Linda Ben-Zvi notes that the author conveys the constricting sense of a woman's isolation with the symbolism of the exploded preserves jars. A summer's worth of canning suddenly destroyed represents a form of outburst; it is a suggestion that something may have erupted. Ben-Zvi reads the cracked jars as a symbol for a break in Minnie's composure. That "preserves explode from lack of heat" is an indicator that any violent expression on Minnie's part may be caused by the lack of warmth she received from her own husband, "a punning reminder of the causal relationship between isolation and violence." The women's compassion for Minnie's lost preserves is a form of sympathy or understanding for her isolated, fractured marriage. Perhaps without realizing it, they are reading her kitchen as a text for her life.

Critic Judith Fetterley describes the kitchen as a text, one the men cannot or will not read because they fail to see it as a text. Fetterley believes the women remove the evidence from the scene because they understand that the men could learn to read the text of women's experience. It is not impossible for men to see it, but their unwillingness makes it unlikely. One reason why the men refuse to read or see the text could be that they also have ulterior motives. The evidence might reveal that John was a brutal man who, in addition to being miserly and curt, was also capable of murdering an animal out of spite. As Fetterley claims, they may not want to uncover any evidence that, although it proves Minnie's guilt, also implies that John Wright, fellow husband, may have been the kind of man whose wife would want to murder him. Perhaps admitting that John was partly to blame for his own murder would be accepting responsibility for the injustices they may have perpetrated against their own wives. It might justify their own possible murders.

Fetterley's interpretation of the kitchen investigation implies that the definition of a good man or a good husband is as much at stake as the definition of a good woman or a good wife. In the beginning, all attention is on what a poor housekeeper Minnie is, a

What Do I Read Next?

- *Trifles* (1916), the one-act play by Susan Glaspell, upon which "A Jury of Her Peers" is based, was written and performed for the Provincetown Players, a theater troupe founded in Cape Cod by Glaspell and her husband, fellow playwright George Cram Cook. It is considered to be her best play by many critics and is frequently included in anthologies of American literature.
- "The Yellow Wallpaper" (1892), by Charlotte Perkins Gilman, is the first-person account of a young woman committed to bed rest and psychiatric care by her husband, who believes that her intellectual pursuits, such as reading and writing, are ruining her health.
- *Their Eyes Were Watching God* (1937), a novel by Zora Neale Hurston, tells the story of Janie Crawford, an African-American woman in the South who struggles with her grandmother's lessons that a woman should not marry for love alone. After years of following this advice, Janie decides to marry Tea Cake, the only man she has ever loved. Their romance ends when Tea Cake dies and Janie is tried for his murder.
- *The Awakening* (1899) by Kate Chopin is a short story of Edna Pontellier, a young married woman struggling to discover her own individuality. After a series of events that try her own sense of sexuality, womanhood, motherhood, and freedom, she asserts herself by taking her own life.
- "Lamb to the Slaughter," a short story by Roald Dahl published in 1953, is a black comedy about a woman who murders her husband and successfully disposes of the evidence with the unwitting help of the police.

criticism that draws attention away from the possibility that John was a poor companion. In maintaining a focus on what a woman should be, there is a lack of focus on what a man should be. This fact clearly works in favor of the male characters.

Literary scholar Karen Stein also agrees that the women come away from the farm with a conclusion—while the men do not—because the women apply a more subjective approach to the crime rather than the standard detective formula that the men do. "[T]hey become personally involved, and throughout their successful investigations they gain human sympathy and valuable insights into their own lives. This growth, rather than the sleuthing process, is the play's focal point." These valuable insights are not available to a person when they maintain objectivity.

Stein points out that the mark of shared insight and similar experience can also be a common goal. She says, "For these women, solving the murder is not a disinterested act, but a cooperative endeavor which leads them to a knowledge essential for their survival as females in a hostile or indifferent world." To allow a fellow housewife to be convicted of murdering her neglectful and abusive husband might also be a crime against themselves. They not only share common experience, but also a common responsibility to ensure that they and other women like them do not have to suffer the consequences of defending themselves. To let Minnie go to jail would be to condone the crimes against her, other housewives, and themselves.

Mrs. Peters identifies with Minnie's violent tendencies. She recalls for Mrs. Hale a childhood incident of violence in which a boy killed her kitten with an ax. She bitterly reflects, "If they hadn't held me back I would have . . . hurt him." Her bitter understanding of the urge for revenge and "female violence" is gained through an experience she then applies to the situation at hand. Ben-Zvi notes that "an understanding of female violence in the face of male brutality" is key to Mrs. Peter's realization of the connection she shares with Minnie. From this point on, Mrs. Peters appears to be more forgiving of any crime against a man as brutal as they imagine John Wright might have been.

Mrs. Peters continues to identify with Minnie by recalling yet another traumatizing experience. She solemnly admits, "I know what stillness is . . . [w]hen we homesteaded in Dakota, and my first baby died—after he was two years old—and me with no other then . . . I know what stillness is." Mrs. Peters understands the suffering of a woman who is left alone all the time. Her memories evoke a sense that her baby's death was more than the loss of a child, it was also the loss of a companion. Mrs. Hale also applies her own sense of what loneliness is when she imagines what it might be like for Minnie to miss the singing of the canary if it was the only thing that broke the stillness of her home. The canary's death represents the same kind of loss of companionship as Mrs. Peters's tragedy.

The women's subjective interpretation of the murder also points to the fact that the men do not see the domestic sphere as a source of information about the murder of a man. Recognizing that there are several definitions of justice operating in the story opens up the possibility that there is more than one crime in the story. Ben-Zvi views the strangling of the John Wright as "a punishment to fit his crime." In her reading, justice prevails because the women envision that Minnie has taken revenge upon her husband. This "eye for an eye" definition of justice is more apparent than another form proposed by Mrs. Hale. When she cries, "Oh, I wish I'd come over here once in a while! . . . That was a crime! That was a crime! Who's going to punish that," she suggests that she may have contributed to Minnie's abandonment. That she sees herself as culpable of a crime reflects yet another level of subjectivity.

A woman's subjectivity becomes the binding force which causes the women to render their own brand of justice. As a kind of "jury," although unrecognized and ridiculed by the law men, the women try Minnie. Although they find her guilty of the crime of murder, they justify the crime through a female solidarity built on the knowledge that women suffer from crimes of loneliness, abuse, and neglect not recognized by the American legal system. Their knowledge that the system, represented by their husbands and Mr. Henderson, does not view these predicaments as crimes, or even as legitimate concerns, causes them to assume responsibility for factoring these concerns into their analysis. They are charged with the responsibility for reading their "verdict" like no one else is able to do. As Fetterley points out, "Women can read women's texts because they live women's lives; men cannot read women's texts because they don't lead women's lives."

Source: Lisa Ortiz, for *Short Stories for Students,* Gale, 1998.

Judith Fetterley

An American educator, Fetterley is the author of The Resisting Reader: A Feminist Approach to American Fiction *(1978). In the following essay, she discusses how "A Jury of Her Peers" can be interpreted as a story about reading and that the women in the story are more adept at "reading" Minnie Wright's situation than are the men.*

As a student of American literature, I have long been struck by the degree to which American texts are self-reflexive. Our "classics" are filled with scenes of readers and readings. In *The Scarlet Letter,* for example, a climactic moment occurs when Chillingworth rips open Dimmesdale's shirt and finally reads the text he has for so long been trying to locate. What he sees we never learn, but for him his "reading" is complete and satisfying. Or, to take another example, in "Daisy Miller," Winterbourne's misreading of Daisy provides the central drama of the text. Indeed, for James, reading is the dominant metaphor for life, and his art is designed to teach us how to read well so that we may live somewhere other than Geneva. Yet even a writer as different from James as Mark Twain must learn to read his river if he wants to become a master pilot. And, of course, in *Moby Dick,* Melville gives us a brilliant instance of reader-response theory in action in the doubloon scene.

When I first read Susan Glaspell's "A Jury of Her Peers" in Mary Anne Ferguson's *Images of Women in Literature* I found it very American, for it, too, is a story about reading. The story interested me particularly, however, because the theory of reading proposed in it is explicitly linked to the issue of gender. "A Jury of Her Peers" tells of a woman who has killed her husband; the men on the case can not solve the mystery of the murder; the women who accompany them can. The reason for this striking display of masculine incompetence in an arena where men are assumed to be competent derives from the fact that the men in question can not imagine the story behind the case. They enter the situation bound by a set of powerful assumptions. Prime among these is the equation of textuality with masculine subject and masculine point of view. Thus, it is not simply that the men can not read the text that is placed before them. Rather, they literally can not recognize it as a text because they can not imagine that women have stories. This preconception is so powerful that, even though, in effect, they know Minnie Wright has killed her husband, they spend their time trying to discover their own story, the story they are familiar with, can recognize as a text, and know how to read. They go out to the barn; they check for evidence of violent entry from the outside; they think about guns. In their story, men, not women, are violent, and men use guns: "There was a gun in the house. He says that's what he can't understand." Though Mrs. Hale thinks the men are "kind of *sneaking* . . . coming out here to get her own house to turn against her," in fact she needn't worry, for these men wouldn't know a clue if they came upon it. Minnie Foster Wright's kitchen is not a text to them, and so they can not read it.

"Perhaps admitting that John was partly to blame for his own murder would be accepting responsibility for the injustices they may have perpetrated against their own wives. It might justify their own possible murders."

It is no doubt in part to escape the charge of "sneaking" that the men have brought the women with them in the first place, the presence of women legitimating male entry and clearing it of any hint of violence or violation. But Mrs. Hale recognizes the element of violence in the situation from the outset. In Sheriff Peters, she sees the law made flesh. "A heavy man with a big voice" who delights in distinguishing between criminals and noncriminals, his casual misogyny—"not much of a housekeeper"—indicates his predisposition to find women guilty. Mrs. Hale rejects the sheriff's invitation to join him in his definition and interpretation of Minnie Wright, to become in effect a male reader, and asserts instead her intention to read as a woman. Fortunately, perhaps, for Minnie, the idea of the woman reader as anything other than an adjunct validator of male texts and male interpretations ("a sheriff's wife is married to the law") is as incomprehensible to these men as is the idea of a woman's story. With a parting shot at the incompetence of women as readers—"But would the women know a clue if they did come upon it?"—the men leave the women alone with their "trifles."

Martha Hale has no trouble recognizing that she is faced with a text written by the woman whose presence she feels, despite her physical absence. She has no trouble recognizing Minnie Wright as an author whose work she is competent to read. Significantly enough, identification determines her competence. Capable of imagining herself as a writer who can produce a significant text, she is also capable of interpreting what she finds in Minnie Wright's kitchen. As she leaves her own house, Martha Hale makes "a scandalized sweep of her kitchen," and "what her eye took in was that her kitchen was in no shape for leaving." When she arrives at Minnie Wright's house and finds her kitchen in a similar state, she is prepared to look for something out of the ordinary to explain it—that is, she is in a position to discover the motive and the clue which the men miss. Identification also provides the key element in determining how Mrs. Peters reads. From the start, Martha Hale has been sizing up Mrs. Peters. Working from her perception that Mrs. Peters "didn't seem like a sheriff's wife," Martha subtly encourages her to read as a woman. But Mrs. Peters, more timid than Mrs. Hale and indeed married to the law, wavers in her allegiance: "'But Mrs. Hale,' said the sheriff's wife, 'the law is the law'." In a comment that ought to be as deeply embedded in our national folklore as are its masculinist counterparts—for example, "a woman is only a woman but a good cigar is a smoke"—Mrs. Hale draws on Mrs. Peters's potential for identification with Minnie Wright: "The law is the law—and a bad stove is a bad stove. How'd you like to cook on this?" At the crucial moment, when both motive and clue for the murder have been discovered and the fate of Minnie Wright rests in her hands, Mrs. Peters remembers her own potential for violence, its cause and its justification: "'When I was a girl,' said Mrs. Peters, under her breath, 'my kitten—there was a boy took a hatchet, and before my eyes—before I could get there—' She covered her face an instant. 'If they hadn't held me back I would have'—she caught herself, looked upstairs where footsteps were heard, and finished weakly—'hurt him'."

At the end of the story, Martha Hale articulates the theory of reading behind "A Jury of Her Peers": "We all go through the same things—it's all just a

> "Glaspell's fiction is didactic in the sense that it is designed to educate the male reader in the recognition and interpretation of women's texts, while at the same time it provides the woman reader with the gratification of discovering, recovering, and validating her own experience."

different kind of the same thing! If it weren't—why do you and I *understand?* Why do we *know*—what we know this minute?'' Women can read women's texts because they live women's lives; men can not read women's texts because they don't lead women's lives. Yet, of course, the issues are more complicated than this formulation, however true it may be. A clue to our interpretation of Glaspell's text occurs in a passage dealing with Mrs. Peters's struggle to determine how she will read: ''It was as if something within her not herself had spoken, and it found in Mrs. Peters something she did not know as herself. 'I know what stillness is,' she said, in a queer, monotonous voice.'' Obviously, nothing less than Mrs. Peters's concept of self is at stake in her decision. The self she does not recognize as ''herself'' is the self who knows what she knows because of the life she has lived. As she reads this life in the story of another woman, she contacts that self from which she has been systematically alienated by virtue of being married to the law and subsequently required to read as a man.

When I was in high school and first introduced to literature as a separate subject of study, I was told that one of the primary reasons people read, and, thus, one of the primary justifications for learning how to read, is to enlarge their frame of reference through encountering experiences that are foreign to them which are not likely to happen in their own lives and, thus, to enrich and complicate their perspective. Since as a young woman reader I was given to read primarily texts about young men, I had no reason to question the validity of this proposition. It was not until I got to college and graduate school and encountered an overwhelmingly male faculty intent on teaching me how to recognize great literature that I began to wonder about the homogeneity of the texts that got defined as ''classic.'' But of course it took feminism to enable me finally to see and understand the extraordinary gap between theory and practice in the teaching of literature as I experienced it. If a white male middle-class literary establishment consistently chooses to identify as great and thus worth reading those texts that present as central the lives of white male middle-class characters, then obviously recognition and reiteration, not difference and expansion, provide the motivation for reading. Regardless of the theory offered in justification, as it is currently practiced within the academy, reading functions primarily to reinforce the identity and perspective which the male teacher/reader brings to the text. Presumably this function is itself a function of the sense of power derived from the experience of perceiving one's self as central, as subject, as literally because literarily the point of view from which the rest of the world is seen. Thus men, controlling the study of literature, define as great those texts that empower themselves and define reading as an activity that serves male interests, for regardless of how many actual readers may be women, within the academy the presumed reader is male. . . .

The reading of women's texts has the potential for giving women a knowledge of the self, for putting us in contact with our real selves, which the reading of male texts can not provide. Which, of course, brings us back to Mrs. Peters and ''A Jury of Her Peers'' and to a final question that the story raises.

Just as the women in the story have the capacity to read as men or as women, having learned of necessity how to recognize and interpret male texts, so are the men in the story presumably educable. Though initially they might not recognize a clue if they saw it, they could be taught its significance, they could be taught to recognize women's texts and to read as women. If this were not the case, the women in the story could leave the text as they find it; but they don't. Instead, they erase the text as they read it. Martha Hale undoes the threads of the quilt that, like the weaving of Philomel, tells the story of Minnie Wright's violation and thus provides the clue to her revenge; Mrs. Peters instinctively creates an alternate story to explain the missing bird and then further fabricates to explain the absent cat; and Mrs. Hale, with the approval of Mrs. Peters, finally hides the dead bird. Thus, we must revise somewhat our initial formulation of the story's point about reading: it is not simply the case that men can not recognize or read women's texts; it is, rather, that they will not. At the end of the story, the county attorney summarizes the situation ''incisively'': ''It's all perfectly clear, except the reason for doing it. But you know juries when it comes to women. If there was some definite thing—something to show. Something to make a story about. A thing that would connect up with this clumsy way of doing it.'' But why, if it is all so perfectly clear to them, have the men made so little intelligent effort to find that ''something'' that would convince and convict? Why, in fact, has this same county attorney consistently deflected attention from those details that would provide the necessary clues: ''Let's talk about that a little later, Mr. Hale''; ''I'd like to talk to you about that a little later, Mrs. Hale.'' This is the question that ''A Jury of Her Peers'' propounds to its readers, making us ask in turn why it is more important for the men in this story to let one woman get away with murder than to learn to recognize and to read her story? . . .

When men ask women to read men's texts under the guise of enlarging their experience and perspective, they are in fact asking women to undergo an experience that is potentially inimical to them; and when men insist that men's texts are the only ones worth reading, they are in fact protecting themselves against just such an experience. If we examine ''A Jury of Her Peers'' with this hypothesis in mind, we may find in the story an answer to the question that it propounds. For what is the content of the text that Minnie Wright has written and that the men are so unwilling to read? It is nothing less than the story of men's systematic, institutionalized, and culturally approved violence toward women, and of women's potential for retaliatory violence against men. For the men to find the clue that would convict Minnie Foster Wright, they would have to confront the figure of John Wright. And if they were to confront this figure, they would have to confront as well the limitations of their definition of a ''good man,'' a phrase that encompasses a man's relation to drink, debt, and keeping his word with other men but leaves untouched his treatment of women. And if a man's treatment of women were to figure into the determination of his goodness, then most men would be found not good. Thus, for the men in the story to confront John Wright would mean confronting themselves. In addition, were they to read Minnie Wright's story, they would have to confront the fact that a woman married to a man is not necessarily married to his law, might not in fact see things ''just that way,'' might indeed see things quite differently and even act on those perceptions. They might have to confront the fact that the women of whom they are so casually contemptuous are capable of turning on them. For, of course, in refusing to recognize the story of Minnie Wright, the men also avoid confrontation with the story of Mrs. Hale and Mrs. Peters—they never know what their wives have done alone in that kitchen.

Male violence against women and women's retaliatory violence against men constitute a story that a sexist culture is bent on repressing, for, of course, the refusal to tell this story is one of the major mechanisms for enabling the violence to continue. Within ''A Jury of Her Peers,'' this story is once again suppressed. Mrs. Hale and Mrs. Peters save Minnie Foster Wright's life, but in the process they undo her story, ensuring that it will never have a public hearing. The men succeed in their refusal to recognize the woman's story because the women are willing to let the principle stand in order to protect the particular woman. Thus, if the men are willing to let one woman get away with murder in order to protect their control of textuality, the women are willing to let the men continue to control textuality in order to save the individual. The consequence of both decisions is the same: Minnie Wright is denied her story and hence her reality (What will her life be like if she does get off?), and the men are allowed to continue to assume that they are the only ones with stories. So haven't the men finally won?

Glaspell, of course, chooses differently from her characters, for ''A Jury of Her Peers'' does not suppress, but, rather, tells the woman's story. Thus, Glaspell's fiction is didactic in the sense that it is designed to educate the male reader in the recognition and interpretation of women's texts, while at the same time it provides the woman reader with the gratification of discovering, recovering, and validating her own experience. For ''A Jury of Her Peers,'' I would argue, from my own experience in teaching the text and from my discussion with others who have taught it, is neither unintelligible to male readers nor susceptible to a masculinist interpretation. If you can get men to read it, they will recognize its point, for Glaspell chooses to make an issue of precisely the principle that her characters are willing to forgo. But, of course, it is not that easy to get men to read this story. It is surely no accident that ''A Jury of Her Peers'' did not make its way into the college classroom until the advent of academic feminism.

Source: Judith Fetterley, ''Reading about Reading: 'A Jury of Her Peers,' 'The Murders in the Rue Morgue,' and 'The Yellow Wallpaper','' in *Gender and Reading: Essays on Readers, Texts, and Contexts,* edited by Elizabeth A. Flynn and Patrocinio P. Schweickart, The Johns Hopkins University Press, 1986, pp. 147–64.

Elaine Hedges

An American critic and educator, Hedges is the author of Land and Imagination: The Rural Dream in America *(1980; with William L. Hedges) and* In Her Own Image: Women Working in the Arts *(1980; with Ingrid Wendt). In the following excerpt from a longer essay, she discusses the reality of women's lives in the nineteenth century, thereby explaining the significance of the events and ''trifles'' that figure in the plot of Glaspell's ''A Jury of Her Peers.''*

Susan Glaspell's ''A Jury of her Peers'' is by now a small feminist classic. Published in 1917, rediscovered in the early 1970s and increasingly reprinted since then in anthologies and textbooks, it has become for both readers and critics a familiar and frequently revisited landmark on our ''map of rereading.'' For Lee Edwards and Arlyn Diamond in 1973 it introduced us to the work of one of the important but forgotten women writers who were then being rediscovered; and its characters, ''prairie matrons, bound by poverty and limited experience [who] fight heroic battles on tiny battlefields,'' provided examples of those ordinary or anonymous women whose voices were also being sought and reclaimed. For Mary Anne Ferguson, also in 1973, Glaspell's story was significant for its challenge to prevailing images or stereotypes of women—women as ''fuzzy minded'' and concerned only with ''trifles,'' for example—and for its celebration of female sorority, of the power of sisterhood. More recently, in 1980, Annette Kolodny has read the story as exemplary of a female realm of meaning and symbolic signification, a realm ignored by mainstream critics and one, as she urges, that feminist critics must interpret and make available. Rediscovering lost women writers, reclaiming the experience of anonymous women, reexamining the image of women in literature, and rereading texts in order to discern and appreciate female symbol systems—many of the major approaches that have characterized feminist literacy criticism in the past decade have thus found generous validation in the text of ''A Jury of her Peers.'' The story has become a paradigmatic one for feminist criticism. . . .

In Glaspell's story, Mrs. Hale and Mrs. Peters comprise an ideal (if small) community of readers precisely because they are able to bring to the ''trivia'' of Minnie Wright's life just such a ''unique and informing context.'' That context is their own experience as midwestern rural women. As a result they can read Minnie's kitchen trifles with full ''recognition and acceptance of . . . their significance.'' For contemporary readers, however, who are historically removed from the way of life on which Glaspell's story depends, such a reading is not so readily available. Superficially we can of course comprehend the story's details, since women's work of cooking, cleaning, and sewing is scarcely strange, or unfamiliar, either to female or to male readers. But to appreciate the full resonance of those details requires by now an act of historical reconstruction. Glaspell's details work so effectively as a symbol system because they are carefully chosen reflectors of crucial realities in the lives of 19th and early 20th century midwestern and western women. The themes, the broader meanings of ''A Jury of her Peers,'' which are what encourage us to rediscover and reread it today, of course extend beyond its regional and historical origins. Women's role or ''place'' in society, their confinement and isolation, the psychic violence wrought against them, their power or powerlessness vis-a-vis men, are not concerns restricted to Glaspell's time and place. But these concerns achieve their imaginative force and conviction in her story by being firmly rooted in, and organically emerging from, the carefully observed, small details of a localized way of life. . . .

''A Jury of her Peers'' is set in the prairie and plains region of the United States. The story itself contains a reference to the county attorney's having just returned from Omaha, which would literally locate the action in Nebraska. And a further reference to ''Dickson County,'' as the place where the characters live, might suggest Dixon County, an actual county in the northeastern corner of Nebraska where it borders on Iowa. In the narrowest sense, then, given Glaspell's own Iowa origins, the story can be said to refer to the prairie and plains country that stretches across Iowa into Nebraska—a country of open, level or rolling land, and few trees, which generations of pioneers encountered during successive waves of settlement throughout the nineteenth century. More broadly, the story reflects the lives of women across the entire span of prairie and plains country, and some of the circumstances of Minnie Wright's life were shared by women further west as well. While emphasizing Iowa and Nebraska, therefore, this paper will draw for evidence on the autobiographical writings by women from various western states. . . .

When a male pioneer registered his sense of the land's emptiness, it was often to recognize that the emptiness bore more heavily upon women. Seth K. Humphrey wrote of his father's and his own experiences, in Minnesota territory in the 1850s and in the middle northwest in the 1870s, and he remembered that "the prairie has a solitude way beyond the mere absence of human beings." With no trees, no objects to engage or interrupt the glance, the eyes "stare, stare—and sometimes the prairie gets to staring back." Women, he observed, especially suffered. They "fled in terror," or "stayed until the prairie broke them." Women themselves reported that it was not unusual to spend five months in a log cabin without seeing another woman, as did a Marshall County, Iowa woman in 1842; or to spend one and a half years after arriving before being able to take a trip to town, as did Luna Kellie in Nebraska in the 1870s. The absence both of human contact and of any ameliorating features in the landscape exacerbated the loneliness felt by women who had often only reluctantly uprooted themselves from eastern homes and families in order to follow their husbands westward.

Minnie Wright is not of course living in circumstances of such extreme geographical isolation. By the time of Glaspell's story, established villages and towns have replaced the first scattered settlements, and networks of transportation and communication link people previously isolated from one another. But John Wright's farm, as we learn, is an isolated, outlying farm, separated from the town of which it is, formally, a part. Furthermore, he refuses to have a telephone; and, as we also learn, he has denied his wife access to even the minimal contacts that town life might afford women at that time, such as the church choir in which Minnie had sung before her marriage. Minnie Wright's emotional and spiritual loneliness, the result of her isolation, is, in the final analysis, the reason for her murder of her husband. Through her brief opening description of the landscape Glaspell establishes the physical context for the loneliness and isolation, an isolation Minnie inherited from and shared with generations of pioneer and farm women before her.

The full import of Minnie's isolation emerges only incrementally in Glaspell's story. Meanwhile, after the characters arrive at the Wright farm, the story confines itself to the narrow space of Minnie's kitchen—the limited and limiting space of her female sphere. Within that small space are revealed all the dimensions of the loneliness that is her mute message. And that message is of course conveyed through those "kitchen things," as the sheriff dismissingly calls them, to which Mrs. Hale and Mrs. Peters respond with increasing comprehension and sympathy.

One of the first "kitchen things" or "trifles" to which Glaspell introduces us is the roller towel, on which the attorney condescendingly comments. Not considering, as the women do, that his own assistant, called in earlier that morning to make up a fire in Minnie's absence, had probably dirtied the towel, he decides that the soiled towel shows that Minnie lacked "the homemaking instinct." The recent researches of historians into the lives of 19th century women allow us today to appreciate the full ironic force of Mrs. Hale's quietly understated reply: "There's a great deal of work to be done on a farm." One of the most important contributions of the new social history is its documentation of the amount of work that pioneer and farm women did. The work as, as one historian has said, "almost endless," and over the course of a lifetime usually consisted of tasks "more arduous and demanding than those performed by men." Indoors and out, the division of labour "favored men" and "exploited women." Sarah Brewer-Bonebright, recalling her life in Newcastle, Iowa in 1848, described the "routine" work of the "women-folk" as including "water carrying, cooking, churning, sausage making, berry picking, vegetable drying, sugar and soap boiling, hominy hulling, medicine brewing, washing, nursing, weaving, sewing, straw platting, wool picking, spinning, quilting, knitting, gardening and various other tasks. . . ." Workdays that began at 4.30 a.m., and didn't end until 11.30 p.m., were not unheard of. Jessamyn West's description of her Indiana grandmother—"She died saying, 'Hurry,

> "In Glaspell's story, Mrs. Hale and Mrs. Peters decide that they, and not the men, are Minnie's true peers. They take the law into their own hands, appoint themselves prosecuting and defense attorneys, judge and jury, and pass their merciful sentence."

hurry, hurry,' not to a nurse, not to anyone at her bedside, but to herself''—captures an essential reality of the lives of many 19th and early 20th century rural women.

The work involved for Minnie Wright in preparing the clean towel that the attorney takes for granted is a case in point. Of all the tasks that 19th and early 20th century women commented on in their diaries, laundry was consistently described as the most onerous. . . .

In her recent study of housework, *Never Done,* Susan Strasser agrees that laundry was woman's ''most hated task.'' Before the introduction of piped water it took staggering amounts of time and labor: ''One wash, one boiling, and one rinse used about fifty gallons of water—or four hundred pounds—which had to be moved from pump or well or faucet to stove and tub, in buckets and wash boilers that might weigh as much as forty or fifty pounds.'' Then came rubbing, wringing, and lifting the wet clothing and linens, and carrying them in heavy tubs and baskets outside to hang. It is when Mrs. Peters looks from Minnie's inadequate stove, with its cracked lining, to the ''pail of water carried in from outside'' that she makes the crucial observation about ''seeing into things . . . seeing through a thing to something else.'' What the women see, beyond the pail and the stove, are the hours of work it took Minnie to produce that one clean towel. To call Minnie's work ''instinctual,'' as the attorney does (using a rationalization prevalent today as in the past) is to evade a whole world of domestic reality, a world of which Mrs. Hale and Mrs. Peters are acutely aware.

So too with the jars of preserves that the women find cracked and spoiled from the cold that has penetrated the house during the night. It is the preserves, about which Minnie has been worrying in jail, that lead Mr. Hale to make the comment Glaspell used for the title of the dramatic version of her work. ''Held for murder, and worrying over her preserves . . . worrying over trifles.'' But here again, as they express their sympathy with Minnie's concern, the women are seeing through a thing to something else: in this case, to ''all [Minnie's] work in the hot weather,'' as Mrs. Peters exclaims. Mrs. Hale and Mrs. Peters understand the physical labor involved in boiling fruit in Iowa heat that one historian has described as ''oppressive and inescapable.'' By the same token, they can appreciate the seriousness of the loss when that work is destroyed by the winter cold. . . .

Hard as the work was, that it went unacknowledged was often harder for women to bear. The first annual report of the Department of Agriculture in 1862 included a study of the situation of farm women which concluded that they worked harder than men but were neither treated with respect as a result nor given full authority within their domestic sphere. And Norton Juster's study of farm women between 1865 and 1895 leads him to assert that women's work was seen merely as ''the anonymous background for someone else's meaningful activity,'' never attaining ''a recognition or dignity of its own.'' Indeed, he concludes, women's work was not only ignored; it was ridiculed, ''often the object of derision.'' Mr. Hale's remark about the preserves, that ''women are used to worrying over trifles,'' is a mild example of this ridicule, as is the attorney's comment, intended to deflect that ridicule but itself patronizing—''yet what would we do without the ladies.'' It is this ridicule to which Mrs. Hale and Mrs. Peters especially react. When Mr. Hale belittles women's work we are told that ''the two women moved a little closer together''; and when the attorney makes his seemingly conciliatory remark the women, we are further told, ''did not speak, did not unbend.'' Mrs. Hale and Mrs. Peters, who at the beginning of the story are comparative strangers to each other, here begin to establish their common bonds with each other and with Minnie. Their slight physical movement towards each other visually embodies that psychological and emotional separation from men that was encouraged by the nineteenth century doctrine of separate spheres, a separation underscored throughout the story by the women's confinement to the kitchen, while the men range freely, upstairs and outside, bedroom to barn, in search of the "real" clues to the crime. . . .

In "A Jury of her Peers" John Wright's murder is discovered because Mr. Hale and his son stop at the Wright farm while travelling to town with their potato crop. Once in town, men had places to congregate—the market, the country store, the blacksmith shop, the saloon. That "women really did little more than pass through the masculine haunts of the village," as Faragher concludes, was a reality to which at least one 19th century male writer was sensitive. "The saloon-keepers, the politicians, and the grocers make it pleasant for the man," Hamlin Garland has a character comment in his story of midwestern rural life, "A Day's Pleasure"; "But the wife is left without a word." Garland wrote "A Day's Pleasure" to dramatize the plight of the farm wife, isolated at home, and desperate for diversion. Mrs. Markham has been six months without leaving the family farm. But when, over her husband's objections and by dint of sacrificed sleep and extra work to provide for her children while she is gone, she manages to get into town, she finds scant welcome, and little to do. After overstaying her leave at the country store, she walks the streets for hours, in the "forlorn, aimless, pathetic wandering" that, Garland has the town grocer observe, is "a daily occurrence for the farm women he sees and one which had never possessed any special meaning to him."

John Wright's insensitivity to his wife's needs parallels that of the men or Garland's story. Lacking decent clothes, Minnie doesn't travel into town. What she turns to in her isolation is a bird, a canary bought from a travelling peddler. It is after her husband strangles that surrogate voice that, in one of those "intermittent flare-ups of bizarre behavior," as one historian has described them, which afflicted rural women, she strangles him.

Here again Glaspell's story reflects a larger truth about the lives of rural women. Their isolation induced madness in many. The rate of insanity in rural areas, especially for women, was a much-discussed subject in the second half of the 19th century. As early as 1868 Sarah Josepha Hale, editor of the influential *Godey's Lady's Book,* expressed her concern that the farm population supplied the largest proportion of inmates for the nation's insane asylums. By the 1880s and 1890s this concern was widespread. An article in 1882 noted that farmer's wives comprised the largest percentage of those in lunatic asylums. . . .

That the loss of her music, in the shape of a bird, should have triggered murderous behavior in Minnie Wright is therefore neither gratuitous nor melodramatic, as is sometimes charged against Glaspell's story. In the monotonous expanses of the prairie and the plains, the presence of one small spot of color, or a bit of music, might spell the difference between sanity and madness. . . .

There is no spot of beauty in Glaspell's description of Minnie's kitchen, which is presented as a drab and dreary space, dominated by the broken stove, and a rocking chair of "a dingy red, with wooden rungs up the back, and the middle rung was gone, and the chair sagged to one side." When the women collect some of Minnie's clothes to take to her in prison, the sight of "a shabby black skirt" painfully reminds Mrs. Hale by contrast of the "pretty clothes" that Minnie wore as a young girl before her marriage.

Unable to sing in the church choir, deprived of her surrogate voice in the bird, denied access to other people, and with no visible beauty in her surroundings, Minnie, almost inevitably one can say, turned in her loneliness to that final resource available to 19th and early 20th century women—quilting. Minnie's quilt blocks are the penultimate trifle in Glaspell's story. The discovery later of the strangled bird and broken bird cage explain the immediate provocation for Minnie's crime. But it is with the discovery of the quilt blocks, to which the women react more strongly than they have to any of the previously introduced "kitchen things," that a pivotal point in the story is reached.

The meaning of quilts in the lives of American women is complex, and Glaspell's story is a valuable contribution to the full account that remains to be written. Quilts were utilitarian in origin, three-layered bed coverings intended to protect against the cold weather. But they became in the course of the 19th century probably the major creative outlet for women—one patriarchically tolerated, and even ''approved,'' for their use, but which women were able to transform to their own ends. Through quilting—through their stitches as well as through pattern and color—and through the institutions, such as the ''bee,'' that grew up around it, women who were otherwise without expressive outlet were able to communicate their thoughts and feelings.

In ''Trifles'' Glaspell included a reference she omitted from ''A Jury of her Peers,'' but which is worth retrieving. In the play Mrs. Hale laments that, given her husband's parsimony, Minnie could never join the Ladies Aid. The Ladies Aid would have been a female society associated with the local church, where women would have spent their time sewing, braiding carpets, and quilting, in order to raise money for foreign missionaries, for new flooring or carpets, chairs or curtains for the church or parish house, or to add to the minister's salary. Such societies, as Glenda Riley has observed, provided women with ''a relief from the routine and monotony'' of farm life. They also provided women with a public role, or place. And through the female friendships they fostered they helped women, as Julie Jeffrey has noted, to develop ''feelings of control over their environment,'' mitigating that sense of powerlessness which domestic isolation could induce.

Denied such associations, Minnie Wright worked on her quilt blocks alone, and it is the effect of that solitude which the women read in her blocks and which so profoundly moves them. It is, specifically, the stitches in Minnie's blocks that speak to them, and particularly the ''queer'' stitches in one block, so unlike the ''fine, even sewing,'' ''dainty [and] accurate,'' that they observe in the others. Nineteenth century women learned in childhood to take stitches so small that in the words of one woman, it ''required a microscope to detect them.'' Mothers were advised to teach their daughters to make small, exact stitches, not only for durability but as a way of instilling habits of patience, neatness, and diligence. But such stitches also became a badge of one's needlework skill, a source of self-esteem, and of status, through the recognition and admiration of other women. Minnie's ''crazy'' or crooked stitches are a clear signal to the two women that something, for her, was very seriously wrong.

Mrs. Hale's reaction is immediate. Tampering with what is in fact evidence—for the badly stitched block is just such a clue as the men are seeking: ''Something to show anger—or sudden feeling''—she replaces Minnie's crooked stitches with her own straight ones. The almost automatic act, so protective of Minnie, is both concealing and healing. To ''replace bad sewing with good'' is Mrs. Hale's symbolic gesture of affiliation with the damaged woman. It is also the story's first intimation of the more radical tampering with the evidence that the two women will later undertake.

In so quickly grasping the significance of Minnie's quilt stitches, Mrs. Hale is performing yet another of those acts of perception—of seeing through a detail or trifle to its larger meaning—on which Glaspell's dramatic effects depend throughout her story. As she holds the badly stitched block in her hand, Mrs. Hale, we are told, ''feels queer, as if the distracted thoughts of the woman who had perhaps turned to it to try and quiet herself were communicating themselves to her.'' Resorting to needlework in order to ''quiet oneself,'' to relieve distress, or alleviate loneliness, was openly recognized and even encouraged throughout the 19th century, especially in the advice books that proliferated for women. . . .

Minnie's stitches speak with equal directness to Mrs. Peters. It is she who first discovers the badly stitched block, and as she holds it out to Mrs. Hale we are told that ''the women's eyes met—something flashed to life, passed between them.'' In contrast to the often outspoken Mrs. Hale, Mrs. Peters has been timid, self-effacing, and ''indecisive,'' torn between sympathy for Minnie and resigned submission to the authority of the law, which her husband, the sheriff, represents. She has evaded Mrs. Hale's efforts to get her more openly to choose sides. The flash of recognition between the two women, a moment of communication the more intense for being wordless, is, as one critic has said, ''the metamorphizing spark of the story.'' It presages Mrs. Peter's eventual revolt against male authority. That revolt occurs when she snatches the box containing the dead bird—the evidence that could condemn Minnie—in order to conceal it from the men. Her defiant act is of course the result of the effect on her of the accumulated weight of meaning of all of the ''trifles'' she has perceived and interpreted throughout the story. But it is here, when she reads Minnie's stitches, that she is first released from her hesitancy into what will later become full conspiratorial complicity with Mrs. Hale.

In examining Minnie's quilt blocks Mrs. Hale observes that she was making them in the ''log cabin pattern.'' The log cabin pattern was one of the most popular in the second half of the 19th century, frequently chosen for its capacity to utilize in its construction small scraps of left-over fabric. For Minnie in her poverty it would have been a practical pattern choice. But there accrued to the pattern a rich symbolism, which would not have escaped a farm woman like Mrs. Hale and which adds yet another rich layer of meaning to Glaspell's exploration of women's place. The log cabin quilt is constructed of repetitions of a basic block, which is built up of narrow overlapping strips of fabric, all emanating from a central square. That square, traditionally done in red cloth, came to represent the hearth fire within the cabin, with the strips surrounding it becoming the ''logs'' of which the cabin was built. As a replication of that most emotionally evocative of American dwelling types, the log cabin quilt came to symbolize both the hardships and the heroisms of pioneer life. More specifically it became a celebration of women's civilizing role in the pioneering process: in the words of one researcher, ''women's dogged determination to build a home, to replace a wilderness with a community.'' . . .

That Minnie is making a log cabin quilt—and the women find a roll of red cloth in her sewing basket—is, both in this historical context and in the context of her own life, both poignant and bitterly ironic. The center of her kitchen is not a hearth with an inviting open fire but that stove with its broken lining, the sight of which, earlier in the story, had ''swept [Mrs. Hale] into her own thoughts, thinking of what it would mean, year after year, to have that stove to wrestle with.'' In Glaspell's story the cult of domesticity has become a trap, Minnie's home has become her prison. Minnie has asked Mrs. Peters to bring her an apron to wear in jail, a request the sheriff's wife at first finds ''strange.'' But when Mrs. Peters decides that wearing the apron will perhaps make Minnie feel ''more natural,'' we can only agree, since in moving from house to jail she has but exchanged one form of imprisonment for another. . . .

Throughout much of the 19th century married women were defined under the law as ''civilly dead,'' their legal existence subsumed within their husbands, their rights to their own property, wages, and children either nonexistent or severely circumscribed. Nor did they participate in the making and administering of the law. In 1873 Susan B. Anthony had challenged that legal situation, in a defense that was widely reprinted and that would have been available to Glaspell at the time of the final agitation for the vote. Arrested for having herself tried to vote, and judged guilty of having thereby committed a crime, Anthony had argued that the all-male jury which judged her did not comprise, as the Constitution guaranteed to each citizen, a ''jury of her peers.'' So long, she argued, as women lacked the vote and other legal rights, men were not their peers but their superiors. So, in Glaspell's story, Mrs. Hale and Mrs. Peters decide that they, and not the men, are Minnie's true peers. They take the law into their own hands, appoint themselves prosecuting and defense attorneys, judge and jury, and pass their merciful sentence. . . .

As the characters prepare to leave the Wright farm, the county attorney facetiously asks the women whether Minnie was going to ''quilt'' or ''knot'' her blocks. In having Mrs. Hale suggest that she was probably going to knot them (that is, join the quilt layers via short lengths of yarn drawn through from the back and tied or knotted at wide intervals across the top surface, rather than stitch through the layers at closer intervals with needle and thread) Glaspell is using a technical term from the world of women's work in a way that provides a final triumphant vindication of her method throughout the story. If, like Mrs. Hale and Mrs. Peters, the reader can by now engage in those acts of perception whereby one sees ''into things, [and] through a thing to something else,'' the humble task of knotting a quilt becomes resonant with meaning. Minnie has knotted a rope around her husband's neck, and Mrs. Hale and Mrs. Peters have ''tied the men in knots.'' All three women have thus said ''not,'' or ''no'' to male authority, and in so doing they have knotted or bonded themselves together. Knots can entangle and they can unite, and at the end of Glaspell's story both men and women are knotted, in separate and different ways, with the women having discovered through their interpretation of the trifles that comprise Minnie's world their ties to one another. One 19th century woman described quilts as women's ''hieroglyphics''—textile documents on which, with needle, thread, and bits of colored cloth, women inscribed a record of their lives. All of the trifles in Glaspell's story together create such a set of hieroglyphics, but it is a language we should by now begin to be able to read.

Source: Elaine Hedges, ''Small Things Reconsidered: Susan Glaspell's 'A Jury of Her Peers','' in *Women's Studies,* Vol. 12, 1986, pp. 89–110.

Sources

Ben-Zvi, Linda, ed. *Susan Glaspell: Essays on Her Theater and Fiction,* University of Michigan Press, 1995.

Davidson, Cathy and Linda Wagner-Martin, eds. *Oxford Companion to Women's Writing in the United States,* Oxford University Press, 1995, pp. 355, 954, 956, 958, 966, 968.

Fetterly, Judith. "Reading About Reading: 'A Jury of Her Peers,' 'The Murders in the Rue Morgue,' and 'The Yellow Wallpaper'," in *Gender and Reading: Essays on Readers, Texts, and Contexts,* edited by Elizabeth A. Flynn and Patrocinio P. Schweickart, Johns Hopkins University Press, 1986, pp. 147-64.

Gilbert, Sandra and Susan Gubar, eds. *The Norton Anthology of Literature By Women: The Tradition in English,* Norton, 1985, pp. 1216-1242, 1388-1389.

Hallgren, Sherri. "'The Law Is the Law—and a Bad Stove is a Bad Stove': Subversive Justice and Layers of Collusion in 'A Jury of Her Peers'," in *Violence, Silence, and Anger: Women's Writing as Transgression,* edited by Deirdre Lashgari, University Press of Virginia, 1995, pp. 203-18.

Makowsky, Veronica. "American Girl Becomes American Woman: A Fortunate Fall?," in *Susan Glaspell's Century of American Women; A Critical Interpretation of Her Work,* Oxford University Press, 1993, pp. 13-28.

O'Brein, Edward, ed. *The Best of Short Stories of 1917,* Small, Maynard & Co., 1918, pp. 256-82.

Papke, Mary E. *Susan Glaspell; A Research and Production Sourcebook,* Greenwood Press, 1993, pp. 15-27.

Shafer, Yvonne. *American Women Playwrights, 1900-1950,* Peter Lang, 1995, pp. 36-57.

Stein, Karen F., "The Women's World of Glaspell's *Trifles,*" in *Women in American Theatre: Careers, Images, Movements, An Illustrated Sourcebook,* Crown, 1981, pp. 251-54.

Further Reading

Makowsky, Veronica. "American Girl Becomes American Woman: A Fortunate Fall?," in *Susan Glaspell's Century of American Women; A Critical Interpretation of Her Work,* Oxford University Press, 1993.

An essay on the actual trial upon which "A Jury of Her Peers" and *Trifles* are based and the historical context and other circumstances which led to their being written.

Mustazza, Leonard. "Generic Translation and Thematic Shift in Susan Glaspell's 'Trifles' and 'A Jury of Her Peers'," in *Studies in Short Fiction,* Vol. 26, No. 4, Fall, 1989, pp. 489–96.

Argues that in adapting *Trifles* to the short story form in "A Jury of Her Peers," Glaspell changed the focus away from the elements of women's lives judged as trivial by men toward women's lack of power in the American legal system.

Waterman, Arthur. *Susan Glaspell,* College and University Press, 1966.

A comprehensive biography of the author.

The Lady, or the Tiger?

Frank R. Stockton

1882

When "The Lady, or the Tiger?" was first published in the popular magazine *Century* in 1882, it was a resounding success. Although Frank R. Stockton had already published a novel and some other stories and would continue to publish for many years, "The Lady, or the Tiger?" remained his most famous story. Originally, he wrote the story, which he called "In the King's Arena," to provoke discussion at a literary party. The story sparked heated discussion, so Stockton expanded it and submitted it to *Century* magazine, where it was accepted and retitled by the editor.

"The Lady, or the Tiger?" is a fantasy story that resembles a fairy tale. However, it is considered more whimsical and open-ended than most fairy tales. It involves a jealous princess, a vindictive king, and an ardent suitor—long the staple elements of fairy tales. In discussing romantic relationships, passion, self-interest, and reason, Stockton puts the princess at the center of a terrible conflict: whether she will send her lover to his death or let him live and marry another woman. Her decision is left unresolved at the story's conclusion. The story's power and popularity was gained by its abrupt ending, which leaves the reader to ponder the princess's decision, and her lover's fate.

Author Biography

Stockton was one of the most famous American writers of the 1880s and 1890s. Known for his fantastic settings, realistic characters, and sly humor, he has been compared to Mark Twain, Joel Chandler Harris, Edward Eggleston, and Bret Harte as an American humorist. Critically admired in his day, Stockton had many fans who were writers themselves, including Twain, Edmond Gosse, and Robert Louis Stevenson. In the twentieth century, Maurice Sendak, Edmund Wilson, and Gertrude Stein have admired and been influenced by his work.

Stockton was born into a large family in Philadelphia in 1834. After he finished high school, he was apprenticed to a wood-engraver, a position arranged for him by his father. Stockton soon turned to writing, and his first short story was published in 1855. In 1864 he started editing and writing for a newspaper, the Philadelphia *Press and Post,* where he remained for twenty years. Stockton enjoyed writing children's fantasy stories and saw his own first stories in that genre published in magazines during the 1860s. In 1873 he began editing a periodical for children, *St. Nicholas Magazine.* He also published stories, articles, and poetry in the magazine under his own name and under pseudonyms.

Stockton's eyesight and health began to fail in 1878. To accommodate this decline he took a part-time job at *Scribner's Magazine,* but eventually he was compelled to give up even limited editorial work completely. Because his doctors told him not to avoid reading or writing, he dictated his stories to his family from then on.

Stockton's story "The Lady, or the Tiger?" appeared in the July, 1882, issue of the *Century* magazine. It had originally been written for a literary group to which he belonged, and the group's members discussed it so much that he decided to publish it. "The Lady, or the Tiger?" proved widely popular, in part because of the open-ended question around which the story is based. Initially, however, Stockton was to some extent oblivious to the story's success, because he and his wife went travelling in Europe in the autumn of 1882 and did not return until 1884. Upon his return he discovered that, in fact, he had succeeded almost too well with this story; magazine publishers now wanted nothing from him unless it was just as good as "The Lady, or the Tiger?" For years he had trouble finding publishers for his new works.

Despite ongoing health problems and the demands of publishers, Stockton continued to write and publish prolifically. By the end of his life he had published six collections of short stories, eight novels, and two collections of fairy tales. He died in 1902 in Washington D.C.

Plot Summary

"The Lady, or the Tiger?" begins with a description of a "semi-barbaric" king who rules his kingdom with a heavy hand. For punishing criminals, he has built an arena featuring two doors. The criminal must choose his own fate by selecting one of the two closed doors. Behind one door is a hungry tiger that will eat the prisoner alive. Behind the other door is a beautiful lady, hand-picked by the king, who will be married to the accused on the spot. The people of the kingdom like this system of justice, because the uncertainty of the situation is very entertaining.

The king has a beautiful daughter whom he adores. She secretly loves a young man who is a commoner. When the king discovers her illicit affair, he throws the young man in jail to await his judgment. For a commoner to love the king's daughter is a crime, so the king searches for the most ferocious tiger and the most attractive lady (but not the princess, of course) for the young man's trial in the arena.

The day of the courtier's "trial" comes, and the young man walks into the arena, his eyes fixed on the princess. He looks to her for guidance, because he suspects that she has learned which door conceals the lady, and which the tiger. Indeed, the princess does know the identity of the young lady behind the door. She has been jealous of her for some time, thinking that she has sought to steal her lover from her. The princess signals for him to choose the right-hand door. Without hesitation, he moves to open the right-hand door.

Stockton does not reveal what waits behind that door; he leaves readers to come to their own answer. As the narrator of the story explains, the answer

> involves a study of the human heart which leads us through devious mazes of passion, out of which it is difficult to find our way.

Characters

Courtier

The courtier is a young man whose love affair with the princess results in his imprisonment and trial. Though of lower birth than the princess, he is ''handsome and brave to a degree unsurpassed in all this kingdom.'' He trusts absolutely in his power to charm the princess, and realizing that she knows what is behind each door, he opens the one she indicates ''without the slightest hesitation.''

King

The king is a ''semi-barbaric'' man with an implacable will. As part of the system of justice he has established in his land, the king sets up a system of choice for criminals. They must enter an arena and pick a door; the door may lead to their freedom or to a terrible death.

Furious when he discovers his daughter's affair with a courtier, the king condemns the young man to the arena, taking great care to select the fiercest tiger to place behind one door and the most respectable marriage candidate from among the ladies of the court behind the other.

Lady

The lady is a young courtier, picked by the king to be the young man's bride, should he open the correct door. She is beautiful, charming, and known to both the courtier and the princess.The princess perceives the lady as a rival for the young man's love, and thus she is an object of the princess's hatred and jealousy.

Lover

See Courtier

Princess

The princess loves a young courtier ''with an ardor that had enough of barbarism in it to make it exceedingly warm and strong.'' The couple is very happy together until the princess's father, the king, discovers the affair and imprisons the courtier. His punishment is to determine his own fate by selecting one of two doors in an arena. One leads to a hungry tiger, the other to a respectable young lady to whom he will be immediately wed should he open that door. The princess learns which door leads to which fate, and thus exercises godlike control over the courtier's fate.

Frank R. Stockton

The tension in the story centers around the choice made by ''that hot-blooded, semi-barbaric princess, her soul at a white heat beneath the combined fires of despair and jealousy.'' She knows that, whichever door her lover opens, he will never be hers again. She believes that the woman picked by the king to be the courtier's wife (if he chooses that door) has flirted with the courtier in the past. She also knows that the hungry tiger will rip him apart if he chooses the other door. After days of anguish, the princess decides which door to indicate. It is left to the reader to ponder which fate she has chosen for her lover.

Themes

Choices and Consequences

The ''semi-barbaric'' king has set up the arena in such a way that the prisoner's choice will determine his fate, regardless of his guilt or innocence. Either he will be eaten by a hungry tiger or he will instantly marry a beautiful girl. This element of choice absolves the king from any responsibility in the situation and intrigues the audience, who eagerly anticipate the prisoner's fate. Not knowing whether they will witness a bloody spectacle or a wedding

Media Adaptations

- "The Lady, or the Tiger?" was adapted as a three-act operetta on May 7, 1888, in Wallack's Theatre, New York, with Stockton present in the opening-night audience. Another company in London opened the play that same night at the Elephant and Castle Theatre. Neither production lasted long, though the American version was revived for a short time during the 1890s.
- "The Lady, or the Tiger?" was adapted for film in 1970 by the Encyclopedia Britannica Educational Corporation. The story was set in the space-age, and a separate 11–minute discussion of the story by Clifton Fadiman was produced at the same time. Both short films are distributed on videotape by Britannica Films.

puts them in a state of suspense. Because the young man is allowed to make his own choice, all others are absolved of guilt. Whether or not his choice and its consequence are just never occurs to them.

The king himself is described as one who likes "to make the crooked straight, and crush down uneven places." In the case of the young man, the king exercises an arbitrary judgement. Because the young man has chosen to fall in love with the princess, he must now face the consequence, which is to make another choice—one that means either life or death.

The princess has made a major choice as well: whether to direct her now-unattainable young man to the tiger who will destroy him or to the lady she hates. She has agonized about her decision and imagined the consequences of both choices in vivid detail. Stockton leaves it to the reader to ponder which choice she makes for the young man, who trusts the princess completely.

Betrayal

The princess *may* betray the man in the arena because she is jealous of the young woman behind the door. Not only does she suspect that her lover may be interested in this attractive female courtier, but she is also deeply troubled by the certainty that their marriage will be compulsory if he chooses the "right" door. Whether she will be loyal to her lover or betray him and send him to his death is the main conflict of the story, and one that is not resolved.

Beauty

In typical fairy-tale terms, the young man is described as "of that fineness of blood and lowness of station common to the conventional heroes of romance who love royal maidens . . . he was handsome and brave to a degree unsurpassed in all this kingdom." The young woman chosen by the king as his potential bride is also "one of the fairest and loveliest of the damsels of the court," someone the princess (who is not described physically) thinks he has noticed before. In mentioning the characters' physical characteristics, Stockton calls to mind familiar tales of beautiful princesses and handsome princes, evoking the fairy-tale tradition.

Love and Passion

Until the king discovers their affair, the young man and the princess love each other and are very happy—or so it seems. In reality, the princess is deeply jealous of a young female courtier she perceives as being attracted to the young man. This perception arouses her passionate hatred for the young woman. In contrast, the young man places his fate in the princess's hands by unquestionably trusting her indication to choose the right-hand door. His love for her is unflinching, even though she may be sending him to his death. The narrator also relates that the king loves his daughter very much. But can this declaration be trusted? If the king truly loves his daughter, would he impose such a sentence on the man she loves?

Style

Point of View

The story is told in third-person omniscient point of view. This means that the narrator knows the thoughts and actions of all the characters. The narrator sets the story in fairy-tale mode—"In the very olden time"—and then addresses the reader directly, in the first-person mode, after the young man makes his choice. The narrator comments on the story, elaborating on the princess's role, and challenging the reader to consider wisely, because "it is not for me to presume to set myself up as the one person able to answer [the question of her decision]. And so I leave it with all of you." The purpose of this address is to place the responsibility for analyzing the story and answering the question posed in the story's title squarely upon the reader's shoulders.

Setting

The story is set in an imaginary time and place, in a kingdom whose king is "semi-barbaric." His autocratic style is described in detail, and the narrator comments at length on his splendid arena. It has tiers upon tiers, galleries, and doors at and below ground level, with curtains round them so that no hint of what is behind them is revealed. If the tiger eats the prisoner, mourners await, and if the lady marries the prisoner, priests are ready to perform the marriage ceremony. The setting bears many similarities to the Coliseum in Rome, which was the scene of elaborate and bloody gladiatorial games for centuries.

Topics for Further Study

- Discuss the concept of religious predestination versus free will as it relates to the roles of the king and the princess in "The Lady, or the Tiger?"
- In answer to queries about the ending of "The Lady, or the Tiger?," Stockton made the following comment: "If you decide which it was—the lady, or the tiger, you find out what kind of a person you are yourself." What do you think he meant by that?
- How can a kingdom be "semi-barbaric"? What sort of practices would you consider barbaric? Are there instances in which it is okay to be barbaric?
- Compare a short story by the American writer O. Henry, whose work is famous for trick endings, to "The Lady, or the Tiger?" Which story do you find more clever, and why?

Structure

Written with many conventions of a fairy tale, "The Lady, or the Tiger?" is divided into three parts. The first part presents the background of the princess and the courtier's particular dilemma, describing the king's justice system and acclimating the reader to this odd kingdom. The second part of the story concerns the love affair, the king's discovery of it, and the young man's sentencing to trial in the arena. In the third part, the narrator focuses on the princess's decision-making process and describes the moment of crisis in the arena, when the reader must decide what is behind the fateful right-hand door.

The obvious climax of the story should come after the lover opens the door indicated by the princess. But Stockton plays with the reader's expectations by refusing to tell what is behind that door. He directly challenges readers to make up their own minds based on their knowledge of the princess. In doing so, the story never reaches its climax and contains no resolution. By subverting the traditional story structure with this open ending, Stockton places responsibility for the story's interpretation completely with the reader.

Fairy Tale

In order to highlight their timeless messages, fairy tales usually take place in an indeterminate time and place. Such is the case with "The Lady, or the Tiger?," which takes place in a kingdom, though no country or year is specified. Fairy tales also rely on stock characters, many of which are represented in Stockton's story, including the vengeful king, the beautiful princess, and the handsome suitor. A handsome but unworthy man falling in love with a vengeful king's daughter is a typical fairy-tale situation, and how their love will transcend the king's wrath is a typical fairy-tale conflict. Unlike a traditional fairy tale, though, the story does not end "happily ever after," and it is the shock of its abrupt ending that jars readers who were expecting a more traditional outcome.

Historical Context

American Humorists in the Nineteenth Century

Popular American literature in the decades preceding the twentieth century included plenty of adventure novels, like those of Robert Louis Stevenson, and humorous works, like the novels of Mark Twain, which often parodied the emerging American culture. Another popular form was the simple short story with a trick ending, like O. Henry's "The Gift of the Magi," in which a young couple's good intentions result in a debacle of Christmas gift-giving. Stockton was considered a humorist, and his stories often combined elements of humor with the trick ending. His children's collection, *Tin-a-ling,* was widely regarded to have brought children's literature into a new era, with his reliance on plots that did not have happy endings even though they were styled after Grimm's fairy tales and bore some similarity with Lewis Carroll's writings.

In his time, Stockton was hailed as the equal of Mark Twain; in 1899 he came in fifth in a poll listing the best living American writers. He used humor for illustrative purposes: "Many of his stories virtually cry out in stifled screams against the cozy suffocation of civilized conduct," said Henry Golemba in the *Dictionary of Literary Biography.* In the 1860s, Stockton's first published works appeared in *Punchinello, Hearth and Home,* and *Puck,* all humor magazines that had a wide following in an era before other forms of mass media became available. Writers often got their start in these magazines, or in newspapers, as Mark Twain did as a reporter. Magazines presented new stories every week or every month, and they often serialized novels, printing a chapter each issue to get readers hooked on the magazine. Such publications were important in a time before the establishment of public libraries or the proliferation of bookstores.

The Pre-Raphaelites Influence Literature

The Pre-Raphaelites were a group of British artists, led by Gabriel Dante Rossetti and Edward Burne-Jones, who gained influence during the 1850s. Their paintings were known for their fairy-tale-like settings that were often influenced by literature—especially poetry—and music. The Pre-Raphaelites' name was intended to display their preference for the idealized art reminiscent of the era before Raphael, an Italian master of the High Renaissance. Their paintings often depicted beautiful women in sweeping gowns, maidens courted by valiant knights, and damsels surrounded by overgrown English gardens. This artistic movement influenced writers as well. In literature, writers who were familiar with the Pre-Raphaelites gained popularity through works that had strong elements of fantasy to it, like Lewis Carroll's *Alice in Wonderland,* and J.M. Barrie's *Peter Pan.*

Stockton's "The Lady, or the Tiger?" can be seen as being a part of the Pre-Raphaelite tradition, with its fairy-tale overtones of a kingdom, a princess, and a valiant suitor. Stockton's stories for children also fit this pattern. Unlike the Pre-Raphaelite's paintings, however, the fantasy literature of the day often included elements of absurdity or irony, as any reader of Lewis Carroll knows. Golemba summarized one of Stockton's children's stories: "after the heroine is beheaded inadvertently by the hero, her head is magically reattached to her body—but backwards." Such irreverence was typical of American humorists, whose displeasure of the modern, mechanized world was to resort to absurdity rather than evoke a long bygone era of art and literature, as was the practice of the Pre-Raphaelites.

As the twentieth-century dawned, and as Stockton feared, his work became a relic of a fast-disappearing age. New tensions that eventually erupted into World War I brought about new styles of literature—especially modernism—and new styles of art, such as cubism and expressionism. The comical, slightly detached view of the world as exercised by Stockton, Twain, and other American humorists came to be seen as quaint and not relevant enough to people dealing with the tragedies of modern life.

Critical Overview

Shortly after Stockton published "The Lady, or the Tiger?," he and his wife left on an extended European vacation. Thus, he missed much of the initial debate that swirled around his story. Martin Griffin in his 1939 biography of Stockton said that "notices

Compare & Contrast

- **1881:** Animals are not protected from human exploitation. P. T. Barnum and his partner, James Bailey, form the Barnum & Bailey Circus, whose main attraction is Jumbo, an African elephant they bought in London. Their traveling show delights thousands across the United States.

  1990s: Tigers and other animals are protected as endangered species. Tigers are frequently raised in captivity and live in zoos or are trained as circus animals. Several breeds of tigers became extinct during the twentieth century. By 1996, there are only twenty to thirty remaining South China tigers.

- **1880s:** Capital punishment is practiced throughout the world and in the United States, though public executions are not as common as they once were. However, some efforts to abolish the death penalty have succeeded. By the 1880s, the state of Michigan and the countries of Venezuela and Portugal have outlawed capital punishment.

  1990s: Many states have reinstated the death penalty. By 1997, it is allowed in all but thirteen states and the District of Columbia. Accepted methods for carrying out death sentences include hanging, electrocution, the gas chamber, the firing squad, and lethal injection. Capital punishment has been abolished in Europe and many other countries, with the United States, China, and Japan the world's most prominent death penalty proponents.

of the strange dilemma proposed by the story began to appear in newspapers and critical reviews.'' The poet Robert Browning believed the man chose the door with the tiger, and Griffin suggested that Stockton weighted the story towards that conclusion. Many other readers, famous and not-so-famous, debated the ending in various public and literary forums. The controversy was so vibrant that when Stockton returned to the United States he was deluged with letters. In response to the story's popularity, he wrote a similar story with a trick ending called ''The Discourager of Hesitancy.'' In another story, ''His Wife's Deceased Sister,'' Stockton tells the story of a writer who writes a wildly popular story and is never able to achieve that level of success again.

Critic Henry Vedder wrote in his 1895 book, *American Fiction To-Day,* about how the story became a social fad and commended Stockton on his commercial shrewdness and his skill as a writer of short fiction. As tastes changed in the twentieth century and modernism exerted its hold over literature, stories like Stockton's became antiquated and were considered relics of an earlier, less relevant time. Stockton had worried about this all along, yet the story itself has remained popular as an example of literature from an earlier era.

Fred Lewis Pattee in his 1923 book, *The Development of the American Short Story: An Historical Survey,* discussed Stockton's mastery of the marvellous, the way he posed his humor in brief, well-written stories that are not overburdened with explanations, and compared him to Lewis Carroll and Mark Twain. In 1925 Sir Arthur Quiller-Couch mentioned that although people had read ''The Lady, or the Tiger?,'' few considered the story appropriate for serious criticism. As one of the first British critics to deal with Stockton, Pattee compared him to Daniel Defoe and wrote about his prominence as a writer of short fiction that is wholly American.

Proving the story's durability, Henry Golemba wrote about Stockton for the *Dictionary of Literary Biography* in 1981, and suggested that ''The Lady, or the Tiger?'' was still worthy of extensive critical analysis. He analyzed Stockton's use of cosmic metaphors in the story: the hero represented an everyman figure and the arena was a symbol of life itself. This interpretation lends itself to more serious themes, an observation that led to Golemba's comment that Stockton's "reputation as a widely popular author in the late nineteenth century has eclipsed the fact that he was also a serious writer, just as his fame as a humorist has made people blind to his serious statements."

Criticism

Tanya Gardiner-Scott

Gardiner-Scott is an associate professor of English at Mount Ida College in Newton, Massachusetts. Her areas of special academic interest include fantasy and science fiction, the British novel, gothic and medieval literature, and women's fiction. In the following essay, she provides a general introduction to "The Lady, or the Tiger?"

When critics today think of American humorists of the nineteenth century, Mark Twain readily comes to mind. But one of his prolific contemporaries was Frank R. Stockton, a writer of fairy tales, children's books, science fiction, and whimsical stories, such as the one which is his most famous, "The Lady, or the Tiger?" In an age in which realism, romanticism, naturalism, and other literary styles were emerging in Western literature, he refused to be categorized in any particular literary group, leading to his reputation as a maverick writer. He considered himself primarily a humor writer, but believed, as he confided to a friend, that "the readers of today do not care for them [humorous stories]; the public taste has altered; humor is no longer fashionable." Although Stockton's style may be dated (having received much more praise from late nineteenth-century and early twentieth-century critics than from later critics), "The Lady, or the Tiger?" remains a work with bite and wit, and the conundrum of the ending remains as fresh as ever.

In 1895 Henry C. Vedder wrote that Stockton's stories "violate certain conventions of literary art. They seldom have a plot; they frequently have no dialogue, consisting wholly or mainly of narrative or monologue; there is not much description, and no apparent attempt at effect." "The Lady, or the Tiger?" indeed has a slight plot, relatively little description, and is told through an omniscient third-person narrator, who, in the manner of early nineteenth-century fiction, addresses the audience directly at the end. Vedder fails to note that the human interest of Stockton's stories is strong, particularly in "The Lady, or the Tiger?" *because* of the epilogue, which directly engages the reader. Biographer Martin I. J. Griffin has argued, "It is this . . . which raises the story above the level of the 'trick,' and invests it with the dignity of an exposition of human strength and human frailty . . . [in which] the conflicting fundamental motives of love and hate and self-preservation are given full play." The central question—what did the princess choose?—was debated fiercely in Stockton's lifetime among thousands of readers, making the author extremely popular, so much so that editors refused to accept any other short fiction from him unless it came up to the same standards as "The Lady, or the Tiger?"

When we turn to the story itself, we may find the tone difficult and the language unfamiliar. It is written in a mannered style, and it seems from the very beginning to expect from the reader a certain knowledge of the Romantic genre, of the human condition, and of political satire. The kingdom setting could be anywhere and nowhere, and it is up to readers to make of this what they will. The king is depicted as whimsically godlike, not only through the biblical language he uses; for, as Henry Golemba has noted, the king is "a Christian god whose nature is 'bland and genial'." This is an interesting interpretation in light of the fact that the king constructs an arena in which free choice determines the young man's fate under certain preset conditions, a life-or-death choice which brings to mind the ongoing debate concerning divine predestination versus so-called free will. The young man cannot evade being put into the arena, and he knows the consequences of either choice, but he has to make the choice itself and then abide by the consequences.

If this interpretation is valid, then Stockton is indeed banking on a certain amount of religious sophistication on the part of the reader, and the implications of the story become more jokingly cosmic. What is Stockton saying about human nature? Is he calling it "semi-barbaric" in its responses to a transcendent order? Does he believe that we humans have moved very far at all from the animal kingdom, "red in tooth and claw"? After all, the king expects that "by exhibitions of manly and beastly valor, the minds of his subjects were refined and cultured." Here Stockton seems to be suggesting—and these suggestive connotations are part of the power of the story—that we as humans have, in fact, not advanced far beyond barbarism.

Stockton presents his characters in shorthand descriptions. The young man falls within the general parameters of the handsome romantic hero who

What Do I Read Next?

- Stockton wrote "The Discourager of Hesitancy" in 1885, in response to questions about "The Lady, or the Tiger?" The story begins in the arena of the earlier story, with one of the audience members leaving just as the young man opens the right-hand door. The departing spectator then poses another open-ended question to the readers.
- "The Knife That Killed Po Hancy" is a story published by Stockton in 1889 about a lawyer who cuts himself with a knife that had earlier killed a Burmese bandit. Once cut, the lawyer alternates between being mild-mannered and being daring and powerful.
- "The Catbird Seat," published in 1945, is a humorous story by James Thurber about a man who plots the dismissal of a loud, overbearing woman in his workplace in such a way that nobody can believe that he has instigated her departure.
- "The Celebrated Jumping Frog of Calaveras County" by Stockton's contemporary, Mark Twain, is the story of a gold miner who spins a fantastic tale of a jumping frog to an incredulous Northerner.
- "The Most Dangerous Game," written by Richard Connell in 1924, has in common with Stockton's story that it was well-regarded when it was published, though most of the author's other works have since been forgotten. An adventure tale that pits two men against each other in a hunt to the death, its sudden ending culminates its deft development of suspense.

loves above his station in life, "a young man of that fineness of blood and lowness of station common to the conventional heroes of romance who love royal maidens." On the other hand, the princess is a jealous, judgmental, mini-god figure who is described in emotional rather than physical terms, a position reinforced by the attitude of supplication the young man assumes as he looks to her for guidance as to which door to open: "He understood her nature, and his soul was assured that she would never rest until she had made plain to herself this thing, hidden to all other lookers-on, even to the king. The only hope for the youth in which there was any element of certainty was based upon the success of the princess in discovering this mystery." For it is through her power and her money that she has found out even more than the king himself knows: which door hides the lady, and which the tiger.

The beautiful young girl is not described in detail. Only the descriptions of the potential consequences have much detail—and the princess's imagination of the consequences:

> "How often, in her waking hours and in her dreams, had she started in wild horror, and covered her face with her hands as she thought of her lover opening the door on the other side of which waited the cruel fangs of the tiger!
>
> But how much oftener had she seen him at the other door! How in her grievous reveries had she gnashed her teeth, and torn her hair, when she saw his start of rapturous delight as he opened the door of the lady! How her soul had burned in agony when she had seen him rush to meet that woman, with her flushing cheek and sparkling eye of triumph; when she had seen him lead her forth, his whole frame kindled with the joy of recovered life; when she had heard the glad shouts from the multitude, and the wild ringing of the happy bells; when she had seen the priest, with his joyous followers, advance to the couple, and make them man and wife before her very eyes; and when she had seen them walk away together upon their path of flowers, followed by the tremendous shouts of the hilarious multitude, in which her one despairing shriek was lost and drowned!"

Our narrator is reliable, and we trust his voice, but he puts us on our guard through his portrayal of the princess as a compromised heroine, a jealous object of adoration. The narrator makes much of her

> "Stockton seems to be suggesting—and these suggestive connotations are part of the power of the story—that we as humans have, in fact, not advanced far beyond barbarism."

similarities to her father in her strong feelings and vivid imagination. Much is also made of her directing her lover to the right-hand door. The phrase "without the slightest hesitation" is repeated to describe the actions of both lovers at the moment of choice. But while it is not surprising that the earnest young man trusts the princess, it is surprising that the princess does not trust him equally, whatever her jealous feelings are for the lady behind the door. Her perceptions of the other young lady, and of his possible interest in her, color her entire decision-making process, and, as Griffin points out, Stockton seems to be giving us an underlying pointer as to the tiger-ward direction her thoughts are taking.

An interesting sidelight on this point is that the story was originally titled "In the King's Arena." Stockton allowed an editor to change the title to "The Lady, or the Tiger?" This shifted the focus from the king, controller of the man's fate, to the princess, the story's romantic interest. In this editorial decision, as Golemba has commented, Stockton "was treated as whimsically as he trapped his blameless, foolish, anonymous hero."

As readers, then, we are placed in the position of the audience, unsure whether to grieve or rejoice until the door opens and the consequences of the choice are clear. The fact that Stockton does not tell us outright what the princess chooses for her lover has for years "stung its reader and then injected an irritating drop that lingered," as Fred Lewis Pattee put it. That Stockton put the burden of interpretation on us, inviting us into the princess's thought processes, "the study of the human heart which leads us through devious mazes of passion," makes us examine our relationship to reading and interpretation and our analysis of what it means to be human. But this seems too heavy an interpretation for the story to bear. Yet, the interpretation is suggested, showing Stockton's power as an American humorist who can pack his slight story with meaning far beyond its seeming bounds.

Source: Tanya Gardiner-Scott, "Overview of 'The Lady, or the Tiger?'," in *Short Stories for Students,* Gale, 1998.

Sarah Madsen Hardy

Madsen Hardy has a doctorate in English literature. In the following essay, she discusses Stockton's satirical revision of the traditional fairy-tale form as a rebellion against the cultural dominance of European literature in the turn-of-the-century United States.

One of the most useful questions that a student reader can ask is: "What kind of expectations do I have for this work?" When one starts to read, one cannot help but bring certain assumptions and expectations to the experience. Authors count on readers for this and often help them along, leading them to believe that their stories will follow a certain course and obey certain rules about how a story works. Upon picking up Frank R. Stockton's "The Lady, or the Tiger?," readers will probably have general expectations something along these lines: This will be a short story. It will introduce its characters, place them in a situation of conflict, describe how the conflict changes the characters, and come to a resolution. Immediately upon reading the first line of the story—"In the very olden times, there lived a semi-barbaric king"—readers will spontaneously refine that initial expectation to one that is much more specific. Merely knowing that the story takes place in "the very olden times" and concerns a king will lead readers to expect that "The Lady, or the Tiger?" will be similar to a fairy tale, a kind of story that is familiar to most of us since childhood. That is, this single line generates expectations that the story will have traditional fairy-tale characters like just kings and demure princesses. The conflicted situations in which they are placed may involve magic or violence, and the outcome will bring complete resolution and impart a universal lesson or moral.

But wait a minute, right away something seems wrong. The king is "semi-barbaric" and his ideas, "though somewhat polished and sharpened by the progressiveness of distant Latin neighbors, were still large, florid, and untrammeled, as became the half of him which was barbaric." This language sounds different from that of a fairy tale. In traditional fairy tales, characters are not described in such a strange and complicated way. Fairy-tale kings are never "semi-barbaric," let alone "florid and untrammeled." They tend to be simple types and to directly represent abstract qualities, such as civilization, justice, and authority.

Thus, it is very important to follow up that first question with another one that is just as useful: How did the story fulfill *or change* my expectations as I read along? Sometimes, as in the case of a traditional fairy tale, a reader's expectations are completely fulfilled (the same thing goes for conventional romantic comedies, horror films, and action movies). But sometimes, as in the case of "The Lady or the Tiger?" a reader's expectations are challenged when the author breaks the rules he or she seemed to have set up. While there is a certain kind of gratification that comes with having one's expectations fulfilled, rule-breaking narratives have their own pleasures. While traditional stories tend to offer conventional morals or views of society, stories that challenge literary conventions often also challenge conventional views. There is something daring and original about Stockton's story. One gets only a hint of this when reading the first lines, but by the "trick" ending, it is clear that Stockton is a literary rebel.

Authors may break with storytelling conventions to create a humorous effect and/or a satirical one. While Stockton was best known as a humorist, reading "The Lady, or the Tiger?" as a satire—an indirect attack on folly, vice, or corruption through irony and wit—offers the best avenue for exploring the cultural context of Stockton's "rebellion" against fairy-tale conventions. While it takes place "in the very olden time," the story reflects issues that were current and pressing in 1882. The United States had gained its political independence from Britain more than a century earlier, but Americans were still insecure about their *cultural* independence—their ability to create their own art in their own style. British writers of the period objected to Americans' use of the English language, claiming that Americans took a civilized language and made it barbaric. Many American artists agreed, believing that Europe represented all that was finest in culture and arts, and trying in their own work to imitate European traditions. While at first Stockton appears to be imitating a traditional form, by the end it is clear that he is really interested in inventing something brand new.

In 1871, eleven years before "The Lady or the Tiger?" was published, Walt Whitman (an American poet who rebelled against traditional forms of poetry wrote a book of prose called *Democratic Vistas.* In it, Whitman calls American writers to action, asking them to leave European art behind and to invent new forms that reflect the best and most unique aspects of American democratic society.

> **"Through his portrayal of a hapless king, Stockton expresses great doubt about the justice rendered through monarchy and shows that it is utterly out of keeping with the values of American culture."**

> America has as yet morally and artistically originated nothing. She [America] seems singularly unaware that the models of persons, books, manners, etc., appropriate for former conditions and for European lands, are but exiles and exotics here.

Whitman is saying that imitating European artistic conventions—say, by writing stories about kings—does not allow Americans to express their own unique ways of living and thinking. While in a European fairy tale a king fits in perfectly, in the context of the United States—which never had kings, being formed as a republic as opposed to a monarchy—a character like a king would be an "exile," and "exotic," or perhaps "semi-barbaric." In "The Lady, or the Tiger?" Stockton makes fun of the idea of trying to use European conventions to express American values and experiences. Answering Whitman's call to action, Stockton shows the absurdity of American writers slavishly depending on European literary traditions.

Instead of just stating that a king has no place in American literature, or simply writing about some other kind of character, Stockton playfully shows what happens to a fairy-tale king when he is "exiled" to an American story:

> When every member of his domestic and political systems moved smoothly in its appointed course, his nature was bland and genial; but whenever there was a little hitch, and some of his orbs got out of their orbits, he was blander and more genial still, for nothing

pleased him so much as to make the crooked straight, and crush down uneven places.

In European history and thus, fittingly, in European fairy tales, kings represent for their subjects the absolute power that establishes social order and holds them together as a people. Conventional fairy-tale kings act decisively in the face of trouble; they determine ways to resolve conflict and bring about justice, even if that justice is sometimes harsh and violent. Stockton's king is instead "bland and genial," and, in the face of conflict, he becomes more bland and genial still. He completely lacks the authority and wisdom characteristic of fairy-tale kings and leaves judgment to the "decrees of an impartial and incorruptible chance," which bring about a 'justice' that is sometimes harsh and violent nevertheless—if one is so unlucky to choose the door behind which is a bloodthirsty tiger, instead of the one where a blushing bride awaits. This figure of supreme authority is shown as a man with little sense or strength. He is not a bad guy; he simply has too much power. Through this portrayal of a hapless king, Stockton expresses great doubt about the justice rendered through monarchy and, furthermore, shows that it is utterly out of keeping with the values of American culture.

As the story progresses, there is indeed a "little hitch" in the domestic and social system of our semi-barbaric king: his daughter falls in love with a "man of that fineness of blood and lowness of station common to the conventional heroes of romance who love royal maidens." When her father punishes her suitor for his illicit love by presenting him with the choice between the two doors, the lovely young princess—who shared the king's tinge of barbarism—takes control of the judicial system, upsetting any remaining expectations a reader might have that "The Lady or the Tiger?" will follow the conventions of a fairy tale. She intervenes in her father's "decree of an impartial and incorruptible chance" and finds out the secret of the doors, which gives her the power to use a supposedly impartial system for her own personal ends. In a traditional tale, the king/father's authority is never interfered with and its ultimate justice renders a moral for the story that reinforces his authority. In Stockton's satirical revision, the king's authority is unseated by his own daughter, and—more unconventional still—the question of what she chooses to do with her power is left unanswered. The princess gestures to her suitor to tell him what door to go through, and he strides to the door and opens it. Here the reader is left quite unexpectedly hanging, and the story ends without disclosing the hero's wonderful or terrible fate.

"The question of her decision is one not to be lightly considered," Stockton writes, suggesting that a moral is, in fact, crucial to the tale. But in providing no resolution, does he not leave his readers helpless to draw a lesson from the dramatic events? The authorial narrator then steps in to decline his control over the climactic resolution of his own story. "It is not for me to presume to set myself up as the one person able to answer it." Here Stockton (who—as author to story is like king to kingdom—would be expected to be a figure of absolute power) simply declines to assume authority. Why should one single person, the kingly author, decide how a story ends? The relinquishment of the author's power provides, perhaps, the moral that readers crave, if not the resolution, Why should readers not make up their own minds, based on their own experiences, beliefs, and knowledge? "And so I leave it all with you," Stockton writes, "Which came out of the door,—the lady, or the tiger?" In an individualist and democratic style, Stockton places the responsibility for this question squarely upon the shoulders of his readers, whose heated public discussions and debates about the answer made the story a brand new and distinctively American kind of literary phenomenon.

Source: Sarah Madsen Hardy, "Tradition or Rebellion?: 'The Lady, or the Tiger?' and American Culture," for *Short Stories for Students,* Gale, 1998.

Martin I. J. Griffin

In the following excerpt, Griffin provides a plot synopsis of "The Lady, or the Tiger?" and an analysis of its central theme of choices and consequences.

The essence of the popularity of "The Lady, or the Tiger?" lay solely in the unanswered, perhaps unanswerable, human problem which Stockton propounded. In a semi-barbaric kingdom, in an unspecified olden time, a monarch of quixotic humor tries offenders against the royal dignity, or against the law, by chance. In a great arena, behind different doors through which no sound can travel, are placed a beautiful woman and a ferocious tiger. The offender is thrust alone into the arena, and permitted to choose which door he shall open. If, happily, the accused man chooses the door behind which the beautiful girl is concealed, then, amid pomp and flowery circumstance, he is promptly married to her, to the accompaniment of the cheers of the multitude. If, however, he opens the door behind which the tiger chafes, his execution is immediate, and the king's dignity is avenged.

In such an unhappy court a personable young member of the king's retinue was tried because he had had the impudence to fall in love with the king's beautiful but impulsive daughter. Since he was not of noble blood, there could be no question of marriage. But the princess loved the helpless young courtier, and by methods which are open only to princesses, she obtained the secret of the doors. The young lover, who was not as ignorant of the ways of maids as he appeared, knew that she would discover behind which door was the lady, and behind which door was the tiger. As he made the traditional salute to the king, who was seated in the royal box, the youth looked quickly to the princess for the signal he knew she would give. The princess motioned toward the right. Without hesitation, he turned, walked briskly across the arena, and opened the door on the right.

At this anxious moment the story ends. Stockton appends an epilogue which explains the dilemma which the princess had had to solve before she gave her signal. It is this epilogue which raises the story above the level of the "trick," and invests it with the dignity of an exposition of human strength and human frailty. It is in this epilogue that the conflicting fundamental motives of love and hate and self-preservation are given full play. The exposition is fair; the solution is left to the reader: The young lover opens the door on the right.

Now [Stockton says], the point of the story is this: Did the tiger come out of that door, or did the lady?

The more we reflect upon this question, the harder it is to answer. It involves a study of the human heart which leads us through devious mazes of passion, out of which it is difficult to find our way. Think of it, fair reader, not as if the decision of the question depended upon yourself, but upon that hot-blooded, semi-barbaric princess, her soul at a white heat beneath the combined fires of despair and jealousy. She had lost him, but who should have him! . . .

The problem of "The Lady, or the Tiger?" as Stockton presented it, was so fundamentally human, so fine a representation of universal emotions and conflicting human desires that it was everywhere discussed. So many thousands of letters poured in to him demanding, begging the answer, that Stockton,

"The epilogue raises the story above the level of the 'trick,' and invests it with the dignity of an exposition of human strength and human frailty."

who at first had stubbornly refused to give any answer, was forced to make a statement. His reply was no more satisfactory. He said, "If you decide which it was—the lady, or the tiger—you find out what kind of a person you are yourself." It is obvious that Stockton was wise in refusing to give his own solution to the problem, but, consciously or unconsciously, he seems to have given his solution—the tiger—in the story itself. In describing the princess, Stockton writes [italics mine]:

> This semi-barbaric king had a daughter as blooming as his most florid fancies, and with a soul as *fervent and imperious* as his own.—This royal maiden was well satisfied with her lover, for he was handsome and brave to a degree unsurpassed in all this kingdom, and she *loved him with an ardor that had enough of barbarism in it to make it exceedingly warm and strong.*

Stockton pictures an *imperious, semi-barbaric* princess who is in love with a brave man, but who is *not* convinced that her love is fully returned. . . .

> *She had lost him, but who should have him?*

The sentence seems to be the unconscious revelation of Stockton's own belief. The same notion in favor of the tiger was expressed by Robert Browning when the problem was presented to him. He replied:

> According to your desire I read the story in question last evening, and have no hesitation in supposing that such a princess, under such circumstances would direct her lover to the tiger's door; mind, I emphasize *such* and *so* circumstanced a person.

It is, however, the sheer human interest of the problem that Stockton proposed which gives "The Lady, or the Tiger?" its valid claim as one of the world's great short stories.

Source: Martin I. J. Griffin, in *Frank R. Stockton: A Critical Biography,* University of Pennsylvania Press, 1939, pp. 64–8.

Henry C. Vedder

In the following excerpt, Vedder comments on Stockton's use of language and wit in an analysis of the style of his short fiction.

American humor has now a world-wide repute, and is enjoyed if not appreciated by an international audience. The goddess of fame has been more lavish than discriminating in the distribution of her favors to American humorists. It is a single type of humor that has become known to foreign readers as distinctively American,—the type of which Artemus Ward and Mark Twain (in a part of his writings) are the best representatives. This humor is broad; it deals largely in exaggeration; it produces gales of merriment by a fortunate jest; it lacks delicacy, constructive power, and literary form. Foreign critics, who are more distinguished for refined taste than for profound knowledge of things American, seldom speak with much respect of American humor. It may be well adapted, they concede, to tickle the ears of the groundlings, but it makes the judicious grieve. We who are to the manner born know the weak spot in this criticism. We know that America has produced another type of humor, and appreciate at its true value the courtly polish of Irving, the catholic and urbane manner of Lowell, the playful, half-bantering earnestness of Warner. To this school belongs the subject of this paper, and he alone would redeem our humorists from the charge of coarseness and want of literary charm. . . .

[In "The Lady or the Tiger?," the] artful way in which [Stockton] led his readers up to the crucial problem and then betrayed their confidence by refusing to solve it, cloaking this refusal under a pretext of inability to decide the question he had raised, was a stroke of humor that showed genius. It also showed commercial shrewdness, and had its reward. Curiosity was piqued, discussion was provoked, and debate on the merits of the question became quite a social "fad." When one thinks on what a slender basis literary fame is sometimes built, how fortuitous the gaining of it generally is, how frequently the public admires an author for that which is not best and most characteristic in his work, the stir that followed the publication of this story becomes more humorous than anything in the story itself. Since that time there has been not only a ready market, but an eager public, for whatever Mr. Stockton might write. He has not been tempted, however, to over-production. He has never shaken from the tree the unripe fruits of his imagination merely because they would sell, but has left them to grow and ripen and mellow.

As no reader will have failed to infer, Mr. Stockton is first of all a clever writer of short stories. Collections of his magazine stories have been made at various times since 1884: *The Lady or the Tiger?, The Christmas Wreck, The Bee Man of Orn, Amos Kilbright, The Clocks of Rondaine,* and *The Watchmaker's Wife,*—each volume containing, besides the title story, several other tales. These volumes show Mr. Stockton's peculiar powers at their best, and they give him an unquestioned place in the front rank of American story-writers. It is true that these tales of his violate certain conventions of literary art. They seldom have a plot; they frequently have no dialogue, consisting wholly or mainly of narrative or monologue; there is not much description, and no apparent attempt at effect. One would say that stories constructed on such a plan could hardly fail to be tedious, however brief, since they lack so many of the things that other story-tellers rely upon for effects. Mr. Stockton's method is vindicated by its success, not by its *a priori* reasonableness. There is such a thing, no doubt, as "good form" in every performance that demands skill; but, after all, the main point is to do the thing. David's smooth stones from the brook seemed a very ineffective weapon with which to encounter a giant, and every military authority of the age would have pronounced his attempt hopeless; but Goliath found, to his cost, that the shepherd's sling was mightier than the warrior's sword and spear. The Western oarsmen who rowed by the light of nature, and nevertheless beat crews trained to row scientifically, explained that theirs was called the "git thar" stroke. Mr. Stockton's method of story-telling may be similarly defined; it succeeds with him, but in another's hands it would very likely be a failure.

It must not be inferred that these stories lack literary merit. The contrary is the fact, as a critical study of them discloses. . . . From one point of view Mr. Stockton may almost be said to have no style. There is nothing, one means, in the mere turn of his sentences, in his method of expression, that can be seized upon as characteristic, and laid away in memory as a sort of trademark by which the author's other work may be tested, judged, and identified. It is very plain, simple, flowing English, this style of Stockton's, the sort of writing that appears to the inexperienced the easiest thing in the world to do—until they have tried. The art that conceals art, until it can pass for nature itself,—that, we are continually told, is the highest type, and the secret of that Mr. Stockton has somehow caught.

These tales stamp their author as one of the most original of American writers. Though his style lacks mannerism or distinctive flavor, it is not so with the substance of his work. That has plenty of flavor, flavor of a kind so peculiar that his work could never by any accident be mistaken for that of any other writer. It might be not the easiest of tasks to tell whether an anonymous essay or story should be fathered upon Mr. Howells or Mr. Aldrich; but it requires no such nicety of literary taste to recognize a story of Mr. Stockton's. One who has sufficient accuracy of taste to distinguish between a slice of roast beef and a raw potato, so to speak, will know the savor of his work wherever it is met. Other writers may be as original, in the strict sense of that term, but few, if any, are so individual, so unmistakably themselves and nobody else.

Source: Henry C. Vedder, ''Francis Richard Stockton,'' in *American Writers of To-day,* Silver, Burdett, and Company, 1895, pp. 288–300.

William Dean Howells

In the following excerpt, Howells examines the elements and style of Stockton's short stories, commenting particularly on Stockton's wit and delineation of plot.

Mr. Stockton's readers have a right to look a little askance at the title and general air of the two volumes, recently published, bearing his name. Is it intimated that this story-teller, having developed into a novelist, finds it a convenient time to bring together in a complete form all his short stories, and thus to take leave of the company? It is quite true that the short story is for most writers a desirable trial flight before they essay the bolder excursion of the novel, and that many short stories are only imperfectly developed novels. It is also true that a prudent intellectual workman may well consider if he be studying a proper economy of his resources, when he uses a dozen different *motifs* in as many stories, instead of making one serve for a single story in a dozen chapters. But, after all, the short story *par excellence* has its own virtue, and is not itself an expanded anecdote any more than it is an arrested novel; and where a writer like Mr. Stockton has shown that his genius has its capital exhibition in the short story, his readers justly take alarm when he makes sign of abandoning it for a form of literature which, though possessed of more circumstance and traditional dignity, is not intrinsically

"Mr. Stockton, more, perhaps, than any recent writer, has helped to define the peculiar virtues of the short story. He has shown how possible it is to use surprise as an effective element, and to make the turn of a story rather than the crisis of a plot account for everything."

more honorable. Or, rather, if we are comparing two cognate forms, it is correcter to say that while larger powers may go into one than into the other, a unique excellence in the minor form justifies a claim to be a genuine artist, and comparisons in that respect are futile; the sphericity of a bubble does not quarrel with the sphericity of a dewdrop.

Mr. Stockton, more, perhaps, than any recent writer, has helped to define the peculiar virtues of the short story. He has shown how possible it is to use surprise as an effective element, and to make the turn of a story rather than the crisis of a plot account for everything. In a well-constructed novel characters move forward to determination, and, whatever intricacy of movement there may be, it is the conclusion which justifies the elaboration. We are constantly criticising, either openly or unconsciously, a theory of novel-writing which makes any section of human life to constitute a proper field for a finished work; however many sequels may be linked on, we instinctively demand that a novel shall contain within itself a definite conclusion of the matter presented to view. But we do not exact this in a short story; we concede that space for development of character is wanting; we accept characters made to hand, and ask only that the occasion of the story shall be adequate. . . . It may be said in general that Mr. Stockton does not often rely upon a sudden reversal at the end of a story, to capture the reader . . . , but gives him a whimsy or caprice to enjoy, while he works out the details in a succession of amusing turns. . . .

There is . . . in his stories a delicious mockery of current realistic fiction. He has an immense advantage over his brother realists. They are obliged to conform themselves to the reality which other people think they see, and they are constantly in danger of making some fatal blunder; making the sun, we will say, strike a looking-glass hung upon a wall in a house so topographically indicated as to be easily identified by the neighbors, who concur in testifying that the sun by no possibility could touch the glass, day or night. Mr. Stockton, we repeat, has an immense advantage over other realists. His people are just as much alive as theirs, and they are all just as common-place; they talk just as slouchy English, and they are equally free from any romantic nonsense; but they are living in a world of Mr. Stockton's invention, which is provided with a few slight improvements, and they avail themselves of these with an unconcern which must fill with anguish those realistic novelists who permit their characters to break all the ten commandments in turn, but use their most strenuous endeavors to keep them from breaking the one imperious commandment, Thou shalt not transgress the law of average experience. Mr. Stockton's characters, on their part, never trouble themselves about the ten commandments,—morality is a sort of matter of course with them,—but they break the realist's great commandment in the most innocent and unconscious manner. . . .

We may observe here that Mr. Stockton falls easily into the autobiographic form, and that his peculiar gift gains by this device. In actual life we listen to a man who can tell a wonderful story of his own experience, and our incredulity vanishes before the spectacle of his honest, transparent face and the sound of his tranquil, unaffected voice. Thus Mr. Stockton, in his ingenious assumptions, brings to bear upon the reader the weight of a peculiarly innocent, ingenuous nature, for the figures that relate the several stories carry conviction by the very frankness of their narratives. They come forward with so guileless a bearing that the reader would be ashamed of himself if he began by doubting, and the entire absence of extravagance in the manner of the story continues to keep his doubts out of the way.

This low key in which Mr. Stockton pitches his stories, this eminently reasonable and simple tone which he adopts, is the secret of much of his success. One discovers this especially by reading "A Piece of Red Calico," and then fancying how Mark Twain would have treated the same subject. Both writers take on an air of sincerity, but one retains it throughout, and never seems to be assuming it; the other allows his drollery to sharpen, and before he is done his voice is at a very high pitch indeed. . . .

We began with the expression of a fear lest these two volumes were an informal announcement that their author had abandoned short stories for novels. A re-reading of the books and an inquiry into the secret of Mr. Stockton's well-won and honorable success reassure us. Whatever ventures he may make in the field of novel-writing, and however liberal may be his interpretation of the function of the novel, we cannot believe that he can escape the demands of his genius. The short story, either by itself or as an episode in a novel, so completely expresses his peculiar power, it makes such satisfactory use of his intellectual caprice, and it avoids so easily the perils which beset one who builds a novel upon a whim that, for his own pleasure, we are sure that Mr. Stockton will go on entertaining the public in a style where he is his only rival.

Source: William Dean Howells, "Stockton's Stories," in *The Atlantic Monthly,* Vol. LIX, No. CCCLI, January, 1887, pp. 130–32.

Sources

Golemba, Henry L. "Frank R. Stockton," in *Dictionary of Literary Biography,* Vol. 74: *American Short-Story Writers Before 1880,* Gale, 1988, pp. 341-47.

Pattee, Fred Lewis. *The Development of the American Short Story: An Historical Survey,* Harper & Bros., 1923, pp. 296–98.

Quiller-Couch, Sir Arthur. "Mr. Stockton," in *Adventures in Criticism,* Putnam, 1925, pp. 211-15.

Further Reading

Golemba, Henry L. *Frank R. Stockton,* Twayne, 1981, pp. 144-46.

Offers useful criticism on "The Lady, or the Tiger?," including sections on its themes and techniques.

Howells, William Dean. "Stockton's Stories," in *The Atlantic Monthly,* Vol. LIX, No. 351, January, 1887, pp. 130-32.

Reviews two of Stockton's short story collections, praising the author's accomplishment as a writer of short fiction.

Howells, William Dean. ''Fiction, New and Old,'' in *The Atlantic Monthly,* Vol. LXXXVII, No. 69, January, 1901, pp. 136-38.

A general discussion of the narrative technique in Stockton's short stories.

May, Jill P. ''Frank R. Stockton,'' in *Dictionary of Literary Biography,* Vol. 42: *American Writers for Children Before 1900,* Gale, 1985, pp. 332-38.

A useful critical biography, linking Stockton's life with his literary career.

Rosenberg, Ruth, revised by Jean C. Fulton. ''Frank R. Stockton,'' in *Critical Survey of Short Fiction,* Detroit: St. James Press, 1994, pp. 2225–29.

A biographical sketch of Stockton, with a list of his major works and further criticism.

The Man Who Lived Underground

Richard Wright

1942

''The Man Who Lived Underground,'' Richard Wright's story about a man who makes a home in city sewers after he is falsely accused of a murder, was first published in the journal *Accent* in 1942. It was originally written as a novel, but Wright could find no publisher for it and shortened the story to a length that would be suitable for a magazine. Two years later, the editor Edwin Seaver, a friend and admirer of Wright, included a longer version in an anthology, *Cross Section.* In 1960 the anthologized version of the story was included in Wright's collection *Eight Men.* Since that publication, the story has been consistently and widely anthologized and discussed. Wright did not live to see the ultimate success of his story, having died two months before *Eight Men* appeared.

The story concerns Fred Daniels, an African American falsely accused of killing a white woman. As he attempts to make a new life in the sewers, he examines his assumptions about guilt and innocence and comes to believe that people are inherently guilty and isolated from one another. These themes, as well as the exploration of life in a large city, are common in Wright's work.

Many readers have seen in ''The Man Who Lived Underground'' influences of Russian writer Fyodor Dostoyevsky's 1864 philosophical novella ''Notes from Underground.'' Others compare the sewer scenes to those in Victor Hugo's classic French novel, *Les Miserables.* Wright, largely self-educated but widely read in world fiction, used the themes and settings of these important European works to present a story that had not yet been told: the story of urban African Americans.

Author Biography

Richard Wright was born September 4, 1908, on a farm near Natchez, Mississippi. His father was a sharecropper and his mother was a teacher. Extreme poverty and family disintegration made it impossible for Wright to attend school regularly, so he was largely self-taught. He did well in school, especially in reading and writing, but he often had to leave school for weeks at a time to beg or work to supplement the family's income. In 1924, when he was only fifteen, he published his first short story, "The Voodoo of Hell's Half Acre," in an African-American newspaper. He continued writing and read whatever major magazines of the day he could find—as well as any books he could manage to check out of the whites-only library on a borrowed card.

In 1927 he left the South for Chicago, where he took a job as a postal clerk. When the Great Depression cost him that job, he found work with the Federal Negro Theater and the Illinois Writers' Project, both government-subsidized organizations. He continued writing. Although his themes were controversial, Wright's talent as a writer was instantly recognized. His first published book was *Uncle Tom's Children* in 1938, a collection of four novellas. This was followed by *Native Son* in 1940, which became one of the twentieth century's most well-known novels by an African American and established Wright's reputation as a major writer. It was made into a film in 1951, with Wright himself playing the leading role; another version of the film was produced in 1986.

Wright had joined the Communist Party in 1932, believing the Party could help bring about a social revolution in the United States. The Communist Party involved him in an intellectual community that transcended race and gave him opportunities to write and edit for Party publications. In his most famous work, the novel *Native Son,* the protagonist Bigger Thomas is defended in court by a Communist lawyer, who speaks eloquently about racial inequality. Wright remained a member of the Party until 1944.

Through his adult life, Wright wrestled with his roles as a black man, an artist, and an American. For most of the 1940s he lived in Mexico, where he wrote the first volume of his autobiography, *Black Boy,* in which he explored the artist's role in society, and the ways in which African Americans contribute to their own oppression. Shortly after *Black Boy* was published, Wright moved to Paris, where he lived for the rest of his life.

In 1953 he published another violent novel dealing with an urban African-American victim of poverty and oppression, *The Outsider.* This was followed by other novels, another volume of autobiography, and political nonfiction. He died in Paris in 1960, after several years of illness.

Plot Summary

As the story begins, a unnamed man is hiding from the police. He is tired of running and has decided that he must either find a hiding place or surrender. At that moment he sees a manhole cover in the street. He lifts the cover; the water below is deep and fast. His fear of the police is stronger than his fear of the water and the darkness, so he enters and is nearly swept away and killed by the water before he finds his footing. As he explores the tunnels, he knows that he is in danger, but an "irrational impulse" prevents him from leaving. Instead he moves forward, looking for a dry hiding place or a safe way out.

Following a faint sound he cannot identify, he comes to a section of the tunnel that is taller and has fresher air. He gropes along, using a pole to test the depth of the water in front of him and occasionally lights a match for a brief bit of light. He finds a dirt cave off to one side, and then comes to a brick wall, through which he can plainly hear a group of people singing Christian hymns. Pulling himself up on some old pipes near the ceiling, he can see through a crevice that black people in white robes are holding a church service. It seems to him that what they are doing is wrong, that asking for forgiveness is obscene.

The man moves on, feeling his way through the water. By the faint light from another manhole cover, he sees a dead baby floating in the water; it has gotten snagged on some debris. With his eyes closed he uses his foot to push the body free, but in his mind he sees it swept away by the current. The nightmarish quality of this episode, and his sense

Richard Wright

that the men and women in the church are as insignificant as this baby, makes him think again about his own guilt.

Returning to the cave, he sleeps. When he wakes, cold and hungry, he knows he should leave the sewers, but knowing that the police have a signed confession from him convinces him to stay. To pass the time, he idly pokes a brick wall with a jagged pipe, eventually loosening enough bricks so he can squeeze through into a dark basement room. The building he has entered turns out to be an undertaker's office, and through a keyhole he can see into a lit room where a dead man is being embalmed. He takes some tools from the coffin-maker's supply and uses a crowbar to open passages to other connected basements.

In a furnace room, he finds a sink with drinkable water and a workman's lunch box. He digs another hole in the bricks, and enters the furnace room of a jeweler's shop. Through a tiny crack he can see a white hand in the next room opening a combination safe full of money and gems. He determines to watch carefully next time so he can decipher the combination.

He miscalculates his place on the wall, and digs into the basement of a meat and fruit market instead. After the store closes, he enters and finds a meat cleaver that holds a strange attraction for him, more fresh water, and an array of fruit which he eats until full. While he is in the store, a white couple come into the store to buy grapes and mistake him for the shop assistant. They do not notice anything unusual about the man, although he must be wet and disheveled after his time in the sewer. When they leave, the man follows them outside. There he finds a newspaper, and the headline is about him. Fear sends him back underground.

He finds a way into the room with the safe. While the watchman sleeps, the man takes money and gems from the safe, then walks over to a typewriter. He tries to type his name, "freddaniels"; this is the only time his name is mentioned in the story. He adds the typewriter to his sack of booty, and returns to the cave. There, he rigs up an electric light and radio he has collected from the basements, and on a whim wallpapers his cave with money and sprinkles the floor with diamonds. He tells himself that what he has done is not equivalent to stealing, because the things he has taken mean nothing to him.

Daniels makes another round of the basements, and once again is drawn toward the sound of hymn singing. He watches a boy get beaten for stealing the radio that is in the man's cave. He watches the police interrogate, threaten, and beat the jewelry store watchman. These policemen are the same ones who forced Daniels to confess to a crime he did not commit. The watchman, however, does not confess but instead hangs himself, confirming the policemen's suspicions of his guilt.

Finally, Daniels accepts that all people share an inherent guilt, and he returns above ground to tell what he has learned. He finds the policemen who beat him, and begs them to come with him to his cave. They have found the real killer and have no further use for him. They burn his false confession, and as he descends back into the manhole, they shoot him. Like the dead baby before him, he is swept away down the sewer.

Characters

Fred Daniels

Fred Daniels is the African-American protagonist of the story, the man who lived underground.

He is an Everyman, whose name is not revealed until he attempts to type it out on the typewriter in the jewelry shop. A few hours later, when he tries to type his name again, even he cannot remember it. He is hiding in the sewer to escape the police, who have forced him to confess to murdering a white woman. (He had been employed at the home of a Mrs. Wooten, a neighbor of the murdered woman.) As the story unfolds and he travels through the sewer tunnels and through a series of connecting basements, little more is learned about him. He recognizes but rejects Christian hymns (in fact, he knows ''most of the churches in the area''), and he is able to use carpentry tools and run wiring. For the purposes of the story, his former life above ground is insignificant. It is what he learns underground, and his return as a new man to the world above, that matter. Ultimately, people with his newfound knowledge cannot be absorbed into society. Daniels is murdered, and there is no mention of anyone who will notice his disappearance.

Johnson

Johnson is one of the three police officers who beat a confession out of Fred Daniels and attempt to do the same to the night watchman, Thompson. Of the three, he is the most tentative, allowing Lawson to do his thinking for him.

Lawson

Lawson is the leader among the three police officers. His name is ironic, because he is not a ''son of the law,'' but a man who has corrupted the law for his own purposes. Under his direction, Johnson and Murphy have beaten two innocent men, leading to one false confession and one suicide. When he orders them to say nothing about Daniels's emergence and about burning the false confession, they agree with no questions. They do not even question why they are following Daniels to the sewer and seem genuinely surprised when Lawson shoots Daniels in cold blood. One of them asks Lawson why he shot Daniels. He replies, ''You've got to shoot his kind. They'd wreck things.''

Murphy

Murphy is another of the three police officers and the one who has the most sympathy for the protagonist. When Daniels appears at the police station after his time underground, Murphy tries to tell him that his name has been cleared, but he is silenced by Lawson. He believes Daniels is harmless but insane.

Media Adaptations

- In 1993, the City Theatre on the South Side of Pittsburgh, Pennsylvania, produced a stage version of ''The Man Who Lived Underground.''

Thompson

Thompson is the night watchman in the jewelry shop. He is sound asleep, with a picture of his wife and children at his head and his gun on the floor beside him, when Daniels empties the safe and also takes the gun. The next day, he is accused of the robbery by the same policemen who accused Daniels, and they beat the watchman as they earlier beat the protagonist, trying to get him to confess. When he is left alone for a few minutes, he kills himself.

Themes

Guilt and Innocence

One of the most important themes in ''The Man Who Lived Underground,'' the idea that Fred Daniels keeps exploring as he moves through the story, is the idea of guilt and innocence. In nearly every episode, Daniels wrestles with guilt. When he hears the churchgoers singing hymns, he wants to laugh, but immediately he is ''crushed with a sense of guilt.'' Contemplating the scene, he comes to believe that they are wrong to be asking forgiveness of God. The contrast is significant: he is ''crushed'' with guilt over the simple act of almost laughing, yet he feels that others should ''stand unrepentant'' for their own sins.

As he moves through the tunnels underground, his exploration of the meaning of guilt appears even more confused. He gradually comes to understand

Topics for Further Study

- Read the sections of Wright's autobiographical *Black Boy* that deal with his strict religious upbringing. To what extent do you think his own religious background influenced the church scenes in "The Man Who Lived Underground"?
- Find some other short stories about racial, ethnic, or gender-based oppression. Do you think Wright demonstrates more or less anger in this story than the writers of the other stories you found? Explain.
- Investigate the laws and policies that govern police officers as they carry out their duties, and the U.S. Supreme Court decision in the 1966 *Miranda v. Arizona* case. How likely would a Fred Daniels of today be coerced to confess to a crime he had not committed?
- "The Man Who Lived Underground" was written during the 1940s. Based on the evidence in the story and other things you can learn about that decade, do you think the United States has moved forward or backward in terms of providing equal opportunities for all its citizens since the 1940s? Have any "wrong turns" been made along the road to equal opportunity? If you believe so, explain.
- In 1993 the City Theatre on the South Side in Pittsburgh, Pennsylvania, presented a stage play version of "The Man Who Lived Underground." How easy do you think it would be to capture the atmosphere of the story visually? What scenes would have to be changed or omitted in a stage version? How well do you think an adaptation for radio would work? What about a film version? Which elements of the story would be best captured by each medium?

---

that everyone is equally guilty, or equally not guilty. Guilt does not prevent him from taking tools, food, a radio, money, or the other items he collects. He is unconcerned over the punishment the boy and the watchman receive because of his own actions, or over the watchman's suicide. He has to hold back another laugh while the boy is beaten for taking the radio, and hopes the beating will make the boy understand "the secret of his life, the guilt that he could never get rid of."

Daniels first enters the sewer soon after making a false confession, that is, after asserting his guilt when he is in fact innocent. At the end of the story, he tries to tell the policemen that he is guilty after all, but now they insist that he is innocent. He knows that the policemen do not understand what he is trying to tell them, but he knows what he has seen: "All the people I saw was guilty."

Alienation and Loneliness

Fred Daniels's alienation, his separateness from the rest of humanity, plays an important role in the story. His is not just a case of mistaken identity. By the middle of the story he has no identity at all, and cannot even remember his own name. Throughout the story he is repeatedly mistaken for someone else. The police think he is the murderer, the movie theater usher thinks he is a patron, the woman at the market thinks he is a shop assistant. For whatever reason the police made their mistake, the usher and the shopper simply must not be looking carefully, not considering Daniels as a human being; neither seems to notice that he is wet and smelling of the sewer, because they do not really notice him at all. Because he is invisible, thus anonymous, he is able to move freely both underground and above.

As he remembers his life above ground, Daniels makes no mention of family or friends, and he does not include family or friends in his playacting with the typewriter, the money, or the gun. Below ground, he is one man standing alone watching groups of people in church, in a theater, at work. He lives out the most common metaphor for separation: instead of figurative walls between himself and others, he and the people he watches are literally separated by brick walls.

Race and Racism

Although it is not the major theme of the story, race and racism are important to understanding what happens to Fred Daniels. An African-American male, he is accused of murdering a white woman, and history tells him that his chances of obtaining justice from white police officers and a white judicial system are slim. Indeed, the police officers have already beaten him, though they know he is innocent of the crime. The newspaper headline, ''Hunt Negro for Murder,'' demonstrates that Daniels's race is more significant to his accusers than his individual identity. Racism, therefore, is a part of what causes Daniels's fear and drives him underground in the first place.

Not everyone treats him terribly, however. The theater usher calls Daniels ''sir,'' and the woman buying grapes is civil enough. But when Daniels returns to the police station, he is called ''boy'' and laughed at. When the three arresting officers cannot make sense of Daniels's strange and incoherent talk, one of them, Lawson, speculates, ''Maybe it's because he lives in a white man's world.'' Wright, who chose to live most of his adult life outside the United States, believed that racist institutions can cause more harm than can be counteracted by well-meaning or morally neutral people. In Daniels's case, the very laws of the society—the police officer is named Law's Son—oppress those people they are supposed to protect. Daniels is an alienated everyman, whose race removes him even further from those around him.

Style

Images and Imagery

Through the many episodes of ''The Man Who Lived Underground,'' Wright weaves imagery of light and darkness, repeating, reinforcing, and inverting the imagery to heighten the sense that the world is chaotic and ultimately unknowable. For the most part, the underground is the world of darkness, and the world above ground is the world of light. The faint light that there is underground is strangely colored, from the ''lances of hazy violet'' coming through the holes in the manhole cover, to the light from the man's matches, ''glowing greenishly, turning red, orange, then yellow,'' to the ''red darkness'' of the furnace room, and to the ''yellow stems'' from another manhole that reveal the floating baby. These odd colors heighten the nightmarish quality of life underground, but also highlight the fact that in this place the man is learning a new way to see.

After just a short time underground, the man loses his ability to live in normal white light. From his dark refuge he can see clearly those people who are still above ground: the people singing in the church, the dead man on the embalming table, the workers in the jewelry shop. In many senses, he can see them more clearly than they can see themselves, and they—although they are standing in the light—cannot see him at all. But when he turns on an electric light in the mortician's basement a ''blinding glare'' renders him ''sightless, defenseless.'' By the end of the story, when he comes back out of the manhole, light and darkness have been inverted. He cannot see well (one harasser calls him ''blind''), and the lights of approaching cars cast him into ''a deeper darkness than he had ever known in the underground.'' As he realizes that the police officers will not listen to his revelation, the light of his new knowledge is extinguished: ''the sun of the underground was fleeting, and the terrible darkness of the day stood before him.''

Setting

The setting of the story, the sewer where Fred Daniels hides from the police, is also an overarching symbol of the darkness and slime in the depths of the human heart. Just as the stinking, filthy sewer lies just beneath the surface of the vibrant city streets, so do evil and rot lie just beneath the surface of society, and of individual people. Unless humankind can transform itself and climb out of the sewer, it will be doomed to everlasting fear, isolation, and blindness. Although he is not himself ''cleansed,'' Fred Daniels nearly succeeds in escaping the sewer, but the world is not yet ready for him or his message of universal guilt.

Naturalism

Wright's earliest autobiographical writings show that he was fascinated with the great novels of naturalism of the late nineteenth and early twentieth centuries, especially the work of Theodore Dreiser.

The foundation of naturalism is the belief that people are a part of the natural world, just as animals are. They are acted upon by forces in their environment which they cannot understand or control. Actions that appear to be acts of will are really reactions to external forces.

Fred Daniels is, as the saying goes, a victim of circumstance. He is accused of murder because of situations entirely out of his control: he is a man of the wrong color in the wrong place at the wrong time. Like many naturalistic protagonists, he is like an animal, living underground and compared by the narrator to a rat or a dog. Daniels is repeatedly driven to act by forces he cannot understand or control. Resting in his cave, he feels an ''irrational compulsion to act.'' As he climbs out of the manhole at the end of the story, the narrator observes, ''His mind said no; his body said yes; and his mind could not understand his feelings.'' Against his own will, he finds the policemen, who have more control over him than he does himself. They, too, are forced by circumstance; they have ''got to shoot his kind.'' When Daniels meets the cruel death that is the fate of most naturalistic protagonists, he is not even a man any longer, but ''a whirling object rushing alone in the darkness, veering, tossing, lost in the heart of the earth.''

Historical Context

The Great Migration

When the Industrial Revolution changed the economy of the United States from predominantly agricultural to predominantly industrial at the end of the nineteenth century, new opportunities opened up for African Americans who were former slaves or the descendants of slaves. Over the first several decades of the twentieth century, African Americans by the hundreds of thousands moved from rural areas in the South to the big industrial cities in the North in what came to be called the Great Migration. These migrants hoped to leave behind increasingly oppressive Jim Crow laws and mob violence directed against African Americans, as well as a poor agricultural economy worsened by a boll weevil infestation. World War I created a greater need for factory workers, because many workers were fighting and because it takes material goods to conduct a war, and many factories that had previously banned black workers now welcomed them.

The new black workers did not find utopia, however. Most were offered only nonskilled or semiskilled jobs, and they were paid less than white employees doing the same work. Poverty was still widespread, and most African Americans lived in ghettos in the inner cities. White violence against the newly arrived blacks led to riots that left many dead in the 1920s. A race riot in Chicago had to be suppressed by federal troops. Still, the migration continued. Between the end of World War I and the 1960s, more than six million African Americans left the South for what they hoped would be a better life in the North.

Wright was a part of this migration. He had been born on a plantation in Mississippi and lived in Tennessee, Arkansas, and again in Mississippi before arriving in a black ghetto in the South Side of Chicago in 1927 at the age of nineteen. There, he found a variety of menial jobs, but also had the opportunity to read widely and develop his writing. He saw that racism was as active in the North as in the South. When the Great Depression forced staff reductions at factories, for example, black workers were the first to be let go, regardless of length of service. Wright observed carefully, gathering what would become details and anecdotes for his writing. Ten years after moving to Chicago he moved to Harlem in New York City, where he was living when he wrote ''The Man Who Lived Underground.'' As he continued to write, he became the first major author to document the experiences of urban black men in the United States, and among the first to present African-American stories to a white audience.

The Communist Party

In 1932, Wright joined a group called the Chicago John Reed Club, a group of radical writers and artists organized by the Communist Party. He soon came to feel that this group of intellectuals, white and black, were interested in him as an individual, regardless of his race. He joined the Communist Party and became its local secretary. He wrote poems and essays about the proletariat, the lowest social class of workers who have no control over the factories in which they labor. As he worked

Compare & Contrast

- **1940s:** Jim Crow laws make life difficult for African Americans. They have a restricted legal right to vote, to ride public transportation, to eat in public restaurants and stay in hotels, to receive a fair wage for their work, to attend public colleges and universities, and no right to rent or buy homes where they wish.

  1990s: With the passage of the Civil Rights Bill in 1964 and the Voting Rights Act in 1965, along with subsequent civil rights legislation, the United States has attempted to remove all legal barriers preventing any citizen from achieving full benefits of American citizenship. However, extralegal economic and social barriers still remain, and the dream of equality for all is still unfulfilled.

- **1940s:** ''Negro'' is a neutral term describing a person of a particular race and is a term the members of the race use to describe themselves. The use of the word is not an insult or an attack. Wright himself had written an essay titled ''Blueprint for Negro Writing'' in 1937, and had helped create an international Congress of Negro Artists and Writers in 1955.

  1990s: The term ''Negro'' is rarely used, except in the names of older organizations like the United Negro College Fund. Successive generations have adopted different terminology, often rejecting earlier systems. The term now preferred by many is ''African American,'' which reflects African heritage and American citizenship. ''African American'' is used as either a noun or an adjective; the word ''black'' is also sometimes used as an adjective.

- **1940s:** When a white person calls a black man ''boy,'' it is a pointed and deliberate insult, denying that the black man has the dignity and stature of an adult. A man insulted in this way feels the strong impact of having been belittled.

  1990s: The term is rarely heard, and does not carry the power it once did. As an insult, ''boy'' has passed from fashion and does not resonate with speakers or hearers with anything approaching its old force.

- **1940s:** The Communist Party has some political influence in the United States and attracts many intellectuals who, like Wright, are disillusioned with inequalities in American society or simply want to align themselves with a cause they deem daringly fashionable. (A case in point here is the rise of Alger Hiss, a key State Department official during Franklin Roosevelt's administration.) To most Americans, however, ''Fifth Columnists,'' or organized subversives, are cold-blooded centralizers and planners trying to overthrow the republic in favor of an omnicompetent state.

  1990s: Since the end of the Cold War in 1990, the national obsession with eradicating communism has abated. Although the Communist Party still exists, the term ''Fifth Columnist'' has been largely forgotten.

with the Party in Chicago and Harlem, he came to consider that African Americans were not the only oppressed people in the United States, and that class was sometimes as big a factor as race in determining who thrived and who failed.

By the time he wrote ''The Man Who Lived Underground,'' Wright had become disillusioned with the Communist Party. He felt that they had manipulated him, turning his art into propaganda, and he no longer believed that the Party's agenda for African Americans was in their best interest. Edward Margolies, in his *The Art of Richard Wright,* finds that ''Fred Daniels' adventures suggest something of Wright's own emotions after ten years in the Communist underground.'' The tone of the story, he believes, is one of ''compassion and despair—compassion for a man trapped in his underground nature and despair that he will ever be able to set himself free.''

Critical Overview

When "The Man Who Lived Underground" was published in the anthology *Cross Section* in 1944, there was not yet a large reading public accustomed to reading works by African-American authors. It was assumed that a black writer could write only about race, from only one point of view, and for a primarily black audience. In Wright's case, his early reviewers had read *Native Son,* and most approached "The Man Who Lived Underground" with the assumption that they already knew what it was about. In a 1944 review in the *Chicago Sun,* Sterling North wrote, "As an enthusiastic Wright fan of several years standing I may perhaps be permitted to point out that Wright is still doing variations on the same theme." Most reviewers read the story as one of a black man suffering under white oppression, and went about supporting that view. A rare exception was Harry Hansen of the *New York World Telegram,* who read Fred Daniels's flight as a "symbolic mission" transcending merely racial or political intent.

Over the next fifteen years, *Cross Currents* went out of print, and Wright published several more books and stories. "The Man Who Lived Underground" faded from public consideration until it was published again in Wright's posthumous collection *Eight Men.* All of the significant criticism of the story follows its publication in *Eight Men.* While the volume as a whole was not as well received as much of Wright's earlier work, "The Man Who Lived Underground" was immediately and nearly consistently hailed as a masterpiece. Of all of Wright's short fiction, this story has been the most studied and the most admired.

For critics in the second half of the twentieth century, the factor of Fred Daniels's race is less important than his humanity. For these readers, Daniels's struggle transcends race and the social climate for African Americans in the United States. Comparing the story to Wright's novel *Native Son,* Shirley Meyer writes in *Negro American Literature Forum* that "While Bigger Thomas gains his identity . . . by defying white society, Fred Daniels gains his identity on a universal level by identifying with all men." Earle V. Bryant agrees that the story "is essentially concerned with personality and its transfiguration" in an essay in *CLA Journal,* but he reminds readers that it is racism that drives Daniels underground.

Critics during the 1960s and 1970s struggled with the question of whether "The Man Who Lived Underground" was a naturalistic or existentialist work. As the drive to categorize literature so strictly waned in the 1980s and 1990s, criticism of the story acknowledged that part of the story's strength comes from Wright's deft handling of material of both traditions. Patricia D. Watkins, writing in *Black American Literature Forum,* explains the paradox of "the story's simultaneous existence as a naturalistic (thus deterministic) fable and an existential (thus anti-deterministic) fable." Yoshinobu Hakutani finds, in effect, that all of the critics who admire the story for different reasons are correct. He finds both a story of one man's struggle with racism and a universal story of identity, both naturalism and existentialism, in a "subtle fusing of various intentions" that "has an affinity with Zen-inspired writing." In short, he finds that Wright knew what he was doing, and that "he succeeds in making his racial and universal themes intensify each other."

Criticism

Cynthia Bily

Bily has written for a wide variety of educational publishers, and directs an interdisciplinary college program for talented high school students. In the following essay, she discusses the strategies Wright uses to present Fred Daniels both as a representative African-American man in a racist society and as an Everyman whose crisis transcends race.

When a writer produces a story that becomes an overnight sensation, it is usually because she or he has written something that touches a nerve in the audience, often one that the readers did not even know was raw and exposed. This is what happened with Richard Wright's *Native Son,* which became a Book-of-the-Month Club selection and sold 200,000 copies in three weeks. Many found in Wright's novel their first exposure to what life was like for African Americans in the Northern cities. Certainly, most of the book's white readers had no intimate acquaintance with African Americans, and only the slightest general knowledge of their circumstances. They read the novel as much for information as for art. Richard Gilman, writing in *Commonweal* twenty years later, remembers that the book "jolted [him], as it did so many others, [but] it

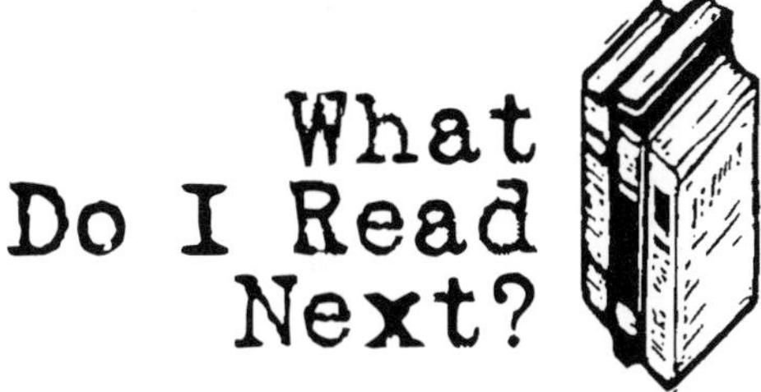

- *Black Metropolis: A Study of Negro Life in a Northern City* (1945) by St. Clair Drake and Horace R. Cayton, a classic sociological study of economic and social conditions on the South Side of Chicago in the first half of the twentieth century. This book has been revised and enlarged three times, most recently in 1993. The original introduction is by Richard Wright.
- *The Interpretation of Dreams* (1900) by Sigmund Freud, the Austrian psychiatrist who founded psychoanalysis. Wright was fascinated by Freud's theories about the connections between dreams and the unconscious, and may have been influenced by Freud's interpretations when he included imagery of stairs, tunnels and walls in his writing.
- *Invisible Man* (1952) by Ralph Ellison, an African-American novelist. Ellison's invisible man, who is never named, is a black man struggling to find his own identity, first in his Southern hometown, and then in a Black National group in New York City. Like Fred Daniels, the Invisible Man is a black man in a racist world, but his struggle to find meaning and purpose transcends race.
- *Native Son* (1940) by Wright. A young African American, Bigger Thomas, commits two murders, stands trial with the assistance of a Communist attorney, and is sentenced to death. Although he has committed serious crimes, Thomas is clearly presented as a victim himself, because of the racial oppression which Wright clearly and convincingly reveals.
- "Notes from Underground" (1864) by Fyodor Dostoyevsky, a Russian novelist and short story writer. This long story is told in two parts: a monologue in which the underground man argues against the notion that material progress leads to social progress, and a series of anecdotes playing out the narrator's ideas. Most critics believe that Wright was influenced by this story in creating his own.
- *Their Eyes Were Watching God* (1937) by Zora Neale Hurston, an African-American novelist and folklorist of the rural South. The novel tells the story of Janie Crawford, who struggles to find her identity through a series of relationships with men. The characters speak in dialects of the African-American South, a literary convention that caused Wright to reject the book as a "minstrel" novel.
- *The Trial* (1925) by Franz Kafka, an Austrian existential novelist. A bank assessor, Joseph K., finds himself accused by an unnamed judicial authority for a crime he knows nothing about. He struggles in vain for justice and is killed. Many critics have seen this story as an allegory of existential guilt.

---

is also true that the jolt was more of the sociological order, not the esthetic."

On the other hand, when a story appears that does not cause a sensation but is quietly and steadily read and talked about for decades, it is often because it contains themes and ideas that are universal, not specific to a particular place and time. This is the case with "The Man Who Lived Underground." Although it has much in common with *Native Son* in terms of situation, plot, character, and theme, Wright took deliberate pains in "The Man Who Lived Underground to present a story which both addresses and transcends issues of race.

Certainly, race is an important factor in the story. Fred Daniels is a black man accused of murdering a white woman. Because he is black and they are white, the three police officers feel free to beat him until he confesses to the crime, and the reader is made to understand that they are indifferent to whether or not he is actually guilty. When Daniels returns to the surface to tell the world what he has realized, he is called "boy" and "nigger" by

> "For Wright, color and color-based oppression are a surface problem—a symptom. Below the surface, in the human heart, is where corruption dwells. Some people are racist, but all people are guilty."

the people he encounters, and Lawson guesses that Daniels's confusion might be "because he lives in a white man's world." It is racism that sends him down into the sewer, and racism that prevents the police officers from listening to his story.

But this is not only a story of how white racism oppresses African Americans. After nearly a decade with the Communist Party, and years of reading fiction, psychology, and sociology from around the world, Wright came to believe that racism was just one symptom of an oppressive and corrupt human nature. Although he is an African-American author writing about an African-American protagonist—he is following the old dictum to "write what you know"—it would be a mistake to read the story as a message from one racial group to another. *Native Son* was a deliberate attempt to change white readers' minds about African Americans and bring about social change—a piece of propaganda. This short story is more than that. It is because Wright broadened his vision when he wrote "The Man Who Lived Underground" that the story retains much of its power more than fifty years after it was written.

If Wright wanted the reader to be constantly aware of Daniels's skin color, he could have easily and naturally made more reference to it. In fact, there are very few references to Daniels's appearance. When he has gone down into the manhole and thinks the police have discovered him, he sees "a white face" hovering above the opening before the lid is replaced. Is this the first hint that the man is not white himself, or is it meant only as a contrast to the opening that turns to black in the next sentence? When he watches "black men and women, dressed in white robes" singing in the church, he does not think that he has been one of them or make any reference to his own skin color. The scene in which he washes his hands in the furnace room sink would have been a natural place to describe the man's skin as he washed it—the man notices the color of everything else in this scene, including his urine. But even though the scenes underground are told in great detail, with nearly every important object described, the man himself is never described. The reader does not know whether he is tall or short, old or young, bearded or clean-shaven. And as long as the man remains underground, there is almost no evidence to settle the question of his color.

During the days he lives underground, the people he encounters do not pay much attention to his color, either. The usher in the theater is polite, and twice calls Daniels "sir." The couple buying grapes are cold, but civil. The woman whom Daniels frightens in the jewelry shop office is frightened because she saw "a man" in the window, but she never mentions his race, as she easily might have if Wright's point were to highlight racism. Again, if Wright's point were to call attention only to racism, he would have made these scenes more racially charged. Since strangers on the street go out of their way to shout insults at Daniels when he resurfaces at the end of the story, why should these white people be an exception? As long as he is living underground, Daniels has no particular identity—no name, no past, and no race. However, as soon as he returns to the surface to live, nearly everyone he meets notices his skin color and treats him badly because of it.

While Daniels is underground, most of the people he meets are "colorless" as well. The dead baby floating in the sewer, the dead man on the embalming table, the night watchman, the usher, the man who stokes the furnace, all are described without reference to their appearance. This is not consistently true: the hand that opens the safe is white, as are the couple in the market and the woman at the file cabinet, and the churchgoers are black. But for the most part, skin color is ascribed only to people above ground, while for those below color is not important. For Wright, color and color-based oppression are a surface problem—a symptom. Below the surface, in the human heart, is where corruption dwells. Some people are racist, but all people are guilty.

In fact, even the racist police officers are more than just racist. Their corruption goes beyond their treatment of Daniels, so that they are seen to mistreat everyone over whom they have power. When Daniels comes to confess to his guilt, Murphy tells him, "We caught the guy who did the Peabody job. He wasn't colored at all. He was an Eyetalian." It is all the same to him. The race of the night watchman is never revealed, but he is beaten and pushed to suicide by the police officers. Their evil, Wright says, is not just racism. They have the power to harm others because they are white, but their whiteness is not the source of evil—it just provides them with the opportunities for it to flourish.

Daniels is more like the other people in the story than he is unlike them. For most of the story he has no name, as most of the characters have no names. When his name is finally revealed, typed in lowercase letters with no space between the words, it is as featureless a name as "Johnson," "Murphy," "Lawson," or "Alice." They may as well all be named John or Jane Doe.

On the surface there are (or there seem to be) distinctions to be made among people. Below the surface, distinctions fade. Wright makes this clear with a series of images of the sewer current carrying away flotsam. First the man finds and kills a rat: "the grizzly body splashed into the dun-colored water and was snatched out of sight, spinning in the scuttling stream." Soon after, he finds the nude body of a dead baby and kicks it loose. "He kept his eyes closed, seeing the little body twisting in the current as it floated from sight." Both scenes involve twisting, and disappearing. At the end of the story, after all he has been through, the man is no different from a dead rat, or a dead baby: "He sighed and closed his eyes, a whirling object rushing alone in the darkness, veering, tossing, lost in the heart of the earth."

In modern literature, a rat is a symbol of evil; a baby stands for innocence. Daniels, the Everyman, is both—or neither. Underground, in the human heart that Wright compares to a sewer, the distinctions do not apply. Light and dark, wakefulness and sleep, guilt and innocence are impossible to determine. The world is chaotic, unknowable, terrifying. It is not a happy story, or an optimistic one, but it is a universal story that still speaks to readers a half century after Wright created it.

Source: Cynthia Bily, for *Short Stories for Students,* Gale, 1998.

J. F. Gounard

In the following essay, Gounard calls "The Man Who Lived Underground" an "existentialist parable" in which the protagonist is "the symbol of loneliness and anonymity surrounding man in a materialistic and unfeeling society."

During the summer of 1941, Richard Wright read an article in the August issue of *True Detective* which assumed a special significance for him. This article, "The Crime Hollywood Couldn't Believe," was about a 33-year-old man, Herbert C. Wright. Unemployed and aimless, Richard Wright's namesake had lived for more than a year in the sewers of Los Angeles. His subterranean existence had enabled him to get whatever he wished by entering stores through their sewer systems and helping himself. A close watch by the police eventually led to his arrest.

Fascinated by this story, Richard Wright noted a parallel between Herbert C. Wright's dilemma and the problems faced by the Black man in American society. Herbert Wright, who was a white man, was looking for a place in a society that rejected his attempts to establish himself as a responsible citizen. During his underground stay, he tried to develop a role, albeit peripheral to the mainstream of society, in which he could function and be himself. This theme was rapidly exploited by Richard Wright who held that the Black American had always played the same hidden role in a society that rejected him.

During the fall of 1941, Richard Wright wrote a short novel based on the *True Detective* story. Of the three sections of the novel, only the third, entitled "The Man Who Lived Underground," was published. It was later included in a collection of short works entitled *Eight Men.*

"The Man Who Lived Underground" tells the story of a Black man forced to hide in the sewers of a city because he is accused of a murder he has not committed. The underground world in which he lives for a while makes him discover that man is guilty by nature. The discovery of human guilt gives him the strength to leave his subterranean refuge to turn himself in to the police. But he is told that the murderer has been apprehended and that he is free. Convinced of his guilt as a man, he insists that police detectives follow him into the sewers to visit his underground world. Thinking he is a raving maniac, one of the detectives shoots him in cold blood when he is halfway down into a manhole. His body is abandoned to the dark and dirty kingdom of the sewers.

The long underground pilgrimage that changes the personality of the main character is used by Wright to illustrate the ideas he had about the essential nature of man. The author wants to show that the position of his protagonist is never stable. If this Black man escapes his racial condition by living in an underground world, he is guilty of abandoning his society. Even though his life enables him to become a man fully aware of his humanity, such a life led in the sewers, caves, and dark passages in which he wanders cannot be considered an ideal existence. It seems to be the existentialist metaphor of man's existence.

Through a series of experiences encountered during his forced isolation in the sewers, Wright's character develops a new perspective that transcends racial concerns and allows him to acquire a new understanding of human existence.

On one occasion, he observes a Black congregation singing in a church and people watching a film in a movie theater, and reaches the conclusion that man must feel guilty. His reasoning is that if man were satisfied with his fate, he would not be looking for an escape in religion or entertainment. On other occasions, he experiments with the liberty afforded by his new existence and begins to steal objects that have no value to him. From the cleaver taken in a grocery store to the diamonds found in the safe of a jewelry store, he sees only the tangible proof of his boundless power. He wants to show that he can do whatever he wants in this new and free world. He begins to feel that: "Maybe anything's right," that circumstances alone determine the rightness or wrongness of a man's actions. Certainly the material goods belonging to his former society are drastically altered in value in his new world. He plays like a child with the *worthless* items from the jewelry store. Dollar bills become wallpaper for his hideaway and rings and watches are hung as decorations. The diamonds are scattered on the ground and trampled.

It is interesting to note that Wright never refers to the main character by name in "The Man Who Lived Underground." It is only by chance that we learn his name when he finds a typewriter in the jewelry store and pecks out "freddaniels." As the story progresses, we again find Daniels seated before a typewriter, this time in the cave where he has made his underground home. Now, however, he tries in vain to recall his own name. Wright shows that the character's identity from his former existence has lost its meaning in his new life. His present condition represents that which is human and universal, and thus devoid of the most significant identifying feature of an individual man.

The choice of a Black man as the protagonist in this story made it easier for Wright to convey his ideas, since the white characters are blinded by racial prejudice that prevents them from knowing Daniels as a man. The condition of this Black man is not only symbolic of all Black Americans, but also of anyone who is oppressed. His life underground allows him to freely express the feelings of the human race that he represents.

Wright underlines that even when Daniels is outside his subterranean universe, he remains totally unknown to the people he meets. If this situation is caused by the color of his skin, it is also a result of human apathy. When he wanders in the halls of a movie theater, he is surprised to be told where the men's room is by an usher used to a tedious job. When he steps out of the grocery store to get some fresh air, a white couple mistakes him for a clerk and buys a pound of grapes from him. Neither the usher nor the white couple can imagine for a second that Daniels has created a fantastic world for himself underground. To them, he is only a person permitted to play certain given roles by society. Daniels' subterranean world is very different from the one above him. Everything is new, including the notion of time that is unimportant. He winds up the stolen watches without worrying about what time of the day or night it is.

A major attraction of "The Man Who Lived Underground" lies in the constant alternation between the mysterious and the commonplace. Apparently mysterious events abound when Daniels emerges from his underground world. The consequences, however, are most basic in terms of human experience. Daniels appears to exert an infinite power in his ability to reveal that man's behavior is founded on guilt and that a realization of this must be reached. A young worker in a radio shop is beaten by his boss and accused of stealing the radio taken by Daniels. Startled by Daniels' sudden appearance, the secretary of the jewelry store screams out in fright. After checking everywhere, her employers think she is mentally deranged because they have not found anything. The night watchman of the jewelry store commits suicide since everybody is convinced of his guilt after the safe has been emptied of its contents. Unable to understand why such a thing has happened to him, he puts an end to his life by shooting himself in the head. This suicide will serve as proof of his guilt to the police. Wright demonstrates that, dead or alive, the night watchman has no hope of proving his innocence to a blind and pitiless society.

If Daniels' invisibility causes brutalities and a suicide, it also enables him to observe and judge the world he has left. Conscious of the guilt of man, he knows that sometime during his life every man must face the mystery of his existence. After seeing someone steal money in the safe of the jewelry store, Daniels tells himself that the thief will pay for his act in the future.

Even though he is not responsible for the murder he was accused of committing, Daniels wants to turn himself in to the police because of a deep feeling of human guilt. He wants to insist on his guilt and also try to make its origin known to all. By doing this, he hopes men will acknowledge the existence of their original guilt and will therefore learn how to improve the lot of mankind. But his good intentions are squelched by suspicious police detectives who feel he would endanger the established order of things. The name of the one who shoots him, Lawson, is symbolic of his profession. He is supposed to protect society by enforcing the law.

''The Man Who Lived Underground'' is an existentialist parable since the protagonist develops his identity through his relationships with other people. Before Sartre or Camus had entered the literary scene, Wright had already grappled with the philosophy they later expressed. The author had tried to define the position of the individual in relation to modern society. Daniels is the symbol of the loneliness and anonymity surrounding man in a materialistic and unfeeling society.

Source: J. F. Gounard, ''Richard Wright's 'The Man Who Lived Underground', A Literary Analysis,'' in *Journal of Black Studies,* Vol. 8, No. 3, March, 1978, pp. 381–86.

Shirley Meyer

In the following essay, Meyer examines the events that lead to the protagonist's identity formation in ''The Man Who Lived Underground.'' The story's lesson, Meyer indicates, is that self-realization occurs only upon ''acceptance of one's responsibility in an absurd world.''

In Richard Wright's short story ''The Man Who Lived Underground'' the hero's quest for identity involves his struggle for meaning in an absurd

"'The Man Who Lived Underground' is an existentialist parable since the protagonist develops his identity through his relationships with other people. Before Sartre or Camus had entered the literary scene, Wright had already grappled with the philosophy they later expressed."

world which, although covered with pretensions of order and meaning, is more fundamentally marked by chaos, disorder, and blind materialism. The hero achieves his identity, however, only when his experiences underground convince him both that it is futile to expect to find meaning in an irrational world and that he must accept social responsibility despite the absurdity of human existence. Fred Daniels finds his identity when he realizes that all men are guilty because they possess an inherently evil nature and when he accepts the responsibility for his own implication in this evil nature.

''The Man Who Lived Underground'' differs from *Native Son,* which was written earlier; while the latter was a naturalistic novel exhibiting a deterministic philosophy and social protest against societal racism, the former (i.e., ''The Man Who Lived Underground'') is a work which is motivated by the existential vision. *Native Son* carries the message that the black man cannot achieve true identity through peaceful methods because societal forces prevent self-realization. ''The Man who Lived Underground,'' on the other hand, goes beyond social protest and says that all men are faced with a meaningless world for which they are in some measure guilty. To be sure, the black man is able to recognize the irrational character of the world more rapidly than others, for he has been driven underground by racism. But, more importantly, ''The Man Who Lived Underground'' carries the universal message that only the acceptance of one's responsibility in an absurd world can result in self-realization. The primary act which acceptance of one's responsibility entails is the act of communicating the existential vision to others. Whereas in *Native Son* Bigger Thomas' rebellious violence gains him his identity, it is not the answer for Fred Daniels. Rather than this, the black man (as representative of every man) must come to grips with an absurd world and must make the most of it by accepting his share of the guilt that characterizes human nature.

Fred Daniels' struggle begins when he is forced to flee from the police for a crime (murder) which he did not commit. He takes refuge by escaping through a manhole into the city sewer. It is here, beneath the superficial elements of the outer world, that he begins to discover the true nature of reality and of human nature. In the depths of the sewer Daniels gropes through the darkness until he finds that he has entrance to the basements of buildings adjacent to the sewer tunnels. In these buildings and in the sewer he sees people in grotesque and different roles, symbolic of the base human nature that underlays outer respectability. He first observes a Negro church service, next discovers a naked, dead baby caught in some debris in the sewer slime, and then goes on to view the people in a mortuary, a movie theatre, a jewelry firm, a radio repair shop, and a meat market. These incidents are significant because the people do not realize they are being observed, and Daniels is seeing them from a unique vantage point, from the level of the unconscious evil and despair which motivate man.

When Daniels first approaches the Negro church service and hears the people imploringly singing

> Jesus, take me to your home above
> And fold me in the bosom of Thy love. . . .

his impulse is to laugh at their blindness. The author tells us,

> Pain throbbed in his legs and a deeper pain, induced by the sight of those black people groveling and begging for something they could never get, churned in him. A vague conviction made him feel that those people should stand unrepentant and yield no quarter in singing and praying. . . .

Daniels sees another side of the human circus as he finds his way into a movie theater:

> Sprawling below him was a stretch of human faces, tilted upward, chanting, whistling, screaming, laughing. Dangling before the faces, high upon a screen of silver, were jerking shadows. . . .
>
> These people were laughing at their lives, he thought with amazement. They were shouting and yelling at the animated shadows of themselves. . . . Yes, these people were children, sleeping in their living, awake in their dying.

In this passage one cannot help seeing echoes of Macbeth's famous speech in which he asserts that

> Life's but a walking shadow; a poor player,
> That struts and frets his hour upon the stage,
> And then is heard no more: it is a tale
> Told by an idiot, full of sound and fury,
> Signifying nothing.
>
> (*Macbeth,* V. v.)

The next symbolic episode occurs as Daniels finds a jewelry firm in which he sees a man opening a huge safe filled with more money than he has ever seen. He feels compelled to get the combination and steal the money. Finally he does get the combination, and with no one around except the sleeping night watchman, he steals nearly all the money, jewelry, and diamonds.

It was with the discovery of the safe and his desire to get the money that "he had a reason for staying here in the underground." It is around this incident that Fred Daniels becomes aware of the evil nature and absurdity of the real world and the guilt of all mankind. He does not desire the money and jewels for any material gain, but merely as a symbol of defiance because he realizes their worthlessness. The symbolic nature of his stealing is again emphasized as Daniels is waiting to get the safe combination. However, when someone finally does open the safe, Daniels is angered to see that that person is also stealing the money.,

> He's stealing, he [Daniels] said to himself. He grew indignant, as if the money belonged to him. Though he had planned to steal the money, he despised and pitied the man. He felt that his stealing the money and the man's stealing were two entirely different things. He wanted to steal the money merely for the sensation involved in getting it, and he had no intention whatever of spending a penny of it; but he knew that the man who was now stealing it was going to spend it, perhaps for pleasure.

All the articles which Daniels plunders become for him his mockery of materialism:

> There was in him no sense of possessiveness; he was intrigued with the form and color of the money, with the manifold reactions which he knew that the men above-ground held toward it. . . .

> He did not feel he was stealing, for the cleaver, the radio, the money, and the typewriter were all on the same level of value, all meant the same thing to him. They were the serious toys of the men who lived in the dead world of sunshine and rain he had left, the world that had condemned him, branded him guilty.

And back in his cave in the underground, Daniels reflects upon his experiences:

> . . . he remembered the singing in the church, the people yelling in the movie, the dead baby, the nude man stretched out upon the white table. . . . He saw these items hovering before his eyes and felt that some dim meaning linked them together, that some magical relationship made them kin. He stared with vacant eyes, convinced that all of these images, with their tongueless reality, were striving to tell him something. . . .

And indeed they are telling him something, for when Daniels retraces his journey to revisit the people whom he has seen, he finds that a boy is being accused of taking the radio which Daniels himself had taken from the radio shop and that the night watchman is being beaten for stealing the money and jewels. Although they are not guilty of these particular crimes, they are guilty, as all men are guilty, by virtue of their humanity.

> Why was this sense of guilt so seemingly innate, so easy to come by, to think, to feel, so verily physical? It seemed that when one felt this guilt one was redesigned long before: it seemed that one was always trying to remember a gigantic shock that had left a haunting impression upon one's body which one could not forget or shake off, but which had been forgotten by the conscious mind, creating in one's life a state of eternal anxiety.

Daniels feels that he must act—he must return to the aboveground and proclaim his discovery to the world. He feels that if he tells them they will surely understand and see as he has seen. He returns to the police station to confess his guilt only to learn that the real murderer has been caught. Daniels insists upon his guilt, however, and takes the police to the sewer to show them what he has seen. The story ends ironically, however, as Daniels steps down into the sewer and is shot to death by the police officer. When asked by one of his fellow officers why he shot Daniels, the policeman replies, "You've got to shoot this kind. They'd wreck things."

Fred Daniels does achieve his identity through his act of leaving the sewer to tell the world the truth about a meaningless existence and an evil human nature, facts from which men in the outer world are hiding. He realizes that all men are responsible for their actions in a world of evil and absurdity, and that men must accept responsibility for their existence nevertheless. Fred Daniels becomes a symbol of true humanity in this story of paradoxes. For by running away he runs into the truth and discovers that the outside world of sunshine is really covered with the darkness of evil and that the dark world underground is really lightened with truth.

"Fred Daniels finds his identity when he realizes that all men are guilty because they possess an inherently evil nature and when he accepts the responsibility for his own implication in this evil nature."

While Fred Daniels is a black man, and Wright does make a few subtle comments about the racist society which drove him beneath ground, Wright does not absolve Daniels of guilt because of his oppression by a hostile society. Whereas Bigger Thomas in *Native Son* is inexorably driven by society to commit murder, and hence is not held responsible for his crime (as Max's speech seems to indicate), Fred Daniels is guilty of murder, and not because he actually committed it but only because of the evil nature which all men possess and which bind them together in all crimes committed by man. While Bigger Thomas gains his identity (via his "creative act" of murder) by defying white society, Fred Daniels gains his identity on a universal level by identifying with all men.

The story then is more than a mere social commentary, for it questions the nature of good and evil, and puts problem of identity to all mankind.

Source: Shirley Meyer, "The Identity of 'The Man Who Lived Underground'," in *Negro American Literature Forum,* Vol. 4, No. 2, July, 1970, pp. 52–5.

Sources

Bryant, Earle V. ''The Transformation of Personality in Richard Wright's 'The Man Who Lived Underground,''' in *CLA Journal,* Vol. 23, No. 4, 1990, p. 379.

Gilman, Richard. ''The Immediate Misfortunes of Widespread Literacy,'' in *Commonweal,* Vol. 74, No. 5, April 28, 1961, p. 130.

Hakutani, Yoshinobu. ''Richard Wright's 'The Man Who Lived Underground,' Nihilism, and Zen,'' in *Mississippi Quarterly,* Vol. 47, No. 2, Spring, 1994, p. 213.

Hansen, Harry. A review of *Cross Section* in *New York World Telegram,* May 31, 1944.

Margolies, Edward. *The Art of Richard Wright,* Southern Illinois University Press, 1969, p. 81.

North, Sterling. A review of *Cross Section* in *Chicago Sun,* June 4, 1944, sec. 5, p. 2.

Watkins, Patricia D. ''The Paradoxical Structure of Richard Wright's 'The Man Who Lived Underground,''' in *Black American Literature Forum,* Vol. 23, No. 4, Winter 1989, p. 767.

Further Reading

Aaron, Daniel. *Writers on the Left: Episodes in American Literary Communism,* Avon Books, 1961.

Examines the political and social twentieth-century American authors, especially those, including Wright, who joined the Communist Party. Wright was a member of the Party during the time he wrote ''The Man Who Lived Underground.''

Fabre, Michel. ''Richard Wright: The Man Who Lived Underground'' in *Studies in the Novel,* Vol. 3, No. 2, Summer 1971, pp. 165-89.

Describes the series of mysterious burglaries committed by a man living in the sewer that inspired Wright to write his story, and shows how Wright manipulated the facts of the actual case to present his own themes.

Fabre, Michel. *The Unfinished Quest of Richard Wright,* William Morrow, 1973.

The definitive biography, written by a leading Wright scholar. Fabre interviewed scores of people who knew Wright at various stages of his life, and presents a great deal of information that will never be superseded.

Felgar, Robert. *Richard Wright,* Twayne, 1980.

A solid starting point for studying Wright's life and writings. Felgar insightfully comments on the story in the context of Wright's full body of work and in the context of social history.

Ridenour, Ronald. ''The Man Who Lived Underground: A Critique,'' in *PHYLON: The Atlanta University of Race and Culture,* Vol. 31, No. 1, spring, 1970, pp. 54–7.

A general explication of ''The Man Who Lived Undergound,'' written in a time in which race relations were hotly debated.

Wright, Richard. *Black Boy: A Record of Childhood and Youth,* Harper, 1945.

The first volume of Wright's autobiography. The book reveals what life was like for many African Americans in the first half of the twentieth century. Of special interest are the sections dealing with Wright's extensive reading of naturalistic novels and how this reading shaped his own work.

On Discovery

Maxine Hong Kingston

1980

''On Discovery'' was first published in 1980 in Maxine Hong Kingston's second book, *China Men.* Along with another vignette, ''On Fathers,'' ''On Discovery,'' serves as a prologue to the family stories and histories contained within the volume. A blend of history, fiction, myth, and autobiography, *China Men* is a companion volume to Kingston's groundbreaking 1976 work, *The Woman Warrior: Memoirs of a Girlhood among Ghosts.* The story of a Chinese sojourner, or traveler, who makes several ironic discoveries in his search for an idealized America called Gold Mountain, ''On Discovery'' was highly acclaimed, as was the rest of *China Men.* Nominated for the 1980 Pulitzer Prize, *China Men* won both the American Book Award and the National Critics Circle Award.

Born in Stockton, California to Chinese immigrants, Kingston often integrates autobiographical elements with Chinese myths and fictionalized history to explore cultural conflicts confronting Americans of Chinese descent. Her work draws upon several sources: the ordeals of the Chinese immigrants who endured exploitation as they labored on American railroads and plantations; the ''talk-stories,'' or oral tales of mythic heroes and family histories told by her mother; and her own experiences as a first-generation American. *China Men* is an attempt to understand her silent father, who never spoke of the past, and to tell the story of what happened to him and other Chinese men who immigrated to America. ''What I am doing in this new

book is claiming America,'' explained Kingston in a 1980 *New York Times Book Review* interview. Written as part fairy tale and part history, ''On Discovery'' not only foregrounds the discrimination that faced Kingston's father and his forebears in America, but it also hints at the complexities of American racism and Chinese cultural misogyny that would be explored throughout *China Men.*

Author Biography

Born on October 27, 1940, in Stockton, California, Maxine Hong Kingston is the daughter of Chinese immigrants. One of six children, Kingston was not supposed to be a writer at all: her mother wanted her to be an engineer. However, after a few semesters at the University of California at Berkeley, Kingston decided to major in English. She graduated from Berkeley in 1962 and taught English and mathematics to high school students before publishing her first book, *The Woman Warrior: Memoirs of a Girlhood Among Ghosts* in 1976. A blend of memory and family stories, fiction and personal experiences, myth and history, *The Woman Warrior* won the 1976 National Book Critics Circle Award for nonfiction and was included in *Time* magazine's top ten list of books for the year. In 1980 Kingston published *China Men,* which features ''On Discovery'' as its first story. *China Men* was nominated for the 1980 Pulitzer Prize and received the American Book Award and the National Book Critics Circle Award. Her 1989 novel, *Tripmaster Monkey: His Fake Book,* won a PEN West Award for Fiction. Kingston has also written *Hawaii One Summer: 1978,* a collection of essays and short stories about Hawaii (where she has lived for many years), as well as numerous essays, articles and short stories. Kingston has received many awards and honors; the State of Hawaii recently declared her to be a living treasure.

Kingston's work draws from a variety of sources and genres—Chinese and American literature and myth, contemporary feminism, family stories, and folktales—to explore the experiences of Chinese American men and women in America. Because her books are interdisciplinary—they contain history, fiction, biography and myth—they are taught in history, women's studies, ethnic studies, and American culture classes as well as in English literature classes. A major theme of all of Kingston's work is claiming America, and each of her books demonstrate that American history contains many different stories. In *Tripmaster Monkey,* Kingston's protagonist, Wittman Ah Sing (named after Walt Whitman and his famous poem, ''I Sing America''), creates not the Great American Novel but the Great American Play.

Kingston is married to Earll Kingston, an actor, and has a son, Joseph, a musician. She currently resides in California, where she is a Chancellor's Distinguished Professor at the University of California at Berkeley. When asked by *SSfS* to comment on the story ''On Discovery,'' she stated that it ''is but the introduction and prologue to an epic novel, *China Men.* Anything mysterious and strange that you don't get should become clear to you when you read the rest of the book.'' Further commenting on the novel, she said that through it, ''I mean to claim America for myself. If America belongs to the 'discoverers' who got here first, Chinese explorers got here a thousand years before Columbus.'' Lastly, she noted: ''I mean 'On Discovery' to be a feminist story.''

Plot Summary

''On Discovery'' begins with the words of a fairy tale: ''once upon a time.'' The story opens with a Chinese explorer named Tang Ao, crossing an ocean in search of the Gold Mountain. Gold Mountain is what Chinese immigrants called the United States because of the gold discovered in California in 1849. Instead of Gold Mountain, Tang Ao discovers the Land of Women. Because he does not expect women to capture him, they easily take him prisoner.

The women lock him in a women's bedroom filled with canopies, makeup, mirrors, and women's clothing. They tell Tang Ao that he needs to get ready to meet the Queen. After they take off his coat, some women shackle his wrists behind him. The women then kneel before him to remove his boots and chain his ankles together.

When the door opens, Tang Ao expects the Queen to appear. Instead, he finds two old women with sewing boxes who tell him not to resist. Two other women sit on him to prevent his moving, and another holds his head while one old woman traces his ear, scraping her fingernail on his neck. He asks what they are doing. As she sterilizes the needle in a candle flame, the old woman jokes that she will sew his lips together. The women all laugh as the old woman pierces his ears using needle and silk thread. Although the women do not literally sew Tang Ao's lips together, after that moment he does not speak.

But the ritual is not over. The women bind his feet, bending his toes back and cracking the arches of each foot. Then they squeeze his feet, breaking many little bones along the sides. They wrap his toes so tightly that Tang Ao weeps with pain. The old women seem not to notice; they wind the bandages tighter and tighter around his feet and try to distract him by singing.

The women keep Tang Ao prisoner for several months. During this time they feed him "women's food." Every day, the women put new thread through the scabs that have grown in his earlobes the previous night until one day they put gold hoop earrings in his ears. Every night, the women remove the bandages with which they have bound his feet, but Tang Ao begs to leave the bandages on. Because his veins have shrunk and the blood flowing through them throbs unbearably, Tang Ao now prefers to have his feet wrapped tightly in the bandages. The final indignity comes when the women force Tang Ao to wash his own bandages. Embroidered with flowers, the bandages are attractive on the outside, but they smell of rotting, moldy cheese from his decaying and infected feet. Tang Ao is embarrassed because the dirty bandages seem like soiled underwear.

One day, the women put jade studs in his ears. They unwrap his bandages and strap his feet to shoes that "curve like bridges." They pluck every hair from his face, powder his face white, and paint eyebrows, lips and cheeks. Finally, Tang Ao is ready to serve a meal at the Queen's court. His hips sway and his shoulders swivel because of his deformed feet. Everyone at court marvels at how beautiful he is. They especially admire his feet as he bends to place their dishes before them. The diners call Tang Ao "she": "She's pretty, don't you agree?"

The narrator adds a postscript to the preceding "fairy tale," explaining that in the Land of Women there are no taxes or wars. The narrator says that sources disagree about when Tang Ao discovered the Land of Women. Some scholars say that the Land of Women was discovered during the reign of Empress Wu (A.D. 694-705), but others claim that it was much earlier than that, A.D. 441. The narrator also suggests that the Land of Women was in North America.

> "It is extemely difficult if not impossible for an author to say what a story means in other words. Everything you need in order to understand the story is already in the story."
>
> —Maxine Hong Kingston

Characters

Tang Ao

The main character of "On Discovery" is Tang Ao, a Chinese explorer in search of riches in the Gold Mountain (America). Instead of finding the Gold Mountain, however, he finds the Land of Women, where he is captured and made into a woman. His feet are bound, his ears pierced, his facial hair plucked, and his face painted. Through his transformation, Tang Ao learns that one can "discover" new lands and ideas without conquering. The source of "On Discovery" is an early nineteenth-century Chinese novel written by Li Ruzhen called *Flowers in the Mirror* In the original version, Tang Ao is a scholar who travels the world in order to find and save twelve flower fairies who have been banished from the Heavenly Court.

Narrator

The narrator of "On Discovery" is, like many of Kingston's narrators, a trickster who plays jokes on the reader by being elusive about the genre and narrative of the story. A trickster narrator allows the author to tell several versions of a story at once, thereby questioning the authority of the canonical, or commonly accepted, versions of a tale. The narrator begins "On Discovery" with the words of a fairy tale: "Once upon a time." The narrator then

Maxine Hong Kingston

tells the fantastic story of how Tang Ao, an explorer, is captured in the Land of Women, all the while encouraging the reader to interpret the story as a fairy tale.

At the end of the story, however, the narrator suddenly suggests that the story is a true history by presenting the reader with ''facts'' in guise of dates, rulers, and geographic locations. Perhaps the Land of Women is not mythical after all, the narrator says: ''Some scholars say that the country was discovered during the reign of Empress Wu (A.D. 694-705), and some say earlier than that, A.D. 441, and it was in North America.'' The narrator suggests a historical basis to the narrative, but presents readers with several historical choices—is the narrative a fairy tale, or did it take place under the reign of the Empress Wu, or did it take place in the fifth century? Who are those who say one thing over the other, and how can readers tell which source to believe? The Empress Wu is a historical Chinese ruler; however, in an essay in *College Literature,* Ning Yu notes that ''two of the three dates that Kingston cites here are inaccurate, and deliberately so.'' The authority and reliability of Kingston's trickster narrator is questionable, and the narrator's tricks lead the reader to question the authenticity of the story.

The Women

An unknown number of women from the Land of Women capture, strip, shackle, pierce, pluck, paint, and bind Tang Ao. Kingston does not make it clear how many women remake Tang Ao in their image, but her descriptions of their activities convey that the women are strong, independent, and cheerful. When one woman jokes that she means to sew Tang Ao's lips together, the other women laugh, and they try to calm Tang Ao's suffering by singing traditional footbinding songs. The women are quite pleased with the result of their labor; they declare that Tang Ao is very pretty.

Themes

''On Discovery'' metaphorically foreshadows the injustice and oppression facing Chinese immigrants to America addressed in *China Men.*

Discovery

An important theme of ''On Discovery'' is discovery. Kingston has said she wrote the story to claim America for herself, for her father, and for her Chinese-American forebears. Tang Ao discovers the Land of Women just as Christopher Columbus discovered America, but significantly earlier. In Tang Ao's discovery, however, no conquest is made. Rather, his discovery is a result of a shift in perspective. At the beginning of the story, he winks at the women who capture him, but by the story's end he has become one of them. Discovery is an important theme in Kingston's work: for Kingston, writing itself is an act of discovery, and certainly she ''discovers'' new things in her Chinese and American source material that readers might not have seen before.

The American Dream

One of the most important themes in ''On Discovery'' is the elusiveness of the American Dream for the Chinese immigrants who came to build the railroads and work the cane fields of the United States. Seeking wealth and social mobility, the Chinese immigrants in America found instead institutionalized racism that prohibited them from becoming American citizens. As Kingston explained in ''The Laws'' section of *China Men,* although the Fourteenth Amendment, adopted in 1868, stipulated that naturalized Americans had the same rights as native-born Americans, the Nationality Act of 1870 said that only whites and "African aliens" could apply for U.S. citizenship. Since the Chinese immigrants were not white, they could not apply for citizenship and thus were not eligible for same rights as citizens. Laws in California prevented the Chinese immigrants from owning property or businesses. In 1882, the U.S. Congress passed the Chinese Exclusion Act, which banned Chinese laborers from entering the country. In 1924, Congress explicitly excluded Chinese women from entering the United States. It was not until 1943, when the U.S. and China signed a treaty of alliance against the Japanese, that the Exclusion Act of 1882 was repealed.

Expecting great riches in his quest for the Gold Mountain, Tang Ao finds himself instead in emasculated servitude. He is hobbled in his mobility by the foot binding just as the Chinese immigrants to America were by anti-Chinese laws. Chinese immigrant men, like Tang Ao, were forced to do "women's work" that white Americans did not want to do. Just as Tang Ao must wash his dirty bandages and serve the wealthy people at the Queen's court, many Chinese immigrants, shut out of other kinds of employment by discriminatory laws, worked long hours in laundries and restaurants for low wages.

Sex Roles and Sexism

In "On Discovery," there is a reversal of stereotypical sex roles. As a man, Tang Ao travels the world seeking treasure. In the Land of Women, he is conquered and made into a woman whose feet are bound and who is locked in a beautiful room. As a woman, Tang Ao finds himself in great pain; he cannot move without help, and he must perform menial tasks he finds embarrassing. Yet the diners at the Queen's court declare his feet beautiful as he bends to serve them. The torture that Tang Ao undergoes in the Land of Women is actually the process of the traditional foot-binding of Chinese noblewomen. Historically, to have one's feet bound was a sign of nobility and beauty, and men admired the effect on women. But for Tang Ao in the Land of Women, he finds the ritual to be the worst sort of torture imaginable.

Constricted by female traditions, Tang Ao is no less strong or smart than he is as a man. The women capture him effortlessly, and they use Tang Ao's own assumptions about women to do so. The women are strong: they sit on him, pierce his ears, and break the little bones in his feet even though he cries out in pain. Women themselves are not weak; they only appear that way because of the social roles

Media Adaptations

- *Maxine Hong Kingston Reading "The Woman Warrior," "China Men,"* was released as an audiocassette in 1987 by American Audio Prose Library.
- *China Men* was recorded unabridged as a series of nine audiocassettes by Books on Tape in 1995. It is performed by Kay Reading and is available through Books on Tape.

forced upon them, as Tang Ao—a discoverer—appears weak once those social roles are forced on him.

At the beginning of the story, Tang Ao does not take women seriously. In "On Discovery," Kingston writes, "[I]f he had male companions, he would've winked over his shoulder" when the women ask him to follow them. To him, the women are sexual objects who exist for his amusement. By the end of the story, however, Tang Ao's perspective has changed. As a prisoner in the Land of Women, he comes to understand how it feels to be a woman in a sexist culture.

Identity and Transformation

In "On Discovery" Tang Ao is transformed from a man into a woman. As a prisoner in the Land of Woman, Tang Ao's very identity changes. Through this act of transformation, Kingston challenges readers' understanding of the dichotomies of male versus female and victim versus victimizer. Although these ideas are often understood to be opposites, Kingston suggests that they are not. In "On Discovery," Tang Ao is simultaneously a man and a woman. Biologically, he is a man; socially, he is a woman. He is both a victim (the women take him hostage) and a victimizer (historically, Chinese men have inflicted these painful constrictions on women).

Through her fable, Kingston suggests that the position occupied by Chinese men in America re-

Topics for Further Study

- Kingston has said that "On Discovery" is the introduction to an epic novel. What connections do you see between "On Discovery" and the other stories in *China Men*? Do you agree with Kingston that *China Men* is an epic?
- Do some research on popular stereotypes of Asian Americans in twentieth-century America. How and why do you think stereotypes get started? Do you think Kingston deals with stereotypes effectively in "On Discovery," or do you agree with Frank Chin that her story allows readers to believe these stereotypes?
- *The Woman Warrior* is characterized as "autobiography" and *China Men* is characterized as "history." Read both works and think about whether you would put them in different categories. What do you think the necessary qualities of a history are? An autobiography? A novel? How can these genres overlap?
- Kingston's work is often discussed in the context of Asian-American literature. Read some fiction by other Asian-American writers and compare it to Kingston's, looking for similarities and differences. Are there many similarities among the stories? Are there just as many differences? Do you think that Asian Americans share a culture, or are there are many different Asian-American cultures?
- Kingston has said that she wrote "On Discovery" to tell the stories that her father would not tell. Why do you suppose Kingston's father would choose not to tell his stories? What good comes from telling stories of the past? Might there be a good reason to keep silent about the past?

sembles the position held by Chinese women in traditional China. Segregated in Chinatowns for much of the last two centuries, Americans of Chinese descent came, like Tang Ao, to occupy a "woman's" role in U.S. society, doing work that white men would not do. In both nineteenth- and twentieth-century American stereotypes of Asians, Asian-American men are depicted as being "womanly" and not masculine.

But Kingston goes further. Having been transformed into a woman, Tang Ao now has a different understanding of how his own culture treats women. Through the transformation of Tang Ao, Kingston suggests that all forms of oppression—including racism and sexism—are linked, and that to eradicate oppression, people must understand the ways in which they themselves have participated the oppression of others. Through Tang Ao's transformation (and throughout *China Men* and *The Woman Warrior*), Kingston demonstrates that men and women are not so different from each other and that the battles against racism and sexism must be fought together at the same time.

Silence and Speech

Although only touched upon in "On Discovery," an important theme in all Kingston's work, including *China Men* is the difficulty and necessity of putting silenced stories into speech. Historically, Chinese Americans have been silenced by discrimination and fear of deportation; their stories do not appear in conventional history books.

In "On Discovery," the women joke that they will sew Tang Ao's lips together. A few pages later, in the story "The Father from China," Kingston writes of her father's "wordless male screams" and "silences." The principle motivation for writing *China Men,* Kingston tells the reader, is to speak her father's stories and to get her father to speak for himself: "I'll tell you what I suppose from your silences and few words, and you can tell me that I'm mistaken. You'll just have to speak up with the real stories if I've got you wrong.''

Style

Setting

The setting of ''On Discovery'' is the Land of Women, which is, the narrator suggests, North America. The Land of Women is run by women, and there are no taxes or wars. The dates, too, are difficult to pin down: the narrator initially places the story in a timeless setting of long ago in a place far away, but by the end, the narrator is fairly certain that the events of this story occurred either during the reign of the real-life Empress Wu (A.D. 694-705) or in the fifth century; in either case, long before Christopher Columbus sailed to America.

Point of View and Narration

''On Discovery'' is narrated in the third person. The narrator presents a limited point of view, staying on the surface of the story and not allowing readers access to Tang Ao's or the women's unspoken thoughts. Tang Ao therefore remains a flat, or undeveloped, character about whom the readers do not learn much.

The narrator is an unreliable narrator in that it is difficult for readers to know whether or not to believe what the narrator is saying. The narrator says that ''On Discovery'' is both fairy tale and fact, fantastic yet true. The form of the story, too, mixes genres, beginning as a fairy tale and ending as a historical document. The subject of ''On Discovery'' is clearly epic—the discovery of a new land by a brave Chinese adventurer—but the narrator's treatment of the subject is decidedly not.

Parody and Allegory

While ''On Discovery,'' like *China Men* mixes genres, it most relies heavily on both parody and allegory. A parody imitates the style and features of a ''serious'' story in order to make fun of it. Parody often makes fun of something that is usually taken quite seriously. In her story, Kingston parodies the myth of the discovery of America.

An allegory is a narrative in which the plot, characters, and sometimes setting not only tell a coherent story on the surface, but also tell a second, hidden story. There are two types of allegory: historical/political allegory and the allegory of ideas. Kingston's story (and much of her other work) incorporate both. ''On Discovery'' functions as a historical allegory as it outlines in broad strokes many Chinese immigrants' experiences in America: they arrive hoping for importance and wealth but find mostly poverty and discrimination. Through a number of discriminatory laws, the Chinese in America were emasculated, which is just one metaphorical step away from being made into women.

''On Discovery'' is also an allegory of ideas. Like Lemuel Gulliver in Jonathan Swift's *Gulliver's Travels* who travels to outlandish lands only to discover the disgusting habits and foibles of the British in each, Tang Ao travels to the Land of Women only to discover, in grotesque parody, the sexist practices of the Chinese nobility. ''On Discovery'' is an allegory of ideas in which Kingston suggests that men of Chinese descent in America need to recognize the ways in which their treatment in America mirrors their own treatment of women. By having Tang Ao, the allegorical Chinese man in America, systematically tortured by being made into a woman, Kingston argues against both racist and sexist oppression.

Symbolism and Metaphors

Because ''On Discovery'' is an allegory, almost every aspect of it has some symbolic significance. Allegorical symbols pair a particular instance with a general concept, so that the character of Tang Ao represents all the Chinese sojourners who went to the Gold Mountain (America) in search of wealth, the foot binding symbolizes the ways in which the Chinese in America were systematically hobbled and emasculated, the soiled bandages that Tang Ao is forced to wash suggest the kind of degrading and devalued labor the Chinese in America performed.

An important metaphor in ''On Discovery'' is that of discovery. In the story, Kingston claims America for herself and the Chinese immigrants who first found it long before Columbus. For Kingston, discovery does not involve conquest but a change in perspective that allows for new understanding. Another important metaphor that is more present elsewhere in Kingston's work is silence. The women threaten to sew up Tang Ao's lips; the men in Kingston's book do not tell their stories readily. Also, the stories of the Chinese Americans who settled here have been silent far too long.

Poetic License

In her work, Kingston often employs Chinese myths, family stories, history, and her own experience in her narratives, including "On Discovery." Rather than tell the stories the way they have always been told, however, she adapts them for her own purposes, a technique called poetic license. Poetic license applies to the ways in which poets and writers are permitted to change the *literal* truth in order to convey a metaphorical or deeper truth. In "On Discovery," she borrows from Li Ru-zhen's nineteenth century novel, but she does not stay true to the original story line. In Kingston's version, Tang Ao is not explicitly a scholar; in Li's version, it is Tang Ao's brother who goes exploring; Li's explorer was searching to rescue fairy women, whereas in Kingston's, the explorer is seeking gold and is captured by women.

Kingston's sense of poetic license is not limited to adapting written stories; she often adapts her own experiences or family stories to get to a larger truth. In a 1980 *New York Times Book Review* interview, Kingston told Timothy Pfaff: "I wrote from stories I remembered because I knew if I asked them again, they would just tell me another version. Besides, I feel that what is remembered is very important. The mind selects out images and facts that have a certain significance."

Postmodernism

With its unreliable, trickster narrator and its blending of history, fiction and myth, Kingston's work, including "On Discovery," is an example of postmodern fiction. Postmodern literature like Kingston's blends literary genres such as the fairy tale and the historical narrative. It also plays with cultural and stylistic levels; although not very prominent in "On Discovery," Kingston often uses phrasing reminiscent of the oral tradition, suggested by the "once upon a time" of the story's opening, with the high culture of classical Chinese myths. Postmodern literature, like Kingston's, resists easy categorization. Readers wonder whether it is fiction or fact, biography or myth.

Much postmodern literature attempts to subvert accepted modes of thought and experience. Kingston in particular attempts to "break the silence" and put into words histories and experiences that have seldom made it into canonical literature or history. Kingston explains in her 1980 *New York Times Book Review* interview that through *China Men* she "is claiming America . . . in story after story Chinese-American people are claiming America."

Historical Context

The Gold Mountain and the Chinese in America

Though "On Discovery" takes place in the timeless domain of legends and myths, it can be useful to explore the history of Chinese in the United States to see parallels between history and Kingston's writing. The California Gold Rush of 1849 attracted immigrants from all over the world. Three Chinese immigrated to California in 1848; by 1851, there were 25,000; and by 1884, fully half of the farm laborers in California were of Chinese ancestry. The phrase *Kim Sum* or "Gold Mountain," which the Chinese called (and still call) America, summarized their dreams of striking it rich and returning home to China. Despite their dreams of wealth and their desire to return home drenched in gold, many of these Chinese travelers to America stayed and made America their home.

Laws in the nineteenth century made sure that the Chinese in America would have inferior status compared to other immigrant groups. Although the Burlingame Treaty of 1868 permitted free immigration of Chinese people to the United States, it explicitly forbade Chinese immigrants the right to become American citizens. The Chinese Exclusion Act of 1882 and the Geary Act of 1892 soon followed. The Chinese Exclusion Act of 1882 banned the entrance of Chinese laborers into the United States, both skilled and unskilled, for ten years; and the Geary Act of 1892 extended the 1882 Exclusion Act for another ten years. In 1904, the Chinese Exclusion Acts were extended indefinitely and made to include Hawaii and the Philippines as well as the continental United States.

Exclusionism was a U.S. policy at both the state and national levels well into the twentieth century. In 1924 Congress passed an Immigration Act that specifically excluded Chinese women and wives from entering the United States. Furthermore, any American who married a Chinese immigrant lost his or her citizenship. In 1943, when the United States and China became allies against Japan in World War II, Congress repealed the Exclusion Act of 1882, though immigration continued to be limited to a quota of 105 immigrants a year. During the war, the Japanese killed more than ten million Chinese civilians. Nevertheless, Chinese immigration to the United States did not rise.

After Congress passed the 1946 War Bride Act, which allowed soldiers to bring foreign-born wives

Compare & Contrast

- **1980s:** Vincent Chin, a Chinese American, is murdered in Detroit in 1982 by two unemployed white men who, enraged over the influx of Japanese automobile imports and the depressed state of the American economy, mistake Chin for a Japanese man.

  1990s: Millions of Americans admire the accomplishment of Maya Ying Lin, a Chinese-American sculptor, who designed the Civil Rights Memorial for the Southern Poverty Law Center in Montgomery, Alabama and the Vietnam Veterans Memorial in Washington, D.C. Both of these huge public sculptures are noted for their emphasis on healing past wrongs.

- **1890s:** The Chinese in America are, economically and politically, among the weakest and poorest of the nation's minorities.

  1990s: In 1997, President Bill Clinton comes under attack for allegedly accepting large campaign donations from wealthy Asian businessmen in exchange for influence in the administration's policies. Spokesmen for Clinton respond by denying any wrongdoing and hinting that the president's critics are simply anti-Asian bigots. At the end of 1997, Clinton appoints Bill Lann Lee, an Asian American, to serve as interim head of the U.S. Justice Department's Civil Rights Division.

- **1980:** In *Fullilove v. Klutznick,* the Supreme Court rules that Congress has the right to instill affirmative action quotas in awarding government contracts as a way to redress generations of racial discrimination against minorities.

  1990s: In a public referendum in 1996, the citizens of the State of California vote to approve Proposition 209, which bans public-sector affirmative action programs for women and minorities in favor of color-blind admission and hiring policies. Since the passing of Proposition 209, the number of African-American and Latino students admitted to state universities has decreased significantly. The number of Asian-American students admitted has risen slightly.

---

to the United States, the government finally permitted the wives and children of Chinese Americans to enter the country. When the Communist government took over China in 1949, Congress passed refugee laws which allowed non-Communist Chinese refugees to seek asylum in the States. It was not until 1965, 1968, and 1978 that new Immigration and Nationality Act and amendments defined "national origin" to mean "country of birth" rather than "race" and the Western and Eastern hemisphere were allotted more equitable quotas of immigrants to the U.S.

Writing Against Stereotypes

In addition to writing in the context of a history of institutionalized racism, Kingston is writing against stereotypical images of Asian Americans that have pervaded American popular culture for over 150 years. The Chinese in American culture were synonymous with opium dens, tong wars, coolie labor, the "yellow peril," laundries, and low wages. Basically, these stereotypes fall into two categories, "bad" Asians and "good" Asians. The "bad" Asians are villains like Fu Manchu or brute hordes that cannot be controlled and therefore must be eradicated. Stereotypes of "good" Asians present Asian Americans as loyal, lovable allies, sidekicks, and servants. Asians are represented as being comical, nonthreatening, noncompetitive, and asexual servants of white men. In stereotypical thinking, Asian men are shown as having no sexuality at all, whereas Asian women are depicted as extremely sexual "dragon ladies" and "geisha girls."

The purpose of both these dichotomous Asian stereotypes is to show the goodness of white Americans. When the Asian caricature is heartless and treacherous, by comparison, the white person is shown as having great integrity and humanity. When the Asian is depicted as cheerful and docile, the white person is shown as a benevolent master. Behind both these stereotypical caricatures is the idea of irreparable difference, with the assumption of Anglo-American superiority. As in ''On Discovery,'' Kingston often exploits a stereotype to make the reader aware of its painful impact on Chinese-American men and women and to metaphorically suggest the ways in which Chinese men in America were legally and culturally emasculated.

Sources for ''On Discovery''

Kingston has said that ''On Discovery'' draws from two sources: Jonathan Swift's eighteenth-century novel, *Gulliver's Travels* and Li Ru-zhen's nineteenth century novel, *Flowers in the Mirror.* Both novels concern voyagers who travel to imaginary lands. ''On Discovery'' adapts the characters and plot of *Flowers in the Mirror* and the allegorical intent of *Gulliver's Travels.*

In *Flowers in the Mirror,* Tang Ao decides to join his brother on a voyage. A god comes to him in a dream and tells him to search for twelve flower fairies (called ''high ladies'') and to bring them back to China. Lin Zhi-Yang, Tang Ao's brother-in-law, travels to the Land of Women, where he plans on selling cosmetics to the Queen and her concubines. The Queen decides that Lin Zhi-Yang should be her concubine, and the women pierce his ears and bind his feet to prepare him for his new role. With his superior command of technology, Tang Ao impresses the Queen by stopping the flooding waters, thus saving his brother-in-law and demonstrating Chinese ingenuity.

In *Gulliver's Travels,* Lemuel Gulliver travels from imaginary land to imaginary land, only to discover in each exotic locale the worst traits of the British, represented allegorically by the Lilliputians' pettiness, the Yahoos' brutishness, and other unsettling characteristics among the strange races he encounters. Gulliver travels far and wide to gain new insight about the human condition. Through allegorical satire, Swift criticizes the arrogance and pettiness of the British—and of people in general.

Both *Gulliver's Travels* and *Flowers in the Mirror* are written in the historical context of empire. Swift, an Irishman, criticizes Britain's imperialism, and Li Ru-zhen celebrates China's. When *Flowers in the Mirror* was first published, China was a great imperial power with colonies of its own. The original story of Tang Ao is a tale of imperial conquest, but Kingston subverts the original story of colonization and conquest so that the potential conqueror finds himself in the position of the conquered. Discovery, she suggests, is not an act of conquest but of insight and understanding.

Family Stories

In addition to historical facts, American stereotypes, and Chinese fables, Kingston's work incorporates idiosyncratic family stories and personal experiences. Like Tang Ao, Kingston's father was a scholar and a teacher in China; thus ''On Discovery'' can be read on yet another level, as a metaphor for the author's father's experience in America. Like Tang Ao, Kingston's father came to America in search of material wealth but found himself stripped of his previous social status, obliged to work in Chinese laundries, rendered speechless and illiterate because he could not speak or read English. The myth of ''On Discovery'' takes on a deeper significance as *China Men* progresses and each individual ''China Man's'' story gets told. The reader gets a sense of the ways in which for Kingston ancient and modern, factual and metaphorical, public and private narratives are inextricably interrelated.

Kingston has also said that she draws upon a tradition of ''talk-story,'' oral versions of classical myths that get passed down from generation to generation. In traditional China, many peasants were illiterate, and so stories would be preserved through repeated tellings.

Critical Overview

China Men, in which ''On Discovery'' appears, was highly acclaimed. Nominated for the 1980 Pulitzer Prize, it won the American Book Award and the National Critics Circle Award. The title of the book comes from the derogatory term ''chinaman,'' which is considered an ethnic slur. Kingston divides the word into its two parts, ''china'' and ''men,'' thus restoring the dignity of her forebears who came to America as she prepares the reader to listen to the stories of men of Chinese descent in America.

Upon its publication, *China Men* received impressive reviews from all the major literary reviewers. In the *New York Times Book Review,* Mary

Gordon observed that "*China Men* is a triumph of the highest order, of imagination, of language, of moral perception." John Leonard wrote in the *New York Times,* "Four years ago, I said [Kingston's] *The Woman Warrior* was the best book I'd read in years. *China Men* is, at the very least, the best book I've read in the four years since." Henrietta Buckmaster, writing in the *Christian Science Monitor,* found Kingston "brilliant. Her sense of words is magical." Anne Tyler called the book "a history at once savage and beautiful, a combination of bone-grinding reality and luminous fantasy." While historical events seem "robbed of factual precision," observed Tamar Jacoby in the *San Francisco Review of Books,* they "are somehow brightened and clarified." In an essay in the literary journal *MELUS,* Linda Ching Sledge declared, "It already seems apparent that for sheer literary talent, originality of style, and comprehensiveness of vision, Kingston is a major American writer and the most formidable Asian-American writer in this nation's history." Sledge further suggested that "*China Men* is neither novel nor history but represents that transmutation of 'oral history' into cultural literary epic."

"On Discovery" in particular has been singled out for praise as well. In *American Literary History,* David Leiwei Li wrote that "Kingston has exercised her cross-cultural imagination to its fullest potential." In *Conflicts in Feminism,* King-Kok Cheung wrote admiringly that "I cannot but see this legend as double-edged, pointing not only to the mortification of Chinese men in the new world but also to the subjugation of women both in old China and in America. . . . The opening myth suggests that the author objects as strenuously to the patriarchal practices of her forefathers in their adopted country." And in *Reading the Literatures of Asian America,* Donald Goellnicht noted that through the figure of Tang Ao, "Kingston seeks to redress this wrong of stereotyping and historical erasure, not by a simple reversal . . . but by a disruption of this gendered binary opposition."

Although *China Men* won many awards and was considered by many newspapers and journals to be one of the best ten books of 1980, Kingston's rewriting of Chinese myths has been criticized by a few. In an early review of *China Men* in the *New York Review of Books,* Frederick Wakeman, an expert on Chinese language and literature, criticized the ways in which Kingston altered and popularized classic Chinese literature such as *Flowers in the Mirror.* He wrote that Kingston's stories, including "On Discovery" "are only remotely connected with the original Chinese legends they invoke; and sometimes they are only spurious folklore, a kind of self-indulgent fantasy that blends extravagant personal imagery with appropriately *voelkisch* [folk-like] themes." In an interview with Jean Ross in *Contemporary Authors,* Kingston responded that because Wakeman studies classical literature, "he sees me as one who doesn't get it right, and who takes liberties with it. In actuality, I am writing in the peasant talk-story Cantonese tradition ('low' if you will), which is the heritage of Chinese Americans." She also told Timothy Pfaff in the *New York Times Book Review* that "I can't help but feeling that people who accuse me of misrepresenting the myths are looking at the past in a sentimental kind of way. It's *so easy* to look into the past. It's harder to look into the present and come to terms with what it means to be alive today."

Chinese-American novelist and playwright Frank Chin suggested that Kingston's manipulation of myths reinforces American stereotypes of Asians. In his introduction to *The Big Aieeeee!* Chin accused Kingston, along with writers such as Amy Tan and David Henry Hwang, of writing "fake" Chinese-American literature that primarily caters to the racist fantasies of white Americans. By exaggerating Chinese patriarchal attitudes and practices and by deliberately misrepresenting Chinese history and legends, Chin observed, Kingston reinforces American racist ideas that Chinese society is more misogynistic than, and therefore inferior to, American culture. Chin's discomfort with Kingston's and Tan's popularity with "mainstream" audiences has much in common with some African-American critics who feel that writers such as Toni Morrison and Alice Walker are anti-male in their focus because they expose problems in African-American communities to Anglo-American audiences.

Kingston explained that while she intended "On Discovery" and her other works to be feminist, her fiction neither attacks men nor allows ugly stereotypes to remain unquestioned. In an interview with Paula Rabinowitz in the *Michigan Quarterly Review,* Kingston said, "I think . . . that the men have had a very bad time." But, still, she continued, "Their anger is misplaced. They aren't reading us right. Instead of being angry with us—I mean, it takes a lot of words to write articles against us—they ought to be home working on those novels." Many critics have been quite impressed with

Kingston's treatment of anti-Asian stereotypes. In the *South Dakota Review,* Alfred Wang wrote that the "brutalization and mass emasculation of the Chinese-American male in America have not been dealt with honestly or profoundly in belles-lettres until the publication of . . . *China Men.*" Donald Goellnicht noted that "Kingston can both deplore the emasculation of China Men by mainstream America *and* critique the Confucian patriarchy of traditional family life." In light of the battle between Kingston and Chin, it is interesting to note that whereas *The Woman Warrior* told a woman's story and *China Men* told of the men's experiences in America, her 1989 novel, *Tripmaster Monkey: His Fake Book* contains a male central character and a female narrator.

Criticism

Jean Leverich

Leverich has a doctorate in English literature from the University of Michigan. She has taught writing and literature at Michigan, New York University's School of Continuing Education, and Georgetown University. In the following essay, she discusses feminism and history in "On Discovery."

When Maxine Hong Kingston began writing her first novel, she found that she was really writing two books. In an interview with Paula Rabinowitz in the *Michigan Quarterly Review,* Kingston said:

> At one time, *The Woman Warrior* and *China Men* were supposed to be one book. I had conceived of one huge book. However, part of the reason for two books is history. The women had their own time and place and their lives were coherent; there was a woman's way of thinking. My men's stories seemed to interfere. They were weakening the feminist point of view. So I took all the men's stories out, and then I had *The Woman Warrior.*

Because she felt that the stories of *China Men* undermined the feminist perspective of *The Woman Warrior,* Kingston separated the stories that comprised *China Men* from those included in her first book. Yet she has said elsewhere that she intends "On Discovery" to be a feminist story. Certainly, Li Ru-zhen, the author of *Flowers in the Mirror,* a source for "On Discovery," was a feminist who championed women's rights in nineteenth century China. This essay explores the ways in which "On Discovery" is a feminist narrative that also presents the hitherto silenced stories of men. Furthermore, "On Discovery" demonstrates that the women's and men's stories do not have to be separated; in fact, it stresses the importance of recognizing the ways in which men's and women's stories are similar and connected.

When Tang Ao arrives in the Land of Women and is captured, his first impulse is to wink at an imaginary male companion. He thinks it is funny to be taken prisoner by ladies, and therefore he is not on his guard. Because he does not suspect women as potential attackers, he is easily caught. In short order, the women make him feminine. The feminization of Tang Ao is a rather brutal process, involving footbinding, ear piercing, hair plucking, and face painting. The women's treatment of Tang Ao can be read as a story of feminist revenge. Although the tortures suffered by Tang Ao seem cruel, many Chinese women had for centuries been forced to undergo similar mutilation. The footbinding of Tang Ao can be read as a kind of revenge fantasy against the Chinese patriarchy in which the residents of the Land of Women do to Tang Ao what men have done to women in China for centuries. By having a man go through these ordeals, as King-Kok Cheung observes in *Conflicts in Feminism,* "On Discovery" clearly suggests that Kingston objects as strenuously to the patriarchal practices of her ancestral culture as she does to the racist treatment of her forefathers in America.

Under Confucianism, a philosophy followed by many Chinese, women did not have as much status in the family as men. Kingston's earliest memories involve hearing her father curse women. In "The Father From China," a short story in *China Men,* she seeks to understand how her father, who clearly loves her very much, could say terrible things about women. She wrote: "What I want from you is for you to tell me that those curses are only common Chinese sayings. That you did not mean to make me sicken at being female. 'Those were only sayings,' I want you to say to me. 'I didn't mean you or your mother. I didn't mean your sisters or grandmothers or women in general'."

Kingston describes in meticulous detail the process by which those in the Land of Women make Tang Ao a woman. The language is colorful and lush, aesthetically pleasing to the reader. Like the embroidery on the cloth bandages used to bind Tang Ao's feet, Kingston's narrative is intricate and delicate even as it contains great pain. Though Tang Ao cries out in agony at the torture of footbinding; for the women, this torture is a normal part of their everyday lives. They try to soothe Tang Ao with songs but continue to bind his feet. When Tang Ao's feet are appropriately small, they dress him in high platform sandals in which he can barely walk and make him serve food at the Queen's court. Once Tang Ao is in this state of submissive servitude, they pronounce him "pretty." Through Tang Ao's ordeal, "On Discovery" criticizes ideals of beauty that are predicated on pain and subservience.

By transforming Tang Ao into a woman, Kingston does not mean to suggest that women are in any way unequal to men. Quite the opposite, in fact. Kingston reverses male and female sex roles as a way of redefining heroism. As Linda Ching Sledge writes in *MELUS,* "Like the crafty Odysseus biding his time in the land of the nymph Calypso, the Chinese hero's strength consists of an ability to find new methods by which to endure, in this case to acquiesce and hence outlast his captivity." In other words, Tang Ao's ability to adapt and survive is heroic. Adaptation and survival are not what readers would normally consider "heroic"; traditionally, conquest and wars are heroic. Kingston plays with this idea in "On Discovery" because Tang Ao initially thinks that discovery is a heroic act of conquest. The narrator lets the reader know that in the Land of Women, this definition of heroism does not apply: "In the Women's Land there are no taxes and no wars." If there are no wars, then what is commonly understood to be heroic needs to be re-evaluated. Given what the Chinese immigrants endured in America, Kingston suggests, their very survival is a sign of strength and heroism.

To understand how enduring the transformation into becoming a woman might be considered heroic, readers need to understand the historical context against which Kingston sets "On Discovery." Kingston provides much of this context herself in "The Laws," a chapter in *China Men* that lists U.S. laws that discriminated against Chinese immigrants from the mid-nineteenth to the mid-twentieth centuries. These range from the 1882 Chinese Exclusion Act which prevented Chinese immigrants from legally immigrating to the United States, to laws that forbade Chinese immigrants from becoming American citizens, owning property or businesses, voting, testifying in court, to the 1924 Immigration Act which excluded Chinese women and declared that any American citizen who married

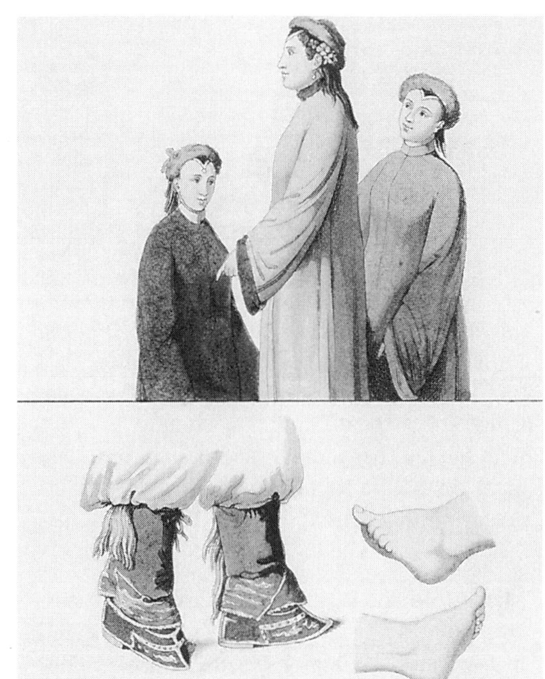

An illustration depicting Chinese foot binding.

a Chinese person would lose his or her citizenship. Although the Chinese Exclusion Act of 1882 was finally repealed in 1943, its damaging effects continued to be felt among Chinese-American communities.

Deprived of the right to bring their wives to the United States or to marry American citizens, the Chinese immigrants lived an isolated existence, working in service professions—in laundries, in restaurants, as servants to wealthy white people—that Americans considered "women's work." The backbreaking labor of the Chinese immigrants as they built a portion of the transcontinental railroad in the nineteenth century and worked in the cane fields was not respected. Instead, it was stereotyped as "coolie labor" for "slave wages." In *Asian-American Literature,* Elaine Kim cites a poem by Daniel O'Connell that was popular in the 1870s. Note how the following portion of the poem describes a swarm of unassimilable "chinamen" who are taking over America:

> We will make a second China by your
>   pleasant Western seas;
> We will swarm like locusts that scourged the East
>   of old. . .
> We can do your women's labor at half a
>   woman's rate . . .

What Do I Read Next?

- *The Woman Warrior: Memoirs of a Girlhood Among Ghosts* (1976), by Maxine Hong Kingston. In her first book, considered a companion book to *China Men,* Kingston writes about a young Chinese-American woman's coming to terms with herself, her mother, and her cultural heritage. Winner of the 1976 National Book Critics Award for nonfiction.
- *Tripmaster Monkey: His Fake Book* (1989), by Maxine Hong Kingston. In Kingston's first nonbiographical novel, Wittman Ah Sing, a beatnik fifth-generation Chinese American in San Francisco in the 1960s follows through on his namesake Walt Whitman's goal of creating a lively, raucous, inclusive, truly multicultural American literature.
- *Flowers in the Mirror* (1828), by Li Ru-zhen. This classic Chinese novel contains the original adventures of Tang Ao and is a source for Kingston's short story, "On Discovery."
- *Gulliver's Travels* (1726), by Jonathan Swift. In this classic allegory, a source for "On Discovery," Lemuel Gulliver travels to the lands of the Lilliputians and Brobdingnags, Laputans, Yahoos, and Houyhnhnms as Swift mercilessly and wittily skewers the faults of the British—and humanity at large.
- *Orlando* (1928), by Virginia Woolf. A fantastical "biography" of a young nobleman whose life encompasses several centuries. Born a man during the European Renaissance, Orlando later is transformed, like Tang Ao, into a woman and thus learns compassion and empathy for women. Kingston has said that the historical sweep and mix of fantasy and history in Woolf's novel influence her own works.
- *The Joy Luck Club* (1989), by Amy Tan. This novel of four Chinese-American women and their complex relationships with their Chinese-born mothers has been compared to Kingston's work.
- *Yankee Dawg You Die* (1991), by Philip Kan Gotanda. Two Chinese-American actors confront stereotypical roles in Hollywood in this hilarious yet pointed play.
- *M. Butterfly* (1988), by David Henry Hwang. A subtle exploration of the orientalist themes in Puccini's opera *Madame Butterfly.* This play is based on a true account of a French diplomat who is so blinded by his prejudices he cannot see what is really going on around him.
- *Obasan* (1981), by Joy Kogawa. A poetic novel about the internment of the Japanese Canadians during World War II, this novel resembles Kingston's both in its mixture of historical documents, poetic images, and personal experiences and in its exploration of different kinds of silences.

We'll monopolize and master every craft upon
your shore,
And we'll starve you out with fifty—aye, five
hundred thousand more!

In the period that this poem was circulated, over 40,000 Chinese immigrants were driven out of towns along the West Coast of the United States. In the 1870s, a series of anti-Chinese riots broke out in the West, from Seattle to Wyoming. Chinese farm laborers were massacred, their living quarters and laundries were burned, and employers of the Chinese were threatened. Because Chinese laborers could not testify in court, they had no legal recourse. For the Chinese in America to endure such discrimination and to live to tell their stories, Kingston suggests, is an act of heroism. If the Chinese male immigrants are heroes, so too are the women, who experienced all that the men suffered in addition to sexism.

Yet the stories of these men and women often were not heard or even spoken out loud. "On

Discovery'' is feminist in its insistence on the necessity of putting silenced stories into speech. Historically, Chinese Americans have been silenced by discrimination and fear of deportation. In ''On Discovery,'' the women joke that they will sew Tang Ao's lips together. A few pages later, in ''The Father from China,'' Kingston writes of her father's ''wordless male screams'' and ''silences.'' The principle motivation for writing China Men, Kingston suggests, is to speak her father's stories and to encourage her father to speak for himself. In ''The Father From China,'' the narrator tells her father, ''I'll tell you what I suppose from your silences and few words, and you can tell me that I'm mistaken. You'll just have to speak up with the real stories if I've got you wrong.''

Another way in which Chinese Americans have been silenced is through stereotypes. In American popular culture, Asian men have been represented as having no sexuality (historically, they did ''women's work'' and lived alone because miscegenation laws forbade them to marry) whereas Asian women have been coded as being ultrafeminine. These stereotypes can silence the individuality of Asian-American men and women; in addition, these stereotypes can get in the way of white audiences from carefully listening to the words of individual Asian-American writers. To counteract the effects of stereotypes, in the 1970s, some Asian-American writers founded a group that was dedicated to publishing writing by Asian-Americans that portrayed Asian-Americans in nonstereotypical ways.

One such voice which arose at mid century, Chinese-American writer Frank Chin, has suggested that stories like Kingston's ''On Discovery'' represent Chinese-American men as feminine and emasculated and thus cater to white audience's preconceived stereotypes of Asian men. According to Elaine Kim in the *Michigan Quarterly Review,* Chin calls for a ''singing, stomping and muscular'' reclamation of Asian-American manhood against hurtful stereotypes. Although Chin's position is admirable, Kim observes that it is marred by his tendency to code ''creativity, courage, and 'being taken seriously' as 'masculine'.'' In his emphasis on reclaiming Asian-American masculinity, Chin oversimplifies Kingston's feminism, assuming feminism to be mean ''anti-male.'' While it is true that Kingston is criticizing sexism in Chinese and Chinese-American culture, to criticize is not the same as to attack. As Donald Goellnicht observes in *Reading the Literatures of Asian America,* ''Kingston can both deplore the emasculation of China Men by

"'On Discovery' is a feminist story that asserts men's as well as women's needs to be represented fairly and redeemed from cultural stereotypes and historical obscurity. Kingston's creative re-visioning of the Tang Ao myth at the beginning of her book dramatizes the structural identity and similarities of sexism and racism."

mainstream America *and* critique the Confucian patriarchy of traditional family life.'' In other words, to be a feminist is not the same thing as to be anti-male; one can be supportive and still give constructive criticism. Metaphorically, depicting the transformation of a traveler into a Chinese woman does not suggest that Kingston believes the stereotypes to be true; in fact, turning what is commonly perceived as ''masculine'' (an adventurer in search of conquest) into what is considered ''feminine'' encourages readers to question exaggerated caricatures of both gender roles.

Seen in its literary, historical, and social context, ''On Discovery'' foreshadows the male Chinese-American experience in America. It is a metaphor of the fact that anti-Chinese exclusion laws forced the Chinese immigrants into confinement and isolation, the social equivalent of having one's feet bound so that one has no mobility. ''On Discovery'' is a feminist story that asserts men's as well as women's needs to be represented fairly and redeemed from cultural stereotypes and historical obscurity. Kingston's creative re-visioning of the Tang Ao myth at the beginning of her book dramatizes the structural identity and similarities of sexism and racism.

Source: Jean Leverich, for *Short Stories for Students,* Gale, 1998.

Ning Yu

Yu is an assistant professor American literature at Western Washington University. He has published critical essays on Henry David Thoreau, Fanny Fern, and Sui Sin Far. In the following essay, Yu discusses the contrast between "high culture" and "low culture" in Asian-American literature and delves into the historical and literary influences of Kingston's "On Discovery."

The Orient, Edward Said postulates, is a "European invention" of the "Middle East" as a "place of romance, exotic beings, haunting memories and landscapes, remarkable experiences." Orientalism is a Eurocentric and hegemonic discourse that "can be discussed and analyzed as the corporate institution for dealing with the Orient—dealing with it by making statements about it, ruling over it: in short, Orientalism as a Western style for domination, restructuring, and having authority over the Orients." But America's concept of the Orient, according to Said, is different from that of Europe, for it is "much more likely to be associated . . . with the Far East (China and Japan, mainly)." I would argue that upon closer scrutiny, however, the process in which Euro-America constructed the "Far East," or more specifically, China, is not very different from Europe's own "invention" of the "Middle East." Like European orientalism, American orientalism is a hegemonic discourse that constructed China as Euro-America's Other, preventing Chinese American as well as Chinese voices from forming and emerging. . . .

American Orientalist discourse is so powerful and so omnipresent that Chinese Americans can still feel its oppressive force today. Despite differences among themselves, Chinese American authors work consensually to replace the American Orientalist discourse with their own voices. To achieve that, some start by rejecting their hyphenated status: these writers and their ancestors either never had a mainstream status in Chinese culture or lost it long ago because of emigration. In America, the hyphenated status tends to marginalize Chinese American authors, excluding their works from mainstream literature; it insinuates that their achievements are somehow compromised, or even "low," their works read for anthropological curiosity rather than literary merit. . . .

Amy Tan, another well-known writer of Chinese American descent, resists the same pigeonholing in similar language. She hopes that people stop calling her "an Asian American writer," because, she insists, "I'm a writer of American literature." Both authors' resistance can be regarded as a frontal engagement with the hegemonic American Orientalist discourse: they forthrightly reject the lowness implied by the hyphenated label that marginalizes them through the sediments of the American orientalist discourse. For them, the high-low dichotomy is not between the low "bitter labor" and the high Confucian scholar, but between the low "heathen Chinee" stereotype and the high "just American" mainstream status. Seeing through the label that veils the high-low dichotomy, they reject the low and claim the high.

Maxine Hong Kingston, however, deals with the implicit low status imposed on Chinese American writers in a different way. Her second book, *China Men,* especially her unusual use of the "high" Chinese classics in it, has aroused criticism from both mainstream American and Chinese American communities. More relevant to my argument in this essay are the remarks of Frederick Wakeman, Jr., who is displeased with Kingston's treatment of Chinese "high culture" because "many of the myths are largely her own reconstructions . . . a kind of self-indulgent fantasy." He argues that Kingston's "pieces of distant China lore often seem jejune and even unauthentic—especially to readers who know a little bit about the original *high culture* which Kingston claims as her birthright." Wakeman's ironic tone is made clear by his status as a top U. S. sinologist who has spent most of his life reading and absorbing Chinese "high culture" with the diligence characteristic of T. S. Eliot's "individual talent" assimilating the "whole of the literature of Europe from Homer." The combination of his status and tone suggests that he knows more than "a little bit about the original high culture," perhaps more than most Chinese immigrants in America and obviously more than Kingston. People familiar with Eliot's essay (almost all of those trained in the New Criticism) would also smile at Wakeman's capturing Kingston in the act of claiming Chinese high culture "as her birthright," for they know that a cultural tradition "cannot be inherited, and [that] if you want [the tradition] you must obtain it by great labor." In Eliot's model, in order to belong to the high culture, either European or Chinese, you must be a member of the cultured class first. You must have the leisure to read the "whole of the literature." A daughter of Cantonese peasants doesn't seem to belong here.

Nevertheless, in a sense, Wakeman is right: in *China Men* Kingston's version of the Chinese classics is by no means accurate. She takes liberties with the classics in every episode, from Tang Ao's discovery of the Land of Women to the life and death of Chu Yuan. Yet, Kingston may have labored harder with Chinese literature than Wakeman believes; her deviation from the Chinese originals is the consequence of deliberate revision rather than, as Wakeman suggests, inaccurate reading of the sources. Indeed, I read her treatment of Chinese sources as a carefully planned move rather than "self-indulgent fantasy." This is supported by Kingston's response to Professor Wakeman: "In actuality, I am writing in the peasant talk-story Cantonese tradition ('low,' if you will), which is the heritage of Chinese Americans. Chinese Americans have changed ancient, scholarly ones from the old country." Here Kingston accepts her status as a Chinese American writer and exposes the hidden "lowness" associated with that term. However, the rhetorical structure in which she announces the acceptance reveals a more subtle denial: first, she acknowledges that she deliberately writes in the Chinese American tradition; next she suggests that to label (explicitly or implicitly) it as low is the consequence of someone else's will. Thus, Kingston's apparent acceptance of the low estate works as a strategy to resist marginalization, not by forthrightly rejecting the "low" status of a Chinese American author, as Jen and Tan do, but by suggesting that the high-low binary opposition is originally a hegemonic construct imposed on Chinese Americans. The economy and effect of this strategy can be better illustrated with a close reading of *China Men,* especially the opening short episode, "On Discovery," where Kingston makes her boldest experimental reconstruction of an early nineteenth-century Chinese novel, *The Romance of Flowers in Mirror.*

"On Discovery" adapts chapters thirty-two through thirty-seven of *Jing Hua Yuan (The Romance of Flowers in Mirror),* a novel of a hundred chapters by Li Ru-zhen, written before 1820 and first published in 1828. A summary of the Chinese original prepares us for an in-depth examination of Kingston's reconstruction of the adventures of Tang Ao, the protagonist of the novel:

> The story is set in the twenty-one years' reign (684–705) of the usurping Empress Wu which interrupted the continuity of the great T'ang dynasty—an era of the ascendancy of women, or rather of one woman. Being of indomitable will, the Empress commanded the hundred flowers in the Imperial Shang-lin Park to blossom on a winter's day: they obeyed, thus disrupting the harmony of the seasons, and for their pains the hundred fairies in charge of the flowers were banished from the heaven, to be born as girls in families all over the empire and even in lands across the seas (chapters 3–6; chapters 1 and 2 take place in heaven). T'ang Ao, a graduate recently deprived of his hard won title of "T'an-Hua" (literally, Seeker of Flowers) because of his earlier association with the empress's political enemies, decides to join his brother-in-law, Lin Chih-yang, on a voyage; being advised by a temple god in a dream to search for twelve famous flowers and transplant them back to China. . . .

"'In actuality,' Kingston has said, 'I am writing in the peasant talk-story Cantonese tradition ("low," if you will), which is the heritage of Chinese Americans. Chinese Americans have changed ancient, scholarly ones from the old country'."

In the original novel Tang Ao, the unhappy scholar, is a "T'an Hua" (a Chinese word with a literal meaning, the seeker of flowers, and a cultural meaning, the official title for the scholar who scores the third highest in the imperial examination). Li Ru-zhen's novel plays on both meanings of the title. As an extraordinarily talented scholar of "high" culture, Tang Ao wins an elite third-place in the imperial examination in which tens of thousands of talented scholars participated; with the mandate of heaven, he travels over the oceans with the "high" romantic purpose of finding and saving the incarnations of a dozen flower fairies, "high ladies" banished from the Heavenly Court. In Kingston's reconstruction, however, Tang Ao's high estate codified in both meanings of his title disappears as he is transformed into a seeker of the Gold Mountain, a Chinese stereotype of the rough and mundane forty-niner. By making this general change in the character of Tang Ao, Kingston suggests a social stepping-down that accompanies the geographic movement of a Chinese scholar from China to North America.

The few chapters on which Kingston particularly draws to write "On Discovery" further reveal the purpose of her rendition. In Li Ru-zhen's

Kingdom of Women, Lin Zhi-yang, Tang Ao's brother-in-law, planned to make a fortune by selling cosmetics to the queen and her "royal concubines." Impressed by Lin's "beauty," the queen decided to make him her new "concubine." Suffering so much from the ear-puncturing and foot-binding and many other humiliating preparations for the marriage, Lin almost killed himself before the queen installed him as a new concubine in her harem. When Tang Ao learned of his brother-in-law's miserable predicament, he decided to risk his life to save Lin Zhi-yang. He made a deal with the queen: if the queen would release his brother-in-law, he would subjugate the flooding rivers that were devastating the country, knowing, though, he would lose his life if he failed to tame the waters. However, because of his superior knowledge and command of advanced technology, Tang Ao finally succeeded in his river project, saved his brother-in-law, and left the land for new adventures.

In the classic novel, it was Lin Zhi-yang, the low merchant, not Tang Ao, the high scholar, who was almost turned into a royal "concubine." As the queen's new favorite, Lin Zhi-yang did not do any of his own washing—all his things were washed by the maids. Thus Tang Ao's humiliating foot-bandage washing is Kingston's invention added to underscore the low estate of the fallen scholar. Similarly, in the original, Tang Ao achieved high heroic deeds, saving the life of his brother-in-law and creating engineering wonders to control the flooding rivers; whereas in Kingston's version, Tang Ao was frustrated, humiliated, and forced to do work traditionally assigned to women, washing his foot-bandages and serving at the queen's banquet table.

In a sense, the original novel was an early nineteenth-century version of Chinese colonialist discourse about conquering overseas colonies with superior technology and knowledge. It is interesting to note that the land of women does not exist in actual geography but reflects the Chinese imperialist fantasy of subduing an "other," a "low" culture whose danger lies in its overwhelming sexuality symbolized by the flood. Tang Ao, the exile from the "high" culture of the "central empire," partially regains his elite status by subjugating the dangerous sexuality and by saving the "low" merchant Lin Zhi-yang. However, the irony of history ushered in the decline of the Celestial Empire within two decades of the publication of the novel. Faced with the faster ships and bigger guns of the West, the traditional Chinese high culture represented by Tang Ao is rendered powerless, the boundary between Tang Ao the high scholar and Lin Zhi-yang the low entrepreneur erased; with the fall of the Chinese scholarship, the fall of the Chinese scholars becomes the rule rather than the exception. Kingston's father, for instance, falls neatly into this pattern as his emigration transforms him from the privileged scholar in China into the illiterate laundry-man in the United States. Kingston's literary reconstruction is an imaginative representation of a social phenomenon: politically constructed opposition between a high scholar and a low laborer can be politically deconstructed or displaced over time (a couple of decades in this case) and space (the Pacific Ocean). By dramatizing the fall of the "high" scholar, Kingston rejects the high-low binary structure constructed by both Chinese and American imperialist discourses.

Kingston's problematization of the high-low opposition is not only demonstrated through her thematic reconstruction of an older text, but also highlighted through an apparent stylistic tension in her own text. "On Discovery" begins with the phrase "Once upon a time" and ends with "A.D. 441 . . . in North America." Placed in between the discourses of fairy-tales and history, is Kingston's story of the humiliating feminization of a Chinese scholar-traveller. Since in the Confucian tradition, as in the Platonic tradition of Western metaphysics, history as the "representation" of facts and truth is always given higher status over fairy-tales, over fiction and fantasy, the genre of Plato's lying poets, it appears justifiable for us to read the tension between the discourses of history and fairy-tales as an appropriate stylistic reflection of the high-low dichotomy. Thus, Kingston seems to begin her story of the American discovery as a fairy-tale, a vivid yet perhaps unreliable account of a Chinese Columbus, and then she switches her tone and confirms the "truth" of her story by appealing to a "high-culture" genre. If this generic transformation is at work, then Kingston's style seems to reinforce the binary opposition between high and low cultures that her thematic revision undermines. However, this apparent contradiction between style and content vanishes when readers examine closely Kingston's historical discourse at the end of the episode: "Some scholars say that that country was discovered during the reign of Empress Wu (A.D. 694–705), and some say earlier than that, A.D. 441, and it was in North America."

Two of the three dates that Kingston cites here are inaccurate, and deliberately so. The first time-frame Kingston offers for the discovery of Women's Land is a half truth: it is true that Empress Wu died in A.D. 705, but Kingston's date for the start of Wu's reign is a fiction. In his late years, Emperor Gao Zong, Wu's husband, was too ill to run the government, and in his stead Empress Wu made important national policy decisions. Immediately after Gao Zong's death in 683, the Empress set up her third son as Emperor Zhong Zong in 684, only to banish him in a few months; in the same year, she crowned and then again banished her fourth son, Emperor Rui Zong. Finally, before the year 684 expired, she announced herself the official ruler of the Tang Dynasty, but she ruled the empire under the old title of Empress. In 690, she announced herself the Emperor of China, changed the name of the country into the Zhou Dynasty, and relocated the imperial capital from Chang An to Luo Yang. In the actual sense, Wu started her reign in 684; in the formal sense, her own dynasty began in 690. Kingston's date 694 is a fictional construct that not only blurs the boundary between fiction and history, but also challenges the distinction between content and style.

In addition to the half truth, Kingston invents a fictional date for her discovery story. The source of her earlier date, A.D. 441, is impossible to identify. The only clue we have is that it is earlier than Wu's reign, and the only known pre-Tang text that mentions the Land of Women is *Shan Hai Jing (The Classic of Mountains and Seas),* a book of mythology and rituals compiled over an incredibly long period ranging from the East Zhou Dynasty (770 B.C.-256 B.C.; much earlier than Wu's Zhou) all the way through the Warring States Period and the Qin Dynasty to the West Han Dynasty (206 B.C.-25 A.D.). Many episodes from Li Ru-zhen's novel, including the story of the Women's Land, are based on the sketchy legends in *Shan Hai Jing.* Obviously, Kingston's date is much too late for that book, yet there is no other identifiable source for the legend of Women's Land before Wu's time.

Even if Kingston does provide accurate dates for Empress Wu's reign and the production of the earlier Women's Land text, the authority of Kingston's historical discourse is still questionable. The source for her discovery story is a novel, and that Empress Wu could order the flowers to bloom in winter is exactly the stuff of fairy-tales. Dates drawn from a romantic novel based on a mythical book which itself is a marvelous mixture of myths and facts accumulated over a millennium in an obscure past, even if Kingston cites the dates faithfully from them, would not lend historical authority to her book. Yet Kingston deliberately mixes the dates from unreliable sources and dresses them up in a seemingly authoritative discourse to make them sound historical. Furthermore, neither *The Classic of Mountains and Seas* nor *The Romance of Flowers in Mirror* places the Land of Woman in North America, but readers somehow assume it to be in North America simply because Kingston says so in a factual tone. The interesting thing here is that although many readers know that both historical texts and fairy-tales are language-mediated interpretations of an irretrievable past, some still seem unwilling to take Kingston's exaggerated form of fictional history itself as a parody exposing the groundlessness of another binary opposition, the binary between high history and low fairy tale. Thus, despite Wakeman's concern with Kingston's use of the Chinese "high culture," what is really important for us is not to challenge Kingston's "inaccuracy" in using sources, but to identify and discuss the rhetorical effect of her deliberate revision. . . .

Source: Ning Yu, "A Strategy Against Marginalization: The 'High' and 'Low' Cultures in Kingston's *China Men,*" in *College Literature,* Vol. 23, No. 3, October, 1996, pp. 73–87.

Mary Slowik

Slowik teaches literature and writing at Pacific Northwest College of Art in Portland, Oregon. She has published critical essays on Leslie Marmon Silko, Adrienne Rich, and Robert Bly. In the following essay, Slowik compares Kingston's stories "On Discovery" and "On Fathers," noting the difficulties inherent in writing on immigrant history and how they become apparent in the stories' narratives.

Maxine Hong Kingston begins *China Men,* her history of the Chinese immigration to America, with two peculiar chapters that suggest such a book is not easily written. The first chapter, "On Discovery," is the legend of Tang Ao, a Chinaman who sets off for America, the Gold Mountain, the land of infinite riches. Instead of finding America, he discovers rather the "Land of Women" where, in a grotesque parody of Chinese traditions, his feet are broken and bound, his ears are pierced, he is fed nothing but rice cakes and he enters into female enslavement. So much for discovery. For the Chinaman who thinks he can leave China, any sailing away from China is a sailing into China, its tradition enforced with a vengeance. . . .

Maxine Hong Kingston places *China Men* in the middle of this gap between generations and

> "'On Discovery' is not only a story about an aborted emigration, it is also a parable of fixed meanings."

countries. Her opening chapters ask two questions: Did the Chinese ever leave China culturally, and if so, can we ever know their story? The way these chapters are written, however, suggests even more difficult problems. At issue is not only a serious break in historical continuity, but the possibility of writing immigrant history at all. ''On Discovery'' is a folktale, evoking the authority of oral tradition, as it is revered, remembered, passed on, but also as it imprisons and ultimately destroys its characters.

Let us look more closely at the narrative problems posed by Kingston in the opening chapters of *China Men.* ''On Discovery'' is not only a story about an aborted emigration, it is also a parable of fixed meanings. In a time outside of time, an omniscient voice speaking with the authority of fairy tale (''once upon a time''), historical document (''in the Women's land, there are no taxes and no war''), and scholarship (''some scholars say . . .'') recounts the story of Tang Ao. There is an acknowledged agreement between narrator and audience. Everyone accepts without question the story to be told. The heroes and victims are unchanging in an unchangeable world. Their lives are fated as the story drives them unerringly to their pre-conceived ends. There are no alternatives to this story—for its characters or for its audience. Not only is ''On Discovery'' about a cultural paradigm gone tyrannical, it is also about a narrative form as enclosed and imprisoning as the story it tells.

On the other side of the self-enclosed omniscience of ''On Discovery,'' however, is the self-enclosed subjectivity of ''On Fathers.'' Although this chapter is particular, personal, and surrounded by the mystery of movement and flux (Participles, ''waiting,'' ''hastening,'' ''pressing,'' replace the tense-less ''once upon a time,'' of ''On Discovery.''), the story nonetheless doubles back on itself; its ending is its beginning—the children are forever running out to meet the father who retreats from them only to approach again in another guise, only to retreat another time. Despite the particularity of the story and the idiosyncrasy of the speaker, the story's subject is as condemned as the fated heroes of the legends. If all beginnings and endings are known to the omniscient voice, there are no beginnings or endings for the first-person speaker of this father's story, only a condemned ''in medias res.'' And what authority can the child/first person command in order to grab that approaching man by his lapels and ask him who he is? Apparently none, for the mother in the story only concurs that the man was that kind of father easily mistaken and the children can only return to waiting.

The story of Tang Ao and the little girl could be taken as two conflicting but typically post-modern versions of history, both fatally self-enclosed, both representing the polarities of relativity and objectivity. ''The formulations,'' Clifford Geertz tells us, ''have been various: 'inside' versus 'outside,' or 'first person' versus 'third person' descriptions; 'phenomenological' versus 'objectivist' or 'cognitive' versus 'behavioral' theories; or, perhaps most commonly, 'emic' versus 'etic' analyses.'' Kingston, however, explores the problem narratively. ''On Discovery'' is in the hands of an omniscient authority, understanding the full patterns of life and condemning all characters in the story to pre-ordained fates and the audience to silent complicity in the tale. Such authority represents a radically objective point of view. ''On Fathers,'' on the other hand, is the stuff of radical historical and cultural relativism where the ephemeral motion of a present moment and the rich though self-limited ''I'' preclude any transcendence. There are no larger structures beyond the self-constructed one, so there is no way of seeing above and beyond the present moment into a past radically different from the present. Tang Ao, the prisoner of omniscience, needs freedom from stories with fixed beginnings and endings. The little girl and her sisters, the prisoners of solipsism, need the means to discover these new stories. Both need a history that will connect them. *China Men* is just that history. By overlaying post-modern and pre-modern methods of storytelling, Kingston makes the connections for Tang Ao and the little girl. She also discovers the connections our forefathers have made for us.

The first thing Maxine Hong Kingston does to release both Tang Ao and the young girl from their respective isolations is to take their stories out of the hands of singular narrators and make those stories the possession and invention of the audience. Retold by many different speakers, stories can carry people like Tang Ao of "On Discovery" back into time with all its unpredictability and introduce the lonely first person, the little girl of "On Fathers," to a group of people to whom she can listen and from whom she can speak. To use the term from oral history (and with apologies to auto mechanics), audience-generated tales can re-link the first-person speaker to a "chain of transmission." Thus, Kingston opens the post-modern story's dilemmas to the pre-modern methods of storytelling. . . .

Kingston, the twentieth-century writer, is not simply a child in the rice field frightened by the story, however, nor is she a distant relative at the end of the generational line. She is now an adult re-telling that story, making it again immediate—alternating the language with the whip strokes, noting the sap still fresh in the branch, and then placing all the subsequent generations in a dramatic final present moment of the story. Thus, inter-textual reading, for Kingston, is not a kind of sophisticated source study that starts with the last version of the story and works backward. Rather, she recalls the story with urgency, as if witnessing it for the first time. We are once again at the moment of the original event looking forward in time through all its subsequent re-tellings. In this story we are momentarily meeting all fathers, mothers, sons and daughters at once.

Bringing the past into such immediacy is possible for Kingston because, for all the self-consciousness of her story, she, nonetheless, takes on the storytelling mentality of her ancestors. A story is told and remembered only in relation to the immediate demands of life. A story is a moral tale intended to teach a lesson not only with ethical content, but with practical content about family and livelihood crucial to physical and cultural survival. Bibi's story, for instance, tells us how to grow rice, how to organize a family, and how to raise children. It is called forth not simply by literary or ethical concerns, but by immediate, physical concerns. Although the story will not be written down, "published," housed and passed on by bookstores and library systems, it will be remembered and re-told by family members as each generation teaches and learns the art of survival. Even though rice has disappeared and children are allowed more rebellious thoughts, the basic narrative frame will still house our ancestors's voices giving us advice on livelihood and children. Thus, a story breaks out of omniscient self-enclosure because an audience, whose lives are never as final as any story's, continually re-tells and re-interprets the tale, connecting their limited, "first person" experiences to the directives of the oral tradition. . . .

Kingston, however, does not deny the fact that she lives in late twentieth-century America. She is not a grandfather. Invoking an oral narrative authority is not easy. As a historian, she is faced with the breaks in continuity between her time and her grandfathers's time. Many of the old stories have been lost, the old China inaccessible, the immigrant Chinese dispersed (in many instances forcibly) once the railroads have been constructed, the mining camps closed. Kingston faces the end of overlapping generations, the death of the listening performer/audiences we have been speaking of.

Furthermore, as a late twentieth-century historian, Kingston approaches her fathers with a faith in language and history more fragile and vulnerable than their own. The two hundred dollar suitcoat and wing-tip shoes are as elusive for Kingston, the historian, as they are for the little girl waiting at the gate in the opening chapters of *China Men.* Unlike her pre-literate fathers, Kingston is trapped by a literate culture. She is *writing* her story, not *telling* it. Pages of type not the sets of a world-encompassing stage make up her novel. Already distanced by a 1977 copyright, Kingston, the author, is indeed removed from her text in the same way her fathers are "removed" from their history. "'Writing,' Jacques Derrida says, '"in the common sense is the dead letter, it is the carrier of death because it signifies the absence of the speaker. . .'". So, too have the fathers long abandoned the slim pieces of evidence they have left behind. . . .

Source: Mary Slowik, "When the Ghosts Speak: Oral and Written Narrative Forms in Maxine Hong Kingston's *China Men,*" in *MELUS,* Vol. 19, No. 1, Spring, 1994, pp. 73–88.

Shu mei Shih

In the following excerpt from a longer essay, Shu mei Shih discusses the "intertext" of "On Discovery," which concerns the exile of the Chinese from China and their emasculation in the West.

In this first intertext which begins [*China Men*], Kingston relates a tale about a certain Tang Ao who finds himself banished to a world where sex roles are reversed, where he is forced to become a woman. This poignant fable about Tang Ao's forced feminization in the Land of Women is taken from the Ch'ing Dynasty novel *Flowers in the Mirror* by Li Ju-chen (c. 1763–1830). The book is commonly read as a social and political allegory; the chapters

> "By revealing the politics of Center and Margin, Kingston shows how being exiled in America has created a common fate for both Chinese men and women. We may call this the moral of the fable."

which deal with the trips of the protagonists (Tang Ao and Lin Chih-yang) to the Land of Women present a satire on social injustice in general and the suppression of women in particular. In Li Juchen's version, genders are reversed in the Land of Women: men are called women and play the roles of women, and women are called men, wear men's clothes and act like men. It is a women-centered society. The King (who is a woman) becomes infatuated with Tang Ao's companion, Lin Chih-yang, because of his "face like peach blossoms, waist like slender willows, eyes that contain autumn waters and eyebrows like distant mountains" and proceeds to make him a concubine. After Lin is subjected to a series of physical tortures normally required of women (his ears are pierced, his feet bound and all the hair on his face plucked out), he is proclaimed ready to become an imperial concubine. But at the crucial moment on the nuptial night, he pretends that he has lost his virility and thus dissuades the King from consummating the marriage. The episode ends with Lin's final rescue by the ingenious Tang Ao and Lin's reunion with his family.

Kingston makes various changes in the original fable. In her version, it is Tang Ao, not Lin Chih-yang, who is taken captive in the Land of Women when he is searching for "the Gold Mountain," which is the name early Chinese immigrants gave to San Francisco. He is put into chains, unlike Lin Chih-yang who is confined to a well-furnished room in *Flowers in the Mirror,* but like early Chinese laborers who were locked below decks in the ships on route to America as described in "The Great Grandfather of the Sandlewood Mountains," another section of the book. Again different from Lin Chih-yang in *Flowers in the Mirror,* Kingston's Tang Ao is turned into a woman to serve meals at the queen's court. In Tang Ao's case, there is no heroic friend to save him, and escape from this woman's land is not feasible at all.

Kingston's fable is an allegorical rendering of the exile situation of China Men in America. Tang Ao is the representative China Man who comes to America in search of the "Gold Mountain" during the Gold Rush in the nineteenth century. But instead of reaching the "Gold Mountain," he is captured and deprived not only of his freedom (enslaved in chains) but also of his manhood (he is turned into a woman and forced to do woman's work—serving meals). Kingston is clearly commenting on the effeminization of China Men by the dominant American culture that has created the stereotype of the Asian man as feminine and submissive, and she thereby echoes the critiques of such stereotypes by male Asian-American writers such as Frank Chin and Jeffery Paul Chan.

Kingston further reinforces her fictional elaboration of China Men's emasculation with historical evidence in "The Laws" section of the book. It is a factual account of Chinese American legal history, a history of segregation and discrimination which witnessed the enactment of such laws as the Chinese Exclusion Act of 1882 and the anti-miscegenation laws of 1924, according to which Chinese men were banned from becoming citizens of the United States and barred from marrying white women. In this way, Chinese men were symbolically castrated and emasculated. They were not allowed to be men since most of them came to America without women. Denied the right to marriage and the legal status of residency, they were relegated to "womanly" professions such as laundry and restaurant work

Tang Ao's forced effeminization is thus a direct commentary on that of the China Men, simultaneously victimized by the mechanisms of racism and sexism. Social, economic, and legal circumstances beyond their control forced them to do womanly work and in turn they were looked down upon even more because of this involuntary femininity. Sexism saw femininity as a negative quality and racism imposed that negative quality on them.

Alongside Kingston's condemnation of the dominant society's racism and sexism is also her ironic treatment of the issue of sexism in the Chinese context. The physical tortures that Tang Ao must endure are the same ones traditionally suffered by Chinese women in order to enhance their "beauty."

Traditional Chinese standards of beauty were defined by men and helped to ensure the subservient position of women in society and the family. The bound feet that epitomized women's imprisonment and subservience in traditional China become the fate of China Men in America. Kingston ironically observes how China Men have become objects of the same kind of sexism which they themselves practiced on their own women at home. Here we see Kingston's characteristic feminist touch. Although she sympathizes with the emasculation of China Men, she at the same time protests against their oppression of Chinese women. In this double-edged criticism, one side turned against racism, the other against traditional patterns of patriarchy, Kingston again operates in a double reality befitting our characterization of her exilic imagination.

Kingston's first book, *The Woman Warrior,* explores the ramifications of female marginality in the male-centered societies of both China and America; but *China Men,* as exemplified by this opening section, investigates the meaning of China Men's marginality in white-centered America, while at the same time retaining a feminist perspective. In the sections that follow, Kingston writes of the various contributions China Men made to the welfare of the country that denied them, and how their blood and sweat enriched the American soil. Arguing against the essentialism of the white-centered discourse which defines China Men as feminine and thus marginalizes them, Kingston complements Julia Kristeva's view that marginality is not a matter of essence, but one of positionality in a given society. Like Kristeva, Kingston is concerned with the imposed marginality of women in patriarchal societies, but she goes a step further by describing how men of a different race can become victims of the same Center/Margin bifurcation that they themselves perpetuate in their treatment of women. Kingston's appropriation of the fable from *Flowers in the Mirror* drives this point home. By revealing the politics of Center and Margin, Kingston shows how being exiled in America has created a common fate for both Chinese men and women. We may call this the moral of the fable. It is the discovery of a true knowledge of the politics of the self and the Other, and the mechanism of subordination and imprisonment. . . .

Source: Shu mei Shih, ''Exile and Intertextuality in Maxine Hong Kingston's *China Men,* in *Studies in Comparative Literature: The Literature of Emigration and Exile,* No. 23, Texas Tech University Press, 1992, pp 65–78.

Sources

Buckmaster, Henrietta. ''China Men Portrayed with Magic,'' in *The Christian Science Monitor,* August 11, 1980, p. B4.

Chan, Jeffrey Paul, and Frank Chin et al. *The Big Aieeeee!: An Anthology of Chinese American and Japanese American Literature,* Penguin, 1990, pp. 1-92.

Cheung, King-Kok. ''The Woman Warrior versus The Chinaman Pacific: Must a Chinese American Critic Choose Between Feminism and Heroism?,'' in *Conflicts in Feminism,* edited Marianne Hirsch and Evelyn Fox Keller, Routledge, 1990, pp. 234-51.

Goellnicht, Donald. ''Tang Ao in America: Male Subject Positions in *China Men,''* in *Reading the Literatures of Asian America,* edited by Shirley Geok-lin Lim and Amy Ling, Temple University Press, 1992, pp. 191-212.

Gordan, Mary. ''Mythic History,'' in *The New York Times Book Review,* June 15, 1980, pp. 1, 24-5.

Jacoby, Tamar. A review of *China Men,* in *The San Francisco Review of Books,* September, 1980, pp. 10-11.

Kim, Elaine. *Asian American Literature: An Introduction to the Writings and their Social Contexts,* Temple University Press, 1982.

Kim, Elaine. '''Such Opposite Creatures': Men and Women in Asian American Literature,'' in *The Michigan Quarterly Review,* Vol. 29, No. 1, Winter, 1990, pp. 68-93.

Leonard, John. A review of *China Men,* in *The New York Times,* June 3, 1980, p. C9.

Li, David Leiwei. ''*China Men:* Maxine Hong Kingston and the American Canon,'' in *American Literary History,* Vol. 2, No. 3, Fall, 1990, pp. 482-502.

Pfaff, Timothy. ''Talk with Mrs. Kingston,'' in *The New York Times Book Review,* June 15, 1980, pp. 1, 25-27.

Rabinowitz, Paula. ''Eccentric Memories: A Conversation With Maxine Hong Kingston,'' in *The Michigan Quarterly Review,* Vol. 26, No. 1, Winter, 1987, pp. 177-87.

Ross, Jean W. An interview with Maxine Hong Kingston in *Contemporary Authors New Revisions Series,* Vol. 13, edited by Linda Metzger, Gale Research, 1984, pp. 291-93.

Sledge, Linda Ching. ''Maxine Kingston's 'China Men': The Family Historian as Epic Poet,'' in *MELUS,,* Vol. 7, No. 4, Winter, 1980, pp. 3-22.

Wakeman, Frederick, ''Chinese Ghost Story,'' in *The New York Review of Books,* August 14, 1980, pp. 42-44.

Wang, Alfred. ''Maxine Hong Kingston's Reclaiming of America: The Birthright of the Chinese American Male,'' in *South Dakota Review,* Vol. 26, No. 1, Spring, 1988, pp. 18-29.

Yu, Ning. ''A Strategy Against Marginalization: The 'High' and 'Low' Cultures in Kingston's *China Men,''* in *College Literature,* Vol. 26, No. 3, October, 1996, pp. 73-87.

Further Reading

Cheung, King-Kok. *Articulate Silences: Hisaye Yamamoto, Maxine Hong Kingston, Joy Kogawa,* Cornell University Press, 1993.

A literary study of Kingston's work that compares her to a Japanese-American and a Japanese-Canadian writer, Cheung's analysis focuses on the themes of silence in all three women's novels.

Foner, Philip S., and Daniel Rosenberg, eds. *Racism, Dissent, and Asian Americans from 1850 to the Present: A Documentary History,* Greenwood Press, 1993.

Contains copies of anti-Asian legislation from the nineteenth and twentieth centuries, along with documents about Asians in America from the perspectives of African Americans, labor organizers, and sympathizers of Asian Americans.

Hagedorn, Jessica, ed. *Charlie Chan Is Dead: An Anthology of Contemporary Asian-American Fiction,* Penguin, 1993.

A hip, well-reviewed anthology of fiction by the younger generation of Asian-American writers, edited by the Filipino-American writer of *Dogeaters.*

Kim, Elaine. *Asian American Literature: An Introduction to the Writings and their Social Contexts,* Temple University Press, 1982.

The first academic study of Asian-American literature, Kim's book focuses on images of Asians in Anglo-American literature, early Asian immigrant writers, the second generation, and contemporary writers.

Takaki, Ronald. *Strangers from A Different Shore: A History of Asian Americans,* Penguin, 1989.

Takaki's comprehensive look at Asian Americans in the nineteenth and twentieth centuries covers those of Japanese, Korean, Filipino, Vietnamese, Indian, and Chinese descent. Takaki takes special care to consider the ways in which, for example, Korean-American experiences differ from Filipino-American experiences.

The Outcasts of Poker Flat

Bret Harte

1869

''The Outcasts of Poker Flat'' was first published in the January, 1869, issue of the *Overland Monthly* magazine, which Bret Harte edited. At the time, Harte was on the threshold of national fame. The success of his short story ''The Luck of Roaring Camp'' the year before had elevated the twenty-nine-year-old writer to a position of literary prominence. Critics praised ''The Outcasts of Poker Flat'' as a suitable follow-up that confirmed Harte's stature as one of the most promising new authors in the United States. By 1871 Harte was not only the highest paid writer in the country, but also one of the most popular. He was a regular contributor to the *Atlantic Monthly,* one of the most popular magazines of the day.

Although both Harte's popularity and critical admiration for his work have declined in subsequent years, ''The Outcasts of Poker Flat'' remains an important piece of American literature and one of the best tales of the rough-and-tumble days of the California Gold Rush. In his use of the Western setting and local color, Harte proved to be a model for other authors, including Mark Twain, whose career he helped launch. Indeed, the familiarity of many of Harte's characterizations—the quick-witted gambler or the prostitute with a heart of gold—attest to the durability of his impact on popular culture. Harte first journeyed to the American West in 1854 and was advantageously positioned to observe one of the key events of the nineteenth century, the California Gold Rush. This setting in ''The

Outcasts of Poker Flat'' is used as a forum to explore themes of tolerance and forgiveness, appearance and reality, and the ominous power of nature.

Author Biography

Best remembered as the author of a handful of short stories depicting the rigors of life during the California Gold Rush, Bret Harte enjoyed a lengthy literary career working variously as a journalist, poet, and playwright. Although at one time he was the highest paid author in the United States and a popular lecturer, his work receives relatively less attention today. The sentimental nature of his style, coupled with the conspicuous repetition of his plots, has resulted in Harte being dismissed or overlooked by many modern readers.

The son of an academic, Francis Brett Harte was born August 25, 1836, in Albany, New York. He developed an interest in literature early in life, reading the classics and composing poetry while still a child. In 1854, Harte moved to San Francisco. During the next four years, he was primarily employed as a teacher and tutor but also worked a series of jobs that placed him in contact with the rugged world of the Gold Rush prospector. Although biographers generally regard him as more of an observer than a participant in the rough-and-tumble culture of Gold Rush California, these experiences provided Harte with a valuable glimpse of frontier life and eventually inspired his most successful writings.

Harte began his professional literary career in 1857 when his essays and poems were published in *Golden Era,* a San Francisco weekly. During the next nine years, Harte worked for several local newspapers and magazines as a typesetter, editor, reporter, and contributor of essays and poetry. In addition, his service as correspondent for two papers published in Boston brought his name to the attention of readers in the East.

Early in 1868, Harte became the editor of the *Overland Monthly,* a new publication designed to showcase the literary talent of California. In the magazine's second issue, Harte included an unsigned story of his own composition, ''The Luck of Roaring Camp.'' By September the story had been reprinted in the East and Harte had been identified as the author. Due to its bawdy characters and overtones of religious parody, ''The Luck of Roaring Camp'' elicited considerable controversy at the time of its publication. Despite its critics, the story elevated Harte to a position of national prominence. During the next two years, he continued to edit the *Overland Monthly* and contribute more short stories to it. His writings from this period, such as ''The Outcasts of Poker Flat'' and ''Tennessee's Partner,'' are widely judged to be his most enduring achievements. He also fostered the talents of a young unknown writer named Mark Twain and published some of his first stories. Twain publicly declared his gratitude to Harte, but in later years he was also known to have derided his mentor's stories as unoriginal.

By 1871 Harte was at the height of his career. He had returned to the East to work as a contributor for a national magazine, the *Atlantic Monthly.* Among other distinctions, Harte was a key speaker at the commencement ceremonies at Harvard University in June. However, his success proved to be fleeting. His new writings failed to achieve the acclaim of his earlier stories, and he was no longer able to command premium prices for his work. To compensate for the decline in income, Harte began a career as a public speaker, giving lectures to Eastern audiences about life in California during the Gold Rush.

Throughout the 1870s, Harte continued to write short stories and also authored two plays, one in collaboration with Twain, titled *Ah Sin.* However, much of his work from this period was produced quickly and carelessly. At times he simply recycled old plots and provided new titles. With his literary reputation foundering, Harte left the United States for a new career in foreign service. From 1880 to 1885 he served as the American Consul to Scotland. Despite this move, Harte did not abandon writing. Throughout the 1890s, he remained prolific and authored critical essays, stories, and an additional play, *Sue,* in 1896. He died in England of throat cancer on May 5, 1902.

Plot Summary

''The Outcasts of Poker Flat'' is set near a California mining community during November of 1850.

Experimenting with the effectiveness of vigilante justice, the residents of Poker Flat hope to improve the town by expelling a group of undesirables. Among these objectionable characters are professional gambler John Oakhurst; a prostitute known as Duchess; her madam, Mother Shipton; and Uncle Billy, the town drunkard and a suspected thief. The foursome is escorted to the edge of Poker Flat and "forbidden to return at the peril of their lives." With no apparent alternative, the group heads toward the next settlement, Sandy Bar. However, the journey requires passage over a difficult mountain trail. Less than midway to their destination, the group becomes exhausted and decides to camp for the night. Oakhurst argues that they should continue on because they lack the provisions to stop safely. The party is unconcerned, ignores him, and opts to consume its supply of liquor.

Later, a horseman from Sandy Bar arrives at the camp. His name is Tom Simson, and he is also referred to as the Innocent. He is traveling with his fifteen-year-old fiance, Piney Woods. The two have eloped and are on their way to Poker Flat to be married. Simson is an acquaintance of Oakhurst, having once lost forty dollars to him in a poker game. However, Oakhurst had taken pity on the Innocent and returned his money, advising him never to gamble again. As a result, Simson perceives Oakhurst as a genuine friend and quickly offers to share his provisions with the foursome. Simson directs the party to an abandoned cabin nearby, and they take shelter there for the night.

The next morning Oakhurst is the first to rise and discovers that Uncle Billy has stolen their mules during the night. Furthermore, the winter snows have begun and left the party trapped in the valley. To avoid frightening Simson and Piney, Oakhurst persuades the Duchess and Mother Shipton to keep Billy's theft a secret. Simson has enough food to last the party ten days and enthusiastically offers to share. Unaware of the gravity of the situation, he envisions the group enjoying a happy camp until the snow melts. During the next week, the party remains trapped in the valley. Simson and Piney not only remain naive about their chances of survival, but also about the reputations of the outcasts. They view the other women with respect and admiration. Unaccustomed to such kindness, the prostitutes become motherly toward Piney and are moved by the sincerity of the couple's love. After ten days in the cabin, Mother Shipton dies of starvation. She had been saving her rations and makes a final request for Oakhurst to give them to Piney.

Bret Harte

Realizing they are probably doomed, Oakhurst instructs Simson to attempt a hike to Poker Flat to get help. The gambler then gathers a supply of firewood for Duchess and Piney and disappears. Several days later a rescue party arrives, only to discover the frozen bodies of the women huddled together inside the cabin. Oakhurst is found nearby with a pistol by his side and a bullet through his heart, and with a suicide note written on a playing card pinned to a tree above his body.

Characters

Duchess

Duchess, a prostitute, is one of four individuals expelled from Poker Flat when the townspeople there decided to evict the "undesirables." As the group of outcasts are making their way to Sandy Bar, she complains constantly, causing the group to stop short of their destination. When Piney Woods and Tom Simson join the group and they become trapped by the snow, Duchess becomes more cheerful and nurturing toward Piney. When the rescuers finally reach the group, they find Duchess and Piney

Media Adaptations

- Several film versions of "The Outcasts of Poker Flat" have been made. The earliest adaptation was a 1919 silent film produced by Universal Studios. In 1937, RKO-Radio Pictures remade the picture with Van Heflin portraying John Oakhurst. In 1952, Twentieth Century-Fox produced a version starring Dale Robertson, Anne Baxter, and Cameron Mitchell.
- "The Outcasts of Poker Flat" became an opera in 1959, with music by Jonathan Elkus and libretto by Robert Gene Bander. Perry Edwards created a one-act play based on the story published by Dramatic Publishing in 1968.
- A one-act play written by Perry Edwards and based on "The Outcasts of Poker Flat" was published by Dramatic Publishing in 1968.
- Several filmstrip versions of "The Outcasts of Poker Flat" are available. A 1973 version by Brunswick Productions utilizes captions, while a 1977 filmstrip from Listening Library includes a cassette recording.
- Listening Library released an audiocassette in 1973, *The Best of Bret Harte: "The Outcasts of Poker Flat," "The Luck of Roaring Camp,"* in which the stories are read by Ralph Bell.

huddled together, dead, and by then it is impossible to determine "which was she that had sinned."

Innocent, The

See Tom Simson

John Oakhurst

John Oakhurst is one of four individuals who were expelled from Poker Flat when its townspeople decided to run out the "undesirables." Oakhurst is a professional gambler noted for his "coolness, impassiveness, and presence of mind." When young Tom Simson and Piney Woods join the outcasts, the reader learns that Oakhurst once returned to Simson forty dollars that he won from the youth in a poker game, advising him to stay away from cards. When the outcasts are trapped by a snowstorm, Oakhurst assumes leadership of the group. After putting together a makeshift pair of snowshoes, he gives them to Simson, instructing him to go to Poker Flat and bring help. When the rescue party finally arrives, Oakhurst has killed himself, revealing himself to be "the strongest and yet the weakest of the outcasts of Poker Flat."

Mother Shipton

Mother Shipton, presumably the madam of the prostitute Duchess, is one of four individuals expelled from Poker Flat when the townspeople decided to rid the community of "undesirables." Although she is accused of immorality, Mother Shipton displays her true qualities when the outcasts are trapped in the snowstorm. Hoping to save Piney Woods, Mother Shipton hoards her own share of the food instead of eating it. Shortly before she dies of starvation, she tells Oakhurst to give her rations to the bride-to-be so that she will have a better chance of surviving.

Tom Simson

Tom Simson is a "guileless youth" who is traveling to Poker Flat with his bride-to-be, Piney Woods, when they encounter the outcasts. On the basis of an earlier encounter with Oakhurst, Simson decides to assist the outcasts, whom he treats with respect, ignorant of their undesirable status. Simson is the lone survivor of the ordeal that ensues.

Uncle Billy

Uncle Billy, a suspected thief and confirmed drunkard, is one of the "undesirables" cast out of Poker Flat. Unlike the others, Uncle Billy scoffs at the innocence of Tom Simson and Piney Woods. During the night he makes off with the group's horses and mules, stranding them as it begins to snow.

Piney Woods

Piney Woods, "a stout, comely damsel of fifteen," is Tom Simson's bride-to-be. Piney has no understanding of the outcasts' unsavory reputations and treats them with courtesy and respect. In response to this kindness, they develop an affection for her that intensifies as they observe her love for Simson. She and Duchess freeze to death before rescuers can reach them.

Themes

"The Outcasts of Poker Flat" tells the story of four individuals exiled from a frontier town because of their alleged immorality. A blizzard traps them and a pair of innocent young lovers, leading to tragic consequences.

Appearances and Reality

At the beginning of the story, the four outcasts are described as "improper persons," and their initial actions suggest that, except for Oakhurst, they are foul-mouthed, lazy, and prone to drunkenness. However, because they come from another settlement, Tom and Piney know little about these strangers, and their perceptions are not clouded by the prejudices of the people in Poker Flat. In a previous brief encounter with Oakhurst, Tom had found him to be kind and gentlemanly, so Tom treats him as a gentleman rather than as a shifty card shark. The young couple assumes that the prostitute Duchess is "Mrs. Oakhurst," and Piney imagines that the women from Poker Flat must be ladies of a high social standing who are "used to fine things."

The discrepancy between appearance and reality becomes most apparent when the party is trapped in the snowstorm. Mother Shipton may indeed be a madam, but she also shows herself to be compassionate and heroic when she sacrifices her life in an effort to save Piney. Likewise Duchess, the "soiled sister," evolves into a companion and protector for Piney. By the end of the story, observers cannot determine "which was she that had sinned." Oakhurst, the member of the party who appeared the most calm during the ordeal, eventually cannot play against unfavorable odds any longer and commits suicide. Throughout the story, Harte demonstrates that where human nature is concerned, reality is often more complex than appearances indicate.

Change and Transformation

Related to the themes of appearance and reality are the issues of change and transformation. During their period of confinement, the outcasts, particularly the two prostitutes, experience a type of metamorphosis. At first the women appear self-centered and dismissive of Tom and Piney and contemptuous of their naivete. But as the group grows closer, these feelings shift to motherly affection, particularly toward Piney. One suspects the sincerity of the young lovers allows Duchess and Mother Shipton openly to display aspects of their personalities they had previously chosen to conceal.

Oakhurst also undergoes a transformation, though a less uplifting one. Until the end of the story, Oakhurst is portrayed as others see him and as he sees himself, as a person noted for "coolness,

Topics for Further Study

- Harte explains that the outcasts are expelled from Poker Flat by a "secret committee." Research the prevalence of vigilante justice in the American West and attempt to determine the extent to which such activities were viewed as a necessary element of the settlement process.
- Although Harte is often described as a "frontier humorist," this story reads as a tragedy. Discuss how a writer may appeal to conflicting emotions, and identify other authors who embrace a similar contradiction in style.
- Considering the historical events of the 1860s, what messages in Harte's story would have been considered controversial to readers in that era?
- Read "The Celebrated Jumping Frog of Calaveras County" by Harte's protege, Mark Twain. Discuss possible influences of Harte's writing on Twain's. Which story do you like better, and why?
- Think of some recent Western movies, television shows, or books. Do any of the characters in them remind you of the characters in "The Outcasts of Poker Flat"? Write an essay comparing and contrasting characters in contemporary Western stories to those in stories from the nineteenth century.

impassiveness, and presence of mind.'' He is the first to grasp the group's predicament and quickly assumes command in the emergency. Tom's earlier experience with him shows that he has always had a streak of kindness and protectiveness toward those younger and weaker than himself, and in the isolated community of outcasts this quickly develops into a thoughtful solicitude for his companions. When it is revealed that he killed himself, it is hard to say whether this represents a change in him or simply reveals a weakness that has always been hidden beneath his apparent strength.

Fate and Chance

Chance plays a critical role in the demise of the stranded travelers. Many developments within the narrative rely on random occurrences. Among the many examples, one can argue that if the outcasts did not stop for the night or had begun their journey one day earlier, they would have missed the snow and reached Sandy Bar. Similarly, if Tom and Piney had continued on their way rather than staying with the outcasts, they could have avoided the storm. However, one could also argue that if Oakhurst had sent Tom for help earlier, or had struggled to keep the fire lit rather than killing himself, most of the group might have survived.

Harte uses the character of Oakhurst to develop the theme of fate. As ''too much of a gambler not to accept fate,'' Oakhurst explains that with luck ''all you know for certain is that it's bound to change.'' Once the party is stranded, Oakhurst's gambling philosophy creates a dilemma for him. Having experienced ''a streak of bad luck'' since the group left Poker Flat, the gambler's experiences suggest that eventually this misfortune should pass. However, it is also the gambler's prerogative to opt out of the game if he does not like the odds, and Oakhurst estimates their odds of surviving as one in a hundred. His suicide note, declaring that he ''struck a streak of bad luck'' and ''handed in his checks,'' attests to his inability to resist despair when the odds on their fate seem stacked against him.

Heroism

To many readers, an important message of the story is that society often fails to recognize the true heroes and heroines in its midst. One can certainly argue this is the case with the sacrifice of Mother Shipton as well as the selfless devotion of Duchess. In both cases, women condemned by society prove themselves to be morally superior to their judges. The suicide of Oakhurst provides further comment on the nature of heroism. Throughout the story, he appears to be the leader of the party and the individual most likely to devise their escape, but ultimately he gives up the struggle and fails to save either the group or himself.

Style

Setting

The setting of ''The Outcasts of Poker Flat'' is of major importance. The story occurs in November, 1850, during the heyday of the California Gold Rush. At that time, law and order on the mining frontier was often synonymous with vigilante justice, in which townspeople took matters into their own hands. Communities such as Poker Flat generally operated outside the reach of established judicial systems, and the type of vigilante activity Harte depicts was an accepted part of everyday life.

The story is set in the foothills of the Sierra Nevada mountains, a remote area in eastern California where the sudden occurrence of a winter storm could easily result in death for travelers. The most famous example of such a misfortune is the ill-fated Donner Party of 1846, in which twelve travelers starved to death and the remaining members resorted to cannibalism. This tragedy was highly publicized for years afterwards and was undoubtedly familiar to the original readers of this story. In an era before automobiles, or extensive railways, the fear of being stranded while traveling was real and vivid.

Genre

Genre is the term used to denote a category of literature. ''The Outcasts of Poker Flat'' is above all, a Western story. Other types of genre literature are science fiction, horror, and romance. Genre works can be identified by their conventions; some of the conventions of Westerns are that they take place on the frontier, they contain ''good'' guys and ''bad'' guys, female characters are either virtuous or ''fallen,'' and conflicts that result in showdowns or gunfights often end in death. All of these elements are prominent in Harte's story; one might say that the "showdown" is the battle between the travelers and Mother Nature.

Comic Relief

Although Harte's story is essentially a tragedy, the narrative contains moments of humor. Rather than the story containing a humorous character per se, the story's levity arises from the narrator's understatement and sometimes condescending tone towards the characters. As an example, the narrator comments that "notwithstanding some difficulties attending the manipulation of this instrument, Piney Woods managed to pluck several reluctant melodies from its keys." Elsewhere, the narrator evaluates Tom's recitation skills by stating he had "thoroughly mastered the argument and fairly forgotten the words." Critics often cited Harte's ability to balance the tragic and the comic as one of his strongest skills as a writer.

Historical Context

Gold Fever and the Manifest Destiny

During the late 1860s, Harte's tales of the California Gold Rush elevated him to a position of national fame. For the remainder of his career, he utilized the West as the setting for his stories and the inspiration for his lectures on life in the gold mines. Americans throughout the country were fascinated by the expansion of the country and tales of the wild West became part of the national consciousness. At the time of their publication, Harte's stories were primarily an idealized vision of an era that had recently passed. By the 1870s, the West was becoming more and more settled, and the vigilante justice of the frontier days was fast fading. While the settlement of the West remained an important topic for books and magazines, it is important to note that "The Outcasts of Poker Flat" appeared less than four years after the end of the Civil War. For a nation exhausted by war, Harte's story of heroics and tolerance recalled a happier period of innocence and opportunity.

It is difficult to exaggerate the importance of the Gold Rush as a historical event; within two years, the sparsely settled territory of California had become the fastest growing state in the union. As aspiring miners arrived from Europe, Asia, South America, and virtually every American state, the population of San Francisco leaped from approximately 800 people in 1848 to over 40,000 in 1850. Although the frenzy for prospecting subsided by the late 1850s, California was left with an infrastructure for industry, transportation, and agriculture that would have taken decades to develop under normal circumstances. For Americans of the day, the rapid settlement of California validated the doctrine of Manifest Destiny: the belief that it was God's will for the nation to expand across the continent.

However, romanticized depictions of the Gold Rush often overlook the unhappy outcome of the event for many prospectors. Relatively few of the '49ers managed to accumulate genuine wealth. Although most prospectors were successful in locating gold, the high cost of living in California prevented miners from pocketing much of their newfound riches. An additional consequence of the Gold Rush was the near-destruction of California's Native American population. The area contained dozens of autonomous Indian tribes, most of which resided in the regions which were the primary centers for mining activity. As a result, these cultures were the victims of both disease and military attacks and were nearing extinction by the 1870s.

Country Longs for a More Simple Time

Harte's fiction was not only a depiction of the past, but it was also a reaction to contemporary events. The American Civil War had halted westward migration from 1861 to 1865. Once the hostilities had ended, though, the nation was anxious to resume its expansion. Although the Pacific shore had been transformed into a center for industry and commerce, the vast area of the Great Plains remained largely unsettled by whites. Like 1849, the late 1860s was an era of movement into new lands.

Even though the post-bellum years were perceived to be a time of imminent opportunity, much of the nation was suffering from the effects of the war. The South was in ruins and resentful of the policies of Reconstruction. The country as a whole experienced a series of financial depressions as the economy readjusted to peacetime conditions. Ulysses S. Grant's 1868 election to the presidency marked the beginning of an era of widespread and highly

Compare & Contrast

- **1850s:** The United States embraces the concept of "Manifest Destiny," a phrase coined in an article in the July-August, 1845, issue of *United States Magazine and Democratic Review.* The phrase imparts the view that it is God's will that the young nation expand across the continent. In the resulting expansion, settlers race west to California in search of gold in 1849.

  1997: Although no longer claiming that expansionism is God's will, the United States continues to explore new frontiers. U.S. astronauts work side-by-side with their Russian counterparts aboard the Russian space station *Mir* in an effort to investigate the prospects of long-term cooperation in space.

- **1850s:** American society at large perceives gambling at cards and other games of chance, in which money changes hands, as the domain of drifters, con-men, and prostitutes.

  1997: Casino gambling is no longer confined to Las Vegas or Atlantic City, having come to be seen as a route to financial reinvigoration in large American cities. Candidates for municipal office often stake their political prospects on their success in bringing casino "gaming" to town, while political figures who oppose casinos are publicly vilified as out-of-touch prigs and Puritans.

---

publicized governmental corruption. Therefore it is not surprising that Harte's vision of a Western society populated with shrewd but valorous individuals such as John Oakhurst would resonate with readers of the day. Anxious to overlook their own shortcomings and to escape the troubles of the present, audiences looked to authors such as Harte to evoke a noble past to which they could hope to return in the future.

Critical Overview

When "The Outcasts of Poker Flat" first appeared in the January, 1869, issue of the *Overland Monthly,* the story was an immediate critical and popular success. Critics such as Emily S. Forman, writing for *Old and New,* praised Harte's use of "novel vernacular" and "vivid portraiture" to "thrill the very depths of the heart and soul." Harte's critical stature declined in subsequent years as people's tastes in literature changed. Despite this shift in tastes, "The Outcasts of Poker Flat" is continually recognized as one of Harte's best stories and is widely anthologized and read today.

As late as 1936, Arthur Hobson Quinn argued in *American Fiction: An Historical and Critical Survey* that the tale was "a masterpiece." But within seven years, Harte's reputation was seriously challenged by Cleanth Brooks and Robert Penn Warren's seminal text *Understanding Fiction,* which was published in 1943. In their analysis of Harte's "Tennessee's Partner," Brooks and Warren cited what later became standard criticisms of the author's work in general: inconclusive plots, lack of realism , and a reliance on melodrama and sentiment.

Such charges are interesting for they are essentially denouncing the traits that were responsible for Harte's initial success. In his heyday, Harte was celebrated for providing a realistic picture of the West. However, later generations possessing the advantage of historical hindsight were quick to label the author as a fraud. In 1973 Kevin Starr categorized Harte's work as "pseudo-history" complete with "comforting memories of finite human comedy and civilizing human sentiment." Given such attitudes it is not surprising that literary critics often take the position that Harte's stories lack artistic merit but are significant because of their influence on others. As an example, James K. Folsom cautioned, "In any discussion of Bret Harte one must begin by making a clear distinction between *importance* and *quality.*''

Other critics argue that is important to understand Harte in the context of nineteenth-century literature. In an article for *American Literary Realism,* Patrick Morrow suggested an alternate approach that sidesteps the issue of whether or not Harte's writing qualifies as great literature and focuses on its importance as a product of the culture in which it was written. Morrow points out that although Harte quickly fell from favor with critics, his work remained immensely popular with the public well into the twentieth century. Rather than denouncing him as a ''hack'' or ''servant of the masses,'' scholars should recognize his stories as a major component of nineteenth-century popular culture and utilize them as a tool to help understand the past. This idea is closely related to the observations of Donald E. Glover, who argued in *Western American Literature* that Harte's later fiction, a body of work traditionally dismissed by literary scholars, is qualitatively similar to his early stories. Glover believed the calibre of Harte's writing did not decline; rather, the audience for his work changed and his style shifted accordingly.

In his interpretation of ''The Outcasts of Poker Flat,'' Harold H. Kolb, Jr. suggested another explanation for the author's declining appeal. Kolb claimed that critical misunderstanding has long undermined an appreciation of Harte's work and that too much emphasis has been placed on the notion of Harte as a realist. Arguing that ''Harte is not concerned with an impression of actuality, his interests lie elsewhere,'' Kolb pointed to Harte's reliance on juxtaposition, such as the contrast between the crudeness of his characters and the sophistication of the narrator, as a form of humor. Despite its somber ending, ''The Outcasts of Poker Flat'' was designed to be read as a comedy. But as Kolb explained, ''the irony of his ironic style is that, for a century, he has had to be content with the enjoyment of his own fun.''

Pioneers on the Yukon Trail in Alaska, c.1897. The harsh climate of the West often made travel difficult and treacherous in the days of the Gold Rush.

Criticism

Allen Barksdale

Barksdale is a Ph.D. candidate in American Culture Studies at Bowling Green State University and teaches at Owens Community College. In the following essay, he argues that Harte satirizes conventional ideas about frontier life in ''The Outcasts of Poker Flat.''

During the late 1860s, Bret Harte was widely regarded as one of America's most promising authors. Such tales of life during the California Gold Rush as ''The Outcasts of Poker Flat,'' ''The Luck of Roaring Camp,'' and ''Tennessee's Partner'' were applauded for exploring the romance and adventure of

What Do I Read Next?

- *The Best of Bret Harte,* edited by Wilhelmina Harper in 1947, contains the author's most famous short stories, including "The Luck of Roaring Camp."
- Franklin Walker's 1939 study *San Francisco's Literary Frontier* details the development of American writers in the West and evaluates Harte within the context of his peers.
- *Roughing It,* Mark Twain's 1872 memoir, is an account of life in Virginia City, Nevada, during the silver mining boom of the 1860s. At one time Twain and Harte were close friends and both men worked as journalists on the mining frontier. Stylistically, they shared an ability to utilize local color and vernacular to create works of enduring fiction based on fact.
- Kevin Starr's 1973 history, *Americans and the California Dream 1850-1915,* is an excellent study of nineteenth-century California and the role it has played in defining the American dream.
- *The Shirley Letters From the California Mines 1851-1852* is a collection of writings by Louise Clappe. Using the pseudonym Dame Shirley, Clappe authored a series of letters to her sister in the East about life during the Gold Rush. An important book as a historical source and an interesting companion to the fiction of Bret Harte.

---

recent American history. Harte's greatest gift was considered to be a masterful ability to create setting by employing local color and regional dialects. Although his detractors complain that the author's depictions of life in the mining camps and gold fields are riddled with inaccuracies, one cannot deny that Harte's style was a powerful influence on subsequent fiction dealing with the American West.

While the majority of Harte's work has been forgotten, "The Outcasts of Poker Flat" has retained a place within the literary canon. Such scholars as James K. Folsom suggest that Harte's lingering presence is due to importance rather than quality, arguing that his writing remains of interest because of its impact upon others rather than from any intrinsic merit. While this is not entirely false, it does not explain why readers return to this tale as opposed to "Found at Blazing Star," "A Waif of the Plains," or any other of the dozens of Harte's works that have faded into obscurity. Perhaps the saga of the doomed outcasts contains some special quality that allows us to appreciate its subtleties more than a century after it was written.

One possible approach in examining "The Outcasts of Poker Flat" is to place the story within the context of writing about the American frontier experience. In Harte's narrative, four individuals are ejected from the relative security of a Gold Rush boom town. Marooned in the wilderness of the California mountains, they experience a confrontation with nature. Although this event is ultimately destructive, the encounter also allows some of the party to be morally rejuvenated by the escape from civilization.

This literary theme of insight through isolation was well established by Harte's time. One can look to Nathaniel Hawthorne's short story "Young Goodman Brown," in which a man's walk through the woods alerts him to the hypocrisy present in Puritan New England, to find a possible precursor to Harte. Indeed, Harte is clearly locating duplicity within Poker Flat; the members of the "secret committee" that banishes the outcasts have gambled with Oakhurst and have been "familiar" with Duchess.

For American writers, before and after Harte, the frontier setting has played the part of an ethical testing ground, providing a space in which individuals have no choice but to reveal their true moral caliber. An early example of this motif is Mary

Rowlandson's 1682 account of her captivity by Indians in colonial America. Widely read in its day, Rowlandson's account describes her ordeal as a reaction by an angry God to her earlier sins. Her captivity functions as a divine test that eventually restores her to grace with her Creator. Central to this experience is her isolation from peers and society, an event that fosters a degree of introspection that would have been otherwise impossible.

Similarly, the ejection of the outcasts from Poker Flat provides them with an opportunity for self-reflection. Clearly this is the case with Oakhurst. "As he gazed at his recumbent fellow-exiles," the reader is told, "the loneliness begotten of his pariah-trade, his habits of life, his very vices, for the first time seriously oppressed him." This self-examination eventually leads the gambler to conclude that his luck has finally run out. From this perspective, his suicide merely hastens an end that he considers inevitable.

"The Outcasts of Poker Flat" also contains the appealing message that given the opportunity, anyone might prove a hero. Although Oakhurst rejects his chance, Duchess and Mother Shipton clearly rise above their disreputable social positions in their efforts to care for Piney. The Innocent bravely confronts the snowstorm trying to save the party. Likewise, through her attempts to distract the outcasts from their misfortune as well as in her final comforting of Duchess, Piney can also be considered heroic.

The popularity of heroic figures in American fiction was well established by the time Harte began to publish. A generation earlier, James Fenimore Cooper's tales of frontier hero Natty Bumppo, including *The Pioneers* and *The Last of the Mohicans,* were among the best-selling works of the day. Harte's familiarity with Cooper's work is easily verified by a look at his *Condensed Novels,* a collection of parodies of popular books that was published two years prior to "The Outcasts of Poker Flat." In one of the selections, *Muck-a-Muck: A Modern Indian Novel,* Cooper is the target of Harte's satire. In recalling this work from his journeyman years, one cannot help but wonder if Harte's melodramatic tale of the snowbound outcasts is also a humorous take on the American fascination with the frontier as site of heroism and moral regeneration.

At least one Harte scholar, Harold H. Kolb, argues that an inordinate amount of attention has been given to the author's talents as a regional writer and local colorist. Kolb suggests that Harte's

"While Harte's initial rise to fame was a direct result of his presence within California's emerging literary community of the 1860s . . . he left this cultural outpost at the earliest opportunity and never returned."

greatest gift is that of humor. "The irony of his ironic style," Kolb comments, "is that, for half a century, he has had to be content with the enjoyment of his own fun." There are numerous asides and comments within "The Outcasts of Poker Flat" that are designed to elicit a grin from the reader. Piney Woods, the character who is often interpreted as a symbol for the purity of love, is described as "a stout, comely damsel." Even the dire circumstances of the outcasts' confinement are diluted by the presence of an accordion's "fitful spasms" and the recitation of Homer "in the current vernacular of Sandy Bar."

In his argument that Harte is a frequently misunderstood humorist, Kolb bases his argument on the relation between author and audience. Another way of looking at this story is to view the proceedings as a satire on the near-sacred status bestowed on the relationship between Americans and the frontier in popular culture. A major difference between this story and most other sagas of the West is that despite some powerful transformations among the outcasts, none of these heroes survive unscathed. While the reader may conclude, since a rescue party does eventually reach the camp, that The Innocent safely reached Poker Flat, his reward is the corpse of his bride-to-be. Of the four outcasts from Poker Flat, the only apparent survivor is the unregenerate Uncle Billy, who steals the groups' mounts. Such an outcome leads one to suspect that Harte was at least somewhat cynical about the possibilities of renewal on the frontier.

The narrative structure of the story, a balance between authenticity and improbability, further alerts the reader that Harte's intentions may stretch beyond a warning against the perils of vigilante justice. When not labeling him a purveyor of melodrama, critics wishing to dismiss Harte are quick to point out major breaches of realism in the story. People rarely starve to death in a matter of days as does Mother Shipton, and Oakhurst's ability to produce a pair of snowshoes from a pack saddle seems at least unusual in a professional gambler. However, such lapses into the unlikely do not equal flaws if one reads ''The Outcasts of Poker Flat'' as a satire, rather than a realistic account, of frontier conditions.

If one looks at the author's career, it is easy to envision him ridiculing popular beliefs about the glorious West. While Harte's initial rise to fame was a direct result of his presence within California's emerging literary community of the 1860s and his ability to commodify his experiences in the West, he left this cultural outpost at the earliest opportunity and never returned. If one reads his tale as a travesty not just of the West, but of the entire national vision of regeneration through confrontation with nature, there is additional significance in Harte's decision to reject the simplicity of the New World and spend the last twenty years of his life in Europe.

While ''The Outcasts of Poker Flat'' is justifiably credited with influencing generations of subsequent writing about the West, one should also consider the work as a variation on themes that were firmly embedded in the American consciousness by the second half of the nineteenth century. Although on the surface Harte delivers a clear message on the dangers of judging others, he also suggests the reader should think twice before accepting certain parts of our cultural consciousness.

Source: Allen Barksdale, ''An Overview of 'The Outcasts of Poker Flat',''in *Short Stories for Students,* Gale, 1998.

Jason Pierce

Pierce is a Ph.D. candidate at the University of South Carolina. In the following essay, he examines Harte's treatment of questions of morality and corruption in ''The Outcasts of Poker Flat.''

When ''The Outcasts of Poker Flat'' appeared in the January, 1869, issue of the California journal *Overland Monthly,* it was widely praised as yet another example of Bret Harte's literary genius. The periodical *Fun* considered it ''worthy of Hawthorne,'' while the *New Eclectic* magazine thought it ''droll and humorous, and at the same time deeply pathetic.'' When it appeared in a collection entitled *The Luck of Roaring Camp and Other Sketches,* William Dean Howells, editor of the *Atlantic Monthly* and one of the most influential American critics of the time, singled out ''The Outcasts'' for particular praise, noting Harte's ''very fine and genuine'' style of representing life in the American West, particularly California. However, not all the reviews were completely complimentary. The *New York Times,* while praising its ''picturesque style,'' upbraided Harte for portraying the marginal members of society in a positive light. Similarly, the *Spectator* applauded Harte's ''originality of style'' but thought his characters ''improper.'' This was the sort of criticism that would dog Harte's fiction well into the twentieth century; though his work was original and demonstrated admirable style, its characters were not compatible with contemporary morals.

When considered, such a reaction is hardly surprising, but the modern reader has grown accustomed to the conventions of the Western genre. We have come to expect that stories set in the ''wild West'' of the mid-nineteenth century will be peopled with gamblers, drunkards, cattle rustlers, whores, and all manner of dissolute individuals. Such characters appear to us as the norm rather than the exception, but Harte's contemporaries saw things very differently. To them, the John Oakhursts and Mother Shiptons of the world were immoral characters who had placed themselves at the margins of society and should be obliged to stay there. Indeed, this is exactly what happens to Oakhurst and the three others when Poker Flat's ''secret committee'' decides ''to rid the town of all improper persons.'' For that matter, such moral exclusion continues today; even in a society burdened by crime and accustomed to vice, modern gamblers, hookers, and thieves are hardly considered socially acceptable. Rather, they are on the outskirts of society, pushed to our equivalent of ''the gulch which marked the uttermost limit of Poker Flat.''

Why, then, are we so willing to accept—and even applaud—such figures in works of fiction? How is it that we can look past the characters' vices and find their virtues when our forebears often could not? Part of the answer is that Western fiction has desensitized us to Western fact. Raised on a steady diet of John Wayne, *Gunsmoke,* and *Doctor Quinn,* we are no longer in touch with what really happened in the nineteenth-century American West.

We have been brought up to consider such character types as the town drunk, the self-sacrificing madam, and the generous gambler to be somehow representative of life in the West during that time period. While I surely do not mean to imply that such people did not exist in the "Old West," we can hardly consider them representative. Indeed, though we often skip over it, the title of Harte's story reminds us that most of its characters are indeed *outcasts,* persons in whom society cannot abide.

That said, what little we see of the characters paints most of them in a positive light. For that matter, there seem to be two types of outcasts: those who encourage vice, and those who are themselves vicious. Only one character, Uncle Billy, truly fits into the latter category. A "suspected sluice-robber"—that is, a thief who steals from gold miners—"and a confirmed drunkard," Uncle Billy is the only character who is truly without morals. He is forced out of Poker Flat because he is a leech upon society, an individual who takes without giving in return. Though we may not approve of the professions of John Oakhurst, the Duchess, or Mother Shipton, they assuredly contribute to the society of Poker Flat: Oakhurst by putting up his money in poker, the women by offering their bodies to paying customers. Though criminals, they participate in victimless crimes; the poker-players and solicitors with whom they associate are fully as criminal as these characters. Uncle Billy, though, is truly profligate. His crimes—assuming, that is, that the town's suspicions are not unfounded—have victims. Whereas the other characters might be considered immoral, Uncle Billy is actively antisocial; his crimes threaten the foundations of society. It should come as no surprise, then, that he steals the mules and horses while the others sleep. It is this act that ultimately leads to the destruction of the "society" of the camp. It is he, if anyone, who is the "villain" of Harte's story.

The other outcasts, despite being socially unacceptable (unacceptable, that is, in Poker Flat, but acceptable in Sandy Bar, a settlement that "not having as yet experienced the regenerating influences of Poker Flat, consequently seemed to offer some invitation") are actually quite admirable in ways not normally associated with gamblers and hookers. Indeed, it was this method of characterization for which Harte drew the greatest criticism. So common were his positive portraits of "fallen" individuals that one anonymous reviewer for the *Spectator* suggested that the author had suffered from "an attack of Dickens-on-the-brain," a reference to the English novelist's propensity to depict such characters in a similar sentimental light. Here, then, is the source of our modern tendency to look at the nineteenth-century American West and see a land of harmless and even noble immorality, a time and place where vice was common but viciousness was rare. Before Harte, there really were no stories that attempted to paint what life was like in California. Other writers had written about the "frontier," but the frontier kept moving west, and writers had a hard time keeping up. Harte's writings filled a void, and, as there was nothing to dispute what he wrote, the character types with which he peopled his stories established themselves as the stock-in-trade of future writers of stories in the Western genre. Towards the end of his life, by which time his writings were generally considered outdated and cliched, he was disparagingly remembered as the writer who had created "the hooker with a heart of gold."

"Harte was not advocating prostitution, gambling, or thievery as modes of moral living; rather, he was arguing that morality is a matter of individual behavior and conscience rather than a societal construct."

Such reproachful remarks, however, ignore the implicit social commentary of Harte's fiction. Though hardly a treatise on society's problems, "The Outcasts of Poker Flat" undoubtedly makes certain critiques of life in early California. The outcasts are set in opposition to the town of Poker Flat, "a settlement unused to Sabbath influences" that, nonetheless, has recently undergone "a change in its moral atmosphere." That change, though, has not come about through any newfound interest in public ethics; rather, the townspeople who cast out "all improper persons" are themselves guilty of similar improprieties. Jim Wheeler, the most vocal member of the "secret committee," wishes to get rid of Oakhurst not because he is a gambler but because he is a *successful* gambler. Wheeler's sense of morality is based on his being a poor loser rather than on any spiritual awakening. He, like the rest of the self-righteous secret committee members, is a hypocrite, and his self-proclaimed morality is in truth nothing more than greed.

In contrast, most of the outcasts—Uncle Billy being the lone exception—have admirable qualities. Oakhurst is the first to show his true colors when he gives the Duchess his horse, Five Spot, in exchange for her ''sorry mule.'' He stays with the other outcasts when the Duchess insists on stopping, and, even though he seems capable of continuing alone, the ''thought of deserting his weaker and more pitiable companions never perhaps occurred to him.'' Later we learn that, in an earlier encounter with Tom Simson, Oakhurst returned poker winnings of forty dollars to ''the Innocent'' with a warning to avoid cards in the future. Mother Shipton, despite her occasional uses of ''bad language,'' is in fact a good and caring person who sets aside her portion of the rations to give Piney Woods a greater chance at survival. The Duchess, a fallen woman and yet an ingenue, tries to comfort Piney in their last hours. Though their professions make them socially unacceptable, all three are good people.

Indeed, this assessment is supported when the Innocent and Piney—the two most wholesome, honest, forthright characters the story offers—arrive and perceive the outcasts as anything but the sinners they supposedly are. Only the reprobate Uncle Billy finds any humor in Tom's mistaking of the Duchess for Oakhurst's wife, his own wickedness having warped him into a sneering, cynical cur. The others are quite willing to let Tom and Piney persist in their mistaken beliefs, to let them remain innocents as regards the outcasts' true natures. When they become snowed in and death seems imminent, the remaining outcasts still do not reveal their ''true'' selves as ''there's no good frightening them [Tom and Piney] now.'' These, though, *are* their true selves. Oakhurst, the Duchess, and Mother Shipton are not the degenerate miscreants that the secret committee of Poker Flat deemed them; rather, they are honest, caring people whose professions conflict with Poker Flat's recent spate of false morality.

This conflict between a corrupt society and its virtuous outcasts is the central theme of Harte's story. By developing characters like the ''hooker with a heart of gold'' that would become Western stereotypes, Harte was not advocating prostitution, gambling, or thievery as modes of moral living; rather, he was arguing that morality is a matter of individual behavior and conscience rather than a societal construct. Though the secret committee of Poker Flat can exile the characters from the town, they have no right to pass judgment on them—the characters' actions, save those of Uncle Billy, show them to be as moral as, if not more moral than, the committee members. Ultimately, in ''The Outcasts of Poker Flat,'' society destroys rather than enforces morality.

Source: Jason Pierce, ''Overview of 'The Outcasts of Poker Flat',' ' in *Short Stories for Students,* Gale, 1998.

Michael Oriard

A former professional football player with the Kansas City Chiefs (1970–74), Oriard is an English professor who has focused much of his study upon the relationship between sports and American culture. He has gone so far as to say, ''To understand America, understand American games and play.'' In the following excerpt from a recent book on that relationship, Oriard explores the character of John Oakhurst as an emblem of ''sporting fatalism'' and discusses the effect on Harte's narrative strategy.

The major sporting figure in Harte's fiction, the frontier gambler, juxtaposed nobility and moral outrage in a similar way. In Harte's three most famous tales—''The Luck of Roaring Camp'' (*Overland Monthly,* August 1868), ''Tennessee's Partner'' (*Overland Monthly,* October 1869), and ''The Outcasts of Poker Flat'' (*Overland Monthly,* January 1869)—the professional gambler emerges as a gamesman by trade but a transcendent sportsman by instinct and action. He is a fatalist in a world dominated by chance, but his absolute commitment to honor and fair play lead to an ambiguous sentimental salvation. . . .

The quintessential emblem of sporting fatalism in these stories is the death of John Oakhurst, which concludes ''The Outcasts of Poker Flat.'' Having been banished from Poker Flat, together with two prostitutes and a thief, Oakhurst ''was too much of a gambler not to accept Fate. With him life was at best an uncertain game, and he recognized the usual percentage in favor of the dealer.'' When the four exiles and an innocent young couple that joins them are trapped in a snowstorm, Oakhurst coolly surveys ''the losing game before him'' then slips away to play out his hand his own way. On a deuce of clubs pinned to a tree with a bowie knife, the rescuers who arrive too late discover his scrawled epitaph:

> BENEATH THIS TREE LIES THE BODY OF JOHN OAKHURST WHO STRUCK A STREAK OF BAD LUCK ON THE 23D OF NOVEMBER, 1850, AND HANDED IN HIS CHECKS ON THE 7TH DECEMBER, 1850

In the story's final line the narrator calls Oakhurst ''at once the strongest and yet the weakest of the outcasts of Poker Flat.'' This self-conscious ambivalence—the gambler as self-sacrificing hero, the gambler as blind fatalist—both typifies Harte's narrative strategy and signals the uneasiness with which genteel culture came to terms with this figure. Readers could be charmed or shocked by Bret Harte's stories, assured of the capacity for goodness in even the least likely souls, left uncertain whether proper values had in fact been affirmed after all, or convulsed with laughter at the moralism his fiction might have seemed to puncture. . . .

Source: Michael Oriard, ''Play, Sport, and Western Mythmaking,'' in *Sporting with the Gods: The Rhetoric of Play and Game in American Culture,* Cambridge University Press, 1991, pp. 40–81.

"In the story's final line the narrator calls Oakhurst 'at once the strongest and yet the weakest of the outcasts of Poker Flat.' This self-conscious ambivalence—the gambler as self-sacrificing hero, the gambler as blind fatalist—both typifies Harte's narrative strategy and signals the uneasiness with which genteel culture came to terms with this figure."

Horace Spencer Fiske

In the following excerpt, Fiske provides a short, synoptic overview of the plot and characters of ''The Outcasts of Poker Flat.''

A unique and striking figure among the ''Outcasts of Poker Flat'' is Mr. John Oakhurst, type of the imperturbable, smooth, daring and irresistible Western gambler, who, under unexpected conditions, develops unexpected qualities,—the qualities of practical sympathy and heroic self-sacrifice. He had been included among those who were destined to leave Poker Flat, for the community had recently lost several thousand dollars, two valuable horses, and a prominent citizen. Two of those destined for exile were already hanging to the boughs of a sycamore in the gulch; a secret committee had even considered the hanging of Mr. Oakhurst, one of the minority contending that ''it's agin justice to let this yer young man from Roaring Camp—an entire stranger—carry away our money.'' The minority of the committee, however, was overruled, and Mr. Oakhurst was included in the ''deported wickedness'' that was escorted to the outskirts of Poker Flat by a body of armed men. In this expatriated company were a young woman familiarly known as the ''Duchess,'' another called ''Mother Shipton,'' and a third person, ''Uncle Billy,'' a suspected sluice-robber and confirmed drunkard. At the outermost edge of Poker Flat this company was set adrift, with the implicit injunction not to return, at the peril of their lives.

The ''outcasts'' decided on Sandy Bar for their destination, a camp that lay over a steep mountain range, a hard day's travel distant. At noon the Duchess refused to go farther, and the party halted, although scarcely half the journey to Sandy Bar was accomplished and provisions for delay were lacking. Mr. Oakhurst, the gambler, called it ''throwing up their hand before the game was played out.'' But they were provided with whisky, if not with any adequate supply of provisions, and they were all soon in a helpless state of stupor—all except the gambler, who never drank,—it interfered, he said, with his profession and he ''couldn't afford it.'' His thought seemed never to be that of deserting his feebler and more pitiable companions, as they lay in a drunken stupor amid the encircling pines,—precipitous cliffs of naked granite rising above them on three sides, and the crest of a precipice in front overlooking the valley. They were suddenly reenforced by an eloping couple going to Poker Flat to be married, and as the prospective bridegroom had once lost money to Mr. Oakhurst and had it

"A unique and striking figure among the 'Outcasts of Poker Flat' is Mr. John Oakhurst, type of the imperturbable, smooth, daring and irresistible Western gambler, who, under unexpected conditions, develops unexpected qualities,—the qualities of practical sympathy and heroic self-sacrifice."

considerately returned, he greeted the gambler as a genuine friend and was insistent on camping with his party, assuring Mr. Oakhurst that he had an extra mule loaded with provisions, and that there was a rude attempt at a log house near the trail. That night the women spent in the log house and the men lay before the door. Waking benumbed with cold, the gambler stirred the dying fire and felt on his cheek the touch of snow! Turning to where the thieving Uncle Billy slept he found him gone, and the tethered mules with him. At dawn the gambler recognized that they were "snowed in," with all that implied in the loss of the trail and the cutting off of provisions and rescue.

In his unsuspected kindliness of heart Mr. Oakhurst, the gambler, was unwilling that Tom Simson and Piney, the eloping couple, should know the real rascality of Uncle Billy, and implied that the latter had wandered off from the camp and stampeded the animals by accident. And through the gambler's request the Duchess and Mother Shipton also gave out the same impression as to Uncle Billy's whereabouts. But Tom seemed rather to look forward to a week's camping with his sweetheart, and his gayety and Mr. Oakhurst's professional calm "infected" the others. From some unaccountable motive Mr. Oakhurst *cached* the whisky, and concealed his cards. And Tom somewhat ostentatiously produced an accordion from his pack, from which his sweetheart, Piney, succeeded in plucking a few reluctant tunes to the accompaniment of Tom's bone castanets. The lovers sang, too, a rude camp-meeting hymn, joining hands as they did so, and the defiant covenanters' swing of the chorus finally led the others to join in the somewhat prophetic refrain:—

> "I'm proud to live in the service of the Lord, And I'm bound to die in His army."

And above these doomed singers the pines rocked and the storm eddied.

In dividing the watch that night with Tom Simson, Mr. Oakhurst somehow managed to take upon himself the greater share of the duty, explaining that he had "often been a week without sleep" when luck at poker ran high. "When a man gets a streak of luck . . . he don't get tired. The luck gives in first. Luck," continued the gambler meditatively, "is a mighty queer thing. All you know is that it's bound to change. And it's finding out when it's going to change that makes you."

The nights were filled with the reedy notes of the accordion, but music failed to fill the aching void of insufficient food, and story-telling was suggested by Piney. However, Mr. Oakhurst and his female companions were hardly willing to relate their personal experiences in the presence of the Innocent, as they called Tom, or of "the child," as the Duchess and Mother Shipton called Piney; and this plan of diversion would have fallen through had the Innocent not been able to recall some of Mr. Pope's translation of the "Iliad," which he had chanced upon a few months before. He told the exciting incidents of the epic in the current vernacular of Sandy Bar. And he got an enthusiastic hearing, while the great pines in the canyon seemed to bow to the wrath of the son of Peleus. Mr. Oakhurst was especially interested in the fate of "Ash-heels," as the Innocent insisted on calling the "swift-footed Achilles."

A week passed over the heads of the outcasts, the sun again abandoned them, and the leaden skies sifted swiftly down upon them great banks of snow, till they stood more than twenty feet above the cabin. It became increasingly difficult to replenish the fires, and yet no one complained. The lovers looked into each other's eyes and were happy, but Mother Shipton seemed to sicken and fade. At midnight of the tenth day she called the gambler to her side, and said, in a querulous weakness of voice: "I'm going, but don't say anything about it. Don't waken the kids. Take the bundle from under my head and open it." It contained the rations she had saved for a week. ''Give 'em to the child,'' she said, pointing to Piney. Starvation through self-sacrifice was the unexpected ending of this abandoned woman's life.

With another unselfish motive coming to the surface, Mr. Oakhurst took the Innocent aside and showed him a pair of snow-shoes he had fashioned from the old pack-saddles. The gambler announced that if by the aid of these Tom could reach Poker Flat in two days, his sweetheart could be saved. Oakhurst pretended to accompany Tom as far as the canon, unexpectedly kissing the Duchess good-by before he went. It stirred her with emotion and amazement; but the gambler never came back. The Duchess, feeding the fire during the fierce storm of wind and snow on the following night, found that some one had quietly piled beside the hut enough fuel to last a few days longer; and it was not difficult to surmise that it was due to the thoughtfulness of Oakhurst. The second night the two women were frozen to death in each other's arms—the soiled Duchess and the virgin Piney. ''And when pitying fingers brushed the snow away from their wan faces, you could scarcely have told, from the equal peace that dwelt upon them, which was she that had sinned.''

At the head of the gulch the searchers found on one of the largest pine trees the deuce of clubs pinned to the bark with a bowie knife; and on it was written in pencil, with a firm hand, ''Beneath this tree lies the body of John Oakhurst, who struck a streak of bad luck on the 23d November, 1850, and handed in his checks on the 7th of December, 1850.'' And underneath the snow, with a bullet through his heart and a derringer by his side, lay the calm-faced gambler, whose hard life was softened and ennobled at its close by thoughtful sympathy and sublime self-sacrifice. . . .

Source: Horace Spencer Fiske, '''The Luck of Roaring Camp' and Other Stories,'' in *Provincial Types in American Fiction,* by Bret Harte, 1903. Reprint by Kennikat Press, Inc., 1968, pp. 241–64.

Sources

Brooks, Cleanth, Jr. and Robert Penn Warren. ''Tennessee's Partner,'' in *Understanding Fiction,* pp. 219–20. New York: F. S. Croft, 1943.

Folsom, James K. ''Bret Harte,'' in *Critical Survey of Short Fiction,* edited by Frank N. Magill, Salem Press, 1981, pp. 1129–35.

Glover, Donald E. ''A Reconsideration of Bret Harte's Later Works,'' in *Western American Literature,* Vol. 8, Fall, 1973, pp. 143–51.

Kolb, Harold H., Jr. ''The Outcasts of Literary Flat: Bret Harte as Humorist,'' in *American Literary Realism,* Vol. 23, Winter, 1991, pp. 52- 63.

Morrow, Patrick. ''The Predicament of Bret Harte,'' in *American Literary Realism,* Vol. 5, Summer, 1972, pp. 181-88.

Quinn, Arthur Hobson. In *American Fiction: An Historical and Critical Survey,* New York: D. Appleton-Century Co., 1936.

Starr, Kevin. *Americans and the California Dream: 1850-1915,* New York: Oxford University Press, 1973.

Further Reading

Gardner, Joseph H. ''Bret Harte and the Dickensian Mode in America,'' in *Canadian Journal of American Studies,* Vol. 2, Fall, 1971, pp. 89-101.

Primarily a comparison between Bret Harte and Charles Dickens which also summarizes many reviews of Harte's writing from 1870 to 1902.

May, Ernest R. ''Bret Harte and the *Overland Monthly,*'' in *American Literature,* Vol. 22, November, 1950, pp. 260-71.

A valuable account of Harte's early career and the important magazine he helped to found.

Scharnhorst, Gary. *Bret Harte,* Twayne, 1992.

A brief but comprehensive volume on the author's life and career. Includes a bibliography.

Rape Fantasies

Margaret Atwood

1977

Margaret Atwood's "Rape Fantasies" was first published in the Canadian version of *Dancing Girls and Other Stories* in 1977 but was omitted from the American edition of the collection. It has become one of Atwood's best-known works, particularly after its inclusion in the 1985 edition of *The Norton Anthology of Literature by Women.* The story, a first-person narration in which a woman discusses her concerns about being raped, exhibits many of the qualities often associated with Atwood's work, including biting humor, vivid characterizations, and an exploration of the power struggle between men and women. Furthermore, it highlights many women's fears of crime and victimization in an urban environment where safety depends on striking a delicate balance between trust and suspicion.

Although "Rape Fantasies" is one of Atwood's most popular stories, little criticism of her work focuses on it specifically. Several critics have noted that Estelle seems to be a naive protagonist, but that view is rejected by an equal number of reviewers. Estelle and her female coworkers have very different ideas on what romance is and how to obtain it without falling prey to the insidious forces in society. The story is often used as a starting point for discussing the gap between men's and women's perceptions of each other.

Author Biography

Margaret Atwood was born in Ottawa, Ontario, Canada, on November 18, 1939. She started reading and writing at an early age and was particularly drawn to the Brothers Grimm fairy tales because of their active female characters. Greek mythology and its themes of metamorphosis, rebirth, and transformation further excited the young girl's imagination. Atwood's father was an entomologist and an avid nature lover. The young Atwood spent much time discovering nature in the wilds of Canada while she was growing up, a fact that is evident in much of her writing. In the book *Conversations,* Atwood discussed the impact her father's work had on her: "The most transformative thing you can study is insects. They change from one thing into another, and the thing they change into bears no relation to what they were before."

As a high school student in Toronto, Ontario, in the 1950s, Atwood began to take writing seriously. In school, she studied mostly British writers, and the idea of a particularly Canadian literature was not common, a fact that she has successfully sought to change throughout her career. After receiving a degree from the University of Toronto in 1961, Atwood came to the United States to study at Radcliffe and Harvard. Cultural differences between Canada and the United States first became an issue when she was attending Harvard University. She discovered that many Americans had only the vaguest notion of Canada. "They seemed to want to believe that my father was a Mounted Policeman and that we lived in igloos all year round, and I must admit that after a while I took a certain pleasure in encouraging these beliefs," Atwood once said.

Atwood's first published work was a collection of poems, *Double Persephone,* which was published in 1961. It was not until 1970 that her first novel was published, *The Edible Woman,* the story of a reluctantly engaged woman who becomes infatuated with a mysterious man utterly unlike her fiance. As her affair progresses, she becomes unable to eat. Over the years, Atwood has published many collections of poetry, stories, and essays in addition to her novels, and has won acclaim for all the genres in which she writes. No matter what form her writing takes, it often incorporates irony, symbolism, and self-conscious narrators. Her themes usually explore the relationship between humanity and nature, the unsettling aspects of human behavior, and power as it pertains to gender roles.

Now considered one of Canada's foremost writers, Atwood continues to write novels and stories to wide public acclaim. In 1996 she published *Alias, Grace,* a fictionalized account of a real-life murder that took place in Canada in the eighteenth century. Other works by Atwood that have proved popular include *Cat's Eye,* the story of a Toronto-based artist who is haunted by the memory of a cruel childhood friend; *The Handmaid's Tale,* a dystopian novel that takes place in the future, when childbearing women are rare and forced into servitude as breeding machines; and *The Robber Bride,* in which three very different women lose the men in their lives to the scheming, preternaturally beautiful Zenia. In addition to her fiction, Atwood contributes to the body of contemporary literary criticism through her frequent reviews and essays on literature and writing. She continues to live in Canada with her husband, the writer Graeme Gibson, and their daughter, Jess.

Plot Summary

The first-person narrator of "Rape Fantasies" is Estelle, a young office worker who notes how popular the topic of rape has become in women's magazines. According to Estelle, articles on the subject seem to be everywhere; titles like "Rape, Ten Things To Do About It" appear in capital letters on the magazine covers, "like it was ten new hairdos or something." She recounts a conversation that took place during her lunch hour between herself and her coworkers after Chrissy, a receptionist in Estelle's office, has read one of these articles. Chrissy interrupts her coworkers' bridge game to ask if any of them ever fantasize about rape. Each character's response defines her personality: Estelle would rather continue playing cards, Chrissy and Sondra are interested in trading stories, and Darlene, the oldest and the only divorced woman in the group, finds such fantasies disgusting and turns her back on the women to go to the coffee machine.

Greta fantasizes about a handsome man coming through her balcony doors, a fantasy that draws on romantic television shows and movies. Chrissy relates that her fantasy is for a man to break into her apartment while she is taking a bath. Estelle re-

Margaret Atwood

sponds to both women by saying "those aren't rape fantasies. I mean, you aren't getting raped, it's just some guy you haven't met formally. . . . and you have a good time. Rape is when they've got a knife or something and you don't want to." Her comments, however, are not met with enthusiasm, and her jokes are considered inappropriate. When prodded by Chrissy, Estelle describes a rape fantasy that involves being accosted on a dark street by a short, ugly man who is "absolutely covered in pimples." Once he pins her to the wall, his zipper gets stuck. He starts to cry and she ends up feeling sorry for him. Abruptly, Estelle interjects that she thought moving to Toronto "was going to be such a big adventure and all, but it's a lot harder to meet people in a city. But I guess it's different for a guy." This is the reader's first indication that Estelle is addressing her remarks to a listener within the story, rather than to the reader.

She then resumes her original narrative, launching into another rape fantasy. This time, she is bedridden with a terrible cold, and a man who, coincidentally, has a cold too, climbs through her window. "I'b goig do rabe you," is what he says. Eventually, they end up taking some medication and watching television together. Revealing her awareness of the seriousness of the topic, Estelle then offers a more realistic rape fantasies: she is accosted by a man with an axe in her mother's basement. She talks to him about the voices in his head, insisting that she hears them too. Her conversation confuses the would-be criminal, and eventually he leaves. Estelle doesn't like to think too much about this particular fantasy, since, as she says: "Dwelling on [unpleasant things] doesn't make them go away. Though not dwelling on them doesn't make them go away either, when you come to think of it." Vaguely aware that her rape fantasies may be no more realistic than those of her coworkers, Estelle acknowledges that "the funny thing about these fantasies is that the man is always someone I don't know, and the statistics in the magazines . . . say it's often someone you do know." Her monologue takes a serious turn when she goes on to talk about her personal life. She says she is not a drinker, but does not mind going to a nice bar by herself. Yet she obviously worries about the risks involved: "It's getting so you can hardly be sociable any more. . . . You can't spend your whole life . . . cooped up in your own apartment with all the doors and windows locked and the shades down." A crucial statement that hints at Estelle's motive for her lengthy speech about rape is directed at her listener, who is a customer, presumably male, in the bar she frequents: "I don't know why I'm telling you all this, except I think it helps you get to know a person, especially at first, hearing some of the things they think about." Getting to know a person is, at least in Estelle's view, a woman's best defense against rape, since she doesn't understand "how . . . a fellow [could] do that to a person he's just had a long conversation with . . ."

Characters

Chrissy

Chrissy is Estelle's coworker who initiates the lunchroom discussion by asking, "How about it, girls, do you have rape fantasies?" Estelle describes Chrissy as "a receptionist and she looks like one; she's pretty but cool as a cucumber like she's been painted all over with nail polish, if you know what I mean. Varnished." Chrissy dreams of a rapist who breaks into her apartment while she is taking a bath. Chrissy represents a passive personality, someone who is easily influenced by novels, movies, televisions, and magazines.

Darlene

Darlene, who is 41, is the oldest woman in the office, "though you wouldn't know it and neither does she," Estelle comments. She is divorced and does not participate in the discussion about fantasies. She claims that she never thinks about such things and that the topic is disgusting. Darlene says, "I don't think you should go out at night, you put yourself in a position," a comment that insinuates that she does not approve of Estelle's behavior. She says she would scream if she were accosted by a rapist, and she tells Chrissy that she should do the same thing. These two comments indicate that Darlene is a cautious and somewhat judgmental individual.

Estelle

Estelle is the first-person narrator of "Rape Fantasies." She works in the filing department of a large company in Toronto, Ontario. She was brought up Catholic in a smaller town and has only recently moved to the city to be on her own. She is described as tall and clever, and her comments indicate that she has a good sense of humor and that she is adept at sizing up other people.

Her coworker Darlene comments that Estelle has the "mark of an original mind" and that "she's a card" since once at an office party, Estelle danced under a table instead of on top of it. Along with her sense of humor, she is cautious. Though her monologue reveals that her "rape fantasies" have happy outcomes, the reason for her monologue appears to be more dire. Twice she asks if things are different for men, indicating that the person to whom she is speaking is receiving a thinly veiled warning: "the waiters all know me and if anyone, you know, bothers me. . . ." She also states that her coworkers consider her a worry wart. That assertion is somewhat borne out by her monologue. At the end, she reveals that all her talk about rape is an attempt to start a dialogue. "How could a fellow do that to a person he's just had a long conversation with?" Her last statement, "I know it happens but I just don't understand it," is an indication to some critics that Estelle is a naive narrator, but others interpret her words as merely the conclusion to a long conversation in which Estelle reveals that she is very aware of the issues of power involved in rape.

Themes

Gender Roles and Stereotypes

Estelle's narration is filled with stereotypes of both men and women. For instance, she describes Chrissy as a receptionist who "looks like one." Atwood relies on the power of the stereotype for readers to envision Chrissy's appearance; the only details readers are given are that she wears lots of makeup, blushes at the thought of discussing rape fantasies, and "looks like she was painted all over with nail polish." Some of the story's humor also lies in stereotypes. When discussing Chrissy and Greta, who wants to be a receptionist, Estelle describes them as blondes who "try to outdress each other." Estelle is also cognizant of male gender roles, and feels sympathy for the men in her rape fantasies because they do not live up to her preconception of the ideal man, a "Clint Eastwood" type. "I mean there has to be something *wrong* with them," she says, after explaining that she imagines rapists to have bad skin or to exhibit symptoms of either physical or mental illness. To Estelle a rapist is a man who does not live up to the ideal of a virile, tall, handsome man able to win a woman by the sheer power of his masculinity. She invokes an age-based stereotype when she states that her boss could not possibly be a rapist because "he's over sixty . . . poor old thing." Even in her sympathy, Estelle tends to stereotype people.

Estelle does recognize that even though all her fantasies concern strangers, a rapist is more likely to be someone the victim knows casually. With that in mind, she imagines that a man at work, whom she calls Derek Duck, would be a likely rapist because he wears elevator shoes and has a "funny way of talking." In the end, Estelle is trying hard to reject the traditional female gender role of being a victim. She fights back in her rape fantasies, or she averts the crime by commiserating with the would-be perpetrator. Both scenarios show her to be an active woman in control of her life and thoughts, rather than a passive observer. The fact that she is probably in a bar by herself hints that she rejects some

Topics for Further Study

- Compare ''Rape Fantasies'' with another first-person narrative addressed to a silent listener, Robert Browning's poem ''My Last Duchess.'' Discuss how both authors develop their characters by what they have their characters say.
- Who do you think has a greater chance of being raped, Estelle or her coworkers? Why? Do you think your answer is influenced by stereotypes in any way?
- Examine rape statistics in the United States from 1977 to today. What kind of trends do you see? How does the United States compare with other countries? Give some possible explanations for the discrepancy between U. S. statistics and those of other countries.
- What do psychologists and sociologists have to say about the underlying causes of rape? Do you agree with them?
- Think of some television shows that utilize stereotypes of men and women. Do you think they are accurate? Do you find these stereotypes offensive? Discuss whether or not you think stereotypes should be restricted in the media.

traditional female gender roles: ''I'm with Women's Lib on that even though I can't agree with a lot of other things they say.''

Victim and Victimization

Though not evident at first, Estelle's monologue becomes an exploration of victims and victimization. She recounts her fantasies of being a victim, yet the reason she does so is to possibly prevent herself from becoming a victim. Though her coworkers claim she is a worry wart, she sees her fantasies as simply a way of ''figuring out what you should do in an emergency.'' The fantasies also reveal that Estelle considers her imagined rapists to themselves be victims—of bad skin, of mental illness, or of leukemia. In the end, Estelle's best defense against victimization is a strong offense. In her fantasies, she actively initiates conversations with her would-be rapists in order to establish their common humanity. ''How could a fellow do that to a person he's just had a long conversation with, once you let them know you're human, you have a life too,'' she wonders.

Though she criticizes women's magazines' preoccupation with the topic, the detailed accounts she provides of her own rape fantasies prove that she herself thinks about rape a great deal. Estelle has taken to heart the dangers of living alone in an urban area in the 1970s; her predicament is one that many single women identify with. ''It's getting so you can hardly be sociable any more, and how are you supposed to meet people if you can't trust them even that basic amount?'' she asks. Her last comment is deceiving: ''I know it happens but I just don't understand it, that's the part I really don't understand.'' Though her confusion could be mistaken for naivete, a trait that would leave her vulnerable to victimization, her tactic of initiating such a conversation in the first place suggests otherwise.

Style

Monologue and Narration

A monologue is a speech given by one person in a performance or work of literature. The entire narrative of ''Rape Fantasies'' is a monologue by Estelle. By creating a story in which the point of view is first person and everything, including the descriptions, actions, and words of the other characters are filtered through the narrator's perception, Atwood creates a highly subjective story in which much of the interpretation is up to the reader. This is one reason why criticism on first-person stories, including ''Rape Fantasies,'' often focuses on whether or not the narrator is reliable. If the narrator is reliable, then his or her words can probably be taken at face value, and little other interpretation of events need take place. If, however, the narrator is not reliable, readers must exercise caution in interpreting the events of the story. Atwood provides few clues to suggest how reliable a narrator Estelle is. While she seems to give biting and accurate character descriptions—describing Chrissy as ''varnished,'' and even commenting negatively on herself as someone who cries at movies, ''even the ones that aren't all that sad''—there is no alternate point of view in the story to corroborate the things she says.

Many readers can identify with Estelle's predicament about moving to a big city, further adding to her credibility as a narrator: "I thought it was going to be such a big adventure and all, but it's a lot harder to meet people in a city." In addition, her speech patterns make her sound like many of the people readers encounter every day. Her speech is not studied or formal; her words sound like everyday conversation: "My mother always said you shouldn't dwell on unpleasant things and I generally agree with that, I mean, dwelling on them doesn't make them go away. Though not dwelling on them doesn't make them go away either, when you come to think of it." By creating a narrator whose speech cadences are familiar and colloquial, and having her give a monologue that is full of everyday experiences, Atwood implies that the topic of rape should not be taboo. Just like Estelle, Atwood infers that "it would be better if you could get a conversation going." Once men and women are able to discuss the politics of rape, it might become less common.

Comic Relief and Black Humor

Comic relief is the use of humor to lighten the mood of a story, and black humor is the juxtaposition of humorous elements and grotesque elements used to shock the reader. Both comic relief and black humor are evident in the story; Atwood is known for her biting, sarcastic humor, and "Rape Fantasies" is no exception. From the beginning of the story, Estelle jokes about a serious topic: "Rape, Ten Things to Do About It, like it was ten new hairdos or something." From the start, it is apparent that not only is the topic of the story rape, but also it is going to be treated irreverently. Black humor is comedy that coexists with horror. This is shown in Estelle's fantasies. When she is accosted on a dark street by a potential rapist, she rummages through her purse to find a plastic lemon so she can squirt the man in the eye, but her purse is so cluttered, she can't find her "weapon." She must ask the rapist to assist her, which he obligingly does. In another instance of black humor, Estelle fantasizes about a rapist who has leukemia, from which, coincidentally, she suffers too. On its own, the topic of serious illness is not funny, but in the context of Estelle's exaggerated fantasies, the elements of rape, illness, and pathos combine to form an absurd—and humorous—fantasy in which she and her attacker decide to live out their remaining days together.

But despite the sarcasm and black humor, the tone of the story turns somber at the end—and the seriousness of the conclusion becomes even more compelling than if the story had been told seriously from the start. With no trace of sarcasm or irony, Estelle addresses her listener purposefully: "I think it would be better if you could get a conversation going. Like, how could a fellow do that to a person he's just had a long conversation with." Her seriousness is in stark contrast with her normally irreverent sense of humor, and therefore becomes all the more poignant. Humor is a valuable device, she realizes (and so does Atwood), but it serves a serious purpose—to break down taboos and begin a dialogue that, Estelle hopes, will prevent violence against women in general and herself in particular.

Rhetorical Question

A rhetorical question is a question used for dramatic effect, one that is not meant to be answered directly or literally. At the end of the story, Estelle queries her listener: "How could a fellow do that to a person he's just had a long conversation with, once you let them know you're human, you have a life too, I don't see how they could go ahead with it, right?" Her comment is rhetorical, that is, she does not expect an answer. She has argued persuasively through her rape fantasies that if a man and woman come to understand one another, crime and pain will be averted due to their mutual sympathy. Her monologue is an attempt to practice this theory. She has revealed much about herself in the hope that she will not become a victim. However, what Estelle may not understand when she says "I just don't understand it, that's the part I really don't understand," is that rape is a crime of power, not lust. According to the way Estelle sees it, a person would not want to rape someone he has just had a long conversation with. But date rape and marital rape, which Estelle never mentions, are serious problems, and operate contrary to her logic. Thus, her attempt at cautious sociability may miss the mark, because attaining familiarity with someone does nothing to address the issues of power that often underlie violent or sexual crimes.

Historical Context

Feminism and the Single Woman

At the time "Rape Fantasies" was first published in 1977, the women's movement had been, for a solid decade, asserting equality for women in many facets of society. Many women entered the

Compare & Contrast

- **1978:** John Rideout, the first U. S. man to be charged with marital rape, is acquitted by an Oregon circuit court.

  1997: A 35-year-old female teacher in Seattle is convicted of second-degree child rape for having an affair with a 13-year-old former student and is sentenced to six months in jail after she gives birth to their daughter.

- **1977:** The U. S. Bureau of Justice Statistics reports that there are 2.33 rapes for every 1,000 people in the country.

  1997: The U. S. Bureau of Justice Statistics reports that incidents of rape have fallen drastically in the past twenty years, reaching an all-time low in 1996 at .90 rapes per 1,000 people.

- **1977:** *Looking for Mr. Goodbar* is a controversial and popular movie, in which a young teacher is murdered after picking up a man in a bar.

  1997: *Push* by Sapphire is a controversial novel, telling the story of a young woman who has been beaten, abused, and raped for most of her life.

work force during the decade, more and more were attending college and postponing marriage and child-bearing, and they began to enter traditionally male occupations, such as law and medicine, in greater numbers than before. As women gained more economic and social independence, some unforeseen effects began to emerge. Traditional rules of courtship began to wither. It was no longer a given that men would ask women out, and if they did, men and women both were unsure of what the expectations of such an arrangement were supposed to be. The so-called ''sexual revolution,'' spawned by available and reliable birth control and the legalization of abortion, led to supposedly higher levels of sexual activity among single people. Sometimes, the dictates of the ''me decade,'' namely, ''if it feels good, do it,'' had tragic consequences. Judith Rossner's 1975 novel *Looking for Mr. Goodbar* told the story of a young teacher who explores her freedom with abandon after a sheltered upbringing. Her social life revolves around singles bars, where she meets a variety of men. Her indiscriminate encounters eventually cost her her life.

During the 1970s, Helen Gurley Brown was the editor-in-chief of *Cosmopolitan* magazine, the type of magazine that, as Estelle says, not only prints articles about rape, but also acts like ''it's something terrific, like a vaccine for cancer. They put it in capital letters on the front cover.'' Brown got her start as the author of the 1962 best-seller, *Sex and the Single Girl,* which became one of the earliest literary works celebrating the independent, career-minded woman who knows how to take care of herself. In the 1970s, Brown corralled this image into the formation of *Cosmopolitan* magazine's ''Cosmo girl,'' a sort of female counterpart to the readers of *Playboy.* The Cosmo girl encompassed all the changes attributable to the youth culture; she was young, attractive, fashionable, independent, sexually active, and interested in politics, art, and current events. By the late 1970s, however, Brown was the target of backlash against the ''Cosmo girl,'' a stereotype that feminists claimed was nothing more than the fulfillment of male fantasies. Outspoken in her opinions on the changing roles of women in society, Brown countered feminists' attacks on the ''Cosmo girl'' by stating that ''a feminist should accept it if a woman doesn't want to realize her potential.'' In sharp contrast was *Ms.* magazine, founded by Gloria Steinem in 1972. The magazine, a handbook of the feminist movement, proved enormously popular upon publication of its first issue, and Steinem subsequently became a leading spokesperson for the women's movement. Part of Steinem's popularity stemmed from the fact that she advocated liberating men as well as women from gender stereotypes. According to her logic, only after both gender roles are sufficiently examined can society truly move forward toward equality.

By this time, though, others had found ways to capitalize on the progress of the women's movement as well. Advertisers formed ad campaigns that celebrated women's newfound independence and their increased power as consumers. Virginia Slims cigarettes proclaimed ''You've come a long way, baby,'' and suggested that women were asserting their equality by taking up smoking, a habit that was once the sole domain of men. A television commercial for perfume praised women's ability to compete in the workforce all day, earn their own money, and still find time to cook dinner and lavish attention on the men in their lives. Many women, like Estelle, agreed with many components of feminism, but were uncomfortable with others. In 1979, women's wages were an average of 57 percent of men's, a fact that angered even conservative women. Obtaining the right to equal pay and equal jobs became a crusade for many, even for those who could not abide the more radical elements of the women's movement, such as bra-burning and urging the armed services to make women eligible for combat duty.

Representing the milder forces of feminism on television was Mary Richards on the *Mary Tyler Moore Show.* Mary was single and independent, and worked as a television news producer. Most importantly, however, Mary did not tie her self-worth to marriage, men, or family. In the early 1970s, Mary Richards was somewhat an anomaly, but by the end of the decade she had much company on television. Strong women characters ran the gamut from *The Bionic Woman* to those high-fashion, female crime-fighters, *Charlie's Angels.* The women's movement had enough popular support to urge Congress to pass the Equal Rights Amendment in 1973, but support faltered by mid-decade, and the amendment failed the ratification process in the early 1980s.

Critical Overview

''Rape Fantasies'' is frequently anthologized and is commonly taught in high schools and colleges, but critics often tend to ignore this story and focus on Atwood's novels. The writers who have commented on the story, however, often note the humorous tone of the story, which seems to be at odds with the serious topic of rape. Lee Briscoe Thompson in her essay ''Minuets and Madness: Margaret Atwood's *Dancing Girls,*'' notes that in ''Rape Fantasies,'' ''the cutting edge seems thoroughly dulled by the sheer zaniness of the dialogue.'' Another Atwood critic, Sherrill Grace, in *Violent Duality: A Study of Margaret Atwood* commends the story for ''offering moving, indeed profound, insights into human nature and the problems of human relationships, without over-burdening the story form.''

The most controversial point of the story concerns the narrator, Estelle. Some commentators take her to be a naive woman, while others laud her tactical maneuvers in self-defense. Barbara Hill Rigney claims that Estelle is a ''naive narrator'' who believes rape can be avoided ''by simply reasoning with the rapist.'' Sherrill Grace and Lisa Tyler, however, assert that Estelle is just the opposite. In her essay, '''I Just Don't Understand It': Teaching Margaret Atwood's 'Rape Fantasies',''' Tyler discusses how students often find the story too ''provocative,'' others ''sail through the story blithely,'' and yet others are ''scandalized'' or ''indignant'' that rape is spoken about in such a cavalier fashion. Tyler notes that through the technique of a dramatic monologue, the reader must first sympathize with the speaker in order to understand the work; then and only then can the reader judge the speaker's character or even recognize the pathology of emotions presented. Thus, readers must sympathize with Estelle before judging her. Estelle does not withdraw from human connection; she struggles to establish connections in spite of her vulnerability and fear.

Critic Sally A. Jacobsen admits in an essay for *Approaches to Teaching Atwood* that ''Atwood acknowledges that rapport is no defense,'' especially considering that date rape or acquaintance rape—relationships in which conversational rapport has presumably been established—is more common than rape by a stranger. Jacobsen's students have also agreed ''the term rape fantasy is dangerous, for it fosters the mistaken perception that women want to be attacked and 'ask for it' in dress or behavior.'' Her students did ''credit Atwood with dramatizing the absurdity that women desire rape.''

Frank Davey, in *Margaret Atwood: A Feminist Poetics*, notices that Atwood portrays the rapists as inept men, and he argues that Estelle ''insists naively, on the essential humanity of even a rapist.'' Furthermore, Estelle's fantasies are closer to the ''nurse romance'' variety, Davey says, since she sends one rapist to a dermatologist and takes care of the other's cold. In this characterization, Atwood highlights how some women want to save men from themselves and even to improve or fix their destructive tendencies. Jacobsen best reveals the most common dilemma of reading ''Rape Fantasies,'' that is, the importance of understanding that ''Estelle is performing an intellectual exercise, or devising a heuristic, to demonstrate the impossibility of a female 'rape fantasy'—showing that rape is an act of power, not of sexual attraction, and that one can refuse 'victimhood'.''

Criticism

Catherine Walter

Walter is an instructor of English at Pennsylvania State University. In the following essay, she discusses the difficulties in determining the character of Estelle on the basis of her monologue.

With her usual caustic wit, Margaret Atwood uses humor to examine women's power and powerlessness and to exploit the distinction between fantasy and fear in her story ''Rape Fantasies.'' Atwood, through the voice of the narrator Estelle, shows readers how hard it is for women to laugh at themselves when they have been conditioned by the media to take themselves and their desires far too seriously and their safety not seriously enough. It is implied that only a rare woman like Estelle analyzes what her ''rape'' fantasies mean and how they have originated, suggesting that television and magazines help inspire a woman's fantasies of submissiveness to a strange male. Estelle especially condemns magazines that

> have these questionnaires like the ones they used to have about whether you were a good enough wife or an endomorph or an ectomorph, remember that? with the scoring upside down on page 73, and then these numbered do-it-yourself dealies, you know? Rape, Ten Things To Do about It, like it was ten new hairdos or something.''

This playfully sardonic line suggests that women must suffer many subtle indignities and condescending attitudes that are publicly sanctioned. The magazines prey on women's feelings of inadequacy but in a seemingly inoffensive, snappy format. Yet Estelle reveals how her intelligence is insulted by the magazine's fashionable coverage of such a devastating topic: ''You'd think it was just invented . . . I mean what's so new about it?'' she asks. She recognizes rape is an ancient violation and exposes the sensationalist way the magazine article presents the issue. Estelle appears to resent the idea that women are often not in control of their own bodies, whether it is in preventing a forcible entry, or preventing society's forced perception of how that body should look.

Because of her awareness, Estelle realizes how different she is from her coworkers: Chrissy, the varnished receptionist, and gullible Greta. Greta and Chrissy are excellent foils for Estelle and she sums them up this way—''They're both blondes, I don't mean that in a bitchy way but they do try to outdress each other.'' Estelle's comment highlights the superficial values the two women have. Their fantasies reveal their acceptance of the magazine's views of women. Chrissy can avidly quote the magazine to support her views: ''It says here all women have rape fantasies.'' Clearly, the magazine's generalization of ''all women'' is damaging since Chrissy accepts fantasy as fact. The magazine's pop-psychology can be dangerous when, for example, in Chrissy's fantasy she is attacked, but she does not defend herself, even by screaming. Chrissy mentions, ''But who'd hear me? Besides, all the articles say it's better not to resist, that way you don't get hurt.'' It is significant that Chrissy is helpless in her fantasy since the magazine condones her helpless passivity. ''I can't very well get out of the bathtub. The bathroom is too small and he's blocking the doorway, so I just lie there.'' Chrissy believes in the image of women as desirable only when they are defenseless.

Magazines are not the only medium to exploit women. When Chrissy discloses her fantasy about a man all dressed in black wearing black gloves, Estelle says, ''I knew right away the [TV] show she got the black gloves off, because I saw the same one.'' Both TV and magazines encourage the idea that unreality is better than reality. Estelle finds her coworkers' fantasies impossibly silly after listening to one fantasy story about a man who climbs eighteen floors with a hook and a rope. The media can become a double-barreled shotgun aimed at women, especially when the fantasies seem like innocent little dreams; ''and then he, well, you know,'' and the magazines and shows do not describe the violent, unwilling sex, but rather only inspire romantic fantasizing. Overall, though Estelle blames not only magazines and TV for their marketing-inspired nonsense, but also the women themselves who buy into the fantasy.

Estelle points out the harm of these fantasies with humor, but her coworkers do not laugh at her teasing jokes. Estelle describes their reactions: ''I swear all four of them looked at me like I was in bad

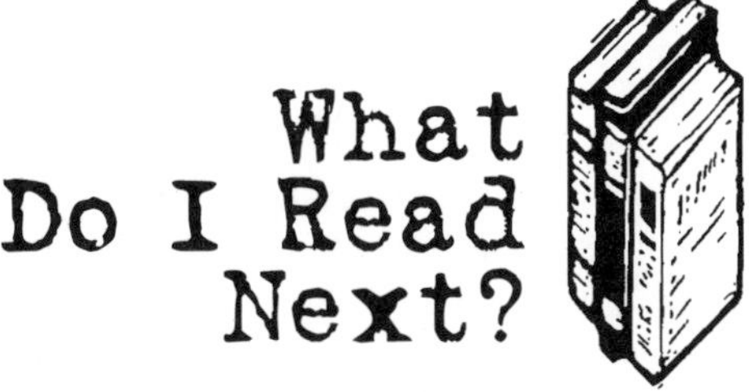

- *The Edible Woman* (1969), Atwood's first novel, concerns a young, recently engaged woman who finds herself paralyzed by the decisions she must make about her future.
- Judy Brady Syfer's classic essay, "I Want a Wife" (1971), often provokes strong reactions from both men and women in its definition of what the duties of a wife entail.
- Jamaica Kincaid's "Girl" (1978) and *Annie John* (1983) are works that explore how women socialize each other into subservience to men.
- May Swenson's poem "Bleeding" (1970) looks at power plays between victim and victimizer.
- Deborah Tannen's *You Just Don't Understand* (1996) explores the differences between how men and women communicate.
- Marge Piercy's poems "The Token Woman" (1976) and "Barbie Doll" are acidic comments on what it means to be female.
- Angela Carter's story "The Company of Wolves" (1979) reworks the fairy tale of Little Red Riding Hood and explores the relationship between romanticism and violence. It was also made into a movie.
- Robert Browning's famous poem "My Last Duchess" (1842) dramatizes one man's perceptions of women.

taste, like I'd insulted the Virgin Mary." Here, Atwood slyly reinforces that the public worships the image of women in a peaceful, but mostly passive, role. After all, part of the Virgin Mary's myth is that she also did not resist. Estelle recognizes that saintly women are somewhat safer than the average woman. This is illustrated in her fantasy in which she tells her rapist that she will "be giving birth to Saint Anne, who will be one day giving birth to the Virgin Mary." If a woman is to be narrowly seen only as a sex object or a saint, it is much safer to be saintly. Estelle tells her coworkers their "rapes" are too safe to be actual rapes.

Only Estelle defines the difference between a fantasy and an actual rape, telling her coworkers that their fantasies are not true rapes: "You aren't getting *raped,* it's just some guy you haven't met formally . . . and you have a good time. Rape is when they've got a knife or something and you don't want to." To Estelle rape is about anxiety, panic, confusion, loss of will, disgust, and fear. Estelle may feel she needs to remind her coworkers to believe this negative side of sexuality still exists in a civilized, modern time when sexual and gender roles are changing. Women have the right to say no, but do they have the power to be believed? Greta knows she will not, so she will not even try to say no.

In sharp contrast to passive Greta, Estelle likes power; she is not helpless in her fantasies. Her fantasies of being a Kung-Fu expert demonstrate her wish for control over her body and her safety. Estelle can outwit, confuse, and fool her fantasy rapists; in fact, she hopes *she* is not too vicious to them. By calmly listening to her rapists or starting a conversation with them, she attempts to assert herself. She can relate to and give advice to her rapists. They can even watch the late show together. Truly, Estelle's rapists are as unrealistically obliging and polite as her coworkers' rapists were romantically accommodating. These fantasy men are definite failures at raping Estelle, but they are more successful at having a relationship with a woman than the "successful" rapists. Ironically, the men even leave her feeling sorry for their unsuccessful attempts at rape. For example, Estelle mentions one rapist who gets his zipper stuck as he starts to undo himself and begins to cry, at "one of the most significant moments in a girl's life, it [rape]'s almost like getting married or having a baby or something." So Estelle dismantles the traditional view of rape and rapists. The rapists in her six fantasies get cancer and colds. Some even have suicidal wishes. They are vulnerable. Estelle might not want to admit it, but she humanizes her rapists, so that she does not have to live in terror. It is her way of imagining control and of having power over them.

Despite her earlier ridicule, Estelle reveals that she does consider the magazine's statistics: ''the funny thing about my fantasies is, that the man is always someone I don't know, and the statistics in magazines say it's often someone you know at least a little bit [like Estelle's boss, who, she is sure]. . . couldn't rape his way out of a paper bag, poor old thing.'' It becomes clear that the only way this narrator can discuss the fearsome topic is with defensive humor. She may not want to believe a rapist could be someone she knows.

Estelle also cannot completely successfully laugh off her fears of rape through her humorous fantasies. Her reputation as the ''office worry wart'' seems to contradict her jovial verbal portrayal of herself. Overall, this makes Estelle an entirely believable, well-rounded, all-too-human character. At first, although she appears merely an intelligent observer of human nature, Estelle morphs into a talkative and nosy person who investigates her coworkers' personnel files. Still, Estelle enjoys a good time and she is quite witty, so surely she cannot be a neurotic, hysterical woman afraid of being raped? Readers may hesitate to shift their opinions and view her in a negative light because in judging Estelle too harshly, we could be looking too closely at our own human foibles and learn that our fears can unbalance and unnerve us. In a sarcastic modern society, Estelle's coping mechanism of denying her fears by making fun of them, so as not to submit to advertising's brainwashing or live out her life in paralyzing fear, is clearly recognizable.

Despite her fears, a woman like Estelle wants her independence as well as her safety. Estelle says, ''You can't spend your whole life in the Filing Department or cooped up in your apartment with all the doors locked.'' Estelle hopes to be able to go for a drink in a nice place, even if she is by herself. But, when Estelle casually mentions, ''I'm with Women's Lib on that, even though I can't agree with a lot of other things they say,'' we begin to wonder to whom she is speaking. Estelle appears afraid of being thought too militant or even unfeminine by her listener. Furthermore, she nonchalantly says that the waiters in the bar know her. Through such nervous chatter, Estelle reveals her situation; she is talking to a stranger who could harm her—possibly to a man she fears could be a rapist.

Thus, the entire story is revealed as her one-way conversation. That we never hear from the man Estelle is talking to may show Atwood feels Estelle needs defensive measures and has a fear of opening up. Estelle may be ambivalent about her independence since she knows the high price of freedom is responsibility for her actions. Entering a bar and having a drink with a strange man might allow some to blame her and say she deserved the rape. There is also a lot of dialogue in her fantasies, which are often mere attempts to get a conversation going since ''once you let them know you're human, that you have a life too, I don't see how they could go ahead with it. I know it happens, but I just don't understand it.'' We realize that Estelle seems to have been manipulating the man into this conversation, so that she will feel safer with him, although she declares, ''I don't know why I'm telling you all this.'' Thus, even though Estelle says, ''I'm totally honest and I always am and they know it,'' at this point in the story, we may suspect that Estelle may not be as entirely honest as she would have us believe. She is not being entirely honest about herself and her fear of being raped. Atwood, however, has honestly portrayed the vulnerability that even strong independent thinkers can have as well as the fear that can occur between unacquainted men and women.

Estelle is the ultimate unreliable narrator. She laughs, but she is a seriously hypocritical clown. Critical of her female coworkers for not fearing rape, she then takes those fears too seriously herself. In Estelle, Atwood asks which is better—to be powerless or powerful, to be a victim or victimizer? For Estelle, it may be good to have some fear, but she may be at the risk of being consumed by it.

One other final aspect that makes this story so powerful is it is not written by man condemning women's fears and fantasies, but rather it is written by a woman who sees—and makes us see—the flaws of one imaginary woman's psyche and that makes this story more believable and frightening, that Atwood, a woman writer, exploits the fears of some women and exploits the way women are themselves exploited.

Source: Catherine Walter, ''The Unreliable Feminine Narrative Voice in 'Rape Fantasies,''' for *Short Stories for Students,* Gale, 1998.

Lisa Tyler

Tyler is an Associate Professor of English at Sinclair Community College in Dayton, Ohio. In the following essay, she warns that students must balance sympathy with judgment when interpreting the inflammatory content of Estelle's dialogue.

Margaret Atwood's "Rape Fantasies" is an unusually provocative short story. Atwood or her publisher perhaps judged the short story *too* provocative for American audiences, since it was omitted from the American hardback edition of the collection *Dancing Girls and Other Stories.* Whoever made that decision may have been right. While some students in my introductory literature classes sail through the story blithely and enjoy its offbeat humor, others are scandalized.

In the story, the first-person narrator, a woman named Estelle, recounts that she and her coworkers shared their rape fantasies over a bridge game in the women's lunch room. The other women's fantasies involve sex with a romantic stranger. In Estelle's, she asks the rapist to hold the contents of her purse while she hunts through her purse for a plastic lemon—which she promptly uses to squirt him in the eye. The lunch group breaks up, but Estelle nevertheless goes on to recount several other, equally ludicrous fantasies involving unusually cooperative would-be rapists.

Indignant female students scold Atwood and her narrator, Estelle, for treating rape too lightly, for not taking it seriously enough. Some readers classify Atwood's story with the magazine articles Estelle criticizes in the story's opening paragraph, those which glamorize rape. No woman who had experienced rape could discuss it in such a cavalier fashion, some of them angrily say in class discussions—and a handful speak from painful personal experience.

In her brief critical study of Atwood's works, feminist critic Barbara Hill Rigney echoes this judgment, referring in passing to "the naive narrator of 'Rape Fantasies,' who believes that rape always happens to someone else and is an event that might be avoided by simply reasoning with the rapist." Jerome Rosenberg makes a related observation, noting Estelle's "curiously benevolent voice." Edgar V. Roberts and Henry E. Jacobs describe Estelle as "bright but superficial" and add, "The actual violence and brutality of rape, in short, are unreal for her." Similarly, Lee Briscoe Thompson criticizes Estelle's "simplistic and determined optimism" and lambastes "the sunny normalcy of this lady's world view"; Thompson later comments that in this story, "it becomes apparent that the naive narrator's innocent premise is the power of the word."

But *is* Estelle naive? She scornfully dismisses her friends' romantic fantasies of sex with strangers as having nothing in common with real rape: "Rape is when they've got a knife or something and you don't want to." She elsewhere describes a short fantasy in which she physically disables a would-be rapist and goes on to remark: ". . . in real life I'm sure it would just be a conk on the head and that's that, like getting your tonsils out, you'd wake up and it would all be over except for the sore places, and you'd be lucky if your neck wasn't broken or something . . .". That hardly suggests naivete; Estelle is obviously cognizant of the violence and fear associated with rape. Far from being blithely naive, Estelle is clearly terrified by rape and consequently obsessed with it: ". . . it's getting so you can hardly be sociable any more, and how are you supposed to meet people if you can't trust them even that basic amount?" She feels guilty or at least self-conscious about her dating, as her sensitivity to her coworker Darlene's comment demonstrates:

> "I don't think you should go out alone at night," Darlene said, "you put yourself in a position," and I may have been mistaken but she was looking at me.

Estelle acknowledges that the "girls" at the office consider her a "worrywart," and she obliquely suggests that her mother does, too: "My mother always said you shouldn't dwell on unpleasant things and I generally agree with that, I mean, dwelling on them doesn't make them go away. Though not dwelling on them doesn't make them go away either, when you come to think of it." But Atwood elsewhere endorses what some readers might see as Estelle's irrational fear:

> . . . [I]n a society like ours where people are pretty much out there on their own hook, there's no real social support system for them, no small tribe or clan or integrated structure that's going to support an individual in it; so fear is a real motivating factor. And because you don't really know where the danger is coming from, fear takes the form often of a generalized anxiety or paranoia. You don't know who the enemy is. You don't know what direction you'll be attacked from. So everybody ends up constantly swivelling around, looking for the next threat. People are afraid of whatever's out there. And rightly so.

This is precisely Estelle's situation; she specifically comments on how difficult it was for her to negotiate the urban environment of Toronto: "I'm telling you, I was really lonely when I first came here; I thought it was going to be such a big adventure and all, but it's a lot harder to meet people in a city.'' Estelle tries to overcome her fears so that she can comfortably go out on dates, but she remains ''uneasy,'' to use a student's apt term.

In trying to encourage students to judge Estelle less harshly, I sometimes point to the story's final two paragraphs, where she says:

> I'm not what you would call a drinker but I like to go out now and then for a drink or two in a nice place, even if I am by myself, I'm with Women's Lib on that even though I can't agree with a lot of the other things they say. Like here for instance, the waiters all know me and if anyone, you know, bothers me. . . . I don't know why I'm telling you all this, except I think it helps you get to know a person, especially at first, hearing some of the things they think about.

Students rarely notice the clues in this passage on their own, but if I point them out, they are able to interpret them. ''Who is she talking to?'' I ask. When, I ask them, does a woman go to a restaurant or bar (a place with waiters) to spend time with a man whom she apparently does not know well? ''A first date,'' they will say, ''maybe even a blind date.'' Perhaps she is picking men up. We know the listener is probably male because Estelle twice wistfully alludes to sexual difference, acknowledging that ''maybe it's different for a guy.''

I then ask them why a woman would tell her date about a series of so-called ''rape'' fantasies in which the rape never occurs. She is warning him, they suggest. She sees him, too as a potential rapist—a contention shared by critics Frank Davey, Sally A. Jacobsen, and Dieter Meindl.

In a sense, ''Rape Fantasies'' is a prose variation on the dramatic monologue associated with the poetry of Robert Browning and Alfred, Lord Tennyson. Atwood, who studied nineteenth-century literature in graduate school, is certainly familiar with the genre; she specifically mentions studying Tennyson, whose dramatic monologues are almost as well known as Browning's. The dramatic monologue traditionally has several characteristics: It involves a speaker and often an at least vaguely identified auditor. More seriously, as Robert Langbaum points out,

> . . . [T]he meaning of the dramatic monologue is in disequilibrium with what the speaker reveals and understands. We understand the speaker's point of view not through [her] description of it but indirectly, through seeing what [she] sees while judging the limitations and distortions of what [she] sees. The result is that we understand, if not more, at least something other than the speaker understands, and the meaning is conveyed as much by what the speaker conceals and distorts as by what [she] reveals.

Langbaum, author of a key study on the dramatic monologue, contends that what distinguishes dramatic monologue is a tension between judgment and sympathy. Confronted with ''the pathology of emotions'' that the speaker demonstrates, the reader must first sympathize with the speaker in order to understand the work; then and only then can the reader judge the speaker's character or even recognize the pathology of the emotions presented. What I attempt to do in class is encourage students to sympathize with Estelle *before* they judge her.

Students unused to reading and analyzing literature sometimes rush to achieve closure and begin interpretation rather than ensuring first that they understand the characters' behavior and motivation as fully as possible. Teachers can aid the latter process by pointing out elements in the text that problematize students' initial readings (or misreadings). It is, I think, incumbent upon us as more experienced readers to slow students down, to point out what they have overlooked in the text in their haste to pronounce a verdict. After reading Tillie Olsen's ''I Stand Here Ironing,'' for example, younger students in particular seem ready to condemn the narrator as a poor mother for neglecting her child—until I point out the line that reads, ''It was the pre-relief, pre-WPA world of the depression.'' Students may not initially understand what the term ''pre-relief'' means or what the Depression meant in terms of unemployment, so we discuss the implications of that sentence in class. If students can slow down in their rush to judgment, if they first try to understand the character, they will gain a better appreciation for the plight of the young mother.

Similarly, if students can be persuaded to suspend their judgments about the apparently inflammatory content of Estelle's fantasies, they may discover that Estelle is a likable character with whom they can readily sympathize. She is frightened at the prospect of dating potentially dangerous strangers, but she is frightened, too, by the prospect of a solitary life. She chooses, caught in this dilemma, to take risks rather than protect herself through isolation. Barbara Hill Rigney contends that in Atwood's novels, ''Atwood argues . . . for a recognition of and a commitment to [the] human condition, no matter how malignant, and for an engagement with life, with reality, no matter how brutal or absurd.'' In this respect, Estelle is admirable. She possesses a sense of humor, and she struggles to cope as cheerfully as possible with her fear of rape. She does not withdraw from human connection; she struggles to *establish* such connections in spite of her vulnerability and fear.

Why, then, do so many readers see her as naive? Her comic fantasies brand her as naive because in those, again and again, she is able with relative ease to dissuade remarkably rational rapists from actually committing the intended rapes. These fantasies, of course, provoke another, more puzzling question: Why does Estelle have rape fantasies in which no rape ever takes place?

One student (who is taking a psychology course) perceptively suggests that fantasies gratify wishes that would otherwise be unfulfilled. Estelle, then, repeatedly fantasizes that she could verbally fend off a rapist—precisely *because* she knows that she cannot protect herself completely in real life. As one critic observes of two of Atwood's novels, ''To see the world and the self as funny, to refuse to take things seriously, is a means of protection against that which threatens and terrifies.'' Estelle knows that she cannot defend herself physically. She can't even manage to keep a plastic lemon in her purse: '' . . . I tried it once but the darn thing leaked all over my chequebook . . .''. She acknowledges her vulnerability when she mentions an improbable fantasy in which she defeats her attacker using kung fu:

> . . . I could never even hit the volleyball in gym, and a volleyball is fairly large, you know?—and I just go *zap* with my fingers into his eyes and that's it, he falls over, or I flip him against a wall or something. But I could never really stick my fingers into anyone's eyes, could you? . . . I feel a bit guilty about that one, I mean how would you like walking around knowing someone's been blinded for life because of you?

In each of her other fantasies, Estelle relies upon conversation to disarm her rapist. She establishes an empathetic connection with her rapist, and once that connection is established, the would-be assailant can no longer go through with the rape. Part of Estelle wants to believe that a man could not rape someone he knew, someone with whom he had talked. In this respect, Estelle may be behaving in a particularly ''feminine'' way—that is, in a way that our culture's construction of femininity fosters. Carol Gilligan, writing about different fantasies, nonetheless makes a point that seems particularly germane here: ''If aggression is tied, as women perceive, to the fracture of human connection, then the activities of care, as their fantasies suggest, are the activities that make the social world safe, by avoiding isolation and preventing aggression . . .''. Estelle gives the rapist her cold medicine, then, or the name of a good dermatologist, in order to forestall his aggression: ''In her imagination she turns constantly to conversation and sympathy as a civilized and sympathetic method of blunting the edge of potential violence.'' In effect, the story as a whole is another variation on the theme of Estelle's various rape fantasies: Estelle is attempting to establish that empathetic connection with the potential rapist she is dating in what she knows is a vain attempt to ensure her personal safety.

"Estelle is obviously cognizant of the violence and fear associated with rape. Far from being blithely naive, Estelle is clearly terrified by rape and consequently obsessed with it."

I identify with Estelle. What she doesn't understand about rape is what an occasional student will eventually admit that *she* (and the student who speaks up is usually a ''she'') doesn't understand:

> Like, how could a fellow do that to a person he's just had a long conversation with, once you let them know you're human, you have a life too, I don't see how they could go ahead with it, right? I mean, I know it happens but I just don't understand it, that's the part I really don't understand.

I don't understand it, either.

Source: Lisa Tyler, '''I Just Don't Understand It': Teaching Margaret Atwood's 'Rape Fantasies',' forthcoming in *Teaching English in the Two-Year College,* 1998.

Sally A. Jacobsen

Jacobsen is on the faculty of Northern Kentucky University. In the following essay, she discusses teaching ''Rape Fantasies'' as a means of opening discussion on the sensitive topic of rape, a topic which students of both sexes find both interesting and disturbing.

Margaret Atwood's poems and short story in Sandra Gilbert and Susan Gubar's *The Norton Anthology of*

Literature by Women (1985) lend themselves to themes of identity that may be discussed in a women's studies or a general studies literature course. My course, American Women Poets, is a women's studies course, but a majority of students of both sexes enroll because it carries general studies credit. Because Northern Kentucky University is largely a commuter college, the average age of students is twenty-six. Displaced homemakers and the occasional grandmother leaven the ideas of recent high school graduates, making class discussions a yeasty mix. Focusing on themes of identity fosters a lively involvement with literature, since students are already engaged in carving out their own identities—whether they were attracted to the course because they are interested in women's studies or want the general studies credit. While poems in *The Norton Anthology of Literature by Women* explore identities brought to the fore in the women's movement—like ''wife,'' ''mother,'' ''daughter,'' and ''feminist activist''—it is easy to give these identities more universal names—like ''spouse,'' ''parent,'' ''child,'' and ''political activist''—so that men in the class see the relevance of these categories to their quests for identity, too. At the same time, men who may not have intended to enroll in a women's studies course benefit from having their consciousness raised to feminist concerns. Male students say that they are gratified by an increased understanding of women that the course gives them.

Every week students select from the assigned reading the poem or story about which they wish to write. The written responses are based on their choice of one of seven identities they feel the work expresses: identity as a parent or child; a spouse, lover, or friend; a ''mover and shaker'' (political activist); a spiritual being; an artist or worker; a sufferer; or a loner. The ''identities'' approach leads to intense discussion of the nuances of the works when students read their responses, either to the class or to a small group responsible for leading the discussion of particular poems. Students keep their responses in a journal to review before examinations, and they submit a few of the weekly writings for evaluation. Students may later trace one of these identities through the work of several writers as an essay choice in examinations or as a term paper topic. Hence, I mention here other poems in *The Norton Anthology of Literature by Women* with which Atwood's may be compared, but these themes of identity would also be useful in taking up Atwood's works in connection with others' in an introduction to literature course. Articulation of these particular identities as topics to explore expands such literary elements as the quest motif, bildungsroman, and antihero—patterns in literature that, as traditionally taught, bear little relevance to the patterns of women students' lives. The identities offer enough variety to speak to the experience and concerns of many kinds of students. . . .

Atwood's story ''Rape Fantasies'' explores female sexual fantasy, a variant of the ''wives and lovers'' identity, and the perversion of that identity in rape. The story is valuable in opening discussion of these sensitive topics; both have intense interest for students, and rape is a particularly troubling subject for both sexes. (*The Norton Anthology of Literature by Women* is the most readily available source for ''Rape Fantasies'' in the United States, because the story was omitted from the United States edition of Atwood's collection *Dancing Girls.*) Students agree that the term *rape fantasy* is dangerous, for it fosters the mistaken perception that women want to be attacked and ''ask for it'' in dress or behavior. Students credit Atwood with dramatizing the absurdity of the idea that women desire rape.

In the story, four working-class women discuss a ''rape fantasies'' quiz in a woman's magazine. Estelle, a wisecracking nonconformist, objects to the quiz's use of the word *rape* to refer to fantasies of erotic encounters with strangers. That isn't rape, she says; ''It's just some guy you haven't met formally. . . . Rape is when they've got a knife or something and you don't want to.'' Students wax eloquent on behalf of Atwood's point about erotic fantasy: ''Atwood shows us the intriguing quality of fantasy and how we are in total control.Many women have been raised to view their sexuality as wrong'' and ''feel comfortable if they can imagine being satisfied without being responsible for it.'' One writer quotes an ''anonymous'' source: ''I can't want sex and still be a good person. It should be his idea—he could even force it on me, gently of course and mostly for my pleasure. After all, it's my fantasy.''

As the story progresses, Estelle humorously tries to fantasize genuine ''rape,'' in which a sense of the threat of rape exists. In each episode, she maneuvers herself out of the victim position by taking power back from the rapist. She identifies in each assailant an element of common humanity—the first displaying gallantry, the second suffering from a winter cold, and the third experiencing mad delusions—and forms a conversational bond with them that allows her to trick them and escape. Many students do not understand that Estelle is performing an intellectual exercise, or devising a heuristic, to demonstrate the impossibility of a female "rape fantasy"—showing that rape is an act of power, not of sexual attraction, and that one can refuse "victimhood." Several students think that because Estelle "wants to have conversations with these 'perverts,'" she must be an exceptionally lonely person ("Even in her fantasies she doesn't meet Mr. Right")—or, in the case of the rapist with a cold, that she is impelled to "mother" in a love relationship. (The idea of the victim "mothering" a rapist is really very funny, most students recognize.) I help students past misunderstandings of the story by outlining the four basic victim positions defined by Atwood in *Survival.* Because Estelle takes action to minimize her victimization, she starts each fantasy in Atwood's "Position Three," "To acknowledge . . . that you are a victim" but to decide how much of the victimization "could be changed if you made the effort"—a "dynamic position" in which anger is applied to effect change. Part of the humor of the story is Estelle's easy success in prevailing over the rapists, her movement to "Position Four": "To be a creative non-victim," in which position the "role of Victim . . . is no longer a temptation." In real life one cannot move to "Position Four" so easily, but there is satisfaction in refusing as much of the victim role as possible.

As in discussions of any aspect of female sexuality portrayed in the works studied, the men in the class sit in gratified silence, drinking in details for their sex education, while women students draw distinctions between "erotic" fantasy and "rape." Male students will join the discussion of rape if they are asked the question with which one student concluded his response to the story: "What about a man fantasizing about rape?" The instructor can remind students of the locker-room bragging in J. D. Salinger's *Catcher in the Rye* and ask if they have witnessed similar boasting about planned rape exploits. Several of Atwood's points about the dangers of indiscriminate use of the term *rape* were driven home in my class when one man answered, "Yes. There is a type of man who, if he is rejected sexually by a woman, will grumble to his friends about what he plans to do to her, the next time he gets her alone—but I assume that's 'just talk.'" The two sexes stared bleakly across the classroom at each other, in a shock of recognition. Even so, students may not see the irony in the ending of "Rape Fantasies" unless their attention is drawn to it. Estelle concludes, "Like, how could a fellow do that to a person he's just had a long conversation with, . . . I don't see how they could go ahead with it, right? I mean, I know it happens but I just don't understand it." This is exactly the situation in "date rape," the most insidious form of sexual assault threatening students. Estelle has built her entire fantasy defense on the establishment of conversational rapport with rapists. Atwood here acknowledges that such rapport is no defense. A further irony lies in Estelle's revelation, at the end of the story, that she has "fantasized" these heuristic rape incidents in a bar, perhaps telling them to a new acquaintance, a potential rapist.

> "Students agree that the term 'rape fantasy' is dangerous, for it fosters the mistaken perception that women want to be attacked and 'ask for it' in dress or behavior. Students credit Atwood with dramatizing the absurdity of the idea that women desire rape."

My undergraduate students' responses reveal the value they find in Margaret Atwood's works, in that the works speak to what really matters to them, and the students' writings demonstrate Atwood's ability to involve readers in literature, a new experience for some of my students. *The Norton Anthology of Literature by Women* (now in its second edition) is the best collection I know for including Atwood in a survey course in the United States. . . .

Source: Sally A. Jacobsen, "Themes of Identity in Atwood's Poems and 'Rape Fantasies': Using *The Norton Anthology of Literature by Women,*" in *Approaches to Teaching Atwood's* The Handmaid's Tale *and Other Works,* edited by Sharon R. Wilson, Thomas B. Friedman, and Shannon Hengen, The Modern Language Association of America, 1996, pp. 70–6.

Lee Briscoe Thompson

In the following brief excerpt, Thompson talks about "Rape Fantasies," specifically the inability of language to allow effective communication between men and women.

. . . The story which best fits the critical stereotype of Atwood's ''bubbleheaded/ladies' magazine fiction'' (vs. her ''serious poetry'') is probably ''Rape Fantasies.'' Agreed, its lower-middle-class diction, full of babbling asides and slang, is far removed from the fine intuitions of the *Power Politics* voices. And the subject matter, the dynamics of a female office/lunch room and the ''girls''' revelations of their extremely unimaginative rape fantasies, hardly seems in the same league as the mythic patterns of *You Are Happy* or the multiple metaphors of *The Journals of Susanna Moodie*. Nevertheless, when the intellectual snobberies are put aside (and appropriately so, since that is one of Atwood's satiric targets here), the narrator does demonstrate an admirable sense of humour, appreciation of the ridiculous, and considerable compassion. For once in Atwood the cutting edge seems thoroughly dulled by the sheer zaniness of the monologue.

One imaginary rapist is ''absolutely covered in pimples. So he gets me pinned against the wall, he's short but he's heavy, and he starts to undo himself and the zipper gets stuck. I mean, one of the most significant moments in a girl's life, it's almost like getting married or having a baby or something, and he sticks the zipper.'' She ends up drawing him out and referring him to a dermatologist. In another incarnation, she and the rapist are both slowed down by ferocious headcolds, which make the would-be assault ''like raping a bottle of LePage's mucilage the way my nose is running.'' The cheerful remedy here is conversation, Neo-Citran and Scotch, plus the Late Show on the tube. ''I mean, they aren't all sex maniacs, the rest of the time they must lead a normal life. I figure they enjoy watching the Late Show just like anybody else.'' As the reader is introduced to these and other alternatives, it becomes apparent that the naive narrator's innocent premise is the power of the word. ''Like, how could a fellow do that to a person he's just had a long conversation with, once you let them know you're human, you have a life too, I don't see how they could go ahead with it, right?'' That we see so easily the flaws in this simplistic and determined optimism serves to underscore a subtle counterpoint Atwood strikes throughout her writing—the actually severe limitations of language, and the doubtfulness of real communication. The sunny normalcy of this lady's world view glosses over a chaotic realm even she must tentatively acknowledge:'' I mean, I know [rape] happens but I just don't understand it, that's the part I really don't understand.''

What is also noteworthy is that this story explicitly draws men into the circle of victimhood that Atwood tends to populate with women. Rapists, yes, but failed rapists; they are betrayed by their jammed flies, their sinuses, their gullibility, their pimples, their inadequacies. And one sees that the filing clerk's rape fantasies are actually scenarios of kinship, friendship with and support of other mediocre, in fact worse-off, human beings.

Source: Lee Briscoe Thompson, ''Minuets and Madness: Margaret Atwood's *Dancing Girls,*'' in *The Art of Margaret Atwood: Essays in Criticism,* edited by Arnold E. Davidson and Cathy N. Davidson, Anansi, 1981, pp. 107–22.

Sources

Davey, Frank. *Margaret Atwood: A Feminist Poetics,* Talonbooks, 1984.

Grace, Sherrill. *Violent Duality: A Study of Margaret Atwood,* Vehicule Press, 1980.

Greenspan, Karen. *The Timetables of Women's History,* Simon & Schuster, 1994.

Ingersoll, Earl G., editor. *Margaret Atwood: Conversations,* Ontario Review Press, 1990.

Olsen, Kirstin. *Chronology of Women's History,* Greenwood Press, 1994.

Further Reading

''Margaret Atwood,'' in *Short Story Criticism,* Vol. 2, edited by Sheila Fitzgerald, Gale, 1989, pp. 1–23.
Contains reprinted criticism focusing on Atwood's stories.

''Margaret Atwood,'' in *Contemporary Literary Criticism,* Vol. 84, edited by Christopher Giroux, Gale, 1995, pp.1–59 .
Contains reprinted criticism covering all of Atwood's work, including stories, novels, and poetry.

''Margaret Atwood,'' in *DISCovering Authors Modules,* CD—Rom, Gale, 1995.
Contains biographical information and critical excerpts on Atwood's work.

Robert Kennedy Saved from Drowning

Donald Barthelme

1968

Donald Barthelme was one of a number of experimentalists writing in the 1960s, and he was heavily influenced by earlier experimental writers, from the eighteenth-century novelist Laurence Sterne to James Joyce and Jorge Luis Borges in the twentieth century. Barthelme and such writers as John Barth, Joseph Heller, Ken Kesey, Vladimir Nabokov, Thomas Pynchon, Ishmael Reed, Kurt Vonnegut, and Tom Wolfe played with fictional forms, language, representation, and established literary norms. Their work was given a variety of labels—black humor, metafiction, surfiction, superfiction, irrealism—that attempted to describe the ways that the authors used language. "Robert Kennedy Saved from Drowning," a story in Barthelme's 1968 collection of short fictions *Unspeakable Practices, Unnatural Acts,* consists of twenty-four scenes, or vignettes, that concern Robert Kennedy, a then-powerful political figure. These vignettes are less "story-like" than they are like the work of Karsh of Ottawa, a famous portrait photographer, who explains in the story's ninth scene that in each portrait sitting there is only one shot that is "the right one." What Barthelme appears to offer, therefore, are a series of disconnected portraits. Indeed, throughout his career, Barthelme was deeply concerned with the fragmentary nature of everyday living, and the extent to which it consisted of so much "dreck" (garbage). Early reviews of his work were mixed. Critics who were searching for grand themes and who were used to more linear, plot-

centered works had a difficult time understanding the seemingly fragmentary and often mundane representations that characterized so much of Barthelme's work. Later critics have found his work to be highly representative of ordinary living in the late twentieth century, so much so that he has even been called a realist, despite the oddities and strange constructions he presents throughout his work.

Author Biography

Donald Barthelme was born in Philadelphia in 1931. His family moved to Houston two years later. Barthelme served in the U.S. Army in Japan and Korea before working as a newspaper reporter for the *Houston Post.* In 1962, at the age of thirty, he moved to New York City, where he edited *Location,* an avant garde literary magazine. The following year, his first published story appeared in the *New Yorker.* In addition to regular contributions to the *New Yorker,* he published subsequent fiction in *Atlantic, Harper's,* and other noted magazines and journals. His first collection of short stories, *Come Back, Dr. Caligari,* was published in 1964. He followed this with the short novel, *Snow White,* in 1967.

In addition to *Snow White,* Barthelme wrote three other novels: *The Dead Father, Paradise,* and *The King.* But the short story was Barthelme's specialty. These stories were collected in eleven volumes, including: *Unspeakable Practices, Unnatural Acts* (in which ''Robert Kennedy Saved from Drowning'' appeared); *City Life; Sadness; Guilty Pleasures;* and *Forty Stories.* Barthelme won a National Book Award and was awarded a Guggenheim Fellowship. He taught at the State University of New York at Buffalo, and at City College of New York. Barthelme died of cancer in Houston on July 23, 1989, at the age of 58.

Barthelme's interest in film, architecture, philosophy, and the arts led him to apply principles from these disciplines in his fiction. Collage—the artistic principle of combining unrelated items to create a new, unsuspected harmony—is one such technique found in the story ''Robert Kennedy Saved from Drowning.''

Plot Summary

The story consists of twenty-four vignettes, or short scenes. What the reader learns about Kennedy is filtered through what the narrator and Kennedy's acquaintances say about the man, as well as what Kennedy says about himself and about his views on the world. The story opens with a description, given by the narrator, of Kennedy at work. The description sets the tone for the rest of the story: these scenes will be brief and will often present contradictory ideas. K., as Kennedy is referred to throughout, is neither abrupt nor kind, or he is abrupt and kind, says the narrator. He uses the telephone both to dominate and to comfort those at the other end.

There is no plot in the traditional sense of the concept. The vignettes are not arranged by a sequence of events that build to a climax and resolve themselves in the falling action. Instead, the vignettes are arranged much as collages are. Therefore, some of their import depends upon what scenes are next to each other. For example, in one scene readers find one of Kennedy's friends speaking about Kennedy's solitary nature and how difficult he is to get to know. The next scene offers Kennedy's own commentary on his relationships with crowds of people. Often, like the narrator's comments in the opening scene, these juxtapositions offer contradictory views of the man.

Many scenes are concerned with the ordinary things that Kennedy does. At a party, he goes behind the bar to make himself a drink only to be asked by the bartender to leave. He receives twelve newspapers a day. He travels through unnamed towns in France and Germany. Later, he wanders unnamed in towns in what is presumably the United States and sees the young people of the country. He reacts emotionally to music on the radio, or to stories he has read in the newspapers. He comments on art. He fails to understand his children. He dreams. He struggles in the water, nearly drowning, though without any emotional reaction whatsoever.

Five of the twenty-four scenes offer direct quotes from Kennedy's friends and employees. His secretaries and administrative assistants, for example, recount stories of his actions. One secretary tells how he personally delivered tulips to her when she was in the hospital; the assistant tells how he resolved a mounting (but unidentified) crisis with a single phone call. His former teacher identifies compassion as perhaps Kennedy's most distinguishing quality.

The remaining scenes introduce Kennedy's own comments on the world and his role in it. Like the narrator's descriptions, these comments are often contradictory, or give multiple facets of the man. He speaks about how he responds to and manages crowds of people. In another, he speculates that he has no effect on the world at all. In all cases, however, Kennedy identifies with what he calls the ''Marivaudian being,'' a person who is always in the immediate present.

In the final scene, the narrator finds Kennedy in the water, drowning. The narrator throws a rope to him and pulls him to safety.

Donald Barthelme

Characters

K

See Robert Kennedy

Robert Kennedy

Robert Kennedy, known in the story by the first letter of his last name, ''K,'' is the subject of the story. The character is drawn from the public figure of Senator Robert Kennedy, brother of President John Kennedy, and is presented in a variety of contexts that might be expected to give a well-rounded portrait of the man. Kennedy dreams, works at his desk, resolves crises, reads to his children, and talks about art in this story. He also gives extended monologues on a French writer, on his role in the world, on how to monitor situations, and on the crowds of young people that are his constituency. Although the story consists of numerous sketches of the man, a fully fleshed portrait never emerges.

Narrator

The unnamed narrator of the story controls what is seen and heard about Kennedy. This narrator recounts the events in half of the scenes with an apparently objective presentation of facts. The selection of facts, however, is often bizarre. In the other scenes, the narrator does not speak, but presents the voices of Kennedy's friends and colleagues or of Kennedy himself. Twice in the story, the narrator comes forward in the first person. The first time, he or she indicates what a ''notoriously poor observer'' he or she is, thereby undermining much of what is presented, especially considering the oddities upon which he or she has focused. The second time the narrator appears in first person is in the final scene when he or she throws a drowning Kennedy a rope. The distance between the narrator and Kennedy begins to collapse when the narrator offers direct descriptions of Kennedy's dreams and thoughts, especially when Kennedy's thoughts repeat what the narrator has just reported.

Others

Barthelme devotes five scenes to characters who are known only by their voices (in most cases, the titles indicate who is speaking). Secretaries, an aide, an administrative assistant, a friend, and a former teacher tell brief anecdotes about Kennedy, anecdotes that highlight something special about him. Often, they stress Kennedy's emotional effect on the people around him. The teacher recalls Kennedy's compassion as his defining and unusual characteristic. One secretary lauds Kennedy's ability to remember his employees and their personal problems, exemplified by his bringing her tulips when she was in the hospital. The administrative assistant tells how Kennedy resolved both a mounting crisis and the general nervousness of his staff with a single phone call. Kennedy's friend explains how difficult it is to know Kennedy, because he does such unexpected things. Ironically, the friend reports, Kennedy has an unshakable faith that things will do what they are expected to do.

Themes

Public vs. Private Life

Robert Kennedy was a very public figure. He came from an important political family, was the brother of President John F. Kennedy, and was himself a candidate for president when Barthelme wrote the "Robert Kennedy Saved from Drowning." One of the questions that emerges from the story is: How much do people know about this man?

The question itself is difficult, for it doesn't specify what kinds of knowledge people are interested in. For those who are interested in the political campaign and whether or not they should vote for Kennedy for President, the knowledge they seek is partially public. They want to know what domestic and foreign policies the man advocates, where he stands on the Vietnam War, or on the civil rights movement, the death penalty—any number of issues. These issues are decidedly absent from the story and reduced to a single mention of "matters" in the scene titled "Matters (from an Administrative Assistant)." In fact, Kennedy's public presence is barely mentioned by the narrator. In "With Young People," Kennedy walks the street, in public, in his public persona. After the opening sentence of the scene, however, Kennedy is no longer mentioned. Nor is his effect on the young people, who are his constituency, mentioned. The narrator notes where the young people gather, what they have with them, and the fact that they are staring, but there is no mention of how or if they react to Kennedy specifically. On policy matters, the story offers even less information. In the scene titled "As Entrepreneur," the narrator reports cost overruns of the North Sea pipeline. Kennedy's response, "Exceptionally difficult rock conditions," serves merely as a description, one that anyone might reasonably make. In "K. on His Own Role," a scene where one might expect something of a policy statement, the subject talks about the need for "careful, reasoned and intelligent action" on the problems in the world. Yet, there is no identification forthcoming from him on the nature of the problems other than the cryptic "In Latin America, for example." Kennedy has merely identified a location of a problem, not the problem itself.

At the other extreme lies the private life. Again, what counts as private is difficult to assess, but there are a couple of moments where the narrator presents such information. Most notably, there is the dream sequence in four images. It is difficult to know someone by his or her dreams alone. Better would be to know his thoughts. But the narrator refuses to enter Kennedy's mind in the story. The closest we come to thoughts is what Kennedy himself has to say. Like his utterances about public policy, his utterances about his private life are often vacuous.

Perhaps the middle ground between the public and private lives is the ground most aptly mined by the narrator. This area includes the realm of the interpersonal relationships and what his friends and acquaintances know about the man. It is also a ground that is full of contradictions. Secretaries report that he both forgets and remembers things. He asks questions like "Which of you has the shirts?" He orders food in restaurants. He is compassionate, says an old teacher. He believes that anchors are anchors, and that they will serve as anchors. His children cry. This area between the public and the private Kennedy is an area that is so ordinary as to be unremarkable.

In the end, the distinction between public and private collapses into this middle ground. Robert Kennedy is neither the mythological superhero that some segment of the public believes he is, nor is he a private person. He is, like everyone else, a human who goes about an ordinary life. How much do people know about the man? Answer: as much as they know about themselves.

The Marivaudian Being

One section in the story finds K. discussing the concept of the Marivaudian Being, a hypothetical character who has no past or future, living only in the present moment. This hypothetical character was invented by the French writer Poulet, based on his reading of the plays of the French playwright Marivaux. The Marivaudian Being, because he has no past experience from which to draw upon, is constantly surprised by events, "overtaken" as K. describes it. This gives the Marivaudian Being a certain fresh quality which Poulet admires. But it also makes the Marivaudian Being inconsistent and sometimes overwhelmed. Barthelme's character K. is presented as a kind of Marivaudian Being who lives his life in brief, unconnected scenes and whose personal characteristics are unstable and contradictory.

Style

Point of View and Narration

The vignettes are presented by a dispassionate first or third-person narrator who only uses the pronoun "I" twice. The difficulty in describing the point of view is compounded by two features. First, there are times when the narrator has access to Kennedy's dreams and thoughts, access that only Kennedy or a third-person omniscient narrator would have. Moreover, the narrator's observations are usually neutral; they don't offer much commentary on the events and characters. Instead, these observations are most often declarative statements or descriptive phrases. In what should be the most dramatic scene of the story, how the narrator saves Kennedy from drowning, the sensory and emotional contents are muted in favor of a distanced, intellectual engagement with the scene. This muting is especially remarkable given that the scene is one of two where the narrator appears explicitly in the first person. Readers might normally expect a more direct involvement with the action, but the narrator refuses to offer personal reactions to the near-drowning. The narratorial access to information is also undermined in the other scene where the narrator appears in the first person. There, after describing Kennedy's wife's clothing, the narrator says "but then I am a notoriously poor observer." This comment calls into question the narrator's reliability as an observer. If he or she cannot adequately describe an outfit, how can he or she possibly represent Kennedy's dreams or thoughts about the world?

The second difficulty in describing the point-of-view lies in the fact that twelve of the twenty-four vignettes present the voices of Kennedy or his acquaintances without any narratorial presence other than the scenes' titles. Although they are marked with quotation marks, which suggest that someone (the narrator) selected and arranged these quotes, fully half of the story is "told" by persons other than the narrator. Readers might legitimately wonder, therefore, how much control the narrator has in developing and describing the events, settings, characters, and themes of the story.

Setting

Many of the vignettes have no setting at all. They are merely the reporting of what people, including Kennedy, have to say about themselves and the world. When there are settings, they are usually so generic that they are stripped of any potential local import. It doesn't matter, for example, whether these scenes take place in Massachusetts or Iowa or Oregon. In the short section subtitled "With Young People," Barthelme deliberately

Topics for Further Study

- Select a current political figure and collect newspaper and magazine articles about him or her from several sources. After reading the articles, do you feel as though you know the *person* any better than you did before? Select one paragraph from each article and cut it out. Arrange your paragraphs in different orders. How does that affect what you know about the person?
- Investigate the social and political issues of the 1960s and what Robert Kennedy's policies were on these issues. Is it necessary to know them to understand Barthelme's story? Why would Barthelme fail to mention the Cuban Missile Crisis, the Vietnam War, poverty, racism, or any of the other important issues of the day?
- Read Barthelme's essay "Not Knowing." What relationship between language and the world does Barthelme argue? Write down what you and your friends say to each other. What things do you do with language besides represent the world? Does language ever get in the way of what you are trying to do?
- Investigate art movements that flourished in the 1950s and 1960s: Abstract Expressionism, minimalism, constructivism, and pop art. Does Barthelme's story share any of the qualities of these movements and their art works?

withholds the names of the town or towns, as though they are unimportant to the story. Similarly, the names of the places in ''France or Germany'' remain unspecified. The generic nature of the settings is also indicated by such subtitles as ''K. at His Desk'' and ''Behind the Bar.'' It matters little where the desks, or bars, or towns are. What matters is Kennedy's relationships to these things, what he does with them or when he is near them.

The lack of importance of the specific settings of the story is mirrored by a similar lack in specific actions. In a scene titled ''Matters (from an Administrative Assistant),'' for example, the assistant reports a series of increasingly more impending problems, yet they are referred to simply as ''matters.''

Structure

One of the most important devices that Barthelme plays with is the structure of the story. Traditional stories tend to follow a sequence of actions through time, through a rising action to a climax. They might involve flashbacks that disrupt or clarify the linear nature of the story, but the basic linearity remains intact. Barthelme rejects this structure in ''Robert Kennedy Saved from Drowning'' by presenting a sequence of scenes that are related to each other neither by a continuity of actions nor by time. This means that there is little opportunity for other literary devices, such as foreshadowing, subplots, or suspense. The structural technique he uses is pastiche, or collage. This technique asks the reader to bring a different set of interpretive strategies to the story. Scenes become important for how they might be associated or related to other scenes. These associations might be symbolic, or they might be topical. In the final scene, the narrator saves Robert Kennedy from drowning. The story's title points to this action.

Postmodernism

Postmodernism describes a period of literary creativity extending roughly from the end of the Second World War to the present day. During this time, many writers have explored types of fiction which dispensed with such traditional elements as plot, character, and narrative structure. These experimental writings focused particularly on how language works to create fictional meaning. The writings were often playful, employing conventional story elements in odd ways and using characters from popular culture, history or the great works of literature. Barthelme, for example, uses the character of Robert Kennedy, an actual politician running for office at the time his story was written, as a fictional character in ''Robert Kennedy Saved from Drowning.'' By using an actual person well known to the public as a fictional character, Barthelme draws attention to how fictional such celebrities actually are and raises questions about the reality of the people and events one finds in the media.

Historical Context

The 1960s: Social and Cultural Upheaval

The 1960s saw more social and cultural upheaval in the United States than any other decade this century, with the possible exception of the 1930s. A major war, race riots, street demonstrations, student protests, greatly expanded federal social programs, the popularization of drug use among the young, and several political assassinations mark the period. A host of people and organizations in the political and popular arenas, including John F. Kennedy, Lyndon Johnson, Barry Goldwater, Richard Nixon, Martin Luther King, Jr., Malcom X, Betty Friedan, the Black Panthers, the Beatles, the Rolling Stones, and Bob Dylan, deeply influenced the nation and served as catalysts for change.

The United States was embroiled in the Vietnam War and saw more and more of its young men drafted to fight in a seemingly endless war in which no clear goals or strategies were defined. Resistance at home to the military draft and a growing division in public sentiment over the conduct of the war led to increasing political tensions, protests and division. At the 1968 Democratic National Convention, television viewers watched as thousands of young protesters confronted Chicago police in bloody street battles. The event saw the birth of the Weather Underground, a factional spinoff of Students for a Democratic Society, which began a campaign of bombings, including attacks on the Pentagon and Congress, on behalf of a revolutionary agenda. On May 4, 1970, the National Guard opened fire on a group of Vietnam war protestors at Kent State University, killing four and wounding nine. With the rise of political violence and the widespread popularity of drugs among the countercultural youth,

Compare & Contrast

- **1968:** Robert Kennedy is assassinated on June 5 after giving a campaign speech in California. Sirhan Sirhan is convicted of the crime and sentenced to life in prison.

  1995: Israeli president Itzak Rabin is assassinated in November after giving a speech at a peace rally.

- **1968:** Many American young people become active in protest causes. College students, in particular, stage many campus protests of the Vietnam War. The voting age is lowered to eighteen in 1971, in response to those who criticize the fact that teenagers are old enough to be drafted into war, but not old enough to vote.

  1990s: In 1994, only 12 percent of 18 and 19-year olds voted. In the presidential election of 1996, only about 49 percent of the country's eligible voters cast ballots, and only 17 percent of those voters were under 30 years old.

- **1960s:** As Attorney General under his brother, President John F. Kennedy, Robert Kennedy is actively involved in decisions that result in the Cuban Missile Crisis, an event that leads the world to the brink of nuclear war in October, 1962.

  1990s: As Attorney General under President Clinton, Janet Reno is widely criticized for her decision to use force to end the siege of the Branch Davidian religious compound in Waco, Texas. The resulting fire on April 19, 1993, claims the lives of more than eighty people.

the so-called "Silent Majority" saw a breakdown of the very values they believed had made America great, values that had seen the country through two world wars and the Great Depression.

The decade seemed fraught with division. By the late 1960s, race riot shook many of America's major cities. President Lyndon Johnson launched the Great Society series of social programs to expand the federal government's role into public housing, school integration, medical care, and welfare. Launched at the same time the government was waging the Vietnam War, the increased spending led to a radical rise in the inflation rate. Women's liberation, the woman's movement for equality in all facets of political, social, and personal life, divided the country along gender lines. Various student movements, with rallying cries not to trust anyone over thirty, divided the young from the old. The passage of the twenty-sixth amendment gave the youth of the nation the right to vote, but not until 1971.

Against this background, Barthelme chooses one of the more celebrated political figures of the time, Senator Robert Kennedy, a man who was brother of the president of the United States, who served as his brother's Attorney General, and who was in the heat of a presidential bid of his own at the time Barthelme wrote the story. (Shortly thereafter, Kennedy was assassinated.) Barthelme patently refuses to mention anything about the political or social climate of the time, except for the cryptic mention of "matters" by his administrative assistant and an oblique reference to the youth movement that contributed to Kennedy's rising popularity. The youth are strangely silent, a far cry from the rallies and protests that characterized the late 1960s.

Critical Overview

Although responses to Barthelme's fictions have been usually positive, John W. Aldridge wrote a particularly severe critique of authors of black humor in general and Barthelme in particular. Titled

''Dance of Death,'' Aldridge's article reviews the 1968 short story collection in which ''Robert Kennedy Saved from Drowning'' appeared, *Unspeakable Practices, Unnatural Acts,* as well as the earlier *Come Back, Dr. Caligari,* and states: ''The stories are quite literally verbal immersions in dreck, the evacuated crud and muck of contemporary life, and they very effectively dramatize the sensations of being suffocated and shat upon and generally soiled and despoiled in soul and mind which accompany our daily experience of contemporary life.''

Aldridge represents an extreme reaction against Barthelme and his fellow experimenters, and picks upon what one of Barthelme's dwarves' says in *Snow White,* which was published a year earlier: ''We like books that have a lot of *dreck* in them.'' Clearly, Aldridge does not appreciate dreck as much as his fellow critics do. These early critics praised Barthelme's playfulness with literary forms and his so-called metafictional impulses. (Barthelme himself denied that he wrote metafiction, or fictions about the status of fiction as fiction.) Later critics recognized that Barthelme was up to something more serious than mere play. Both William Gass and Raymond Carver (themselves fiction writers) have remarked upon Barthelme's innovations with the short story form, but find that the formal experiments are part of a larger investigation into the conditions of how we know the world. One of these conditions is language itself, says Barbara Roe. She reminds us that ''Characters, setting, action, and viewpoint are, after all, creations of language. If language 'alters when inspected closely,' so do its ostensible referents.''

Although these later critics might agree that Barthelme was up to something more than mere play, they do not always agree upon precisely what it was. Charles Molesworth challenges the idea that Barthelme's short story structures are merely rejections of earlier structures, and offers two alternatives: that they reflect the fragmented world and its values, and that they reinstate those same values. A story like ''Robert Kennedy Saved from Drowning,'' therefore, would affirm the values found in the story, assuming they might be discovered amidst the numerous contradictions. Alan Wilde would agree with Molesworth's basic premise when he argues how deeply concerned with morals Barthelme was throughout his writings. Other critics have tried to reconcile the apparent disjunction between the emphasis Roe places on language and its tenuous status, and the affirmations of values and morals asserted by Molesworth and Wilde.

Wayne Stengle offers one solution. He argues that the audience of the story ''contains all those readers who attempt to do as the narrator does in the last of the story's many, short, disconnected segments. There, the narrator tries to rescue Kennedy from the sea of publicity that always threatens to submerge him.'' Here, Stengle appeals to the readers of the story and their responses for the rescue.

Rather than commenting upon what *is* in the story, Thomas Leitch looks at what is not. ''Perhaps the most striking feature of Donald Barthelme's fiction is the number of things it gets along without.'' From a traditional standpoint, this list is long. There may be characters, but they are flat, rather than round. There is little to no plot, in the traditional sense. Setting remains in the background. And yet, Leitch finds Barthelme's work compelling. In an essay written a couple of months after Barthelme's death, John Barth praises the author's minimalism. Contrary to Aldridge's early assessment, Barth honors Barthelme for how he made every word count in his short stories and novels, and for the ''exhilarating'' displays of his verbal art.

Criticism

Richard Henry

Richard Henry is an Assistant Professor of English at the State University of New York at Potsdam. In the following essay, he discusses the collage structure of Barthelme's story ''Robert Kennedy Saved from Drowning'' and argues that it comments on the fictional nature of Kennedy's image.

''Robert Kennedy Saved from Drowning'' consists of twenty-four scenes, or snapshots, of Robert Kennedy, a once powerful political figure. These snapshots are less story-like than they are like the work of Karsh of Ottawa, a famous portrait photographer, who tells us in the ninth scene in the story that in each sitting there is one shot that is ''the right one.'' With this interpretation, the entire story becomes a roll of film, twenty-four exposures, with the hope that one of them is the shot that best captures Kennedy.

Oddly enough, if Karsh of Ottawa is correct, that there is only one "right one," then "Karsh of Ottawa" has to be the one "right scene" in the story. Ironically, this is the one scene in which we learn next to nothing about the man—it is Kennedy's people, not Kennedy himself, who want the sitting and who don't know what his schedule is. In short, Kennedy is *absent.* This absence might be precisely what interests Barthelme in the story.

Only one shot is *the* shot, the rest are reduced to what the author has elsewhere called "dreck." If so, why read, unless the point of reading is the search for the one tidbit of importance. Fortunately, a host of other interesting observations arise if we abandon the single shot theory, and examine the entire roll as a series of scenes that have particular content and that are arranged in very specific ways. A better description of the construction of the story and how it means what it does might be "collage." In a collage, a variety of images, or voices, or characters, or events are juxtaposed; meaning is revealed by their juxtapositions. In this story, the juxtapositions serve to highlight a series of cancellations that leave the reader unable to say she or he knows much more about the Robert Kennedy character (let alone the actual Robert Kennedy) upon completing the story.

Robert Kennedy visiting an impoverished community during the 1960s.

The opening scene, indeed, the opening sentences, set up some of these contradictions. Kennedy is working at his desk. The narrator begins with: "He is neither abrupt with nor excessively kind to associates. Or he is both abrupt and kind." Such contradictions can easily be traced through the story. They are revealed not only within scenes, or within sentences, as in the opening two sentences, but between scenes. For example, among the details readers learn about Kennedy at his desk in the opening scene is that he spends his time sending and receiving messengers (a line initiated by the narrator and repeated by Kennedy himself). The second scene introduces two descriptions by his secretaries. They are seemingly about his memory: Secretary A tells how her boss forgets things, and even does so intentionally; Secretary B recalls how he remembered her when she was sick in the hospital by arriving, smiling, behind a mass of tulips. As in the opening sentences, Kennedy's contradictions are displayed: he neither remembers nor forgets; he both remembers and forgets, as the narrator might say. Equally as important as these secretarial observations, however, is the function Kennedy plays in Secretary B's story. In the first scene, Kennedy sends and receives messengers. Here, Kennedy *is* the messenger, as he delivers, in person, yellow tulips to his secretary. Without the close juxtaposition of the two scenes, this connection might be lost.

The fourth, fifth, and sixth scenes—"K. Reading the Newspaper," "Attitude Toward His Work," and "Sleeping on the Stones of Unknown Towns (Rimbaud)"—reveal a series of contradictions about Kennedy and his relationship to language. Taken individually, and taking their clues from the titles, readers will find three scenes that are about apparently disparate things: a narrator recounting how Kennedy reads newspapers, Kennedy speaking about how he gets things done, and the narrator showing Kennedy in France or Germany where he wanders the towns, streets, and shops. In the first of the three, however, Kennedy is presented as a master of the language and of the stories that the newspapers tell. He is able to read twelve newspapers a day, to clip important stories, and to memorize what he reads. Moreover, he is able to act decisively upon them. The next scene undermines this positive and active relationship with language and stories. Kennedy says of himself that sometimes he *cannot* read: "I can't seem to get the gist of it, it seems meaningless—devoid of life." The

What Do I Read Next?

- *Snow White* (1967) by Barthelme. Barthelme wrote only four novels during his career, though they might better be called novellas for their brevity. This, his first, is a rewrite of "Snow White and the Seven Dwarves" that challenges the structure of fairy tales.
- *Sadness* (1972) by Barthelme. This is a collection of stories, often parodies, that play with emotions and boredom.
- *The Dead Father* (1975) by Barthelme. Barthelme's second novel concerns the father/son relationship, and is deeply involved in the play of words and their representative functions.
- *Yellow Back Radio Broke Down* (1971) by Ishmael Reed. Reed is a satirist and a parodist who often targets literature and literary forms. In this novel, he parodies the Western novel.
- *Slaughterhouse-Five; or, The Children's Crusade* (1969) by Kurt Vonnegut. Vonnegut's novel plays with the premise that its protagonist, Billy Pilgrim, travels back and forth randomly in his own past, present, and future, experiencing episodes from his life as a prisoner of war in Germany during World War II, an optometrist in suburban 1960s America, and an exhibit in a zoo on the planet Tralfamadore.
- *Gravity's Rainbow* (1973) by Thomas Pynchon. Lieutenant Tyrone Slothrop spends the end of World War II monitoring V2 rockets, but begins to suspect a variety of potentially worldwide conspiracies, including secret governments, a series of secret experiments that were conducted upon him when he was a child, and African tribesmen trained as rocket technicians by the Germans during the war.
- *The Atrocity Exhibition* (1969) by J. G. Ballard. A collection of stories structured in collage fashion and telling of a scientist suffering a nervous breakdown, in the process of which media figures from the 1960s play symbolic roles.

reason for this inability is precisely the opposite of what the narrator said in the previous scene. There, his ability to concentrate was strong, here, his "mind is elsewhere." This either/or proposition, one that shows him both able and unable to master language, is undermined in the third scene in this language sequence. Here, it is language itself that is incomprehensible and changing. Even were Kennedy to focus upon it, he would not be able to master it: "The shop signs are in a language which alters when inspected closely, MOBEL becoming MEUBLES," intones the narrator. This third possibility, that of incomprehensibility, suggests that in the previous two scenes language was comprehensible to Kennedy, even if it might be meaningless. Strangely enough, the possibility that Kennedy might be master of an incomprehensible language emerges as one of the possibilities in the either/or, neither/nor scheme that the narrator has established. It is the juxtaposition of these three scenes that calls attention to Kennedy and his contradictory relationships with language.

Once one realizes that many of the significant aspects of the story result from reading scenes against each other, one can begin to contrast noncontiguous scenes. In the scene titled "K. Puzzled by His Children," Kennedy reads to his children from a German reader. Another relationship with language is advanced here—can Kennedy make something happen with it? The answer in this scene is a resounding no. His children are crying both at the beginning of the scene and at the end, despite his attempts to placate them with reading. Two scenes earlier, in "K. on Crowds," however, we find Kennedy talking about how one must speak to a crowd depending upon its mood. Although he asserts his ability to do this, he fails utterly when faced with his children. He has not able to adjust what he says according to the mood of his children. Apparently, Kennedy is neither able to adjust his discourse to the mood of his audience, nor unable to adjust his discourse. He is both able and unable to have an effect on his audience.

There are other points of contrast developed in addition to Kennedy's varied relationships to language. His relationships to crowds is advanced in scenes other than the one entitled "K. on Crowds." In "Behind the Bar," Kennedy reveals his own tendency to consider himself apart from the crowd as he wanders behind the bar. The bartender recognizes the danger. If one person wanders behind the bar, everyone will, so the bartender sends him back to the other side. His ability to manage crowds highlights his separateness from the ordinary people, a separateness that the bartender refuses to recognize. In "A Friend Comments: K.'s Aloneness," Kennedy's friend remarks how much Kennedy is distinctly separated from the rest of the world. But this quality depends on how well one knows the man. The friend suggests that it is impossible to know him; yet others, secretaries, the old teacher, aides and assistants, show that it *is* possible to know something of the man. In many cases, the either/or, neither/nor distinction fails to hold because there is too little attention to the gray areas in between those descriptions that are advanced by the variety of commentators. To the bartender, Kennedy is simply one of the crowd, in part because the bartender knows almost nothing of him. To the friend, Kennedy is always distinct from the crowd because the friend knows so much about him.

One of the most curious juxtapositions occurs with the two final scenes. In the next to last scene, Kennedy discusses a twentieth-century French (actually Belgian) writer and critic, Georges Poulet, who himself was deeply influenced by an eighteenth-century French novelist and dramatist, Pierre Carlet de Chamberlain de Marivaux. The discussion itself is slightly ironic, for in it, Kennedy embraces Poulet's description of the Marivaudian being: "a pastless, futureless man, born anew at every instant. The instants are points which organize themselves into a line, but what is important is the instant, not the line. The Marivaudian being has in a sense, no history. He is constantly being *overtaken* by events. This freshness Poulet, quoting Marivaux, describes very well."

Part of the irony lies in Kennedy's embrace of the "freshness" of the Marivaudian being through

"Barthelme uses the collage as a structure for his short story precisely because it highlights the moment that each scene describes."

another writer who quotes Marivaux. (Attentive readers might recall Kennedy's preoccupation with a different kind of freshness in the short scene titled "Dress.") That is, Kennedy might have come to Marivaux directly, but doesn't. The quotes Poulet offers his readers are by no means fresh, both because they are nearly two hundred years old, and because they are *quotes,* or the words of another. The entire business of quotation is rooted in repetition, in earlier speaking events, and, therefore, rooted in history. This is especially the case when a quote is attributed, that is, when the original source is cited, for the attribution insures the connection to other points in history. Barthelme further plays with the irony of calling something fresh that might indeed be "stale," by putting Kennedy's observations in quotation marks. The narrator quotes Kennedy, who is representing Poulet, who is representing Marivaux. This series of representations have a history and it is highlighted by Barthelme's series of attributions. What is important is the "line," or attributions, that connects these instants or points.

Also ironic is Kennedy's relationship to the "line" as we see it in the final scene. In the Poulet section, Kennedy appears to reject lines in favor of instants, or moments. We see this earlier, as well, when the narrator describes Kennedy in an art gallery. There, Kennedy views geometric paintings and comments, "Well, at least we know [the artist] has a ruler." With the comment comes a dismissal, a rejection of rulers and lines and geometry. (Readers might note that in the laughter that follows, the narrator tells us that people "repeat the remark," that is, they quote Kennedy.) In the final scene, it is Kennedy, perhaps as a Marivaudian being, who is being overtaken by events as he flails in the water. The narrator throws him "a line" to rescue him. After missing it, Kennedy "grasps the line." Once he has "both hands on the line," the narrator begins to haul him out. "Line" is mentioned three times in this short section (not counting the two times it is referred to as "it"). What the narrator has done in this section is made the connection between events, a connection that is unimportant to the Marivaudian being, and a connection that has been unimportant, apparently, to Kennedy. Yet it is this connection that saves him from being overtaken, that saves him from drowning.

Barthelme uses the collage as a structure for his short story precisely because it highlights the moment that each scene describes. The fact that Kennedy needs to be saved, and that the narrator does so by making a connection, challenges the breathlessness and dazzlement that surrounds Kennedy. His friends, acquaintances, and aides are themselves overtaken by their momentary encounters with the man. The narrator reminds readers that connections must be drawn. If not, they, too, will be overtaken by the story. The narrator gives a hint; the astute reader will follow his line.

Source: Richard Henry, "Making Connections: Collage as Structure in 'Robert Kennedy Saved from Drowning'," for *Short Stories for Students,* Gale, 1998.

Stanley Trachtenberg

In the following essay, Trachtenberg discusses the "Marivaudian being" as it relates to "Robert Kennedy Saved from Drowning." The "Marivaudian being" is a term invented by the eighteenth-century French dramatist Pierre Marivaux.

Art proves . . . disappointing as a means of interpreting its subject in "Robert Kennedy Saved from Drowning," in which the narrator records his observations about Kennedy, describes episodes in his life, and provides snatches of conversation or statements he is supposed to have made. Each of the segments is given its own heading; none is accorded more importance than any of the others. They do not build toward some definitive revelation or in their totality establish a definitive portrait. Collectively they serve more as a catalog than a coherent perspective from which to view their subject. . . . Kennedy proves more various, more surprising, even mysterious, finally capable of wide ranges of behavior which seem impossible to reconcile. Gracious as an employer, attentive as a husband and father, compassionate even as a child, he can be abrupt and insensitive, both assured and vulnerable. Though partial to soberly cut suits in dark colors, he is pictured, at length, with a mask, black cape, and sword. This romantic notion is reinforced by Kennedy's large-scale ambitions which, however moral, seem hopelessly naive. "The world is full of unsolved problems," he is quoted as saying, "situations that demand careful reason and intelligent action. In Latin America, for example." The example is so arbitrary, so unfocused, above all so inadequate in its lack of specificity that Kennedy's pronouncement along with the flat, terse assertions he is constantly quoted as uttering make him seem almost a cartoonlike figure of authorial mockery.

Yet Kennedy himself provides a paradigm for responding to the fiction in his erudite discussion of the French writer Georges Poulet's analysis of the eighteenth-century French dramatist Pierre Marivaux. Quoting Poulet, Kennedy identifies a figure he terms the Marivaudian being:

> A pastless futureless man, born anew at every instant. The instants are points which organize themselves into a line, but what is important is the instant, not the line. The Marivaudian being has in a sense no history. Nothing follows from what has gone before. He is constantly surprised. He cannot predict his own reaction to events. He is constantly being *overtaken* by events. A condition of breathlessness and dazzlement surrounds him. In consequence he exists in a certain freshness which seems, if I may say so, very desirable.

Frustrating linear definition, the historical understanding of what follows from the knowledge of what has gone before, the Marivaudian figure perhaps best describes the story itself; yet part of the disturbing effect the story has is the dissatisfaction it projects with its own approach. Reducing Kennedy to the Kafkaesque near invisiblity of the letter *K,* the narrator in the manner of overstuffed biographies in which the subject is figuratively drowned also includes such trivial information as the exact dishes he has ordered in a restaurant or the word-for-word text of an alphabet lesson he read to his children and includes a digressive passage describing the indifferent young people who line the streets along which Kennedy walks.

Source: Stanley Trachtenberg, in his *Understanding Donald Barthelme,* University of South Carolina Press, 1990, pp. 64–6.

Charles Molesworth

In the following essay, Molesworth describes "Robert Kennedy Saved from Drowning" as an example of metafiction, a work whose theme is the conventions of writing itself.

Barthelme's fiction raises many of the questions that plague current literary theory and that seem to be involved in a fitful but widespread feeling of cultural crises. Is there a stable subject, an authorial identity that anchors meaning and intention, or is writing a transpersonal process so involved with models and transgression of models as to be completely without stable reference, let alone verisimilitude? We can easily enough identify Barthelme as a writer of metafiction (I choose this term over other contenders such as *surfiction* and the *new fiction*), as one who writes less obviously about the traditional subjects—love, fame, death—than about the conventions of writing itself. But this easily made identification can serve to blur other issues, issues that have been drawn up by opposing camps and have more or less calcified in the last twenty years or so. Art should deal with life, with ethical values, with people's felt needs and shared experiences, and do so in a common language and with conventional means. So says the traditional camp. No, says the innovative side, fiction's first duty is to show us ourselves; and since we have so utterly changed, in order for fiction to be true or even dutiful, it must also be changed. The problem could easily be transformed into a question of deciding if we have indeed changed, and if so, in what ways. But to pose the question that way is to become too general, too "extraliterary," too far removed from fiction itself. The problem then will be addressed in and through fiction: this is about the only thing on which the two camps agree. . . .

Barthelme's stories, as objects, operate in a realm neither completely objective nor completely subjective, though they implicitly claim the authority associated with both modes. They also hide behind the excuses that each mode implicitly offers: "it speaks for itself," and "I was only playing."

One way to show this is to turn to "Robert Kennedy Saved from Drowning," from *Unspeakable Practices,* one of Barthelme's best-known stories. The theme of this story remains ambiguous, but it involves in part the way a public figure is an invention of public needs and fantasies, and so the public's knowledge of such a person is always imperfect, because partial and factitious, yet perfect, because answerable and cathartic. The story creates, re-creates, and exposes a variety of presentations, using a series of short passages in which the main character, K., is shown in several situations. In the story's title a real-life, historical individual is named; thoughout the story proper, he is called only K., as if a character in a Kafka novel. So from the beginning, history and fiction are conflated. The paragraphs variously try to "humanize" K., showing him at home with his children, for example, and to mythologize him, by showing how he exists in the imagination of others. And both attempts are themselves subject to parody.

Here is one paragraph, in which K. can be seen as either human, because he is vulnerable, nervous, and yet witty, or inhuman, because the whole incident sounds like a press agent's gossip item.

> *Gallery-going*
>
> K. enters a large gallery on Fifty-seventh Street, in the Fuller Building. His entourage includes several ladies and gentlemen. Works by a geometricist are on show. K. looks at the immense, rather theoretical paintings.
>
> "Well, at least we know he has a ruler."
>
> The group dissolves in laughter. People repeat the remark to one another, laughing.
>
> The artist, who has been standing behind a dealer, regards K. with hatred.

K.'s remark objectifies the paintings, turns them into mere exercises in construction and the use of tools (some would say the paintings invite just such a response). But then the remark itself is turned into an object of sorts as it is repeated, "passed around," serving as a marker of K.'s wit. The paragraph ends with the irruption of "genuine" emotion, but it remains concealed. In fact, the physical position of the hate-filled artist would almost suggest he is cowering, ironically enough behind the dealer who serves to publicize his work. The Fuller Building is a real building on Fifty-seventh Street, and does in fact house several galleries. The incident has been described by Barthelme as the only "real" fact in this story.

What, then, are we to make of the following item, from *The New York Times* of May 1, 1981 (about thirteen years after the Barthelme story first appeared), entitled "A Wisecracking Prince Charles Tours Washington"? The item begins like this:

> Sipping orange juice, the Prince of Wales stood studying a modernistic bronze sculpture titled "Icarus" at the National Air and Space Museum.

> "The theme of this story remains ambiguous, but it involves in part the way a public figure is an invention of public needs and fantasies, and so the public's knowledge of such a person is always imperfect."

Finally, he turned away from the oddly misshapen work of art. "I'd love to have seen it," he remarked drily, "before it melted."

Is Barthelme ghostwriting for the House of Windsor as he once did for the president of a Texas university? Or has Prince Charles been dabbling in metafiction? This would seem to prove one point that metafictionists want to impress on us: no matter how much artificial structure exists in a work of fiction, "real life" is equally ridden with formulae, stances, rehearsed material and borrowed motifs. Less grandly, we can at least notice that Lynn Rosellini, the reporter whose by-line appears on this item, has read enough fiction to use phrases like "remarked drily" with apparent ease. But what of the apparently parodic bits in this item, how intentional are they? Did the artist create a work for the Air and Space Museum and call it *Icarus* with any but an air of homily and moral irony directed at technological pride? And did Prince Charles know the piece's title before he made his condescending remark? Yet if the artist meant such a warning against pride to those who commissioned the statue, was an abstract sculpture the best way to get his point across? And what are we to make of the overdone phrase "oddly misshapen"? Either modifier would have done, so both together can indicate anxiety on the author's part to vindicate the Prince's reaction, or perhaps it could serve as ironic exaggeration and so reflect against the Prince. (The noun in the phrase after all is "work of art," not "heap of metal" or "thing.")

What such a witticism does is to vindicate the entire situation. Otherwise we would have been left with the "simple" truth that society's leaders don't comprehend modern art, a safe enough "fact," or that their condescension toward such works expresses the otherwise guarded dismissal many people feel in the face of art that doesn't readily declare itself. Effectively the remark reaffirms the politician's or celebrity's identity as one who is baffled but who has the skill to pull through, and it expresses for us a sense of occasion in which our leaders, for a change, accurately speak for us. In either case, the fictional or the real incident, an object signifies (or attempts to signify) some complex cultural experience and the person involved dismisses the signification. But in doing so the person acts mechanically, like an object, responding to the pressures of an entourage and the "dynamics" of a situation in a manner that seems scripted. Both art work and public figure are "on show," and both play out their functions to the evident satisfaction of all viewers. It's easy to dismiss this example (and there are others like it in Barthelme, though none so pointed) by saying that reality has stylizations and fiction can, if it wishes, imitate them. But building up an aesthetic on such an easy formulation still raises questions about fiction's status. . . . The Barthelme paragraph also recalls the structures of fabulation—the character called by his initial, the glowering spectator revealed at the close of the scene—in such a way as to suggest a genuinely playful exercise in tale-telling. . . .

Self-referential fiction traces its lineage back at least to Cervantes and Sterne. If one of the functions of metafiction is to challenge or undercut realist fiction, it has failed, since realism has flourished since Sterne. But there do remain the general lineaments of realism against which metafiction is not only judged but against which it operates. A recent article, besides offering a useful survey of theories of realism, suggests one chief characteristic of the highly developed realism of the later nineteenth century. Characters in such realist fiction are driven not only by outside, heterogeneous forces, but also by an inner necessity. Inner necessity for individual characters is revealed, even defined, by other characters' perception of them, as well as what they are in themselves. This process of revelation, . . . presents an ordering of things that enables us to see "the individual neither dissolving into its other by the ironic play of reflections nor succumbing to forces from outside but being overmastered by something from within." What Barthelme's parody of realism suggests is that if people are overmastered by something from within, that "something" is a lack, an absence, an awareness of their own frustrated desires.

Barthelme's characters are often on the verge of dissolving into the other *and* being overmastered by outside forces, as "Robert Kennedy Saved from Drowning" exemplifies. The very structure of the story reinforces the notion that K.'s inner necessity is totally mysterious. We are forced to see him only as he is reflected in the consciousness of others, and only in reaction to outside forces. He has, in effect, no clear intersubjective reality, or at least none that allows us to see his destiny being revealed. In one paragraph called "A Friend Comments: K.'s Aloneness," we read that this "terrible loneliness . . . prevents people from getting too close to him. . . . He says something or does something that surprises you, and you realize that all along you really didn't know him at all." Then as if to illustrate this principle, the friend tells the story of K. acting as captain in a small boat beset by rough weather. The friend raised the question of whether or not the anchor would hold. And K.'s reaction is in some ways the metonymic reduction of his character: "He just looked at me. Then he said: 'Of course it will hold. That's what it's for.'" This absolute trust in things, their reliability and functionality, is a kind of Weberian rationalism in which means and ends are in perfect accord. Presumably we are to read this incident as showing how K.'s relation to people and events in general is essentially that of an absolute pragmatist, or perhaps more accurately, an *apparatchik.* Yet other paragraphs in the story portray just the opposite sort of character, for example in the "Childhood of K. as Recalled by a Former Teacher," where we are told "what was unusual about K. was his compassion. . . . I would almost say it was his strongest characteristic." The story is parodying the media-constructed biography of a celebrity—a form especially noticeable today every time there is an assassination, an election campaign, or a national scandal—but its method of collage is suggesting something further.

The collage of viewpoints presents a jumble of cliche structures and fantasy items (e.g., "A Dream" and "He Discusses the French Writer, Poulet") which effectively parodies each and so calls into question whether our knowledge of K. (or his of himself) can ever be adequately represented. Yet at the same time the skill, the glibness of presentation in each paragraph indicates that the need to fictionalize is endemic in our society (and in human nature?). We might carry this one step further and say K.'s unknowability is necessary for the endless variety of fictions to continue. The story even suggests that the object of the fictions must be a blank, that the signified must be absent, for the necessary processes of fictionmaking to occur. In this way, K. himself becomes an "anxious object," in that he serves both as the center of all concern and the completely expressive absence. And he also serves as the source of the "blanketing effect" in language, for it is his unknowability that causes people to continue "filling in" what would otherwise be only isolated data of perception and representation.

"The story is parodying the media-constructed biography of a celebrity—a form especially noticeable today every time there is an assassination, an election campaign, or a national scandal—but its method of collage is suggesting something further."

I would suggest that K. is in many ways the paradigmatic Barthelme character. Although his story is one of the best of the entire corpus, the way he exists as a creation of parodic strategies makes him typical. At the heart of the matter, so to speak, is an ambiguity blended out of romance and anti-romance elements. As K. himself puts it, paraphrasing Poulet's description of the French author Marivaux, the character is "a pastless futureless man, born anew at every instant. . . . He is constantly surprised. He cannot predict his own reaction to events. He is constantly being *overtaken* by events. A condition of breathlessness and dazzlement surrounds him." The medieval romance hero and the Little Man of urban mass culture have merged into one person, one object. Perhaps this is the most antirealist of all of Barthelme's strategies, for this character denies the rock of linear chronology on which realist narrative erects its faith. But notice that the character is not simply an object among other objects, for in some sense he reflects, even epitomizes his environment. This reflection is one of the main characteristics of the realist hero. In fact, the syntax of the last sentence quoted is ambiguous, since we can't be sure if the dazzlement is directly the nature of the events, or if it's the character's reaction to those events that overtake him. It can be argued that the character is at one with his environment, or completely victimized by it, and this brings us back to the ambiguity of tones in Barthelme, that mixture of nostalgia and disdain. Also it recalls the mix of total freedom and total determinism brought about by the ambiguous authorial control in Barthelme's metafiction.

Source: Charles Molesworth, in his *Donald Barthelme's Fiction: The Ironist Saved from Drowning,* University of Missouri Press, 1982, pp. 1, 64–70.

Sources

Aldridge, John W. ''Dance of Death,'' in *Critical Essays on Donald Barthelme,* edited by Richard F. Patteson, G. K. Hall, 1992, pp. 25-8.

Barth, John. ''Thinking Man's Minimalist: Honoring Barthelme,'' in *Critical Essays on Donald Barthelme,* edited by Richard F. Patteson, G. K. Hall, 1992, pp. 1-4.

Leitch, Thomas M. ''Donald Barthelme and the End of the End,'' in *Critical Essays on Donald Barthelme,* edited by Richard F. Patteson, G. K. Hall, 1992.

Molesworth, Charles. *Donald Barthelme's Fiction: The Ironist Saved from Drowning,* University of Missouri Press, 1982.

Roe, Barbara. *Donald Barthelme: A Study of the Short Fiction,* Twayne, 1992.

Stengle, Wayne B. *The Shape of Art in the Short Stories of Donald Barthelme,* Louisiana State University Press, 1985, p. 172.

Further Reading

''Donald Barthelme,'' in *Short Story Criticism,* Vol. 2, edited by Sheila Fitzgerald, Gale, 1989, pp. 24–58.
Reprinted criticism on Barthelme's short stories.

Gordon, Lois. *Donald Barthelme,* Twayne, 1981.
Gordon gives an overview of Barthelme's stories and novels published through 1979. She includes his then-unpublished stories, as well as an annotated bibliography of criticism.

Kennedy, Robert F. *Robert Kennedy, in His Own Words: The Unpublished Recollections of the Kennedy Years,* edited by Edwin O. Guthman and Jeffrey Shulman, Bantam, 1988.
Sponsored by the John F. Kennedy Library, this book contains oral interviews with Robert Kennedy conducted from 1964-1967, in which he speaks of his brother John Kennedy's presidency.

Patteson, Richard F., ed. *Critical Essays on Donald Barthelme,* G. K. Hall, 1992.
Patteson has assembled eight reviews of Barthelme's collections and novels and thirteen essays by critics. Also included is an introduction by novelist John Barth examining Barthelme's work.

The Shawl

Cynthia Ozick

1980

''The Shawl'' was first published in the *New Yorker* in 1980. The story was reprinted in Cynthia Ozick's 1989 collection, *The Shawl,* where it was paired with ''Rosa,'' a story that picks up the tale of the same characters some thirty years later. ''The Shawl'' is about the Holocaust, the systematic slaughter of some six million Jews, as well as at least that many gypsies, homosexuals, and other ''undesirables'' by the Nazis during World War II. Although Ozick was born and raised in the United States, she is well-versed in Jewish history and tradition, and her story quickly became one of the best–known stories about the Nazi death camps. ''The Shawl'' is particularly admired for its compactness. In only two thousand words, Ozick manages to evoke the horror of the Holocaust for her readers. The story touches on many themes, including survival, motherhood, nurture, prejudice, and betrayal.

Author Biography

Cynthia Ozick was born on April 17, 1928, in New York City. Her parents, William and Celia (Regelson) Ozick, had come to the United States from northwestern Russia. In addition to his work as a pharmacist, William was a Jewish scholar. Ozick considers herself a feminist and claims she became one at the age of five, when her grandmother took her to heder,

a school for the study of Hebrew and the Torah. The rabbi told Ozick's grandmother to take her home, since "a girl doesn't have to study." Ozick returned the next day and quickly established herself as a good student.

She continued her education at Hunter College High School, then at New York University, from which she graduated in 1949 with a B.A. in English. She received an M.A. in English from Ohio State University in 1950.

Throughout the 1950s, Ozick worked as an advertising copywriter for Filene's Department Store. She also wrote articles and poetry and began work on a novel, which she abandoned several years later. In 1952, she married Bernard Hallote, a lawyer. Her daughter, Rachel, was born in 1965. That year, Ozick had several poems published in *Judaism* magazine.

Ozick's literary career gained momentum in 1966 with the publication of her novel *Trust,* the first of her many works with a Jewish theme. Her next book, *The Pagan Rabbi and Other Stories,* was published in 1971. It won the Jewish Council Book Award and the B'nai B'rith Jewish Heritage Award and was nominated for the National Book Award. Ozick has continued to win many prestigious awards for her fiction. Other works of fiction include *Bloodshed and Three Novellas* (1976), *Levitation: Five Fictions* (1982), *The Cannibal Galaxy* (1983), *The Messiah of Stockholm* (1987), and *The Shawl* (1989). Ozick has also written two nonfiction books: *Art and Ardor,* published in 1987, and *Metaphor and Memory,* published in 1989.

Ozick contributes to the "About Books" column in the *New York Times Book Review,* and writes articles, reviews, stories, poems, and translations from Yiddish for such periodicals as *Commentary,* the *New Republic, Partisan Review,* the *New Leader, Ms., Esquire,* the *New Yorker, American Poetry Review,* and *Harper's.*

Plot Summary

"The Shawl" opens with a description of three people, suffering tremendously, who are walking. The narrator notes that Rosa has a yellow star sewn into her coat, and Magda has blue eyes and yellow hair, like one of "them." Soon it is clear that Rosa and Stella are Jewish women who are being marched to a concentration camp. Magda, an infant, will be killed if she is discovered, so Rosa considers giving Magda to someone by the side of the road. But Rosa fears that she will be shot if she leaves the line, or that the person she tries to pass Magda to might not take her, or might drop her, killing her instantly. She continues to hide the baby inside her shawl.

In the camp, Rosa manages to keep Magda hidden for some time. Rosa knows, however, that Magda will die. She fears that someone, perhaps Stella, will kill Magda to eat her, or that she will be discovered somehow. As Rosa protects Magda, Magda protects her shawl. It is "her baby, her pet, her little sister." She hides in it, laughs at it when it blows in the wind, and sucks on it for sustenance.

One day, Stella steals Magda's shawl to put over herself. Searching for the shawl, Magda toddles into the square outside the barracks, screaming "Maaaa—." Rosa cannot run to Magda or they will both be killed. Instead, she runs to get the shawl, hoping to return to the courtyard in time to catch Magda's attention and stop her screaming before she is discovered. But Rosa is too late. She watches as Magda is carried off by a guard who throws her into the electric fence, killing her. Still, Rosa cannot run to Magda. She cannot scream or do anything else that would indicate that Magda was her child. She stuffs the shawl into her own mouth to keep herself from screaming.

Characters

Magda

Rosa's daughter, Magda, is a nursing infant hidden in her mother's shawl at the beginning of the story, and a fifteen-month-old child when she is killed. Magda is the center of Rosa's existence: Rosa gives Magda most of her own food and focuses much of her energy on worrying about what might happen to Magda and on keeping the child alive. Magda learns as an infant not to cry when she is hungry; instead, she satisfies her hunger by sucking on the shawl. The shawl becomes the center of her existence, her "own baby, her pet, her little sister." She hides under it to keep from being discovered by the Nazis, sucks on it to satisfy her hunger, laughs at it as it blows in the wind. Magda does not cry until Stella takes her shawl away. Her cries then, as she walks out of the barracks during roll call, cause her to be discovered and killed.

Rosa

Rosa is a Jewish woman who, along with her daughter and niece, is imprisoned in a concentration camp. Rosa's one focus in "The Shawl" is how to keep her infant daughter Magda alive for as long as possible, even though she knows the child is doomed to die. As she is marched to the camp, Rosa thinks of passing Magda to a bystander in an attempt to save her, but she fears the person might intentionally or unintentionally drop the baby. She fears that her niece, Stella, is waiting for Magda to die so that she can eat her. Later, Rosa fears that someone in the camp will kill Magda for the same reason. She also fears the Nazi guards, who will kill Magda the moment she is discovered. Rosa knows that Magda will die, but she draws on every resource of her body, mind, and soul to delay that moment.

Cynthia Ozick

Stella

Stella is Rosa's fourteen-year-old niece. She is described as a girl who is "too small, with thin breasts," whose knees are "tumors on sticks, her elbows chicken bones." Such a description hints at the near-starvation conditions under which prisoners lived in the camp. Stella is always cold, always hungry, and jealous of Rosa's baby, who at least has the comfort of her mother and her shawl. Stella also accuses Magda of being an Aryan because the child has blond hair and blue eyes, two features of the Nazi's idealized race. Rosa fears that Stella is waiting for Magda to die so she can eat the child—not an unreasonable fear given the circumstances. Stella's most important action is to cause Magda's death by taking the child's shawl for herself. "I was cold," is all she says later, in explanation.

Themes

Survival

Underlying Ozick's story is the theme of survival. Rosa struggles with this constantly. During the march to the concentration camp, Rosa struggles over whether or not she should pass Magda to an onlooker, possibly ensuring her child's survival. Rosa decides against this, however, realizing that she would risk her own life in doing so and could not guarantee Magda's safety. Rosa chooses survival in the moment for both of them, rather than probable death for herself and uncertainty for her child. As Rosa struggles over what to do about Magda, Stella longs to be Magda: a baby rocked and sleeping in her mother's arms. Rosa also thinks that the starving Stella gazes at Magda as if she wishes to eat the child. Magda, though far too young to have any knowledge of what is happening to and around her, gives up screaming and quietly sucks on the shawl.

Life in the camp is a constant battle for survival. Rosa, apparently caring more about Magda's survival than her own, gives most of her food to her child. Stella, caring mostly about her own survival, gives no food to Magda. Magda herself turns to the shawl for comfort; it is her "baby, her pet, her little sister"; when she needs to be still—and stillness is necessary to her survival—she sucks on a corner of it.

Halfway through the story, Stella takes Magda's shawl because she is cold. It is, perhaps, the only one of her afflictions that she can do anything about.

Media Adaptations

- 'The Shawl'' was adapted as a play by Cynthia Ozick. Directed by the well-known film director Sidney Lumet, the play was performed (as *Blue Light*) in 1994 at the Bay Street Theatre in Sag Harbor, New York, and in 1996 at the Jewish Repertory Theater, New York City.
- An audio version of ''The Shawl,'' read by actress Claire Bloom, is available on the National Public Radio series ''Jewish Short Stories from Eastern Europe and Beyond.''

There is no food to ease her hunger, and there is nothing she can do to escape from the camp; but Magda's shawl might ease her cold. This, too, is a form of reaching for survival. Stella has chosen to bring what small comfort she can to herself, ignoring the potential cost to Magda and Rosa.

Magda, knowing no better, leaves the barracks in her search for the shawl. Again, Rosa has to make a choice about her survival. If she runs to Magda, they will both be killed. If she does nothing, Magda will be killed. The only solution she can think of, however slim, is to get the shawl to Magda before she is discovered by the camp's guards. She runs for the shawl and returns to the square with it, but she is too late. A soldier carries Magda away toward the electric fence at the other side of the camp. Rosa watches her baby fly through the air, hit the fence and die, then fall to the ground. Again, there are choices. If she goes to Magda, she will be shot; if she screams, she will be shot. Rosa chooses survival, using the shawl to mute her scream.

Motherhood and Nurturing

Closely linked to the theme of survival are issues of motherhood and nurturing. Throughout ''The Shawl,'' Stella longs to be nurtured. On the march, she longs to be a baby, comforted by her mother's arms. In the camp, she longs for food, sometimes causing Rosa to think that she is ''waiting for Magda to die so she could put her teeth into the little thighs.'' She takes the only bit of nurturing she can find: warmth from Magda's shawl.

The issues of motherhood are more complex. Because she is a mother, Rosa cannot think only of herself, as Stella does. Each decision must be weighed. What is the possible benefit to her? To Magda? What are the possible costs? With each decision, Rosa must decide whether it is in her best interest to sacrifice herself, her baby, or both of them.

Prejudice and Tolerance

Issues of prejudice and tolerance are also raised in ''The Shawl.'' Rosa, Stella, Magda, and the others are imprisoned or killed in concentration camps simply because they are Jewish. Prejudice exists on their part too—at least on the part of Stella. Looking at Magda's yellow hair and blue eyes, she says ''Aryan,'' in a voice that makes Rosa think she has said, ''Let us devour her.''

The issue of tolerance is raised in the camp itself. Rosa and Magda are not alone in the barracks they occupy. The other occupants are aware of Magda's existence and of Rosa's deception. In the camp, ''a place without pity,'' they cannot know what might happen to them if Magda is discovered in the barracks. Yet no one reports her presence.

Betrayal

Rosa constantly fears that Stella—or someone else—will kill Magda to eat her. While this does not happen, it is Stella's betrayal that costs Magda her life and Rosa her child. ''The Shawl'' points to one reason for this kind of betrayal: the inhuman treatment Stella has received has made her pitiless. ''The cold went into her heart,'' the narrator says. ''Rosa saw that Stella's heart was cold.''

Style

Point of View

''The Shawl'' is written in an omniscient third-person point of view. It is omniscient because the narrator can see things through the eyes of all the characters. For instance, the narrator tells readers that "Stella wanted to be wrapped in a shawl," and that "Rosa did not feel hunger"—things which could only be known by that character. The point of view is said to be third person because the narrator speaks about the characters from the outside, referring to them as "she" or "he."

Dialogue

"The Shawl" is notable for containing almost no dialogue. Rosa says nothing. Stella speaks twice: once when she calls Magda an "Aryan," and again when she says "I was cold" to explain why she took Magda's shawl. Magda screams in the early part of the story, but soon gives that up. She makes no other sound until her shawl is taken from her; Rosa even thinks Magda is a mute. When Stella steals the shawl, however, Magda says what will be the only word she ever speaks: "Maaaa—." The characters' silence may represent the silence they had to maintain during the march and in the camp in order to protect their lives. Had any of them uttered one word or complaint that could have been overheard by a camp official, they would have been killed, as Magda was. Despite their lack of communication through speech, the plot is intense due to their tragic situation.

Topics for Further Study

- Imagine that Rosa and Stella both survived the concentration camps and are alive today. Pick one controversial social issue, such as abortion or welfare. Discuss the position you think each character would take on this issue and why.
- Rosa stuffs the shawl into her mouth to keep herself from screaming when Magda is killed. Discuss the significance of this act.
- "The Shawl" is written from the third-person omniscient point of view. Why do you think Ozick chose that point of view? Do you think that first-person narration might have worked better? Why or why not?
- Read another contemporary Jewish tale, such as Isaac Bashevis Singer's "Gimpel the Fool," or Ozick's "The Pagan Rabbi." How are these stories influenced by Jewish religion, lore, tradition?

Style

Ozick uses an extremely spare style in "The Shawl." The story is only two thousand words long. An important characteristic of this style is how much information Ozick trusts the reader to fill in for him or herself. Ozick does not waste words by stating that Rosa and Stella are being marched to a concentration camp. She simply describes a march. In the process, she mentions the yellow "star sewn into Rosa's coat" and the fact that Magda's blue eyes and blonde hair could cause you to think "she was one of *their* babies." At this point, it becomes evident that Ozick is describing the plight of Jews during the Holocaust, and readers are trusted to bring what knowledge they have of that event to their reading of the story. Ozick does not describe the camp itself until some description of it becomes necessary to the story, and then she describes only what the reader absolutely needs to know. She mentions the square into which Magda has wandered. The one part of the camp that Ozick describes in detail is the electric fence surrounding it, the fence against which Magda will be thrown.

Structure

In the course of the story, Ozick shifts from a narrative mode that consists primarily of exposition to one in which the reader accompanies the character through the action–step by step, thought by thought—in an extended scene. Exposition is when the writer does not take the reader through the action step by step, but allows the narrator to present an overview of what has occurred or is occurring. Approximately the first two-thirds of "The Shawl" is exposition. In a little over a thousand words the narrator succinctly reports the events of several months. The narrator recounts the march and what life was like in the camp. Readers are occasionally told what a character thinks or feels, but these sketchy details do not comprise full-fledged scenes.

With Magda's first word, "Maaaa—," Ozick switches from an exposition to a detailed scene. The narrator moves into the mind of Rosa and remains there until the end of the story. In the first two-thirds of the story, enough time passes for Magda to have grown from a nursing infant to a fifteen-month-old child, old enough to walk. The final third of the story covers only a few moments. Readers see what Rosa sees and hear her thoughts. The narrator recounts Rosa's trek into the barracks to find the shawl and back out to discover she is too late. Readers witness Magda's death through Rosa's eyes.

This switch from exposition to a detailed scene has a powerful effect on the story. During the time when Magda's nearly inevitable death is somewhere in the future, the reader is more distant from the characters. As Magda's death approaches, readers move closer to Rosa's perspective. When Magda is killed, readers witness the scene from the position of a mother watching as her daughter is murdered.

Repetition

Ozick uses repetition to build suspense. Readers know from the beginning of the story that Magda is constantly on the edge of death. Rosa's breasts are dry, so there is nothing for Magda to eat; she could die of starvation at any moment. Or she could be discovered by the soldiers and killed. Rosa also knows that Magda is ''going to die very soon.'' But time moves forward and Magda does not die. Then she begins to walk and the time of her death seems to move closer: ''When Magda began to walk, Rosa knew that Magda was going to die very soon.'' Again, time passes and Magda does not die. Then Stella steals the shawl and Magda walks out into the square. Her death moves even closer: ''Rosa saw that today Magda was going to die.'' Finally, Magda screams and the time of her death is present: Rosa ''saw that Magda was going to die.'' The repetition causes an echo in the reader's mind: Magda is going to die, Magda is going to die. The outcome of the story is never in dispute, the action merely concerns how Magda's death is played out. Along with Rosa, readers see Magda's death growing nearer. And, along with Rosa, they can do nothing to change what will happen.

Symbolism

The most obvious symbol of the story is Magda's seemingly magical shawl. Critic Alan R. Berger, writing in *Crisis and Covenant: The Holocaust in American Jewish Fiction* (1985), claims that the shawl is a literary symbol of the tallit, or Jewish prayer shawl. To wrap oneself in the tallit, he says, is to be surrounded ''by the holiness and protection of the commandments.'' Berger believes that one message of ''The Shawl'' is that ''Jewish religious creativity and covenantal symbolism can occur even under the most extreme conditions.'' According to Andrew Gordon in ''Cynthia Ozick's 'The Shawl' and the Transitional Object'' (*Literature and Psychology,* 1994), Ozick denies having had this in mind when she wrote the story. Critic Suzanne Klingenstein, writing in the Fall, 1992, issue of *Studies in American Jewish Literature,* says that ''the shawl functions in place of speech for both infant and mother and also as a kind of umbilical cord between the two characters. Again, states Gordon, Ozick has denied that this was her intention.

Gordon also believes that the shawl is a ''transitional object,'' an object that helps an infant make the transition from the state of being one with its mother to the recognition that it is an individual, separate from its mother. He states that Rosa, Stella, and Magda, ''in their need to possess the shawl can be considered as infants suffering extreme oral deprivation and in need of a mother.'' Gordon reads ''The Shawl'' as ''a story about delusion as a defense against an overwhelming reality, against loss of control, and against traumatic loss.'' Ozick herself claims that she had none of these ''pop psychology''ideas in mind when writing ''The Shawl.''

Historical Context

The Great Depression Leads to Hitler's Rise

One of the major historical events of Ozick's lifetime was the Great Depression—the period of economic crisis and unemployment that began in the United States in October, 1929, and continued through most of the 1930s. Although she was born in 1928, one year before the start of the Depression, Ozick claims not to have been affected by it. She describes ''the family pharmacy as giving a sense of comfort and prosperity,'' according to Joseph Lowin in *Cynthia Ozick.*

A series of events that seem to have had a far greater effect on Ozick's work occurred in Europe. In 1933, Adolf Hitler became Chancellor of the German Reich. Several months later, he proclaimed a one-day boycott of all Jewish shops, followed quickly by the forced retirement of all non-Aryan civil servants, except soldiers. Hitler's persecution of the Jews had begun. He instituted the use of the

Compare & Contrast

- **1930s:** Adolf Hitler's persecution of the Jews in Germany begins in 1933. Discrimination gives way to the loss of all their rights as citizens. In 1938, the Nazis destroy the country's synagogues and begin imprisoning Jews and others in concentration camps, like the one depicted in ''The Shawl.'' The Final Solution escalates throughout World War II, ending only in 1945 when the camps are liberated by the Allies.

  1980s: The historical reality of the Holocaust is questioned by the largely discredited fringe organization, the Institute for Historical Review, through articles in the Institute's publication, *The Journal of Historical Review.*

  1990s: New information about the Holocaust continues to make headlines. In 1995, the International Committee of the Red Cross (ICRC) admits its ''moral failure'' to come to the aid of the Jews during the Holocaust. In 1997 the organization releases its wartime files. Among the files is an exchange of letters from May, 1940, in which the World Jewish Congress asks the ICRC to investigate reports of the mass murder of Jewish prisoners of war. The ICRC responded several months later that the reports were unfounded. Also in 1997, Swiss banks release information on the dormant accounts opened by Holocaust victims before World War II. The banks are accused of hoarding the money of Holocaust victims.

- **1940s:** The horror of the Holocaust is reflected in the diary of a young Jewish girl who lives hidden away with her family above a shop in Amsterdam. *The Diary of Anne Frank* is published in 1947, two years after she dies in a concentration camp.

  1980s: *Schindler's List* is written by Thomas Keneally in 1982. The story focuses on Oskar Schindler, a German who saves the Jews working in his factory from the gas chambers. Other Holocaust survivor stories are told in works such as *To Save a Life: Stories of Jewish Rescue,* in 1984.

  1990s: The Holocaust becomes a topic of interest to the motion picture industry. *Schindler's List* is made into a movie by Steven Spielberg in 1993. The film wins seven Academy Awards, including Best Picture. In 1997, *The Populist*, a movie about Adolf Hitler's rise to power, which was aided by Ernst Hanfstaegl, the man who introduced Hitler to the wealthy financiers of the Third Reich, is planned.

---

term ''Aryan'' to designate members of what they believed to be a ''master race'' of non-Jewish white people, particularly those with Nordic features. Soon, kosher butchering was outlawed, as was the selling of Jewish newspapers in the street. In 1936, Jews lost the right to participate in German elections. In 1938, Jewish passports were marked with a ''J,'' all Jewish businesses were closed down, Jewish students were removed from German schools, and Jews were no longer allowed to attend plays, movies, concerts, or exhibitions. By 1939, Jews had to hand in their driver's licenses and car registrations, leave the universities, sell their businesses and real estate, and hand over securities and jewelry. By the middle of 1939, more than half of Germany's Jews had left for other countries. Many came to the United States.

By the end of 1939, Jews were beginning to be forced to wear yellow stars of David. Two years later, in 1941, the large-scale deportation of Jews to concentration camps began. Three years after that, only 15,000 Jews remained in Germany—down from over 500,000 eleven years earlier.

Ozick was five years old when Hitler became Chancellor; she was thirteen the year that extermination of Jews in concentration camps began in earnest. She was seventeen in 1945, the year the concentration camps were liberated and World War II ended. She grew up in a Jewish culture: her parents came from northwest Russia and from the Lithuanian Jewish tradition of that region. Her father, aside from being a pharmacist, was a Jewish scholar in Yiddish Hebrew. Ozick herself entered Jewish religious instruction at the age of five. Yet her entire youth was spent in a world where Jews were persecuted, then murdered, in Nazi-dominated countries, and refused sanctuary in most other countries, including her own United States.

Alongside the European events were Ozick's own difficulties with being a Jew in America. She calls the area of the Bronx where she was raised a place where it was "brutally difficult to be a Jew," and describes being called names and having stones thrown at her because she was Jewish. Ozick talks about the influence of history on her first published novel, *Trust.* She describes it has having been transformed from an American novel into a Jewish novel. "It's history as narration," she says, quoted in Lowin's *Cynthia Ozick,* "history as pageant almost." Jewish characters and the history of the Jewish people are at the center of much of Ozick's fiction.

Critical Overview

Both the story "The Shawl" and the later collection by the same name were very well received by critics. In a September 10, 1989, article in *The New York Times Book Review,* Francine Prose finds that Ozick "pulls off the rare trick of making art out of what we would rather not see." Barbara Hoffert, reviewing the story for the August, 1989, *Library Journal,* praises the work as "a subtle yet morally uncompromising tale that many will regard as a small gem." Reviewer Irving Halperin, writing of the collection in the December 15, 1989, issue of *Commonweal,* states that "In a time when the memory of the Holocaust is being trivialized by slick fiction, talk shows, and TV 'documentaries,' . . . Ozick's extraordinary volume is a particularly welcome achievement of the moral imagination."

In "The Shawl," Ozick continues to develop the body of work based on Jewish characters and themes that she has concentrated on for most of her writing career. According to Elaine M. Kauvar in *Cynthia Ozick's Fiction: Tradition and Invention* (1993), however, "The Shawl" represents the first time Ozick tells a tale "directly from the consciousness of a Holocaust survivor." Rosa, Stella, and Magda are fictional characters, but Ozick places them in a story filled with "facts gleaned from history and events derived from memoirs," Kauvar states. Ozick takes the reader into the minds of fictional characters, but these fictional characters walk in shoes we can easily imagine to have been inhabited by Jews living in Europe during Nazi rule. The effect is different from that of reading "about" the Holocaust; it is closer to the effect of walking through it. Kauvar believes that this is one element of "The Shawl" which makes it "undeniably of great importance" to Holocaust literature. Kauvar claims that this basis of history and memoir allows Ozick to penetrate "the individual psyche by apprehending the historical occurrences that shaped it." In another time and place, Rosa, Stella, and Magda might have made different decisions and acted differently than they do in "The Shawl." But they do not live in another time and place. This allows Ozick to demonstrate the extent to which human beings are affected by, even formed by, the time and place in which they live.

Kauvar also discusses the ways in which Ozick merges biography and fiction. Many Holocaust survivors have written biographical accounts of their experiences. Readers approach these accounts with the knowledge that, whatever these people have been through, the events occurred in an increasingly distant past, and the author whose work we are reading survived. While some may empathize with and attempt to understand the writer, the barrier of time makes it difficult for others to walk in the Holocaust survivor's shoes. Biography presents events. It might describe, it might analyze, but it rarely evokes. To evoke is to do what almost anyone who has taken any writing class has been told: to show rather than tell. Ozick does not talk about Rosa; she puts readers in Rosa's shoes. She does the same, though to a somewhat lesser extent, with Stella and Magda. The barrier of time disappears. Readers walk as the victims—both survivors and those who did not survive—walked: step-by-step, facing one decision at a time, never knowing what is to come.

"The Shawl" is often discussed in tandem with "Rosa," its sister story, which picks up on the stories of Rosa and Stella some thirty years later. "Rosa" is, again, evocative, dropping readers into the life of Rosa Lublin in the United States. The two stories share more than characters. They share themes and imagery: as Rosa's life in the camp was hell, her life thirty years later is a different form of hell, and the shawl that sheltered Magda appears again in the latter story. As one might expect, critics have examined the role of the shawl in these stories from the viewpoints of many schools of criticism. Though it plays a lesser role in ''Rosa,'' the shawl as a symbol is, perhaps, the most-discussed aspect of ''The Shawl.''

Criticism

Tery Griffin

Griffin has published several short stories and essays and has taught at Trinity College and at the University of Michigan. In the following essay, she discusses the significance of the shawl in Ozick's story.

There are many ways to approach a work of fiction, to decide what that work has to offer you. You can look at the plot: the events that happen and the order in which they occur. You can examine the characters who people the story: what can you learn from who they are and what they do? You can study the story's language, or the images—both obvious and suggested—that the writer uses.

In Cynthia Ozick's ''The Shawl,'' the images and language the author uses bring certain ideas to mind. This discussion will lead us to one of the things ''The Shawl'' imparts: a suggestion about how strong the human will to survive is and the lengths to which human beings will go to ensure their survival. The first and most obvious thing to consider upon finishing ''The Shawl'' is the shawl itself. It is clearly important, since the story is named after it. The shawl is also one of the most widely discussed parts of the story. It seems as if each critic who considers this story has his or her own interpretation of the shawl.

In his article ''Holocaust Responses I: Judaism as a Religious Value System,'' Alan L. Berger claims that the shawl ''is a literary symbol of the tallit,'' or Jewish prayer shawl. To wrap oneself in the tallit, he says, is to be surrounded ''by the holiness and protection of the commandments.'' Berger believes that one message of ''The Shawl'' is that ''Jewish religious creativity and covenantal symbolism can occur even under the most extreme conditions.'' In his interpretation, the shawl protects first Magda and later Rosa from the horrors that surround them in the same way that the Jewish religion protects the souls of Jews from the horrors of the world.

In an article in *Studies in American Jewish Literature,* Suzanne Klingenstein says ''the shawl functions in place of speech for both infant and mother and also as a kind of umbilical cord between the two characters.'' Klingenstein stresses the mother/daughter relationship in ''The Shawl'' and believes that this relationship is the heart of the story. The shawl is important because it represents the constant link between mother and daughter.

Andrew Gordon believes the shawl is a ''transitional object,'' an object that helps an infant make the transition from the state of being one with its mother to the recognition that it is an individual, separate from its mother. He states that Rosa, Stella, and Magda, ''in their need to possess the shawl can be considered as infants suffering extreme oral deprivation and in need of a mother.'' Gordon reads ''The Shawl'' as ''a story about delusion as a defense against an overwhelming reality, against loss of control, and against traumatic loss.'' In Gordon's interpretation, the shawl represents that delusion: it is an ''illusion'' which ''allows for magical thinking as a defense against anxiety in traumatic circumstances.'' Rosa can believe that the shawl can nourish and hide her baby.

While each of these interpretations has merit, it is possible to view the role of the shawl in the story in a less complicated way and have those views regarded as completely valid. To do this, simply examine what happens in the story and how the shawl relates to those events.

Death is omnipresent in ''The Shawl.'' Death is introduced in the opening paragraph, when the narrator explains that Rosa's breasts do not have enough milk to feed the baby Magda—who sometimes screams because there is nothing for her to suck except air—that Stella is also ravenous, and that Stella has knees that are ''tumors on sticks'' and elbows that are ''chicken bones.'' Later, twice in quick succession it is stated that Rosa thinks Stella is waiting for Magda to die. Readers are repeatedly told that Magda is going to die, and her death moves closer as the story progresses. First, Rosa knows Magda is going to die very soon, then today, then now. Finally, in one long scene that takes up nearly half the story, we watch as Magda dies. Death fills ''The Shawl.''

Survivors of the Nazi concentration camp at Dachau, Germany, greet Allied forces who liberated the camp in April, 1945, toward the end of World War II. Some 32,000 prisoners were in the camp at the time of its liberation.

The role of the shawl when we examine its relationship to death is to thwart death. It saves Magda from starvation. Throughout the story, as long as Magda remains hidden under the shawl, she remains alive. It is only when the shawl is taken from her that Magda dies. When Magda is murdered, Rosa stuffs the shawl into her own mouth, stifling a scream. If Rosa had screamed, the guards would have killed her, too.

Another prominent idea in "The Shawl" is the idea of hell. Hell is brought up in the first sentence, where we are told that Stella feels "cold, cold, the coldness of hell." We do not usually think of hell as being cold. It takes some thought, and perhaps some research, to realize that Ozick might be referring to Dante's *Inferno,* where the coldness at the center of hell is reserved for those who commit the worst of sins: betrayal.

At the opening of the story, Stella's coldness seems external. Her body is cold. As the story progresses, Stella's coldness is one of the things that causes her to steal Magda's shawl. We are told that

- Ozick's works of nonfiction—*Art and Ardor*, published in 1987, *Metaphor and Memory*, published in 1989, and *Fame and Folly*, published in 1996—discuss literature, Ozick's feelings about her art, and her ideas about the relationship between art and history.
- Ozick's story "Rosa," published in *The New Yorker* in 1983, then in a short story collection paired with "The Shawl," picks up the story of Rosa and Stella some thirty years after the final scene of "The Shawl." It carries over some of the themes and images from the earlier story.
- Elie Wiesel's memoir *Night* (1960) portrays Wiesel's own experiences as a teenager imprisoned in two concentration camps, Auschwitz and Buchenwald. At least one critic, Elaine Kauvar, believes there are allusions to *Night* in "The Shawl."
- Anne Frank's *The Diary of Anne Frank* describes the life of a Jewish family trying to elude capture by the Nazis in Amsterdam during World War II. It is written by a young Jewish girl, a girl of about the age that Stella is in "The Shawl."

after the theft and Magda's death, Stella is "always cold, always. The cold went into her heart: Rosa saw that Stella's heart was cold." The repetition of the words "cold" and "always" helps to ensure that the reader notices the coldness. That repetition occurs immediately following the only place in the story where we actually hear Stella's words, as she explains that she stole Magda's shawl because "I was cold." This single short patch of dialogue also serves to draw the reader's attention to the coldness.

Because the coldness is so closely associated with Stella, it might be easy to conclude that the hell only relates to her. But we are also told that the concentration camp they are in is "a place without pity" and that "all pity was annihilated"—a word associated with death—"in Rosa." The hell is all around them and inside them. The closing scene, where we watch step by step as the baby Magda is electrocuted, is surely an image of hell.

The role of the shawl when we examine its relationship to hell is to comfort, and perhaps to make this hell a little less wretched. At the story's beginning, Magda is comforted by being in her mother's arms, "wrapped in a shawl . . . rocked by the march." Rosa is also somewhat comforted, since her baby is safe for the moment. The shawl also represents comfort to Stella, though it is not comforting to her at this moment. She envies Magda for being wrapped in the shawl and rocked in her mother's arms. She wishes the comfort represented by the shawl could be hers.

The shawl's ability to hide Magda at this point saves her life. The shawl saves her life in another way too—it is a magic shawl which can "nourish an infant for three days and three nights." Its ability to stave off starvation is another source of comfort for Magda and Rosa. As Magda becomes older, the shawl comforts the girl in another way. It becomes her "baby, her pet, her little sister." It even causes her to laugh "when the wind blew its corners." Stella still envies Magda's shawl, which she is now not even allowed to touch.

Stella's desperate need for some bit of comforting, however small, is one of the reasons she finally takes Magda's shawl for herself. She covers herself with it—perhaps gaining some tiny measure of warmth along with the security of being covered by the magic shawl—and falls asleep. Magda, having lost her comforter, wanders into the barracks square screaming. She is discovered by the Nazi guards and immediately killed. As this occurs, Rosa runs to the barracks and retrieves the shawl. The thought that she might be able to use it to somehow save Magda comforts her momentarily. But she cannot save Magda. Now the shawl's role of saving people returns: Rosa fills her mouth with the shawl, stifling

> "The shawl can be seen as an object used to show us how strong the human will to survive is."

her scream. If she had screamed, she too would have been killed.

The shawl is not a great or impressive item. Yet, at least in the minds of the characters in this story, the shawl is able to save and to comfort. Perhaps the shawl can be seen as an object used to show us how strong the human will to survive is. It is a small thing, but it is the only thing available to these people in this situation. They turn to it, reaching for whatever chance for survival it might offer.

Source: Tery Griffin, ''Overview of 'The Shawl','' in *Short Stories for Students,* Gale, 1998 .

Andrew Gordon

In the following excerpt, Gordon analyzes the function of the shawl in Ozick's story in terms of concepts drawn from psychoanalysis.

Cynthia Ozick's ''The Shawl'' (1980) is a Holocaust story about a mother struggling heroically but in vain to save her baby in a death camp. Brief and poetically compressed—two thousand words, just two pages in its original publication in *The New Yorker*—it has a shattering impact. Ozick manages to avoid the common pitfalls of Holocaust fiction: on the one hand, she does not sentimentalize, but on the other, she does not numb the reader with a succession of horrifying events. She works largely through metaphor, ''indirection and concentration'' [according to Joseph Lowin, *Cynthia Ozick,* 1988]. For example, the words ''Jew,'' ''Nazi,'' ''concentration camp,'' or even ''war'' are never mentioned; these would arouse the kind of immediate, unearned responses Ozick eschews. We do not know what year it is or what country. As the story opens, we only know that three female characters —Rosa, her fifteen-month-old baby Magda, and a fourteen-year-old girl named Stella (only in a sequel story, ''Rosa'' [1983], do we learn that Stella is Rosa's niece)—are being marched, exhausted and starving, toward an unknown destination. Two details—the word ''Aryan'' and the mention of yellow stars sewn into their coats —allow us to fill in the rest. The historical and political context disappears, and the focus narrows to the feelings of three characters as they struggle to survive moment by moment in extreme circumstances: ''They were in a place without pity.'' Rosa, the central character, could be any mother who wants to keep her baby alive against impossible odds. This is a story about the oppression of women: there is no mention of Magda's father, and the only male referred to is the guard who murders Magda, a faceless monster described in terms of a helmet, ''a black body like a domino and a pair of black boots.''

I want to consider the central symbol of the story, the shawl in which Magda is wrapped, which I believe functions in a way similar to what D. W. Winnicott would call a ''transitional object'' [*Playing and Reality,* 1971]. But the shawl serves not only as a transitional object for the infant in the story but also as the focus of the conflict, and while it passes from hand to hand among the three characters, it becomes a totem or fetish for the teenage Stella and the mother Rosa as well. The shawl suggests the necessity for illusion, for magical thinking as a defense against anxiety in traumatic circumstances, but also the ways in which healthy illusion can easily shift into unhealthy delusion. As Winnicott writes, ''I am therefore studying the substance of *illusion,* that which is allowed to the infant, and which in adult life is inherent in art and religion, and yet becomes a hallmark of madness.'' Rosa, Stella, and Magda form a group on the basis of their shared illusion concerning [what is described in the story as] the ''magic shawl.'' (Although the infant's use of the shawl is understandable, Rosa and Stella's belief in it is a sign of desperation, of regression and the breakdown of rationality in the face of extreme deprivation and loss. Transitional phenomena, Winnicott explains, eventually become diffused and spread ''over the whole cultural field,'' including such generally healthy activities as play, art, and religion, but also such neurotic manifestations as ''fetishism'' and ''the talisman of obsessional rituals.'' The shawl in Ozick's story, I believe, functions as a transitional object which later changes into an infantile fetish for the baby, and for the teenager and the mother it definitely becomes a fetish or magical talisman.

The transitional object, Winnicott explains, is the infant's ''first 'not-me' possession,'' (1) something which is both found and created, both inner and outer, and stands in for the breast. The object, which may be a bit of cloth or a security blanket, comes at an intermediate stage of development between thumb-sucking and attachment to a toy or doll. It exists in an intermediate area "between the subjective and that which is objectively perceived." "The object represents the infant's transition from a state of being merged with the mother to a state of being in relation with the mother as something outside and separate."

If the transitional object is a form of defense against the loss of the breast and separation from the mother [Elizabeth Wright, *Psychoanalytic Criticum: Theory in Practice,* 1984], then all three characters in "The Shawl"—the baby, the teenager, and the mother—in their need to possess the shawl can be considered as infants suffering extreme oral deprivation and in need of a mother. Here is the opening paragraph:

> Stella, cold, cold, the coldness of hell. How they walked on the roads together, Rosa with Magda curled up between sore breasts. Magda wound up in the shawl. Sometimes Stella carried Magda. But she was jealous of Magda. A thin girl of fourteen, too small, with thin breasts of her own. Stella wanted to be wrapped in a shawl, hidden away, asleep, rocked by the march, a baby, a round infant in arms. Magda took Rosa's nipple, and Rosa never stopped walking, a walking cradle. There was not enough milk; sometimes Magda sucked air; then she screamed. Stella was ravenous. Her knees were tumors on sticks, her elbows chicken bones.

The keynotes of oral deprivation, inadequate mothering, and the desire to revert to infancy are established in this opening: Rosa is defined as a mother with sore breasts who can no longer adequately feed her infant. Magda is suffering from forced weaning. Stella too is starving—she has been turned into a thing resembling sticks or the skeleton of a chicken. Stella, a teenager, "in a stage between childhood and adulthood" [according to Margot Martin, in *RE: Artes Liberales,* Spring-Fall, 1989], longs to revert to infancy, symbolized by her desire to be wrapped in and mothered by the shawl that protects Magda.

By the second paragraph, Rosa's milk has entirely dried up and Magda has relinquished the breast and turned to the shawl as a surrogate breast: "The duct crevice extinct, a dead volcano, blind eye, chill hole, so Magda took the corner of the shawl and milked it instead." At the same time, Stella moves from desiring the shawl to seeming to want to devour Magda: "Stella gazed at Magda like a young cannibal. . . . it sounded to Rosa as if Stella had said 'Let us devour her'. . . . She was sure that Stella was waiting for Magda to die so she could put her teeth into the little thighs."

"The shawl suggests the necessity for illusion, for magical thinking as a defense against anxiety in traumatic circumstances."

While the ravenous Stella regresses to a stage of oral sadism, the starving Rosa also seems to regress to infancy: "she learned from Magda how to drink the taste of a finger in one's mouth." The shawl becomes Magda's means of survival: "It was a magic shawl, it could nourish an infant for three days and three nights." Magda grows silent and guarded: she stops crying and never seems to sleep. Her silence and the shawl keep her alive: "Rosa knew Magda was going to die very soon; she should have been dead already, but she had been buried away deep inside the magic shawl, mistaken there for the shivering mound of Rosa's breast." But Rosa fears that Magda has become a deaf-mute from the experience.

For Magda, this shawl has become everything: mother, food, clothing, and shelter.

> She watched like a tiger. She guarded her shawl. No one could touch it; only Rosa could touch it. Stella was not allowed. The shawl was Magda's own baby, her pet, her little sister. She tangled herself up in it and sucked on one of the corners when she wanted to be very still.

At this point, it is appropriate to ask whether this shawl is truly a transitional object for Magda or instead an infantile fetish. According to Phyllis Greenacre, the transitional object is an aid to growth that results from healthy development when the child has a good-enough mother. But the infantile fetish results from a disturbance in development, when the mothering is not good enough or "the infant has suffered unusually severe deprivation" [*International Journal of Psychoanalysis,* 1970]. The fetish "grows out of early inadequate object relations and, through its crystallization, tends to constrict their further development." It has some similarities to "the fetish in adult perversion." Considering the trauma that Magda has suffered—a terrorized mother, exposure to a hostile, constantly life-threatening environment, premature weaning and starvation—and the hysterical mutism that she develops, her attachment to the shawl seems to partake more of the neurotic fetish than of the healthy transitional object.

Greenacre mentions that fetishistic phenomena usually appear after weaning at the end of the first year, which corresponds to Magda's case. The fetish begins "at about the time that the transitional object may be adopted by infants most of whom seem less disturbed. The fetish here seems to represent the feeding function even more strongly than is true of the transitional object," which also holds in Magda's case: because she is starving, she has practically nothing to feed on but the shawl. Greenacre mentions an instance of infantile fetishism which strongly resembles Magda's behavior, in which a blanket was "of great magical effectiveness in quieting severe disturbances of infantile separation anxiety and even of physical pain." When head lice and body lice bite Magda and "crazed her so that she became as wild as one of the big rats that plundered the barracks . . . , she rubbed and scratched and kicked and bit and rolled without a whimper." Her silence is abnormal behavior for an infant, just as her relationship to the shawl seems far more intense than the healthy connection of a baby to a transitional object.

But one sunny afternoon, Stella appropriates the shawl for herself and goes to sleep beneath it in the barracks. She wants some of the mothering power associated with the shawl. "Thus, by losing her magical shawl, Magda loses the magical charm that apparently protects her from death for so long."

Rosa is outside and sees Magda toddling into the sunlight, howling for the lost shawl, screaming "Maaaa—." It is the first sound she has made since Rosa's milk dried up, and the only word she speaks in the story. It seems a cry for both shawl and mother, which for her have become synonymous. "Magda was going to die, and at the same time a fearful joy ran in Rosa's two palms": the joy comes from realizing that her baby can speak, the fear from the ironic fact that the noise has doomed Magda. Only her continued silence would have saved her.

Rosa finds the shawl and tears it away from Stella: the object of struggle has now passed among all three characters. Then, under the influence of "voices" she imagines she hears in the electrified fence (one can take this as another sign of her derangement, although a critic reads these voices as symbolic of the Jewish dead [Lowin 109]), Rosa runs outside again and waves the shawl like a flag to attract Magda's attention. The shawl is now a banner representing life and faith and hope. But it is too late: a guard has already seized the baby, carries her off, and abruptly tosses her to her death against the fence.

The few minutes leading up to Magda's destruction take up over half the narrative. The murder is described in slow motion and beautiful metaphors to intensify both the suspense and the horror. Magda's arms reach out to the shawl and to her mother, but she recedes into the distance, becoming a "speck" and "no bigger than a moth." When she is hurled at the fence, she turns into a floating angel: "All at once Magda was swimming through the air. The whole of Magda traveled through loftiness. She looked like a butterfly touching a silver vine."

Through metaphor, the moment of death becomes a moment of magical transfiguration. As she watches her baby murdered, there is nothing further Rosa can do without endangering her own life. The voices of the fence urge her to run to Magda. But "Rosa's instinct for self-preservation overcomes both her maternal instincts and any heroic urges she may have had" (Lowin 109). The final sentence of the story (which, for the sake of emphasis, is also its longest sentence) shows the shawl now becoming a transitional object for Rosa:

> She only stood, because if she ran they would shoot, and if she tried to pick up the sticks of Magda's body they would shoot, and if she let the wolf's screech ascending now through the ladder of her skeleton break out, they would shoot; so she took Magda's shawl and filled her own mouth with it, stuffed it in and stuffed it in, until she was swallowing up the wolf's screech and tasting the cinnamon and almond depth of Magda's saliva; and Rosa drank Magda's shawl until it dried.

By stifling her screams, the shawl becomes a means of survival for Rosa, as it had been for Magda. And the shawl nurtures her, filling her mouth, just as it had done for Magda. Finally, as the shawl had become a surrogate mother for Magda, so it becomes a surrogate baby for Rosa. "Magda's cinnamon and almond breath has permeated her shawl, which now become synonymous with her spirit." In drinking the shawl, she is devouring her dead infant [according to Barbara Scrafford, *Critique,* Fall 1989], although this is a symbolic cannibalism, unlike the butchery of the death camps or the lethal selfishness of Stella. To put it another way, Rosa is attempting to reincorporate Magda in order to mourn her.

Thus I read "The Shawl" as a story about delusion as a defense against an overwhelming reality, against loss of control, and against traumatic loss. I see it as a story about separation, isolation, death, and thwarted mourning. The three characters are together, yet each suffers alone: Stella separates herself by her selfishness and Magda by withdrawing into the substitute womb of her shawl. Magda dies alone, and Rosa is powerless either to prevent her death or even to embrace her dead baby or mourn aloud her loss. In this environment, simply being human can condemn you to death, so you must suppress your humanity. The isolation and separation are also expressed metaphorically. Characters are never seen whole but reduced to body parts or things: Rosa is "sore breasts" and "a walking cradle," Stella has elbows like "chicken bones," Magda shows "one mite of a toothtip . . . an elfin tombstone of white marble", and the guard is merely a helmet, "a black body like a domino and a pair of black boots." This is a vivid, terrifying world of part objects and fetish objects which never approaches the world of whole object relations.

Any infant is in a condition of helplessness and absolute dependence; through attachment to the transitional object, it begins to come to terms with reality and with the separateness of the mother as an object in her own right. If the mothering is insufficient or the environment hostile, the infant may instead latch onto a fetish object. As prisoners of the Holocaust, the teenage Stella and the grown Rosa are thrust back into the helplessness of infants, infants with a monster parent. The Nazi state becomes a cannibal, annihilating and devouring its offspring. Finally, to survive such intolerable circumstances, these desperately needful characters resort to magical thinking. Each seizes upon Magda's shawl as a magical object, a substitute for the good mother, the only thing on which an assurance of survival or a sense of identity can be grounded. And for all three characters, the transitional object shades over into a fetish object and a healthy *illusion* becomes instead a neurotic *delusion.*

In 1983, Ozick wrote a sequel to "The Shawl" entitled "Rosa." This story takes place in Miami Beach thirty years after the events of "The Shawl"; Rosa has survived the Holocaust but is mentally unstable. She denies her daughter's death and fantasizes that Magda is a married woman, a successful doctor or professor. And she now worships as a religious relic the only object left from her daughter: the shawl. As Greenacre writes, "The relation of illusion to the fixed delusion might be roughly compared to that of the transitional object to the fetish."

Source: Andrew Gordon, "Cynthia Ozick's 'The Shawl' and the Transitional Object," in *Literature and Psychology,* Vol. XXXX, Nos. 1 & 2, 1994, pp. 1–9.

Barbara Scrafford

Scrafford is affiliated with San Francisco State University. In the following excerpt, she discusses the theme of motherhood in "The Shawl" and examines how characterization and imagery contribute to the development of this theme.

In her award-winning short story, "The Shawl," Cynthia Ozick reveals the mind of a mother slogging her way through the ashes of the dead. Set in a Nazi concentration camp, the story does not focus on the political decision to exterminate an entire race, nor on the crimes and their perpetrators, but on the mind of Rosa and her struggle to keep her infant alive, despite the fact that the child's only future is certain death. Ozick's short sentences and concise syntax move quickly and efficiently forward to tell the story with a minimum of rhetoric. The story is only a few pages long, and Ozick exposes Rosa's mind to her reader, capturing what might have been days or even weeks as if it were only a moment. Her succinct story-telling gives us no direct information about Stella's relationship to Rosa and does not tell us explicitly where the story is set. Ozick focuses only on Rosa, Rosa only on Magda, and Magda only on the shawl. Containing no extraneous descriptions, scene-setting, or narration, the story is a skeleton of itself. All that is left is what gives it shape.

The story derives much of its power from ironic contrast. The setting is barbarous, a place built to end lives; the theme—motherhood—implies the continuity of life. Rosa struggles to keep her small daughter alive as long as possible, knowing all the while that the baby will not live. Although it would be easy for a writer to become sentimental with such material, Ozick does not blink in her rendering of the tale. Flowers and turds, butterflies and electric fences, innocence and depravity move the story rhythmically forward to the final crescendo. Ozick never explains the world we enter with her. The reader is pulled into the march without knowing where the writer is taking him or her, just as the Jews marched to their deaths without being told their destination. A young girl's legs are tumors on sticks; a child's hair is as yellow as the star sewn

> "Rosa is reduced to complete primitivity, the voices of instinct growling within her. Like a cornered wild animal, she devours her young in the form of the shawl."

to its mother's coat. Then we know where we are headed.

The characters are Rosa, Magda, and Stella—a mother, her baby, and a young girl. Rosa and Magda take center stage, the shawl winding around mother and child like an umbilical cord.

> Rosa knew Magda was going to die very soon; she would have been dead already, but she had been buried way deep inside the magic shawl, mistaken there for the shivering mound of Rosa's breasts; Rosa clung to the shawl as if it covered only herself. No one took it away from her.

Rosa, of course, symbolizes the maternal instinct. A walking cradle, she desperately hides her baby from its predators, secreting her in the barracks and nursing her with dry breasts—"dead volcanoes."

Through the breast motif, Magda is strongly associated with nourishment. Her mother's breasts extinct, she learns to milk a corner of the shawl and teaches Rosa to drink the taste of a finger. Her mother gives her share of the food to Magda who, in turn, provides spiritual sustenance for Rosa. Magda's hair is like feathers; she is variously described as a moth and a butterfly, and her breath, suggestive of the spirit, is flavored with cinnamon and almond. But Magda is also the center of the ominous theme of cannibalism. Rosa seems obsessed by the idea that "someone, not even Stella, would steal Magda to eat her." "Aryan," Stella says. But Rosa hears, "Let us devour her."

It seems odd, does it not, that the story of Rosa and Magda should begin with a paragraph devoted mainly to Stella?

> Stella, cold, cold, the coldness of hell. How they walked on the roads together, Rosa with Magda curled up between sore breasts, Magda wound up in the shawl. Sometimes Stella carried Magda. But she was jealous of Magda. A thin girl of fourteen, too small, with thin breasts of her own, Stella wanted to be wrapped in a shawl, hidden away, asleep, rocked by the march, a baby, a round infant in arms. Magda took Rosa's nipple, and Rosa never stopped walking, a walking cradle. There was not enough milk; sometimes Magda sucked air; then she screamed. Stella was ravenous. Her knees were tumors on sticks, her elbows chicken bones.

Although Rosa and Magda are also introduced in this paragraph, each reference to the mother and child is countered with comments on Stella's character. Cold Stella. Jealous Stella. Ravenous, tumor-kneed, chicken-elbowed Stella. She says little and seemingly performs only one function in the story—the stealing of little Magda's shawl, which leads to the death of the child. Although she is responsible for Magda's death, she is not in this sense necessary to the story. Anything could have happened to the shawl. Another prisoner could have taken it; it could have blown away on the ash-stippled wind. Why, then, did Ozick include her? Stella does not emerge as a character in the way that Rosa and Magda do. We are not privy to her emotions. She does not laugh, cry, suck. The narrator allows us to see Magda crazed by lice, calmed by the shawl's linen milk, furious when she finally loses her little pet. We see Rosa's dried nipples, see her withered thigh hold the child secure through the night. Usurper of the shawl, tumor-legged Stella is also the focal point of Rosa's fears that Magda will be eaten. Stella—the first word in the story—means "star," but Stella is not a radiant shining star, giving off energy of its own. Ozick tells us that she is cold, and the rhythm of the sentence "Stella, cold, cold, the coldness of hell" has a dirge-like quality. Stella, then, is a burned-out—a dead—star. Rather than giving off light, she reflects the light of others.

Implicit in Stella's name is the idea of reflection. We know so little of her—only through Rosa's perceptions. Stella functions as a mirror of the larger situation. In the first paragraph, Rosa and Magda are described in terms of the struggle of their oppression—the long walk, the sore breasts, and the dearth of mother's milk—while Stella is described in terms of the results of a struggle lost. She has become jealous of an infant, and, while the author speaks of Magda's attempt to suckle and nourish herself, Stella shows the results of starvation: "Her knees were tumors on sticks, her elbows chicken bones."

Twice in the story the narrator refers to the other inmates of the camp through references to Stella. Rosa is afraid that "someone, not *even* Stella, [will] steal Magda to eat her" (emphasis added). Later, when she speaks of her imagined voices in the humming electric fence, Rosa says that "*even* Stella said it was only an imagining" (emphasis added). In both these sentences, the use of the word "even" preceding Stella's name implies the reflection of the other inmates in Stella's impulses and perceptions.

A forerunner of the cannibalism motif is the imagery of nourishment introduced in the first paragraph: thin, dry breasts; a hungry babe; a walking cradle; tiny lips sucking air. Rosa's mother-love forces her to give to Magda beyond her physical and emotional capabilities. She has become lighter than air, a "floating angel . . . teetering on the tips of her fingernails." She is in a trance-like state, a state in which one's intellect is suspended and one's instincts take over. Rosa never considers her own needs but lives only for her child. Although she is afraid of the pitiless Stella, Rosa is also without pity when she looks at the young girl:

> They were in a place without pity, all pity was annihilated in Rosa, she looked at Stella's bones without pity. She was sure that Stella was waiting for Magda to die so she could put her teeth into the little thighs.

Stella is a reflection of the others in the camp, and Rosa's feelings toward her extend to those who share her fate. Her mothering instinct is her only surviving drive. Her milk is gone; her body is going; she is reduced, a "walking cradle," to instinct alone. As her daughter enters the arena screaming for her shawl, Rosa does not react with her mind but with her body. A "tide of commands" hammers in Rosa's nipples, the physical emblem of motherhood. "Fetch," they tell her, "get, bring!," reducing language to its simplest form, suggestive of the way a trainer speaks to animals. The "grainy sad voices crowd her," telling her "to hold up the shawl, high; . . . to shake it, to whip with it, to unfurl it like a flag," in one last attempt to satisfy Magda's needs. At the moment of Magda's impact, the voices of instinct—in a mad, frenzied growling—urge Rosa to the little pile of bones. But this time the voices that signify maternal instinct conflict with another instinct in Rosa, one she is for the first time free to respond to—the instinct of self-preservation. She does not run to her dead child's body "because if she ran they would shoot," and if she screamed, they would also shoot. The wolf's screech ascending through her body and the instinctive reaction of a mother to the death of her young oppose the will to survive as she stifles her scream with the magic shawl. She says she is "swallowing" the wolf's screech, but she also seems to be trying to ingest the shawl, tasting her daughter's saliva, drinking it dry.

In this powerful final picture, all of the story's themes and images coalesce. Rosa is now reduced to a wild animal, a howling wolf, suggesting the previous bestial images: a vulnerable baby squirrel in a nest that becomes a lice-crazed rat, a grinning tiger. We are reminded also of Magda's sucking of the shawl, and "the shawl's good flavor, milk of linen." Rosa sucks the shawl until it dries, just as Magda drinks all that Rosa's withered nipples can offer. Magda's cinnamon and almond breath has permeated her shawl, which now becomes synonymous with her spirit. Stella and the cannibalism Rosa associates with her are also implicitly present in this scene. The young girl symbolizes the ashes of the death camps. She belongs to those who have lost their humanity and who, like biological creatures only, struggle merely to stay alive. These are cold stars, who have no life of their own. They bring only their bodies to their imprisonment. Rosa is obsessed by the fear that Stella will cannibalize Magda, but she also knows that others also want what she suspects Stella of wanting.

As Rosa stuffs the shawl into her mouth, drinking the "cinnamon and almond depth of Magda's saliva," the cannibalism motif is revealed not to be the desperate act of a degraded and debased fourteen-year-old, but a symbolic final frantic attempt by Rosa to protect her offspring. Rosa is reduced to complete primitivity, the voices of instinct growling within her. Like a cornered wild animal, she devours her young in the form of the shawl. Many animals, when cornered by a predator, do the same, for if the mother dies, the young will suffer a far worse fate at the jowls of the attacker. Rosa's motherhood is her total existence. The only parts of her body described for us are her breasts and her thighs. Her every move is dictated by the needs of her child, to the exclusion of all others. She feels no pity for her fellow prisoners, not even Stella. A "walking cradle," she lives only for the survival of her young.

In "The Shawl," Ozick gives us a mother frantically trying to nurture her child in the ashes of the dead. Like a panicked animal, she desperately tries to hide her little squirrel from the predator. She knows Magda will not live, yet she protects her with

> "Ozick strongly implies that the camps, designed to turn Jews into matter and then to destroy that matter, although successful to an awesome and staggering degree, were not able to achieve complete domination of the Jewish soul."

the magic shawl, gives her own meager offerings of food to the silent little mouth, and guards her at night with her own body. Stella and the others, reflections of the massacred six million, fade into the shadows, as the author hones in on Rosa to show us what it is like to be a mother in the time of the hunted.

Source: Barbara Scrafford, "Nature's Silent Scream: A Commentary on Cynthia Ozick's 'The Shawl'," in *Critique: Studies in Contemporary Fiction,* Vol. XXXI, No. 1, Fall, 1989, pp. 11–15.

Alan R. Berger

Berger teaches at Syracuse University. In the following excerpt, he argues that Ozick's use of symbolism in "The Shawl" contributes to the story's theme of Jewish endurance in the face of horrendous suffering

Cynthia Ozick has written that "stories ought to judge and interpret the world." But universal meaning can only be derived from particularistic experience, "Literature," she has written, "is the recognition of the particular." Responding to the Holocaust requires not only an encounter with, but a struggle to redeem from, evil. Ozick's "redemptive literature" is embedded in biblical, rabbinic, and mystical symbolism. . . .

"The Shawl" (1980), . . . is a unique story because it directly confronts the horrors of a death camp experience. The tale, told from the perspective of an omniscient narrator, concerns three Jewesses; Rosa, her infant daughter Magda, and her adolescent niece Stella. The story centers around Rosa's unsuccessful attempt to keep Magda—who is wrapped in a mysterious shawl—alive. In the brief space of two pages Ozick paints the familiar but no less terrifying landscape of death and torment which was the fate of Europe's Jews; forced marches, starvation, dehumanization, the filth of death camps, murder, and the indifference of the world. She spares no detail of Jewish misery. For example, Rosa contemplates giving Magda to a stranger during the course of their march toward certain death. Rosa thinks, however, that if she left the line of prisoners she would be shot. But supposing she managed to hand the shawl-wrapped infant to an unknown woman, would the stranger take the precious package? Or would she drop it, splitting Magda's head open? Countless thousands of Jewish women had to confront this dilemma, one which makes King Solomon's decision seem a pale thing in comparison.

Both on the march and in the camp itself, the shawl provides life-giving sustenance. When Rosa's own sore breasts were dry, Magda sucked on the corner of the shawl and "milked it instead," with the smell of "cinnamon and almonds" emanating from Magda's mouth. Ozick twice describes the nurturer as a "magic shawl"; one which could "nourish an infant for three days and three nights." Although pitifully undernourished, Magda lived long enough to walk. Rosa gave the child almost all of her own food. Stella, on the other hand, was envious of Magda whom she gazed at "like a young cannibal," and to whom she gave no food. Rosa's premonitions about Magda's impending death grew increasingly strong. The Jews were, writes Ozick, "in a place without pity." Toddling across the roll call area without her shawl Magda is murdered by a guard who throws her onto the camp's electrified fence. Rosa, watching from a distance, is helpless; able only to stuff the shawl into her own mouth in order to swallow "the wolf's screech ascending now through the ladder of her skeleton." Rosa tasted "the cinnamon and almond depth of Magda's saliva," drinking the shawl dry.

Ozick has masterfully combined covenant Judaism and a mystical parapsychology as responses to the pervasive hopelessness of the death camps. The magic shawl is a literary symbol of the tallit. Although women were freed from the so-called time-bound *mitzvot* (commandments), such as wearing a prayer shawl, Jewesses have donned this ritual object. The Talmud tells, for example, that Rabbi Judah the Prince, editor of the Mishnah (second century C. E.), affixed *tzitzit* (tallit fringes) to his wife's apron (Menahot 43a). Wrapping oneself in a prayer shawl is tantamount to being surrounded by the holiness and protection of the commandments; as well as conforming to the will of God. The wearer of the tallit is a member of the covenant community. Ozick's shawl/tallit is a talisman which protects both Rosa and Magda when they either wear or hold it. Separated from the shawl, Magda dies.The shawl saves Rosa as well. If she had screamed at her daughter's murder she would herself have been murdered since the Nazis, amplifying the edict of Pharaoh, had decreed that having a Jewish child was an offense punishable by death.

Rosa is also portrayed as being literally above the earth, or able to overcome history. Ozick employs a variety of words to suggest that Rosa, like her subsequent literary heir Feingold in ''Levitation,'' can fly. For example, Rosa, while on the march, was ''already a floating angel.'' Magda's mother ''flew, she could fly, she was only air.'' Magda, for her part, is also described in flight imagery. Riding on the shoulders of her Nazi murderer, she is ''high up, elevated.'' She appeared—hurtling toward the death fence —as a ''butterfly touching a silver vine.'' Rosa is also clairaudient; she hears ''grainy sad voices'' coming from the fence. What do these phenomena signify?

Ozick strongly implies that the camps, designed to turn Jews into matter and then to destroy that matter, although successful to an awesome and staggering degree, were not able to achieve complete domination of the Jewish soul. The peculiar aroma of cinnamon and almonds, itself so out of place in the midst of death, corpses, and wind bearing the black ash from crematoria, evokes a quasimystical image of the *besamim* (spice) box. Jews sniff the *besamim* at the *havadalah* ceremony which marks the outgoing of the Sabbath, thereby sustaining themselves for the rigors and tribulations of the profane or ordinary days of the week. By utilizing the prayer shawl and spice box imagery, and paranormal phenomena usually associated with the mystical element of Judaism, Ozick's tale conveys the message that the bleakness of the historical moment is not the final chapter in Jewish existence. Jewish religious creativity and covenantal symbolism can occur even under the most extreme conditions. . . .

Source: Alan R. Berger, ''Holocaust Responses I: Judaism as a Religious Value System,'' in *Crisis and Covenant: The Holocaust in American Jewish Fiction,* State University of New York Press, 1985, pp. 39–90.

Sources

Halperin, Irving. ''The Shawl,'' in *Commonweal,* Vol. 116, December 15, 1989, pp. 7-11.

Hoffert, Barbara. ''The Shawl,'' in *Library Journal,* Vol. 114, August, 1989, p. 165.

Kauvar, Elaine M. *Cynthia Ozick's Fiction: Tradition & Invention,* Indiana University Press, 1993.

Klingenstein, Suzanne. ''Destructive Intimacy: The Shoah Between Mother and Daughter in Fictions by Cynthia Ozick, Norma Rosen and Rebecca Goldstein,'' in *Studies in American Jewish Literature,* Vol. 11, No. 2, Fall, 1992, pp. 162- 73.

Prose, Francine. A review of ''The Shawl,'' in *The New York Times Book Review,* September 10, 1989, p. 1, 39.

Further Reading

Chartock, Roselle and Jack Spence, eds. *The Holocaust Years: Society on Trial,* Bantam Books, 1978.
One of many histories of the Holocaust, Chartock and Spencer's book is notable for its clear chronology of the events in Europe from 1933 to 1945; its discussions of prejudice and scapegoating, and behavior under stress; and many essays in the words of witnesses and of Nazis themselves.

Cohen, Sarah Blacher. *Cynthia Ozick's Comic Art: From Levity to Liturgy,* Indiana University Press, 1994.
Cohen concentrates on Ozick's use of irony in her work.

Lowin, Joseph. *Cynthia Ozick,* Twayne Publishers, 1988.
Lowin's book provides an excellent overview of Ozick's life and work. It includes a biographical section and sections on many of Ozick's works of fiction , including ''The Shawl.''

Ozick, Cynthia. *Art & Ardor,* Knopf, 1983.
A collection of Ozick's essays about literature and writing, including essays discussing her struggles to discover what it means to be a Jew, and the writer's material—including the Holocaust.

Ozick, Cynthia. *Fame & Folly,* Knopf, 1996.
A collection of Ozick's essays about literature and writing. Includes essays on the relationship of the artist to his or her material, and the relationship of history to literature.

Shiloh

Bobbie Ann Mason

1982

After appearing initially in the *New Yorker* magazine in 1982, Bobbie Ann Mason's story ''Shiloh'' became the title story in her first collection of fiction, *Shiloh and Other Stories,* also published in 1982. The volume was well-received by critics and earned nominations for a National Book Critics Circle Award, an American Book Award, and a PEN/Faulkner Award. Mason also won the 1983 Ernest Hemingway Foundation Award for best first fiction. ''Shiloh'' has been widely anthologized in literature texts, and critics have demonstrated an ongoing interest in the story.

Readers and critics admire ''Shiloh'' for the author's spare, unadorned style and her ear for rural Southern speech patterns. Set in western Kentucky, ''Shiloh'' is the story of a disabled truck driver, Leroy Moffitt, and his wife, Norma Jean. Like Mason's other fictional characters, the Moffitts are rural, working-class Southerners who are affected by the changing culture in which they live. Norma Jean, Leroy, and Mabel Beasley—Norma Jean's mother—are locked in a struggle over the Moffitts' marriage, a struggle that culminates at the Shiloh Civil War battlefield. Through this story, Mason addresses the theme of individual identity in a time of social change. As the landscape of rural Kentucky changes, so do the cultural forces exerting pressure on the Moffitts' marriage.

Author Biography

Bobbie Ann Mason was born on May 1, 1940, and grew up on a farm in western Kentucky outside the small town of Mayfield. She attended Mayfield High School and wrote for the school newspaper, and after graduation she went to the University of Kentucky.

Her first job out of college was writing for fan magazines in New York City. Eventually, she earned a master's degree and then a doctorate before becoming a part-time college journalism professor. Before she began writing fiction, she published two books of nonfiction, one on the writer Vladimir Nabokov and the other titled *The Girl Sleuth: A Feminist Guide to the Bobbsey Twins, Nancy Drew, and Their Sisters.*

Mason had nineteen stories rejected by the *New Yorker* magazine before her story ''Offerings'' was accepted. Mason models her characters on people she sees around her in rural Kentucky. Mayfield, like her fictional settings, is a landscape undergoing transition. In a *Time* review of *Shiloh and Other Stories,* R. Z. Sheppard coined the term ''ruburb'' to describe her settings. A ruburb is a place that is no longer rural but not yet suburban, a place where subdivisions of new houses pop up amongst corn fields.

In a 1985 interview with Lila Havens, Mason said, ''I am generally more interested in the cultural effects on men than I am the women characters in my stories because women are in an incredible position right now. . . . I'm interested in these *men* who are immersed in a culture where they had a certain role, and now all of a sudden these women are going off and going to school, getting strange jobs. They're walking out on the men and the men don't know what to do. I feel there's a lot of pathos in that.'' Mason drew on this interest in her creation of Leroy Moffitt.

Mason has continued to produce a steady stream of well-received literature since her first book of fiction. Her work includes the novel *In Country,* a story about a Kentucky teenager's search for her father who was killed in Vietnam, and her uncle who has been left crippled and haunted by the war. The novel was made into a movie in 1989 starring Bruce Willis and Emily Lloyd. Mason's other works include the novel *Spence + Lilac* (1988) and *Feather Crowns* (1993). She has also written another collection of short stories, *Love Life,* published in 1989.

Plot Summary

''Shiloh'' is told from the point of view of Leroy Moffitt, a recently disabled truck driver. As the story opens, Leroy is watching his wife, Norma Jean, lift weights. Leroy was injured in a trucking accident; now he stays at home, smokes marijuana, and makes things from craft kits. It is unclear whether Leroy will ever return to work as a truck driver. From one of his craft kits Leroy has built a model log cabin. Now he wants to build a real log cabin for his wife. Norma Jean, however, is not interested in a log cabin. She works at a Rexall drugstore and wants to improve her mind and body. Consequently, she goes from a weight-lifting class to an adult education composition class. She also spends time learning songs on the organ Leroy bought her for Christmas. She wants Leroy to find a job; having him home all the time makes her uncomfortable.

Norma Jean's mother, Mabel Beasley, frequently visits Leroy and Norma Jean. On one visit she becomes enraged when she discovers Norma Jean smoking a cigarette. Norma Jean is mortified that her mother has found out that she smokes and becomes increasingly unhappy with her life from this point on. Mabel repeatedly tells the Moffitts about how she and her late husband, Jet, spent their honeymoon at Shiloh, a Civil War battlefield. She can see that Leroy and Norma Jean are having problems in their marriage and nags them about taking a trip to Shiloh. She believes that such a trip will solve their problems.

Through flashbacks in the story, it is revealed that Leroy was rarely home while he was a trucker. He often took speed while he drove, and he continues to smoke marijuana now that he is disabled. The couple got married because Norma Jean was pregnant. They had a baby named Randy who died of sudden infant death syndrome in the back seat of the Moffitts' car, while his parents watched a movie at a drive-in. Leroy and Norma Jean never discuss Randy's death, though Leroy recalls the baby's death and the trip to the hospital. When Mabel makes a comment to Norma Jean about a baby who is mauled by a dachshund because the baby's mother was negligent, Norma Jean knows that her mother is blaming her for Randy's death.

Bobbie Ann Mason

Leroy continues to pester Norma Jean about building a log cabin for her. Mabel continues to pester Norma Jean and Leroy about going to Shiloh. When Leroy discovers that there is a log cabin at Shiloh, he decides to take Norma Jean there. When they arrive at the battleground, it is not what either of them has expected. They have a picnic lunch at the cemetery for the Union dead, and Norma Jean tells Leroy she wants to leave him. Leroy cannot seem to comprehend that his marriage is falling apart. He realizes that he understands very little about his marriage. In the story's last scene, Norma Jean is walking away from him down a "serpentine brick path." Leroy tries to follow, but his leg hurts him. Norma Jean turns back to him and waves her arms from where she stands on a bluff overlooking the Tennessee River. Leroy cannot understand what her wave means.

Characters

Mabel Beasley

Mabel Beasley is Norma Jean's mother and Leroy's mother-in-law. She lives near the Moffitts and often comes over to their house. She frequently enters without knocking and one day surprises Norma Jean and catches her smoking a cigarette. Mabel was displeased when Leroy got Norma Jean pregnant and saw the death of their son as a sort of divine retribution. She lets Norma Jean know that she blames her for the baby's death by telling her a story about a baby who died because of a negligent mother. When she was a bride, Mabel and her husband visited the Shiloh battlefield. She now wants Leroy and Norma Jean to take a trip to Shiloh in hopes that the visit will help them fix the problems in their marriage.

Stevie Hamilton

Stevie Hamilton is the teenaged son of a prominent doctor in Leroy and Norma Jean's town. He is also a drug pusher who supplies Leroy with drugs. When Leroy obtains marijuana from him, the occasion prompts him to reminisce about his own lost son, who would have been about Stevie's age.

Leroy Moffitt

Leroy Moffitt is a disabled trucker living with his wife, Norma Jean, in western Kentucky. The story is told from Leroy's point of view; therefore, readers learn only what he is thinking. After his truck accident, Leroy stays at home, smokes marijuana, and makes things from craft kits. Although Leroy gets along with his mother-in-law by joking with her, he feels that "Mabel has never really forgiven him for disgracing her by getting Norma Jean pregnant."

Leroy knows that his marriage is failing, even if he is slow to accept it. He also realizes that Norma Jean is changing, just as rural Kentucky is changing, but he does not know how to cope with either change. Mostly, he wants to return to how things were in the beginning with Norma Jean, and his plan to build a log cabin is indicative of his tendency to live in the past rather than to look toward the future. Although Leroy loves Norma Jean, he does not know what she thinks about him, about their marriage, or about the death of their infant son, Randy. Mason told Lila Havens in an interview that she is interested in male characters in the midst of cultural change. She stated, "The men don't know what to do." Leroy is such a man. "Nobody knows anything," Leroy thinks. "The answers are always changing."

Norma Jean Moffitt

Norma Jean Moffitt lives in rural western Kentucky with her husband, Leroy Moffitt, who has recently been injured in a trucking accident. She works at a Rexall drugstore, likes to lift weights, play the organ, and cook interesting meals. After many years of seeing her husband so seldom, she is uncomfortable having him home all the time. Norma Jean's efforts at self-improvement demonstrate that she is a forward-looking person who is doing her best to adapt to change.

Norma Jean grows increasingly unhappy with her marriage as the story unfolds. She is not interested in the log cabin that her husband wants to build for her, and she is tired of her mother's meddlesome attitude towards her marriage. When she agrees to visit Shiloh, she finally tells Leroy that she wants to leave him. Her ambiguous gesture at the end of the story serves to further confuse her husband, who cannot accept her for who she is.

Randy Moffitt

Randy Moffitt was the infant son of Norma Jean and Leroy. He died of sudden infant death syndrome while asleep at a drive-in theater with his mother and father. At the time the story takes place, Randy has been dead for fifteen years.

Topics for Further Study

- One critic has called contemporary writers like Raymond Carver, Ann Beattie, and Bobbie Ann Mason ''K-Mart realists.'' What do you think this term means? Do you feel it is accurate?
- The South has inspired many talented women writers. Two of the most popular are Flannery O'Connor and Eudora Welty. Read a story by each of these authors and discuss how their perceptions of the South differ from Mason's.
- Critics Hal Blythe and Charlie Sweet have compared Leroy Moffitt to the Fisher King of the Holy Grail legend. Find out who the Fisher King was, and explain if you think this is a valid comparison.

Themes

The American Dream

For most people, the American Dream is the belief that if one works hard and long enough, one will achieve financial and emotional security. With his accident, however, Leroy is confronted with the truth: he lives in a rented home, he has no child, and his wife has lost interest in him. He attempts to resurrect his idea of the American Dream by making plans to build a log cabin. However, even this dream evaporates as his wife tells him that she wants to leave him. Norma Jean also buys into the American Dream but lives an empty life. She works at a drug store and is confronted with cosmetics and beauty magazines promising to change her life. She lifts weights and writes compositions. She cooks exotic food and plays the organ. She makes lists of things Leroy can do. In spite of her dreams and hard work, however, she too finds the American Dream elusive.

Change and Transformation

In ''Shiloh,'' Leroy and Norma Jean are victims of rapid social change. Subdivisions and shopping malls are quickly changing their formerly rural Kentucky environment. Leroy ''cruises the new subdivisions, feeling like a criminal rehearsing for a robbery. . . . All the houses look grand and complicated. They depress him.'' Leroy resists change, looking backward to an earlier time. He wants to build a log cabin—a traditional dwelling. Furthermore, he wants to start his marriage over again. ''You and me could start all over again,'' he tells Norma Jean. ''Right back at the beginning.'' Norma Jean, however, has no desire to go back to the beginning. She attempts to transform herself in the face of change. Her weightlifting, adult education classes, and exotic cooking are symptomatic of her desire for transformation. She dismisses Leroy's notion of a log cabin; the subdivisions are more to her liking. Leroy embraces tradition, but Norma Jean rejects it. ''You ain't seen nothing yet,'' Norma Jean says to her mother. When she tells Leroy she wants to leave him, she rejects not only Leroy but also the tradition of marriage.

Identity and the Search for Self

Closely related to social change and transformation is the search for new identities by the characters of ''Shiloh.'' Until his accident, Leroy had identified himself with his big rig, which now sits useless in his yard. Now Leroy sits in his house and makes needlepoint pillows. He searches for some way to reestablish himself as the head of the household and finally settles on the idea of building a log cabin. Norma Jean's search for self emerges in her attempts at self-improvement. When she married at eighteen, she had imagined herself as a housewife and mother. With the death of her child and the disability of her husband, however, she finds that she needs a new identity. Norma Jean's movement from one self-improvement project to another suggests that she is not certain about the self she is trying to uncover. During her life, her identity has been defined by her relationship first to her mother and then to Leroy. Although she is uncertain of the identity she wants to assume, she knows that she can no longer allow her mother and Leroy to define her. In response to Leroy's assertion that they could start all over again, she replies, "She won't leave me alone—*you* won't leave me alone." She adds: "I feel eighteen again. I can't face that all over again."

Gender Roles

At least part of the identity crisis that Leroy and Norma Jean face can be attributed to their reversal of traditional gender roles. When Leroy shows Mabel his needlepoint pillow cover, she responds, "That's what a woman would do." Now that Leroy can no longer work, Norma Jean holds down the role of primary breadwinner for the family. Her interest in building her pectoral muscles is also a traditional male preoccupation. Norma Jean points out to Leroy that his name means "the king." However, when Leroy asks, "Am I still the king around here?" Norma Jean responds by flexing her biceps and feeling them for hardness. The term "flexing one's muscles" is often used metaphorically to describe someone who is trying to exert his or her power in a situation. In this case, Norma Jean is getting ready to assert her independence. In the final reversal of the story, it is Norma Jean who drives the car when she and Leroy go to Shiloh. Leroy, the long-distance truck driver, sits in the passenger seat as his wife drives him to the site of the Confederate defeat.

Death

The theme of death weaves its way through the text of "Shiloh." In the background is the death of the infant Randy, the only fruit of the union between Leroy and Norma Jean. Their way of life in rural Kentucky is also dying, buried beneath subdivisions and shopping malls. The critical scene in the story—the breakup (or death) of Leroy and Norma Jean's marriage—takes place in the Union cemetery at the Shiloh battlefield. As Norma Jean walks away from Leroy after telling him that she wants to leave him, Leroy "tries to focus on the fact that thirty-five hundred soldiers died on the grounds around him." Each of the themes discussed above arrives at a kind of death: the death of traditional culture, the death of the American Dream, the death of old selves, identities, and roles, and, finally, the death of the Moffitts' marriage.

Style

Point of View

Although a number of critics see "Shiloh" as a feminist saga of a woman flexing her muscles and taking flight, "Shiloh" is really Leroy's story. The story is told entirely from his point of view. Point of view, sometimes called narrative perspective, is the term used to describe the way in which the writer presents the material of a story to the reader. "Shiloh" is told from a third-person, limited point of view. That is, readers see only what Leroy sees and hear only what Leroy hears. In addition, because the story is told from Leroy's point of view, readers are privy to Leroy's thoughts and memories, but not to Norma Jean's or to her mother's. Because of this, readers' reactions to the others in the story are conditioned by Leroy's perspective.

Narrative

The term "narrative" relates to how events unfold in a story. A narrative can be arranged chronologically, in which the events that occur first are depicted first, or according to any number of plans that the writer might want to follow. The narrative of "Shiloh" is in present tense, which gives readers the sense that the story is unfolding before their eyes. In addition, although the overall narration moves from an earlier point in time to a later point in time, there are flashbacks embedded in the story. Sometimes an event or thought in the present will trigger a memory for Leroy, and this is how readers learn about the Moffitts' past. For example, when Leroy buys marijuana from Stevie Hamilton, he reflects that his infant son, Randy, would have been about Stevie's age had he lived. This thought leads to the memory of the night of Randy's death.

Setting

The setting of a story includes not only the geographical location in which the story is set but the time period of the story as well. The setting can also include the occupations of the characters and their religious, moral, emotional, and social environments. In "Shiloh," the geographic setting is western Kentucky as it existed in the early 1980s, when the story was written. In addition, Mason creates a world of working-class, marginally educated characters. In an interview with Lila Havens, Mason stated, "My characters are members of the shopping mall generation." These characters inhabit a world in transition. In "Shiloh," the old culture of rural Kentucky is being replaced by the suburban, consumer-oriented culture of late twentieth-century America. In addition to the contemporary setting of western Kentucky, Mason also refers to an earlier time in the title of the story and in the placement of its climactic scene. These references to Shiloh invoke the Civil War and the death of the Old South. Placing the breakup of the Moffitts' marriage in the Shiloh battlefield focuses readers' attention on the civil war between Norma Jean and Leroy and the birth of the New South.

Symbols and Imagery

The terms symbol and image are closely related but not identical in meaning. In literature, a symbol is an object that stands for something else, usually an abstract idea. An image is a concrete picture and can function as a symbol. Often a writer will use repeated, similar images to give them symbolic meaning. In a short article in *The Explicator,* Stewart Cooke demonstrates the uses of imagery in "Shiloh." For example, Leroy's wrecked truck, sitting in the yard while Leroy sits in the house, is a symbol for the disabled Leroy himself. In addition, however, Mason describes the truck with this image: "It sits in the backyard, like a gigantic bird that has flown home to roost." A bit later, she describes the way Norma Jean picks at cake crumbs "like a fussy bird." Leroy thinks about the way Norma Jean makes love as he watches birds at the feeder. Finally, in the last scene, Norma Jean stands waving her arms, as if she is about to take flight. As Cooke points out, through the use of bird imagery, Mason warns us that Norma Jean is about to leave Leroy, or, in the popular expression, "fly the coop."

Of course, the most obvious symbol in the story is Shiloh itself, a battlefield on which thousands of soldiers died; it becomes the final battlefield of the Moffitts' marriage. As Robert H. Brinkmeyer, Jr., points out, "In the literature of the Southern renaissance Civil War battlefields and Confederate graveyards are usually extremely significant, often initiating profound meditation and interior probings." He suggests that Mason's story provides "one of the clearest statements of the contemporary loss of historical vision that was once so significant to the Southern mind." The significance of the Shiloh battlefield is lost on Leroy and Norma; they know it only as the spot where Mabel and Jet Beasley spent their honeymoon. Norma Jean and Leroy skirmish amidst the graves of fallen soldiers, yet Leroy fails to recognize the irony of the Moffitt civil war being played out on the site of so brutal a Civil War battle. He admits that he "is leaving out the insides of history." Consequently, just as he is unable to understand the significance of the battlefield, he is unable to understand the significance of this moment in his marriage.

Historical Context

Change Comes to Kentucky

Virtually every reviewer of "Shiloh" notes that the story is set in rural western Kentucky, a location undergoing rapid cultural change. This is the Kentucky in which Mason herself grew up. As a result, she is able to create believable characters caught in the transition between the old, pastoral, rural world of farms and close-knit communities and the modern, anonymous, suburban world of shopping malls and fast-food restaurants. In "Shiloh," for example, Leroy did not notice the change in his hometown while he was on the road as a trucker. However, now that Leroy has come home to stay, "he notices how much the town has changed. Subdivisions are spreading across western Kentucky like an oil slick."

Some of these changes are noticeable from demographic information about the area. For example, in 1980, 73 percent of western Kentucky's residents had completed grammar school, but by 1990, the figure had jumped to 84 percent. This statistic is reflected in Mason's story: Leroy and Norma Jean had little formal education, but Norma Jean comes to realize the value of school and begins taking adult education classes. Similarly, in 1980 only 11 percent of Kentuckians had completed at least one year of college. By 1990, over 19 percent had. Other statistics point to shifting cultural pat-

Compare & Contrast

- **1980s:** Sudden infant death syndrome has been a recognized medical disease since 1970. In 1988, there are 5,476 infant deaths from SIDS in the United States.

  1990s: Estimates regarding the number of deaths caused by SIDS in the United States range from 3,000 to 7,000 per year. Experts determine that putting babies to sleep on their backs can prevent SIDS. In 1994, only 30 percent of babies are put to sleep on their backs. By 1997, the number rises to 79 percent.

- **1980s:** Marijuana use among high schoolers is steadily declining. By 1989, 33 percent of high school seniors report having smoked marijuana, down from 50 percent in 1979. Until the late 1980s, when the federal Drug Enforcement Administration holds hearings on reclassifying marijuana as a legal, prescribable substance, marijuana is quietly used as a medical treatment for some conditions.

  1990s: Many experts still believe that the dangers of marijuana are unknown. Nevertheless, cultivation of marijuana in the United States is on the rise and accounts for nearly 25 percent of the U.S. market in 1990. In 1996, the use of marijuana for medical purposes, typically for glaucoma and to relieve nausea caused by cancer treatments, becomes legal in California and Arizona after voters approve controversial propositions.

- **1980s:** After the introduction of laws in the 1970s that make divorce easier to obtain, divorce rates rise. In 1982, the divorce rate in the United States is 5.1 per 1,000 people.

  1990s: It is widely held that one out of every two marriages ends in divorce. The U.S. Census Bureau notes that from 1970 to 1996, the number of divorced persons has quadrupled. On an average day in the United States, more than 3,000 divorces are finalized.

---

terns in formerly rural Kentucky. In 1985, Graves County (where Mason grew up) per capita income was $10,900, but by 1995 this figure had risen to $18,900. Out of 14,500 homes in the county, 42 percent have been built since the 1970s.

Socially, Leroy and Norma Jean are working-class white people caught in a time of diminishing expectations. When Leroy claims that he plans on building a log cabin for them, Norma Jean responds, "Like *heck* you are.... You'll have to find a job first. Nobody can afford to build now." In the early years of Ronald Reagan's presidency, a severe recession gripped the United States. High interest rates, double-digit inflation, and high unemployment squeezed the working classes, while many wealthy Americans reaped the benefits of Reagan's system of "trickle-down economics." In 1982, unemployment was 10.8 percent—the highest since the Great Depression—and the number of Americans living below the poverty line was the highest in seventeen years. Despite this, the stock market set record highs and traded record numbers of shares.

These economic trends correlate with other social trends, like the rising divorce rate, which peaked in 1981 at 5.3 per 1,000 marriages, as more and more women (like Norma Jean) became financially independent. In 1966, around the time the Moffitts were married, the divorce rate was 2.5 per 1,000 marriages. Additionally, the average length for all first marriages that end in divorce is 11 years, and the average age at divorce for men is 35, for women the average age is 33. These figures closely correspond with the Moffitts' situation. Mason put a human face on statistics in creating the characters of Leroy and Norma Jean.

Mason herself has commented many times on her concern with working-class people. In her interview with Lila Havens, she noted, ''I'm constantly preoccupied with the class struggle and I'm exploring various kinds of culture shock—people moving from one class to another, people being threatened by other people's ways and values—and the way those attitudes come into play with each other, especially when people do leave home or when the outside world comes prancing in via the television.''

Critical Overview

Mason's story ''Shiloh'' became the title story in her first collection of fiction, *Shiloh and Other Stories,* published in 1982. The volume was well-received by critics and earned nominations for a National Book Critics Circle Award, an American Book Award, and a PEN/Faulkner Award. Mason also won the 1983 Ernest Hemingway Foundation Award for best first fiction. ''Shiloh'' has been widely anthologized in literature texts, and critics have demonstrated an ongoing interest in the story.

In a review of *Shiloh and Other Stories* in *Newsweek,* for example, Gene Lyons compared Mason to Arkansas novelist Charles Portis, best known as the author of *True Grit,* for her simple, straightforward prose. In another review in *The New Republic,* noted novelist and short story writer Anne Tyler praised Mason as ''a full-fledged master of the short story.'' She also wrote that although *Shiloh and Other Stories* was Mason's first book of fiction, ''there is nothing unformed or merely promising about her.''

Shiloh and Other Stories was not without its detractors, however. The most common negative comments concerned the characters' lack of development in the stories. Patricia Vigderman, writing in *The Nation,* suggested that the stories end with ''a closeness that seems tacked on.'' She also charged that ''Mason takes us into her characters' new Kentucky homes and then runs a made-for-TV movie. Her people's emotions come across merely as dots on the screen.'' In addition, some early reviewers, while lavish in their praise, nonetheless faulted Mason for the similarity of her stories. Robert Towers in *The New York Review of Books* wrote that ''individually effective as they are, there is a degree of sameness to the collection.''

Beyond reviews of her book printed in the months after its publication, Mason's work has attracted significant scholarly and critical attention. In addition, current criticism is moving in creative and innovative directions. For example, Hal Blythe and Charlie Sweet in an article written for *Studies in Short Fiction,* have attempted to connect Leroy with the mythical Fisher King of the Grail legend. Other critics have concentrated on close readings of ''Shiloh.'' Stewart Cooke examines the uses of bird imagery, connecting Leroy to a large roosting bird and Norma Jean to a bird about to take flight.

Mason has expressed some ambivalence toward feminist examinations of her work. As she commented in an interview with Lila Havens, she is more interested in the changes her male characters undergo. Nonetheless, in a 1989 article for *The Southern Literary Journal,* G. O. Morphew examined Mason's female characters and concluded that ''the downhome feminists of these stories do not want what their city cousins want: equal legal and political rights, equal access to careers, equal pay, government support of child care, and so on. Mason's women simply want breathing space in their relationships with their men.''

Because so many of Mason's stories concern characters caught up in cultural change, some literary critics have focused on this theme in Mason's work. Albert Wilhelm, a critic who has written widely on Mason's stories, studied this in an essay for *The Midwest Quarterly.* Wilhelm views the journey to Shiloh as a rite of passage in which the characters move from an old culture to a newly emerging one. In an essay in *The Southern Literary Journal,* Wilhelm wrote that ''culture shock and its jarring effects on an individual's sense of identity'' is the theme that ''dominates the sixteen pieces in *Shiloh and Other Stories.*

Finally, Mason has been identified as a minimalist—that is, a writer who creates lean, focused prose filled with concrete details. Because of this categorization, her work has been compared and contrasted with that of Raymond Carver, Charles Portis, and Ann Beattie. Barbara Henning undertakes such a study in her essay in *Modern Fiction Studies.* Henning detailed the elements of Mason's work. She argued that both Mason's and Carver's characters ''have managed to survive without protesting in a world with reduced economic and emotional possibilities. Their anxieties and disappointments are instead displaced through drug and alcohol use and through an even more deadening activity: a steady focus on the random details of everyday life.''

Criticism

Bobbie Ann Mason

In the following essay, Mason discusses the evolutionary process of writing ''Shiloh'' as a story that revealed itself to her slowly. She cautions that although the destination of Shiloh may have symbolic overtones, it is integral to the story and should not be separated from its context in any analysis.

I have been pleased and very surprised by the popularity of my story ''Shiloh.'' I could not have imagined when I wrote it that it would be widely anthologized and that students would be discussing it in class. I did not think that far ahead. I couldn't, if I expected to keep my attention on what was unfolding in the story.

In trying to recall how this story came about, I can share with you something of the writing process. As students, you read a finished work, and you try to read it as fully as possible. But from the writer's point of view, during the writing itself, that finished work is far from realized. The writer can only start with a blank page and a sense of wonder. The writer can't guarantee that the story she writes will match the one in her mind. Fiction has a way of happening when you are making other plans.

When I began this story, I had been thinking about two minor characters in another story, a pair named C. W. and Betty. I wondered if I could get closer to C. W. and Betty by writing a story about them. I changed their names to Leroy and Norma Jean. I did not know what to expect. I kept thinking about something I had overheard someone say to a coworker, ''It's amazing that I have strong feet, coming from two parents that never had strong feet at all.''

These were the two inspirations for my story. These two bits did not seem to be anything to build a story on. But I like to start with something that strikes my fancy and then see where it goes. Almost immediately, I wrote the first sentence, ''Leroy Moffitt's wife, Norma Jean, is working on her pectorals.'' Now where was this going? I let that scene go on for a bit, to see if anything interesting would happen. Then I wondered, who are they?

It came to me: Leroy is a truck driver.

I invented this. I made it up. It felt scary, as if I were going to start driving a truck myself. What did I know about driving a truck? Nothing. I wondered what I could do with these characters if I didn't know anything about Leroy's occupation. Should I go out and do research? It occurred to me that maybe he had an accident and was homebound now. Now I was off the hook, and I had found a new direction for the story. The story is not about driving a truck, it's about what happens when Leroy comes home from the road. I started to sense that this story was about a marriage. I kept going, begging my imagination to carry me through. I wondered how Norma Jean spent her time. The Rexall drugstore came to mind, because I had worked in a Rexall at the soda fountain when I was in high school. I wondered what happened to Leroy and Norma Jean in high school. I thought of the baby. The loss of their child, years ago, had defined their marriage. This surprised me. It set the tone for what was to follow. Now that Leroy is home again, they are thrown together again, as if they were starting over. Now the changes around them will appear in sharp focus, and they will have to deal with how they have changed inside.

And so I kept on in this way, taking wrong turns at times, and meandering for long stretches that had to be cut out because they added little interest, direction, or depth to the story. Then a third main character, Norma Jean's mother, whose personality casts a light on the whole story, entered the scene. Mabel is a strong force in Norma Jean's life, especially with Leroy away from home so much. The characters are talking along, when all of a sudden, Mabel suggests that Leroy take Norma Jean to Shiloh. I had not planned this. I thought of it at the same moment Mabel said it. It was as though she—an imaginary character—had said it rather than that I had written it. The word ''Shiloh'' came sailing into my mind, out of a memory long ago of class field trips to the Shiloh battleground. I never went on one of the trips, but there was so much talk of them that the word ''Shiloh'' had a mystique about it. And it seemed appropriate at this point.

Now the story had a focus and a direction. This trip to Shiloh was going to be the setting for determining the outcome of this marriage. I followed Leroy and Norma Jean along, through the domestic scenes, and then to the battleground. I had discovered the story by being open to the characters and being willing to see what they would do, to

Shiloh National Military Park Cemetery in Hardin County, Tennessee.

write down anything that came into my head just to see if I could use it.

I rewrote the story many times, throwing out what was inappropriate and developing parts that were crucial to bringing the story of this marriage to life. As I worked to deepen the story, Norma Jean and Leroy became more real to me, and I began to feel truly the sadness of their situation, their loss, and the dissolving of their marriage. I tried to take account of the changes taking place in their small town, so that I could have some context for understanding what was happening with them. It seemed to me that a great deal had been lost, and that the characters were struggling with how they were going to live their lives in the face of great social changes.

If you are studying literature for the first time, I hope you will read the story for its feelings, its details, the way the characters talk, what kind of world they live in, what things are meaningful to them, and what feelings their lives evoke in you. I don't like to reduce the story to themes and symbols, which may be useful as signposts, but cannot ultimately be separated from the story itself. In this story, Shiloh is a destination, and maybe someone will say it is a symbol of some kind, but there are

- *In Country* is Mason's 1985 novel about eighteen-year-old Samantha Hughes's quest to understand her father's death in the Vietnam War and to understand herself.
- Mason's 1989 collection of short stories, *Love Life*, introduces more characters caught in changing circumstances.
- Shelby Foote's *Shiloh* (1952) is a fictional account of the Civil War battle told from a variety of perspectives.
- *The American Story: Short Stories from the Rea Award* (1993), edited by Michael Rea, offers a selection of stories by such authors as Raymond Carver, Joyce Carol Oates, Ann Beattie, Charles Baxter, and Grace Paley, among others, for the student wishing to further an understanding of the short story genre and of minimalist writing.
- *The War in Kentucky: From Shiloh to Perryville* is James McDonough's 1994 exploration of the importance of Kentucky in the Civil War.
- *New Women and New Fiction: Short Stories since the Sixties* (1986) is a collection of stories by such contemporary women writers as Cynthia Ozick, Toni Cade Bambara, Anne Tyler, Fay Weldon and Ann Beattie, among others.
- Raymond Carver's *Where I'm Calling From: New and Selected Stories* (1988) is widely considered a collection of minimalist masterpieces.

---

many things to say about Shiloh as a destination that can't be simply taken apart from the story. I would like for Shiloh to be so much a part of the story that you can't remove it. I like to feel the images—such as the dust ruffle on the bed, the crinkled-cotton texture of Mabel's face, the crumbs on the cellophane cake wrapper—as if I could hold them between my fingers. I hope such textures make the story real enough that you can believe you are right there with Leroy and Norma Jean on their way to Shiloh.

Source: Bobbie Ann Mason, ''Commentary on 'Shiloh','' for *Short Stories for Students,* Gale, 1998.

Diane Andrews Henningfeld

Henningfeld is an assistant professor of English at Adrian College, in Adrian, Michigan. In the essay below, she offers a general introduction to ''Shiloh.''

Bobbie Ann Mason's short story ''Shiloh'' appeared initially in the *New Yorker* and later became the title story of her first collection. Reviewers praised Mason for her spare realism and her ear for the language of the people of western Kentucky. Several critics have identified Mason's style as an example of minimalism, a literary movement characterized by spare, unornamented prose and use of specific, concrete detail. Minimalist fiction often takes as its subject the small events in the lives of characters. Such writers as the late Raymond Carver, Ann Beattie, and Jayne Anne Phillips, as well as Mason, have been identified with this style of writing. Sometimes, critics use the term ''K-Mart fiction'' to describe the style.

Mason herself is uncomfortable with labels. In an interview with Bonnie Lyons and Bill Oliver which appeared in *Contemporary Literature,* Mason stated, ''I'm not sure what's meant by minimalism. I'm not sure if it means something that is just so spare that there is hardly anything there, or if it describes something that is deliberately pared down with great artistic effect, or if it's just a misnomer for what happens in any good short story, economy.'' Regardless of the label attached to Mason's prose, style is very important to her. She reports that she tries ''to approximate language that's very blunt and Anglo-Saxon.''

In a critical essay appearing in *Modern Fiction Studies,* Barbara Henning details the negative reception that Mason's "blunt and Anglo-Saxon" writing has received in recent years. She reports that both Mason and Raymond Carver have been accused of creating characters who lead "flat and robotic" lives. Henning argues that such stories require a special kind of reading. Rather than trying to interpret the story as we read it, we should "suspend the interpretive moment." By doing so, we can experience the accumulation of details and arrive at an understanding of the situation at the same time as the narrator. Furthermore, according to Henning, "the characters, setting, and situation are revealed in 'Shiloh' through an accumulation of synecdochic details . . . the narrator and Leroy concentrate on the particular as a substitute for the general, emphasizing Leroy's inability and unwillingness to understand his environment and his wife." By "synecdochic detail" Henning means that Mason accumulates details which represent parts of the Moffitts' lives and that these parts, in turn, reveal the whole. A careful examination of the detail and the dialogue of "Shiloh" can demonstrate this argument.

Readers who encounter the fiction of Bobbie Ann Mason through *Shiloh and Other Stories* discover a world of ordinary, working-class Southerners. Mason's characters drive trucks, work at Wal-Mart, eat at Burger Chef, and watch "M*A*S*H" on television. Their English is not always standard, and their education is generally marginal. "Shiloh" is a saga of such individuals. Like Mason's other fictional characters, Leroy Moffitt and his wife Norma Jean are rural Kentuckians who are affected by the changing culture in which they live. The pastoral landscapes around them are quickly being paved into streets for subdivisions and parking lots for shopping malls. Such changes separate the characters from their traditions. They live in a world where "nobody knows anything" and where "answers are always changing."

Not only do Leroy and Norma Jean struggle with cultural change, they struggle with changes in each other. Leroy, a trucker, has been injured in an accident and can no longer drive his big rig. Consequently, he is at home all of time. Norma Jean now lifts weights, works at the Rexall cosmetics counter, and seems uncomfortable around her husband. Mabel Beasley, Norma Jean's mother, frequently visits the Moffitts' house and often criticizes Norma Jean's housekeeping. Her interference adds tension to Norma Jean's search for a new identity. Mabel, however, believes that the couple can solve their marital difficulties by simply taking a trip to the place

"As I worked to deepen the story, Norma Jean and Leroy became more real to me, and I began to feel truly the sadness of their situation, their loss, and the dissolving of their marriage."

where she spent her first honeymoon—the Shiloh battlefield.

The story opens with Leroy watching Norma Jean lift weights. Leroy thinks she looks like Wonder Woman, all pectorals and legs. From the first paragraph, as Norma Jean attempts to build herself up, Leroy attempts to build Norma Jean into the woman he thinks he married. But he fails to realize that, like the changing landscape, Norma Jean has changed over the fifteen years of their marriage.

When Norma Jean sits down to play songs from the 1960s on her electric organ, she complains, "I didn't like those old songs back then. . . . But I have this crazy feeling I missed something." Leroy immediately tells her, "You didn't miss a thing." In doing this, Leroy tries to build a history for Norma Jean in which there are no missing parts. As Leroy continues to watch Norma Jean play the organ, he reflects that he is "finally settling down with the woman he loves." But what does he love about this woman? His reflection continues: "She is still pretty. Her skin is flawless. Her frosted curls resemble pencil trimmings." Again, by attaching the details of Norma Jean's appearance to the thought that this is the woman he loves, Leroy continues to build his model of Norma Jean.

At the same time that Leroy is figuratively building his model of Norma Jean, he is literally building a model of a log cabin. Just as he idealizes Norma Jean, he idealizes the life-size log cabin that he wants to build for her. Although Norma Jean says repeatedly that she does not want to live in a log cabin, Leroy continues to insist that she does.

On one of her visits to her daughter's house, Mabel tells Norma Jean about a baby who has been eaten by a dachshund because the baby's mother

> "Leroy's imagined Shiloh is different than the reality of Shiloh. This discrepancy is rooted in Leroy's habit of seeing only parts of things, not their totality."

was neglectful. Norma Jean sees this as a veiled reference to her own baby, who died in infancy of sudden infant death syndrome. Norma Jean says, "The very idea, her bringing up a subject like that! Saying it was neglect." Leroy's immediate response is: "She didn't mean it." In so doing, he undercuts Norma Jean's attempt to talk about her dead baby and her relationship with her mother. Again, Leroy attempts through the dialogue to control and build Norma Jean into his own image.

Ironically, although Leroy notices that his hometown has changed, he is unable to see, or at least acknowledge, changes in his wife. "Something is happening," the narrator reports, "Norma Jean is going to night school." What is happening are strong shifts in Norma Jean's identity and in the structure of the Moffitt marriage. However, although Leroy senses that Norma Jean is "miles away" and although "he knows he is going to lose her," he seems unable to acknowledge to himself the changes in his wife and the changes in his marriage.

The problem, of course, is that Leroy is attempting to assemble a whole person and a whole marriage using only the flat, surface details of their daily lives. Leroy has been seeing Norma Jean as the composite of her parts rather than as a whole person. As with his sense of history, he has left out the details of his marriage and his wife. Although he tries to create Norma Jean by telling her what to think and what to do, she eludes him; although he tries to build a house that will take Norma Jean back to the beginning of their marriage, he ultimately fails.

In the climactic scene, Leroy and Norma Jean travel to Shiloh, the Civil War battlefield that Mabel has been urging them to visit. Leroy does not recognize the irony of going to a battlefield to try to make peace with his wife. They discover that the battlefield is not as they had expected it. Furthermore, the log cabin that Leroy wanted to see is full of bullet holes. "That's not the kind of log house I've got in mind," says Leroy.

In both cases, Leroy's imagined Shiloh is different than the reality of Shiloh. This discrepancy is rooted in Leroy's habit of seeing only parts of things, not their totality. With Shiloh, for example, he is only aware of one small fact: that it is the place where Mabel and her late husband spent their honeymoon. Although he is vaguely aware that a battle was fought there, he does not realize that it is the site of a Confederate defeat.

Leroy himself is headed for defeat. As Norma Jean and Leroy share a picnic lunch on grounds overlooking the white slabs of a cemetery, Norma Jean says, "I want to leave you."

Leroy's response is that of a man whose building project has suddenly turned out wrong because he has mismeasured the pieces: "Leroy takes a bottle of Coke out of the cooler and flips off the cap. He holds the bottle poised near his mouth but cannot remember to take a drink. Finally he says, 'No, you don't'." He denies that Norma Jean could want such a thing. "I won't let you," Leroy continues. Ironically, Leroy does not see that it is this kind of response that has gotten him into his predicament. However, Norma Jean is through being told what to do by her mother and her husband, and she will no longer let the two of them define her existence with their words.

In a gesture that is symptomatic of the Moffitt marriage—a marriage in which even the death of their infant son is repressed—"Leroy takes a lungful of smoke and closes his eyes as Norma Jean's words sink in." His immediate response to radical change is to close his eyes. With his eyes still closed, he reviews events: "He tries to focus on the fact that thirty-five hundred soldiers died on the grounds around him. He can only think of that war as a board game with plastic soldiers. . . . General Grant, drunk and furious, shoved the Southerners back to Corinth, where Mabel and Jet Beasley were married years later. . . . The next day, Mabel and Jet visited the battleground, and then Norma Jean was born, and then she married Leroy and they had a baby, which they lost, and now Leroy and Norma Jean are here at the same battleground. Leroy knows he is leaving out a lot. He is leaving out the insides of history. History was always just names and dates to him. It occurs to him that building a house out of logs is similarly empty—too simple. And the real inner workings of a marriage, like most of history, have escaped him.''

Leroy finally seems to realize that he has been looking only at the surface details of his marriage, not at the whole, complicated relationship. When he opens his eyes, however, Norma Jean ''has moved away and is walking through the cemetery, following a serpentine brick path.'' As the story closes, Norma Jean is too far away for him to speak to her. Nonetheless, she turns back toward Leroy ''and waves her arms.'' Leroy is uncertain what the gesture means.

The final scene of the story, depicting what could be the final scene of the Moffitts' marriage, is permeated with the theme of death. Leroy's reference to their dead baby, the death of his dream of building a log cabin, and, of course, the realization that he is surrounded by both Union and Confederate dead serve to underscore pain, anguish, and finality. Whether or not there will be a rebirth of the Moffitts' marriage is unclear. In this moment, the past has died, and the future remains ambiguous, just like Norma Jean's wordless gesture.

Source: Diane Andrews Henningfeld, ''Overview of 'Shiloh','' in *Short Stories for Students,* Gale, 1998.

Stewart J. Cooke

Cooke is affiliated with McGill University in Montreal. In the following excerpt, he explores Norma Jean's quest for growth and change in ''Shiloh,'' as well as Mason's use of imagery in the story.

Much of the critical commentary on Bobbie Ann Mason's short stories has focused on the effects of social change on her characters' sense of self. Accordingly, the consensus is that Norma Jean Moffitt, the heroine of ''Shiloh,'' is a ''good example of a character who attempts to construct a new identity'' (Albert E. Wilhelm, ''Making Over,'' *Southern Literary Journal,* 1987, 77). Thus, [Tina] Bucher writes of ''Norma Jean's quest for independence'' (''Changing Roles,'' *Border States,* 1991, 50); G. O. Morphew calls her a ''downhome feminist'' (*Southern Literary Journal,* 1986, 41); [Robert H.] Brinkmeyer describes her ''open-armed embrace of a world promising the potential for growth and freedom'' (''Rocking,'' *Southern Literary Journal,* 1987, 12); and Wilhelm labels her a ''good-old Southern girl'' who ''is definitely striving to be a new woman'' (''Private,'' *Midwest Quarterly,* 1987, 277).

"At the very moment that Leroy has stopped moving, Norma Jean has begun to move forward."

In support of these contentions, one can point to the ending of the story where, having told her husband Leroy that she wants to leave him, Norma Jean walks quickly through the cemetery at Shiloh, pursued by the limping Leroy, who is both literally and symbolically unable to keep up with her:

> Norma Jean is far away, walking rapidly toward the bluff by the river, and he tries to hobble after her. . . . Norma Jean has reached the bluff, and she is looking out over the Tennessee River. Now she turns toward Leroy and waves her arms. Is she beckoning to him? She seems to be doing an exercise for her chest muscles. The sky is unusually pale—the color of the dust ruffle Mabel made for their bed.

The ending brings together a number of motifs that support the critics' claims as well as Mason's own assertion that Norma Jean's ''life is on the way up'' (Wilhelm, ''An Interview with Bobbie Ann Mason,'' *Southern Quarterly,* 1988, 35). At the center of this cluster is the image of a flying bird, represented by Norma Jean's waving arms. Both thematically and structurally, the imagery of birds permeates the story by means of a contrast between Norma Jean, who is ready to end the marriage, to spread her wings and fly, and Leroy, who has returned to the nest and is desperately hoping to start their marriage afresh.

Leroy, a long-distance trucker who has spent most of the last 15 years on the road, has come home to stay after a highway accident that has wrecked his tractor-trailer rig. The rig, emblematic of his former lifestyle, ''sits in the backyard, like a gigantic bird that has flown home to roost.'' Leroy, himself, ''finally settling down with the woman he loves'' yet aware of his wife's dissatisfaction, is obsessed with the idea of building a log house, which he hopes will be ''a real home.'' Norma Jean, on the other hand, is more concerned with ''building herself up,'' with creating a new self-image that will enable her to overcome her dependence on her husband and her mother. She takes a variety of classes, from weight lifting to cooking exotic foods to English composition, in an attempt to become a new woman, to find a new organizing principle for her life. At the very moment that Leroy has stopped moving, Norma Jean has begun to move forward.

It is Leroy who first associates his wife with the birds that he watches at the feeder in the back yard:

> He notices the peculiar way goldfinches fly past the window. They close their wings, then fall, then spread their wings to catch and lift themselves. He wonders if they close their eyes when they fall. Norma Jean closes her eyes when they are in bed. She wants the lights turned out. Even then, he is sure she closes her eyes.

Norma Jean's closing of her eyes in bed, like her staring off into a corner when she chops onions, "as if she can't bear to look," is symptomatic of her ability to avoid the truth of her marriage. There is more to the analogy, however, than Leroy realizes. And among Mason's critics, only Barbara Henning [in "Minimalism," *Modern Fiction Studies,* 1989] asks whether "we [are] to make an analogy between the characters and the feeding birds." Although she suggests that "these details . . . offer the reader a moment to hesitate and to make comparisons within the context, finding a metaphoric framework in which to understand the situation," she does not develop the notion, concluding only that "Mason's juxtaposition of these two images presents Leroy as toying with the idea that Norma Jean might also be floundering."

In actuality, the flight of the birds symbolizes the trajectory of Norma Jean's life. Like the goldfinches, Norma Jean, who found herself pregnant at the age of 18, had closed her wings and fallen into marriage, not because she was in love, but because she wished to spare her mother Mabel the disgrace of having an unwed mother in the family. When the baby died of SIDS while Leroy and Norma Jean were at a drive-in watching *Dr. Strangelove,* a movie in which the world is destroyed, their world was in a sense also destroyed. Their marriage since then has been an empty shell, which has lasted only because Leroy was away from home so often and because, like the "off-white dust ruffle" that Mabel makes for their bed, Norma Jean is adept at covering things up, at hiding the truth.

The accident that keeps Leroy at home forces Norma Jean to confront him and opens her eyes to the emptiness of a marriage made tolerable only by his frequent absence—"In some ways, a woman prefers a man who wanders," she says. Her mother's catching her smoking, however, precipitates her decision to leave—"That set something off," she tells Leroy. The last step in her growing sense of independence is the realization that she no longer needs to submit to her mother's wishes. Nor does she need to continue in a loveless marriage. The final battle in her undeclared war takes place, appropriately enough, at Shiloh, where, "picking cake crumbs from the cellophane wrapper, like a fussy bird," she announces her decision to leave:

> "She won't leave me alone—*you* won't leave me alone." Norma Jean seems to be crying, but she is looking away from him. "I feel eighteen again. I can't face that all over again." She starts walking away.

Faced with the prospect of beginning anew, Norma Jean is not about to repeat her past mistakes. As she stands on the bluff waving her arms under a pale sky, the color of Mabel's dust ruffle, she is no longer hiding the truth. Metaphorically, she has stopped falling, opened her eyes, spread her wings, and lifted herself. Neither Leroy nor Mabel will have the strength to hold her back this time.

Source: Stewart J. Cooke, "Mason's 'Shiloh'," in *The Explicator,* Vol. 51, No. 3, Spring, 1993, pp. 196–99.

G. O. Morphew

In the following excerpt, Morphew analyses the character Norma Jean Moffitt in "Shiloh" and briefly discusses the function of military imagery in the story.

Much has been written about the loss of identity experienced by the characters of Bobbie Ann Mason's short stories; the people of *Shiloh and Other Stories* in particular seem to be confused by the onslaught of pop culture, the media, and other forces of social change. The males, perhaps, seem the more affected, and more ineffectual in their attempts to seize or to create some new center for their lives. The women, at least most of them, react to their frustration and discontent more forcefully; they are or become downhome feminists, and the degree of their feminist responses within their culture is largely determined by education, by economic empowerment, and by age, or by some combination of the three. . . .

It is important to see that the downhome feminists of these stories do not want what their city cousins want: equal legal and political rights, equal access to careers, equal pay, government support of child care, and so on. Mason's women simply want breathing space in their relationships with their men. Sometimes only divorce, always initiated by the women, will provide the degree of change these women seek but sometimes their assertiveness merely aims for a change of pace—casual adultery, for example.

The culture of Mason's Western Kentucky is focused on the lower class, defined by a general lack of higher education, by consumer taste, and, increasingly, by choice of leisure activity. Mason's characters have enough discretionary income to buy such big-ticket items as campers and organs, and enough time to take continuing education classes, or, in the case of Shelby, the preacher in "The Retreat," even the flexibility to follow an avocation which does not support him and his family (he is an electrician during the week). . . .

Like Georgeann [a character in "The Retreat"] Norma Jean, the main female character of "Shiloh," is unhappily married. She, too, is restless, or, as she says, ". . . I have this crazy feeling I missed something." The constant presence of her husband, Leroy, a trucker "finally settling down with the woman he loves" because of an accident, is more than Norma Jean can stand. She also must cope with a domineering mother, Mabel, who spends a lot of time with Norma Jean: "When she visits, she inspects the closets and then the plants, informing Norma Jean when a plant is droopy or yellow." Even though Norma Jean is thirty-four, she still hides her smoking habit from Mabel, until one day Mabel barges in and catches her—as Norma Jean says, "She don't know the meaning of the word 'knock'."

Because she is so dominated by her mother, Norma Jean skirmishes as much with Mabel as with Leroy in her struggle to free herself from a marriage she no longer wants. The struggle is long and difficult because the tradition of the sanctity of marriage in this culture is old and strong. Norma Jean confronts her mother directly as the story develops. At one point Mabel rebukes Norma Jean for saying "for Christ's sake" and Norma Jean retaliates with, "You ain't seen nothing yet." Mabel, sure that Norma Jean will settle down if she will just go on a "second honeymoon," provokes even stronger language during the same conversation: "When are you going to *shut up* about Shiloh, Mama?"

Norma Jean has not used direct confrontation with Leroy; instead, she has sought to create emo-

"Mason's timely usage of military language heightens the marital strife in 'Shiloh.'"

tional distance by taking up a series of activities that pointedly do not include Leroy. First, she tries bodybuilding, then jogging, then night school. Once, Norma Jean hands Leroy a list, "Things you could do," she says but the alliance of Leroy and Mabel is too strong for her to make her move at home.

Mason's timely usage of military language heightens the marital strife in "Shiloh." In response to Norma Jean's list, Leroy discusses his latest project, the log house he wants to build for them. Norma Jean ignores him as she does her exercises, "marching through the kitchen . . . doing goose steps." Also, there is the origin of Norma Jean's name: ". . . from the Normans. They were invaders." This she tells Leroy on their way to Shiloh. Norma Jean's acceptance of her mother's suggestion that she and Leroy go to Shiloh is itself a brilliant tactical move: she has split her enemies. By himself, Leroy is no match for Norma Jean, and, like the Union army of the original battle of Shiloh, she is the aggressor, the invader, and she wins her own battle when she announces she is leaving Leroy.

Certainly Norma Jean has a stronger personality than Georgeann and Mason must allow for this, or else Mason would simply write the same story with the same characters again and again. Still, Norma Jean can support herself—she is a sales clerk at a Rexall drugstore—whereas Georgeann has never worked outside the home. Norma Jean has also had some exposure to higher education through an "adult-education course in composition" and her first paper garners a B, yet another confidence builder. Finally, Norma Jean has had fifteen years of living by herself while Leroy was on the road and this solitude has developed a cherished independence in her, or, as she puts it, "In some ways, a woman prefers a man who wanders."

Source: G. O. Morphew, "Downhome Feminists in *Shiloh and Other Stories,*" in *Southern Literary Journal,* Vol. 21, No. 2, Spring, 1989, pp. 41–9.

Barbara Henning

Henning teaches English at Long Island University. In the following excerpt, she examines Mason's metaphorical use of details to reveal characters and situations in ''Shiloh.''

Mason's story ''Shiloh'' is about two people and a community who are affected by their beliefs in the American dream and the myth of progress: you can succeed and build a happy life for yourself and your family in this country if you keep up with the times and if you work hard. Leroy Moffitt and Norma Jean, a couple who have been married for fifteen years, find their lives disrupted not only by the trucking accident that has rendered Leroy disabled and unemployed but also by the changes that are occurring in their home town in Kentucky. While the community around them is being built up (''Subdivisions are spreading across western Kentucky like an oil slick''), Norma Jean is building muscles and constructing compositions. Leroy, who passes time smoking marijuana, refuses to look for work; instead, he spends his time practicing at building by putting together craft kits. Finally, despite Norma Jean's refusal to live in a log cabin, he orders a full-size cabin in a kit as a built-in old-fashioned solution for saving his marriage. The act of building offers the reader a framework for understanding this story.

Mason foregrounds details to emphasize the static, spatial nature of the characters' lives. By referring nonchalantly to commercial items—using trade names instead of types: Coke, Lincoln Logs, and *The Donahue Show* instead of soda, toy logs, and TV talk shows—Mason, as well as Carver, disrupt the reader's conventional expectations for more universal details, causing us to hesitate and to focus on the day-to-day detail. The characters, setting, and situation are revealed in ''Shiloh'' through an accumulation of synecdochic details such as these; the narrator and Leroy concentrate on the particular as a substitute for the general, emphasizing Leroy's inability and unwillingness to understand his environment and his wife. Norma Jean is also revealed through Leroy's consciousness as a series of anatomical details. The narrator concentrates on her body parts, foregrounding her pectorals, her legs, her arms, her knees, her ankles, her hard biceps, her chest muscles, and on her two-pound weights. Norma Jean is never depicted as a whole person because Leroy and the empathic narrator are unable to see her in that way.

When a scene ends in Mason's work, it almost always ends with a focus on a specific image. After Norma Jean complains to Leroy about comments her mother had made about a baby who was killed by a dog, Mason ends with a detail: ''For a long time, they sit by the kitchen window watching the birds at the feeder.'' Then silence, switch of scene. Leroy does not answer her. Are the birds random details selected so that we can experience his loss of words? Or are we to make an analogy between the characters and the feeding birds? These details are selected out of a whole context and offered to us as lingering details, parts of a whole. This final image stands out, causing the narrative to come to a standstill, displacing Leroy's and Norma's pain about their failing relationship and the earlier loss of a baby to crib death, by concentrating on another aspect of the context. These details also offer the reader a moment to hesitate and to make comparisons within the context, finding a metaphoric framework in which to understand the situation.

Leroy's rig is now ''a huge piece of furniture gathering dust in the backyard.'' His world is disintegrating into details, and he cannot decide what to do, so his wife—who would rather have him on the road—tries to decide for him. She reads from a list: ''Things you could do. . . . You could get a job as a guard at Union Carbide, where they'd let you set on a stool. You could get on at the lumberyard. You could do a little carpenter work, if you want to build so bad. You could—.''

Before Leroy's accident he had taken benzedrine tablets and spent his time ''flying past scenery'' in his truck; after the accident, however, when he is home and high on marijuana, he drives his car and the ''Power steering and an automatic shift make a car feel so small and inconsequential that his body is hardly involved in the driving process.'' The reader cannot help but compare Leroy's driving processes, in both instances, to the way he lives his life, numbly fitting into the system without making connections between details. He is out of date—attempting to move backward in history instead of forward into the future where opportunity supposedly lies for someone who believes in the American dream. Leroy is, like the rig, a random insignificant detail, a useless piece of old furniture. And Norma Jean is cleaning house. As readers, we have a choice. We can read metaphorically, making connections between the deteriorating truck, Leroy's body, Leroy and Norma Jean's relationship, life in the suburbs, and the language used, a language that concentrates on details—or we can pass everything by as part of the setting.

Leroy is an observer who wants desperately to go back in time and make things right, but he is unable to act, unable to make connections between facts and details.

> He sees things about Norma Jean that he never realized before. When she chops onions, she stares off into a corner, as if she can't bear to look. She puts on her house slippers almost precisely at nine o'clock every evening and nudges her jogging shoes under the couch. She saves bread heels for the birds. Leroy watches the birds at the feeder. He notices the peculiar way goldfinches fly past the window. They close their wings, then fall, then spread their wings to catch and lift themselves. He wonders if they close their eyes when they fall. Norma Jean closes her eyes when they are in bed. She wants the lights turned out. Even then, he is sure she closes her eyes.

He watches Norma Jean in the same way that he watches the birds. The birds are not compared to Norma Jean; instead, they are offered as "selected" details in the context. Leroy just happens to be watching the birds as he is thinking about Norma Jean in bed. Mason's juxtaposition of these two images presents Leroy as toying with the idea that Norma Jean might also be floundering; he never confronts the idea directly. When he comes back to his reverie about Norma Jean, after looking at the birds, he wonders if she closes her eyes when she falls, just as he had wondered about the birds. We recognize, by bringing these two metonymies together, that even though Norma Jean is building up her strength, she is a creature of habit who cannot face intimacy in the light.

Finally, Leroy decides to do what Mabel, Norma's mother (who was raised in a log cabin and hates log cabins), has been urging; he plans a trip to Shiloh, Tennessee, where Mabel and her husband had their honeymoon, a place Mabel explains is full of "history," a Civil War battleground. When the couple goes to Shiloh, they find a log cabin, full of bullet holes. Even Leroy has to laugh. Shiloh is not what Mabel had built it up to be, and it does not hold the same meaning or history for them as it does for Mabel. "Norma Jean wads up her cake wrapper and squeezes it tightly in her hand." She has been building up her strength for this one moment in Shiloh when, in the middle of a battlefield, she will demolish in her fist Leroy's hope for unity, his hope to reconstruct their relationship. "Without looking at Leroy, she says, 'I want to leave you'." Again the reader cannot help but make an analogy between

"Leroy is out of date—attempting to move backward in history instead of forward into the future where opportunity supposedly lies for someone who believes in the American dream."

Leroy and Norma Jean's encounter and the battles that were fought in Shiloh, a place where Norma Jean's parents began their marriage, a place where lives were lost, where blood was shed, where the shelter is full of bullet holes, a place where Leroy simply looks in the other direction.

Leroy realizes, near the end of the story, the limited way he has seen the world.

> Leroy knows he is leaving out a lot. He is leaving out the insides of history. History was always just names and dates to him. It occurs to him that building a house out of logs is similarly empty—too simple. And the real inner workings of a marriage, like most of history, have escaped him. Now he sees that building a log house is the dumbest idea he could have had. It was clumsy of him to think Norma Jean would want a log house. It was a crazy idea. He'll have to think of something else, quickly. He will wad the blueprints into tight balls and fling them into the lake. Then he'll get moving again. He opens his eyes. Norma Jean has moved away and is walking through the cemetery, following a serpentine brick path.

It is Leroy who has had his eyes closed, not Norma Jean. She is far away from him, and while he has been concentrating on her parts and building an empty metaphor to hold them, she has left him. He is ready to make new plans, but he has again displaced his anger in details: now she is following a "serpentine" brick path. In the final lines, by focusing on the sky, he further displaces the anxiety he is experiencing because of Norma Jean's announcement: "The sky is unusually pale—the color of the dust ruffle Mabel made for their bed."

Mason offers us one example after another—Leroy's body, the truck, the car, the craft kits—and the use of trade names, anatomical details in place of the whole, foregrounded details, as well as examples, focus our attention on the "part" rather than the "whole." These synecdoches create a kind of "understatement" and at the same time an aura of special shared knowledge between reader and narrator. In Mason's story, the details also regionalize the story, showing the particular culture that is being lost. A concentration on these types of details and a focus on the activity of building serve as displacements for Leroy's feelings about his marriage and his life, emphasizing the pain and alienation Norma Jean and he are experiencing.

To survive in a modern world, Norma Jean is willing to give up the past and any ideas and rituals involved with their heritage, including their marriage. She believes in the American dream. She must move forward, and she perceives the development of technology as a step forward. From Norma Jean's point of view, malls, television shows, and suburbs improve one's style of living. A log cabin, though, is not as valuable as a condominium in the suburbs, so Leroy—with his dream of a log cabin, his unwillingness to get back to work, and his desire to stop speeding by details—is a failure, in terms of the myth of progress. He is caught in the middle. Because of modernization there is no place in Kentucky for Leroy to build his cabin. Besides that, his understanding of history is distorted; living in a cabin was never such a wonderful experience, as Mabel explains to him, and as the bullet-ridden cabin at Shiloh testifies. It is a no-win situation for Leroy. Perhaps his mistake—in the context of this story—is that he orders a "kit" to build the cabin, embracing modernization at the same time as opposing it.

The parallels between building up strength, building a model house, building a meaningful relationship, and building a future do not quite work. Norma does improve her muscle tone, but Leroy's house is never built, and their relationship is deteriorating. She enters the mainstream, but in the process she begins to lose her culture and community. One cannot "build" to improve, especially if the foundation—history, relationships, and community—is being demolished. In this story, in semirural Kentucky, now well on the way to being developed, a newly passive husband with a modern wife and a ready-made log cabin will not fit into a suburban maze. And no one in particular is responsible.

Source: Barbara Henning, "Minimalism and the American Dream: 'Shiloh' by Bobbie Ann Mason and 'Preservation' by Raymond Carver," in *Modern Fiction Studies,* Vol. 35, No. 4, Winter, 1988, pp. 689–98.

Albert E. Wilhelm

In the following excerpts from a longer article about the collection of stories in which "Shiloh" appears, Wilhelm presents his view of the interrelated themes of social change and personal identity in "Shiloh."

She grew up on a small dairy farm in rural Kentucky. A few years later she had migrated to New York City and was writing features on Fabian, Annette Funicello, and Ann-Margaret for *Movie Life* magazine. As a child her favorite reading materials were Nancy Drew and other girl sleuth mysteries. As a young woman she published a scholarly study of Nabokov's *Ada.*

Given these divergent circumstances of her own life, it is hardly surprising that Bobbie Ann Mason should be interested in culture shock and its jarring effects on an individual's sense of identity. This theme dominates the sixteen pieces in *Shiloh and Other Stories,* her major work of fiction which was nominated for the National Book Award in 1983. Throughout this collection Mason dramatizes the bewildering effects of rapid social change on the residents of a typical "ruburb"—an area in Western Kentucky that is "no longer rural but not yet suburban" [R. Z. Sheppard, *Time,* 3 Jan. 1983]. Again and again in these stories old verities are questioned as farm families watch talk-show discussions of drug use, abortion, and premarital sex. Old relationships are strained as wives begin to lift weights or play video games with strange men. In such contexts the sense of self is besieged from all sides and becomes highly vulnerable. As O. B. Hardison has observed [in *Entering the Maze: Identity and Change in Modern Culture,* 1981], "Identity seems to be unshakable, but its apparent stability is an illusion. As the world changes, identity changes. . . . Because the mind and the world develop at different rates and in different ways, during times of rapid change they cease to be complementary. . . . The result is a widening gap between the world as it exists in the mind and the world as it is experienced—between identity formed by tradition and identity demanded by the present" (xi–xii).

Mason's stories document many efforts to bridge such a gap. Although the behavior of her characters is diverse, two basic patterns are apparent. When faced with confusion about their proper roles, they tend to become either doers or seekers. They stay put and attempt to construct a new identity or they light out for the territories in the hope of discovering one. In short, they try to make over or they make off. Both patterns are, of course, deeply entrenched in American history. The former reflects the Puritan emphasis on building a new order through work. The latter repeats the typical response of the wanderer from Natty Bumppo to Jack Kerouac. (The occupations of Mason's characters frequently parallel these basic patterns. For example, many of her male characters are either construction workers or truck drivers.)

One good example of a character who attempts to construct a new identity is Norma Jean Moffitt in the book's title story. Even though her double given name may suggest a typical good-old Southern girl, Norma Jean is definitely striving to be a new woman. Like many of Mason's characters, her days are filled with the contemporary equivalents of what Arnold van Gennep [in *The Rites of Passage,* 1960] has termed sympathetic rites—ceremonies "based on belief in the reciprocal action of like on like, of opposite on opposite, of the container and the contained . . . of image and real object or real being." For example, her efforts to build a new body by lifting weights reveal also her efforts to build a new self. She doesn't know exactly what to make of her husband and her marriage, so she frantically makes all sorts of other things. By making electric organ music she strives for new harmony. By cooking exotic new foods she hopes to become what she eats.

Her husband Leroy (no longer the king of his castle) has to dodge the barbells swung by Norma Jean, but he too is obsessed with making things. He occupies himself with craft kits (popsicle stick constructions, string art, a snap-together B-17 Flying Fortress) as if putting together these small parts can create a more comprehensive sense of order. No doubt he is also seeking *craft* in its root sense of *power* or *strength.* In an effort to create a real home, Leroy is even thinking of "building a full-scale log house from a kit." Having failed to make a family because of the accidental death of their baby, he and Norma Jean must now "create a new marriage." Although Leroy admits that a log cabin will be out of place in the new subdivisions, he apparently sees such a construction as a means of returning to a more stable past. He and Norma Jean could join together in a cabin-raising and revert to the time of those more resourceful Kentuckians like Abe Lincoln or Daniel Boone. . . .

"Even though her double given name may suggest a typical good-old Southern girl, Norma Jean is definitely striving to be a new woman."

Although Leroy and Norma Jean Moffitt in "Shiloh" are both avid makers, this story also ends with a futile journey. Actually Leroy has spent many days on the road. Before his accident he drove his tractor-trailer rig "to kingdom come and back," but he realizes that he never took time "to examine anything." Now, at the urging of his mother-in-law, he embarks with Norma Jean on a journey of reconciliation to Shiloh. In an effort to find peace, they ironically go to a battlefield. Since Leroy is interested in building a log home, they go to see an old cabin in the park. When they arrive, however, it is surrounded by tourists looking at bullet holes in the walls. The final irony which caps this ill-fated trip is that Leroy and Norma Jean discuss their failing marriage while sitting in a cemetery. . . .

The characters in Mason's stories are a cast of valiant strugglers. They attempt to create order through various sympathetic rites, but their magic is frequently powerless. They journey through wide expanses without ever finding a real sense of place. In spite of all their efforts they repeatedly find themselves caught in the dilemma described by Orrin Klapp [in *Collective Search for Identity,* 1969]: "In the accumulation of new things, it is possible for society to pass the optimum point in the ratio between the new and the old . . . between innovation and acculturation on the one hand and tradition on the other. Beyond this optimum point, where society is roused to creativity by introduction of new elements, is a danger point where consensus and integrity of the person break down." In her "few square miles of native turf" (Towers, *New York Review of Books,* 16 Dec. 1982), Mason graphically depicts such a society.

Source: Albert E. Wilhelm, ''Making Over or Making Off: The Problem of Identity in Bobbie Ann Mason's Short Fiction,'' in *The Southern Literary Journal,* Vol. 18, No. 2, Spring, 1986, pp. 76–82.

Wilhelm, Albert E. ''Private Rituals: Coping with Change in the Fiction of Bobbie Ann Mason,'' in *The Midwest Quarterly,* Vol. 28, No. 2, Winter, 1987, pp. 271-82.

Sources

Blythe, Hal, and Charlie Sweet. ''The Ambiguous Grail Quest in 'Shiloh','' in *Studies in Short Fiction,* Vol. 32, No. 2, Spring, 1995, pp. 223-26.

Lyons, Gene. A review of *Shiloh and Other Stories* in *Newsweek,* November 15, 1982, p. 107

Mason, Bobbie Ann and Lila Havens. ''Bobbie Ann Mason: A Conversation with Lila Havens,'' in *The Story and Its Writer: An Introduction to Short Fiction,* 2nd ed., edited by Ann Charters, St. Martin's Press, 1987, pp. 1345-49.

Towers, Robert. A review of *Shiloh and Other Stories* in *The New York Review of Books,* December 16, 1982, p. 38.

Tyler, Anne. A review of *Shiloh and Other Stories* in *The New Republic,* November 1, 1982, p. 36.

Vigderman, Patricia. A review of *Shiloh and Other Stories* in *The Nation,* March 19, 1983, p. 345.

Further Reading

''Bobbie Ann Mason,'' in *Short Story Criticism,* Vol. 4, edited by Thomas Votteler, Gale, 1990, pp. 298–311.

Includes reprinted criticism on Mason's short stories.

Brinkmeyer, Robert H., Jr. ''Finding One's History: Bobbie Ann Mason and Contemporary Southern Literature,'' in *The Southern Literary Journal,* Vol. 19, No. 2, Spring, 1987, pp. 20-33.

Concentrates on the sense of history in Mason's work as well as Mason's place in the history of Southern literature.

Mason, Bobbie Ann, Bonnie Lyons, and Bill Oliver. An interview in *Contemporary Literature,* Vol. 32, No. 4, Winter, 1991, pp. 449-70.

Covers Mason's work through 1991 and focuses on her understanding of the themes of her stories as well as her writing process.

Sorrow-Acre

Isak Dinesen

1942

First published in Danish as part of the collection *Winter's Tales,* ''Sorrow-Acre'' is the most frequently anthologized of Dinesen's short stories. Written upon her return to Denmark after more than a decade in Africa, and during the darkest days of World War II, the collection's title has a double meaning, referring to both the cold, northern climate in which Dinesen found herself and to the war raging all around her. As Thomas Whissen writes, ''[D]enied a sword, she took up the only weapon she had—her pen—and wrote *Winter's Tales.* Huddled behind blackout curtains in that draughty old house on the sound, cut off from the world, aware that she was being watched (German soldiers camped in her backyard), she began writing tales again, the first in nearly a decade.''

However, it would be a mistake to read the collection, or ''Sorrow-Acre,'' as nothing more than the effect of these causes. Dinesen was one of the more gifted writers of an abundantly gifted era, and all of her gifts are on display in this collection. Donald Hannah gives one obvious example drawn from ''Sorrow-Acre'' when he observes that Dinesen's ''life-long interest in painting is . . . reflected by the way in which her imagination in the tales frequently operates in visual terms. She writes like a painter. The striking description of the countryside in the opening paragraphs of 'Sorrow-Acre' is but one example of this.'' Throughout ''Sorrow-Acre,'' *Winter's Tales,* and indeed, throughout her entire life's work, she demonstrates the power of

her clearsighted imagination and formal elegance to impressive, often stunning effect.

Author Biography

Isak Dinesen was born Karen Christentze Dinesen at the estate of Rungstedlund, near Rungsted, fifteen miles north of Copenhagen, Denmark, on April 17, 1885. Though she is best known today for her writings about Kenya—works like *Out of Africa* and *Shadows on the Grass*—she in fact spent most of her life at Rungstedlund. She was raised there, returned there after her years in Kenya, and lived there until her death; it is at Rungstedlund that she wrote *Winter's Tales,* the collection in which "Sorrow-Acre" appeared.

Dinesen's parents were from two very different walks of life. Her mother's family, the Westenholzes, were quite wealthy, urbane, liberal, and bourgeois. Judith Thurman, in *Isak Dinesen, the Life of a Storyteller,* writes that the Westenholzes "were also . . . passionate feminists and nonconformists, converts to the Unitarian Church. . . . Their energies went into practical or abstract projects, and mostly to their own moral excellence." Her father's family, the Dinesens, were cut from a different cloth. Although they were also wealthy, her father's family was from the country; they carried no title, but nonetheless had aristocratic, rather than bourgeois sensibilities. In Thurman's words, "the men tended to be virile and opinionated, the women elegant and pretty." Isak navigated through life guided by the magnetism of these two opposite poles, poles Thurman identifies as "Dinesen/Westenholz, freedom/taboo, aristocrat/bourgeois," and finally, "either/or."

Dinesen's life as a writer can be conveniently broken up into three periods. During the first period, as Karen Dinesen, she filled her time with the social life her station in life afforded her—with parties, receptions, balls—but also with writing. During these early years, she succeeded in getting three of her stories published in Danish literary reviews—"The Hermits," "The Ploughman," and "The de Cats Family"—but she did not yet think of herself as a writer. The first period came to an abrupt end in 1914 when she moved to Kenya and married her Swedish cousin, Baron Bror von Blixen-Finecke, who had purchased a large coffee farm near Nairobi with her family's money. The seventeen-year period which followed, recounted in the memoirs *Out of Africa* and *Shadows on the Grass,* was brought to a close when the farm eventually ran into so much debt that she was forced to sell it and leave. The marriage with Blixen had failed also, he being chronically unfaithful to his wife. In 1931 Dinesen, now forty-six, returned to Rungstedlund where she began to write in earnest, publishing the story collections and memoirs for which she is known. The remainder of her life was spent with her international reputation growing greater, while her physical well-being declined. Dinesen died at Rungstedlund in 1962 of emaciation, the result of her long, unendingly painful fight with the syphilis she had acquired from Blixen early in their marriage.

Plot Summary

At his mother's urgent request, a young man named Adam has returned from England to his ancestral home in Denmark at the height of the short Danish summer. He meets his uncle in a beautiful garden on the estate. After an amiable discussion comparing the tasks confronted by the gods of Rome to those of the earlier Norse gods, Adam notes that his uncle seems distracted. His uncle admits that his thoughts are elsewhere and tells Adam the story of Goske Piil.

One week before Adam's arrival, his uncle says, someone burned down his barn at Rodmosegaard. A few days later, the keeper at Rodmose and a wheelwright came to the house with Goske Piil, a widow's son, in tow. They swore that Goske was the person who had set the barn on fire. Both men disliked Goske. The keeper suspected him of having poached on the grounds of Rodmose, while the wheelwright suspected Goske of having relations with his own young wife. The boy swore to his innocence, but he was unable to convince Adam's uncle in conversation with the two men that he was truly innocent. Adam's uncle had Goske locked up, meaning to send him to the judge of the district with a letter. The judge, he explained, is an idiot and would have done whatever he thought the uncle wanted him to do: send the boy to prison, put him in the army as a bad character, or even free him.

During a ride through his fields, Adam's uncle met Anne-Marie Piil, Goske's mother. She protested her son's innocence, saying that her son had indeed been in Rodmose at the time of the barn-fire, but only to visit someone. Still uncertain of what to do with Goske, Adam's uncle had an idea: he told Anne-Marie that if she could mow the rye field in which they stood in a single day, between sunrise and sunset, he would drop the case and free Goske. If not, ''he must go, and it is not likely [she] will ever see him again.'' The task to which Anne-Marie agreed was huge: ''a day's work to three men, or three days' work to one man,'' but Anne-Marie agreed gladly, ''kiss[ing] his boot in gratitude.''

At sunrise, as Adam and his uncle discussed Norse and Olympian mythology, Anne-Marie begins to mow the field. A little later in the morning the narrative focus shifts to Adam's uncle's new wife, Sophie-Magdalena, a seventeen-year-old girl who had been raised at court. Although she is not, as the narrator observes, ideally suited for the role she is to fill as the uncle's wife (''there was probably not in the whole country a creature more exquisitely and innocently drilled to the stately measure of a palace''), she quickly learns to adapt to country life, enjoying the sensual reality of nature in a greater intimacy than life at court allowed. In terms of action, Sophie-Magdalena's scene is quite short. She wakes up, takes her nightdress off and observes her naked form in a mirror, kills a flea on her leg, and dresses.

In the afternoon, after a ride around the bounds of the estate with Sophie-Magdalena, Adam returns to the garden, joining his uncle who continues to watch Anna-Marie's progress across the field. Now, for the first time, Adam begins to understand that Anne-Marie will almost certainly die, whether she succeeds or fails, and begs his uncle to change his mind. But Adam's uncle remains resolute, insisting that his word cannot be broken, and that Anna-Marie is at peace with their agreement. They quarrel, and Adam threatens to leave forever, but shortly thereafter has a change of heart.

As sunset nears, it appears that Anne-Marie may finish the acre and succeed in freeing her son. The whole village gathers around her to watch as she makes her way, ever more slowly, down the last row. The village bailiff has even brought Anne-Marie's son to the field to watch. After she cuts the last handful of corn, the uncle tells her that she has succeeded, that her son is free. She does not seem to hear, so he tells her son to repeat what he has said. Goske tells her. She reaches up, touches his tear-stained cheek, and falls into his arms, dead.

Isak Dinesen

''In the place where the woman had died the old lord later on had a stone set up, with a sickle engraved in it. The peasants on the land then named the rye field 'Sorrow-Acre.' By this name it was known a long time after the story of the woman and her son had itself been forgotten.''

Characters

Adam

Adam, the first character described in the story is also the story's protagonist, or main character. The narrator's initial description of him is external: ''he was dark, a strong and sturdy figure with fine eyes and hands; he limped a little on one leg,'' but it soon becomes clear that Adam is also keenly intelligent and well-traveled. Not only is he familiar with Roman and Danish mythology, but he is well-read in philosophy: from Aristotle's *Poetics,* which provides the structural background to his discussion of tragedy, to then-modern philosophical tracts, most notably Thomas Paine's (1737-1809) ''The Rights of Man'' (1791). He has ''traveled and lived out of Denmark, in Rome and Paris,'' and is appointed to the Court of King George, the same King George from whom the American colonies won their independence in the Revolutionary War.

Anne-Marie Piil

It is Anne-Marie Piil who works herself to death in ''Sorrow-Acre,'' and for whom the acre is subsequently named. Although she says nothing during the course of the story (with the exception of her reported conversation with Adam's uncle), her wordless presence in the story is meant to be an overwhelming demonstration of what Dinesen terms ''an effort too sweet for words'': ''to die for the one you loved.''

Goske Piil

Goske, Anne-Marie's son, is the catalyst for the story's action. Accused of setting a barn on fire, he was to be sent to the magistrate for trial; but Adam's uncle, meeting the boy's mother, Anne-Marie, by chance, agrees to free Goske if she can reap a large field in a day's time. Like Anne-Marie, Goske says little during the story, but he is present at the end of the day, and it is in his arms that his mother dies.

Sophie-Magdalena

Like Adam's uncle, Sophie-Magdalena's full name is never given, and her character remains somewhat incomplete as well. Originally the intended bride of Adam's young, sickly cousin, Sophie-Magdalena marries the bridegroom-to-be's father soon after his son's death. Being from a good family, Sophie-Magdalena will, it is hoped, restore Adam's uncle to good graces with the King. Sophie's appearance on the stage of ''Sorrow-Acre'' is brief; but her nubile, sensuous awakening in her bed-chamber nonetheless provides a striking contrast to the cool, dispassionate intellectualism of the conversation taking place outside between Adam and his uncle.

Uncle

The uncle is both Adam's foil and his future. Adam's uncle is the head of the family estate, the younger man's father having died some time ago. The uncle had wished to leave the estate and his name to a son, but his only son died before the beginning of the story's action, and before he was able to marry and provide Adam's uncle with a grandson. In order to pass his name on, Adam's uncle marries his son's intended bride, Sophie-Magdalena, shortly before the start of the story's action.

Themes

Custom and Tradition

From the opening paragraphs, in which the narrator reminds the reader that ''a human race had lived on this land for a thousand years'' to the closing sentence, in which the reader is told that the place was known as ''Sorrow-Acre a long time after the story of the woman and her son had itself been forgotten,'' Dinesen keeps the power of custom and tradition in the forefront of her narrative. In this fictional world, custom and tradition work hand in hand, reinforcing each other—things are done in a certain way, a customary way, because there is a tradition of doing them that way; the tradition exists because of the adherence to custom. This is, in some sense, the crux of the story, for when Adam returns from England, awakened to the ideas of freedom and equality then sweeping America, France, and England, he finds it difficult to accept the feudal state that still exists in his ancestral home. Interestingly, however, it is only when Adam is confronted with the reality of Anne-Marie's suffering that he becomes upset; this demonstrates the degree to which he has remained a product of his culture.

Duty and Responsibility

Hand in hand with custom and tradition runs the theme of duty and responsibility. In one of the crucial passages in the story, Adam and his uncle articulate their very different visions of what it means to give one's word, and, by extension, the meaning of words themselves. In an allusion to the opening passage of the Gospel of John (''In the beginning was the Word, and the Word was with God, and the Word was God''), the uncle says, ''you have learned in school . . . that in the beginning was the word. It may have been pronounced in caprice, as a whim, the Scripture tells us nothing about it. It is still the principle of our world, its law of gravitation. My own humble word has been the principle of the land on which we stand, for an age of man. My father's word was the same, before my day.'' The uncle's argument maintains that the word, once given, is irrevocable; it creates a responsibility for both the giver and receiver, so that neither the uncle nor Anna-Marie can be freed from the might of the word.

Adam, on the other hand, sees the word in more Joycean terms ("in the virgin womb of the imagination the Word was made flesh"), arguing that his uncle is wrong, that the word "is imagination, daring and passion," sentiments more in keeping with the present day than with the "thousand year old" precedents the uncle is fond of quoting. Nonetheless, despite the appeal of the sentiments Adam voices to contemporary readers, one must think carefully about the implications of the uncle's undoubtedly correct assertion that, while he and Adam—and by extension, modern readers—"do not, perhaps, quite understand one another," he is "in good understanding" with "[his] own people."

Religion

Though religion does not play as prominent a place in this story as one might expect it to, Christian and pagan gods are a recurrent theme. As the narrator explains early on in describing the country house, the class of people from which Adam comes is less concerned with the hereafter than with the here: "The country house did not gaze upward, like the church, nor down to the ground like the huts; it had a wider earthly horizon than they. For these people, as Adam and his uncle demonstrate, God may be useful, but the gods of old are more useful, at least as a starting point for a discussion of absolute power, its workings, and its pitfalls. While Adam believes that the Norse gods were morally greater than the Greco-Roman gods because they possessed the sublime human virtues of righteousness, trustworthiness, benevolence and chivalrousness, his uncle argues that virtue came more easily to these gods because their power was not absolute. "'And does power,' Adam again asked, 'stand in the way of virtue?'" "'Nay,' said his uncle gravely, 'Nay, power is in itself the supreme virtue.'"

Topics for Further Study

- What is the significance of the sickle engraved on the stone marker at the end of "Sorrow-Acre"? Does the sickle have a symbolic function?
- Evaluate the arguments Adam's uncle gives in favor of making the widow Piil finish the entire field. Are they persuasive? Would your opinion be different if she had lived?
- Adam decides not to go to America. How would the reader's impression of the uncle be affected if Adam had made good on his threat and left?
- The reader learns that Sophie-Magdalena is unhappy, then she disappears from the story. Why? Is her story complete?
- What is the purpose of the many allusions to the Bible in "Sorrow-Acre"?
- How does the material Dinesen added to the uncle's speech change your understanding of the story? (See the essay by David Kippen.)

Style

Point of View and Narration

"Sorrow-Acre" is told from a consistent third-person, or "he said/she said," point of view, and from a strikingly even narrative distance. The narrator is partially omniscient; that is, she can tell the reader what Adam and Sophie-Magdalena are thinking when the alternative would be unwieldy. (Imagine, for example, how awkward it would appear if Sophie-Magdalena had to say everything she thinks aloud to herself or someone else). But generally the narrator prefers to present narrative commentary ("the low, undulating Danish landscape was silent"; "a young man walked") and report speech. At the same time, this narrator clearly has a personality distinct from the personalities of the story's characters, and seems to view the characters with occasional irony and complete detachment. The narrative voice, not to be confused with the personal voice of the author, is similar to the voice Dinesen utilizes in some of her longer works; compare, for example, the first-person voice and tone in the opening lines of *Out of Africa* to the narrative tone at the outset of "Sorrow-Acre."

Setting

The story is set in an almost feudal Denmark in the late eighteenth century, but the England of George III—a nation on the cusp of modernity—is a powerful, albeit offstage, force. Adam, the story's protagonist, tries to bridge the impossible gulf between these two but must eventually choose either to flee to America, or to be a Dane in Denmark.

Structure

Although "Sorrow-Acre" can be read as a story, it works better when read as an allegory. As is often the case in the heavily stylized, nuanced allegorical form, the action takes place during a single day, from sunrise to sunset. During that interval, two characters, one young, the other old, engage in a genteel battle between feudalism and modernity, which in turn can be read as a commentary on the far-from-genteel battle between the democratic Allied forces and the quasi-feudal Axis forces fighting for control of Europe during the early years of World War II, when Dinesen's *Winter's Tales* collection was written and published. (One of the advantages of allegory over many other fictional forms is that one can talk about controversial things in oblique language, which makes allegory more difficult to censor and perhaps even safer than thinly disguised narrative).

Fairy Tale

"Sorrow-Acre" exhibits many characteristics of a fairy tale or fable. The story is set in a timeless agrarian place where nobles, the gentry, and the yeoman peasantry interact along clearly drawn class lines. There is a palatial estate upon which the action takes place, specifically the undertaking of a challenge which, if met, will mean the difference between life and death. There is an inflexible tyrant in the uncle, a beautiful young woman longing for more from life than she is experiencing, a traveler from afar (Adam) to challenge the tyrant's prerogative, and an earnest old peasant woman who accepts a challenge which seems beyond her ability to fulfill.

Historical Context

In order to fully understand the critique of Dinesen's "Sorrow-Acre," one must first examine three very different historical moments and places: late eighteenth-century Europe, early twentieth-century Kenya, and mid twentieth-century Denmark.

Eighteenth-Century Europe

The first, most obvious point of inquiry is the late eighteenth-century during which the story's action takes place. The story's physical setting is Denmark, but in light of Adam's preoccupation with the intellectual currents sweeping England, France, and the newly independent United States, it is clearly important to consider what is happening in these places as well. Although changes during this period are many, the most significant are that the French Revolution and the American War of Independence have ushered in a new age of individual rights. The once clear divisions between the landed nobility and the landless peasantry now became increasingly complicated. One complicating factor is the emergence of a "middle" class—a consequence of the fledgling Industrial Revolution. Another is the contradiction between "the divine right of kings" and the "inalienable rights of men." It is important, however, to keep in mind that these new, liberal ideas are not embraced by the landed aristocracy in England, France, or anywhere else; they are a threat to the very idea of traditional aristocratic rights. In Denmark, to this point, the eighteenth century has seen a gradual, but nonetheless substantial, erosion in the rights of the peasantry. But as England's needs for grain outstrip its ability to supply its needs, it turns to Denmark (among others) to fill the gap. In turn, the rise in the prices for grain and other agricultural commodities ushers in a period of increasing economic advantage for the farmworker that lasts until the end of the Napoleonic Wars in 1809. So the period during which "Sorrow-Acre" is set is not one of stasis, but instead, an historic moment in which the pattern of centuries is dramatically revised.

Twentieth-Century Kenya

Less obvious, but no less essential to understanding Dinesen's point of view, is an understanding of Kenya in the early twentieth century. It is in Kenya that Dinesen learns to be her own person and—more importantly—to begin to empathize with people who do not share her fortunate station in life. It is also here that she gathers the material which is to become *Out of Africa,* the collection of stories for which she is best known today. Like the rest of sub-Saharan Africa, the record of Kenya's twentieth century is greatly influenced by the colonial power which ruled it—in Kenya's case, Britain. Early twentieth-century British policy in Kenya centered around the Uganda railway: first building it, then making it profitable. The building done, Britain encouraged settlement and farming of the Kenyan highlands in the hope that transporting the agricultural produce of this largely uninhabited, good land would be sufficiently lucrative to support

Compare & Contrast

- **1940s:** Breaking its promise of non-aggression, Germany invades and occupies Denmark in 1940. Although active resistance is futile, a powerful passive-resistance movement soon emerges. The Nazis occupy Denmark throughout World War II. Denmark is liberated at the war's end and joins the alliance of Western nations called NATO (North Atlantic Treaty Organization) four years later.

  1990s: Denmark is considered one of the world's nations most open to free expression and personal autonomy.

- **1940s:** Dinesen enjoys a generally positive critical reaction to her writings, including *Winter's Tales,* becoming increasingly confident in herself as a public intellectual and in the issues surrounding women's intellectual advancement.

  1990s: After the popular and critical success of Sydney Pollack's film version of *Out of Africa* (1985), Dinesen's literature enjoys a revival among a new generation of readers; today it is widely read and the source of much critical interpretation.

the line. It is in these highlands that Dinesen settled and about them that she writes in the beginning of *Out of Africa:* ''I had a farm in Africa, at the foot of the Ngong Hills.'' In an ironic parallel to Europe's gradual democratization from the late eighteenth century onward, white hegemony, or control, in Kenya is questioned with increasing frequency and insistence during the years of Dinesen's tenure there. For many, this questioning culminates in 1938 with the publication of Jomo Kenyatta's *Facing Mount Kenya,* a book whose effect on Kenyan politics of this period is similar to the effect of Thomas Paine's *The Rights of Man* on the politics of the English-speaking world of the late eighteenth-century Revolutionary era.

Denmark and World War II

Knowing something about what Denmark was like during the late 1930s and early 1940s is also quite important. One cannot pass over these years without making reference to the reality of World War II and the conflict between freedom-loving nations and nations bent upon conquest of other people and their lands. If the motion of the prior 150 years has been toward greater individual freedom, Hitler's invasion—and Denmark's acquiescence—signaled the elimination of individual freedoms and the advent of totalitarianism. The physical contest between nations is therefore of less concern to Dinesen at this point than is the threat of totalitarianism—which seeks to control the minds of others—that she sees in Hitler's National Socialism. *Winter's Tales,* the collection containing ''Sorrow-Acre,'' can perhaps be best understood, therefore, in the context of the fairly successful passive-resistance movement in Denmark.

Critical Overview

Critical reaction to *Winter's Tales* must be seen through two lenses: present and past. Although she is now considered a major twentieth-century writer, Dinesen was, for a time, essentially forgotten. The revival of interest in her as a writer can be attributed in large part to Sydney Pollack's film version of *Out of Africa.* As a result, one cannot speak of a single critical reaction, but must instead consider two reactions: those of her contemporaries and those of the post-revival critics. Interestingly, each group seems to have seized upon very different facets of her writing as most worthy of comment. For the most part, earlier critics were more interested in her stylistic accomplishments, for example, Orville Prescott, writing in the *New York Times,* called her style ''elaborately artificial, formal, suave, and beautiful,'' while William Sansom wrote in the *Saturday*

Review that she "gives us tales of blood and doom and honor in the old grand manner." Later critics seem more interested in understanding the significance of her stories' content.

However, there are some points at which all critics seem to agree. Although they understandably see many different things in *Winter's Tales,* they are unanimous in their praise for the literary accomplishment the stories demonstrate. David Richter pointed out in the *Journal of Narrative Technique* that "Sorrow-Acre" "invokes many of the persistent themes that haunt Dinesen's work: the contrast between the cruel beauty of the *ancien regime* and the more prosaic humanitarian ethos of modern democracy that will inevitably displace it; the inextricable connections between men and the land they live on; the arcane routes by which men seek and find their destiny; the perverse and terrible costs which love extracts."

Criticism

David Kippen

Kippen is an educator and specialist on British colonial literature and twentieth-century South African fiction. In the following essay, he discusses "Sorrow-Acre" as an allegory.

Like fable, allegory describes one thing—usually something quite specific—to talk about something else that shares similar features or characteristics. So, for example, Aesop's fable "The Tortoise and the Hare" isn't really "about" a tortoise or a hare; instead, it is about plodding perseverance and mercurial quickness—the tortoise and the hare are merely physical manifestations of these moral attributes. Similarly, Dinesen's "Sorrow-Acre" is neither about a young man named Adam nor about the fate of the widow Piil. These characters are representations of—or standing in for—what turns out to be a complex use of history. Unlike fable, however, allegory rarely presents a clearly discernible moral. While "slow and steady wins the race" neatly summarizes both the story of the race run by the tortoise and underscores the (moral) value of perseverance, it is difficult to draw a single, clear moral from Dinesen's story. This difficulty is due both to the complexity of the ideas the characters manifest and to the greater length and larger cast of allegory in general and Dinesen's story in particular. However, while one may not be able to reduce the meanings of "Sorrow-Acre" to a single phrase, it is nonetheless clear that the story has as its focal point Adam's question at daybreak, and the landscape's answer at dusk.

Returning to Denmark after an extended stay abroad, Adam finds his homeland deeply familiar, but his absence gives him new vision, enabling him to stand outside this familiarity. He sees his homeland, and his hereditary place in it, as natural, but not inevitable. He sees the windmill, the church, the manor—all of these give evidence of a process by which the land and the people who live on it have worked upon and shaped one another, in much the same manner as sea and seashore exist in simultaneous opposition and partnership, each defining itself against, but also through, the other. As the omniscient narrator observes, "a human race had lived on this land for a thousand years, had been formed by its soil and weather, and had marked it with its thoughts, so that now no one could tell where . . . the one ceased and the other began."

However, though Adam returns as "nominal" heir to his manor and estate, his stay in England coincides with the powerful emergence of a set of ideas that throw into question doctrines arguing that the rights of kings and lords over their subjects represent the will of God, and are therefore the divine intention: "[H]e had come in touch with the great new ideas of the age: of nature of the right and freedom of man, of justice and beauty. The universe, through them, had become infinitely wider to him." Thomas Paine's "The Rights of Man" (1791), the French Revolution (1789), and the American Revolutionary War had in common a theme most forcibly articulated in the second paragraph of the American colonies' Declaration of Independence:

> We hold these truths to be self-evident, that all men are created equal, that they are endowed by their Creator with certain unalienable rights, that among these are life, liberty and the pursuit of happiness. That to secure these rights, governments are instituted among men, deriving their just powers from the consent of the governed. That whenever any form of government becomes destructive to these ends, it is the right of the people to alter or to abolish it, and to institute new government, laying its foundation on such principles and organizing its powers in such form, as to them shall seem most likely to effect their safety and happiness.

Perhaps it is the dissonance between this strident call of the future—a call for rulers to be accountable to the ruled—and the feudal, thousand-year past through which Adam finds himself walking that morning, that makes Adam speak to the

A still from the film Out of Africa, *depicting the expanse of Dinesen's farm in Kenya, which brings to mind the vast field that Anne-Marie Piil was forced to mow.*

land "as to a person, as to the mother of his race." He asks: "Is it only my body that you want . . . while you reject my imagination, energy and emotions? If the world might be brought to acknowledge that the virtue of our name does not belong to the past only, will it give you no satisfaction?"

His question, asked "half in jest," receives no answer that morning, but it holds within it the conflict at the heart of Dinesen's story between the uncertainty of feudal authority, and the verdant, certain fructiveness of democracy. As Susan Hardy Aiken observes, "Sorrow-Acre" "constitutes a fundamental interrogation of patrilineal primacy both cultural and textual, not only on the literal level of its narrative 'events,' but also on the symbolic level, where it functions as an oblique, mythopoeic parable about its own origins and its 'illicit' position in the lineage of male texts."

It would be wrong, of course, to argue that this conflict between feudalism and democracy, between the powers of paternity and maternity is the *only* important theme in "Sorrow-Acre." Although most of her other thematic concerns are ultimately subordinate to this one, as noted earlier, Dinesen's story has a number of other well-developed thematic threads, as well as some important parallels to other texts. A useful discussion of these relationships could easily be the subject of several essays and is therefore beyond the scope of the present study, but the most important parallels—to the Bible and to Shakespeare's *Hamlet*—should not be passed over without mention.

Dinesen is not light-handed when she wishes to have her reader note an allusion to another text. While another author might be content to name his protagonist "Adam" and, having done so, expect his reader to look for simple symmetry between the contours of his text and the Old Testament, Dinesen creates an elaborate parable-in-parallel between the Bible and her text. She invokes an "old Adam," in the person of the Uncle, who personifies commandments brought into question (or up to date) by the arrival of the "new Adam," in youth like Christ; she sets their meeting in a garden "which is as fresh as the Garden of Eden, newly created," and she thereby invites her readers to link the relationship of the divine right of kings and the Rights of Man. Similarly, when she wishes to invoke *Hamlet* Dinesen is not content to create a young Danish protagonist who has been called back to his ancestral home—now under the reign of "his father's brother"—by the death of a relative and the incestuous marriage

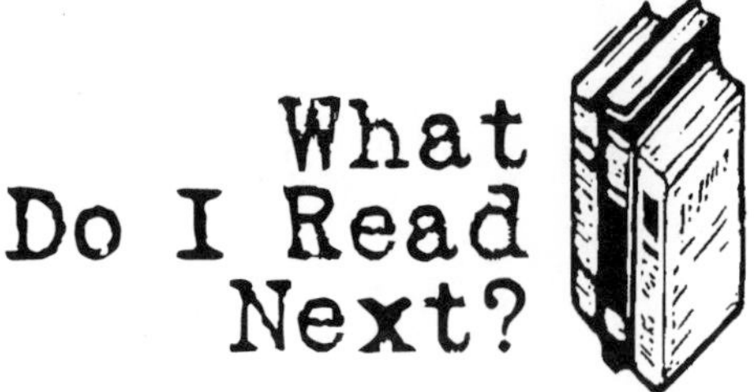

- Judith Thurman's *Isak Dinesen: The Life of a Storyteller* (1982) is the most comprehensive biography of Dinesen's life in print. Thurman writes in a clear, straightforward, readable style, and her work is accepted by most as the definitive biography of Dinesen.
- *Winter's Tales* (1942) is the collection in which "Sorrow-Acre" first appeared. The other stories in the book, according to critic Marcia Landy, "are structured around dominant Shakespearian motifs—the relationship between art and nature, loss and recovery, and the pastoral elegiac vision as a vehicle for exploring these motifs."
- *Out of Africa* is Dinesen's best-known work. Loosely adapted and mixed with parts of *Shadows in the Grass,* it was made into a movie by Sydney Pollack in 1982. Both novel and film chronicle an Africa of dangerous, arduous beauty.
- In terms of economy and insight, Guy de Maupassant is considered by many to be a short story writer without equal. Like the stories in Dinesen's *Winter's Tales* his *Day and Night Stories* deal with moral issues. They are short, concise, and—like Dinesen's—offer a clear-sighted vision of Everyman confronting the challenges of circumstances for which he is not entirely prepared.

of his uncle. As if this might not yet be clear, she peppers the rest of her text with unveiled references to the play: "a Rosenkrantz . . . at Rosenholm"; "He remembered the old servants who had taught him; some of them were now in their graves"; "the stage of this world." While exploration of these parallels is not possible here, it is certainly worth noting that the unquestioned authority of paternity is the central focus of each of them: God, the Father of man; Hamlet, his father's avenger.

Dinesen engages with authority, but particularly paternal authority, at a number of levels, some abstract, seemingly far-removed from the story's action, others quite concrete. At Adam's first meeting with his uncle, for example, they enter into an obscure, lengthy discussion whose primary subject is a comparison between the Norse gods and the gods of Greece and Rome. As Adam's uncle explains, the primary distinction between these gods (at least for Dinesen's purposes) comes down to this: the Norse gods were not omnipotent; the Greco-Roman gods were. One is tempted to understand this discussion as a framework for the rest of the story, to create an equation between Adam and the Norse gods' impotence, on one hand, and his Uncle and the Greco-Roman gods' omnipotence on the other. This line of thought would seem to be borne out by the quick shift in their discussion from this highly abstract terrain to the fate of the widow Piil, and it is reasonable to assume that—at least on the surface of the allegory—Dinesen's intention is to be understood in just this manner.

Near the end of the day, Adam again joins his uncle, who has spent the morning and afternoon steadfastly watching the widow's progress. Adam, who until this point seems to have understood that day's events in an academic, or philosophical framework, is now close enough to the widow to see her as a suffering individual; he is finally moved to beg his uncle to break his word and release the widow from their agreement. His uncle refuses, saying "my own humble word has been the principle of the land on which we stand, for an age of man. My father's word was the same, before my day." Adam responds: "you are mistaken. . . . The word is creative, it is imagination, daring and passion. By it the world was made." But Adam is unable to move his uncle, who says "you are young . . . I am old-fashioned, I have been quoting to you texts a thousand years old. We do not, perhaps, quite understand one another.'' In the American edition, he then says ''But with my own people I am, I believe, in good understanding.'' The uncle seems to end the discussion here, saying in essence: ''I'm not going to argue any more. I'm going to do what I wish.'' But this is not Dinesen's final word.

According to Olga Anastasia Pelensky (author of *Isak Dinesen: The Life and Imagination of a Seducer,* 1991), the following passage was added when Dinesen rewrote the story in Danish, then added to the British edition, but was never incorporated into the American edition. After ''we do not, perhaps, quite understand each other,'' Dinesen later added:

> ''But if, to your ears, my orthodoxy does now sound antiquated, remember that within a hundred years both mine and your own speech will sound antiquated to the generations then discoursing upon word and life. Have patience, let me explain myself to you.
>
> ''Believe me, I have the public welfare as much at heart as you yourself. But should we, in our concern, for *le bien commun,* gaze only at those human beings who happen to be about us today, and look neither before or after? When we consider the matter rightly we will find the past generations to be in majority—Well,'' he interrupted himself, as Adam made a gesture of impatience, ''let them rest as they deserve to. But the coming generations, you will agree, must ever be in majority. And when we speak of the welfare of the many we must needs let them have the last word. King Pharaoh, I have been told, made a hundred thousands of his subjects slave for him and suffer great hardships, in order to build him a pyramid. He might at the same cost, have distributed bread and wine amongst his people, have fed and clothed them, and have been blessed by them. Still even so things would have been with them, today, what they are now: they would all be dead and gone. And a hundred generations have, since the days of King Pharaoh, lifted their eyes to the pyramids with pride and joy, and acclaimed them their own. A great deed, my nephew,—be it even brought forth with tears, even with blood,—is a fund of resource, a treasure for the coming generations to live on, it is, within hard times and the hour of need, bread to the people.
>
> ''But the true insight into these matters,'' the old lord went on, ''you will never find, and can never reasonably expect to find, with the common people, to whom the chief concern in life is their daily bread, and who are living, mentally as well as physically, from hand to mouth. Nay, my nephew, it is our affair and our responsibility, we, who have inherited from the past and who know that we are to live on, in name and blood, through the coming centuries. These humble peasants, whose life is one with the life of the earth, and of whom you have spoken with so much fervency, what good are we to them but this: that they may trust you to look after *le bien commun,* not at the moment only, but in the future? And see you now, my good nephew, you and I may find it a little difficult to see eye to eye.''

"What does the thunder say? That it is not the world deciding for the individual, but the individual who must decide for himself whether his virtue is to be found in his 'imagination, energy and emotions' or in the possession of a thousand-year-old name with the power to rule."

Then follows the line, ''but with my own people I am, I believe, in good understanding.''

Why, one wonders, did Dinesen add this passage? It complicates the uncle's position with regard to Anne-Marie Piil, suggesting that she is not only the author of her fate, but that there exists a grander order of things in which it is more important to *le bien commune* (''the common good'') that there someday be a place called ''Sorrow-Acre'' than that justice be done today. What does the story gain by this addition?

In order to answer this question—which is another formulation of Adam's question (''Is it only my body that you want . . . while you reject my imagination, energy and emotions?'')—one must recall both the function of allegory and the historical moment during which Dinesen composed ''Sorrow-Acre.'' As I observed at the beginning of this essay, allegory describes one thing to talk about something else that shares similar features or characteristics. To this point, I have discussed the correspondence between Adam and one nexus of ideas—Paine's ''Rights of Man,'' the Norse gods, etc., and the correspondence between his uncle and an opposite nexus—feudalism, Greco-Roman gods, etc. But Dinesen's allegory works on another level as well: as a critique of Hitler's paternalistic, feudal National Socialism.

Unable to attack National Socialism directly (Denmark was invaded in 1940, two years before

Winter's Tales was published), Dinesen was forced to choose a more oblique line of approach, one that revisits the past to illuminate the present. While the uncle is not a clearly-recognizable Hitler figure, this fact is essential to Dinesen's critique, for it shifts the reader's focus away from the uncle's person toward the customs and traditions that make him do what he does. For Dinesen, the interesting question is not "why Hitler," but why do otherwise good people do bad things, or in Adam's case, fail to stop others from doing them? Dinesen's answer, it would seem, is that good people do, or allow, bad things because they remain susceptible to the powerful allure of custom and tradition.

Adam has a chance to escape the tradition of arbitrary punishment masquerading as justice by leaving Denmark for America, but in order to do so, he would have to sacrifice not only his ancestral home but also a conceptual framework that, at the most profound level, makes sense to him. All day long, as Anne-Marie makes her slow passage back and forth across the Rye field, the landscape silently waits for him to decide between the freedom of the unknown and the security of the morally repugnant known, and to declare his decision. Finally, he says to his uncle "If you wish it I shall not go. I shall stay here." A wordless peal of thunder immediately reverberates through the hills: "the landscape [has] spoken." What does the thunder say? That it is not the world deciding for the individual, but the individual who must decide for himself whether his virtue is to be found in his "imagination, energy and emotions" or in the possession of a thousand-year-old name with the power to rule.

Source: David Kippen, "What the Thunder Said," in *Short Stories for Students,* Gale, 1998.

David H. Richter

A professor of English at City College of New York—Queen's College, Richter is the author of Fable's End: Completeness and Closure in Rhetorical Fiction *and* Ten Short Novels. *In the following essay, he discusses what he calls the "covert plot" of "Sorrow-Acre," stating that Dinesen encrypted the secret meaning into her story in a gesture of cultural elitism.*

Perhaps none of Isak Dinesen's novellas has been more admired, and certainly none has been more widely anthologized, than "Sorrow-Acre," originally published with her *Winter's Tales* in 1942. This lyrically tragic tale, set in Denmark in the 1770s, invokes many of the persistent themes that haunt Dinesen's work: the contrast between the cruel beauty of the *ancien regime* and the more prosaic humanitarian ethos of modern democracy that will inevitably displace it; the inextricable connections between men and the land they live on; the arcane routes by which men seek and find their destiny; the perverse and terrible costs which love exacts. These themes have been sensitively and eloquently elucidated in the published criticism on Dinesen, particularly the studies by Langbaum, Johannesson and Hannah; what these critics, and others, seem to me to have misunderstood about Dinesen's "Sorrow-Acre" is not her themes but her plot. Or her plots, rather. For it is my basic thesis that "Sorrow-Acre" is informed by two interlocking plots, one overt and obvious, which no reader can conceivably miss, the other merely hinted at through foreshadowing allusions which previous commentators have misread or read but in part. The brief essay that follows will concern itself with the covert plot of "Sorrow-Acre," its relation to the more visible plot, and why Dinesen may have adopted the apparently risky strategy she chose of structuring a story around a plot so enciphered that it might easily remain a mystery.

The open or visible plot of "Sorrow-Acre"—which to my mind is the subordinate one of the two—has its source in a Jutland folk-tale collected by Ohrt and retold by Paul la Cour in 1931; Hannah has found the latter, more literary version to have been Dinesen's most direct inspiration. The story, as it appears in "Sorrow-Acre," concerns a widow, Anne-Marie, whose only son Goske has been accused of setting fire to a barn belonging to the "old lord" on whose landed estate they work. Anne-Marie pleads with the old lord to save her son, and the old lord offers her a bargain: if she will mow in one day a rye-field that would be work for three men, he will let her son go; if she fails, the boy will be sent away to be judged and she will never see him again. On the day set for the ordeal, Anne-Marie begins mowing the field, quickly at first, then ever more slowly as her strength ebbs and as the heat of the day takes its toll. In the presence of a crowd of peasants gathered to commiserate with and encourage her, and in the presence of the son for whom she made the bargain, Anne-Marie finishes the field just at sunset, only to collapse, dead from exhaustion.

While this story occasionally occupies the foreground of Dinesen's narrative, particularly at the denouement, for the most part it forms the backdrop against which a very different figure is traced. This takes the shape of a debate between the old lord and his young nephew, Adam, whom most commentators correctly take to be the focal character of the story. On the day set for the mowing, Adam has just returned to his ancestral estate from England, where he has absorbed the liberal and humanitarian values current there in intellectual circles, and which we today would associate with Jefferson or Rousseau. As he walks to the mansion at the centre of his uncle's feudal estate, Adam experiences a recrudescence of intense love for the soil of his forefathers, which he senses wishes to claim him, body and soul; these feelings are qualified, however, by his awareness of how alien his values have become to the hierarchical structures of autocracy physically emplanted in the topography of the manor. As Adam stands listening, in the morning, to the old lord's exposition of the bargain he has made with Anne-Marie, he says nothing to challenge his uncle's decree, but as the day wears on the drama being played out in the rye-field weighs ever heavier upon his conscience, and he is driven to remonstrate with his uncle: "'In the name of God . . . , force not this woman to continue.'" The old man answers Adam calmly and reasonably from within his aristocratic and feudal values: that Anne-Marie chose to accept the ordeal as freely as he chose to offer it; that his word, once given, is to him as sacred as that Word out of which the world was created; that his decree, if cruel as those of the Greek gods, at least allows the woman the beauty of a tragic destiny to which gods themselves cannot aspire; finally, to the prediction of Nemesis foreseen by Adam, the old lord responds with a shrugging "Amen," accepting whatever fate history will bring to him and his class. The old lord is immovable, his fortress of reasons impregnable, and Adam is finally driven to declare that, rather than stay in a land where such brutality must be, he will leave Denmark and go, not to England, where the feudal structures are incompletely eradicated, but to America, in whose fields and forests his more modern ideas reign supreme.

But this is not where Dinesen leaves the matter. In a long passage of interior monologue written with an intensity that marks it as the emotional climax of the story, Adam reverses his decision and decides to stay on his uncle's estate. The passage begins with the old lord's bitter benediction upon Adam's choice to go to America: "'Take service, there, . . . with the power which will give you an easier bargain than this: That with your own life you may buy the life of your son.'" This refers, most obviously, to the bargain the old man had concluded with Anne-Marie, but it also alludes to the uncle's private sorrow—the death of his only son, who was to inherit the manor. Though the old man has married himself the bride intended for his dead son, and may, Adam thinks, have children by her, Adam sees as he had not before the old man's suffering, and his ever-present dread of "the obliteration of his being" through the failure of his direct line. And as Adam contemplates his uncle with pity and forgiveness, he recognizes that beneath his liberal values was a stronger, universal vision which determines him not to leave but to stay. To make this vision comprehensible it must be quoted at some length:

> He saw the ways of life, he thought, as a twined and tangled design, complicated and mazy; it was not given him or any mortal to command or control it. Life and death, happiness and woe, the past and the present, were interlaced within the pattern. Yet to the initiated it might be read as easily as our ciphers—which to the savage must seem confused and incomprehensible—will be read by the schoolboy. And out of the contrasting elements concord arose. All that lived must suffer; the old man, whom he had judged hardly, had suffered, as he had watched his son die, and had dreaded the obliteration of his being. He himself would come to know ache, tears and remorse, and, even through these, the fullness of life. So might now, to the woman in the rye-field, her ordeal be a triumphant procession. For to die for the one you loved was an effort too sweet for words.
>
> As now he thought of it, he knew that all his life he had sought the unity of things. . . . Where other young people, in their pleasures or their amours, had searched for contrast and variety, he himself had yearned only to comprehend in full the oneness of the world. If things had come differently to him, if his young cousin had not died, and the events that followed his death had not brought him to Denmark, his search for understanding and harmony might have taken him to America. . . . Now they have been disclosed to him today, in the place where he had played as a child. As the song is one with the voice that sings it, as the road is one with the goal, as lovers are made one in their embrace, so is man one with his destiny, and he shall love it as himself.

As Adam decides to stay, he feels the hour "consecrated . . . to a surrender to fate and to the will of life," and as he speaks of his altered plans to his uncle a roll of Jovian thunder signals the fateful choice. But Adam is not afraid: he thinks, in his present *amor fati,* that "he had given himself over to the mightier powers of the world. Now what must come must come."

But just what is it that "must come"? What is the fate that Adam has accepted with such gravity? This is what I have called the covert plot of "Sorrow-Acre,'' for it is not so much told to us as it is enciphered by Dinesen in the loose and stray details surrounding the visible story. One common view is that expressed by Robert Langbaum: ''It is the destiny of Anne-Marie and the old lord to die, and it is the destiny of Adam to inherit the lord's estate and marry his young wife.'' Another view is that of Johannesson, who speculates that Adam will cuckold his uncle; the latter, we are told, ''is a comic figure because . . . he will have a son produced for him by his wife and Adam.'' Now while there is evidence to support elements of both these views, neither is very congruent with the tone Dinesen uses to describe Adam's acceptance of his fate, or Adam's reflection, a little later on, that ''Anne-Marie and he were both in the hands of destiny, and destiny would, by different ways, bring each to the designated end.'' The sombre tone of Adam's vision, and his foresight of a link with Anne-Marie's tragic destiny, suggest a very different fate for Adam than the inheritance of a valuable estate or a sexual romp with his uncle's beautiful young bride. Contemplating either destiny would require little in the way of *amor fati.* I believe, however, that when Dinesen's hints are read as a whole, the story in which one infers Adam will play the role of protagonist would be more like that of Tristan and Isolde than like Chaucer's ''Merchant's Tale.'' There will indeed be a love-affair between Adam and his youthful aunt, a love-affair that will culminate in the birth of a child; but Adam's fate will be to die, at the hands or his uncle or his minions, sacrificing himself to save the woman and their son.

The common ground of all three interpretations is the future connection between Adam and his uncle's seventeen-year-old bride, and indeed this is the element of Dinesen's covert plot that is most difficult to miss. Our inferences are primarily cued by the lengthy digression Dinesen makes from the visible story to portray this girl, who plays no explicit part either in Anne-Marie's tragedy or in Adam's fateful decision. Dinesen's language is somewhat coy here, but the portrait clearly enough indicates her sexual frustration. We are told, somewhat ambiguously, that ''she was given an old husband who treated her with punctilious respect because she was to bear him a son. Such was the compact. . . . Her husband, she found, was doing his best to fulfill his part of it, and she herself was loyal by nature and strictly brought up,'' Such mild hints that the old lord may be impotent are validated by the bride's dreadful ''consciousness or an absence'' in her life, her longings for ''the being who should have been there'' in her embrace, ''and who had not come.'' This absence is quite clearly sexual, for it is when examining her nude and lovely body in the looking-glass that she most intensely feels ''a *horror vaccui* like a physical pain. That Adam will be the one to fill this vacuum, to complete her inchoate longings, is first hinted at when the bride tears herself from her unpleasant meditation by thinking instead about ''her new nephew arrived from England,'' with whom she plans to ''ride out on the land.'' The activities of Adam and his aunt on the day the narrative is set are chaste enough, of course, but their thoughts about each other, their ride together, and their collaboration in a musical duet as the curtain is drawn upon them symbolize even as they presage the love-affair we can foresee.

That his will be an illicit affair, rather than a more staid romance that will wait upon the death of Adam's uncle, is largely implicit in the sexual urgency of the bride's physical frustration, taken together with the absence of any suggestion that the old lord is soon to die. But there are other hints as well. The young bride's middle name, for one thing, is Magdelena, traditionally identified with the fallen woman of the seventh chapter of the Gospel according to Luke. For another, there is the prophecy made to Adam back in England: ''When at Ranelagh an old gypsy woman looked at his hand and told him that a son of his was to sit in the seat of his fathers.'' If we take the prophecy seriously, and in the literal way such foreshadowing is generally to be taken in tragedies and folk-tales, it suggests that, while a son of his will possess the manor, Adam himself will *not* be its inheritor. Thus one must reject the Langbaum interpretation, and accept the Johannesson, as far as it goes. But Johannesson's notion that the covert plot of ''Sorrow-Acre'' is a cuckold comedy is unsatisfactory for quite a number of reasons.

The first and perhaps most unanswerable reason is that already mentioned: that the tone of ''Sorrow-Acre'' is tragic, not merely in the section devoted to the destiny of Anne-Marie but in that devoted to Adam and his fateful decision to remain on his uncle's manor. Here Adam foresees that ''he himself would come to know ache, tears and remorse,'' which is far from suggesting that his love-affair will be a bedroom farce devoid of serious consequences. Second, Johannesson's formulation is structurally off kilter, for his view takes the old lord to be the protagonist of this comedy, whereas it is clear from the narrative point of view that it must be Adam that is the protagonist of the novella's covert plot. Finally, there are a great many subtle hints within the text that death, rather than birth or love, is the focus of Adam's fate.

First off, there is Adam's name, recalling the Biblical Adam, our once innocent forefather who was betrayed by woman into death. Second, there is Adam's sense, on his first approach to the manor house, that he has been invited there by the dead (''Dead people came towards him and smiled upon him. . .''). Next, there is the tragedy by Johannes Ewald which Adam brings with him and leaves with his uncle. It is not named in the text, but the conversation it kindles suggests that it must be the 1775 verse drama of *Baldurs Dod,* which centers upon a young god who dies, driven by his passion for a mortal woman. Fourth, there is the sinister aspect to the young bride's sexual fantasies, which imply that loving her would be a most dangerous thing:

> A sudden, keen itching under her knee took her out of her reveries, and awoke in her the hunting instincts of her breed. She wetted a finger on her tongue, slowly brought it down and quickly slapped it to the spot. She felt the diminutive, sharp body of the insect against the silky skin, pressed the thumb to it, and triumphantly lifted up the small prisoner between her fingertips. She stood quite still, as if meditating upon the fact that a flea was the only creature risking its life for her smoothness and sweet blood.

Fifth, there is the recurrent pair of lines from Gluck's *Alceste,* repeated three times within the novella: ''Mourir pour ce qu'on aime, C'est un trop doux effort.'' These lines about dying for the one you love are not only translated within Adam's interior monologue, they are alluded to as the curtain is discreetly drawn upon him and his aunt, for it is Alceste's aria which the two are playing and singing together. They apply, obviously, to Anne-Marie, who sacrifices herself for her son, but in his interior monologue Adam apparently applies them to his own case. Finally, there is Adam's sense, already alluded to, that his fate and that of Anne-Marie are somehow linked, that they are ''both in the hands of destiny'' which will bring each of them to ''the designated end''; in the context this makes even more ominous Dinesen's guarded statement, ''Later on he remembered what he had thought that evening.''

Arching over all these details, and marshalling them into perspective, is the reader's desire to make the fullest possible sense of Dinesen's story, to take this ''twined and tangled design'' and find in it a ''pattern,'' to unify this work of literature and participate in its harmonies in the same way that Adam wants to decipher the hidden unity and harmony of life. It is this aesthetic sense that has dictated Adam's decision to stay, just as it is the old lord's aesthetic sense that has made him stage-manage the tragedy of which Anne-Marie is the protagonist. And I suspect that Dinesen trusted the aesthetic sense of her readers to complete, to stage-manage in their own minds, the tragedy linked to the visible one of which Adam is the protagonist. And, if we have been following her implications correctly, a single denouement, the completion of Anne-Marie's sacrifice and death, will serve as the katharsis for both. Anne-Marie, as a peasant-woman, is the heroine of a tragic folk-tale; Adam, as befits his higher birth and station, will be the hero, not of a folk-tale or a fabliau, but of a variant of the tragic myth of Tristan.

> **"If we take the old gypsy woman's prophecy seriously, and in the literal way such foreshadowing is generally to be taken in tragedies and folk-tales, it suggests that, while a son of his will possess the manor, Adam himself will not be its inheritor."**

It is in fact a misapplication of Dinesen's aesthetics that led Johannesson and Hannah to posit a cuckold-comedy as the covert plot of ''Sorrow-Acre.'' Their argument is based upon the old lord's view that, just as the omnipotent Greek gods could not be tragic, so too the aristocrats of Denmark ''who stand in lieu of the gods'' should ''leave to our vassals their monopoly of tragedy.'' But it is only the old lord himself who, in his omnipotence and amorality, like the Greek gods, is beyond the reach of the tragic. His nephew is no Zeus; he is more like the Norse gods of Asgaard who, the old lord tells us, ''had, at all times, by their sides those darker powers which they named the Jotuns, and who worked the suffering, the disasters, the ruin of our world''; and like the Norse gods, like the Baldur of Ewald's drama, Adam in his limitations possesses the capacity for tragedy. The old lord quite explicitly identifies Adam with Baldur: the new age, which Adam represents ''has made to itself a god in its own image, an emotional god. And now you are already writing a tragedy on your god.'' To put it another way, the old lord, from his Olympian perspective, may indeed view himself as a comic figure, a deceived Vulcan whose Venus has strayed. But from Adam's perspective—and given the point of view it is his angle that we share—his destiny to love the young bride, to father her son, and to die sacrificing himself for them is indeed a tragic fate, which his uncle characterizes as the highest human privilege.

I have tried to show how the demands of tone, of parallel structure, of point of view, and of details and verbal allusions all collaborate to convey the covert tragic plot of ''Sorrow-Acre.'' But if we can agree that Dinesen has succeeded in organizing her story in such a way, then we must also paradoxically admit that she has failed. She has failed, at least, to convey her covert story to five sensitive readers whose studies I have cited, and therefore, one suspects, to most of those who have perused her novella. To the initiated, Adam says in his interior monologue, the pattern of life, that complicated and mazy design, ''might be read as easily as our ciphers—which to the savage must seem confused and incomprehensible—will be read by the schoolboy.'' And yet Dinesen has so enciphered the primary plot of her story that few of her readers are likely to make it out. For those who succeed, the pleasures of tacit collusion with the author are intense and refined indeed; for those who fail—and here is Dinesen's insurance policy—most will have not sense of what they have missed.

The fact is that Isak Dinesen was an elitist in more ways than one. The reception of *Seven Gothic Tales* had suffered in Denmark, critic Tom Kristensen remarked, from the common readers' reaction to ''their too aristocratic tone, verging on snobbery.'' Though Kristensen felt that the *Winter's Tales* had more ''humanity'' than the earlier book, it is clear that her defense of the *ancien regime,* her contempt for democratic vistas, are by no means absent from the later collection, which includes ''Sorrow-Acre.'' And as an elitist, Dinesen was very unlikely to have been averse to reserving some of her work's secret pleasures for a select group of kindred souls capable of following her indirections and allusions. Like Joyce's *Finnegans Wake,* whose meaning is encrypted in thousands of puns in dozens of living and dead languages, like Nabokov's ''The Vane Sisters,'' whose hidden denouement is encoded in the initial letters of the last paragraph's words, and like Dinesen's own ''The Roads Round Pisa,'' whose ending requires the reader to decipher an obscure symbolic passage in Dante, ''Sorrow-Acre'' is a story that is also part puzzle, a reflection of its author's intellectual snobbery and a challenge, moral as well as intellectual, to the reader's own.

Source: David H. Richter, ''Covert Plot in Isak Dinesen's 'Sorrow-Acre','' in *The Journal of Narrative Technique,* Vol. 15, No. 1, Winter, 1985, pp. 82–90.

Eric O. Johannesson

Johannesson has written distinguished studies of Dinesen and the novels of August Strindberg. In the following excerpt, he discusses ''Sorrow-Acre'' as a story that expresses Dinesen's elitist views and aristocratic sympathies.

The most dramatic illustration of the aristocratic philosophy of life is found in ''Sorrow-Acre.'' This story, which is set in Denmark, seeks, in Milton's words, to justify the ways of God to man. It seeks to answer several related questions: Why is life so dear? Why is life so pitiless? Is there not a God who can temper the laws of necessity with mercy?

The central incident concerns a crime. Anne-Marie, a peasant woman, has a son who is accused and probably guilty of having set fire to a barn, and for this crime he is to be punished. When Anne-Marie pleads for her son the lord of the estate makes a stipulation: if she can mow a field of corn in one day, her son will be set free. Normally this is a task for three men. Anne-Marie succeeds, however, and the son is set free, but she dies from exhaustion.

This incident, and particularly the role which the lord plays in it, is very shocking to his nephew, the young hero of the tale. Adam has been living in England and has been imbued with a number of the new liberal ideas: ideas about nature, justice, and the rights and freedoms of man; he even has some notions of going to the United States. To him the uncle, who has always been an embodiment of ''law and order, the wisdom of life and kind guardianship,'' now appears as ''a symbol of the tyranny and oppression of the world.'' At one point he tells the uncle to stop ''this terrible thing,'' and he decides to leave the estate and go to the United States. Before evening, however, he has changed his mind. The reasons for this change are to be sought, I think, in his three conversations with the uncle, and in certain events which put the figure of the uncle in a new light.

These conversations are central to the story. They concern the nature of comedy and tragedy. Adam has been reading a tragedy by the Danish poet Johannes Ewald (1743–81), entitled *Balder's Death* (1775), and at his suggestion the uncle also reads it during the course of the day.

During the first conversation Adam suggests "that we have not till now understood how much our Nordic mythology in moral greatness surpasses that of Greece and Rome." Adam feels that the gods of Greece and Rome were "mean, capricious and treacherous," while "the fair gods of Asgaard did possess the sublime human virtues; they were righteous, trustworthy, benevolent and even, within a barbaric age, chivalrous." The uncle disagrees with this statement: it was easier, he insists, for the Nordic gods to be virtuous because they were not as powerful as the gods of classical antiquity. The Nordic gods, he says, had at all times "by their side those darker powers which they named the Jotuns, and who worked the suffering, the disasters, the ruin of our world." The omnipotent Greek and Roman gods had "no such facilitation. With their omnipotence they take over the woe of the universe." Jove is superior to Odin because he "avowed his sovereignty, and accepted the world which he ruled."

The second conversation occurs after the uncle has read *Balder's Death.* This conversation concerns the nature of comedy and tragedy. Adam suggests that tragedy is, "in the scheme of life, a noble, a divine phenomenon." The uncle agrees that tragedy is a noble phenomenon, "but of the earth only, and never divine." "Tragedy," he says, "is the privilege of man, his highest privilege." As such it "should remain the right of human beings, subject, in their conditions or in their own nature, to the dire law of necessity. To them it is salvation and beatification." The gods, on the other hand, are not subject to necessity. As a result they can have no knowledge of the tragic: "When they are brought face to face with it they will, according to my experience, have the good taste and decorum to keep still, and not interfere."

"The true art of the gods is the comic," the uncle insists. "In the comic the gods see their own being reflected as in a mirror, and while the tragic poet is bound by strict laws, they will allow the comic artist a freedom as unlimited as their own." The comic artist may even mock at the gods.

On earth the aristocrats stand in lieu of the gods and have likewise emancipated themselves "from the tyranny of necessity." For this reason they must also "accept the comic with grace." And no master will "make a jest of his servants' necessity, or force the comic upon them." The aristocrat will not fear the comic: "Indeed," says the uncle, "the very same fatality, which, in striking the burgher or peasant, will become tragedy, with the aristocrat is exalted to the comic. By the grace and wit of our acceptance hereof our aristocracy is known."

"Adam learns to accept tragedy—not as a misfortune—but as a human privilege, because it confers on us ordinary human beings a greatness which is denied the gods and the aristocrats, denied those who are liberated from necessity."

The third conversation occurs after Adam has told the uncle to stop the terrible tragedy that is being enacted on the cornfield. The uncle answers that he is not at all forcing the old woman to go on. Adam's animadversions that the woman's death will come upon the uncle's head leave the uncle unperturbed. He says he has given Anne-Marie his word, and in his world the word is still the principle, the law of gravitation. Adam speaks for imagination, daring, and passion as greater powers of the word than those of any restricting or controlling law, but the uncle answers that it is impossible for him to stop Anne-Marie now without making light of her exploits, which would be making her into a comic figure. Adam's statement that he might go to the United States the uncle answers as follows: "Take service, there, with the power which will give you an easier bargain than this: That with your own life you may buy the life of your son."

The conversations between Adam and his uncle are evidently designed to illustrate the differences between two worlds: the world of the eighteenth century and the world of the postrevolutionary and romantic nineteenth century; between the feudal and aristocratic eighteenth century and the sentimental and humanitarian nineteenth century. The uncle represents a firm and well-defined order based on law, form, style, and continuity, and within this order his word is law. He has unlimited freedom within this order, but it is a freedom of the same kind as that possessed by the composer of a fugue or a symphony: it is circumscribed by certain rules. The uncle cannot break his word, and he must accept responsibility for the world he rules. Thus he is an aristocratic figure.

Adam, the rebel, cannot accept at first the inhumanity of the uncle's forcing Anne-Marie to sacrifice her life for her son. At last he does so, however. Two things make him change his mind. He realizes that his uncle, too, is a tragic figure who has suffered as other human beings must suffer. The uncle has suffered because he has lost his only son. Thus the whole world that he represents is in danger of perishing, because it is based on the principle of continuance. Adam also comes to realize that the uncle is a comic figure, a representative here on earth of the comic-amoral divinities. He is a comic figure because, as a gypsy had prophesied, he will have a son produced for him by his wife and Adam. This is clearly indicated in the story. At the very outset it is suggested by the author that the real power in this aristocratic world is held by the women, because they alone can attest to the legitimacy of the sons who are to inherit the estates. When we are introduced to the wife of the uncle, she is standing naked in front of the mirror, admiring herself, while thoughts of a sexual nature flit through her mind: she thinks of the bulls and the stallions; she is conscious of an absence of some kind, and when a flea bites her she thinks it silly that only a flea should have the courage to risk its life "for her smoothness and sweet blood." In the afternoon she and Adam ride together in the field. Finally, it is said about Anne-Marie that to save her son is a sweet effort. This line also occurs in a popular tune, the words of which flit through the minds of both Adam and the wife: *"C'est un trop doux effort."* The sweet effort referred to in this connection, although obviously of another nature, is to the same end as that of Anne-Marie: to save a son.

Thus Adam is able to accept the feudal-aristocratic world, and his acceptance is based on a kind of religious experience: he realizes that all which lives must suffer, and that, consequently, there are no easy bargains in life. Adam realizes the unity of all things and accepts the world as it is. He also realizes that suffering brings greatness. By letting her play her role the uncle has conferred immortality on Anne-Marie: the field is forever after known as "Sorrow-Acre." Adam learns to accept tragedy—not as a misfortune—but as a human privilege, because it confers on us ordinary human beings a greatness which is denied the gods and the aristocrats, denied those who are liberated from necessity. . . .

Source: Eric O. Johannesson, in his *The World of Isak Dinesen,* University of Washington Press, 1961, pp. 99–104.

Sources

Aiken, Susan Hardy. "Dinesen's 'Sorrow-Acre ': Tracing the Woman's Line," in *Isak Dinesen: Critical Views,* edited by Olga Anastasia Pelensky, Ohio University Press, 1993, pp. 174-98.

Hannah, Donald. *"Isak Dinesen" and Karen Blixen: The Mask and the Reality,* Putnam & Co., 1971, p. 12.

Pelensky, Olga Anastasia. *Isak Dinesen: The Life and Imagination of a Seducer,* Ohio University Press, 1991, pp. 178-79.

Thurman, Judith. *Isak Dinesen: The Life of a Storyteller,* St. Martin's Press, 1982, pp. 6, 8.

Further Reading

Green, Howard. "Isak Dinesen," in *The Hudson Review,* Vol. XVII, No. 4, Winter, 1964–65, pp. 517–30.

Examines "Sorrow-Acre" as an example of a "divine art" that brings the reader "face to face with the extraordinary, the unique, the inexplicable, the unpredictable."

"Isak Dinesen," in *Short Story Criticism,* Volume 7, edited by Thomas Votteler, Gale, 1991, pp. 159-210.

Reprinted criticism on Dinesen's short stories. Included is criticism by Mark Van Doren, Eric O. Johannesson, Donald Hannah, and several other scholars.

"Isak Dinesen," in *DISCovering Authors Modules,* CD-Rom, Gale, 1995.

Includes personal information, a bibliography, and reprinted criticism on Dinesen's works.

Vengeful Creditor

Chinua Achebe

1971

Chinua Achebe's story ''Vengeful Creditor'' first appeared in 1971 in the inaugural issue of *Okike: A Nigerian Journal of New Writing,* a magazine that Achebe founded, and it was later reprinted in his collection of stories, *Girls at War, and Other Stories.* The story focuses on the gap between the wealthy and the poor in the tumultuous environment of a haphazardly modernizing African country. The overt political issue at stake is the government's institution of free primary education for children, a policy the well-to-do Emenikes resent because it means they will have difficulty keeping their servants. In order to obtain a nurse for their baby, the Emenikes promise an impoverished girl that she will eventually be able to go to school—her only chance at obtaining a better life for herself. As it becomes clear that the Emenikes are not going to make good on their promise, the young servant, Veronica, becomes increasingly resentful and acts out her frustration on the Emenikes and their child.

Achebe is known primarily as a novelist, and his 1958 novel *Things Fall Apart* is considered one of literature's most important African novels. He has written relatively few short stories in his career, but his collection *Girls at War, and Other Stories* like his novels, has received overwhelming positive reviews from critics. ''Vengeful Creditor'' in particular is noted for its satirical qualities in depicting ''women and their aspirations, blighted . . . by the society and the circumstances that surround them,'' according to C. L. Innes in her book *Chinua Achebe.*

Author Biography

Albert Chinualumoga Achebe (Chinua Achebe) was born in the village of Ogidi in eastern Nigeria in 1930. His parents, members of the Ibo people, were missionary teachers. By the time Achebe was fourteen, he could speak English and he was sent to study at the Government College at Umuahia, one of the best schools in West Africa. Continuing on to college, Achebe matriculated at University College, Ibadan, a new school affiliated with the University of London, and studied English literature. While in school, Achebe published stories in the *University Herald,* and upon graduation he decided to be a writer. In 1954, Achebe obtained a job with the Nigerian Broadcasting Corporation, where he worked until the Nigerian government began persecuting the Ibo people in 1966. He then resigned and relocated to Biafra, the region in which many massacres of the Ibos were taking place.

Things Fall Apart, his first novel, appeared in 1958 and almost instantly gained renown. A portrait of traditional village life in Nigeria at the beginning of the colonial era, it reminded Nigerians about their heritage at a time when independence from British rule was imminent. In the novel, Achebe told *Nigeria Magazine,* he tried to remind his nation, and all Africans, that they "did not hear of culture for the first time from Europeans; that their societies were not mindless but frequently had a philosophy of great depth and value and beauty, that they had poetry and, above all, that they had dignity."

Achebe followed *Things Fall Apart* with two other novels about the meeting of the British colonial and the Nigerian indigenous cultures, *No Longer At Ease* (1960) and *Arrow of God* (1964). Both explore the waning colonial days of the country and its independence from British rule. In his other novels, he has examined issues related to self-rule and to the corruption and mismanagement that have often characterized the Nigerian government as well as many other African governments.

Although Achebe is primarily known as a novelist, he is a master of all forms of writing. During the two and a half years of the Biafran civil war that began in 1967, Achebe was not inclined to concentrate on long fiction. He did write poetry, much of which was later published in the collections *Beware, Soul Brother, and Other Poems* (1971) and *Christmas in Biafra and Other Poems* (1973). He also produced a number of short stories, many of which—including "Vengeful Creditor"—appear in his 1972 collection *Girls at War, and Other Stories.* Achebe has since published several stories for children and collections of essays. He returned to the novel in 1988 with the publication of *Anthills of the Savannah.* Set in an imaginary African country, it tells the story of three childhood friends who all rise to positions of political power. Emeritus professor at the University of Nigeria since the early 1970s, Achebe has also held a number of visiting fellowships and professorships at universities in the United States and England.

Plot Summary

Set in an unnamed independent African country, "Vengeful Creditor" opens as Mrs. Emenike, an educated and well-to-do African woman, is checking out of the supermarket. She is irritated at the decline in the standards of service in the store ever since the government instituted free primary education. She complains that her household servants have been quitting lately, returning to their native villages to go to school. She wonders how "a working woman with a seven-month-old baby" is expected to cope.

The newspaper has published many letters written by highly educated people who are critical of the government's policy. The Emenikes are representative of these critics: he is a mid-level bureaucrat, while she is a social welfare officer. They oppose the program and are affected by it directly when several of their servants quit to go to school. The defection of their baby-nurse makes Mrs. Emenike particularly angry. However, since more than twice as many children have enrolled in school as the government had anticipated, financing for the scheme falls through and after a single school term, the program is suspended.

In an impoverished village, one of the people who is "broken-hearted" at the suspension of free education is Veronica, a ten-year-old girl whose widowed mother, Martha, is struggling to care for four children. Martha has some education, having attended a missionary school, but the death of her carpenter husband has left her destitute and unable to pay school fees for her children. Veronica had enjoyed her brief term in school as a respite from her responsibilities taking care of her younger siblings while their mother worked in the fields. Martha's children spend their time foraging for grasshoppers and palm-kernels to take the edge off their hunger.

One day Mr. Emenike, who was born in the village, visits Martha's hut. He wants to hire Veronica to take care of the baby. Martha is reluctant to let her daughter go, despite the family's desperate need for the annual payment of £5. She recalls that she once assumed all her children would go to college and now laments her inability even to send them to primary school. In the course of their discussion, Mr. Emenike comments that if Veronica is a good nurse, "what stops my wife and me sending her to school when the baby is big enough to go about on his own?" Martha and Mr. Emenike understand this to be "only a manner of speaking." Veronica, however, overhearing the conversation, goes off happily to work for the Emenikes thinking she will soon be able to return to school.

Veronica proves so competent and efficient that Mrs. Emenike nicknames her "Little Madame." But Veronica gradually becomes dissatisfied with her situation. At first she simply envies the older children when she watches them leave for school in the morning, but as time passes she increasingly covets those "little daily departures in fine dresses and shoes and sandwiches and biscuits wrapped in beautiful paper-napkins in dainty little school bags." Veronica channels some of her frustration into inventing songs that she sings to quiet the baby.

One day Mrs. Emenike discovers that Veronica has painted her lips with red ink from Mr. Emenike's desk. In scolding the girl she warns her that red ink is poisonous. Soon afterwards Mrs. Emenike comes home to discover the baby's dress stained red. She whips Veronica "until her face and arms [run] with blood." The girl then admits to making the baby drink red ink.

Mr. Emenike hastily loads Veronica into his Mercedes and returns her to the village. Martha returns from a hard day of labor, listens to her daughter's story, and insists that they go at once to see the Emenikes, who are still in the village. When Martha realizes that her daughter meant to kill the baby she attempts to whip Veronica herself, but when Mrs. Emenike implies that Veronica's upbringing is at the source of her actions Martha is shocked and denies the charge. Mrs. Emenike then remarks sarcastically, "Perhaps it's from me she learnt." Mr. Emenike tries to quiet the dispute by blaming the girl's action on "the craze for education." As Martha and Veronica return home, Martha at first berates her daughter. Her anger is slowly redirected, however, as she realizes the unfairness of Mr. Emenike's comment and of a situation in which her daughter thinks she has to kill in order to have a chance to go to school.

Chinua Achebe

Characters

Mark Emenike

Mark Emenike is a Permanent Secretary, a mid-level bureaucrat in the postcolonial government of an African nation. Although his family enjoys such economic privileges as private schooling for the children, a car, and a houseful of servants, Mr. Emenike is constantly made aware of his own lowly status in comparison to those who are wealthier and more powerful. As a civil servant, he is not permitted to express his views on education in the local newspaper and must be content to comment on his friend Mike Ogudu's letter to the editor. In Cabinet meetings, he must refrain from any participation in the debate; even laughter is prohibited for a civil servant, and when he violates this strict protocol, he receives a ''scorching look'' from the Prime Minister. Nevertheless, he is an important man in his home village and is easily able to persuade Martha that Veronica will be happy in his comfortable home in the nation's capital.

Mr. Emenike

See Mark Emenike

Mrs. Emenike

Mrs. Emenike, the middle-class employer of the story, is the mother of five children and a social welfare officer. She is self-absorbed and sees people and events only in terms of how they will affect her own life. Free primary education, for example, which means so much to the poor people of her country, is viewed as a major inconvenience and a threat to her comfort. Young people who are in school are unavailable to serve her needs, both at the market, where the only person left to carry her groceries to the car is a forty-year-old ''grumbling cripple,'' and at home, where she depends on a staff of poorly paid domestic servants, most especially a nurse for her infant son. Mrs. Emenike is oblivious to the needs and desires of those who serve her. When Veronica composes a song about her longing to go to school with the other children in the family's noisy little Fiat, Mrs. Emenike interprets this as support for her own desire for a new sports car.

Madam

See Mrs. Emenike

Martha

Martha, Veronica's mother, is a widow with four children. She works long hours on a farm and in the market to eke out a meager living—so meager that the children must scramble for palm-kernels and grasshoppers to eat. Martha's early life had held great promise; she was educated by white missionaries so that she might serve as a cleric's wife but was instead urged by her teacher to marry a trade school student, a future carpenter. Her husband was never as prosperous as any of the teachers and evangelists she might have married and worse yet, he was partially paralyzed for the last five years of his life. His death has left Martha and the children destitute. Furthermore, since the couple had been married for twenty years before they were able to have children, Martha is an older widow trying to support very young children. Reluctantly, she must abandon her dream that her children will achieve a higher level of education than she herself did. At one point she had hoped they might attend college, but Veronica's entry into domestic service forecloses that possibility. When the Emenikes bring Veronica home, beaten and disgraced, Martha is at first inclined to beat the child again but, in a flash of insight, she realizes that the more appropriate targets for her anger are Mr. Emenike for his refusal to honor his pledge and the rigid class system that makes it all but impossible for the poor to obtain an education and a way out of their misery.

Mary

Mary is Veronica's one-year-old sister for whom Veronica must care before she goes to work for the Emenikes. The girl is undernourished and cannot even chew her food, although she is always hungry.

Vero

See Veronica

Veronica

Veronica is a girl of ten who temporarily escapes the grim poverty of her mother's home by going to school during the brief period when free primary education is available in her country. She is a bright child who loves school and misses it terribly when she is forced to resume her duties watching her younger siblings while her mother works. She takes up similar duties in the Emenike household, caring for their baby in exchange for room, board, and the £5 her mother receives for Veronica's services for one year. Veronica is so anxious to resume her education that she misinterprets Mr. Emenike's suggestion that he might send her to school when the baby is older. Although this is merely small talk offered by Mr. Emenike to Veronica's mother, the girl takes it at face value and becomes impatient when the baby does not grow fast enough to suit her plans. In her eyes, the baby stands between her and an education, and finally, in desperation, she tries to poison the infant. At that point she becomes the vengeful creditor of the title, trying to make the Emenikes pay the debt they owe her. When her employer discovers what she has done, Veronica is severely beaten and sent home in disgrace.

Themes

Class Conflict

In "Vengeful Creditor" the interests of the middle class are pitted against those of both the rich and the poor. The Emenikes, with their civil service jobs, are certainly comfortable enough, although they are neither as wealthy as Mr. Emenike's friend Mike Ogudu, who owns a shipping line, nor as powerful as the Cabinet Ministers whom Mr. Emenike serves as a Permanent Secretary. Compared with the poor, however, who have barely enough to stay alive, the family is extremely well off. Because of the desperate poverty of the majority of the country's people, the Emenikes are easily able to exploit their unfortunate servants. Veronica's mother, for instance, is paid only £5 for the girl's services for an entire year, although another more knowledgeable applicant for the baby-nurse position demands a salary of £7 per month. Similarly, Mrs. Emenike feels cheated by one of the young males in the family's service who should, according to her, forfeit a month's pay in lieu of his notice to quit. Yet when the gardener tries to give notice, she refuses it and finds another excuse to deny him the wages she owes him.

One of the most glaring consequences of class difference involves access to education. The middle class and the rich can afford to pay school fees, and, of course, all of the Emenike children attend school. The poor, however, are unable to pay these fees; the only educational opportunity they enjoy is the "free primadu" briefly offered by the government and then subsequently withdrawn. The middle class refuses to support this program because it would necessitate a tax increase that would confer no benefits on their own group and also because education for poor children would eliminate the vast pool of cheap, unskilled labor that serves the middle class.

The Emenikes, particularly Mrs. Emenike, are barely able to contain their contempt for the poor. Mrs. Emenike is disgusted by the "grumbling cripple" who carries her packages at the market. She disapproves of "old men running little boys' errands," and seems to feel that a youngster in that position would not be complaining about having to do "monkey work" and would perhaps be more grateful for the meager tip she dispenses. When a member of the domestic staff outwits her and disappears with a full month's pay, Mrs. Emenike refers to him as a "little rat" and vows to avoid treating future servants with kindness, since in her experience, it simply does not pay. But this contempt is returned by Martha at the story's end when she expresses, if only to herself, her rage at Mr. Emenike, "that thing that calls himself a man."

Morality and Ethics

"Vengeful Creditor" explores the relationship between public ethics and private actions. A cynical government establishes a program of free education as a means of currying favor with the poor, but then withdraws it a few months later because it is too successful. The only way to maintain the program would be to raise taxes, which the officials are unwilling to do because it would adversely affect their chances of remaining in office. As for the poor children who must leave school, the Finance Minister is unconcerned about their situation. They are expendable.

Topics for Further Study

- Investigate the history of Nigeria since 1970. What complaints do the people of Nigeria have against the government? How have the Nigerian government and other countries responded to these complaints? Is there hope for change?
- How do people benefit when they are allowed to have an education? Examine the economic effects of free public education in a developing country. Does it make the workforce more or less productive? Do wages go up or down?
- When did the United States introduce free public education? Research the decision to institute public education, and look at some of the arguments offered for and against it.
- The novella "A Simple Heart" by nineteenth-century French writer Gustave Flaubert also concerns the fate of a young, uneducated woman who goes to work in a middle-class household. In what ways are the two stories similar? How are they different?

The Emenikes regard their domestic workers in a similar fashion. If free education is available to the masses, then the pool of inexpensive labor will disappear, causing serious inconvenience to the family. The implications for the million and a half individuals who must give up their dreams of an education are lost on the Emenikes, whose personal comfort takes precedence over everything.

It seems only logical, then, that Veronica should learn from the actions of her government and her employers that impediments to personal goals must be eliminated. Mr. Emenike himself believes that ''any sacrifice'' should be made in order to secure an education. Since little Goddy seems to be the primary impediment to Veronica's education, she quite naturally wishes to eliminate him.

Education

Formal education in this story is essential to the development of the plot and emblematic of class differences. Also important, though, are issues of informal education—those lessons passed, often by example, from parent to child or from employer to employee. For example, Mrs. Emenike's first baby-nurse was an ignorant young woman who had to be educated, not only on the duties of her position, but also on the most basic elements of personal grooming and comportment. Once Mrs. Emenike transforms Abigail into a ''lady,'' though, the ungrateful girl abandons her position in order to continue to better herself, this time by taking advantage of free primary education.

When Veronica paints her lips and fingernails with red ink, Mr. Emenike says the girl ''is learning fast,'' and reminds his wife of a proverb that seems to apply to the situation: When mother cow chews giant grass her little calves watch her mouth. His wife, however, is not amused by the comparison between herself and a cow, and the issue of what exactly Veronica has learned from Mrs. Emenike's example becomes important at the story's end when Martha and Mrs. Emenike accuse each other of having taught the girl to murder.

City vs. Country

The Emenike family lives in the capital, although they are originally from the same rural village where Martha and her children live. The contrast between the prosperous life of a civil servant and the grim conditions of life in the countryside are apparent when Mr. Emenike comes calling to recruit Veronica into domestic service. His Mercedes 220S cannot make it up the narrow path to Martha's hut, so the ''great man'' must park on the main road and cover the remaining five hundred yards on foot.

For Veronica, the difference between country life and city life is nowhere near as great as she had hoped it would be. Although she leaves behind a diet of palm-kernels and bitter-leaf soup, her position is virtually the same in both locations. At the Emenikes' home, the other children go off to school and leave Veronica behind to watch little Goddy, just as in her mother's home she is left in the hut to care for her siblings. Her chances of obtaining an education are equally dismal in both situations.

Style

Point of View

''Vengeful Creditor'' is told by a third-person narrator who focuses on the viewpoints of various characters at different points in the narration. The story opens with Mrs. Emenike doing her marketing in a modern supermarket. She is pleased by the deference accorded her by the staff; the checkout clerks compete for the privilege of serving her, and even the paper receipt politely thanks her for her patronage. But when the only ''boy'' available to carry her groceries to her Mercedes is less than eager to serve and less than grateful for the tip she offers, Mrs. Emenike displays her impatience and irritation with members of the lower class. Although the reader is given Mrs. Emenike's version of these events, she is not presented in a favorable light. For example, the narrator's description of Mrs. Emenike's painstaking search through the many coins in her wallet for a three-penny piece to confer on the waiting bag boy, or the ''grumbling cripple'' as she refers to him, makes the reader sympathize with him rather than her.

Midway through the story, the narration shifts to Veronica's point of view. Again the narrator is not completely objective, but in this case the evaluation of the character is positive. The girl's destitute condition combined with her enthusiasm for education make her a very sympathetic character, especially when her hardships are contrasted with the relatively minor ''problems'' of the Emenike family. These contrasts are emphasized by the narrator's shifting perspective, between Mrs. Emenike's ''nightmare'' when Abigail leaves and Veronica's impatient calculations of how long it will take an infant to

The modern city of Ibadan in the southwestern part of Nigeria. Ibadan has a population of over one million and is home to a large university.

achieve independence. At the end of the story, Martha's point of view is presented. Although she initially blames Veronica for trying to poison the baby, Martha slowly becomes aware of the horrible injustice of a system that has driven her daughter to such a desperate state.

Setting

The story's setting is an unnamed African country in the postcolonial period, though the description of the government's "free primadu" is reminiscent of Nigeria's education policy in the mid-1950s. The British colonial government has been replaced by native officials and bureaucrats who have adopted their predecessors' love of privilege and contempt for the poor. Government policies and programs, therefore, are based on expediency and self-interest rather than on the welfare of the citizens. The story also makes use of the contrast between city and country.

Dialect

One of the ways in which Achebe indicates the deep class divisions in his story is through the use of dialect. The Emenikes speech is depicted as standard English, while the poor speak a dialect that combines elements of their native language and English. Martha, who has been educated, is the exception. Although desperately poor, she uses the language taught to her by the white missionaries. Her daughter Veronica is fluent in both, as is the supermarket clerk, who speaks one way to Mrs. Emenike and another to John, the bag boy. Mr. Emenike, too, seems to be bilingual, using native dialect when he grills the servants, but also when he speaks of Mike Ogudu, whose position is superior to his own. ''Too much money is bad-o,'' he tells his wife, referring to his rich friend.

Irony and Satire

Irony and satire are important stylistic elements in ''Vengeful Creditor.'' The reader's evaluation of the characters is dependent on seeing through the pretensions of the Emenikes, who seem to believe the lower class's happiness should be found in faithful service to their superiors. Thus, when Mrs. Emenike switches to a different checkout line at the market, the narrator refers to the clerk at the first machine as ''the cheated girl,'' ironically suggesting that it is such a privilege to wait on Mrs. Emenike that the ''loser'' regrets not being chosen. Mrs. Emenike consoles the girl with a promise to pick her on the next visit. The reference also foreshadows Veronica's status as ''the cheated girl,'' although the Emenikes will deprive her of something far more important than the privilege of serving them.

The narrator repeatedly satirizes the self-absorbed attitude of the middle class that fails to see the limited options available to the poor. For example, the debate over free education is conducted in the local newspaper with several ''responsible citizens'' insisting the time is not right for the country to offer such a program. They, of course, are all professionals who can afford the fees to send their own children to school. Mr. Emenike, although forbidden as a civil servant from writing to the newspaper, believes that free education is unnecessary. ''Parents know the value of education and will make any sacrifice to find school fees for their children,'' he tells his wife. ''We are not a nation of Oliver Twists,'' he claims, associating himself with the former colonizers of his country by this reference to a British novel about a poor orphan. Mr. Emenike's statement reveals his failure (or refusal) to notice that, with the exception of the privileged classes, they are indeed a nation of Oliver Twists. The Finance Minister is equally oblivious to the plight of the poor, insisting that school fees, unlike taxes, are entirely voluntary in a democratic society. As he sees it, if a parent chooses not to pay school fees, ''the worst that can happen is that his child stays at home which he probably doesn't mind at all.'' Again, this suggests that the poor can ''choose'' whether or not to pay for their children's education.

The story's ending turns on a doubly ironic statement by Mrs. Emenike who sarcastically suggests that perhaps Veronica learned to murder while in her service. Of course she means to blame Veronica's mother by pointing out how absurd it would be to teach a child in one's service to kill, but in truth that is exactly where the young girl was taught that people could be sacrificed in the pursuit of one's own interests.

Symbolism

The most obvious use of symbolism in ''Vengeful Creditor'' is the red ink. When Veronica appropriates Mr. Emenike's ink and uses it in apparent imitation of Madame's use of cosmetics, she is chastised and told that the ink is poisonous. In the business world, red ink indicates debt, and here, when the girl later attempts to eliminate little Goddy by making him drink the red ink, she is, in effect, using it to call in her debt. She is the vengeful creditor of the story's title, the creditor who is owed an education by her employers. She is, in effect, bathing the child in red ink, an image that is echoed soon afterward when Madame beats Veronica until she is bloody. Besides signifying debt, the ink also serves as a symbol for Veronica's desire for education and literacy—a desire to be able to use ink for its intended purpose, to write, just as Mr. Emenike does.

Historical Context

History of Nigeria

Achebe belongs to an ethnic group known as the Ibo, who have had a civilization in West Africa for centuries. Unlike many other African civilizations, the Ibo were a decentralized people who maintained a largely village-based culture rather than one governed by a king or an emperor. Achebe has based much of his writing on the Ibo culture and its interactions with the British colonial administrations, as well as its conflicts with the central Nigerian government.

Compare & Contrast

- **1974:** In the heavyweight boxing title bout, Muhammad Ali defeats the younger George Foreman in Kinshasa, Zaire, bringing big-time Western sports to sub-Sahara Africa. With his charisma and fast-talking persona, Ali charms the people of Africa, and becomes probably the best-known Westerner on the continent.

  1996: Former heavyweight boxing champion Evander Holyfield regains the title by defeating the much-feared Mike Tyson—then successfully defends his title in a rematch held in June, 1997. Ironically, an aging George Foreman still holds a rival boxing organization's heavyweight title after making a comeback in the early 1990s.

- **1966-72:** After persecution of the Ibo people in northern Nigeria commences, Achebe resigns from his post in the Nigerian Broadcasting Corporation and moves to the breakaway province of Biafra. He becomes a spokesman for the eventually defeated Biafran cause.

  1995: Writers in the Third World experience increased danger for their political views. In 1990, the Iranian government issues a "fatwa," or death sentence, against the Indian writer Salman Rushdie for the purported blasphemy of his book *The Satanic Verses.* Nobel Prize-winning Egyptian writer Naghib Mafouz has his life threatened by Islamic militants. In Nigeria, writer Ken Saro-Wiwa is executed by the government for his political activities.

- **1971:** The Democratic Republic of Congo in Africa becomes the Republic of Zaire on October 27th. Mobutu Sese Seko assumes political power and declares himself president.

  1997: Zaire once again becomes the Congo after Mobutu is overthrown. After years of a bloody reign in which he executed enemies and friends alike, Mobutu is weakened by cancer and dies in September.

In the early 1800s, British traders interested in palm oil began to travel to the region that later became known as Nigeria, and there they encouraged the slave trade. The British maintained their influence in the area until 1914, when the British government assumed direct control of the land (which up until then had been under the administration of the Royal Niger Company). They united the northern and southern halves of the country and administered the territory from the city of Lagos, which remains the capital.

Ethnic differences made governing the country difficult, and the three regions developed at different paces. The British granted Nigeria independence in 1960, but not until they set up a constitution that guaranteed the rights of minority ethnic groups. After a honeymoon period of approximately two years, in which Nigerians celebrated their newly-won independence, the country began to have political troubles. Elections were disputed and boycotted, and in 1965 a group of military officers attempted a coup. Ethnic tensions began to rise, and much anger was directed against the Ibo people in the north of the country.

In 1967, three of the eastern states of Nigeria seceded from the country and named their new country Biafra. After two and a half years of bloody civil war in which many thousands were killed and many more civilians starved, the Biafrans surrendered in 1970. Since then, the country has endured numerous military dictatorships and failed civilian administrations.

Nigeria, the most populous country in Africa, is also potentially one of the wealthiest. Its abundant natural resources—which include large oil reserves—indicate that the country should enjoy prosperity and development. However, corrupt administrations have ensured that the prosperity is only enjoyed by a tiny segment of the population.

The poor are crowding into the cities, and Lagos is now the second largest city in Africa (after Cairo). Nigerian artists and writers have been persecuted for speaking out against the government and against what they see as the environmental depredations of foreign countries, and one prominent writer, Ken Saro-Wiwa, was executed for his political activities.

Education in Nigeria

The temporary program of free primary education represented in "Vengeful Creditor" has as its basis actual events in Nigeria in 1957. The Eastern Region attempted to establish such a program, modeled after a similar venture in the Western Region two years earlier. Just as in the story, free education had to be withdrawn because demand quickly exceeded the government's resources. Workers who had left their menial jobs to attend school were forced to return to them since they could not afford to pay the reinstated school fees. Not until 1976, five years after Achebe's story was initially published, did the universal primary education program begin again. Compulsory primary education was in place after 1979.

Critical Overview

Primarily known as a novelist, Chinua Achebe has published relatively few short stories. His only collection of stories, *Girls At War, and Other Stories,* appeared in 1973 and brought together stories written over the preceding twenty years. "Vengeful Creditor," which appears in this collection, had first been published in the inaugural issue of the journal *Okike: A Nigerian Journal of New Writing. Okike* itself was founded by Achebe , and he has continued to edit the magazine throughout his stays in the United States.

In general, critical opinion on Achebe is overwhelmingly positive. He has claimed a place as one of Africa's leading writers, and *Things Fall Apart* is now considered a classic of African literature. Critics laud Achebe's ability to meld his pride in his own culture with a deep respect for Western literary traditions. *Things Fall Apart,* for instance, is a story of a traditional African village in which the intrusion of British influence is an important theme, but by no means the defining characteristic of the story.

Critics have noted Achebe's allusions to Western classics in his novels, specifically the epics of Greek mythology and the modernism of Eliot and Yeats (from whose poem "The Second Coming" the title of *Things Fall Apart* is taken). The primary importance of Achebe's works, to many critics, is his simple dictum that Africans had a deep and complex culture before the arrival of the colonizing powers. Achebe does not reject the Western tradition in favor of a strictly Afrocentric viewpoint; nor does he attempt to graft Western intellectual structures onto supposedly "primitive" African traditions. He shows that the two traditions are of equal value and importance, and his writings often depict what happens when these sometimes-opposing forces meet. Achebe is also known for his willingness to criticize the conduct of the ruling classes in postcolonial Africa.

The story "Vengeful Creditor" has received little critical attention apart from general reviews of the collection, *Girls at War, and Other Stories.* Most critics point out its satirical critique of middle-class Africans, its use of irony, and its realistic narrative voice. According to John Carr in the *Critical Survey of Short Fiction,* it "appears to be a story about class struggle and then, as the reader sees layer after layer of meaning stripped away and one theme leading directly to another, it seems to be—and is—about something really quite different than either education or the class system." David Carroll, in his book *Chinua Achebe,* focuses on the story's examination of "the corruption of both private and public morality." In an article published in the journal *Comparative Literature Studies,* F. Odun Balogun notes numerous stylistic and thematic similarities between this story and the story "Sleepy," written by the nineteenth-century Russian writer Anton Chekhov.

Criticism

David Kippen

Kippen is an educator and a specialist on British colonial literature and twentieth-century

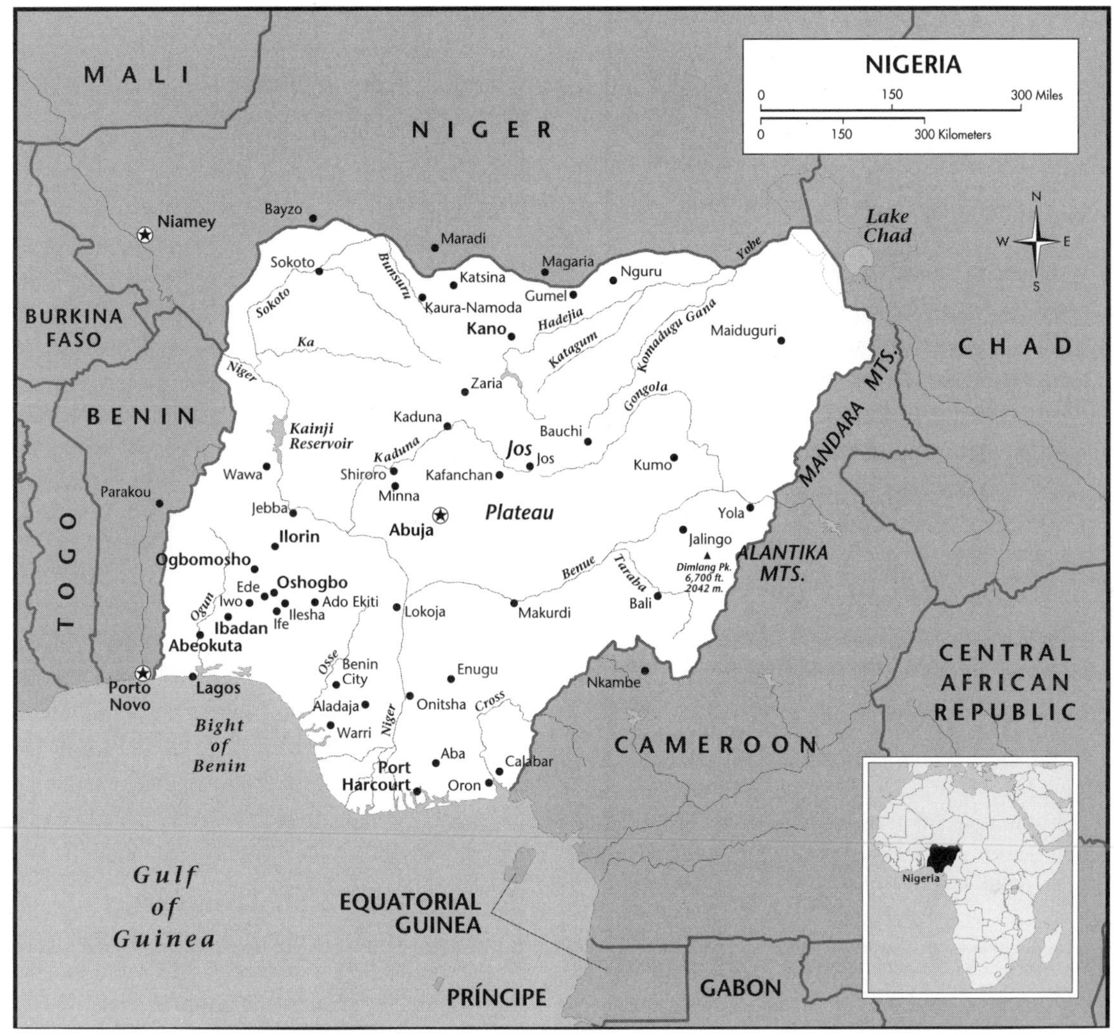

A map of Nigeria, showing the country's location on the coast of Central Africa.

South African fiction. In the following essay, he explores the satirical intent of "Vengeful Creditor."

In the story "Vengeful Creditor," Chinua Achebe presents a situation similar to that of post-independence Nigeria, in which an African country's administrative class has maintained the worst attributes of the departed British colonial system. His depiction of the class conflict between the rich and the poor centers around whether or not free primary education (called universal primary education, or UPE, in Nigeria) should be implemented, and if so, how it should be paid for. Achebe's exploration of this matter becomes a scathing satire of the failures of traditional (i.e., European) solutions, both liberal and conservative, to the problems of governance and inequality between classes, problems that emerged as African nations achieved independence.

Everyone has lost something by the story's conclusion. Mrs. Emenike has lost her baby nurse, as well as any willingness to consider the merits of "free primadu." Mr. Emenike has certainly lost peace of mind and, at least for the moment, status, since he was playing "the great man" to Veronica by holding the promise of an education out to her. Martha, herself once a pioneer mission-school

What Do I Read Next?

- *Things Fall Apart* (1958), Achebe's first and most famous novel, traces the life of a man in an Ibo village. Okonkwo tries to overcome the shameful legacy of his father, Unoka, by rejecting everything his father stood for. The book is not just a story of a man, though, but of traditional Ibo culture preparing to come into contact with the colonizing forces of Britain and the West.
- *No Longer at Ease* (1960) and *Arrow of God* (1964) continue the story begun with *Things Fall Apart.* In these two novels, Achebe tells the story of two later generations in the same family as they deal with British rule and with Nigerian independence.
- *A Forest of Flowers,* by the murdered Nigerian writer Ken Saro-Wiwa, is a collection of stories that convey the vitality of everyday Nigerian life. Characters live in close-knit families, and their lives are dominated by tradition, superstition, and the corruption of the country's politics; the collection was highly praised by critics when it was published in 1986.
- ''The Train from Rhodesia,'' written by Nadine Gordimer and first published in 1952 is a story that examines the differences between the British ruling class and the African cultures they govern.
- ''Sleepy,'' a story by Russian writer Anton Chekhov written in 1888 bears some similarity to ''Vengeful Creditor.'' It is about an exhausted child who kills the infant in her charge so that she can finally sleep.
- Ayi Kwei Armah's *The Beautyful Ones Are Not Yet Born* (1968) examines another West African country, Ghana. In this novel, Armah follows a typical Ghanaian worker, a man with a job on the railroad, and delves into the anomie and alienation of the man (who is never named) as he negotiates his way between African tradition and Western expansion.

student, had already lost her husband before the story begins; by the story's conclusion she has also lost her one remaining hope: that her daughter will have a better life than she had. Veronica, of course, has lost more: the luxuries of the well-appointed home she had become accustomed to and the promise of a good future which is contingent upon membership in the educated elite. Given the abysmal state of things at the story's conclusion, given that this is satire and not tragedy, the first question confronting the reader must surely be ''why doesn't Achebe offer solutions?'' The answer has to do both with the restrictions of satire and the uncomfortable position Achebe occupies as a novelist from a postcolonial state.

Satirical fiction is unique in that it identifies a problem, adopts a clear position in regard to it, but rarely offers a concrete solution. Were the satirist to offer solutions, he or she would be exchanging the thick mantle of outrage for the thin and self-serving cape of advocacy, hopelessly weakening the force of the satire. In some cases—the most famous being Jonathan Swift's *A Modest Proposal,* in which the eating of babies is suggested as the solution to a number of ills—the satirist may even go one step further and suggest a spurious solution, one that clearly cannot and should not be implemented. In short, satire does not solve problems; it proclaims their existence. So, for example, James Joyce wrote *Dubliners* in a spirit of ''scrupulous meanness'' to alert Ireland's residents to their condition (which he identified as paralysis), but he did not blaze a path for them to follow.

Once people see themselves in the satire, it is the satirist's hope that they will change themselves appropriately.Therefore, that Achebe's satire offers no solutions is not coincidental, but central to its success as story and effectiveness as satire. And, since satire is based upon the assumption that the reader will generalize from the particulars of the satire to the problem at large, the subjects of satire are easily recognizable types, not fully individuated characters. Thus, the Emenikes, their various servants, the Ministers of Education and Finance, etc., are two-dimensional, lacking emotional complexity. If Mrs. Emenike, the social welfare officer who receives the bulk of Achebe's animosity, surprises the reader it is with her meanness or with the irony of her unintended self-revelations (''Perhaps it's from me she learnt''), not with shows of unexpected compassion or introspection. Mr. Emenike is created from a similar mold, playing the great man about the village to his perceived subordinates, while laughing too loudly in town, in servile, disingenuous support of his superiors. He also is not immune to the revealing irony, responding to Mrs. Emenike's ''perhaps it's from me she learnt'' in proverb: ''when the mother cow chews giant grass her little calves watch her mouth.''

In addition to working within the form of satire as an internationally recognized member of Nigeria's intelligentsia, Achebe must also contend with the possibility that his writing will be of consequence. Put another way, what he says is certain to be heard. While this may be true of every writer who captures the imagination of the reading public and becomes, however unwittingly, the spokesperson for others, this carries added weight for African writers. As James Booth observes in his *Writers and Politics in Nigeria,* ''conceptual problems unknown in Europe and North America confront the political thinker and the imaginative writer in an independent African state. . . . The first step of political emancipation having been achieved he is wary of re-enslaving himself by a kind of cultural neo-colonialism to non-African concepts and ideals whose relevance to his situation is questionable.'' Satire's genre restrictions aside, Achebe cannot easily come down in favor of the solutions offered by either the Minister of Finance or the Minister of Education because, simply put, the solutions they have to offer do not fit the problem they are trying to solve. This is not to say that questions of taxation and education, issues of rights and responsibilities, or a basic disagreement over the value of a free market mean any less in Nigeria than they do elsewhere. Quite the contrary—they mean at least as much, and perhaps more, arising as they do against a national backdrop that still remains to be painted. The important issue is neither a question of who should pay or who should attend (since everyone loses in the end anyway), but of what the core values of ''the new Nigeria,'' the post-colonial Nigeria, will be. Follow the example of the Emenike family, and Nigeria looks disturbingly like it did before the British began their gradual retreat, except that people are now divided along the lines of class rather than race. Follow the path trod by Veronica, and the future looks more bleak than it did for her mother, and the severe malnourishment of Veronica's youngest sister Mary promises an even deeper decline for the yet-unborn poor.

"Once people see themselves in the satire, it is the satirist's hope that they will change themselves appropriately."

This is not to say that the questions surrounding UPE do not also address core values, but these are tangential to Achebe's main target—the educated elite. In one of the more ironic passages in the story, Achebe identifies a chorus of the educated and shows their solidarity in their meanspirited oppression of the less fortunate: ''responsible citizens—lawyers, doctors, merchants, engineers, salesmen, insurance brokers, university lecturers, etc.—had written in criticism of the scheme. No one was against education for the kids, they said, but free education was premature.'' This selfish declaration is central to the irony surrounding Veronica's short career in the Emenike household. Mr. Emenike seems oblivious to the irony of recognizing Veronica's genius while denying her schooling, or of telling her mother that destiny is all written in the hand when his own destiny and ongoing success are so clearly the result of a patronage system. Achebe underscores the dichotomy between the educational haves and have-nots by alternating between standard English and pidgin English.

In focusing almost exclusively on the Emenikes' disdain for their less fortunate countrymen, Achebe simplifies the issue to sharpen his satire. In fact, the educated elite stood to benefit considerably from UPE. In *The Political Dilemma of Popular Educa-*

tion: An African Perspective, David Abernathy argues that the promise of UPE would solve a number of problems for this elite and help them to gain and consolidate power. "Colonial rulers . . . had created a three-way struggle for legitimate authority among the British . . . the chiefs . . . and the educated elite. Initially this elite lacked the prestige that came from having substantial political or administrative power. . . . The political leaders of the early 1950's could expect to gain popular support only by promising certain benefits that neither the British nor the chiefs were likely to provide. Universal primary education was an admirable aid in resolving 'the legitimacy crisis.'" Though UPE was successfully implemented in 1976, followed in 1979 by a law requiring compulsory education for six years, the division between educational haves and have-nots and the corresponding imbalance between powerful and powerless remain today much as Achebe described them in 1971. In terms of social equality, Veronica's credit still exists while the educated classes' debt continues to mount.

Source: David Kippen, "Overview of 'Vengeful Creditor'," in *Short Stories for Students,* Gale, 1998.

Elisabeth Piedmont-Marton

Piedmont-Marton has a Ph.D. in English and teaches American literature and coordinates the Writing Center at the University of Texas at Austin. In the essay below, she offers a general introduction to "Vengeful Creditor," focusing upon issues related to class struggle.

"Vengeful Creditor" was first published in 1971 and two years later was included in the short story collection *Girls at War, and Other Stories.* Long before, following the publication of his first novel, *Things Fall Apart,* in 1958, Chinua Achebe established himself as Nigeria's best-known novelist. The subsequent publication of four more novels and several volumes of poetry has expanded his reputation to the point where he is now widely recognized as one of the preeminent writers of Africa. Achebe has also written many essays and delivered numerous speeches in which he discusses the role and responsibility of the modern African writer in the turbulent postcolonial period characterized by military dictatorship, civilian misrule, and civil war. "Vengeful Creditor" takes place during the period when the new government had established and then discontinued an experimental program in free primary education for all. Achebe uses this situation as an opportunity to examine the way this abortive democratic initiative affected the lives of a variety of people. Achebe treats his subject with his characteristic tone of detached irony, but his social critique is serious and well-aimed.

The world that Achebe describes in this story, and in all his fiction, is one still struggling with the legacies of colonialism. The departure of the British in 1960, Achebe acknowledges, created the modern nation state of Nigeria and provided all Nigerians with a language they could use to communicate with others beyond their immediate tribes. Independence, however, created a cluster of new problems and failed to solve those that existed under colonial rule. One of the most pernicious of these social problems is the gap between a prosperous governing class, represented by the Emenikes, and a poor, rural, uneducated underclass, represented by Veronica and her mother. Achebe points out in his fiction the painful irony that those who sought freedom from the bigotry and oppression associated with British rule quickly assumed the same condescending posture towards the lower class once they were in power. Critic C. L. Innes noted that this story marks a shift in focus in Achebe's fiction, away from portrayals of the limitations of traditional village life, toward a concern for "the importance of class interest in the denial of individual fulfillment" for modern Africans. It is clear from the opening scene of "Vengeful Creditor" that Mrs. Emenike is going to bear the brunt of Achebe's satire. Her cruel and patronizing attitude toward the workers in the supermarket is characteristic of members of her class who are "willing to sacrifice the poor and relatively helpless so that their own lives may not be discomforted," Innes further stated.

Achebe finds many rich veins of irony to expose in Mrs. Emenike and her husband. While she is certainly a modern Nigerian woman with a career outside the home, her attitudes derive from the "old" days of colonial rule. In addition, her professional identity as a social worker is comically at odds with her behavior; she is a government official whose duty it is to improve the lives of the people, but her major complaint is that the promise of free education makes it difficult for her to get good servants. At the grocery store she is upset that free schooling has depleted the ranks of the help and she must settle for a surly forty-year-old to grudgingly carry her bags to the car. Both she and her husband are supposedly disinterested civil servants, but in fact, they are motivated only by self-interest. After blaming the free education experiment for the defection of their household staff, Mr. and Mrs.

Emenike exploit Veronica's desire to attend school in order to hire her at low wages to care for their baby.

In his portrayal of Martha's family, Achebe offers further ironic commentary on the Christian missionaries who have professed to help the poor. Veronica's father had believed the missionaries' promises when he became a carpenter and assumed he would continue to have employment, but "carpentry never developed much," and the family was not prosperous. When he died, the Christians offered to the widowed Martha and her children only the useless reassurance that "he had been called to higher service in the heavenly missions by Him who was Himself once a Carpenter on earth." Martha and her children are powerless in the face of a system that denies them even basic education and that employs people like Mrs. Emenike as Social Welfare Officers. It is no wonder, then, that when Mr. Emenike shows up in his big Mercedes to offer Veronica a job, Martha feels that she has no choice but to accept even though she does not believe his promise to send her daughter to school.

A further irony emerges when Veronica proves to be so good at her job that Mrs. Emenike praises her by calling her "little Madame." Achebe's point is that Mrs. Emenike can joke about the likeness between the two of them only because she is quite certain that they have nothing in common. This ironic contrast becomes more extreme as Veronica earns praise and recognition for her intelligence. According to Mr. Emenike, the child is a genius despite her lack of schooling. The couple seems to find in Veronica's natural abilities justification for their beliefs that universal education is unnecessary, and they are quite willing to exploit her for their own ends. The two worlds are poised to collide in Achebe's surprisingly dark ending.

Veronica finally decides to collect the debt she believes the Emenikes owe her by eliminating what she sees as the obstacle to her attendance at school, the baby. Veronica's plan is literally to take the baby's place at school and the weapon she employs to eliminate him, red ink, resonates with the ironies characteristic of the story as a whole. In the first place, Mrs. Emenike herself gives Veronica the idea by telling her that red ink is poisonous, and Veronica is smart enough to learn the lesson well. Furthermore, red ink is the medium of creditors and Veronica is using it to write the debt-due notice large on the body of the child. Finally, the choice of ink as a weapon signifies Veronica's violent appropriation of the means of education. If the Emenikes and their kind will not give her access to education, she will take it anyway.

"Mrs. Emenike's professional identity as a social worker is comically at odds with her behavior; she is a government official whose duty it is to improve the lives of the people, but her major complaint is that the promise of free education makes it difficult for her to get good servants."

The discussion between Martha and the Emenikes that closes the story contains one final, ominous irony. After Martha insists that Veronica could not have learned to become a murderer from her, Mrs. Emenike says sarcastically, "Perhaps it's from me she learnt." Readers know that on a literal level, she is right; she taught Veronica that red ink could poison the child. On a larger symbolic level, she is also right, but does not know it. The governing class's politics of exclusion have taught the underclass that they will have to seize their fair share. Veronica learns how to be a murderer from Mrs. Emenike and she learns how to collect the debt that is due her. Mr. Emenike's final pronouncement, that he had "always known that the craze for education in this country will one day ruin all of us," is a chilling and ironic prediction.

Source: Elisabeth Piedmont-Marton, "Overview of 'Vengeful Creditor'," in *Short Stories for Students,* Gale, 1998.

F. Odun Balogun

In the following excerpt from his book-length study of African short stories, Balogun examines how "Vengeful Creditor" exposes various inadequacies in Nigeria's political, social, and religious systems, focusing on class differences, education, power, and the distribution of wealth.

"Mrs. Emenike is a good example of the crass materialism and insensitivity that characterize members of the modern elite who are totally Machiavellian in the tactics they adopt to safeguard their privileges."

Materialism and hypocrisy remained with the church even after it had survived infancy in Nigeria, and as Achebe's stories reveal, these evils have continued to survive today. . . .

The inadequacy of the new faith is . . . evident in "Vengeful Creditor." A close examination of this story shows that religion is callous where it needs most to be sympathetic and understanding. Martha's pathetic fate is dismissed with easy platitudes. Her husband who dies prematurely, leaving her and their children in miserable poverty, is said to have been called to "higher service," when it is obvious that his "higher service" actually lay in remaining alive to cater to the needs of his family. His death plunges his dependents into misery and subjects them to degradation and callous exploitation at the hands of the modern elites, represented in this story by the Emenike family. The much vaunted advantages of Christian and colonial education are revealed in this story not to be the result of a conscious plan for the advancement of the black man, but the accidental byproducts of a basically paternalistic objective: Martha's husband was trained "by white artisan-missionaries at the Onitsha Industrial Mission, a trade school founded in the fervent belief that if the black man was to be redeemed he needed to learn the Bible alongside manual skills.". . .

It is obvious from all this that the Christian missionaries and colonial administrators were not the right people to select and train modern replacements for the elites of traditional African societies. It is the misfortune of Africa, however, that it was precisely the task these missionaries and administrators were morally ill-equipped to perform that they actually performed. It was therefore a foregone conclusion that modern elites, be they in the bureaucracy, business, politics, religion, or the academics, were going to misuse power perhaps even worse than did their predecessors in the traditional society. . . .

Achebe's stories show that the modern elite, as a rule, is not idealistic. . . . The joint exploitation of Martha and her daughter, Vero, by the permanent secretary, Mr. Emenike, and his wife in "Vengeful Creditor" is a classic example. The way the elites collaborate not only between themselves but also with foreign neocolonial forces to protect their privileges at the expense of the exploited masses is also a major subject in "Vengeful Creditor." The controversy surrounding the withdrawal of the free primary education scheme exposes the fraud, hypocrisy, and deceit that characterize the collaboration existing between the business, bureaucratic, and political elites and their neocolonial external sponsors represented respectively here by Mike Ogudu, Mr. Emenike, the finance minister, and the newspaper, *New Age.*

With her love for cars, public displays of affluence, array of five house maids and servants, her superficiality, lack of interest in serious issues of public concern, and her callousness to her maids, Mrs. Emenike is a good example of the crass materialism and insensitivity that characterize members of the modern elite who are totally Machiavellian in the tactics they adopt to safeguard their privileges. They lie and falsify facts as happens, for instance, during the debate on free primary education. The truth is that free education encroaches on the privileges of the elites by depriving them of easy access to housemaids and servants. It provides opportunities for the common men to elevate themselves through education and thus become competitors with the members of the elite class. Moreover, it threatens the chances of the reelection of the political elites because it requires increased taxation, which the population resents. Rather than admit these facts openly, the elites—"lawyers, doctors, merchants, engineers, salesmen, insurance brokers, university lecturers, etc."—use the *New Age* (the platform provided by their external neocolonial sponsors) to publish vicious criticisms of the scheme. For instance, Mike Ogudu, the business tycoon, claims that "free primary education is tantamount to naked communism"; the *New Age* calls the proposal a "piece of hare-brained socialism" that is "unworkable in African conditions"; the finance minister pretends he is protecting "our long-suffering masses'' from further taxation by advocating the cancellation of the program; and Mr. Emenike is all regrets that civil servants are prohibited from writing to the papers—otherwise, he would have liked to make it known that ''we are not a nation of Oliver Twists'' for whom free education has to be provided.

Both ''Vengeful Creditor'' and ''The Voter'' give a good picture of how the modern political elites operate. To win elections they use false promises, bribes, thugs, and tribal sentiments. After elections they rob the national coffers both ''to retire'' their ''election debts'' and to provide themselves with luxuries. . . .

Source: F. Odun Balogun, ''Tradition and Modernity in the African Short Story: Achebe and lo Liyong,'' in *Tradition and Modernity in the African Short Story: An Introduction to a Literature in Search of Critics,* Greenwood Press, 1991, pp. 57–64.

C. L. Innes

Innes is a Senior Lecturer in English, African, and Caribbean Literature at the University of Kent at Canterbury, England. In the following excerpt, she focuses on the theme of social conflict in ''Vengeful Creditor.''

There could scarcely be a sharper contrast with the traditional setting and mode of ''Akueke'' than ''Vengeful Creditor,'' published almost a decade later in the first issue of *Okike.* Opening not in a small rural village hut but in a busy urban supermarket, and characterizing a confident, wealthy working woman who is also a wife and mother, we seem to have moved a long distance from the world of Akueke and the psychological isolation that was her lot. Nor is there the compassion and suspended judgement which hovers over the dilemma of all the characters in the earlier story, male and female alike; here the satire and judgement is directed sharply against Mrs. Emenike, along with her husband and others of their class who are so willing to sacrifice the poor and relatively helpless so that their own lives may not be discomforted. The difference between the two stories marks a more general change in Achebe's fiction from concern with those such as Unoka, Nwoye and Akueke for whom the cultural and psychological conventions and norms of their society do not allow adequate fulfillment, to an increasing recognition (seen in *A Man of the People*) of the importance of class interest as a factor in the denial of individual fulfillment.

> "The red ink spilt over the baby's front is a potent image of the bloody vengeance that the poor may take upon the middle classes who blindly and selfishly exploit them."

As a means of focusing on the ways in which private and public concerns converge, Achebe uses the issue of free primary education and its abortive introduction by the Western and Eastern Regional Governments in 1955–57. Mrs. Emenike, a social worker, and her civil servant husband, are quickly disillusioned with its introduction when their servants begin deserting them in order to attend school. On one of their brief and infrequent visits to Mr. Emenike's home village, they secure the services of ten-year-old Veronica for a wage of £5 a year and, more importantly as far as Veronica is concerned, the vague promise of schooling for her when their youngest child no longer needs a 'baby-nurse'. As Veronica watches the Emenike children escape each day from the world of her household duties and the moment of her own return to schooling seems ever more distant, she tries to eliminate the baby whom she sees as the obstacle to her own education, by giving him red ink to drink.Her choice of ink has been made credible by a previous warning from Mrs. Emenike, who has found her playing with it, that red ink is poisonous, but the ink is also a symbol of the education she so avidly desires. Veronica is no passive resister like Akueke, or like her tired and harassed mother, and the red ink spilt over the baby's front is a potent image of the bloody vengeance that the poor may take upon the middle classes who blindly and selfishly exploit them and frustrate their aspirations to share in those things the Emenikes so complacently take for granted as their right—bountiful food, work and good wages, and education for their children. As David Carroll points out in his discussion of this story, Mrs. Emenike's response, 'Perhaps it's from me she learnt', when Veronica's horrified mother protests that she could not have learned such things from home, is doubly ironic. For Veronica *has* learned by example from the Emenikes that the welfare and rights of others can be dispensed with if they stand in the way of her getting what she wants. And the remark also epitomizes Mrs. Emenike's smug certainty that she is blameless, a blind complacency which suggests little hope of change from the top.

Source: C. L. Innes, "Marginal Lives: 'Girls at War' and Other Stories," in *Chinua Achebe,* Cambridge University Press, 1990, pp. 121–33.

F. Odun Balogun

Balogun is affiliated with the University of Benin, Nigeria. In the excerpt below, the critic compares "Vengeful Creditor" with Anton Chekhov's "Sleepy." Noting similarities in the political and social backdrops of the two narratives, the critic also discusses stylistic and thematic parallels, particularly with regards to class conflicts, wealth and poverty, and morality.

In "Vengeful Creditor," Achebe also denounces man's inhumanity to man by exposing the deceit and callousness characterizing the attitude of contemporary Nigerian educated elites towards the poor. Mr. Emenike, a permanent secretary in the civil service, engages Vero as a baby-nurse with the promise to send her to school as soon as his baby grows up. Every morning Emenike's older children, beautifully dressed in uniforms, are driven to school; and each morning Vero is full of admiration and anticipation. She becomes anxious and wants "little Goddy," the baby she is tending, to grow up quickly so she too can join in these beautiful daily departures which guarantee escape from the poverty of her mother to the comfort of the Emenikes. Vero's passionate desire to resume schooling, which she had stopped because of her mother's inability to pay fees, intensifies and becomes an obsession, but the Emenikes' baby, it appears to Vero, refuses to grow up fast enough. Time passes and the situation does not change; in fact, the baby tends to become even more dependent on her. Vero concludes that "little Goddy" refuses to grow on purpose so as to deprive her of the opportunity to go to school, which promises the only avenue of escape from the poverty that looms menacingly in her future. She becomes desperate and decides to eliminate the obstacle preventing her from going to school. She gives the baby red ink to drink in the belief that it would kill him, having once been told by Mrs. Emenike that red ink is poisonous. The baby is unhurt, but Mrs. Emenike is horrified, beats Vero with bestial ferocity, and sends her back to the poverty of her mother, Martha, in the village.

Obviously, one cannot equate Varka's deprivation [in Chekhov's "Sleepy"] of a basic physical human necessity—the need to sleep—with Vero's "dispensable" desire for education; nonetheless, the two deprivations are comparable since they each act as a catalyst for tragedy in the stories. Moreover, in the context of a developing nation like Nigeria, education makes all the difference between a decent living and a poverty-stricken existence. For Vero, therefore, the choice of going or not going to school is a choice between an abject, cruel existence and a happy, meaningful life, which, ultimately, is a no-choice situation.

However comparable the situations might be, the fundamental difference needs to be stressed. Vero's action lacks the compelling immediacy which eliminates moral and ethical considerations and justifies Varka's action and makes the reader see her decision as absolutely inescapable and accept the baby's murder as a necessity to preserving her own life. Varka's choice is not one between a meaningful and purposeless existence as is the case with Vero, but an absolute case of no-choice, for no human being who has not slept for days can resist indefinitely the overwhelming urgency to sleep at last. This is why the reader is in total sympathy with Varka whereas Vero's action takes him a little by surprise.

Each of these stories was conceived by the author as a critical response to an existing social anomaly of the time it was written. . . .

Achebe on his part . . . based his story on a specific historical fact. In 1957 the government of the Eastern Region of Nigeria introduced a non-paying primary education scheme following the successful example of the government of the Western Region which started the program in 1955. Unlike the latter, however, the former had had to stop the venture after only one year of implementation for financial reasons. Part of the problem was that enrollment had outstripped anticipated figures because both school-age and post-school-age children as well as children from neighboring regions had registered to take advantage of the scheme. After the reintroduction of fees, children of the poor who could not pay came to grief as they were compelled to withdraw from school which had suddenly opened new prospects of a better life to them. The disappointed would-be pupils drifted back to either the farms or to urban markets for domestic servants—places from which they had only recently hurriedly withdrawn their services in the rush to acquire education. The urban middle class who had experienced an acute shortage of domestic servants during the one year the experiment lasted once more were able to engage as many household helpers as they wanted.

Achebe not only remains faithful to the details of this historical fact but also renders the story more pungent by an effective contrasting presentation of two families representing the middle class and the poor. Not that Achebe needed prototypes to successfully represent a common reality such as the relationship between the Emenike family and that of Martha, but the factual details of this relationship as presented in the story strongly suggest that the initial impetus for its composition goes beyond the mere observation of a general fact. The account brims with such evidence of concretely observed details that it seems safe to assume that the story's characters, especially Martha, had living prototypes.

Just like Chekhov in "Sleepy," Achebe in "Vengeful Creditor" portrays the callous indifference and selfishness of the master to the servant. The shoemaker and his wife in Chekhov's story are duplicated by Mr. Emenike and his wife, who are likewise unaware of the humanity of their domestic servants whom they see as objects good only to be exploited in the process of guaranteeing their elitist comfort and happiness. The inhumanity as expressed in selfishness, hypocrisy, callousness, and exploitation which characterize the relationship of the Nigerian elite with the poor is what Achebe has exposed to satiric ridicule in his story.

"The inhumanity as expressed in selfishness, hypocrisy, callousness, and exploitation which characterize the relationship of the Nigerian elite with the poor is what Achebe has exposed to satiric ridicule in his story."

It is evident from what has been said so far that a specific historical circumstance dictated to Achebe the subject of "Vengeful Creditor." There are, however, a number of coincidences which seem to adduce some degree of direct influence of Chekhov on Achebe in matters of details. Chekhov's heroine is a thirteen-year-old orphan named Varka, a diminutive for Varvara. Achebe's heroine is a ten-year-old orphan with a surviving mother and her name is Veronica, but more often she is referred to by the diminutive, Vero. Both Varka and Vero are employed by exploitative, callous masters as baby-nurses. Both heroines compose lullabies although for slightly different reasons: Varka to pacify a baby whom the mother said must be bewitched for never stopping screaming, and Vero both to pacify her ward and to intimate her masters of her burning desire to go to school. Both girls find their cruel exploitation, not intellectually, but physically and emotionally unbearable and decide on murder as the only way out. Varka's murder of the baby cannot be said to be willful in as much as she makes her decision in a hallucinatory state of mind induced by over-exhaustion. Vero's decision, though taken consciously, also cannot be regarded as willful since such a young girl is not fully aware of the implications of her action.

The styles of the two stories are more different than alike, although similarities exist in aspects of characterization and language. In each, there is a contrasting set-up of characters with the master representing the class of callous exploiters and the teenage baby-nurse symbolizing the class of the oppressed poor. Each gives details showing the misery and abject poverty in which lives the family of the baby-nurse. Also in each case there is some detail provided about the circumstances surrounding the death of the baby-nurse's father in order to reveal the predicament of the widowed mother and orphaned daughter.

The master and mistress in each story are also negatively portrayed. . . . Vero's mistress is depicted as vain, shallow, materialistic, and callous. Varka's master, the shoemaker, is inconsiderate, insensitive, cruel, and crude; while Mr. Emenike, Vero's master and a permanent secretary, is in fact selfish, hypocritical, and inhumane even though he pretends to be a refined, decent gentleman. In each of the stories also, the poor are portrayed as morally superior to their social masters by virtue of their humility, patience, forbearance, and the courage with which they carry on in the face of extreme, adverse conditions.

The most significant difference in characterization is that Chekhov is very sparing in providing details concerning the lives of his characters. Achebe, on the other hand, gives elaborate details of the world of Vero's masters. The story is in fact structurally presented in two unseparated halves. The first half is generously spiced with ironic humor as the hypocrisy, callousness, and inhumanity of the masters are exposed to satirical ridicule. The second half, devoted to Martha and Vero, is humorless as it reveals the tragic details of the lives of these two.

Thus while the first part of Achebe's story fits Gogol's formula of "laughter through tears," for being "gay in appearance but sad in substance" [D. S. Mirsky, "Chekhov," *Anton Chekhov's Short Stories,* 1979], the second half is much the reverse: "tears through laughter" [Renato Poggioli, "Storytelling in a Double Key," *Anton Chekhov's Short Stories,* 1979], because in spite of its tragic sadness there is some ironic humor, such, for example, as emanates from Vero's naivete which makes her think she could kill by administering red ink as poison. . . .

Although brevity in characterization enhances the over-all artistic effect of Chekhov's story, the same quality makes the characters one-dimensional, flat: the masters are bad, the nurse is simple-hearted. By contrast, Achebe is able to portray multi-dimensional characters by using more details. Although the masters in Achebe's story are still negative, some extenuating circumstances are introduced into their motivations to ameliorate their badness. We are made to sympathize, for instance, with their plight when they had no one to take care of their children; and also, unlike the shoemaker and his wife in Chekhov's story, the Emenikes cater to the basic needs of their servants.

The most outstanding difference in the styles of the two stories is the brevity of one and the relaxed, unhurried tempo of narration of the other. . . . Achebe, who is also a master of conciseness as attested to by the majority of the stories in his collection, has elected to present a detailed narration in "Vengeful Creditor." It should be noted, however, that in spite of its detailed narration, "Vengeful Creditor" is composed with a linguistic terseness that permits Achebe to compress into fewer pages what a lesser talent would have expressed in several more. . . .

Although Achebe's "Vengeful Creditor" cannot compare as a poetic composition with Chekhov's "Sleepy" or even with Achebe's own story entitled "The Madman," it nonetheless shows a conspicuous, conscious effort on the part of the author to produce a rhythmic prose. The first page of the story, for instance, sustains a poetic cadence based on the repetitive use of parallel syntactical units with built-in variations along with a regular recurrence of words such as "Madame," "sang," and "cash." The second half of the first page and the whole of page two of the story are structured rhythmically on the recurrence of parallel coordinating sentences repeatedly using the same coordinating conjunction, "and." A brief passage much later in the text again repeats the same formula of recurring words, phrases, and parallel sentences. The poetic rhythm of Achebe's story as a whole is further reinforced on one hand by the songs composed by Vero and on the other by the rhythm inherent in dialogue which frequently punctuates the text.

Both stories are narrated in the third person with objective detachment, but there is greater distancing in Chekhov's story. This is not to say that Achebe's story is for that reason less successful. Indeed, the satirical irony, with which the world of the middle class is portrayed and which reveals the narrator's sympathy with the exploited poor, adds a humorous dimension to Achebe's story which is lacking in Chekhov's. . . .

Chekhov achieves his brevity and "the very limit of the detachment which he prizes so highly in a writer" in two ways. Firstly, as already pointed out he completely leaves undescribed the world of Varka's masters and by so doing forestalls the exposure of his sympathy, which is obviously on the side of Varka. Secondly, he portrays events not through his own perception as narrator but through the consciousness of his heroine, who is permanently in a hallucinatory, dream-like state of mind. Thus the story comes to us as if totally unmediated. This is particularly evident in the different ways the two authors use flashbacks. While past events are recalled in "Sleepy" through Varka's dreams and hallucinations, incidents in the past are remembered in "Vengeful Creditor" not by Vero or any of the characters but by the narrator himself. Consequently, the role of objective narrator is more convincingly sustained in ''Sleepy'' than in ''Vengeful Creditor.''

Indeed, nowhere else is the ''subjective objectivity'' of Achebe's narrator more evident than when telling about the calamities which have befallen Martha, who appears to be the victim of cosmic irony. Martha, the narrator says, ''was a hard-luck woman'' who in spite of early promise as a pioneer pupil in a girls' mission school had turned out an abject failure. Her marriage, we are told, ''had been a bad-luck marriage from the start.'' She accepted without bitterness the misfortune of having children only when ''she was virtually an old woman . . . and little strength left for her task.'' But ''what she nearly did grumble about was the disease that struck her husband and paralysed his right arm for five years before his death. It was a trial too heavy and unfair.''

Even though the last sentence appears to be a direct rendering of Martha's thoughts, there is some ambiguity that makes it possible for it to be interpreted as the narrator's own conclusion. In any case, Martha is conscious of divine unfairness, ''injustice,'' in the way she has been treated. That she holds God responsible for her plight is evident in her conversation with Mr. Emenike:

> Yes I pray God that what is written for these children will be better than what He wrote for me and my husband.

Her hope did not materialize, rather her tragedy worsened. In the end, she loses patience and cries out in revolt:

> ''*Oh, God, what have I done?''* Her tears begin to flow now. ''If I had had a child with other women of my age, that girl that calls me murderer might have been no older than my daughter. And now she spits in my face. *That's what you brought me to,''* she said to the *crown of Vero's head,* and jerked her along more violently (emphasis mine).

It is obvious, of course, that Martha is addressing Vero when she says ''That's what you brought me to.'' However, the syntactical arrangement of the quoted passage as a whole, beginning with an exclamatory query to God: ''Oh, God, what have I done?'' introduces an ambiguity into Martha's last complaint; and it therefore becomes equally applicable to Vero as to God: ''That's what you brought me to.'' This ambiguity is intentional at least on the part of the narrator who out of sympathy seems to have edged Martha into her revolt.

Martha's revolt recalls the religious doubts and questioning of God's fairness by both Dimitri and Olesha, and even to some extent Ivan's atheistic revolt against God, in Dostoevsky's *The Brothers Karamazov.* Martha's revolt may lack the intensity and intellectual motivations of Dostoevsky's characters, but it certainly springs from the same emotional source, and even more importantly from the bitterness of personal experience. Thus, in Achebe's hands, a Chekhovian theme has been consciously or unconsciously given a Dostoevskian twist.

The purpose of this study has not been to pitch Achebe's talents against Chekhov's since such an exercise is uncalled for; rather its objective has been to demonstrate how writers of different countries and periods do sometimes share similar concerns as a result of their common humanism. Furthermore, the aim has been to illustrate how similar socioeconomic and political set-ups in different regions of the world and at different periods can sometimes promote similar literary responses.

Source: F. Odun Balogun, ''Russian and Nigerian Literatures,'' in *Comparative Literature Studies,* Vol. 21, No. 4, Winter, 1984, pp. 483–95.

Further Reading

Innes, C. L., and Bernth Lindfors. *Critical Perspectives on Chinua Achebe.* Washington, D.C.: Three Continents Press, 1978.

A collection of essays on Achebe that concentrates primarily on his novels. However, many of the essays provide interesting context for Achebe's work, detailing the cultural and political events on which he is commenting.

Bonetti, Kay. ''An Interview with Chinua Achebe,'' in *The Missouri Review,* Volume 12, No. 1, 1989, pp. 63-83.

An interview with Achebe, conducted in the United States, in which he delineates his view on art and on his place in world literature.

Rowell, Charles H. ''An Interview with Chinua Achebe,'' in *Callaloo,* Volume 13, No. 1, Winter, 1990, pp. 86–101.

Interview in which Achebe discusses what texts he would include in an introductory twentieth-century world literature course. His combination of traditional authors such as T. S. Eliot and Ernest Hemingway with more ''exotic'' authors such as Nadine Gordimer and Raja Rao provides an example of how one might ''open up'' the literary canon .

Wren, Robert M. *Achebe's World: The Historical and Cultural Context of the Novels of Chinua Achebe.* Washington, D.C.: Three Continents Press, 1980.

Although this work concentrates on Achebe's novels, it provides a detailed context for his work. Many of the issues that Achebe discusses in his novels recur in the short fiction and in ''Vengeful Creditor.''

Where I'm Calling From

Raymond Carver

1982

Raymond Carver was at the height of his career when "Where I'm Calling From" first appeared, in the March 15, 1982, issue of the *New Yorker.* The story was included in *The Best American Short Stories, 1983* and was published in Carver's prize-winning collection *Cathedral,* appearing also in the author's 1988 collection *Where I'm Calling From: New and Selected Stories.* The story, about a man struggling to overcome his alcohol problem in a "drying out facility," appears to have some autobiographical elements that harken back to an earlier period in Carver's life when he struggled to overcome a drinking problem which left him unable to work for long periods of time. The story is set in a rehabilitation center in which the unnamed narrator finds himself listening uncomfortably to a fellow patient relate the history of his marriage. Carver, who had been sober for nearly five years by the time he wrote the story, emphasizes the characters' vulnerability and the uncertainty of their futures. In the story's ambiguous ending, the narrator is not certain what he will say if he actually reaches his estranged wife or his girlfriend on the telephone, but the very fact that he is motivated to even make these calls may provide some hope for an end to his numbing isolation.

Carver helped lead what many critics saw as a renaissance of the American short story in the 1970s and early 1980s. At a time when literature seemed to be dominated by highly self-conscious experimental writing, Carver wrote starkly realistic fiction in a sparse style reminiscent of Ernest Hemingway. Along with writers like Bobbie Ann Mason and Tobias Wolff, Carver came to be seen as a leader of a new "minimalist" school which sought to use language as economically as possible and to depict the lives of ordinary people without sentimentality. Though some dismissed this type of writing as "K-Mart realism" or "TV fiction," Carver won widespread popular and critical acclaim for his work.

Author Biography

Raymond Carver was exposed at a young age to many of the darker aspects of family life and the working world. He was born on May 25, 1938, in Clatskanie, Oregon, into a working-class family that was dominated by his alcoholic, sometimes-violent father. Carver started working immediately after high school in the same sawmill as did his father. By age 20, he had a wife, two children, and was heavily in debt. The pressures he faced climaxed when his father was admitted to a psychiatric ward in a hospital—one floor below the room in which his wife was to give birth to their second child.

In 1958, Carver enrolled part-time at Chico State College in northern California and took a literature course from then-unpublished novelist John Gardner, who would become a major influence on his writing. Carver himself commented, however, that during the first half of his career one of the strongest influences on him was alcohol. Carver's literary reputation grew slowly as he published short stories, poems, and essays throughout the 1960s and early 1970s, but his chronic alcoholism was disrupting his personal life. He was able to work only sporadically and twice filed for bankruptcy. He was hospitalized four times and nearly died of alcohol poisoning. He and his wife divorced in 1978.

Carver often said that the most important day in his life was June 2, 1977, when he finally stopped drinking. He considered it a miracle that alcoholism had not killed him and regarded the remaining years of his life as "pure gravy." His newfound sobriety coincided with a remarkable acceleration in his rise to literary fame. In 1976 his first major press book, a collection of short stories entitled *Will You Please Be Quiet, Please?* was published by McGraw-Hill and received a National Book Award nomination the following year. Carver finally attained some financial stability by winning a Guggenheim Fellowship in 1978, which was soon followed by several other prestigious awards. During these years, he wrote many prize-winning stories and published two highly acclaimed collections—*What We Talk About When We Talk About Love* and *Cathedral.* Carver's domestic life also improved as he began a long-term relationship with fellow writer Tess Gallagher.

Carver continued to hold "the dark view of things," as he called it, even in happier times. "In this second life, this post-drinking life," he told an interviewer, "I still retain a certain sense of pessimism." He continued to draw on experiences from his "bad Raymond days" for the subject matter of his stories, and while some critics believe that Carver's writings after 1981 display a slightly less fatalistic viewpoint, he has consistently been identified as a chronicler of the alienated and the dispossessed. By the time he died of cancer at age 50 in 1988, he was among the most celebrated writers in the world, credited for having breathed new life into the tradition of realistic short fiction in America.

Plot Summary

The story takes place over three days at a residential treatment center for alcoholics—a "drying out facility," as the unnamed narrator calls it. For most of the story, the narrator sits on the front porch with a fellow patient named Joe Penny, or J.P., whom he has just met. J.P. is around 30 years old and has never stayed at such a facility before. The narrator is a little older and on his second stay.

Anxious and distracted, the narrator tries to listen to J.P., who has begun rambling about the trauma he had experienced at age 12 when he fell down a dry well and waited for his father to rescue him. Encouraged by the narrator, J.P. then launches into the story of his stormy relationship with Roxy, his wife. He describes his first encounter with her during an afternoon of beer drinking at his friend's house: Roxy, dressed in a work uniform that includes a top hat, has come to clean the chimney. For J.P., it is love at first sight. J.P.'s tale-within-a-tale moves quickly through his courtship with Roxy; the couple soon gets married and has children. He also learns chimney-sweeping from Roxy and becomes a partner in her family's business.

Raymond Carver

J.P.'s happy domestic situation disintegrates rapidly as his drinking escalates. He and Roxy have violent fights which leave physical scars on both of them. When J.P. discovers that Roxy is having an affair, he goes "wild," forcibly removing her wedding ring and shredding it with a wire-cutter. The next morning he is arrested for drunk driving on his way to work and loses his license. Having hit rock bottom, he does not protest when his wife's father and brother drop him off at the treatment facility.

J.P. falls silent when the proprietor of the treatment facility joins them on the porch. A robust, cigar-smoking man named Frank Martin, the proprietor points to a hill visible from the porch and announces that the famous writer Jack London used to live there. "But alcohol killed him," he adds. "Let that be a lesson to you."

The narrator then reveals a little about how he came to the facility, though he is less open than J.P. On his first visit, his wife (now estranged) brought him in. This time, he was brought in by his girlfriend after a drinking binge that the two of them began on Christmas Eve.

The day after the narrator's first chat with J.P. is December 31, New Year's Eve. The narrator tries to call his wife, but no one answers. At the treatment center's New Year's Eve dinner, the narrator seems to be the only patient with an appetite. After dinner, the narrator again tries in vain to call his wife and then starts to dial his girlfriend's number. He decides not to complete the call, however, because he knows she has recently been tested for cancer, and he does not want to hear any bad news she might have gotten from her doctor.

After breakfast on New Year's Day, the narrator again sits on the porch with J.P., who is expecting a visit from Roxy. When she arrives, J.P. introduces the narrator as "my friend." Watching the couple's warm interaction and remembering J.P.'s account of their first meeting, the narrator asks for and receives a kiss from Roxy, saying "I need some luck." (According to tradition, it is lucky to kiss a chimney-sweep.) Rather than succumb to depression, he thinks again of J.P. and Roxy. This triggers an oddly humorous, bittersweet memory from early in his own marriage.

In the story's ambiguous closing passage, the narrator resolves to call his wife and his girlfriend. He remembers reading a Jack London story, "To Build a Fire," concerning a man who is lost in the frozen Yukon and must build a fire in order to survive. In the story, a branch-full of snow falls and puts the fire out, and the man freezes to death. Perhaps deciding that reaching out to the women in his life is necessary for his own survival, the narrator fantasizes about presenting himself in an honest and direct fashion on the phone. He imagines calling his wife simply to wish her a happy New Year and to tell her "where I'm calling from" without raising his voice or making unrealistic promises. If he reaches his girlfriend, he plans only to say, "Hello sugar. It's me."

Characters

Frank Martin

Frank Martin is the proprietor of a residential treatment facility for alcoholics. A short, heavy-set, cigar-smoking man, he advises his patients to consider the example of Jack London, the famous writer who died of alcoholism. His rather "macho" approach seems simplistic in the context of the complex human problems J.P. and the narrator have been discussing.

Narrator

The unnamed narrator of the story is an alcoholic, probably in his late thirties or early forties, who has checked into a residential treatment facility for the second time. He is estranged from his wife and seems unable to cope with the news that his girlfriend may have cancer. Sitting on the facility's front porch, the narrator listens to a fellow patient named J.P. describe his own turbulent marriage. The narrator seems genuinely touched by J.P. and by his wife, Roxy, when she comes to visit. Seeing the warmth of this couple's interaction, the narrator is motivated to reach out to his own wife and to his girlfriend. It is uncertain whether the narrator will ever overcome his alcoholism or establish healthy emotional bonds with the women in his life. There may be some hope in the story's open-ended closing, however, as the narrator imagines the warm greetings he will offer if he does manage to reach either his wife or his girlfriend on the telephone.

Joe Penny

J.P. is an alcoholic in his thirties on his first stay at a residential treatment facility. Sitting on the front porch with the narrator, J.P. shares his anxieties and much of his life story. He was married at a fairly young age to a woman named Roxy and became a partner in her family's chimney-cleaning business. As his drinking escalated, so did his violent fights with Roxy. After losing control upon discovering that his wife was having an affair, he allowed his wife's father and brother to bring him to the treatment center. J.P.'s openness with the narrator, as well as the warmth he shares with his wife when she comes to visit, seems to touch and inspire the narrator in new ways.

J.P.

See Joe Penny

Roxy

Roxy, J.P.'s wife, is a generous and earthy woman who shows support for her husband despite the far-from-ideal history of their relationship. She strikes the narrator as "a tall, good-looking woman . . . who can make fists if she has to." She is evidently strong enough to hold her own in physical brawls with her husband, and passionate enough to conduct an extramarital affair when her husband's drinking comes between them. She is also forgiving enough to embrace her husband again when she visits him at the treatment facility.

Media Adaptations

- An audiocassette entitled "Where I'm Calling From" includes a reading of this story and four others written by Carver. It was produced for Random House in 1989. All the stories are read by actor Peter Riegert.
- The 1993 feature film *Short Cuts*, directed by Robert Altman and released by New Line Cinema, was based on several of Raymond Carver's stories. Although "Where I'm Calling From" is not specifically included, the film does manage to convey much of the tone and many of the themes found in that story and in all of Carver's work.

Tiny

Tiny is another alcoholic patient at the treatment facility. "A big, fat guy . . . from Santa Rosa," Tiny is outgoing, jovial, and confident in his belief that he will be back home with his family before New Year's Eve. However, a horrifying seizure one morning abruptly puts an end to these plans and greatly disturbs his self-confidence.

Themes

Alienation and Loneliness

In a review of *Cathedral* for the *New York Times Book Review,* Irving Howe identified an important theme in Carver's work when he called the collection "stories of our loneliness." The setting for "Where I'm Calling From" is a "drying out facility," which is by design a place of isolation. Its residents are deliberately kept apart from family, friends, and society as a part of their cure. Yet, the characters have been plagued by an inability to connect with others since long before they checked into the facility. Both the narrator and J.P., for example, come to the facility from failed or failing marriages. The narrator's current relationship with his girlfriend seems to have suffered a complete breakdown in communication: neither has called the other since she dropped him off at the facility, and the narrator admits that he does not want to hear whether she has received any bad news regarding her medical tests. Perhaps most alienated of all is the patient who denies being an alcoholic, even though he is unable to remember how he arrived at the facility. The narrator refers to him as "a guy who travels," and though his business takes him all over the world, the man is out of touch with the reality of his situation and seemingly without a home.

Friendship and Intimacy

The phone calls that the narrator never quite succeeds in making to his wife and girlfriend symbolize his loneliness and isolation. At the same time, they also reflect his fundamental need for connection to others. Interwoven throughout the story's portrayal of lonely, isolated men are parallel themes of friendship and intimacy—perhaps best illustrated by the relationship between J.P. and the narrator. J.P. displays a natural tendency to seek intimacy. He reaches out to Roxy, for example, asking for a kiss almost as soon as he meets her. Sitting on the porch with the narrator, J.P. has a need to communicate and to share information about himself. The history of the narrator's relationships suggests that intimacy and friendship do not come easily to him, but J.P. calls him "friend" or "pal" three times during Roxy's visit near the end of the story. He begins listening to J.P. mostly out of a desire to be distracted from his own worries, but in the end J.P.'s story seems to help the narrator become more clearly aware of himself and his problems. He is inspired to reach out—first by asking Roxy for a kiss, and then in a more important and challenging way—by calling his wife and girlfriend.

Identity and the Search For Self

As much as "Where I'm Calling From" is about the narrator acknowledging his need for others, it is also about turning inward and searching for one's own identity. Two of the other patients at the facility are presented as cautionary examples of what happens without sufficient self-awareness. Tiny, the jolly "fat guy" from Santa Rosa, prematurely believes himself to be ready to go home to his family on New Year's Eve. When his sudden and terrifying seizure exposes his repressed vulnerability, he becomes feeble and depressed—"not the same old Tiny." The "guy who travels" denies the obvious fact that he is an alcoholic. He verges on paranoia as he worries that being accused of alcoholism might "ruin a good man's prospects," and when he insists that his blackouts are caused by the ice "they put into your drink."

The question of identity is raised in a sarcastic way by the narrator's girlfriend when she first drops him off at the treatment facility. "Guess who's here," she says. Becoming more aware of who he is, it turns out, may be an important key to the narrator's recovery. Toward the end of the story, while thinking about what J.P. has told him, the narrator recalls an event from his own past. The memory, an embarrassing but minor incident in front of a new landlord, includes a significant moment of contentedness: "And a wave of happiness comes over me that I'm not him—that I'm me and that I'm inside this bedroom with my wife." The story ends as the narrator, perhaps hoping to recover some of that lost happiness, plans to call his wife and girlfriend simply to present himself as straightforwardly as he can. He is not sure what to say to these women if and when he reaches them, other than being honest (at least to his wife) about "where [he's] calling from."

Style

In his essay "On Writing," Carver explained that he tries to write realistic stories without calling unnecessary attention to the method of their construction or to his own presence: "I hate tricks. At the first sign of a cheap trick or a gimmick in a piece of fiction, a cheap trick or even an elaborate trick, I tend to look for cover." On the other hand, many aspects of Carver's writing style—the short and simple sentence structures, clipped dialogue, and sparse descriptions—often instantly identify stories as his work.

Point of View and Narration

"Where I'm Calling From" is told in the first person by an unnamed narrator. The present tense is used almost exclusively, even in scenes that are memories or accounts of earlier events. The narrator tends to be blunt, informal, and brief. In the first paragraph, for example, he describes J.P. as "first and foremost a drunk." He frequently uses run-on sentences and sentence fragments, as in the description of one of the worst fights between J.P. and Roxy: "He manages to get Roxy's wedding ring off her finger. And when he does, he cuts it into several pieces with a pair of wire-cutters. Good, solid fun.'' Most of the narration consists of matter-of-fact physical description, rarely offering analysis of motivation or psychological states beyond simple statements like ''he's scared.'' Whether out of inarticulateness or a lack of insight, the narrator seems at a loss to explain his drinking problem or the reason for his return to the treatment facility for a second time: ''What's to say? I'm back.'' Similarly, he wonders ''who knows why we do what we do?'' in retelling the story of the escalation of J.P.'s drinking. This ''surface-only'' approach invites readers to play a more active and creative role, leaving them to make their own deductions about the internal workings of the characters.

Setting and Narrative Structure

The principal setting of the story—the porch of the treatment facility—is used as a kind of narrative frame. The story begins and ends there; in between, stories-within-the-story describe events out of chronological sequence. The stories J.P. tells are presented, for the most part, as paraphrased by the unnamed narrator rather than as direct quotations of J.P.'s words. This filtering tactic keeps the story focused on the narrator and encourages readers to see the impact which J.P. has on the narrator. Carver also seems to use the setting of the porch to reflect certain aspects of the characters' lives. At one point, a bank of clouds on the horizon visible from the porch seems to mirror the impending doom in the story J.P. is telling. Sitting on the porch, the narrator and J.P. are also on another kind of threshold: a turning point in their relationships with others and in their struggles with alcoholism. The prospects they face seem very much like a choice between retreating inside—back into the relative warmth of the bottle—or venturing forth into the chilly unknown to mend their shattered lives.

Allusion

One of the most interesting and subtle aspects of the story is Carver's use of allusion to illuminate characters and events. The proprietor of the treatment facility makes a reference to the famous writer Jack London and his book *The Call of the Wild.* Associated with an outlook of ''rugged individualism,'' London wrote adventure stories that described heroic men struggling alone in the wilderness. The concept of ''making it on one's own'' implied by the proprietor's reference stands in contrast to the more collaborative form of healing taking place between the narrator and J.P. The narrator thinks of Jack London again at the end of the story, as he recalls a London story he once read about a man struggling to survive in an arctic environment. (The story is called ''To Build a Fire.'') Remembering that the man in the story ends by dying alone, the narrator decides that his own survival in the cold world outside the treatment facility will depend on his ability to connect with others.

Other, less explicit references to various aspects of popular culture are scattered throughout the story, helping to convey the atmosphere of boredom and banality in which the characters live. Television is almost omnipresent: residents at the treatment facility look up from the television when a new

Topics for Further Study

- Research the common symptoms of alcoholism and approaches to its treatment. How do the characters in the story ''Where I'm Calling From'' exhibit the symptoms you read about? Based on your research, what do you think will happen to the narrator after he leaves the facility? Citing evidence from what he reveals about himself in the story, do you think he will recover? How does his prognosis compare to J.P.'s?
- Raymond Carver is called a minimalist, yet the author himself often said he disliked the term. How well do you think it applies? Open a copy of the winter, 1985 issue of the *Mississippi Review,* a special issue that was devoted to commentary on minimalism. Which of the various definitions of minimalism offered in the journal, if any, do you feel accurately describes ''Where I'm Calling From''?
- Find studies that have been conducted on the effects of living with an alcoholic and then rewrite the story from the point of view of the narrator's wife or girlfriend. What might they say about the narrator that he is unaware of himself? What might they tell us about themselves that the narrator has overlooked?

patient arrives, J.P. and Roxy drink in front of their television, and the narrator imagines that he and his girlfriend are watching the same TV show when he decides not to finish dialing her number. The narrator also mentions the annual New Year's Eve broadcast from Times Square, which he is watching with his fellow patients. Critic Randolph Paul Runyon has even argued that the story contains allusions to other stories written by Carver, pointing to a number of similarities between the narrator and the main character of the story immediately preceding "Where I'm Calling From" in the collection *Cathedral.* Carver's borrowing from diverse aspects of American life invites readers to draw connections between the story and whatever personal or cultural experiences they find meaningful.

Historical Context

Reagan Era Pageantry and Polarization

Many people have interpreted the early 1980s as an unusually image-conscious era in the United States. After the election of former movie star and California governor Ronald Reagan as president, the elaborate black-tie festivities surrounding his inauguration in January, 1981, were watched with fascination on televisions around the country. Reagan's inauguration served as an important symbol to many, representing sweeping changes promised by the new conservative Republican leader and ushering in a new era of prosperity. The previous president, Jimmy Carter—who had worn a plain business suit to his inauguration—had tried to project a more down-to-earth image. Many felt that the country's prestige had been diminished in recent years, and Carter's popularity had waned especially in the preceding 14 months, during which 53 Americans had been held hostage by Islamic fundamentalists in Teheran, Iran. On the very day of Reagan's inauguration, the hostages were released and images of Iranians holding Americans at gunpoint finally disappeared from nightly news broadcasts. Given the disastrous American economy under Carter, as well as his poor performance during a debate with Reagan shortly before the 1980 election and the latter's genial optimism about the abilities of the American people to accomplish great things (contrasted with Carter's gloomy public assertion that the American people suffered from spiritual malais), it was not surprising that Reagan won the election handily.

The patriotic makeover Reagan offered, however, was at odds with other people's images of the country, especially among the president's many partisan critics in the broadcast media. By November of 1982, in part because of poor decisions enacted at the Federal Reserve, unemployment reached 10.8 percent, its highest rate since 1940. The number of people living below the poverty line was the highest in 17 years. Many women and minorities claimed to feel excluded from Reagan's vision, which harkened back to a perhaps-romanticized past—especially when he proposed cutting funding for federal programs from which they benefited. Members of the gay community, which was being ravaged by the deadly new AIDS epidemic, felt overlooked by the Reagan Administration as they pleaded for more research and education about the disease. Although Reagan consistently did well in public opinion polls, he also had many vocal critics who felt that his policies glossed over—and even exacerbated—a growing list of social ills in America, including homelessness, drug abuse, violent crime, pollution, educational underachievement, and income disparity. For his part, Reagan believed that all these problems were essentially "private-sector" issues, related to personal choices (moral, spiritual, and relational), private association, family life, and small-business endeavor, areas in which federal "assistance" was irrelevant and inappropriate.

Just Say No

Reagan, along with his wife Nancy, soon chose to focus special attention on the growing problem of drug abuse. Crack, a highly addictive, relatively inexpensive crystallized form of cocaine that could be smoked, was opening new mass markets among young people, particularly in poor urban neighborhoods. As crack was tied to increasing violent crime, disintegration of families and communities, and proliferating health emergencies, President Reagan announced a "war on drugs" in October, 1982. Shortly thereafter, Nancy Reagan began a media campaign to combat drug use, adopting the slogan "Just Say No."

These efforts had many critics, including those who argued that the First Lady was only trying to improve her image. Nonetheless, in the early 1980s a number of drug abuse prevention movements gained momentum. Though the overall rate at which young people used drugs continued to rise until the 1990s, there were small signs of progress. Treatment programs, many based on the twelve-step approach developed by Alcoholics Anonymous, reported increased enrollment and improved recovery rates. Among the most successful anti-drug efforts in the 1980s were those aimed at raising awareness about alcohol as an addictive drug and preventing drunk driving. MADD (Mothers Against Drunk Driving) was founded in 1980 by a small group of women in California after a 13-year-old girl was killed in an accident caused by a drunk driver. By the end of the decade, MADD had grown into a large national organization with nearly 600 local chapters. Working to raise public awareness and lobbying for stiffer penalties for driving under the influence of alcohol, the agency played a leading role in reducing alcohol-related accidents and helped to slow the escalation of teenage drinking.

Reading and the Arts In the "Information Age"

As personal computers became common household and office equipment, some observers announced the arrival of a new "Information Age." Schools began to include more computer classes in their curricula to better prepare young people to compete in a new information-based global economy. Fundamental changes did occur in the way Americans obtained news and information, but critics charged that in some ways information was becoming less accessible, not more. Local newspapers, once the country's primary source for news, were losing in their competition with television news. Many folded or were purchased by national chains. On September 15, 1982, the Gannett newspaper chain began publishing *USA Today.* Keeping stories brief and making more use of color, the new national daily almost instantly won a huge readership, placing even more pressure on local independent newspapers.

Commentators of diverse political persuasions pointed fingers at each other in assigning blame for declining literacy rates in America's schools. In his controversial 1987 book, *The Closing of the American Mind,* conservative scholar Allan Bloom accused liberals of "dumbing down" America in the name of equality. Liberal thinkers like Marian Wright Edelman blamed Reagan administration "cutbacks" in public school funding and neglect of students from poor neighborhoods for the declining test scores. Similar disputes arouse in the arts world, which was increasingly criticized for its insularity and for being out of touch with the mainstream. Controversial artists—like performance artist Karen Finley, whose work many people considered obscene, or at least unworthy of taxpayer support—were threatened with the possibility of being denied the government grants on which they depended.

In the literary world, a group of authors that included Raymond Carver, Bobbie Ann Mason, Tobias Wolff and others, began using more traditional, realistic techniques in their writing. Their stories, appearing in a handful of long-established magazines like the *New Yorker* and the *Atlantic Monthly,* began to reach a wider audience than most serious literature had in recent years. Their understated and accessible approach to writing stood in contrast to that of the previous generation of postmodernist writers, who were known for extravagantly experimental works that were long and hard to understand. The new writers shared an interest in depicting the lives of contemporary "ordinary" people, often in identifiable regional settings within the United States. Because these writers tried to avoid intrusive storytelling gimmicks and made an effort to use language as efficiently as possible, they came to be known as minimalists.

Critical Overview

Carver was already considered one of America's premier short story writers when "Where I'm Calling From" was first published, in the *New Yorker* in 1982. The story was chosen for inclusion in the *Best American Short Stories, 1983* published by Houghton Mifflin. Carver's story "Cathedral" had been chosen for the preceding year's edition. Both of these stories were a part of Carver's 1983 collection entitled *Cathedral,* which was nominated for both a National Book Critics' Circle Award and a Pulitzer Prize.

Carver's work, however, has not been without controversy. Many critics believed that Carver—along with other minimalist writers—were outmoded in their realism and simplistic in their characterizations. James Atlas, for example, wrote in the *Atlantic* that he found Carver's prose "so aggressive in the suppression of detail that one is left with a hunger for richness, texture, excess." Minimalists' work in general has suffered under a long list of unflattering labels, including "K-Mart realism," "hick chic," "TV fiction," and "lo-cal literature." The avant-garde postmodernist writer John Barth even suggested in a *New York Times Book*

Review article that the popularity of the minimalists was actually due to the declining literacy levels of the American public. Critic Charles Newman, writing in the journal *Salmagundi,* went so far as to describe minimalists' work as "the classic conservative response to inflation—under-utilization of capacity, reduction of inventory and verbal joblessness." In an otherwise negative review of *Cathedral,* in the *Hudson Review,* Michael Gorra praised "Where I'm Calling From": "It is easily the best story of this collection, and makes me think that if he confronted his subject he might in fact manage to turn the alcoholic into Everyman."

Probably the most prominent early defender of the new generation of writers was Carver's former professor and mentor, novelist John Gardner. For Gardner, the trend toward realism in fiction, after a generation of postmodernist experimentation with narrative forms, was a return to a kind of literary "morality." Gardner saw the minimalists as part of an inevitable cycle in the progress of cultural development. As he wrote in his landmark 1978 book *On Moral Fiction,* "Art rediscovers, generation by generation what is necessary to humanness." Another influential critical assessment appeared in the *Mississippi Review* in 1985, in a special issue devoted entirely to the new American minimalists. In his introductory commentary, guest editor Kim Herzinger argued that minimalism was a continuation of postmodernist ideas about language and narrative form, rather than a rejection of them. He also pointed to several crucial distinctions between the minimalists' work and traditional realism, including the minimalists' "distaste for irony" (i.e., the distance between the implicit viewpoint of the author and that of the characters) and their refusal to define characters through location and setting.

When Carver's collection *Cathedral* appeared, initial reviewers noted a new direction in Carver's work. In his previous stories—most of which were collected in *Will You Please Be Quiet, Please* (1976) and *What We Talk About When We Talk About Love* (1981)—he had seemed to be condensing his writing, paring down the narrative structures of his stories to their barest essentials. His characters lived unremittingly bleak and spiritually barren lives. In *Cathedral,* critics saw a change in Carver's work—"an increase in vitality," as Anatole Broyard described it in the *New York Times Book Review,* Also writing in the *New York Times,* reviewer Irving Howe noted "a greater ease of manner and generosity of feeling," and compared Carver's work to that of painter Edward Hopper in his effort to explore "the far side of the ordinary."

By the time of Carver's death in 1988, he had won a large array of critical honors and secured his influence on American literature. Since then, biographers have examined the relationship between his life and work, and a number of book-length studies of his writings have been published. Most have taken Herzinger's approach and placed Carver in a continuing postmodernist tradition. In 1992, for example, Randolph Paul Runyon's *Reading Raymond Carver* examines Carver's use of repeated motifs and references to his own stories, suggesting that "Carver is in fact a self-reflexive metafictional writer." Kirk Nesset's 1995 study, *The Stories of Raymond Carver,* gives a very thorough "full-scale critical investigation" of all Carver's major prose works, including an examination of themes of "insularity and self-enlargement" in the stories included in *Cathedral.*

Criticism

Michael Sonkowsky

Sonkowsky has taught college English and written on a wide range of topics in education. He is currently involved in the creation of alternative educational programs that take an intergenerational approach to learning. In the following essay, he examines images of supportive older men in "Where I'm Calling From" and discusses their implications about the role of father figures in personal growth and development.

> We feel one thing one minute,
> something else the next.
>
> —Raymond Carver, from a poem entitled "Romanticism"

The stories in Raymond Carver's 1983 *Cathedral* collection include possibilities for characters' growth and development not found in his earlier stories. Carver commented in interviews that he was aware of something "totally different" about the stories as he was writing them—something which, as he put it, "reflects a change in my life." Reflections of two of the biggest changes in the author's life—quitting drinking in 1977 and sharing a home with writer

What Do I Read Next?

- *Will You Please Be Quiet, Please?* (1976), Carver's first major book, a collection of stories written over thirteen years. This book marked a turning point in its author's career when it was nominated for a National Book Award in 1977. The stories document the development of Carver's minimalist writing style and bleak outlook on modern life.
- *Where Water Comes Together with Other Water* (1985), Carver's best-known collection of poetry. His poems address familiar topics from daily life in a "prose-like" way, often incorporating narrative elements. This prize-winning collection has been praised for the highly distilled slices of American life it contains.
- *Back In the World* (1985), by Tobias Wolff, Carver's friend and fellow writer. The ten stories in this collection reveal Carver's influence in their tone and subject matter. Wolff's characters, like Carver's, tend to be alienated and dispossessed, but they are perhaps also somewhat more eccentric in their fantasy lives.
- *Shiloh and Other Stories* (1982), by Bobbie Ann Mason, another writer associated with the minimalist revival of the short story in the late 1970s and early 1980s. Her stories chronicle the lives of lower middle-class, rural Southerners. In the title story, a couple attempts to rekindle their faltering marriage by taking a trip to see a Civil War battlefield.
- *Winesburg, Ohio* (1919), by Sherwood Anderson, seen as one of Carver's literary progenitors. This collection of short stories, all set in the same small Ohio town, was controversial when it was first published, mostly due its references to human sexuality and its satirical portrayal of some religious characters. Anderson broke new ground for the realistic American short story form and had tremendous influence on generations of writers who followed him.
- *At the Owl Woman Saloon* (1997), by Tess Gallagher, Carver's second wife and sometime collaborator. This collection of stories includes one entitled "Rain Flooding Our Campfire," which is a retelling of Carver's story "Cathedral."

Tess Gallagher since 1979—can certainly be found in "Where I'm Calling From." The story concerns an alcoholic narrator who befriends a fellow alcoholic named J.P. at a treatment center they have both checked into. Much of the hope for change in the lives of the two main characters seems to lie in establishing better relations with women: at the story's end, J.P. is embraced by his wife and the narrator resolves to call his wife and his girlfriend.

For the most part, however, women in "Where I'm Calling From" remain off stage. The story's setting, "Frank Martin's drying out facility," is a decidedly male place. "Just about everyone at Frank Martin's has nicks on his face," as the narrator points out, from shaving. A key to understanding the characters' potential for growth lies in the images of helpful—or potentially helpful—older men that appear throughout the story. Carver presents a series of interactions between males of different ages that depict personal transformations in various ways and seem to hint at the importance of father-like figures.

J.P. begins his communication with the narrator by sharing a boyhood memory of falling down a dry well and being rescued by his father. The most vivid aspect of the memory seems to be the fear and sense of isolation J.P. experiences looking up from where he landed: "In short, everything about his life was different for him at the bottom of that well." It is easy to imagine that J.P.'s reminiscence has been triggered by the parallels between the bottom of that well and his current situation—isolated from loved ones, in another "dry" place, after having "hit bottom," looking out at a midday sky from the porch. The memory of being rescued by his father, then, comes as a kind of infantile wish, a fantasy of the personal transformation which both J.P. and the narrator want to undergo.

J.P. is brought to Frank Martin's at a point when he has started falling again—falling off roofs while drunk at work. It is interesting to note that he is handed over to Frank Martin's care by male escorts, his father-in-law and brother-in-law, and that "the old guy signed him in." Frank Martin, however, proves to be a much less nurturing substitute father. The proprietor of this treatment facility for men exhibits exaggerated masculine characteristics: he is physically large, smokes cigars, and stands "like a prizefighter." In an abrupt "sermon," he advises J.P. and the narrator to consider the famous writer Jack London, who, though "a better man than any of us," died of alcoholism. The "rugged individualist" model of manhood embodied by Jack London's adventure tales—and by the brusque Frank Martin—does seem deadly to J.P. and the narrator, who are more in need of support from others. In J.P.'s childhood memory, his father rescues him from a hole where young J.P. "was thinking of insects"; Frank Martin's effect on J.P. is only to make him "feel like a bug."

Toward the end of the story, the narrator experiences a flash of memory and has a hard time explaining its trigger: he suggests that maybe J.P. the chimney sweep reminded him of a house in which he used to live, but then dismisses the notion, adding "That house didn't have a chimney." A more likely explanation concerns the "old guy" at the center of the memory. The narrator remembers getting out of bed with his wife to investigate a noise that had awakened them early one morning and encountering his landlord, who had come to paint the house. Staring through a window at the old man, the narrator experiences a moment of unusual contentedness: "Goddamn it, I think, if he isn't a weird old fellow. And a wave of happiness comes over me that I'm not him—that I'm me and that I'm inside this bedroom with my wife." The encounter ends as the narrator notices that he had forgotten to put on a robe before opening the window curtain and that the landlord could see his nakedness. Returning to his wife in bed, the narrator imagines the old man saying, in fatherly fashion, "Go on, sonny, go on back to bed. I understand." In the closing image of narrator's memory, the old man "starts climbing the ladder," moving upward.

The memory of encountering this "weird old fellow" appears to be the narrator's fantasy about the personal transformation he needs to undergo in order to recover any happiness. For J.P., being rescued by his father meant being transported from where "everything" is "different" to "back in the world he'd always lived in." For the narrator, the sight of his landlord somehow brings him back to himself—back to being happy with his own identity. The "old fart" outside his window reveals something to the narrator about himself in a way that his wife cannot. It makes sense, of course, for older men to embody growth and development for a male narrator and a male writer: an older man is what a younger man will become. The narrator's landlord appears to understand because as an older person he has perhaps experienced aspects of life the narrator is currently experiencing. Looking at the old man through his window, the narrator is getting a glimpse of himself.

The narrator has been cast as the older man all along, since introducing J.P. in the story's first paragraph: "He is about 30 years old. Younger than I. Not much younger, but a little." The narrator's treatment begins as he conceals his own fears and adopts the role of the more experienced protector of J.P., reassuring him that "the shakes will idle down" and encouraging him to talk. The final step in recovery, which both J.P. and the narrator have yet to take, may be acknowledging their own roles as father figures. J.P. will eventually have to confront the children he forbids his wife to bring along on her visit to Frank Martin's. The narrator, by the same token, will have to be ready to talk to his girlfriend's "mouthy kid" if he is the one who answers the phone.

When J.P. and the narrator reach that point, at which they can talk to the women and children in their lives without rage and can "stay dry" (like the unfortunate man in the London short story cited by the narrator) on a long-term basis, they will be ready to assume their place as fathers and protectors in the world.

Source: Michael Sonkowsky, "Grown Men in 'Where I'm Calling From'," for *Short Stories for Students,* Gale, 1998.

Thomas J. Haslam

In the following essay, Haslam compares the original story, published in the New Yorker, *to the version published in Carver's collection* Where I'm Calling From.

Raymond Carver liked to revise his stories. He won critical acclaim from reviewers and academics alike for rewriting "The Bath" from *What We Talk About When We Talk About Love* (1981) into "A Small, Good Thing" for *Cathedral* (1983); and he published in *Fires* (1984) a selection of revised stories as well as an essay on his practice. It is hardly surprising that there are three published versions of Carver's "Where I'm Calling From." The story initially appeared in the *New Yorker* (15 March 1982); it was significantly revised for Carver's highly praised *Cathedral;* and, with a few slight changes, was reprinted in his new and collected stories, *Where I'm Calling From* (1989). There are substantial differences between the first and last published versions of the story. These revisions—not all of which are improvements—are also a sort of commentary, providing both new matter and means for a critical appreciation of "Where I'm Calling From." Reading both story versions for their strengths and weaknesses, I comment on five key differences between *New Yorker* text and the *Where I'm Calling From* text. In doing so, I hope to foreground (and later argue for) Carver's understanding of people as intrinsic story-tellers, as dialogic selves who find their meaning, value and identity through and by interaction with other selves, other stories. Of course, the textual findings I present are better understood as illustrating rather than proving my basic claim about Carver and the narrative self.

The first difference between the two story versions concerns the narrator's description of a rival for his girlfriend's attention and affection. The *New Yorker* text reads:

> She tried to explain to her son that she was going to be gone that afternoon and evening, and he'd have to get his own dinner. But right as we were going out the door this Goddamned kid screamed at us. He screamed, "You call this love? The hell with you both! I hope you never come back. I hope you kill yourselves!" Imagine this kid!

The revised *Where I'm Calling From* text reads:

> She tried to explain to her kid that she was going to be gone for a while and he'd have to get his own food. But right as we were going out the door, this mouthy kid screamed at us. He screamed, "The hell with you both! I hope you never come back. I hope you kill yourselves!" Imagine this kid!

The final version is less blatant, but subtlety is not the highest virtue. In favor of the *New Yorker* text, the "Goddamned" Oedipal "son" carries more weight than the revised gender-neutral "mouthy kid"; and positioned as the narrator's male rival, the teenaged son provides both a moral and practical reference lacking from the revised version. His parting shot—"You call this love? To hell with you both"—condemns his mother and the narrator for their bleak, clearly dysfunctional relationship centered on alcohol abuse, careless—rather than casual—sex, and a shared indifference that seems more like mutual contempt. In favor of the final version, however, the changes from "that afternoon and evening" to "a while" and from "dinner" to "food" brilliantly underscore the chaotic and harmful aspects of the lovers' relationship: the kid is left to fend for himself—and not just miss dinner—for an indefinite period as his mother disappears with her boyfriend into the void.

> **"Carver presents a series of interactions between males of different ages that depict personal transformations in various ways and seem to hint at the importance of father-like figures."**

The second difference between the two story versions concerns the narrator's drinking blow-out just before checking into Frank Martin's treatment center. In the *New Yorker* text, the narrator recalls: "I didn't eat anything except cashew nuts"; and "I bought us three bottles of champagne. Quality stuff—Piper." In the final version these descriptive details are effaced: "I didn't eat anything but salted nuts"; and "I bought us the champagne." The deletion of these details, the champagne brand and type of snack, seem trivial. But an alcoholic narrator in quest of recovery, telling his own story the best he can, might find a curious importance in recollecting and reconstructing the contingencies of his experience. In comparison with the *New Yorker* narrator, the *Where I'm Calling From* narrator lacks memory and seems flatter and less colorful.

Less is not always more. The third difference brings this into relief for higher stakes. In describing himself and J.P. leaving the porch, the *New Yorker* narrator comments:

> J.P. and I get out of our chairs slowly, like old geezers, and we go inside. It's starting to get too cold on the porch anyway. We can see our breath drifting out from us as we talk.

This, in the first published version, is a moment of subdued but powerful insight. Due to their excessive alcohol abuse, J.P. and the narrator are prematurely (although perhaps only temporarily) "like old geezers"; and sitting together on the porch, they watch their breath—archetypally, their life-force or souls—drifting out or dissipating as death approaches. The final version all but annuls this moment, since the clause "like old geezers" has been deleted (otherwise the narrator's description reads exactly the same).

There are yet further consequences to Carver's deletion of a mere three words. In the *New Yorker* text, the narrator's self-depiction as an "old geezer" sets up a dialectic with his later reflection on the "old duffer" Mr. Venturini, his former landlord. The narrator recalls his thoughts when disturbed early one morning by Mr. Venturini painting the outside of the house:

> God damn it, I think, if he isn't a weird old hombre, then I've never seen one. And at that minute a wave of happiness comes over me that I'm not him—that I'm me and that I'm inside this bedroom with my wife.

This memory gains significance through the narrator's realization that he, a dispossessed and virtual "old geezer," is presently in far worse shape than Mr. Venturini, and yet may still have a chance to regain some of his former happiness and stability. Inspired by his recollection of a better time, the narrator tentatively plans a comeback:

> Maybe later this afternoon I'll try calling my wife again. And then I'll call to see what's happening with my girlfriend.

These reverberations are missing from the *Where I'm Calling From* text, since there is no interplay between the narrator's earlier insight into his own condition and his later recollection of Mr. Venturini. Also, the *New Yorker* descriptions of Mr. Venturini as an "old duffer" and "a weird old hombre" are changed in the final version to the more mundane "old guy" and "weird old fellow."

The fourth difference results from Carver's most extensive revision. In the *New Yorker* text, Frank Martin encounters J.P. and the narrator sitting on the porch and offers them a sermon about real men and the need to reach out:

> "Jack London used to have a big place on the other side of the valley. Right over there behind that green hill you're looking at. But alcohol killed him. Let that be a lesson. He was a better man than any of us. But he couldn't handle the stuff, either. . . . You guys want to read something while you're here, read that book of his *The Call of the Wild.* You know the one I'm talking about? We have it inside, if you want to read something. It's about this animal that's half dog and half wolf. They don't write books like that anymore. But we could have helped Jack London, if we'd been here in those days. And if he'd let us. If he'd asked for our help. Hear me? Like we can help you. *If. If* you ask for it and *if* you listen. End of sermon. But don't forget it. If," he says again. Then he hitches his pants and tugs his sweater down. "I'm going inside," he says. "See you at lunch."

In the final version, a less pontifical Frank states:

> "Jack London used to have a big place on the other side of the valley. Right over there behind that green hill you're looking at. But alcohol killed him. Let that be a lesson to you. He was a better man than any of us. But he couldn't handle the stuff, either. . . . You guys want to read something while you're here, read that book of his, *The Call of the Wild.* You know the one I'm talking about? We have it inside if you want to read something. It's about this animal that's half dog and half wolf. End of sermon," he says, and then hitches his pants up and tugs his sweater down. "I'm going inside," he says. "See you at lunch."

The *Where I'm Calling From* sermon strikes me as far superior. It makes little sense for Frank, as he does in the *New Yorker* version, to weaken his case by belatedly reclaiming Jack London. It is the dismal death of Jack, "a better man than any of us," that drives home Frank's point that alcohol abuse kills, and kills regardless of machismo or merit. Otherwise laconic with the deportment of "a prize fighter, like somebody who knows the score," Frank in either version seems not the type to cant repetitious "if, if, if" verbiage to men who know better.

For similar reasons, I think the revised characterization of Frank is superior as well. In the *New Yorker* version, Frank diminishes in stature by prissily prattling grandiose. Talkiness bleeds authority. In the revised version, Frank remains in character as a tough, shrewd handler of men. Indeed, after smacking the narrator and J.P. on the head with Jack London as an object lesson, the revised Frank proffers them a vicarious thrill of positive reinforcement to let them know that it is their behavior—and not them—that is bad. First the stick and then the suggestion of a carrot: a good way to deal with naughty boys and men. The *New Yorker* text is painfully heavy-handed; the *Where I'm Calling From* text, direct and assured.

The fifth difference between the two versions—and arguably Carver's best revision to the story—

concerns the narrator's encounter with J.P.'s wife, Roxy. The *New Yorker* text reads:

> He's embarrassed, too. I'm embarrassed. But I keep looking at her. Roxy doesn't know what to make of it. She grins. "I'm not a sweep anymore," she says. "Not for years. Didn't Joe tell you? What the hell. Sure, I'll kiss you. Sure. For luck."

Some of the narrator's comments are superfluous. It is obvious, for example, from the way the incident is described and framed that he and J.P. are embarrassed. The slimmer and trimmer *Where I'm Calling From* text reads:

> But I keep looking at her. Roxy grins. "I'm not a sweep anymore," she says. "Not for years. Didn't Joe tell you that? But sure, I'll kiss you, sure."

In favor of the final version, the revised Roxy is stronger and sharper, more in character as the "tall, good-looking woman" who deeply loves J.P. and yet "can make fists if she has to." The revision also emphasizes Roxy's kiss as an act of deliberate compassion and not—unlike the *New Yorker* version—a "what the hell" lark. In both texts, Roxy's last words to the narrator are "Good luck" ; in the final version, her single anointment of good fortune is more poignant and powerful. Given the quality of Carver's revisions concerning Roxy and Frank Martin, I moderately favor the *Where I'm Calling From* text over the *New Yorker* text. No doubt one could reach a different judgment based on the same revisions. More importantly, I think that the differences in question bring into relief the complex interplay of desire, memory, and dialogue that distinguishes Carver's view of the narrative self. The best example of this interplay seems to me the turning point common to both versions of the story, the narrator's flirtation with Roxy. It is the narrator's desire for Roxy, and the kiss she gives him in turn, that cause him to reflect on his own history of relationships. His recapitulation of the past is both a recovery and a reweaving of the self. A person, Caroline Whitbeck argues, should be understood

> as a relational and historical being. One becomes a person in and through relationships with other people; being a person requires that one have a history of relationships with other people, and the realization of the self can be achieved only in and through relationships and practices.

Relationships and practices are made possible and realized, of course, through and within the intersubjective means of language. That is why to recover himself, to tell his story, the narrator must engage in a dialogue with others—he must rejoin the larger society from which he has been alienated. In short, he must resume a normal life. The narrator considers doing just that at the story's end as he tentatively plans to call either his wife, girlfriend, or both.

But "dialogue" is easy to say and quite often difficult to achieve. We speak because we desire and lack; our conversations are a form of commerce; and yet our "dialogues" may oscillate from automatic and impersonal exchanges to colliding and conflict-ridden soliloquies. Likewise, the social practices and values that define and maintain normality work as well to define and police—and thus in a very different way to maintain—abnormality. What you are able to say and do, what dialogues you can engage in, very much depend on your position as a social subject: where you are calling from. I think that Carver's story explores rather than resolves these concerns, since the closure to "Where I'm Calling From" is problematized and deferred in two fairly distinct ways. Although these two demarcations will always overlap, Carver uses ordinary and literary language to necessitate the reader's collaboration.

By ordinary language I mean, simply enough, a fairly literal reading of the narrator's final statements. He intends "maybe later this afternoon" to call his wife. He would like to call his girlfriend but does not "want to get her mouthy son on the line." Reflecting for a moment on Frank Martin's earlier sermon about Jack London and the need that even real men occasionally have for help, the narrator thinks about the one London story he knows, "To Build a Fire," in which the rugged individual alone in the wilderness freezes to death. Graced with sudden insight, the narrator yet again decides to "try his wife first"; but after considering what she might say, he thinks about calling his girlfriend first. Once more, however, he pauses at the specter of her son answering the phone. These hesitations and reversals show that the narrator does not quite know what he wants or what he will do. As readers, we do not quite know either.

Nor do we obtain a resolution beyond the "surface" of the narrator's final remarks. The literary language, and by that I mean the recognizable use of such conventions as allusion and enplotment, works against closure. More simply and specifically, the narrator's reflective summary of Jack London's "To Build a Fire" is not fortuitous. The story offers an ironic parallel to his own:

> This guy in the Yukon is freezing. Imagine it—he's actually going to freeze to death if he can't get a fire

> "What you are able to say and do, what dialogues you can engage in, very much depend on your position as a social subject: where you are calling from."

> going. With a fire he can dry his socks and clothing and warm himself. He gets his fire going, but then something happens to it. A branchful of snow drops on it. It goes out. Meanwhile, the temperature is falling. Night is coming on.

The narrator, too, is trying to build a fire. Like the protagonist in London's story, who, after a few desperate efforts, seems to have triumphed against dire odds, the narrator makes some false starts as well—the two failed attempts to call his wife on New Year's Eve. If he successfully reaches his wife or girlfriend this time around, and this we as readers will never know, we are still left wondering whether all his efforts—like those of London's protagonist—will come to nothing. The narration ends in anticipation of a yet-to-be realized event. The story achieves resolution—if at all—through the imposition of our expectations and desires.

In stressing the non-teleological aspect of "Where I'm Calling From," I am not asserting that the text "deconstructs itself." Nor does a text read itself. We participate in a Carver story because we must—but also because we are meant to. Consider it one-half of an ongoing dialogue. We read to listen; we react to speak; we talk about Raymond Carver and his world, our world. By offering us a vision of the self as a narrative agent, a social and relational being always already in dialogue with other selves and other histories—some good, some harmful, Carver keeps alive our hopes for human solidarity and for better ways of speaking, acting, living. The open-endedness of "Where I'm Calling From" (and other Carver stories) works to sustain the conversation between the reader, the text, and the world. Reviewing the collection *Where I'm Calling From,* David Lipsky cogently remarked:

> Reading [this collection], one realizes that Carver has been not a minimalist but a precisionist, setting down, as precisely as possible, the exact words for things. He has brought news of his world into ours. One imagines that the title does not so much highlight the story of that name as reflect Carver's whole enterprise. We now know where Raymond Carver has been calling from—it's a place that would have gone unremarked, in a style that would have gone unnoticed, had it not been for him.

I should let Lipsky have the last word since I cannot improve on what he has said. Instead, I will end with the hope that this essay may help to provoke more and better writing about Raymond Carver.

Source: Thomas J. Haslam, "'Where I'm Calling From': A Textual and Critical Study," in *Studies in Short Fiction,* Vol. 29, No. 1, Winter, 1992, pp. 57–64.

Claudine Verley

In the following essay, Verley analyzes the narration in "Where I'm Calling From," using it to deduce the character traits of the story's protagonist.

The short story can be read in the following way: two alcoholics meet up in a rehabilitation centre, one of them tells his life story while the other—the narrator—listens and is then reminded of some of his own personal adventures. Life in the centre on December 31st is briefly portrayed and the narrator is trying in vain to telephone his wife while his friend, J.P., is actually visited by his wife, Roxy, the following day. The narrator's name remains a mystery as do any personal details, except for the fact that he is separated from his wife while at the same time he is not particularly interested in his girlfriend. He is afraid of having a heart attack and has clearly not recovered from his addictive state. This is all and it is not a great deal.

Only by making an implicit comparison between J.P. and the narrator can such a narrative, which is as bare of actual events as many other of Carver's works, form any consistent unity. However we cannot grasp the richness of it if we limit ourselves to declaring that Roxy has no equivalent life-force in the narrator's existence since he remains alone at the end. We are plunged into a melodrama of alcoholism and conjugal life if we remain on the surface of things, with the dullness of the present and the pitiful shallowness of the lives depicted. Carver could thus be described as a minimalist or a miniaturist and the critics who use these terms are not paying homage to his talent by doing so.

On the contrary I would like to suggest that there is a true depth to be found in Carver's work but not in those areas where it is usually sought: neither in a psychological complexity nor in the polysemy of the themes, nor even in the intricacies of a rich style. Carver's interiority is not so much described as staged and the depth is produced by the different layers of the retrospections, the overlapping of the focalisations, the alternating and sometimes even the blending of the voices and finally the use of techniques which allow both for the diversification of narrative sources and the extension of tenses far beyond their traditional uses. The story which I have chosen to analyse here provides a good example of this hidden depth.

To begin with I am going to limit myself to a brief study of the structure of the story and of the mirror effect which it sets up between J.P. and the narrator as characters since this will help to define the lines along which the analysis will be developed.

The story is made up of nine sequences separated by spaces. It is easy to distinguish a very well knit first section from sequence one to four, due to the unity of time, place and action. It is centered around J.P. who is telling his "story" to the narrator. Time breaks and fleeting minor characters (Frank Martin, Roxy, the "traveller") typify the sequences of the second section which mainly concern the narrator and his own story. J.P. is still present but remains in the background. The accent is therefore placed on the need for a comparative and contrasting reading of the two stories which are not developed in a parallel fashion but with a gap between them. Sequence four, which marks a turning point, is particularly interesting in this respect. Firstly because the final analepsis, in the present tense, reinforces the unity of the first section by referring to a moment previous to the beginning of the narrative—J.P. is getting ready to start his story—hence the perfect circularity of this section. More particularly it stresses the parallel between the two characters by portraying, in retrospect, their arrival at the centre one after the other even if the specific circumstances are completely different. Finally because it contrasts the inverted chronology of the two stories. The narrator's story starts off in the present with his arrival at the centre in sequence four and recedes back towards the past, whereas J.P's, begun by his fall into the well, progresses up to the present with his arrival at the centre. Neither this contrast nor the gap between the two stories are to be interpreted negatively for the time being. It appears that J.P. and the narrator each dominate in a section made up of roughly the same number of sequences and that their fates as characters are comparable in many ways.

A closer examination of these fates or rather of what shows on the surface, confirms this similarity. They are both about the same age, married, alcoholics, and J.P's stay in the centre seems to duplicate the first stay of the narrator who thus describes it. "That's when we were still together, trying to make things work out." Yet here again there is another gap since this is the narrator's second visit and he has already experienced the "shakes" which are bothering J.P. He himself suffers from them a little later, on the day when Roxy comes to visit her husband which gives the narrator the chance to ask her for the chimney sweep's kiss, which is supposed to bring good luck. And here the gap widens immensely compared to the kiss Roxy gave J.P. when they first met years earlier. The narrator's request, which surprises everyone, including himself, can only be seen as a cry for help ("I need some luck", p. 387). A childish cry but one which betrays the same anguish as that felt by J.P. at the bottom of the well. It is impossible not to link this request with the constant telephone calls made in vain by the narrator and also with the cries of little J.P. "hollering for help". The title itself, "Where I'm Calling From," plays on this double meaning and the repetition of these words in the last paragraph: "She'll ask me where I'm calling from" is merely another example of the circularity of the text.

However the young J.P. is saved by his father with the help of a rope that is far more effective than the telephone wires. Will anybody save the narrator by rescuing him from the vicious circle of alcoholism? It is now no longer a question of a gap between the two characters but a decisive opposition. Big Tiny's seizure is related at the very start of the story, Jack London's death is mentioned in sequence four, while that of his hero is brought up on the last page. Death is recurrent and threatening for those such as J.P. and the narrator who are half-way between the ordinary world and the mythical universe beyond the hills. One seizure means that another one is likely, one stay at the centre does not prevent another (again this circularity) and when, in the second paragraph, the narrator thinks to himself: "I know something's about to happen" we are not surprised to read on the last page that "something happens to it." The vital fire of London's hero is put out by an absurd fall of snow as absurd as Tiny's seizure or the incipient alcoholism of J.P.: "Who

"At the end of the story, it seems that the character can also find his salvation in discourse, which allows the greatest freedom and the most authentic truth, just as before it lent itself to a false mastery and a hypocritical detachment."

knows why we do what we do?'' A blind fate seems to weigh upon the existence of Jack London killed by alcohol which he did not manage to control, upon Tiny reduced to silence and fasting by an uncontrollable fear and upon the narrator who seems to be waiting for something: the warning signs of a seizure? someone's help? his wife's voice on the telephone? J.P. goes into the centre with Roxy while he stays alone with his memories and plans to make an umpteenth phonecall.

The gaps and contrasts between J.P. and the narrator are thus meaningful and they seem to suggest the accidental bringing together of two antithetical characters. Their alcoholism is a common point but their routes seem to differ. J.P. is ahead by a length (his ''shakes'' stop just before the narrator's start), one could almost say ahead by a story and thanks to Roxy he takes up with life and the outside world again. At the end the narrator shows the symptoms of his dependence, he seems obsessed by a fate which is condemning him and constantly goes back in time to his two arrivals at the centre. This assessment seems completely negative and is no doubt accurate if J.P. and the narrator are put on the same level, that is to say considered as characters.

But the narrator is also a narrator and the validity of this rather too systematic contrast could be called into question if the narration itself is taken into account. Does the narrator have the same relationship with J.P. as a narrator that he has with him as a character? His narrative function could lead to some alterations in the conclusions which have just been reached.

Let us start from the obvious fact this is a simultaneous narration in the present tense. Only five occurrences of the preterite (traces of a standard narrative?) can be found in the first narrative—leaving aside the retrospections and memories of the past brought up in the ''stories'' of J.P. and the narrator. With the present tense the temporal distance is abolished and both story and narration coincide. According to Genette, this type of narration can work in two opposite directions, ''depending on whether the stress is placed on the story or on the narrative discourse,'' in other words in a purely factual narrative (objective literature, Ecole du regard) or conversely in interior monologue narratives. ''Where I'm Calling From'' is written in both the present tense *and* the first person, and it presents an especially interesting exploitation of the dual function of the narrator as narrator and as character. It is first and foremost a factual narrative in which the narrator appears as a character but in certain passages resembling an interior monologue, the character completely controls the discourse. One would thus find the two directions indicated by Genette, together with the presence of a narrator who comments on the action, informs the reader and keeps the distance which his function allows. This relative complexity and the unequal distribution of the different roles of the narrator seem to suggest a much more subtle interpretation than the one previously put forward.

In the very first paragraph of the story, in fact in the first two sentences we find two examples of the simple present, one factual, the other expressing the narrator's comments on J.P.:

> J.P. and I are on the front porch at Frank Martin's drying-out facility. Like the rest of us at Frank Martin's, J.P. is first and foremost a drunk. But he's also a chimney sweep. . . .

This alternation continues throughout the paragraph and is a constant feature of the first sequences.

The narrator should also be credited with the more or less detailed presentation of minor characters: Frank Martin or the narrator's girlfriend or the ''traveller'' who is described in a paragraph detached from the factual context where the present tense has an iterative value: ''One of the guys here . . . he says . . . he also says . . . he tells us. . . .'' A similar control of time is shown by the narrator in the analepses which correspond to a temporal break and through which he artificially inserts an earlier part of the narrative. Finally the narrator intervenes once as organiser of the narrative when the retrospective episodes about Tiny is preceded by ''J.P. can wait a minute.'' He thus interrupts his narrative to introduce this incident which has been brought to his mind by the mention of J.P.'s shakes and his own fears.

The shift towards the interiority of the character which is expressed by the inner monologue, becomes more pronounced in the last lines of the story:

> I'll try my wife first. If she answers I'll wish her a Happy New Year. But that's it. I won't bring up business. I won't raise my voice. Not even if she starts something. . . .

However, it is already in evidence in sequence six, in the paragraph which follows the account of the narrator's arrival at the centre, and which is characterized by a strong modalisation with the repetition of ''maybe'', by contradictions with ''then again'' and ''but'', by very short sentences, paratactic structures and spoken language. A similar shift is noticeable at the end of the seventh sequence with the repetition of ''I don't want to talk to her''. These examples are all located in the second part of the story but two others are equally to be found in the first sequence (in the second and final paragraphs) which thus appears extremely diversified since here the narrator is present as a narrator (comments, analepsis and control of the narrative), as a character (factual present) and also as a character-narrator if this taking over of the discourse by the character—just as there is a taking over of power—can be so expressed. However here it could simply be considered as a limited instance of conjunction, as it were introductory, since there are no other examples of interior monologue before the end of sequence six. The development of this form of discourse is therefore characteristic of the second part. On the other hand the predominance of the narrator lies almost exclusively in the first part (in the whole of the fourth sequence and the majority of the first, second and third sequences). He is absent from the last two sequences and can only be credited with one paragraph in sequence seven and two lines in sequences five and six. There is thus an extremely clear division between the narrator dominating as a narrator in the first part and as a character in the second part, as well as a shift of this narrator-character towards what I have termed the character-narrator to take advantage of the relationship between the two functions. Although this appears clearly, the pinpointing of the various functions contradicts what has been suggested before, that is the importance of J.P. in the first part as he tells his story and achieves, in theory, the role of narrator and the similar importance of the narrator in the second part. . . .

The emergence of a form of discourse resembling an interior monologue which is found in sequence seven and especially in the last paragraph of the short story completes the evolution of the narrator. This is the third stage following the superiority of the narrator and the ordeal of the character. The character finally takes over and tries to control the discourse, moving from dishonesty and belief in his distinctiveness towards truth and acceptance of his identity. Our analysis of the narrator-character relationship—whether this character be J.P. or the narrator himself—therefore leads us to a very different interpretation from that suggested first of all by merely taking into account the similarities and differences between J.P. and the narrator. . . .

In order that I, too, should conform to the law of recurrence and circularity which governs the structure of ''Where I'm Calling From,'' I should like to conclude by using the same terms with which I initially defined the story while drastically altering the original suggestions. If it is indeed a question of two stories with a gap between them, they do not stand in opposition to each other; on the contrary they depict a parallel evolution which becomes noticeable when one takes into account the dual status of the narrator as a narrator and as a character. The weaknesses of the character in the second part should be analysed as following on from the rather suspect authority shown by the narrator in the first part and leading to an attempt at sincerity which leaves the final conclusion open. I would be tempted to see a symbol of this openness in the centre itself, a transitory location par excellence, but also in the well (''nothing closed off that little circle of blue'') and of course in the chimneys as channels or passages from one point to another, from the inside to the outside. It is probably not mere chance that Roxy teaches J.P. his job as a chimney sweep after his father saved his life by getting him out of the well. We do not know whether the narrator benefited from similar help, whether his wife can still represent a fountainhead of life or whether he has to help himself. However, at the end of the story, it seems that the character can also find his salvation in discourse, which allows the greatest freedom and the most authentic truth, just as before it lent itself to a false mastery and a hypocritical detachment. In contrast to Jack London's character who submits to the destiny decided by his author, in contrast to Jack

London himself who succumbed to something stronger than himself, the character of the narrator only depends on the narrator which he, in fact, is. This at least is what is suggested with a certain amount of optimism by the narrative.

Source: Claudine Verley, ''Narration and Interiority in Raymond Carver's 'Where I'm Calling From',' ' in *Journal of the Short Story in English,* No. 13, Autumn, 1989, pp. 91–102.

Sources

Atlas, James. ''Less Is Less,'' in the *Atlantic Monthly,* Vol. 246, No. 6, June, 1981, p. 97.

Barth, John. ''A Few Words about Minimalism,'' in *The New York Times Book Review,* December 28, 1986, p. 1.

Broyard, Anatole. ''Books of Our Times: Diffuse Regrets,'' in *The New York Times Book Review,* September 5, 1983, p. 27.

Carver, Raymond. ''On Writing,'' in *Fires: Essays, Poems, Stories,* Capra, 1983, p. 14.

Gardner, John. *On Moral Fiction,* Basic Books, 1978, p. 6.

Gentry, Marshall Bruce and William Stull. *Conversations with Raymond Carver,* University Press of Mississippi, 1990, p. 44.

Gorra, Michael. ''Laughter and Bloodshed,'' in *The Hudson Review,* Vol. XXXVII, No. 1, Spring, 1984, pp. 151–64.

Howe, Irving. ''Stories of Our Loneliness,'' in *The New York Times Book Review,* September 11, 1983, p. 1.

Nesset, Kirk. *The Stories of Raymond Carver: A Critical Study,* Ohio University Press, 1995, pp. 7, 51.

Newman, Charles. ''The Post-Modern Aura: The Act of Fiction in an Age of Inflation,'' in *Salmagundi,* Vol. 63-64, Spring-Summer 1984, p. 93.

Runyon, Randolph Paul. *Reading Raymond Carver,* Syracuse University Press, 1992, p. 4.

Further Reading

Campbell, Ewing. *Raymond Carver: A Study of the Short Fiction,* Twayne, 1992.

In addition to close readings of most Carver's stories, this useful resource includes reprints of Carver's essay ''On Writing,'' an interview of Carver, and short pieces on Carver by three other critics.

Herzinge, Kim, ed. *Mississippi Review,* Vol. 40-41, Winter, 1985.

Articles in this special issue devoted to the new minimalists present a range of views on the works of writers like Carver, Bobbie Ann Mason, Ann Beattie, Tobias Wolff, and others. In his influential essay, ''Introduction: On the New Fiction,'' guest editor Herzinger sees the movement as a continuation of postmodernist trends.

Nesset, Kirk. *The Stories of Raymond Carver: A Critical Study,* Ohio University Press, 1995.

An in-depth analysis of the major themes and stylistic concerns in most of Carver's major stories. This study includes an excellent discussion of themes of ''insularity and self-enlargement'' in ''Where I'm Calling From.''

Saltzman, Arthur. *Understanding Raymond Carver,* University of South Carolina Press, 1988.

The first book-length study on Carver, written shortly before his death, gives insightful close readings of most of his major stories and some of his poetry.

Woman Hollering Creek

Sandra Cisneros

1991

''Woman Hollering Creek'' was first published in Sandra Cisneros's 1991 collection of short stories, *Woman Hollering Creek and Other Stories.* Like her novel, *The House on Mango Street*, published in 1983, which describes the lives of Mexican immigrants in a Chicago neighborhood, ''Woman Hollering Creek'' describes the lives of Mexicans who have crossed the border to live on *''el otro lado''*—the other side—in the American Southwest. Critically acclaimed as a major voice in Chicana and feminist literature, Cisneros has won numerous awards and has established herself as an important voice in the American literary mainstream as well. Cisneros's work is widely anthologized, and her novel, short stories, and poetry are part of many high school and college literature classes.

In ''Woman Hollering Creek'' Cisneros writes of a woman, Cleofilas, who is trapped in a constricting, culturally assigned gender role due to her linguistic isolation, violent marriage, and poverty. Weaving in allusions to women of Mexican history and folklore, making it clear that women across the centuries have suffered the same alienation and victimization, Cisneros presents a woman who struggles to prevail over romantic notions of domestic bliss by leaving her husband, thus awakening the power within her.

Author Biography

Born in Chicago in 1954, Sandra Cisneros grew up with her Mexican father, Mexican-American mother, and six brothers. Her family moved back and forth between Chicago and Mexico City, never staying long enough for her to find the friends she hoped would make up for her lack of a sister. As a child, her defense against loneliness was reading books and writing poetry. In high school, she continued writing, trying to distinguish her own voice from the voices of the literary giants she studied. It was not until a creative writing class in college in 1974, described in ''Ghost Voices: Writing from Obsession,'' that she began to realize that she had not only a unique voice but also a new story to tell that had not been told in American literature. It is the story of immigrant families living on the borders between countries, neighborhoods, social classes, linguistic groups, and races.

In order to reclaim her father's Spanish, Cisneros tells Reed Dasenbrock and Feroza Jussawalla that she ''made a conscious choice to move to Texas.'' Looking back at *The House on Mango Street,* which is written in English, she realizes that ''the syntax, the sensibility, the diminutives, the way of looking at inanimate objects—that's not a child's voice as is sometimes said. That's Spanish!'' Living in San Antonio gives Cisneros the Spanish culture she seeks to enrich her English. ''Everywhere I go I get ideas, something in the people's expressions, something in the rhythm of their saying something in Spanish.''

Writing primarily in English, but English infused with Spanish, Cisneros has published three volumes of poetry: *Bad Boys* (1980), *My Wicked, Wicked Ways* (1987), and *Loose Woman* (1994), in addition to her novel, *The House on Mango Street* (1983) and her short story collection, *Woman Hollering Creek and Other Stories* (1991). She is currently working on a new novel, *Caramelo.*

Plot Summary

Cleofilas Enriqueta DeLeon Hernandez believes she will live happily ever after when her father consents to her marriage to Juan Pedro. She leaves her father and six brothers in Mexico and drives to *''el otro lado''*—the other side—with Juan Pedro to start a new life as his wife in a ramshackle house in a dusty little Texas town. Across a stream called Woman Hollering Creek, Cleofilas soon finds that she has left the boring yet peaceful life she shared with her father and six brothers for the tumultuous, lonely, desperate life of a woman with an abusive husband. Her new life, which was supposed to have been full of the passion she had seen on television soap operas, grows ''sadder and sadder with each episode,'' even though she believes that ''when one finds, finally, the great love of one's life, [one] does whatever one can, must do, at whatever the cost.'' She is trapped with her infant son and widowed neighbors, Dolores and Soledad, along the banks of the creek with the name no one can explain. Cleofilas wonders if it is pain or anger that caused the woman of Woman Hollering Creek to holler. No one can answer; no one remembers.

Pregnant with her second child and promising to hide her most recent bruises, Cleofilas begs her husband to take her to the clinic for a checkup. The physician at the clinic, Graciela, realizes that Cleofilas is an abused woman who speaks no English, is completely cut off from her family, and desperately needs help to escape from her husband. Graciela calls her friend, Felice, who agrees to drive Cleofilas and her baby, Juan Pedrito, to San Antonio where they can get a bus to take them back to her father, Don Serafin, in Mexico. Cleofilas is amazed to learn that Felice drives her own pickup truck and does not have a husband, and she is shocked when, as they cross the bridge over Woman Hollering Creek, Felice opens her mouth and yells ''like Tarzan.''

Characters

Dolores

Dolores, whose name means ''sorrow,'' is Cleofilas' neighbor on the right. She is a widow who lives in a house full of incense and candles, mourning her husband and two dead sons. She grows immense sunflowers and sad-smelling roses to decorate their small graves in the nearby cemetery. She worries about Cleofilas and her baby getting sick if they are ever out in the night air where the ghostly La Llorona might find them.

Felice

Felice is an independent, spirited woman who owns her own truck and who is willing to help other women in distress. Along with the clinic physician,

Graciela, she conspires to help Cleofilas escape from her abusive husband. Felice is a woman who rejects traditional sex roles and fiercely and fearlessly defends women who are trapped in restricted, traditional lives. She tranforms the holler of Woman Hollering Creek from a cry of pain or rage to a shout of laughter and liberation.

Graciela

Graciela, whose name means "grace," is the clinic physician who, like Felice, has rejected traditional sex roles. She takes the initiative to get Cleofilas away from her husband by calling Felice to drive the battered woman to the bus depot in San Antonio.

Cleofilas Enriqueta DeLeon Hernandez

Cleofilas is a young, innocent Mexican woman with much curiosity and a head full of dreams of a life of love and passion derived from her beloved books, song lyrics, and soap operas. When her father offers her in marriage to a man from *"el otro lado"*—the other side of the border, she hastily makes her bridal gown, gathers flowers for her makeshift bouquet, and goes off with the "man she has waited her whole life for" to find "passion in its purest crystalline essence," even the passion women often pay for with "sweet pain."

After her husband, Juan Pedro, begins to abuse her, she stays quiet even though she shudders at the thought of all the dead women she reads about in the newspapers. She realizes how dangerous her situation is, but pride prevents her from returning to her father in Mexico. "Where's your husband?" she knows they would ask. Cleofilas eventually musters enough courage to leave, though she obtains help from Graciela and Felice. Relying on the strength of these women, whom Cleofilas finds fascinating, she leaves Juan Pedro behind and returns to her former life.

Juan Pedro Martinez Sanchez

Juan Pedro is Cleofilas's abusive, alcoholic husband who only wants to marry his young Mexican bride quickly and take her back to his life of poverty in Seguin, Texas. There he can resume his habit of drinking and carousing with his foul-mouthed friends at the local ice house. Soon after their marriage, he reveals himself to be faithless, violent, and quick to cry tears of remorse and shame, which are predictably followed by renewed episodes of physical abuse.

Sandra Cisneros

Juan Pedro is a man who disdains the romance that feeds his wife's fantasies, and hates the music and soap operas she adores. He is short, husky, scarred from acne, and overweight from all of the beer he drinks. Consistent with the gender-role socialization of his youth, he demands that his wife provide dinners like his mother prepared. He also demands that Cleofilas take care of all his needs and those of his children without complaint.

Don Serafin

Don Serafin is Cleofilas' father, who told her as she left his house with her new husband, "I am your father, I will never abandon you." Still, he sends her off to *"el otro lado"*—the other side—with a man neither he nor his daughter really knows. Even as she leaves, he wonders if she will someday dream of returning to her hard life of chores with him and her six brothers. Don Serafin teaches Cleofilas that the love between parent and child is different and stronger than the love between a man and a woman, a lesson she remembers as she looks at her infant son. After his daughter's disastrous, violent marriage, to which he initially consented, he is there to welcome her and her children home.

Soledad

Soledad, whose name means "alone," is Cleofilas's neighbor on the left in Seguin, Texas. Soledad says she is a widow, but rarely talks about her husband. Local gossip claims he either died, ran off with another woman, or went out one day and never came back. Soledad is one of the few people Cleofilas can visit, but she does not offer any hope for relief from the abuse Cleofilas suffers. She frustrates Cleofilas because she cannot explain the name of Woman Hollering Creek, and she is full of warnings about the dangers of walking alone at night.

Themes

Love and Passion

Cleofilas longs for "passion in its purest crystalline essence. The kind the books and songs and *telenovelas* describe when one finds, finally, the great love of one's life, and does whatever one can, must do, at whatever cost." Because, she believes, "to suffer for love is good. The pain all sweet somehow." Unhappily, the passive acceptance of suffering for love that Cleofilas learns as she grows up makes her especially vulnerable to her abusive husband. She had always believed that "she would strike back if a man, any man, were to strike her." Instead, when Juan Pedro first hits her, "she had been so stunned, it left her speechless, motionless, numb." Unbelieving and forgiving when the abuse begins, Cleofilas wonders why her pain goes beyond the sweet pain of her soap opera heroines. Where is the love that is supposed to go along with the pain?

Cleofilas learns that the only love that endures in her life is the love of a parent for a child. When she leaves her father's house in Mexico, he tells her, "I am your father, I will never abandon you." Although he gives her in marriage to a man whose violence is unknown to them, he welcomes her home after she escapes her life of domestic abuse.

Sex Roles

Women, in Cleofilas' culture, are assigned to carefully circumscribed roles, as they are in most cultures. For example, she is given to Juan Pedro by her father, moves from her father's house into her husband's house, does not drive or have access to a car, and is isolated with her child to the small house where she must cook, clean, and care for her family without even the companionship of a television. She is shocked to meet Felice, a woman who drives a pickup truck that is her own, not her husband's, since she does not even have a husband. It is a truck she chose and that she pays for herself. Felice's life is full of freedom that Cleofilas never even imagines. When Felice lets out a loud yell as they cross Woman Hollering Creek, Cleofilas and her baby are both startled by the outburst. Felice explains that the only woman who is revered, or for whom any place is named around their town, is the Virgin, and in fact "you're only famous if you are a virgin."

Men, too, are constrained by the sex roles assigned to them by culture. Nothing in Juan Pedro's world encourages him to be other than he is. His icehouse friends condone violence against women, and even the women near his home who must know his violent ways, do nothing to correct him. His wife forgives him and promises to remain silent about his beatings and even to lie outright if asked about her many bruises by her doctor. She will say "she fell down the front steps or slipped when she was out in the backyard, slipped out back, she could tell him that."

Victimization

Cleofilas is a classic victim of domestic abuse, according to Jean Wyatt in her essay "On Not Being La Malinche: Border Negotiations of Gender in Sandra Cisneros's 'Never Marry and Mexican' and 'Woman Hollering Creek'" (*Tulsa Studies in Women's Literature,* Vol. 14, Fall, 1995). After being battered by her husband, Cleofilas "could think of nothing to say, said nothing. Just stroked the dark curls of the man who wept and would weep like a child, his tears of repentance and shame, this time and each." The cycle of abuse followed by guilt and remorse continues. Like other victims of violence at the hands of men, Cleofilas is isolated, poor, has one child and is pregnant with another, and lives in a climate where violence against women is ignored—even condoned. Her husband and his friends at the ice house joke about Maximiliano "who is said to have killed his wife in an ice house brawl when she came at him with a mop. I had to shoot, he had said—she was armed." Like many women, Cleofilas believes that she must remain with her husband; the *telenovelas* have taught her that "to suffer for love is good. The pain is all sweet somehow." In calmer moments, the drama of passion continues to flair within her: "this man, this father, this rival, this keeper, this lord, this master," she tells herself, "this husband till kingdom come."

Cleofilas is finally able to "slip out back," with help from the women of the clinic, and to escape being victimized by her husband. As Cisneros tells Reed Dasenbrock and Feroza Jussawalla in *Interviews with Writers of the Post-Colonial World,* "There's a lot of victimization but we [Mexican women] are also fierce. Our mothers had been fierce. Our women may be victimized but they are still very, very fierce and very strong."

Style

Point of View and Narration

The majority of "Woman Hollering Creek" is narrated in the third-person omniscient voice. The narrative voice that describes Cleofilas's life in Mexico, her father and brothers, the women friends with whom she gossiped in her town, speaks in longer more lyrical sentences than the narrative voice that describes her life and thoughts in Seguin, Texas. The opening sentence reads: "The day Don Serafin gave Juan Pedro Martinez Sanchez permission to take Cleofilas Enriqueta DeLeon Hernandez as his bride, across her father's threshold, over several miles of dirt road and several miles of paved, over one border and beyond to a town *en el otro lado*—on the other side—already did he divine the morning his daughter would raise her hand over her eyes, look south, and dream of returning to the chores that never ended, six good-for-nothing brothers, and one old man's complaints."

In contrast to her present life, her past life in Mexico does seem more and more lyrical, almost idyllic, as her life in Texas spirals downward into more and more abuse, loneliness, and chaos. The short, choppy, incomplete sentences of the Texas sections reach their crescendo as she sits out on the grass with her baby, by Woman Hollering Creek, listening to a voice she interprets as la Llorona, the mythical Weeping Woman who is alleged to have drowned her children. "La Llorona calling to her. She is sure of it. Cleofilas sets the baby's Donald Duck blanket on the grass. Listens. The day sky turning to night. The baby pulling up fistfuls of grass and laughing. La Llorona. Wonders if something as quiet as this drives a woman to the darkness under the trees."

An abrupt change from the third person narrative voice occurs when Graciela, the clinic physician, speaks in the first person on the telephone to Felice. Suddenly there is action; something happens. Cleofilas' silent life of abuse is now given voice by a woman who will help Cleofilas to escape the cycle of abuse and gain some control over her life for the first time.

Topics for Further Study

- Research the folklore surrounding the mythical woman, La Llorona. How have Chicana writers redefined her as a role model for modern women?
- Compare Gloria Anzaldua's account of the conquest of Mexico by the Spaniards to the account in an encyclopedia or a world history textbook. What defines her point of view? How and why is it distinct?
- Compare the works of Chicano writers (Rudolfo Anaya, Tomas Rivera, Rolando Hinojosa) to Chicana writers (Gloria Anzaldua, Denise Chavez, Ana Castillo, Sandra Cisneros). What characteristics do these works share? How are they different?

Setting

The river named Woman Hollering Creek forms the center of the borderland in which the story unfolds. It marks the crossings of culture, language, gender, marriage, enslavement, and freedom that take place in the story. Cleofilas's Mexican "town of gossips . . . of dust and despair" on the one side, is not so different from Seguin, Texas, another town of "gossips. . . . dust and despair" on the other side, except that in her father's town she is safe from physical harm.

The Texas side of the creek proves to be a dangerous place for Cleofilas. Her immediate environment, her house and the houses of her neighbors, Dolores and Soledad, is a predominately female setting. But it is a dangerous one since Juan Pedro often stays away at night, and because when he is there he is often violent. The ice house, a predominately male setting, is another dangerous place that makes her feel mute and vulnerable. After all, Maximiliano killed his wife there. Even at the clinic

Cleofilas cannot feel safe because her husband is in the waiting room. Only in Felice's truck, in the competent hands of this fierce, independent woman, can Cleofilas allow a ripple of laughter to escape from her throat. She is safe in Felice's care.

Structure

"Woman Hollering Creek," like the *telenovelas* Cleofilas watches, is episodic. It does not follow a linear story line with smooth transitions from one setting or topic to another. "Cleofilas thought her life would have to be like that, like a *telenovela,* only now the episodes got sadder and sadder. And there were no commercials in between for comic relief." Although the story moves back and forth in time, and from setting to setting as Cleofilas thinks back to her life in Mexico, each episode, like soap operas, takes place in one time and one place.

The episodic nature of "Woman Hollering Creek" and Cisneros's novel *The House on Mango Street* is a stylistic choice that links the author to the Chicano writers who preceded her, like Rudolfo Anaya, Tomas Rivera, and Rolando Hinojosa. As Reed Dasenbrock and Feroza Jussawalla write in the introduction to their interview with Cisneros (in *Interviews with Writers of the Post-Colonial World,* 1992), "There are some strong continuities between the two generations and groups of writers: both use a mosaic of discontinuous forms in place of a continuous, linear narrative." Cisneros takes her craft very seriously, as she tells Dasenbrock and Jussawalla, and she believes a writer needs to be a meticulous carpenter of small rooms, small stories, before she can take on building a house.

Symbols and Images

Cisneros employs much symbolism in the names she chooses for her characters. Notably, Cleofilas' neighbors on either side are widowed women named Dolores and Soledad, which mean "sorrow" and "alone," respectively. The two women who come to her aid are Graciela, which is a Hispanic version of the name Grace, and Felice, which means "happiness." Cleofilas's name is clarified by Graciela, who tries to explain it to Felice over the phone: "One of those Mexican saints, I guess. A martyr or something." This point is underscored by Jean Wyatt who notes that Mexican culture reveres women who suffer, as Cleofilas admires the tortured souls on the *telenovelas.*

The borderlands formed by Woman Hollering Creek are important images in Cisneros's story just as they are in the writing of many of her Chicana colleagues, such as Gloria Anzaldua. For people who live on the edges of cultures and languages different from their own, the concept of borders and borderlands is important because it symbolizes places where life is hard and losses are monumental. Yet they are also places where the fluidity of cultures allows new formulations and transformations to occur. For example, Cleofilas did not imagine the changes that would take place in her life on the banks of Woman Hollering Creek when she was a teenager watching *telenovelas* in Mexico. Only by moving across the border through marriage, to the edges of a linguistic community in which she is truly silenced by her inability to speak English, does she find herself in the care and company of two women like Graciela, her doctor, and Felice, her driver to safety. Only through her contact with these women, who have found the space in the fluidity of the borderlands to recreate themselves outside of their assigned sex roles, can Cleofilas imagine a new life where suffering for love is not the central motive.

La Llorona, another important image in "Woman Hollering Creek," is the model for the woman who suffers endlessly for love. La Llorona, the Weeping Woman, has been a well-known character of Mexican folklore for so many centuries that her precise origins are themselves the subject of myth. Most often she is described as a woman who drowned her children and who wanders forever in the night crying. One myth says she killed her children because their father was from a higher social class and abandoned her. The same fate awaits modern-day Maria, the star of the *telenovela* "Maria de Nadie." In other legends, La Llorona merges into La Malinche, the mistress of the conqueror Hernan Cortes, who is alleged to have killed the son she had by Cortes when Cortes threatened to take him back to Spain. In "Woman Hollering Creek," La Llorona, a figure known to Cleofilas since her childhood, appears as a voice calling her as she sits by the bank of the creek with her baby.

La Gritona, which means "woman hollering," may be the new image of La Llorona. Cleofilas wonders why the woman is hollering—is it from anger or pain? Why does such a pretty creek "full of happily ever after" have such a strange name, and why can no one explain its meaning? In the story, Cleofilas begins to think of the image of La Gritona, the Hollering Woman, as La Llorona, the Weeping Woman, and begins to hear the holler as a cry of pain with which she identifies very strongly. Yet in the end, here in the borderlands, the cry of La Gritona is transformed in the throat of Felice, who always laughs and yells "like Tarzan," symbol of great physical power, as she drives her pickup truck over the creek.

Historical Context

Mexico: The Early Years

From the beginning of the fourteenth through the end of the fifteenth century, the Aztec people built an empire in what is now Mexico by conquering other tribes. Under Montezuma II, from 1502 until 1520, the empire reached its peak in the days before the arrival of the Spanish conquistadors. Led by Hernan Cortes, the Spaniards took the Aztec capital city of Tenochtitlan on August 13, 1521. Subsequently, Cortes took as his interpreter and mistress the Aztec woman La Malinche.

Post-Colonial Times

After three hundred years of colonial rule, Mexico, which at that time comprised much of what is now the southwest of the United States, won her independence from Spain, in 1821. In the 1848 treaty of Guadalupe-Hidalgo that ended the Mexican-American war, Mexico ceded all territory north of the Rio Grande and the Gila River to the United States. Mexican President Antonio Lopez de Santa Ana sold land south of the Gila River to the United States in the Gadsden Purchase of 1853.

Changing Borders

Looking at Mexican history, particularly regarding the changing geographical borders between the United States and Mexico, it is clear why Cisneros, Gloria Anzaldua, and other Chicana writers find the metaphor of borders and borderlands such fertile ground for both fiction and nonfiction writing. Borders, like the U.S.-Mexican border, can be changed overnight by government treaty or reprisals of war, and contested areas can become part of a different country in a moment. But people do not change so readily; their culture, language, folklore, and community history cannot be changed by legal treaties. Consequently, people find themselves strangers in their own land, disenfranchised, often powerless residents of a borderland country not their own. Like the Mexicans who lived in Texas or Arizona before those regions were annexed by the United States, they have no "old country" to return to since other states in Mexico were never their homes, and they are not really a part of the new country linguistically, culturally, or historically. They come to inhabit the edges of communities where the contact of divergent cultures produces hybrid races, languages, and cultures.

Critical Overview

Cisneros's *Woman Hollering Creek and Other Stories* received much attention when it was published in 1991. It was explicated in several literary journals, including *Tulsa Studies in Women's Literature, Frontiers,* and *Heresies,* and won acclaim in the mainstream press. Writing in the *New York Times Book Review,* Bebe Moore Campbell gave the collection a favorable review, noting that in all the stories—and particularly the title story—"she uses the behavior of men as a catalyst that propels her women into a search deep within themselves for the love that men have failed to give them." *Newsweek* listed *Woman Hollering Creek and Other Stories* as the first of its seven books recommended for summer reading. Peter S. Prescott and Karen Springen summarized the collection in *Newsweek:* "Noisily, wittily, always compassionately, Cisneros surveys woman's condition—a condition that is both precisely Latina and general to women everywhere.

Jean Wyatt, in an essay for *Tulsa Studies in Women's Literature,* said that in "Woman Hollering Creek," "Cisneros juxtaposes the heroines of contemporary Mexican *telenovelas* with the traditional figure La Llorona to imply that then, now, and always the ideals of femininity that Mexican popular culture presents to its women are models of pain and suffering." Jacqueline Doyle, in an essay titled "Haunting the Borderlands: La Llorona in Sandra Cisneros's 'Woman Hollering Creek'," concentrated on the mythical figure of the Weeping Woman in the story. "Immersed in romance novels and the telenovelas, Cleofilas is initiated into a culture of weeping women, the tale of 'La Llorona' retold in countless ways around her. . . . Cleofilas's own life begins to resemble La Llorona's, as she decodes and erases evidence of her husband's infidelities."

Harryette Mullen, in her essay "'A Silence Between Us Like a Language': The Untranslatability of Experience in Sandra Cisneros's 'Woman Hollering Creek'," concentrates on the author's portrayal of Mexican culture in the story. "Cisneros

Compare & Contrast

- **Texas:** According to 1995–96 U.S. Census Bureau statistics, 17 percent of all people living in the state subsist beneath the poverty threshold, which is defined as $16,036 for a family of four.

  New Hampshire: According to the same statistics, 5.9 percent of all residents in this state live beneath the poverty line.

- **Texas:** According to 1996 statistics, 2.5 million state residents speak Spanish, and 714,958 are defined as ''linguistically isolated,'' meaning that they know little English.

  Maine: According to the same statistics, 4,527 people in this state speak Spanish as their primary language.

- **Texas:** The U. S. Census Bureau states that, according to 1996 statistics, nearly 25 percent of the state's residents speak Spanish.

  California: The Census Bureau states that 30 percent of the state's residents speak Spanish—a total of 4 million people; 2 million of whom are identified as ''linguistically isolated.''

employs throughout the entire text of Woman Hollering Creek a network of epigraphs taken, not from the literary traditions of the United States or Europe or Latin America, but instead from Mexican ballads and romantic popular songs that circulate throughout, and indeed help constitute, Spanish-speaking communities.''

Criticism

Jennifer Hicks and Barbara Smith

Hicks has a Master's Degree in English literature, and has written extensively for academic journals, and is CEO of WordsWork, a freelance writing firm that provides Web site content. Smith has Master's Degrees in both bilingual studies and humanistic and behavioral studies. She has designed and facilitated several multicultural workshops for educators. In the following essay, they discuss multicultural aspects of ''Woman Hollering Creek.''

In her short story ''Woman Hollering Creek,'' Sandra Cisneros demonstrates in her writing the same linguistic and cultural transformations she describes in her narrative. Writing about Mexicans and Mexican-Americans like Cleofilas and her husband Juan Pedro who inhabit the border between the United States and Mexico, Cisneros explores the terrible losses and limitations that exist for people who live in the edges of divergent languages and cultures. These borderlands, as Gloria Anzaldua describes them in her book, *Borderlands/La Frontera: The New Mestiza,* ''are physically present wherever two or more cultures edge each other. . . . It's not comfortable territory to live in, this place of contradictions. Hatred, anger and exploitation are the prominent features of this landscape. . . . However, there are compensations and certain joys. . . . Dormant areas of consciousness are . . . activated, awakened. . . . There, at the juncture of cultures, languages cross-pollinate and are revitalized.'' Borderlands are a place where ''The new mestiza (a Chicana like Felice) reinterprets history and using new symbols, she shapes new myths.''

Along the border language becomes more fluid, and new meanings can be derived as one language infuses another with its vocabulary and syntax. Cisneros talks of the influence of her father's Spanish on her written English. As she tells Dasenbrock and Jussawalla, incorporating Spanish ''changes the rhythm of my writing . . . [and] allows me to create new expressions in English—to say things in English that have never been said before . . . All of a sudden something happens to the English, something really new is happening, a new spice is added

What Do I Read Next?

- *Borderlands/La Frontera: The New Mestiza* (1987) by Gloria Anzaldua, a Chicana writer. This largely nonfiction volume also includes poetry. In it Anzaldua analyzes the experiences of Mexicans/Chicanos in the United States.
- *Latina: Women's Voices from the Borderlands* (1995) is edited by Lillian Castillo-Speed. This collection of writings from 31 Latina writers includes short stories, excerpts from novels, and essays that describe lives on the borders of languages, races, and communities.
- *Cuentos: Stories by Latinas* (1983) is edited by Alma Gomez, Cherrie Moraga, and Mariana Romo-Carmona. These stories describe the lives of Latina women in their struggle to overcome the challenges of living in complex cultural contexts.
- *Chicana Creativity & Criticism: New Frontiers in American Literature* (1996) is edited by Maria Herrara-Sobek and Helena Maria Viramontes. This collection of poetry, prose, criticism and visual art includes literature by and about Chicanas.
- *The Woman Warrior* (1976) by Maxine Hong Kingston. Cisneros has cited this book about the family history, myth, and the memories of an Asian-American woman as an inspiration for writing *The House on Mango Street.*
- *The House on Mango Street* (1983) by Sandra Cisneros. Cisneros describes her first novel as a string of little pearls. Each little pearl, each story, can be read and understood on its own, or the whole collection can be seen as a necklace, to be read as a whole.
- *Storyteller* (1981) by Leslie Marmon Silko. A collection of stories by a Native American writer who explores her Pueblo heritage and weaves myths, autobiography, and the history of her community into her tales that highlight the importance of stories as a form of knowledge.

---

to the English language.'' For example, in ''Woman Hollering Creek,'' all of the characters have Spanish names that are familiar enough in English, but their true resonance derives from their Spanish meanings. In her Texas town, Cleofilas lives between ''Dolores'' and ''Soledad,'' that is, between ''sorrow'' and ''loneliness.'' In the end of the story, she is saved by ''Graciela'' and ''Felice,'' or ''grace'' and ''happiness.'' The term ''compadre'' is also familiar in English, but the term ''comadre'' may not be. Graciela, the physician who identifies Cleofilas' abuse, calls her friend Felice ''comadre,'' but Cisneros does not translate this. Literally, ''comadres'' are a mother and a godmother to a child, and the cultural expectation is that they will be like co-mothers to that child. In ''Woman Hollering Creek,'' Graciela and Felice are the co-mothers that bring Cleofilas to her new birth, her new understanding of her culture's myths, and her release from her role as passive victim of violence.

Just as language can take on new meaning and new formulations in the borderlands, cultural myths, too, can be transformed. The three principal women of Mexican myth that play roles in Cleofilas' life as described by Gloria Anzaldua are: ''The Virgen de Guadalupe, the virgin mother who has not abandoned us, La Chingada/La Malinche, the raped (taken by Hernan Cortes the Spanish conqueror) mother whom we have abandoned, and La Llorona, the mother who seeks her lost children and is a combination of the two.'' The Virgin of Guadalupe, who suffers the loss of her son, Jesus, remains the virgin who is available to her children throughout the centuries in prayer. La Malinche, on the other hand, is traditionally believed to have betrayed her people when she became the mistress of Hernan Cortes. Finally, La Llorona suffers the grief of the loss of her children and her lover for all time. These roles, all passive and long-suffering, are the mythic roles the Mexican culture teaches its daughters.

> "Graciela and Felice are the co-mothers that bring Cleofilas to her new birth, her new understanding of her culture's myths, and her release from her role as passive victim of violence."

In spite of these legends, Cisneros hastens to add in her conversation with Reed Dasenbrock and Feroza Jussawalla that "the traditional Mexican woman is a fierce woman" to have survived at all. In fact, the legends can be reclaimed and reframed to emphasize this fierce instinct for survival. For example, it has long been accepted that the subjugation of a native woman, La Malinche, by Cortes is a cause of great shame to the Mexican people. According to Octavio Paz, author of *Labyrinth of Solitude,* all Mexicans are "sons of La Malinche"; that is, they are illegitimate. And yet in the borderlands, La Malinche can be seen in a new light, not as the passive victim of male violence, but as the Indian mother of the mestizos who survived to create the new race. As Anzaldua writes, "La cultura chicana identifies with the mother (Indian) rather than with the father (Spanish).

In the case of La Llorona, the mythical figure is transformed linguistically and culturally. Renamed La Gritona, and reincarnated as a woman who yells rather than weeps, La Llorona becomes a symbol of power and rebellion, not submission. Jussawalla comments to Cisneros, "[Y]ou've revised the myth in 'Woman Hollering Creek.' La Llorona doesn't kill . . . the children as she does in the stories told here along the border, she gives laughter." Cisneros adds, "This Chicana woman (Felice) could understand the myth in a new way. She could see it as a grito (a yell), not a llanto (a sob). And all of a sudden, [Cleofilas] who came with all her Mexican assumptions learned something. The Chicana woman (Felice) showed her a new way of looking at a Mexican myth. And it took someone from a little bit outside of the culture to see the myth in a new way."

For readers outside of both Mexican and Chicana culture and for readers who do not know Spanish, the subtle connotations of the myths and of Cisneros' language choices might be lost were it not for her ability to both tell and demonstrate the transformations that take place in the story. Cisneros acknowledges in her talk with Dasenbrock and Jussawalla that "the readers who are going to like my stories the best and catch all the subtexts and all the subtitles . . . are the Chicanas. . . . But I also realize I am opening doors for people who don't know the culture." Because it is so well constructed, "Woman Hollering Creek" is a story that can be read in different ways by different audiences. Readers familiar with the Southwestern and Mexican myths and legends of La Llorona, La Malinche, and the Virgin of Guadalupe may see the cultural transformation of women's roles Cisneros describes, while readers unfamiliar with these legends may focus on the particular transformation of the vividly drawn lead character, Cleofilas, the classic battered woman.

Source: Jennifer Hicks and Barbara Smith, Overview of "Woman Hollering Creek," for *Short Stories for Students,* Gale, 1998.

William Rouster

Rouster has a Ph.D. in Composition and Rhetoric and has published a number of pieces in different composition journals and on ERIC. In the following essay, he discusses patriarchy in "Woman Hollering Creek."

"Woman Hollering Creek" by Sandra Cisneros was published in *Woman Hollering Creek and Other Stories* in 1991. This story deals with the pain and suffering of women in a patriarchal, or male-dominated, society. Patriarchy, as defined by Bruce Kokopeli and George Lakey in *More Power Than We Want,* refers to "the systematic domination of women by men through unequal opportunities, rewards, punishments, and the internalization of unequal expectations through sex role differentiation." Patriarchy is evident in a number of ways in the women's world of "Woman Hollering Creek." The women tend to have mundane low-paying jobs, like Trini, the laundromat attendant, or no jobs outside of the house, like Dolores and Cleofilas. The men make all of the decisions and do all of the talking when men and women are present in this story. Further, the men are able to mistreat the women with impunity.

Patriarchy is also seen in the preoccupation these women, particularly Cleofilas, have with finding a man to love, an obsession which seems to dominate their lives. Cleofilas has been anticipating finding the man of her dreams since she can remember:

> But what Cleofilas has been waiting for . . . is passion . . . in its crystalline essence. The kind the book and songs and *telenovelas* describe. When one finds, finally, the great love of one's life, and does whatever one can, must do, at whatever the cost.

As her idol, Cleofilas takes Lucia Mendez, heroine of the popular *telenovela You or No One,* who lives on her show the kind of life described above: "The beautiful Lucia Mendez having to put up with all kinds of hardships of the heart, separation and betrayal, and loving, always loving no matter what, because that is the important thing."

The image of the woman who will keep loving her abusive betraying man no matter what is critical to the maintenance of the patriarchal society. If women can be socialized to believe that "to suffer for love is good," then the men can basically do as they please and women will put up with it because they believe "the pain [will] all [be] sweet somehow. In the end." Thus, the men can be unfaithful and beat their wives with no fear of recrimination. Furthermore, if women put men on pedestals and make their main goal in life loving them no matter what, then the men are automatically given the predominant position in society.

Unfortunately for Cleofilas, who, it is suggested, was named for a Mexican martyred saint, her married life does not contain many of the positive elements of the *telenovelas,* just the negative ones. She envisions herself as being married, living in a nice house, having plenty of money, and buying the kinds of clothes that Lucia Mendez gets to wear. In reality, she ends up having very little money, and the house she moves into is a shabby little place located on Woman Hollering Creek in the desolate town of Seguin, Texas.

None of the women with whom Cleofilas is acquainted knows where the creek got its name: "a name no one from these parts questioned, little less understood. . . . Who knows, the townspeople shrugged, because it was of no concern to their lives how this trickle of water received its curious name." A critical element for keeping a practice in place is that the people do not question it and that it seems as if life has always been that way. The fact that no one questions the name of the creek, but just accepts it as is, represents how they accept patriarchy without question. Just as the creek was always named that and always would be, so men have always been in power and always would be and women would always be hollering. Who cares why women are hollering anyway? Since they have no power, their reasons for hollering are unimportant. Cleofilas, however, wants to find out the story behind the meaning of the creek's name and she wants to know why the women were hollering. Her experience on Woman Hollering Creek leads her to believe that the woman's holler was one of pain and rage.

"The fact that no one questions the name of the creek, but just accepts it as is, represents how they accept patriarchy without question."

This belief is reinforced by the two widows who live next door to Cleofilas, one on each side. To the left lives Soledad, who calls herself a widow, but who will not say how she lost her husband. Cleofilas suspects that he may have simply left her. Dolores, living to the right, keeps altars topped with burning incense and candles for the two sons killed in the war and the husband who died of grief soon after. Every Sunday she leaves fresh flowers on their graves. Across the street lives a man who shot his wife when she attacked him with a mop during a fight at the ice house. The women on Woman Hollering Creek suffer much from their dealings with the men in their lives.

The women in Seguin have no real power; the town was not built to empower women: "the towns here are built so that you have to depend on husbands. Or you stay home. Or you drive. If you're rich enough to own, allowed to drive, your own car." Even if they have cars, the women may not be allowed to drive them. This powerlessness extends to social gatherings at the ice house, the center of the Seguin social world, where the women come and sit in silence next to their men, as the men tried to solve the problems of the world. This is as it should be in patriarchy: the men attempt to take care of the world's difficulties while the women sit in silence, admiring them.

Probably more than in any other place, the reader gets to see the havoc patriarchy can wreak on women. Cleofilas's situation is much like that of Nora's in Henrik Ibsen's *The Doll House:* both go from their father's house to their husband's house and have very little real power in either place. Unlike Nora, though, Cleofilas experiences some of the more overtly physically and emotionally painful aspects of patriarchy. Her husband, Juan Pedro, takes advantage of the power inherent in a man's position in such a society by beating her, and she just takes it: "When the moment came, and he slapped her once, and then again, and again; until the lip split and bled an orchid of blood, she didn't fight back, she didn't break into tears, she didn't run away." She is beaten so often and so severely that by the time she decides to leave him, the lady at the health clinic notes in astonishment that "This poor lady's got black-and-blue marks all over." In a moment full of symbolism, her husband even hits her in the face with a romance novel, leaving a welt on one cheek. The critical element here is that her husband feels free to beat Cleofilas at will, with little or no fear of punishment. In a patriarchal society such as this, men often beat their wives with total impunity because the women are relatively powerless. Many women, such as Cleofilas, have no income apart from their husbands, so where will they go if they leave?

In addition, Cleofilas has no power in the household. She has no transportation of her own and likely cannot drive anyway. She is not allowed to have any contact with her family in Mexico. Furthermore, she has to beg her husband to take her to the doctor in order to ensure that her pregnancy will go well and that she will not be injured in childbirth. She does not even have the power to defend herself when he beats her. When she asks him to fix something, he abuses her emotionally, kicking the refrigerator and shouting:

> He hates this shitty house and is going out where he won't be bothered with the baby's howling and her suspicious questions, and her requests to fix this and this and this because if she had any brains in her head she'd realize he's been up before the rooster earning his living to pay for the food in her belly and the roof over her head.

This man is all too aware of the power he has in the household as the breadwinner. She refers to him as "this keeper, this lord, this master." When she decides to leave him she has to sneak out, in fear that he will catch her, like a dog trying to sneak out of the yard, and beat her again and prevent her from leaving.

It is in leaving Juan Pedro that she learns a new meaning for Woman Hollering Creek other than the rage and anger she has experienced. The woman who picks her up to drive her to the bus station in San Antonio, Felice, whose name means "happy," drives a truck—her own truck—is unmarried, and swears just like a man. She is not controlled by patriarchy, at least not directly. As they are crossing the creek she yells like Tarzan, a victory yell, one of strength. She says she yells like that every time she crosses the bridge because nothing in the area is named after women, except virgins and that one creek, and it makes her want to holler. Passing over the creek with Felice, Cleofilas glimpses a world where a woman can take care of herself and gain control over her life. She is going back to her father's house in Mexico, but she is returning with a new awareness. In telling her father and brothers about Felice's yell, "Felice began to laugh again, but it wasn't Felice laughing. It was gurgling out of her own throat, a long ribbon of laughter, like water."

Source: William Rouster, for *Short Stories for Students,* Gale, 1998.

Harryette Mullen

Mullen is an educator at Cornell University. In the following essay, she discusses the implications of language in "Woman Hollering Creek" in an effort to highlight the unique culture Cisneros writes about, one which is not easily understood within the confines of the English language.

In jests, dreams, magic, poetry, and poetic prose, Sandra Cisneros finds abundant examples of the "everyday verbal mythology" of Mexican-American culture. Language and literacy as sites of cultural and class conflict, or what Paulo Freire and Donaldo Macedo describe as the "antagonistic" yet potentially "positive" relationship of minority to dominant linguistic and cultural codes, are critical matters in *Woman Hollering Creek.* The text includes frequent references to the specificity and difference coded into any and all languages; to the violence of inadequacy of translation and interpretation; to the translator's and, by extension, the writer's unfaithful role as betrayer of the culture's inside secrets; and to the existence of encoded messages, which are more accessible to readers familiar with various insider codes and cryptographic devices deployed in the text.

These attributes Cisneros's text shares with texts by other Chicano, Latino, and minority writers, who implicitly or explicitly refer to their own ambiguous relationships to both dominant and subordinated cultures in their roles as translators and interpreters of minority experience. . . .

Woman Hollering Creek offers stories of a variety of women trying various means of escape, through resistance to traditional female socialization, through sexual and economic independence, self-fashioning, and feminist activism, as well as through fantasy, prayer, magic, and art. Cisneros's most complex characters are those who, like adult Esperanzas, have left and returned to the barrio as artists. For them, art is a powerfully seductive way of ''Making the world look at you from my eyes. And if that's not power, what is? . . .''

In addition to her portraits of the artist as a Chicana, Cisneros is concerned with representing the silenced and marginalized, including children, homosexuals, and working class and immigrant Chicanos and Mexicanos, whose stories have been untold or untranslated. Her particular focus on the silencing of women is signaled in the title story, ''Woman Hollering Creek.'' The creek called ''La Gritona'' is reminiscent of popular folktales about ''La Llorona,'' a nameless tragic woman who drowned herself and her children. The creek, the border, and the *telenovelas* define the mythic spaces given to Cleofilas in her fantasies of escape from a battering husband. The cultural scripts associated with each space offer her different escape fantasies: homicide and/or suicide, like La Llorona; dramatic border crossings, like the escape of an outlaw desperado from the U.S. into Mexico, or the crossings of *mojados* and smuggler *coyotes;* or *telenovelas,* soap operas that provide the escape of entertainment. Cisneros creates a new destiny in a story that revises all three of these cultural scripts, allowing Cleofilas a realistic escape with the help of Chicana feminist activists. Translating from ''La Llorona'' (weeping woman) to ''La Gritona'' (shouting woman) to the English ''Woman Hollering Creek'' allows a greater set of possibilities for interpreting the cry of the restless spirit. With its haunting sound of wind and water, the creek speaks with an enigmatic voice—crying, weeping, wailing, shouting, hollering ''like Tarzan,'' perhaps even laughing—a voice too often denied in traditional representations of Latinas. Paradoxically, ''La Llorona,'' a woman silenced in life, wails her grief in death. Cleofilas learns to decode a feminist message of survival in the haunted voice of the creek that hollers with the rage of a silenced woman. Much as Chicana feminists have revised folklore, legend, and myth to open up possibilities for new representations of women, the activism of Felice and her *companeras* helps Cleofilas to reinterpret the message of La Gritona, translating her voice from a wail, to a holler, to a shout, to laughter; from an *arroyo* associated with a tragic legend to ''a creek . . . full of happily ever after.''

"Much as Chicana feminists have revised folklore, legend, and myth to open up possibilities for new representations of women, the activism of Felice and her companeras helps Cleofilas to reinterpret the message of La Gritona, translating her voice from a wail, to a holler, to a shout, to laughter; from an arroyo associated with a tragic legend to 'a creek . . . full of happily ever after'."

Searching for and validating folk and popular articulations often excluded from ''the literary,'' Cisneros employs throughout the entire text of *Woman Hollering Creek* a network of epigraphs taken, not from the literary traditions of the United States or Europe or Latin America, but instead from Mexican ballads and romantic popular songs that circulate throughout, and indeed help to constitute, Spanish-speaking communities through dissemination of recordings, through jukeboxes located in restaurants and nightclubs located (along with *tortillerias, mercados, cines,* and *botanicas*) in Latino neighborhoods, and through Spanish-language radio stations broadcasting to cities or geographic regions with large Spanish-speaking populations. Cisneros privileges such commercial/cultural sites in which commodities and services are aimed at a culturally specific clientele, such as the cinemas

> "Cisneros's text registers tensions implicit in a community where the border between the U.S. and Mexico is reproduced within the psyche of the individual, and where the 'Mericans' are also the 'Mexicans.'"

devoted to the showing of films from Mexico or *telenovelas,* soap operas, produced for Mexican television and syndicated in the U.S.

The church functions similarly, as a cultural as well as religious site: specifically as a site of origin for insider discourses specific to Mexican-American and other Latino cultures, through the exchange of prayers and religious services for offerings made and thanks given by devout Catholics whose religion syncretically embraces folk beliefs. Cisneros recognizes and acknowledges the prayers of ordinary people addressing the Christian God, Catholic saints fused with Aztec goddesses, and even African deities, as a folk discourse worthy of inclusion in a literary text of an emergent minority literature. As Rosario offers her braid to the Virgin in thanks for the opportunity to become an artist rather than a mother, Cisneros offers her book (with its elaborate list of acknowledgments to family, friends, colleagues, *la Divina Providencia,* and *Virgen de Guadalupe Tonantzin*) as a kind of literary ex voto devoted to Chicano culture. Her text associates this folk genre with the religious articles and folk healing paraphernalia referred to in "Anguiano Religious Articles," "Little Miracles, Kept Promises" and "*Bien* Pretty." These religious or quasi-religious cultural sites, like such fixtures of U.S. commercial culture as Kwik Wash laundromats, K-Mart, Woolworth's, Cash N Carry, Luby's Cafeteria, and flea markets where fire-damaged Barbie doll Dream Houses can be purchased by families who could not afford to buy them even at K-Mart, are markers of class and gender, as well as sites for the reproduction of the dominant culture and the production of a resistant ethnic minority culture, which is neither entirely of the U.S. nor Mexico. . . .

Cisneros's text registers tensions implicit in a community where the border between the U.S. and Mexico is reproduced within the psyche of the individual, and where the "Mericans" are also the "Mexicans." The computer spell checker suggests "Mexican" as a substitute for "Merican," Cisneros's paragrammatic truncation of "American." The alteration, like translation, makes distinct signifiers equivalent. The words are equal in length if not identical in meaning. After all, Mexicans are Americans and, as the North American Free Trade Agreement reminds those who needed reminding, Mexico is part of North America. The spell checker also suggests "Moroccan" as a possible replacement for the unrecognized word, but that is another story.

Source: Harryette Mullen, "'A Silence Between Us Like a Language': The Untranslatability of Experience in Sandra Cisneros's *Woman Hollering Creek,*" in *MELUS,* Vol. 21, No. 2, Summer, 1996, pp. 3–20.

Sources

Anzaldua, Gloria. *Borderlands/La Frontera: The New Mestiza,* Spinsters/Aunt Lute, 1987.

Campbell, Bebe Moore. "Crossing Borders," in *The New York Times Book Review,* May 26, 1991, pp. 6-7.

Candelaria, Cordelia. "La Malinche, Feminist Prototype," in *Frontiers,* Vol. 5, No. 2, 1980, pp. 1-6.

Candelaria, Cordelia. "Letting La Llorona Go, or Re/reading History's Tender Mercies," in *Heresies,* Vol. 7, No. 3, 1993, pp. 111-15.

Cisneros, Sandra. "Ghost and Voices: Writing from Obsession," an excerpt from "From a Writer's Notebook," in *The Americas Review,* Vol. 15, No. 1, Spring, 1987, p. 73.

Doyle, Jacqueline. "Haunting the Borderlands: La Llorona in Sandra Cisneros's 'Woman Hollering Creek'," in *Frontiers,* Vol. 16, No. 1, Winter, 1996, pp. 53-71.

Dasenbrock, Reed and Feroza Jussawalla. *Interviews with Writers of the Post-Colonial World,* University Press of Mississippi, 1992.

Paz, Octavio. *Labyrinth of Solitude: Life and Thought in Mexico,* translated by Lysander Kemp, Grove Press, 1950.

Prescott, Peter and Karen Springen. "Seven for Summer," in *Newsweek,* June 3, 1991, p. 60.

Wyatt, Jean. "On Not Being La Malinche: Border Negotiations of Gender in Sandra Cisneros's 'Never Marry a Mexican' and 'Woman Hollering Creek'," in *Tulsa Studies in Women's Literature,* Vol. 14, No. 2, Fall, 1995, pp. 243-71.

Further Reading

Chavez, Lorenzo. ''Woman Hollering Creek and Other Stories,'' in *Hispanic,* April, 1991, p. 52.

Offers a brief overview of *Woman Hollering Creek,* praising the collection's language, humor, and realistic depiction of barrio life.

Ponce, Merrihelen. ''A Semblance of Order to Lives and Loves,'' in *Belles Lettres: A Review of Books by Women,* Vol. 7, No. 2, Winter, 1991–92, pp. 40, 44.

Laudatory overview of *Woman Hollering Creek,* claiming that, unlike Cisneros's earlier fiction, this collection ''resonates with voices of wiser Mexicanas/Chicanas.''

''Sandra Cisneros,'' in *Contemporary Literary Criticism,* Volume 69, edited by Roger Matuz, Gale, 1992, pp. 143-56.

Reprinted criticism on Cisneros's early works. Included are excerpted essays by Julian Olivares, Barbara Kingsolver, and Bebe Moore Campbell, among others.

Glossary of Literary Terms

A

Aestheticism: A literary and artistic movement of the nineteenth century. Followers of the movement believed that art should not be mixed with social, political, or moral teaching. The statement "art for art's sake" is a good summary of aestheticism. The movement had its roots in France, but it gained widespread importance in England in the last half of the nineteenth century, where it helped change the Victorian practice of including moral lessons in literature. Edgar Allan Poe is one of the best-known American "aesthetes."

Allegory: A narrative technique in which characters representing things or abstract ideas are used to convey a message or teach a lesson. Allegory is typically used to teach moral, ethical, or religious lessons but is sometimes used for satiric or political purposes. Many fairy tales are allegories.

Allusion: A reference to a familiar literary or historical person or event, used to make an idea more easily understood. Joyce Carol Oates's story "Where Are You Going, Where Have You Been?" exhibits several allusions to popular music.

Analogy: A comparison of two things made to explain something unfamiliar through its similarities to something familiar, or to prove one point based on the acceptance of another. Similes and metaphors are types of analogies.

Antagonist: The major character in a narrative or drama who works against the hero or protagonist. The Misfit in Flannery O'Connor's story "A Good Man Is Hard to Find" serves as the antagonist for the Grandmother.

Anthology: A collection of similar works of literature, art, or music. Zora Neale Hurston's "The Eatonville Anthology" is a collection of stories that take place in the same town.

Anthropomorphism: The presentation of animals or objects in human shape or with human characteristics. The term is derived from the Greek word for "human form." The fur necklet in Katherine Mansfield's story "Miss Brill" has anthropomorphic characteristics.

Anti-hero: A central character in a work of literature who lacks traditional heroic qualities such as courage, physical prowess, and fortitude. Anti-heroes typically distrust conventional values and are unable to commit themselves to any ideals. They generally feel helpless in a world over which they have no control. Anti-heroes usually accept, and often celebrate, their positions as social outcasts. A well-known anti-hero is Walter Mitty in James Thurber's story "The Secret Life of Walter Mitty."

Archetype: The word archetype is commonly used to describe an original pattern or model from which all other things of the same kind are made. Archetypes are the literary images that grow out of the "collective unconscious,'' a theory proposed by psychologist Carl Jung. They appear in literature as incidents and plots that repeat basic patterns of life. They may also appear as stereotyped characters. The ''schlemiel'' of Yiddish literature is an archetype.

Autobiography: A narrative in which an individual tells his or her life story. Examples include Benjamin Franklin's *Autobiography* and Amy Hempel's story ''In the Cemetery Where Al Jolson Is Buried,'' which has autobiographical characteristics even though it is a work of fiction.

Avant-garde: A literary term that describes new writing that rejects traditional approaches to literature in favor of innovations in style or content. Twentieth-century examples of the literary *avant-garde* include the modernists and the minimalists.

B

Belles-lettres: A French term meaning ''fine letters'' or ''beautiful writing.'' It is often used as a synonym for literature, typically referring to imaginative and artistic rather than scientific or expository writing. Current usage sometimes restricts the meaning to light or humorous writing and appreciative essays about literature. Lewis Carroll's *Alice in Wonderland* epitomizes the realm of belles-lettres.

Bildungsroman: A German word meaning ''novel of development.'' The *bildungsroman* is a study of the maturation of a youthful character, typically brought about through a series of social or sexual encounters that lead to self-awareness. J. D. Salinger's *Catcher in the Rye* is a *bildungsroman*, and Doris Lessing's story ''Through the Tunnel'' exhibits characteristics of a *bildungsroman* as well.

Black Aesthetic Movement: A period of artistic and literary development among African Americans in the 1960s and early 1970s. This was the first major African-American artistic movement since the Harlem Renaissance and was closely paralleled by the civil rights and black power movements. The black aesthetic writers attempted to produce works of art that would be meaningful to the black masses. Key figures in black aesthetics included one of its founders, poet and playwright Amiri Baraka, formerly known as LeRoi Jones; poet and essayist Haki R. Madhubuti, formerly Don L. Lee; poet and playwright Sonia Sanchez; and dramatist Ed Bullins. Works representative of the Black Aesthetic Movement include Amiri Baraka's play *Dutchman,* a 1964 Obie award-winner.

Black Humor: Writing that places grotesque elements side by side with humorous ones in an attempt to shock the reader, forcing him or her to laugh at the horrifying reality of a disordered world. ''Lamb to the Slaughter,'' by Roald Dahl, in which a placid housewife murders her husband and serves the murder weapon to the investigating policemen, is an example of black humor.

C

Catharsis: The release or purging of unwanted emotions—specifically fear and pity—brought about by exposure to art. The term was first used by the Greek philosopher Aristotle in his *Poetics* to refer to the desired effect of tragedy on spectators.

Character: Broadly speaking, a person in a literary work. The actions of characters are what constitute the plot of a story, novel, or poem. There are numerous types of characters, ranging from simple, stereotypical figures to intricate, multifaceted ones. ''Characterization'' is the process by which an author creates vivid, believable characters in a work of art. This may be done in a variety of ways, including (1) direct description of the character by the narrator; (2) the direct presentation of the speech, thoughts, or actions of the character; and (3) the responses of other characters to the character. The term ''character'' also refers to a form originated by the ancient Greek writer Theophrastus that later became popular in the seventeenth and eighteenth centuries. It is a short essay or sketch of a person who prominently displays a specific attribute or quality, such as miserliness or ambition. ''Miss Brill,'' a story by Katherine Mansfield, is an example of a character sketch.

Classical: In its strictest definition in literary criticism, classicism refers to works of ancient Greek or Roman literature. The term may also be used to describe a literary work of recognized importance (a ''classic'') from any time period or literature that exhibits the traits of classicism. Examples of later works and authors now described as classical include French literature of the seventeenth century, Western novels of the nineteenth century, and American fiction of the mid-nineteenth century such as that written by James Fenimore Cooper and Mark Twain.

Climax: The turning point in a narrative, the moment when the conflict is at its most intense. Typically, the structure of stories, novels, and plays is one of rising action, in which tension builds to the climax, followed by falling action, in which tension lessens as the story moves to its conclusion.

Comedy: One of two major types of drama, the other being tragedy. Its aim is to amuse, and it typically ends happily. Comedy assumes many forms, such as farce and burlesque, and uses a variety of techniques, from parody to satire. In a restricted sense the term comedy refers only to dramatic presentations, but in general usage it is commonly applied to nondramatic works as well.

Comic Relief: The use of humor to lighten the mood of a serious or tragic story, especially in plays. The technique is very common in Elizabethan works, and can be an integral part of the plot or simply a brief event designed to break the tension of the scene.

Conflict: The conflict in a work of fiction is the issue to be resolved in the story. It usually occurs between two characters, the protagonist and the antagonist, or between the protagonist and society or the protagonist and himself or herself. The conflict in Washington Irving's story ''The Devil and Tom Walker'' is that the Devil wants Tom Walker's soul, but Tom does not want to go to hell.

Criticism: The systematic study and evaluation of literary works, usually based on a specific method or set of principles. An important part of literary studies since ancient times, the practice of criticism has given rise to numerous theories, methods, and ''schools,'' sometimes producing conflicting, even contradictory, interpretations of literature in general as well as of individual works. Even such basic issues as what constitutes a poem or a novel have been the subject of much criticism over the centuries. Seminal texts of literary criticism include Plato's *Republic,* Aristotle's *Poetics,* Sir Philip Sidney's *The Defence of Poesie,* and John Dryden's *Of Dramatic Poesie.* Contemporary schools of criticism include deconstruction, feminist, psychoanalytic, poststructuralist, new historicist, postcolonialist, and reader-response.

D

Deconstruction: A method of literary criticism characterized by multiple conflicting interpretations of a given work. Deconstructionists consider the impact of the language of a work and suggest that the true meaning of the work is not necessarily the meaning that the author intended.

Deduction: The process of reaching a conclusion through reasoning from general premises to a specific premise. Arthur Conan Doyle's character Sherlock Holmes often used deductive reasoning to solve mysteries.

Denotation: The definition of a word, apart from the impressions or feelings it creates in the reader. The word ''apartheid'' denotes a political and economic policy of segregation by race, but its connotations—oppression, slavery, inequality—are numerous.

***Denouement*:** A French word meaning ''the unknotting.'' In literature, it denotes the resolution of conflict in fiction or drama. The *denouement* follows the climax and provides an outcome to the primary plot situation as well as an explanation of secondary plot complications. A well-known example of *denouement* is the last scene of the play *As You Like It* by William Shakespeare, in which couples are married, an evil-doer repents, the identities of two disguised characters are revealed, and a ruler is restored to power. Also known as ''falling action.''

Detective Story: A narrative about the solution of a mystery or the identification of a criminal. The conventions of the detective story include the detective's scrupulous use of logic in solving the mystery; incompetent or ineffectual police; a suspect who appears guilty at first but is later proved innocent; and the detective's friend or confidant—often the narrator—whose slowness in interpreting clues emphasizes by contrast the detective's brilliance. Edgar Allan Poe's ''Murders in the Rue Morgue'' is commonly regarded as the earliest example of this type of story. Other practitioners are Arthur Conan Doyle, Dashiell Hammett, and Agatha Christie.

Dialogue: Dialogue is conversation between people in a literary work. In its most restricted sense, it refers specifically to the speech of characters in a drama. As a specific literary genre, a ''dialogue'' is a composition in which characters debate an issue or idea.

Didactic: A term used to describe works of literature that aim to teach a moral, religious, political, or practical lesson. Although didactic elements are often found inartistically pleasing works, the term ''didactic'' usually refers to literature in which the message is more important than the form. The term may also be used to criticize a work that the critic finds ''overly didactic,'' that is, heavy-handed in its delivery of a lesson. An example of didactic literature is John Bunyan's *Pilgrim's Progress.*

Dramatic Irony: Occurs when the reader of a work of literature knows something that a character in the work itself does not know. The irony is in the contrast between the intended meaning of the statements or actions of a character and the additional information understood by the audience.

Dystopia: An imaginary place in a work of fiction where the characters lead dehumanized, fearful lives. George Orwell's *Nineteen Eighty-four,* and Margaret Atwood's *Handmaid's Tale* portray versions of dystopia.

E

Edwardian: Describes cultural conventions identified with the period of the reign of Edward VII of England (1901-1910). Writers of the Edwardian Age typically displayed a strong reaction against the propriety and conservatism of the Victorian Age. Their work often exhibits distrust of authority in religion, politics, and art and expresses strong doubts about the soundness of conventional values. Writers of this era include E. M. Forster, H. G. Wells, and Joseph Conrad.

Empathy: A sense of shared experience, including emotional and physical feelings, with someone or something other than oneself. Empathy is often used to describe the response of a reader to a literary character.

Epilogue: A concluding statement or section of a literary work. In dramas, particularly those of the seventeenth and eighteenth centuries, the epilogue is a closing speech, often in verse, delivered by an actor at the end of a play and spoken directly to the audience.

Epiphany: A sudden revelation of truth inspired by a seemingly trivial incident. The term was widely used by James Joyce in his critical writings, and the stories in Joyce's *Dubliners* are commonly called "epiphanies."

Epistolary Novel: A novel in the form of letters. The form was particularly popular in the eighteenth century. The form can also be applied to short stories, as in Edwidge Danticat's "Children of the Sea."

Epithet: A word or phrase, often disparaging or abusive, that expresses a character trait of someone or something. "The Napoleon of crime" is an epithet applied to Professor Moriarty, arch-rival of Sherlock Holmes in Arthur Conan Doyle's series of detective stories.

Existentialism: A predominantly twentieth-century philosophy concerned with the nature and perception of human existence. There are two major strains of existentialist thought: atheistic and Christian. Followers of atheistic existentialism believe that the individual is alone in a godless universe and that the basic human condition is one of suffering and loneliness. Nevertheless, because there are no fixed values, individuals can create their own characters—indeed, they can shape themselves—through the exercise of free will. The atheistic strain culminates in and is popularly associated with the works of Jean-Paul Sartre. The Christian existentialists, on the other hand, believe that only in God may people find freedom from life's anguish. The two strains hold certain beliefs in common: that existence cannot be fully understood or described through empirical effort; that anguish is a universal element of life; that individuals must bear responsibility for their actions; and that there is no common standard of behavior or perception for religious and ethical matters. Existentialist thought figures prominently in the works of such authors as Franz Kafka, Fyodor Dostoyevsky, and Albert Camus.

Expatriatism: The practice of leaving one's country to live for an extended period in another country. Literary expatriates include Irish author James Joyce who moved to Italy and France; American writers James Baldwin, Ernest Hemingway, Gertrude Stein, and F. Scott Fitzgerald who lived and wrote in Paris; and Polish novelist Joseph Conrad, who lived in England.

Exposition: Writing intended to explain the nature of an idea, thing, or theme. Expository writing is often combined with description, narration, or argument.

Expressionism: An indistinct literary term, originally used to describe an early twentieth-century school of German painting. The term applies to almost any mode of unconventional, highly subjective writing that distorts reality in some way. Advocates of Expressionism include Federico Garcia Lorca, Eugene O'Neill, Franz Kafka, and James Joyce.

F

Fable: A prose or verse narrative intended to convey a moral. Animals or inanimate objects with human characteristics often serve as characters in fables. A famous fable is Aesop's "The Tortoise and the Hare."

Fantasy: A literary form related to mythology and folklore. Fantasy literature is typically set in non-existent realms and features supernatural beings. Notable examples of literature with elements of fantasy are Gabriel Garcia Marquez's story "The Handsomest Drowned Man in the World" and Ursula K. LeGuin's "The Ones Who Walk Away from Omelas."

Farce: A type of comedy characterized by broad humor, outlandish incidents, and often vulgar subject matter. Much of the comedy in film and television could more accurately be described as farce.

Fiction: Any story that is the product of imagination rather than a documentation of fact. Characters and events in such narratives may be based in real life but their ultimate form and configuration is a creation of the author.

Figurative Language: A technique in which an author uses figures of speech such as hyperbole, irony, metaphor, or simile for a particular effect. Figurative language is the opposite of literal language, in which every word is truthful, accurate, and free of exaggeration or embellishment.

Flashback: A device used in literature to present action that occurred before the beginning of the story. Flashbacks are often introduced as the dreams or recollections of one or more characters.

Foil: A character in a work of literature whose physical or psychological qualities contrast strongly with, and therefore highlight, the corresponding qualities of another character. In his Sherlock Holmes stories, Arthur Conan Doyle portrayed Dr. Watson as a man of normal habits and intelligence, making him a foil for the eccentric and unusually perceptive Sherlock Holmes.

Folklore: Traditions and myths preserved in a culture or group of people. Typically, these are passed on by word of mouth in various forms—such as legends, songs, and proverbs—or preserved in customs and ceremonies. Washington Irving, in "The Devil and Tom Walker" and many of his other stories, incorporates many elements of the folklore of New England and Germany.

Folktale: A story originating in oral tradition. Folktales fall into a variety of categories, including legends, ghost stories, fairy tales, fables, and anecdotes based on historical figures and events.

Foreshadowing: A device used in literature to create expectation or to set up an explanation of later developments. Edgar Allan Poe uses foreshadowing to create suspense in "The Fall of the House of Usher" when the narrator comments on the crumbling state of disrepair in which he finds the house.

G

Genre: A category of literary work. Genre may refer to both the content of a given work—tragedy, comedy, horror, science fiction—and to its form, such as poetry, novel, or drama.

Gilded Age: A period in American history during the 1870s and after characterized by political corruption and materialism. A number of important novels of social and political criticism were written during this time. Henry James and Kate Chopin are two writers who were prominent during the Gilded Age.

Gothicism: In literature, works characterized by a taste for medieval or morbid characters and situations. A gothic novel prominently features elements of horror, the supernatural, gloom, and violence: clanking chains, terror, ghosts, medieval castles, and unexplained phenomena. The term "gothic novel" is also applied to novels that lack elements of the traditional gothic setting but that create a similar atmosphere of terror or dread. The term can also be applied to stories, plays, and poems. Mary Shelley's *Frankenstein* and Joyce Carol Oates's *Bellefleur* are both gothic novels.

Grotesque: In literature, a work that is characterized by exaggeration, deformity, freakishness, and disorder. The grotesque often includes an element of comic absurdity. Examples of the grotesque can be found in the works of Edgar Allan Poe, Flannery O'Connor, Joseph Heller, and Shirley Jackson.

H

Harlem Renaissance: The Harlem Renaissance of the 1920s is generally considered the first significant movement of black writers and artists in the United States. During this period, new and established black writers, many of whom lived in the region of New York City known as Harlem, published more fiction and poetry than ever before, the first influential black literary journals were established, and black authors and artists received their first widespread recognition and serious critical appraisal. Among the major writers associated with this period are Countee Cullen, Langston Hughes, Arna Bontemps, and Zora Neale Hurston.

Hero/Heroine: The principal sympathetic character in a literary work. Heroes and heroines typically exhibit admirable traits: idealism, courage, and integrity, for example. Famous heroes and heroines of literature include Charles Dickens's Oliver Twist, Margaret Mitchell's Scarlett O'Hara, and the anonymous narrator in Ralph Ellison's *Invisible Man.*

Hyperbole: Deliberate exaggeration used to achieve an effect. In William Shakespeare's *Macbeth,* Lady Macbeth hyperbolizes when she says, ''All the perfumes of Arabia could not sweeten this little hand.''

I

Image: A concrete representation of an object or sensory experience. Typically, such a representation helps evoke the feelings associated with the object or experience itself. Images are either ''literal'' or ''figurative.'' Literal images are especially concrete and involve little or no extension of the obvious meaning of the words used to express them. Figurative images do not follow the literal meaning of the words exactly. Images in literature are usually visual, but the term ''image'' can also refer to the representation of any sensory experience.

Imagery: The array of images in a literary work. Also used to convey the author's overall use of figurative language in a work.

In medias res: A Latin term meaning ''in the middle of things.'' It refers to the technique of beginning a story at its midpoint and then using various flashback devices to reveal previous action. This technique originated in such epics as Virgil's *Aeneid.*

Interior Monologue: A narrative technique in which characters' thoughts are revealed in a way that appears to be uncontrolled by the author. The interior monologue typically aims to reveal the inner self of a character. It portrays emotional experiences as they occur at both a conscious and unconscious level. One of the best-known interior monologues in English is the Molly Bloom section at the close of James Joyce's *Ulysses.* Katherine Anne Porter's ''The Jilting of Granny Weatherall'' is also told in the form of an interior monologue.

Irony: In literary criticism, the effect of language in which the intended meaning is the opposite of what is stated. The title of Jonathan Swift's ''A Modest Proposal'' is ironic because what Swift proposes in this essay is cannibalism—hardly ''modest.''

J

Jargon: Language that is used or understood only by a select group of people. Jargon may refer to terminology used in a certain profession, such as computer jargon, or it may refer to any nonsensical language that is not understood by most people. Anthony Burgess's *A Clockwork Orange* and James Thurber's ''The Secret Life of Walter Mitty'' both use jargon.

K

Knickerbocker Group: An indistinct group of New York writers of the first half of the nineteenth century. Members of the group were linked only by location and a common theme: New York life. Two famous members of the Knickerbocker Group were Washington Irving and William Cullen Bryant. The group's name derives from Irving's *Knickerbocker's History of New York.*

L

Literal Language: An author uses literal language when he or she writes without exaggerating or embellishing the subject matter and without any tools of figurative language. To say ''He ran very quickly down the street'' is to use literal language, whereas to say ''He ran like a hare down the street'' would be using figurative language.

Literature: Literature is broadly defined as any written or spoken material, but the term most often refers to creative works. Literature includes poetry, drama, fiction, and many kinds of nonfiction writing, as well as oral, dramatic, and broadcast compositions not necessarily preserved in a written format, such as films and television programs.

Lost Generation: A term first used by Gertrude Stein to describe the post-World War I generation of American writers: men and women haunted by a sense of betrayal and emptiness brought about by the destructiveness of the war. The term is commonly applied to Hart Crane, Ernest Hemingway, F. Scott Fitzgerald, and others.

M

Magic Realism: A form of literature that incorporates fantasy elements or supernatural occurrences into the narrative and accepts them as truth. Gabriel Garcia Marquez and Laura Esquivel are two writers known for their works of magic realism.

Metaphor: A figure of speech that expresses an idea through the image of another object. Metaphors suggest the essence of the first object by identifying it with certain qualities of the second object. An example is "But soft, what light through yonder window breaks? / It is the east, and Juliet is the sun" in William Shakespeare's *Romeo and Juliet.* Here, Juliet, the first object, is identified with qualities of the second object, the sun.

Minimalism: A literary style characterized by spare, simple prose with few elaborations. In minimalism, the main theme of the work is often never discussed directly. Amy Hempel and Ernest Hemingway are two writers known for their works of minimalism.

Modernism: Modern literary practices. Also, the principles of a literary school that lasted from roughly the beginning of the twentieth century until the end of World War II. Modernism is defined by its rejection of the literary conventions of the nineteenth century and by its opposition to conventional morality, taste, traditions, and economic values. Many writers are associated with the concepts of modernism, including Albert Camus, D. H. Lawrence, Ernest Hemingway, William Faulkner, Eugene O'Neill, and James Joyce.

Monologue: A composition, written or oral, by a single individual. More specifically, a speech given by a single individual in a drama or other public entertainment. It has no set length, although it is usually several or more lines long. "I Stand Here Ironing" by Tillie Olsen is an example of a story written in the form of a monologue.

Mood: The prevailing emotions of a work or of the author in his or her creation of the work. The mood of a work is not always what might be expected based on its subject matter.

Motif: A theme, character type, image, metaphor, or other verbal element that recurs throughout a single work of literature or occurs in a number of different works over a period of time. For example, the color white in Herman Melville's *Moby Dick* is a "specific" motif, while the trials of star-crossed lovers is a "conventional" motif from the literature of all periods.

N

Narration: The telling of a series of events, real or invented. A narration may be either a simple narrative, in which the events are recounted chronologically, or a narrative with a plot, in which the account is given in a style reflecting the author's artistic concept of the story. Narration is sometimes used as a synonym for "storyline."

Narrative: A verse or prose accounting of an event or sequence of events, real or invented. The term is also used as an adjective in the sense "method of narration." For example, in literary criticism, the expression "narrative technique" usually refers to the way the author structures and presents his or her story. Different narrative forms include diaries, travelogues, novels, ballads, epics, short stories, and other fictional forms.

Narrator: The teller of a story. The narrator may be the author or a character in the story through whom the author speaks. Huckleberry Finn is the narrator of Mark Twain's *The Adventures of Huckleberry Finn.*

Novella: An Italian term meaning "story." This term has been especially used to describe fourteenth-century Italian tales, but it also refers to modern short novels. Modern novellas include Leo Tolstoy's *The Death of Ivan Ilych,* Fyodor Dostoyevsky's *Notes from the Underground,* and Joseph Conrad's *Heart of Darkness.*

O

Oedipus Complex: A son's romantic obsession with his mother. The phrase is derived from the story of the ancient Theban hero Oedipus, who unknowingly killed his father and married his mother, and was popularized by Sigmund Freud's theory of psychoanalysis. Literary occurrences of the Oedipus complex include Sophocles' *Oedipus Rex* and D. H. Lawrence's "The Rocking-Horse Winner."

Onomatopoeia: The use of words whose sounds express or suggest their meaning. In its simplest sense, onomatopoeia may be represented by words that mimic the sounds they denote such as "hiss" or "meow." At a more subtle level, the pattern and rhythm of sounds and rhymes of a line or poem may be onomatopoeic.

Oral Tradition: A process by which songs, ballads, folklore, and other material are transmitted by word of mouth. The tradition of oral transmission predates the written record systems of literate society.

Oral transmission preserves material sometimes over generations, although often with variations. Memory plays a large part in the recitation and preservation of orally transmitted material. Native American myths and legends, and African folktales told by plantation slaves are examples of orally transmitted literature.

P

Parable: A story intended to teach a moral lesson or answer an ethical question. Examples of parables are the stories told by Jesus Christ in the New Testament, notably ''The Prodigal Son,'' but parables also are used in Sufism, rabbinic literature, Hasidism, and Zen Buddhism. Isaac Bashevis Singer's story ''Gimpel the Fool'' exhibits characteristics of a parable.

Paradox: A statement that appears illogical or contradictory at first, but may actually point to an underlying truth. A literary example of a paradox is George Orwell's statement ''All animals are equal, but some animals are more equal than others'' in *Animal Farm.*

Parody: In literature, this term refers to an imitation of a serious literary work or the signature style of a particular author in a ridiculous manner. A typical parody adopts the style of the original and applies it to an inappropriate subject for humorous effect. Parody is a form of satire and could be considered the literary equivalent of a caricature or cartoon. Henry Fielding's *Shamela* is a parody of Samuel Richardson's *Pamela.*

Persona: A Latin term meaning ''mask.'' Personae are the characters in a fictional work of literature. The persona generally functions as a mask through which the author tells a story in a voice other than his or her own. A persona is usually either a character in a story who acts as a narrator or an ''implied author,'' a voice created by the author to act as the narrator for himself or herself. The persona in Charlotte Perkins Gilman's story ''The Yellow Wallpaper'' is the unnamed young mother experiencing a mental breakdown.

Personification: A figure of speech that gives human qualities to abstract ideas, animals, and inanimate objects. To say that ''the sun is smiling'' is to personify the sun.

Plot: The pattern of events in a narrative or drama. In its simplest sense, the plot guides the author in composing the work and helps the reader follow the work. Typically, plots exhibit causality and unity and have a beginning, a middle, and an end. Sometimes, however, a plot may consist of a series of disconnected events, in which case it is known as an ''episodic plot.''

Poetic Justice: An outcome in a literary work, not necessarily a poem, in which the good are rewarded and the evil are punished, especially in ways that particularly fit their virtues or crimes. For example, a murderer may himself be murdered, or a thief will find himself penniless.

Poetic License: Distortions of fact and literary convention made by a writer—not always a poet—for the sake of the effect gained. Poetic license is closely related to the concept of ''artistic freedom.'' An author exercises poetic license by saying that a pile of money ''reaches as high as a mountain'' when the pile is actually only a foot or two high.

Point of View: The narrative perspective from which a literary work is presented to the reader. There are four traditional points of view. The ''third-person omniscient'' gives the reader a ''godlike'' perspective, unrestricted by time or place, from which to see actions and look into the minds of characters. This allows the author to comment openly on characters and events in the work. The ''third person'' point of view presents the events of the story from outside of any single character's perception, much like the omniscient point of view, but the reader must understand the action as it takes place and without any special insight into characters's minds or motivations. The ''first person'' or ''personal'' point of view relates events as they are perceived by a single character. The main character ''tells'' the story and may offer opinions about the action and characters which differ from those of the author. Much less common than omniscient, third person, and first person is the ''second person'' point of view, wherein the author tells the story as if it is happening to the reader. James Thurber employs the omniscient point of view in his short story ''The Secret Life of Walter Mitty.'' Ernest Hemingway's ''A Clean, Well-Lighted Place'' is a short story told from the third-person point of view. Mark Twain's novel *Huckleberry Finn* is presented from the first-person viewpoint. Jay McInerney's *Bright Lights, Big City* is an example of a novel which uses the second person point of view.

Pornography: Writing intended to provoke feelings of lust in the reader. Such works are often condemned by critics and teachers, but those which can be shown to have literary value are viewed less harshly. Literary works that have been described as pornographic include D. H. Lawrence's *Lady Chatterley's Lover* and James Joyce's *Ulysses.*

Post-Aesthetic Movement: An artistic response made by African Americans to the black aesthetic movement of the 1960s and early 1970s. Writers since that time have adopted a somewhat different tone in their work, with less emphasis placed on the disparity between black and white in the United States. In the words of post-aesthetic authors such as Toni Morrison, John Edgar Wideman, and Kristin Hunter, African Americans are portrayed as looking inward for answers to their own questions, rather than always looking to the outside world. Two well-known examples of works produced as part of the post-aesthetic movement are the Pulitzer Prize-winning novels *The Color Purple* by Alice Walker and *Beloved* by Toni Morrison.

Postmodernism: Writing from the 1960s forward characterized by experimentation and application of modernist elements, which include existentialism and alienation. Postmodernists have gone a step further in the rejection of tradition begun with the modernists by also rejecting traditional forms, preferring the anti-novel over the novel and the anti-hero over the hero. Postmodern writers include Thomas Pynchon, Margaret Drabble, and Gabriel Garcia Marquez.

Prologue: An introductory section of a literary work. It often contains information establishing the situation of the characters or presents information about the setting, time period, or action. In drama, the prologue is spoken by a chorus or by one of the principal characters.

Prose: A literary medium that attempts to mirror the language of everyday speech. It is distinguished from poetry by its use of unmetered, unrhymed language consisting of logically related sentences. Prose is usually grouped into paragraphs that form a cohesive whole such as an essay or a novel. The term is sometimes used to mean an author's general writing.

Protagonist: The central character of a story who serves as a focus for its themes and incidents and as the principal rationale for its development. The protagonist is sometimes referred to in discussions of modern literature as the hero or anti-hero. Well-known protagonists are Hamlet in William Shakespeare's *Hamlet* and Jay Gatsby in F. Scott Fitzgerald's *The Great Gatsby.*

R

Realism: A nineteenth-century European literary movement that sought to portray familiar characters, situations, and settings in a realistic manner. This was done primarily by using an objective narrative point of view and through the buildup of accurate detail. The standard for success of any realistic work depends on how faithfully it transfers common experience into fictional forms. The realistic method may be altered or extended, as in stream of consciousness writing, to record highly subjective experience. Contemporary authors who often write in a realistic way include Nadine Gordimer and Grace Paley.

Resolution: The portion of a story following the climax, in which the conflict is resolved. The resolution of Jane Austen's *Northanger Abbey* is neatly summed up in the following sentence: ''Henry and Catherine were married, the bells rang and everybody smiled.''

Rising Action: The part of a drama where the plot becomes increasingly complicated. Rising action leads up to the climax, or turning point, of a drama. The final ''chase scene'' of an action film is generally the rising action which culminates in the film's climax.

***Roman a clef*:** A French phrase meaning ''novel with a key.'' It refers to a narrative in which real persons are portrayed under fictitious names. Jack Kerouac, for example, portrayed his various friends under fictitious names in the novel *On the Road.* D. H. Lawrence based ''The Rocking-Horse Winner'' on a family he knew.

Romanticism: This term has two widely accepted meanings. In historical criticism, it refers to a European intellectual and artistic movement of the late eighteenth and early nineteenth centuries that sought greater freedom of personal expression than that allowed by the strict rules of literary form and logic of the eighteenth-century neoclassicists. The Romantics preferred emotional and imaginative expression to rational analysis. They considered the individual to be at the center of all experience and so placed him or her at the center of their art. The Romantics believed that the creative imagination reveals nobler truths—unique feelings and attitudes—than those that could be discovered by logic or by scientific examination. ''Romanticism'' is also used as a general term to refer to a type of sensibility found in all periods of literary history and usually considered to be in opposition to the principles of classicism. In this sense, Romanticism signifies any work or philosophy in which the exotic or dreamlike figure strongly, or that is devoted to individualistic expression, self-analysis, or a pursuit of a higher realm of knowledge than can be discovered by human reason. Prominent Romantics include Jean-Jacques Rousseau, William Wordsworth, John Keats, Lord Byron, and Johann Wolfgang von Goethe.

S

Satire: A work that uses ridicule, humor, and wit to criticize and provoke change in human nature and institutions. Voltaire's novella *Candide* and Jonathan Swift's essay "A Modest Proposal" are both satires. Flannery O'Connor's portrayal of the family in "A Good Man Is Hard to Find" is a satire of a modern, Southern, American family.

Science Fiction: A type of narrative based upon real or imagined scientific theories and technology. Science fiction is often peopled with alien creatures and set on other planets or in different dimensions. Popular writers of science fiction are Isaac Asimov, Karel Capek, Ray Bradbury, and Ursula K. Le Guin.

Setting: The time, place, and culture in which the action of a narrative takes place. The elements of setting may include geographic location, characters's physical and mental environments, prevailing cultural attitudes, or the historical time in which the action takes place.

Short Story: A fictional prose narrative shorter and more focused than a novella. The short story usually deals with a single episode and often a single character. The "tone," the author's attitude toward his or her subject and audience, is uniform throughout. The short story frequently also lacks *denouement*, ending instead at its climax.

Signifying Monkey: A popular trickster figure in black folklore, with hundreds of tales about this character documented since the 19th century. Henry Louis Gates Jr. examines the history of the signifying monkey in *The Signifying Monkey: Towards a Theory of Afro-American Literary Criticism,* published in 1988.

Simile: A comparison, usually using "like" or "as," of two essentially dissimilar things, as in "coffee as cold as ice" or "He sounded like a broken record." The title of Ernest Hemingway's "Hills Like White Elephants" contains a simile.

Socialist Realism: The Socialist Realism school of literary theory was proposed by Maxim Gorky and established as a dogma by the first Soviet Congress of Writers. It demanded adherence to a communist worldview in works of literature. Its doctrines required an objective viewpoint comprehensible to the working classes and themes of social struggle featuring strong proletarian heroes. Gabriel Garcia Marquez's stories exhibit some characteristics of Socialist Realism.

Stereotype: A stereotype was originally the name for a duplication made during the printing process; this led to its modern definition as a person or thing that is (or is assumed to be) the same as all others of its type. Common stereotypical characters include the absent-minded professor, the nagging wife, the troublemaking teenager, and the kindhearted grandmother.

Stream of Consciousness: A narrative technique for rendering the inward experience of a character. This technique is designed to give the impression of an ever-changing series of thoughts, emotions, images, and memories in the spontaneous and seemingly illogical order that they occur in life. The textbook example of stream of consciousness is the last section of James Joyce's *Ulysses.*

Structure: The form taken by a piece of literature. The structure may be made obvious for ease of understanding, as in nonfiction works, or may obscured for artistic purposes, as in some poetry or seemingly "unstructured" prose.

Style: A writer's distinctive manner of arranging words to suit his or her ideas and purpose in writing. The unique imprint of the author's personality upon his or her writing, style is the product of an author's way of arranging ideas and his or her use of diction, different sentence structures, rhythm, figures of speech, rhetorical principles, and other elements of composition.

Suspense: A literary device in which the author maintains the audience's attention through the buildup of events, the outcome of which will soon be revealed. Suspense in William Shakespeare's *Hamlet* is sustained throughout by the question of whether or not the prince will achieve what he has been instructed to do.

Symbol: Something that suggests or stands for something else without losing its original identity. In literature, symbols combine their literal meaning with the suggestion of an abstract concept. Literary symbols are of two types: those that carry complex associations of meaning no matter what their contexts, and those that derive their suggestive meaning from their functions in specific literary works. Examples of symbols are sunshine suggesting happiness, rain suggesting sorrow, and storm clouds suggesting despair.

T

Tale: A story with a simple plot and little character development. Tales are usually relatively short and often carry a simple message. Examples of tales can be found in the works of Saki, Anton Chekhov, Guy de Maupassant, and O. Henry.

Tall Tale: A humorous tale told in a straightforward, credible tone but relating absolutely impossible events or feats of the characters. Such tales were commonly told of frontier adventures during the settlement of the West in the United States. Literary use of tall tales can be found in Washington Irving's *History of New York,* Mark Twain's *Life on the Mississippi,* and in the German R. F. Raspe's *Baron Munchausen's Narratives of His Marvellous Travels and Campaigns in Russia.*

Theme: The main point of a work of literature. The term is used interchangeably with thesis. Many works have multiple themes. One of the themes of Nathaniel Hawthorne's "Young Goodman Brown" is loss of faith.

Tone: The author's attitude toward his or her audience may be deduced from the tone of the work. A formal tone may create distance or convey politeness, while an informal tone may encourage a friendly, intimate, or intrusive feeling in the reader. The author's attitude toward his or her subject matter may also be deduced from the tone of the words he or she uses in discussing it. The tone of John F. Kennedy's speech which included the appeal to "ask not what your country can do for you" was intended to instill feelings of camaraderie and national pride in listeners.

Tragedy: A drama in prose or poetry about a noble, courageous hero of excellent character who, because of some tragic character flaw, brings ruin upon him or herself. Tragedy treats its subjects in a dignified and serious manner, using poetic language to help evoke pity and fear and bring about catharsis, a purging of these emotions. The tragic form was practiced extensively by the ancient Greeks. The classical form of tragedy was revived in the sixteenth century; it flourished especially on the Elizabethan stage. In modern times, dramatists have attempted to adapt the form to the needs of modern society by drawing their heroes from the ranks of ordinary men and women and defining the nobility of these heroes in terms of spirit rather than exalted social standing. Some contemporary works that are thought of as tragedies include *The Great Gatsby* by F. Scott Fitzgerald, and *The Sound and the Fury* by William Faulkner.

Tragic Flaw: In a tragedy, the quality within the hero or heroine which leads to his or her downfall. Examples of the tragic flaw include Othello's jealousy and Hamlet's indecisiveness, although most great tragedies defy such simple interpretation.

U-Z

Utopia: A fictional perfect place, such as "paradise" or "heaven." An early literary utopia was described in Plato's *Republic,* and in modern literature, Ursula K. Le Guin depicts a utopia in "The Ones Who Walk Away from Omelas."

Victorian: Refers broadly to the reign of Queen Victoria of England (1837-1901) and to anything with qualities typical of that era. For example, the qualities of smug narrow-mindedness, bourgeois materialism, faith in social progress, and priggish morality are often considered Victorian. In literature, the Victorian Period was the great age of the English novel, and the latter part of the era saw the rise of movements such as decadence and symbolism.

Cumulative Author/Title Index

Nationality/Ethnicity Index

Subject/Theme Index

*Boldface terms appear as subheads in Themes section of story.

G

H

I

J

K

L

M

N

O

P